History of Western Civilization
A Handbook

History of Western Civilization
A Handbook
Revised and Enlarged

William H. McNeill

THE UNIVERSITY OF CHICAGO PRESS
CHICAGO/LONDON

THE UNIVERSITY OF CHICAGO PRESS, Chicago 60637
The University of Chicago Press, Ltd., London

International Standard Book Number: 0-226-56138-0
Library of Congress Catalog Card Number: 69-18121

Contents

Illustrations

Maps

Charts

Plates

SHAPERS OF THE MODERN WORLD

Preface

This *Handbook* was written in 1949 for use in the course in the History of Western Civilization at the University of Chicago. It has since been revised in 1951, 1953, 1958, and 1969.

The book was originally written because the College History Staff could not find a satisfactory textbook that dealt with the development of western civilization as a whole and was at the same time sufficiently brief to allow what we considered adequate student time for reading selected primary and secondary materials. To base our course mainly upon a text book, however good, seemed likely to obscure the problematic nature of the study of history, and, we thought, would also detract from the interest which can and should be aroused by direct contact with records of the past. Yet to base our course solely upon selected readings would produce an inevitable disjointedness and fragmentation. Our solution was to provide the students with this *Handbook* as a background base upon which to build their comprehension of the *Selected Readings*.

The author acknowledges with gratitude the assistance he has received from the members of the College History Staff of the University of Chicago who read the entire text in its original form, and who have since given him the benefit of their experience with the book in the classroom when the time came for revision. Illustrations for this revised edition were selected with the help of Mr. Kenneth Irvine, and Mr. David Folmer updated Suggestions for Further Reading. The maps are from the hand of Mr. Vaughn Gray. I wish to thank each of these men for helping to improve the book; but responsibility for the text (with any surviving errors) rests entirely upon the author.

W.H.M.
28 February 1969

To The Student

This book is intended to provide in a convenient form information which will help you (1) to acquire a sense of the sweep and continuity of Western history, and (2) to provide background for a better understanding of collateral readings.

It is a handbook rather than a history. Efforts to explain connections between events have been deliberately minimized. Instead, the task of interpreting the meaning of history has been left to you. This book offers only a part of the raw material for such a task, i.e., a body of information. In class and in collateral readings various ideas and variant views of historical development will be presented to you, as well as additional information. Other courses have no doubt done likewise. From the welter of information and ideas which you have met, you are now expected to set about the task of shaping for yourselves a pattern of belief about the past, a pattern which will be useful to you for the rest of your lives, however much you may find it possible or necessary to modify, enrich, or in some cases perhaps, reconstruct your interpretation.

No one imagines that each of you should arrive at the same view of history. Still less does it seem likely that the views you form from your experience of a course in history will prove certainly or eternally true. Such truth has eluded historians in the past and will probably continue to do so. But this limitation of human powers does not mean that the effort to clarify and refine your understanding of the past is worthless. Decision and action in daily life are largely a consequence of ideas about what has happened before. A capacity to view current events in a long perspective, to compare them with others of former times, and to fit them into a general scheme of historical interpretation will sustain in you a more balanced, stable judgment of the men and ideas which normally compete for your attention and allegiance. In time of political or social crisis such a capacity may provide intellectual solace—it is comforting to know that others have shared similar disaster or disappointment. On the other hand, an informed view of history may inspire you to resolute, even heroic, action, for the greatest religious and political movements of humanity have been associated with and in some measure inspired by a view of history.

Arbitrary principles of ordering and selection must perforce be brought into play in the writing of any account of the past. This book is no exception to the rule. The organization which has been chosen is arbitrary, and others could have been substituted for it. Here you will find three major periods labeled Ancient Oriental, Classical, and European civilization. Possible alternative divisions would be the more traditional Ancient, Medieval, and Modern segmentation of history; or Ancient Oriental, Greek, Roman, Medieval, early Modern, and Modern. Other principles have often been used to organize knowledge of the past. For instance, history might be divided in the light of theological belief into Old and New Dispensations; or epochs of human history might be based upon changes in technology (e.g., the age of iron and wood) or in thought (e.g., the Enlightenment).

The grouping of facts which any organization supplies tends to give the reader a particular view of history. It is, therefore, important for you to realize in reading this book that an artificial organization has been imposed on the unbroken continuity of human affairs; and that the criteria by which these divisions were made are not the only possible ones. Periodization inevitably distorts in greater or lesser degree; and if you allow the device to disguise the wholeness of history, or to obscure the divergencies and differences within the periods marked off, you will have permitted a mechanical scheme to cut you off from the living variety and multifariousness of the past.

In short, you should read this book with all the wisdom and discernment of which you are capable, aware of its limitations and bearing always in mind the question: how does this information fit into my understanding of the past? In other words, this book should provide you with bricks from which to build a structure of your own rather than a pattern into which your understanding should fit itself.

History of Western Civilization
A Handbook

PART I

Western Civilization in World History

During the past four centuries the civilization of Western Europe has undergone an enormous expansion, has destroyed many weaker societies, and has exerted a powerful influence on others, so that no part of the earth today is exempt from its impact. This *Handbook* describes the growth of this Western European civilization from its roots in classical antiquity to the present. But men existed on the face of the earth long before the Greeks invaded Hellas; and other societies and civilizations have flourished independently of the Classical and Western European traditions until relatively recent times. For the sake of a just perspective one must know something of the distant past and be at least aware of the existence of other civilizations.

A. Background of Classical Civilization

1. OLD STONE AGE (*c.* 500.000[?]–8000[?] B.C.)

Members of the biological species, *homo sapiens*, began to scatter their bones on the earth about 500,000 years ago. Skeletons with more or less human characteristics have been found in widely separated regions of the earth: in Java, China, south and east Africa, Palestine and Germany. No clear line of evolution or biological relationship can be traced, however, from the few skeletal fragments that have so far been discovered.

The earliest people whose way of life can be surmised with any accuracy is the Neanderthal, so-called from a valley in Germany where remains of this people were first discovered. Neanderthal skeletons and artifacts have also been found in other parts of Europe, and similar finds have recently been made in Palestine, South Africa and even in far-off Java.

Neanderthal men did not have skeletons identical with those of modern men. Their bones were heavier and their eye ridges and jaws were more

3

prominent. They lived in caves, used chipped stones as weapons for hunting, knew how to control fire, and buried their dead in ceremonial fashion, putting food and implements in the graves, a custom which seems to show a belief in life after death. Neanderthal society was certainly primitive; yet it required the use of skills and knowledge which had slowly accumulated over thousands of years among earlier and still more primitive peoples about whom we know very little.

In Europe, Neanderthal men lived under sub-arctic conditions, and with the last retreat of the great glaciers (12,000 to 20,000 years ago), different peoples, apparently the ancestors of contemporary men, appeared at about the same time in Europe, Africa, China and Palestine. On their first appearance, modern men showed sub-types: tall Cro-Magnon, short Grimaldi, and others. They displaced the Neanderthalers, although some interbreeding between modern and Neanderthal races may have taken place.

The newcomers knew how to make and use a greater variety of tools and weapons than the Neanderthalers. Many different styles of stoneworking developed in various parts of the world, and in some cases it is possible to discern successions: one type of equipment giving place to another, usually more elaborate, type. Such changes may testify to migrations and conquests or to invention and diffusion of new skills. In general the number of special tools and the skill of their manufacture increased as time went by.

Spear and arrowheads, harpoons of bone and ivory, spearthrowers and bows all were known. Shelters constructed of skins or dug into the earth made it easier to follow herds of reindeer and bison onto the tundra where the natural shelter of caves was not available. In southern France and northern Spain a number of cave paintings have been discovered which portray, with an aesthetic appeal still vivid today, the various animals which were hunted. Other remains, such as bracelets and necklaces of shells, show that a decorative effect was striven for and appreciated. Music was made with simple pipes and whistles. Burial practices, the cave paintings, and small statues of men and of animals have been interpreted by archaeologists as evidences of religious beliefs—e.g., the propitiation of the spirits of the animals slain in the hunt.

2. NEOLITHIC AGE (*c.* 8000 [?]–3000 B.C.)

It is worth emphasizing that from the strictly chronological point of view nearly all of man's career on the earth is covered by the Old Stone Age. Cultivation of crops and the domestication of animals—the economic basis of neolithic and of all subsequent societies—began perhaps no more than 8,000 to 10,000 years ago. These great improvements were first developed into a new way of life in the Middle East; that is, in the area south of the Caucasus, east of the Mediterranean, north of the Persian Gulf, and west of the Hindu Kush. From this center, food-producing economy spread over a wide area of Europe, Asia, and Africa. Its spread was doubtless very slow, measured by the developments of historical times, but was nonetheless rapid when compared to changes that occurred during the Old Stone Age.

In the wide grasslands of Central Asia, southern Russia, and northern Arabia, men became nomads, dependent on flocks and herds. In upland regions of Syria, Asia Minor, Persia and Afghanistan, where tough sod did not impede them, men turned rather to agriculture. When fields were exhausted from repeated cropping, neolithic farmers abandoned them and made new fields in virgin soil. If no promising land could be found near at hand, the whole community simply packed up and moved to some place where suitable soil did exist. Use of fertilizer, crop rotation or fallowing to restore or maintain fertility were all unknown.

All the important food crops of modern times were discovered by neolithic agriculturalists (although several, such as corn and potatoes, were known only in the Americas until after the European discoveries). Similarly, most of the important domestic animals, save for the horse and camel, were tamed before civilized societies came into existence. Other useful arts such as the making of pottery, weaving, brewing and baking, and the polishing of stone to produce a cutting edge were also discovered in neolithic times. With the enlarged food supply which agriculture and stock breeding made available, man was no longer the rare animal of earlier times; but nonetheless, villages were small, and isolated from one another by great stretches of uninhabited forest or grassland.

Female figurines and phallic symbols seem to indicate that neolithic peoples engaged in fertility rites, probably connected with the life cycle of the crops. Tombs and temples were built on a great variety of models. Elaborate grave furniture in some of the tombs suggests that their makers believed in a life after death.

Presumably neolithic villages were almost completely self-sufficient, and probably were inhabited by kindred families. There is some evidence of incipient specialization and trade. Flint mines have been found, for example, with shafts sunk many feet into the ground, following seams of flint nodules; while sea shells and special types of hard stone useful for toolmaking were carried long distances, presumably as a result of trade.

Archaeologists have found many different types of tools and weapons on neolithic sites. The variety and richness of the finds is, of course, much greater than for the Old Stone Age. Traces of wars and conquests are unmistakable. Some villages were fortified, and skeletons have been found with arrow heads embedded in the bones—a silent testimony of ancient battles.

3. THE RIVER VALLEY CIVILIZATIONS (*c.* 3000–1750 B.C.)

---

a. Mesopotamia

b. Egypt

Neolithic agricultural methods made permanent settlement of relatively large populations impossible in most parts of the earth. Only in some river valleys, where annual floods fertilized the fields, could tillage be kept up year after year. Within the general area where agriculture was first developed, two great valleys met these conditions: the valley of the Two Rivers—the Tigris and Euphrates—in modern Iraq; and the valley of the Nile in Egypt. But before these regions could be fully exploited, dikes, canals and reservoirs had to be constructed, for both valleys suffer from floods and from an almost complete lack of rainfall in the months when the crop ripens. Unless water could be brought to the fields artificially, the summer sun would parch and destroy the grain.

Other geographical peculiarities of these valleys favored the development of the first civilized societies. In the Tigris-Euphrates valley, or Mesopotamia (Greek for "the land between the rivers") as it is usually called, native stone for the making of tools was lacking and had to be brought from afar; and at the same time, the rivers and their valleys provided natural lines of communication and transport. Thus trade and stimulating contact with other people were both easy and necessary. When once the indispensable irrigation works had been constructed, the richness of the soil facilitated the production of food surplus, and this surplus in turn provided a margin for trade and for the support of various specialists—priests, rulers, craftsmen and merchants.

Partly as a result of these geographical peculiarities, the peoples of Mesopotamia and Egypt became the leaders in what has sometimes been called the urban revolution. With the rise of cities the earliest societies we recognize as civilized came into existence, first in Mesopotamia, and a little later in Egypt.

a. Mesopotamia

Between about 6000 B.C. and 3000 B.C., a series of social changes and technical improvements transformed small neolithic settlements in the valley of the Two Rivers into cities like Ur, Lagash and Erech, which are revealed by the earliest written records of Mesopotamia. The most important technical improvements made during this time were the discovery of writing, of how to smelt and cast copper, the harnessing of animal power

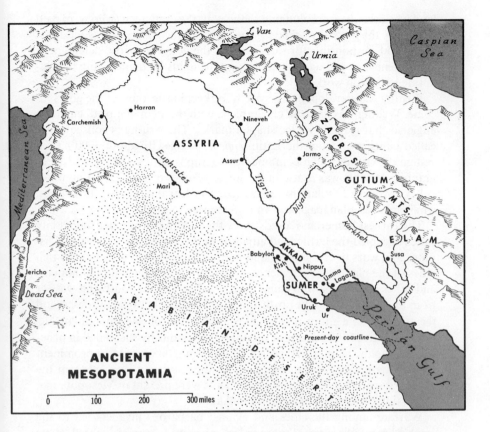

by the development of plows and wheeled vehicles, the invention of the sailing boat, and the invention of the potter's wheel.

The urban revolution depended not only on these technical improvements but also upon a social reorganization which permitted coordination of effort among large numbers of men. Without such coordination, specialization and the development of technical skills (which depended on specialization) could not go very far. Even more important, the irrigation, without which cultivation of the Tigris-Euphrates valley was impossible, could only be undertaken and maintained by large-scale social action.

The steps by which the simple organization of a neolithic village was developed into the social hierarchy of the earliest cities can only be surmised. By 3000 B.C. distinct social classes had been formed, including slaves, tenant farmers (who paid a part of their crop to the god, i.e., to the temple priests, as a sort of rent or taxes), various craftsmen, merchants, priests, and chief-priests who were at the same time governors or kings. Government was carried on in the name of the city's god or gods: the city's land was described as belonging to the god, the craftsmen (who were paid in kind by the priests) worked for the god, and the governor was the agent of the god, responsible for safeguarding the god's property, defending it against enemies and against floods and droughts by maintaining the elaborate irrigation works.

Writing was developed as a system for keeping account of the god's income. Writing was done on clay tablets, with the stem of a reed, cut at an angle so that it made wedge-shaped marks. The writing is consequently called cuneiform, from the Latin, *cuneus*, wedge. By about 3000 B.C., a system of writing which combined pictographs with syllabary and ideographic elements was in use in the lower reaches of the Tigris-Euphrates valley. Modern scholars have succeeded in learning to read this script, which records a language known as Sumerian.

The earliest Sumerian records show that a number of independent city states occupied the fertile land adjacent to the Tigris and Euphrates. Disputes and wars over rights to land and water were frequent, but the rich cities of the plain were threatened even more by the incursion of nomads and other barbarians who came from the desert to the south and west or from the mountains to the north and east. Hostility between the desert and the towns was a more or less constant feature of Mesopotamian life. Groups native to the desert or mountains periodically succeeded in penetrating into the plain, and there set up states of their own. Most prominent among the invaders were Semites from the south; and indeed from the earliest discernible times, Semitic elements were present in Mesopotamia, especially to the north of Sumeria in Akkad.

Warfare among the cities and against barbarous invaders led to the establishment of a series of more or less ephemeral "empires" based on the conquests of some particularly successful ruler. Such empires did not involve central administration; rather the conquered cities recognized the suzerainty of the conqueror and paid tribute, while maintaining their local government and religion as before. The most famous early conqueror was Sargon of Akkad, who succeeded in extending his control from the Persian Gulf to the Mediterranean about 2350 B.C. But new invasions and civil wars destroyed Sargon's empire after a few generations; and others rose in its place. The best known of Sargon's successors was Hammurabi of Babylon (*c.* 1800 B.C.) who ruled the whole valley as well as bordering regions. By this time the original Sumerian population had been submerged, and the predominant language was Semitic.

Nevertheless, the general mode of life which the early Sumerians had worked out remained surprisingly stable. Successive waves of barbarian invaders accepted the civilization of the cities of the plain. They borrowed the cuneiform system of writing and used it to write their own languages. The worship of the ancient Sumerian city gods was maintained, though not without accretions and syncretism between old and new deities and powers. Artistic traditions, such as the engraving of seals in miniature, continued to flourish, as did technical skills such as metal working, fine weaving and pottery making.

Long-distance trade was an important and vital part of Mesopotamian life. Metals and wood and other raw materials had to be imported, coming from Syria, Cyprus, Asia Minor and even more distant regions. Trading posts were established as far away as the Black Sea coast in the time of Sargon, and wars were fought to protect or to open up routes of trade. Law codes, of which that bearing the name of Hammurabi is the best known, show an elaborate development of commercial relations, and recognize a variety of contracts between merchants and their agents, between debtor and creditor, landlord and tenant. Silver, though not in the form of coins, was used as a medium of exchange and measure of value. The Sumerians worked out a system of numerical notation (based on 60) and were able to do ordinary arithmetic. They developed a system of time reckoning by hours, weeks and months which is the direct ancestor of our own system. Careful observations of the stars and planets were made, and records of their movements were kept in the temples. Doctrines about the influence of the stars on human affairs were gradually elaborated, from which present day astrology derives.

The religion of ancient Mesopotamia centered in great temples, built in the form of pyramidal step towers. The biblical Tower of Babel was such a temple. An elaborate mythology was embodied in epic poems which described the creation of the world and the deeds of gods and heroes. Some of the Mesopotamian myths are paralleled in the Old Testament, in particular the story of the Flood. Worship consisted of sacrifices, processionals, chants and other rituals conducted by priestly castes on behalf of the entire city. The number of gods whose names appear in the records is enormous. Some were personifications of the power of earth, water, storms. etc.; others had no recognizable basis in physical nature.

b. Egypt

At about the time when Sumerian cities were forming, the lower Nile valley was inhabited by people who learned how to control the Nile flood and use it to irrigate their fields, how to smelt metal, and how to communicate in writing. In many respects the Egyptian development paralleled that of Mesopotamia, though an important and enduring difference arose from the fact that Egypt was relatively immune from invasion, being surrounded by nearly impassable deserts. Consequently, barbarian invasion was not a serious problem, and warlike activity was correspondingly less prominent in Egypt than in Mesopotamia during the early centuries of civilized history.

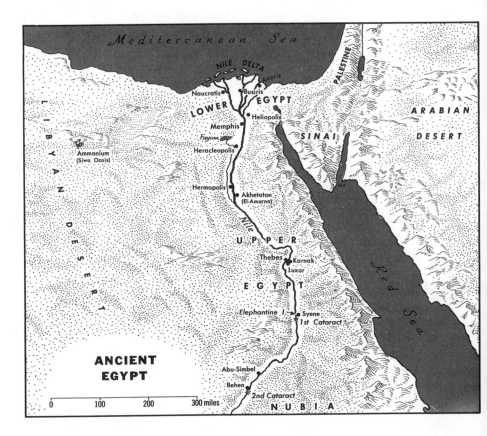

Archaeologists have found traces of independent Egyptian village communities, but before 3000 B.C. the land of Egypt had been united under a
single ruler, the Pharaoh. Unlike the Mesopotamian rulers, the Pharaoh
was considered to be a god himself, not merely the god's agent on earth.
His divinity conferred vast powers. Thus, for example, the Pharaoh owned
all the land of Egypt and merely rented it to its occupiers. This stood in
contrast to Mesopotamian law, which by the time of Hammurabi fully
recognized private property in land, and permitted its sale and lease.

From the beginning of written records (*c.* 3000 B.C.) the Egyptian
government was carried on by a centralized bureaucracy. Political control
was scarcely distinguished from religious direction. Taxes (or rents) were
systematically collected for the Pharaoh from all the cultivated land, and
hundreds of thousands of men were organized to work on great building
enterprises, of which the most famous are the pyramids. The whole coordination of Egyptian society depended on the religious prerogatives of
the Pharaoh and the priests around him.

EGYPTIAN ARCHITECTURE: PYRAMIDS AND TEMPLES

The architectural monuments of the Old Kingdom indicate the profound Egyptian concern for life after death. The *mastaba,* with its flat top and sloping walls, was generally modest in size and reflects the predynastic stage in Egyptian history. The Step Pyramid of Zoser represents a transitional form but was quickly superceded by the simple geometric form of pyramid characteristic of the Old Kingdom. The great pyramids at Gizeh mirror the solidification of royal power in the hands of the Pharaoh. Literally thousands of workmen were required to perform the difficult tasks of dragging the huge stones to the pyramid site and lifting them into place. The Middle and New Kingdoms were marked by the emergence of the priesthood as a dominant force. This shift of emphasis in political power was reflected in the building of numerous temples.

Model of a *Mastaba*
(The Metropolitan Museum of Art)

This cutaway model shows how the *mastaba* design protected the burial chamber from unauthorized entry by filling up the access passage with stone.

Step Pyramid of Zoser, Saqqara
Third Dynasty, *circa* 2700 B.C.
(Hirmer Verlag München)

The Step Pyramid is a large structure with recessed steps, moving from a broad base to a narrow top. It resembles a number of successively smaller *mastaba*s piled on each other.

Pyramids at Gizeh
(Hirmer Verlag München)

Distant view of the pyramids of Menkure (*circa* 2525 B.C.), of Khafre (*circa*
2560 B.C.), and of Khufu (*circa* 2600 B.C.). The pyramid of Khufu
(far right) with base of 756 feet and height of 481 feet is the largest mass
of stone in the world assembled by human hands. The huge and solid
bulk of the pyramids convey a real sense of the monolithic power
of the Pharaoh.

Temple of Amon-Mut-Khonsu, Hall of Amenhotep III
Circa **1390** B.C.
(Hirmer Verlag München)

A sense of enormous mass is still preserved in the monumental size of the columns and lintels of the temple. But the temple celebrates the greatness of the god Amon-re and of the priests who served him, not of Pharaoh.

Economic life was highly centralized. Trade was largely monopolized by the Pharaoh's agents, and craftsmen served mainly the court and temples. No wealthy and independent class of merchants developed as was the case in Mesopotamia.

It is difficult to overestimate the preeminent place which religious practices, ideas and attitudes had in shaping the Egyptian intellectual tradition. The Egyptians worshiped many gods. Some, in animal form, suggest a derivation from clan fetishes. Others were personifications of the Nile, of the sun or of other natural objects. From very early times, the Egyptians were concerned with life after death, and the Great Pyramids were constructed to assure safe and comfortable housing for the Pharaoh's immortal soul. It appears that originally only the Pharaoh could aspire to immortality in his own right. Later influential officials and priests, and still later, ordinary men were believed capable of immortality, if their bodies were properly preserved as housing for their spirits (by mummification) and the appropriate charms were said and ceremonies performed.

Egyptian writing, called hieroglyphics, combined pictographic with syllabary and alphabetic symbols. Like the Mesopotamians, the Egyptians developed a system of arithmetic, and knew some principles of geometry. Priests measured and recorded the movements of sun, moon, stars and planets; and about 2776 B.C. they instituted a calendar of 365 days. We know something of Egyptian medicine, in which charms and magic played a large role. Details of human anatomy were better known than in Mesopotamia, perhaps because of the practice of mummification.

The most obvious difference between Egyptian and Mesopotamian civilization appears in art and architecture. Abundant supply of good building stone in Egypt made possible such monumental structures as the Great Pyramids (built between 2800 and 2400 B.C.). Stone sculpture in the round, often on a colossal scale, and skillful wall painting and bas-relief were characteristic of Egyptian art from the earliest times. Artistic conventions were defined very early (e.g., the statue pose with one foot advanced, arms at the side) and were rigidly adhered to thereafter. The fact that tombs were frequently decorated with scenes from everyday life permits us a vivid glimpse of many details of ancient Egyptian civilization.

The divine status and absolute power of the Pharaoh did not always prevent insubordination on the part of his officials. The remarkable concentration of power which prevailed at the beginning of the so-called Old Kingdom (3000–2300 B.C.) gradually gave way as offices became hereditary. Rival claimants for the Pharaoh's throne arose; and for nearly 300 years Egypt was, in effect, divided into a series of rival states. About 2050 B.C. the rulers of Thebes in upper (i.e., southern) Egypt made good their claim to supreme power and initiated what is called the Middle

Kingdom (*c.* 2050–1800 B.C.). But, as in Mesopotamia, the style of civilization which had emerged at the beginning of Egyptian history remained surprisingly stable through these and subsequent political upheavals.

4. THE DIFFUSION OF URBAN CIVILIZATION

During the centuries when Mesopotamia and Egypt were developing their own peculiar patterns of civilization, neolithic village life, based on agriculture and animal husbandry, continued to spread over ever wider areas of the earth, penetrating into Europe up the Danube valley, and spreading along the north coast of Africa into Spain and adjacent parts of Western Europe. Neolithic techniques also spread eastward to India and China. The Americas, however, did not share in this development. When, much later, agriculture arose in Central and South America, it utilized plants and animals (corn and potatoes, and the llama) different from those of Eurasia and Africa.

Until improvements in agricultural methods made it possible for men to settle permanently on land watered only by rainfall, neolithic farmers could borrow little from the nascent civilizations of Mesopotamia and Egypt. In the course of the fourth millenium B.C., however, farmers in the Middle Eastern area found out how to maintain the fertility of their fields by crop rotation, fallowing, and the use of natural fertilizers like manure, ashes or sea shells. These improvements meant a larger food production and a more sedentary pattern of life in the border lands surrounding the two great river valleys which had pioneered the urban revolution.

Once permanent villages had been formed, cities began to grow up in places where trade routes crossed, or where administrative, religious or tribal centers were established. As a result, cities began to appear in northern Mesopotamia, Syria, Palestine, Asia Minor, and the Iranian plateau soon after 3000 B.C.; and the area became studded with villages and towns during the course of the next thousand years. Throughout these regions, archaeologists can detect varying blends of Mesopotamian and Egyptian influence, together with local peculiarities and traditions.

Two areas deserve special mention. In the lower Indus valley a civilized society appeared before 2500 B.C. which, like Egypt, was substantially independent of Mesopotamian influence, though the Indus peoples had trading connections with the Tigris-Euphrates valley. The civilization which arose on the island of Crete in the third millenium B.C. bore a similar relation to Egypt. Trade was carried on with the Egyptians, but the Cretan (or Minoan) civilization was independent in such things as artistic style, religious cult, and method of writing.

Warlike remains are remarkably lacking from both these civilizations. About 1400 B.C. the Cretan civilization was destroyed, probably by invaders from mainland Greece. The Indus valley civilization disappeared about a century earlier, when barbarous invaders from the north overran the region.

5. THE ANCIENT ORIENTAL EMPIRES (1750–323 B.C.)

---

a. The Indo-Europeans
b. The New Empires (1750–1250 B.C.)
c. Fresh Invasions and Successor States
   (1250–745 B.C.)
d. The Later Empires (745–323 B.C.)
e. Characteristics of Oriental Civilization
f. The Hebrew People and their Religion
   (1400–331 B.C.)

Between about 1750 B.C. and 1550 B.C., the process of diffusion from the civilized centers of Mesopotamia and Egypt was hastened by a widespread migration of peoples, a militarization of Oriental society, and the consequent mixing of populations during a prolonged period of war and conquest. The comparative isolation and security of Egyptian society was shattered about 1750 B.C. by the victorious invasion of a barbarous people known as Hyksos. At about the same time, Mesopotamia was overrun by hill peoples from the north, and Hammurabi's empire came to an end; new waves of Semites penetrated into the fertile agricultural regions from the southern grasslands; and Indo-European tribesmen from the steppes overran extensive territories in Europe, India, and intervening portions of western Asia.

a. The Indo-Europeans[1]

The Indo-Europeans (with extensive immixture of other peoples) were to be the principal bearers of the subsequent classical and western civilizations. During the course of some 1500 years (2000–500 B.C.), wave after wave of these semi-nomadic tribesmen conquered nearly all of Europe, while other groups ruled over shifting areas of the Near East and India. Their early military successes were connected with the fact that the Indo-Europeans had tamed the horse, and used it, with terrifying effect, as an

---

[1] The term "Indo-European" refers to a group of related languages and, by association, to the peoples who spoke them. The name is simply descriptive, since modern speakers of these languages inhabit Europe and India, and countries in between. The Indo-European peoples are sometimes called Aryans, from the name of the Indo-European tribe which invaded India. It is rash to assume any identity between race and language even for very ancient times; in recent centuries, blood and language certainly have no close connection with one another.

The Semites, referred to earlier, are a similar linguistic group whose languages were related to one another, and to modern Arabic and Hebrew.

animal of war. In many areas, the Indo-European conquerors became a
military aristocracy ruling over an indigenous population. In areas where
the arts of civilization had developed, the invaders were regularly absorbed
or ejected after relatively short periods. In Europe, however, where high
civilization had not yet arisen, the Indo-Europeans succeeded in imposing
their language on whatever remnants of the earlier population survived
their conquest. As a result, nearly all the languages of modern Europe (exceptions are Hungarian. Finnish and Basque) are Indo-European.

b. The New Empires (1750–1250 B.C.)

New states arose in the Near East after the long series of invasions.
Mesopotamia was divided between the Kassites in the south and the
Mitanni in the north; in central and eastern Asia Minor, the Hittites
founded an extensive kingdom. Further west, on the Greek mainland and
islands, Cretan gave way to Mycenaean power. Probably all of these new
states were ruled over by Indo-Europeans, though the underlying strata of
society—the tillers of the soil, hewers of wood and drawers of water—were
of different language. The invaders in each of these areas took over to a
greater or lesser extent the civilization they found already established, and
proceeded to develop local variations of their own.

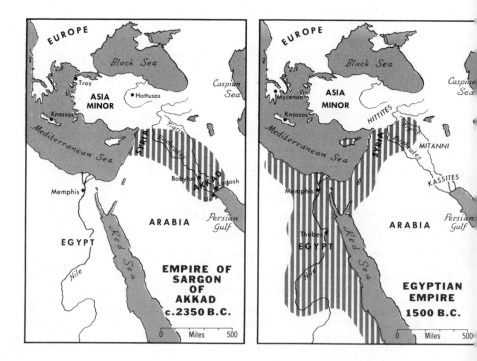

At about the same time, fresh waves of Semitic invaders from the south likewise established themselves in Syria and Palestine—the Phoenicians and Canaanites of the Old Testament. These peoples did not immediately succeed in setting up independent states, however, for they were conquered by Egypt in the course of the sixteenth century B.C. When the native Egyptians succeeded in overthrowing the Hyksos invaders (about 1565 B.C.), the Pharaohs did not rest content with the old boundaries, but embarked on a policy of military expansion through Palestine and Syria. For nearly 200 years the Egyptian Empire, or New Kingdom, enjoyed a predominant position in the Eastern Mediterranean area; but about 1400 B.C. Hittite rulers began to challenge Egyptian control of Syria. A prolonged struggle ensued, ending only with mutual exhaustion and the breakup of both empires (*c.* 1150 B.C.). In the course of these wars, the Mitanni were destroyed, and thereafter the kingdom of Assyria took over the rule of the upper Tigris valley.

c. Fresh Invasions and Successor States (1250–745 B.C.)

As the Egyptian and Hittite empires weakened, fresh movements of peoples took place. A new wave of Indo-European barbarians invaded the old seats of civilization from the north. Dorians pushed their way into Greece, Phrygians into Asia Minor and Medes and Persians into Iran. Simultaneously from the south came new groups of Semitic invaders: the Hebrews (Palestine), Aramaeans (Syria) and Chaldeans (Babylonia). These movements extended over some two hundred years, and involved many secondary displacements of nations and intensive intermixture between old and new peoples. Thus it has been surmised that the Phrygian and Dorian invasions forced peoples native to Asia Minor to migrate from their homes, some of whom set themselves up along the coast of Palestine and were known as Philistines while another group went to north central Italy and were called Etruscans.

Following these great movements, a number of comparatively small states arose in the Near East. In Greece and Asia Minor the invaders overthrew the Mycenaean and Hittite civilizations and these areas entered upon a "Dark Age," from which they only emerged after about 800 B.C. with the rise of the Lydian kingdom in western Asia Minor and the beginning of Classical civilization in Greece. Closer to the center of Oriental civilization, in Syria, Palestine, and Mesopotamia, no such profound eclipse occurred. In Phoenicia the trading cities of Tyre, Sidon, and Byblos entered upon a period of political independence and commercial prosperity. To the south, the Hebrews erected their kingdom after prolonged struggles with the Philistines. Eastward the Aramaean city of Damascus controlled a considerable part of Syria. Babylonia was ruled by a Semitic

dynasty, as was the Assyrian kingdom in the upper Tigris valley. Wars between these states (and many others which have not been mentioned) were
more or less chronic. By degrees the military power of Assyria emerged
preeminent, and when an Assyrian king, Tiglath-Pileser III (745–727 B.C.),
reorganized the Assyrian administration and began to rule rather than
merely to raid neighboring states, the political life of the Near East entered on a new, empire-building, phase.

d. The Later Empires (745–323 B.C.)

As a result of a long succession of campaigns, Tiglath-Pileser III and
his successors conquered almost all the civilized area of the Near East. In
612 B.C., however, the Assyrians were attacked by a coalition of Chaldeans
and Medes; their empire was overthrown, its capital, Nineveh, was sacked,
and the Assyrian people were destroyed. Egypt had successfully asserted
its independence some years before. The rest of the Assyrian empire came
to be divided between the Medes and the Chaldeans. The most famous
ruler of the Chaldean, or Neo-Babylonian, Empire was Nebuchadnezzar
(604–562 B.C.), who figures prominently in the Old Testament. But the
division of power between Media, Babylonia and Egypt did not long e..
dure. A scant sixty years after the overthrow of Assyria, a new conqueror

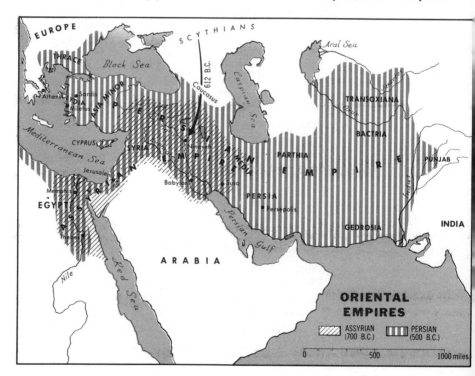

arose—Cyrus, king of the Persians, a people closely related in language and culture to the Medes, whose subjects they had been. When Cyrus revolted against the Median king, he won an easy victory (550 B.C.), and went on to conquer Lydia (546 B.C.) and Babylonia (539 B.C.). His son, Cambyses, added Egypt (525 B.C.); and after a brief period of disorder, Darius the Great (521–484 B.C.) rounded out the vast empire with conquests in India, central Asia and European Thrace. His successor, Xerxes, failed to subdue Greece (480–479 B.C.). Thereafter the Persian power gradually weakened until Alexander of Macedon, in a brilliantly successful campaign, destroyed it (334–323 B.C.).

Alexander's conquest brought a powerful current of Greek cultural influence into the Near East. Yet underlying characteristics and attitudes of Near Eastern civilization did not disappear, though temporarily overlaid with a veneer of Hellenism. Under the late Roman empire an "Oriental [i.e., Near Eastern] reaction" manifested itself; and to this day the lands where this ancient civilization once flourished retain deep marks of the distant past, not only in the form of archaeological monuments, but in the thoughts and habits of living men. Nor is the contemporary influence of the Ancient Orient (as we may call Near Eastern civilization when contrasting it with the civilization of Greece and Rome) confined to the Near East. Not to speak of Judaism and Christianity, both of which took form in a matrix of Oriental civilization, so basic a rhythm of our lives as the seven day week derives from Babylonian ideas and practices, as, indeed, does our whole system of time reckoning by hours, minutes and seconds.

e. Characteristics of Near Eastern Civilization

The long succession of wars and conquests, sketched above, mixed the peoples of the Near East and produced a more or less common pattern of urban and rural life over all the parts of that area where agriculture could flourish. There were of course local differences, and each people combined the common elements in different proportions. Yet it is possible to speak of an Oriental civilization. Its main lines had been worked out by the ancient Sumerians and Egyptians, and later conquerors for the most part merely elaborated upon their ideas and practices.

1. Progress in technology continued. Metal weapons and tools became more abundant, especially when new methods of refining ore allowed ancient smiths to make use of iron. This improvement became general between about 1200 and 1000 B.C. For the first time metal became cheap enough that ordinary farmers were able to use it for plow shares, sickles and other tools. Bronze, the standard metal of earlier times, had always been a strictly aristocratic material because it cost so much.

Transport was speeded by the introduction of horses and camels; and the Assyrian and Persian kings not only built roads, but maintained relays of mounted messengers who were capable of carrying messages more than a hundred miles a day. Seagoing vessels were developed by the Cretans and others, and the sea soon became a highway for both trade and piracy. Coinage of money was introduced by the Lydians, thereby facilitating trade and exchange.

Perhaps the most important single invention was the development of alphabetic writing. This apparently occurred about 1400 B.C., somewhere between the peninsula of Sinai in the south and Syria in the north, and was based on simplified Egyptian hieroglyphs, adapted for a Semitic tongue. Every alphabet used today is derived from this original. Our alphabet passed from the first inventors to Phoenicia, thence to the Greeks, and from the Greeks to the Romans. The invention of a relatively simple method of writing ended the priestly monopoly of learning. Merchants and secular administrators began to keep written records; and even common people sometimes learned to read and write.

2. Trade expanded and came to embrace the whole Mediterranean basin. Raw materials, especially metals, were sought and found as far away as the British Isles. The Phoenician cities, Tyre, Sidon and Byblos, were especially prominent as mercantile centers after about 1250 B.C., and established trading stations and colonies over widely scattered parts of the Mediterranean coast. Carthage, in northern Africa, was the most famous and powerful Phoenician colony. It was founded about 800 B.C.

3. The structure of society remained much as it had been in the days of Hammurabi, with this difference, that the power and influence of the priests tended to be rivaled by groups of professional soldiers and administrators. The soil was cultivated by semifree or slave classes; and slavery among the artisans of the towns was common. In Phoenicia and Babylon wealthy merchants had a prominent place in society, but elsewhere merchants were not important as a distinct class.

4. Governmental technique was greatly improved, especially by the Assyrians and Persians. The latter divided their empire into a series of provinces, called satrapies; and the satraps, appointed by the king, mostly from among noble Persians, were responsible for nipping incipient revolts in the bud, for collecting tribute, and in general for carrying out the orders of the central government. The empire was held together by the system of communications already mentioned, and by a standing army composed of Persians and some of the more warlike subject peoples. The army was organized into regular units, with distinct branches, such as cavalry, bowmen, spearmen, and siege experts.

5. The Hittites, Assyrians, and Persians each developed a distinctive art style, but it is impossible to describe them satisfactorily here. In Egypt, the old artistic traditions were adhered to closely. A monumental style of columnar temple was developed under the Empire; and for a brief time in

the fourteenth century B.C., when traditional religious rules were overthrown, Egyptian artists showed themselves capable of graceful naturalism in wall painting and sculpture. Thereafter reaction set in, and artists
consciously imitated archaic styles.

6. In the field of science the ancient peoples of the Orient made little progress during the imperial age until near its end, when the Babylonians carried the study of astronomy to new levels of minute observation. They
calculated the length of the solar year to within a few seconds of modern
measurement, and detected the precession of the equinoxes.

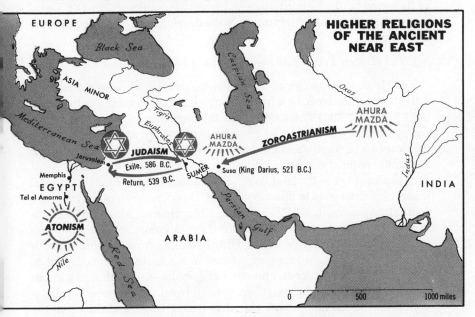

7. Perhaps the most interesting, and for subsequent history, the most
significant, innovations were made in religion. In Egypt in the fourteenth
century B.C., under the Pharaoh Akhnaton, an effort was made to introduce exclusive worship of the sun-god, Aton. But the attempt aroused bitter hostility in priestly circles, and was abandoned soon after Akhnaton's
death. In Mesopotamia, Marduk, the god of Babylon, tended to rise to
greater and greater preeminence; but the old Sumerian mythology and
pantheon remained official, despite such changes in emphasis.

Among the Persians a religious reformer, called Zoroaster or Zara-
thustra, who probably lived in the sixth century B.C., cast the religion of
the Persians in a new form. He taught that Ahura-Mazda, supreme god,
creator of the world and of light, champion of good, truth and mortality,
was in constant contest with the forces of evil and darkness. Men were free
to choose sides between them; those who chose to follow Zoroaster and

obey Ahura-Mazda were rewarded with the hope of immortality. Zoro-astrianism was peculiar among the religions of the ancient Orient in rejecting sacrifices and images. In ancient times, Zoroastrianism scarcely spread beyond the Persian aristocracy; but it helped to shape their character by its ethical teaching which emphasized the military virtues and truthfulness. The religion still survives in modified form in parts of India and Persia.

Far more influential in the subsequent history of the Western world was the religion of the Hebrews. The peculiar importance of their religion and of its sacred books, handed down in Christian tradition as the Old Testament, warrants separate treatment of the development of the Jewish state and religion.

f. The Hebrew People and their Religion (1400–331 B.C.)

The Hebrews were one of many Semitic peoples who filtered into the settled area of the Near East from the grasslands of northern Arabia. They began to move into Palestine in the fourteenth century B.C., when the Egyptian empire was losing its grasp on that country, and in the course of the next two hundred years gradually conquered and partly absorbed the Canaanite population, while adopting many of the more civilized ways of their predecessors in the land. Wars against the Philistines led the original loose tribal federation to unite under Saul, David, and Solomon into a centralized monarchy (c. 1025–930 B.C.). The Hebrew kingdom was administered much as were the numerous neighboring states which arose from the ruins of the Egyptian and Hittite empires. After Solomon's death the kingdom split into two parts: Israel in the north with its capital at Samaria, and the smaller and poorer Judah in the south with Jerusalem as its capital. In 722 B.C. the Assyrians invaded Israel and destroyed the kingdom. Many of the inhabitants were deported or killed, and thereafter the Hebrews of the Northern Kingdom lost their identity. In 586 B.C. Nebuchadnezzar, king of the Neo-Babylonian empire, conquered Judah and carried a large proportion of the population off to exile in Babylon. But in captivity the people of Judah clung to their religion and were able to keep themselves distinct from the peoples round about. When the Persians overthrew the Babylonian empire in 539 B.C., the people of Judah, or Jews, were permitted to return to Palestine. Some of them did so and there set up a semiautonomous theocratic state which lasted until after the Roman conquest.

The political experience of the Hebrews was undistinguished, being very like that of neighboring peoples. What has given them so commanding a place in history is their religion. The history of Jewish religion has been intensively studied, yet scholars are not agreed on how it developed. Some think that monotheism goes back to Moses; others that monotheism only emerged much later in the time of the great prophets. It would be presumptuous to try to reduce such disputes to a formula. All that need be noted here are some of the main periods of Hebrew religious development.

About 1200 B.C. Moses led a group of Hebrew tribesmen out from Egypt. After Moses' death this group joined fellow tribes in invading the land of Palestine. By tradition, it was Moses who first formulated the worship of Jahweh, as the early Hebrews called their God. At the heart of Mosaic religion lay the conviction that God had entered into a covenant with the people of Israel, a covenant which bound the Israelites to observe certain Divine commandments, and in particular, to worship Jahweh and only Jahweh. When the Hebrews occupied Palestine and took up an agricultural mode of existence, the Mosaic religion had to struggle against local fertility gods.

Protest against their worship, and against social injustices which the development of a complex, socially stratified society under the monarchy brought in its train, was voiced by a series of great prophets between about 750 B.C. and the end of the Babylonic exile. The prophets greatly enlarged and deepened the religious concepts of Mosaic religion. On the one hand, they exalted Jahweh by asserting His power over all mankind, not only over the Hebrew people as may (or may not) have been Moses' conception. In addition, the great prophets interpreted the Divine commandments as requiring moral conduct of individual men and of the Hebrew nation as a whole; and they explained the political misfortunes of the Hebrew Kingdoms as a punishment visited by God upon His faithless and unrighteous people. Some of the prophets developed the hope of an eventual purification of the Chosen People through suffering, and looked forward to a Messiah who in the fulness of time would bring deliverance. The Messiah was conceived by some as a man who would restore the vanished Kingdom of David, by others as a supernatural being who would establish the Kingdom of God on earth.

Side by side with the prophets, the Hebrew religious tradition was elaborated by colleges of priests. They collected, edited and added to the sacred books, which we know as the Old Testament. In particular, the priests developed a code of religious ritual and law which had binding force upon the Jewish people, and more than anything else served to keep them distinct from their neighbors.

The prophetic and priestly traditions combined to create Judaism. The definitive formulation of the religion did not occur until about a century after the first return from the Exile, when Nehemiah (*c.* 458 B.C.) and Ezra (*c.* 428 B.C.?) reorganized the Jewish state, and succeeded in persuading the Jews to live more nearly according to the letter of the sacred Law.

Religious thought did not come to a standstill after this time. New sects, new ideas and new emphases were steadily introduced; and books which were eventually incorporated into the Old Testament were written as late as the second century B.C. Nevertheless, the distinctive character of Judaism was fixed by the time of Nehemiah and Ezra, and has remained, despite all of the vicissitudes of Jewish history, to the present day.

Two peculiarities especially distinguished Judaism from nearly all other religions developed in the ancient Near East. First, Jewish law-givers, prophets and priests taught that God revealed himself to His people through historical events, not through natural phenomena such as the lightning flash or the renewal of vegetation each spring. The fact that their religion centered upon an interpretation of history made it possible for the Jews to dissociate religion from locality and even from membership in a particular society or subjection to a particular state. This constituted the second peculiarity of Judaism. It meant that when military events and economic pressures combined to disperse Jews into far corners of the earth—even after the Romans in A.D. 70 finally destroyed the Temple in Jerusalem—Judaism could and did continue to flourish. It had already, by the time of the Babylonian Exile, become a world religion.

B. Independent Civilized Traditions

Several hundred societies exist on the face of the earth at present, and many thousands of others have existed in times past. Yet only a very few have developed the size and complexity, the technical mastery over their environment, and the artistic and intellectual richness that we consider hallmarks of civilization. This *Handbook* makes no attempt to deal with the civilizations which arose and flourished apart from the oriental-classical-European tradition. Yet it seems necessary at least to call attention to their existence.

The slow spread of neolithic herdsmen and village communities through Eurasia and Africa has already been mentioned. As civilized societies arose in the Middle East, in India and in China, influences from each civilized center radiated outward, met and overlapped. From very early times, indeed, an irregular and indirect cross-stimulation between the separate civilized societies of Eurasia was maintained. After the sixteenth century A.D. overland contact was powerfully supplemented by the development of trans-oceanic shipping. European discoverers sailed to the coasts of India, China and the Americas; they were soon followed by swarms of merchants, soldiers, missionaries and adventurers—men who not only brought European ways to others but brought back to Europe plants, techniques and even ideas which they had gathered from distant shores.

In India, the disappearance of the Indus valley civilization after about

1500 B.C. (see above p. 16) was followed by several centuries of retrogression; but in time, the barbarous Aryan invaders constructed a more complex, socially stratified society once more. This society has survived, despite subsequent changes, and despite repeated political-military upheavals, to the present.

Religion played a peculiarly prominent part in Indian history. Of the three principal religions of the sub-continent, Hinduism apparently evolved gradually from age-old neolithic and Aryan roots, and it remains the religion of the majority to this day. Buddhism, on the contrary, was founded in the fifth century B.C. by followers of a teacher, saint and holy man named Gautama Buddha. Like Christianity, Buddhism found its greatest success not in its original milieu, but among alien peoples—principally in China and south east Asia. The third great religion of India, Mohammedanism, was brought by Moslem invaders from the north who first penetrated deeply into India in the eleventh century A.D. By the sixteenth century Moslem rulers consolidated their power over nearly all India; but their Empire was already showing signs of breakup when European traders and soldiers began to play a decisive part in Indian politics. European intervention culminated in the British conquest of India in the eighteenth century. In our own time, British rule in India came to an end (1947) and the peninsula was divided along religious lines between Hindu India and Moslem Pakistan.

In China, a complex society which can properly be called civilized developed from an indigenous neolithic base, and there is no particular date that can be assigned to the beginnings of Chinese civilization. By about 1500 B.C., however, China had developed cities and a relatively complex political system.

China's political history showed an alternation between periods of centralized, imperial government and periods of internal confusion and local rivalries. A number of invasions from the steppe lands which lie north and west of the Chinese river valleys gave China some of her most powerful rulers. The last such invasion, from Manchuria, led to the establishment of the Manchu dynasty, which ruled China from 1644 until 1911. In that year a revolution led by Sun Yat Sen established a republic which has since passed through many tribulations, including chronic civil war, a long struggle with Japan (1937–45) and, more recently, the accession of Communists to power in 1949.

The character of Chinese civilization, like that of India, was powerfully affected by religion. Confucianism, a moral rule rather than a theological-metaphysical system, was decisively shaped by the recorded teachings of the sage Confucius (551–479 B.C.). It later became if not the official religion certainly the religion of officials in China. Buddhism was a more popular religion. It became heavily encrusted with magic and superstition.

Civilized society in Japan arose later than in China, and Japan came very strongly under Chinese influence. One of the most striking differences was the greater development of militarism in Japan, a difference which goes back to very early times. When Europeans first embarked upon commercial and missionary enterprise in the Far East, the Japanese initially welcomed the newcomers and then when they felt their own traditions were in danger reacted by trying to cut off all contact. Eventually, when this policy proved impracticable (Admiral Perry, 1854), the Japanese showed a most remarkable aptitude in adopting European techniques, especially military techniques. As a result, by 1894 Japan was strong enough to make successful war against China; and in 1904–5 the Japanese defeated the Russians in a short but hard fought war. With this victory, Japan abruptly laid claim to the status of a great power in the Pacific.

The civilizations of Central and South America lagged far behind Eurasian developments. Agriculture based on maize seems to have started very early; but the rise of cult centers resembling Sumerian cities came slowly, so that levels of skill and specialization we recognize as civilized were not attained before about 500 B.C. Major centers of civilized life arose in Guatemala and Yucatan (Mayas), in central Mexico (Toltecs, Aztecs and others) and in Peru (Incas and their predecessors). Aspects of the high cultures of these regions spread widely through North and South America before the arrival of Columbus—for example, major ritual centers were beginning to arise in what is now the southeastern United States at the time white men appeared on the scene. But the Spanish conquest of Mexico and Peru abruptly altered the course of New World development, although, of course, important traces of pre-Columbian civilizations survive still in many parts of Central and South America.

Suggestions for Further Reading for Part I

The Cambridge Ancient History. Vols. 1–4. Cambridge: 1923–26.

The Cambridge Ancient History, Volumes of Plates. Vol. 1. Cambridge: 1927.

Albright, W. F. *From the Stone Age to Christianity.* 2d ed. New York: Anchor Books, 1957.

Baron, S. W. *A Social and Religious History of the Jews.* New York: 1952–67.

Bewer, J. A. *The Literature of the Old Testament.* Rev. ed. New York: 1962.

Ceram, C. *Gods, Graves, and Scholars.* New York: 1967.

Chiera, E. *They Wrote on Clay.* Phoenix Books.

Childe, V. G. *Man Makes Himself.* New York: 1952.

Childe, V. G. *What Happened in History.* Penguin Books.

Fakhry, Ahmed. *The Pyramids*. Chicago: 1961.

Finegan, Hack. *Archaeology of the World Religions*. Princeton: 1952.

Frankfort, H. *The Birth of Civilization in the Near East*. Anchor Books, 1959.

Frankfort, H; Wilson, J. A; Jacobsen, T; and Irwin, W. A. *The Intellectual Adventure of Ancient Man*. Chicago: 1959 (most of this book reprinted as *Before Philosophy*. Pelican Books).

Fryre, Richard N. *The Heritage of Persia*. Cleveland: 1963.

Glotz, G. *Aegean Civilization*. New York: 1925.

Heidel, Alexander. *The Babylonian Genesis*. Chicago: 1949.

Kramer, Samuel N. *The Sumerians: Their History, Culture, and Character*. Chicago: 1963.

Lloyd, S. *Early Anatolia*. Pelican Books.

Muller, Herbert J. *Freedom in the Ancient World*. New York: 1961.

Netanyahu, B. gen. ed. *The World History of the Jewish People. Ancient Times*. Vol. 1. *At the Dawn of Civilization, A Background of Biblical History*.

Olmstead, A. T. *A History of Palestine and Syria to the Macedonian Conquest*. New York: 1931.

Olmstead, A. T. *History of the Persian Empire*. Chicago: 1948.

Oppenheim, A. Leo. *Ancient Mesopotamia: Portrait of a Dead Civilization*. Chicago: 1964.

Piggott, Stuart. *Ancient Europe from the Beginnings of Agriculture to Classical Antiquity: A Survey*. Chicago: 1965.

Roebuck, Carl. *The World of Ancient Times*. New York: 1966.

Rostovtzeff, M. *A History of the Ancient World*. Vol. I. Oxford: 1926.

Steindorff, G; and Seele, K. C. *When Egypt Ruled the East*. Chicago: Phoenix Books.

Toynbee, A. J. *A Study of History* (abridged by D. C. Somerville). 2 vols. Oxford: 1947 and 1957.

Wilson, J. A. *The Burden of Egypt*. Chicago: 1951.

Wilson, J. A. *The Culture of Ancient Egypt*. Phoenix Books.

Wooley, L. *Prehistory and the Beginnings of Civilization*. New York: 1963.

Novels

Asch, Shalom. *Moses*. New York: 1951.

Asch, Shalom. *The Prophet*. New York: 1955.

Feuchtwanger, Lion. *Jephta and his Daughter*. New York: 1958.

Gautier, Theophile. *The Romance of a Mummy*. New York: 1886.

Lofts, Norah. *Esther*. New York: 1950.

London, Jack. *Before Adam*. New York: 1907.

Mann, Thomas. *Joseph and His Brothers*. New York: 1934.

Mann, Thomas. *Joseph in Egypt*. New York: 1938.

Mann, Thomas. *Joseph the Provider*. New York: 1944.
Mann, Thomas. *Young Joseph*. New York: 1946.
Schmitt, Gladys. *David the King*. New York: 1946.
Werfel, Franz. *Hearken unto the Voice*. New York: 1938.

Chronological Table for Part I

(NOTE: All dates before about 1500 B.C. are based on guess work, and may be subject to error of several hundred years. The dates assigned below are based on opinions of scholars in the Oriental Institute of the University of Chicago. Even later dates may err by as much as a decade: thus the reigns of the Assyrian or Persian kings can only be said to approximate the dates given below. In this and following chronological tables, asterisks have been placed opposite dates worth memorizing.)

B.C.

500,000 (?)–8000 (?)	Old Stone Age.
18,000 (?)	Appearance of modern man in Europe; displacement of Neanderthalers
8000 (?)–3000	Neolithic culture in Near East, spreading thence through Europe, Asia, and Africa.
*by 3000	Emergence of civilized societies in Mesopotamia and Egypt.
3000–2300	Old Kingdom in Egypt.
2800–2400	Pyramids built in Egypt.
2500–1500	Indus civilization.
2500–1400	Minoan civilization in Crete.
2350	Sargon of Akkad conquered most of Mesopotamia and Syria.
2050–1800	Middle Kingdom in Egypt.
1800	Hammurabi of Babylon united most of Mesopotamia under his rule.
*1750–1550	First general movement of peoples: Hyksos invasion of Egypt; Hittites in Asia Minor; Kassites and Mitanni in Mesopotamia; Mycenaeans in Greece; Aryans in India.
1600–1100	Mycenaean civilization.
1565	Ejection of Hyksos from Egypt; establishment of the New Kingdom or Empire.
1500 (?)	Beginning of civilization in China.
1400	Invention of alphabetic writing.
1400–1150	Struggle between Egyptians and Hittites for control of Syria; mutual weakening and eventual collapse of their respective empires.

1375	Akhnaton, Pharaoh of Egypt, tried to introduce Atonism.
*1250–1050	Second general movement of peoples and invasion of centers of civilization: Dorians in Greece bring on a "Dark Age"; Phrygians in Asia Minor; Medes and Persians in Iran; Hebrews in Palestine; Chaldeans in Mesopotamia; Aramaeans in Syria.
1025–930	United Hebrew monarchy under Saul, David, and Solomon. Divided after Solomon's death between Israel and Judah.
800	Founding of Carthage by the Phoenician city, Tyre.
750–539	Age of the major Hebrew prophets.
*745–612	Predominance of the Assyrian Empire in the Near East.
745–727	Tiglath-Piieser III, King of Assyria, conqueror and organizer of the Assyrian kingdom.
722	Assyrian conquest of Israel; deportation and disappearance of the ten tribes of Israel.
705–688	Sennacherib, King of Assyria; abortive attack on Egypt and Judea.
612	Overthrow of Assyrian empire by Medes and Chaldeans.
604–562	Nebuchadnezzar, King of Babylon.
586	Conquest of Judah by Nebuchadnezzar; the Babylonian captivity.
*550–334	Predominance of the Persian Empire in the Near East.
550–527	Cyrus, King of the Persians.
550	Cyrus overthrew the Median empire.
546	Cyrus conquered Lydia (Croesus).
539	Cyrus conquered Babylon; permitted Jews to return to Palestine.
527–521	Cambyses, King of Persia; conquered Egypt.
521–484	Darius, the Great, King of Persia, conquered parts of the Indus valley, areas of Central Asia and European Thrace.
484–465	Xerxes, King of Persia; failed to conquer Greece.
458–28 (?)	Reforms of Nehemiah and Ezra in Jerusalem.
*334–323	Alexander the Great, King of Macedon, conquered the entire Persian empire.

PART II

Classical Civilization (c. 900 B.C.-A.D. 900)

Classical civilization may be defined as the pattern of social life which grew up in the Greek city states, spread through the Mediterranean basin, reaching its maximum extent in the time of the Roman Empire, and then broke up gradually through a period of barbarian invasions. Such a definition is arbitrary. During the time span of some 1800 years profound changes took place in every aspect of human life. The Frankish warrior of Charlemagne's army would scarcely have recognized Homer's Achilles as a fellow participant in a common civilization; nor would either of these have felt much kinship with an Aristotle or a St. Paul.

Viewed as the rise and fall of certain types of economic and political organization, the whole period nevertheless presents a certain unity. From the point of view of intellect and feeling, however, the rise of Christianity constitutes a tremendous division of what is here lumped together, and many historians have used this criterion to divide the period into two, traditionally labeled Ancient and Early Medieval. If the student prefers this or some other grouping, it should be possible for him, by the use of a little imagination, to impose his chosen pattern on the information here presented.

In a similarly arbitrary way, the major phases through which Classical civilization passed have been marked off as follows: A. Greek city states; B. Hellenistic kingdoms; C. Roman Republic; D. Roman Empire. Following the breakup of the Roman empire three divergent societies divided the territory which had formerly been under Roman sway; Byzantium, the barbarian kingdoms of the West, and the Arab empire. Only very brief notice of the first and last of these has been included in this book, not because they lack interest or importance, but because Byzantine and Arab civilizations are here considered not in their own right, but solely from the point of view of their connection with Classical and their influence upon western European civilization.

33

A. The Greek City States (c. 900 B.C.–336 B.C.)

1. GEOGRAPHICAL SETTING

The Greek world centered around the basin of the Aegean sea, with a secondary center in southern Italy and Sicily. These areas, where the characteristic pattern of classical civilization was first worked out (as the pattern of Oriental civilization first evolved in the great river valleys of the Near East) have a common climate and topography.

The land of Greece is mountainous. Pockets of soil in river valleys, lacustrine and coastal plains are the only areas that can easily be tilled. Inhospitable mountain slopes separate one plain from another and make land communication difficult. As a result, the sea was and remains the main avenue of transport. The sunken coastline of the Aegean provided innumerable harbors for small ships such as those built in antiquity; and the island chains of the Aegean and Ionian seas made navigation relatively easy and safe. These geographical conditions help to explain why the Greeks from very early times took to the sea as pirates, colonists, and traders. Equally, the isolation of the fertile plains from one another contributed to the formation of small independent city states. Barren mountains provided natural boundaries between many of the political units into which ancient Greece was divided.

The Greek city states were very small by modern standards. Attica is not more than forty air miles in its longest dimension, and Attica was one of the larger states of ancient Greece. The whole peninsula is so small that one can see all the way from the Ionian to the Aegean sea from an airplane on a clear day. Moreover, the famous cities of antiquity occupied only a part of modern Greece. The Greek mainland north and west of Boeotia remained semibarbarous when Athens and Sparta were at their height. Classical Greek civilization was closely linked to the coastline and never penetrated far inland. On the other hand, it did spread widely along the Aegean, Black Sea and Mediterranean coastlines, far beyond the confines of the modern Greek state.

The most important of these "colonial" areas were the Asia Minor coast and the coastal fringe of Sicily and southern Italy. The eastern shore of the Aegean is more hospitable than Greece proper. Broad river valleys lead into the interior of Asia Minor, offering natural trade routes to the Orient. Rocky promontories divide one bay from another, however, and make the sea the main avenue of north–south communication. Southern Italy and especially Sicily also offer wider plains and a less rugged topography than Greece itself. In ancient times these areas produced large amounts of grain for export, and were famous for their agricultural wealth.

The climate of the Aegean and of southern Italy is comparatively mild. The seasons are sharply differentiated, however, for in winter the zone of prevailing westerlies covers Greece and Italy, bringing rain, and, occasionally, snow. In summer, the trade winds blow steadily over these lands from the northeast. The summer heat is modified thereby, but the winds are dessicating. As a consequence, it seldom rains between April and October. During this time, the clear skies invite life in the open. This aspect of the climate permitted the frequent outdoor public meetings that were characteristic of the Greek city states.

Agricultural practices had to be adapted to the rainfall. Grain was planted in the autumn, harvested in early summer. Only deep-rooted plants could withstand the summer drought. Two such plants, the grape-vine and the olive tree, became, with grain, the agricultural staples of the Greek world. Fodder crops needed moister summers. Hence, only in the north, where summer rain sometimes fell, could horses be easily raised; and in classical times the possession of horses was always a sign of great wealth. Oxen and donkeys, able to live on less succulent herbage, were the principal draught animals; sheep and goats, pastured on the mountain slopes, provided meat, milk, wool, and leather.

Mineral resources were not abundant. Some silver and gold was mined in classical times, especially in Attica and Thrace; marble and excellent potters' clay abounded almost everywhere. But for some basic raw materials the Greeks had to depend on foreign sources. Local supplies of iron and copper had to be supplemented by imports; and (at least by the fifth century when population had grown and shipping was of prime importance), timber, flax and grain likewise came from abroad.

2. FORMATION OF THE CITY STATES (TO *c.* 750 B.C.)

The Greeks did not begin to use letters for writing until about 700 B.C., and only scraps have survived from before 600 B.C. For earlier times archaeological remnants and the Homeric epics are our only guides. The rediscovery of Cretan and Mycenaean civilization is one of the romances of archaeology; but the problem of the relation of these civilizations to the people whom we, with the Romans, call Greeks, but who called themselves Hellenes, is much disputed. In classical times, the Greeks recognized three great divisions among themselves: Aeolian, Ionian, and Dorian. It is tempting to assume that these divisions correspond to three waves of invasion; but the testimony of Homer and the record revealed by archaeology do not bear out any such simple scheme. Actually, the immigration of the Greek-speaking population into the Aegean basin appears to have been a complicated process, involving many separate conquests and flights, and extensive mixings of populations.

Neolithic development in Greece was greatly accelerated when the influence of Minoan civilization (2500–1400 B.C.) radiated outward from its center in Crete to the smaller islands of the Aegean and to "shore stations" on mainland Greece and the coast of Asia Minor. Remains from such sites are called Helladic. Probably about 1800 B.C. Greek-speaking war bands appeared on the European mainland, at about the time when other Indo-European peoples appeared all along the northern boundaries of the Near Eastern world. (See above, p. 17.) The newcomers seem to have constituted themselves a ruling aristocracy; but they borrowed much from the more civilized ways of their new subjects. The amalgamation of the war-like ways of the conquerors with civilized traditions derived from Crete we call Mycenaean (*c.* 1600–1100 B.C.)

Mycenaean remains are distinguished from Minoan by the much greater prominence of warlike materials. Great fortresses built of large stones were erected at such places as Mycenae, Tiryns, and Orchomenos. In later times the Greeks attributed such masonry to semidivine beings, the Cyclops, for it seemed there mere men could not have handled such blocks. Many of the Greek legends were derived in part from historical events of

Mycenaean times: the stories of Agamemnon and Clytemnestra, Oepidus, the Trojan war, and others. They were later to form the raw material for Homer's poems and for the tragedies of the Attic dramatists. What may be fact and what poetic embroidery in these legends is hard to say. Archaeology has startlingly revealed that Troy may in fact have been besieged and captured by the leagued princes of Greece (*c.* 1184 B.C.); and Homer's picture of a warlike, semibarbarous society, united into a loose confederacy under the leadership of King Agamemnon of Mycenae, is probably substantially accurate.

The political centralization of the Mycenaean age broke up when fresh invaders from the north, the Dorians, appeared about 1100 B.C., overthrew the citadels, and half-depopulated the land. The Dorians did not occupy the whole of Greece, however. In historic times, Dorians inhabited most of the Peloponnese, Crete, the southwestern coastline of Asia Minor, and some of the smaller islands of the Aegean. The Aeolians occupied the northwestern corner of the Peloponnese, the mainland north of the Gulf of Corinth, and the north Aegean coastline of Asia Minor. In between, the Ionians lived along the central coast of Asia Minor (Ionia), populated most of the Aegean islands, and held a corner of the mainland in Attica. The distinction between Dorian, Aeolian, and Ionian was based primarily on language, for each group spoke a distinct Greek dialect. The Aeolians played a relatively small part in classical civilization. Sparta was the leading Dorian city, seconded by Corinth. Athens became the greatest Ionian city; but in early times Miletus and other cities of Asia Minor were of far greater importance.

During the "Dark Age" which followed the Dorian invasion, the rudiments of Greek classical civilization took shape. When the Dorians came into Greece they were organized into tribes, based on real or fictitious blood relationship. Tribes were in turn subdivided into kindreds, brotherhoods and, at the bottom, patrilineal families. At each level, the group protected its members, by force if need be, and was collectively responsible for its members' actions. It is probable that fixed individual property in land was not recognized by custom. Rather, the kindred group exercised a sort of collective ownership, proportioning out shares of cultivable land among its members. A particular plot of land was not cultivated continuously. Instead, after several years' cropping when weeds became too thick, old fields were abandoned and fresh land broken to the plow. As long as population was sparse and abundant wasteland existed, any exact definition of property rights was not necessary. Under such conditions, mobility of population was relatively great. A tribe could easily transfer from one plain to another, displacing its earlier possessors; and indeed the Dorian invasions probably occurred in just such a fashion by a series of movements by many separate groups from one fertile plain to another.

As time passed, population increased and agricultural technique improved so that continuous cultivation of a particular farm became possible and necessary. (Instead of abandoning a field to weeds, it was plowed and left fallow. By plowing at the right time of year, most weeds could be killed before they seeded. Hence, the next year the soil could be planted with grain again, and a good crop secured.) With this development, movements of population became less common, and the ties of locality tended to become more important than those of kinship. The result was not the disappearance of tribal organization, for tribes persisted as religious and political units well into historical times. Rather a new political unit, the city state, or *polis*, as the Greeks called it, began to emerge from the territorial association of various kindred groups. The idea that the citizens of the fully developed *polis* were akin to one another never entirely disappeared. But kinship as a basis for social organization steadily lost ground before the territorial and collective loyalty to the *polis* itself. In fifth-century Athens, for example, tribes survived only as voting units, and blood relationship between fellow tribesmen was almost wholly fictitious.

The *polis* or city state was to be the cell of classical civilization. Even when larger political structures were superimposed, city states remained the vehicle for most of the social and economic, and for much of the political activity, of classical society. It is therefore important to understand clearly what a *polis* was.

A *polis* comprised a town or city with a stretch of surrounding countryside. In early times, a citizen was normally a farmer; later this ceased to be true in some of the more active and important cities, but the feeling that a citizen should own land and only so could fully become a member of the community persisted throughout antiquity. Within the area of the city state, justice was administered by official representatives of the *polis*. Blood feuds, which had been chronic in tribal society, were ended, and the habit of carrying arms decayed as the need for self protection against strangers disappeared. Instead, military enterprise was brought under the control of magistrates, and directed solely toward defense or aggression on behalf of the *polis*. Religious ceremonies, too, were entrusted to representatives of the *polis*, and were conducted on behalf of all the citizens. Private property in land came to be universally recognized as settled agriculture spread. Pasture land, however, remained as a common possession, as did mineral finds.

With the weakening of the tribes and the consolidation of the *polis*, the loyalty of individuals came to be firmly fixed upon the city of their birth. The collective welfare of the *polis* could, and regularly did, demand the sacrifice of the citizens' time, wealth and even life in case of need. Larger loyalties were almost entirely obscured by the passionate attachment each citizen felt toward his native city.

The classical *polis* differed in one important respect from modern territorial states: a *polis* was always a privileged corporation. Not everyone who lived in the territory of the *polis* was a citizen; and in some of them (as Sparta) only a very small minority enjoyed full citizen rights. In every Greek state, slaves were excluded from citizenship by their status, and they were sometimes very numerous. Moreover, strangers who came from some other city were not admitted to citizenship except by special grant. The aristocratic idea that citizens should be ready to fight and to deliberate, but should not have to work for a living was deep rooted in Greek tradition, even in democratic cities like Athens. This ideal presupposed the existence of a slave or politically inferior laboring class.

The steps whereby tribes were transformed into *poleis* can only be surmised. In Attica, legend attached the name of Theseus to the measure which united previously scattered hamlets into a single government and twelve tribes into one political community. Backward regions of Greece retained tribal government into historic times, and there are a few records of the formation of city states in these regions by the deliberate action of the inhabitants. Perhaps the famous city states of classical Greece— Athens, Sparta, Corinth, Thebes, Argos, Megara, and the rest—were similarly formed. In Ionia, on the other hand, it is possible that political organization based upon cities survived unbroken from Mycenaean into classical times.

The Greeks of the Dark Age were rude and barbarous. Skill in stone cutting disappeared, and local variations in pottery styles attest the absence of extensive contact between different parts of the country. Command of the sea was lost to the Phoenicians, and maritime skill seemingly suffered partial eclipse. On the other hand, the use of iron for tools and weapons was generally established in place of the bronze which had served Mycenaean craftsmen and warriors. Iron was cheaper and for some uses better than bronze. Perhaps the most important technical advance made possible by the relative cheapness of the new metal was the introduction of iron plow shares. This made tillage of the soil far more efficient than it had been earlier when plows were made simply of wood. Fallowing became a practicable routine with metal plow shares, as not before.

The decline of civilization in Ionia was in every respect less than in European Greece; and it was from Ionia that the great literary achievement of the Greek Dark Age came: the epic poems of Homer. The authorship and content of the *Iliad* and *Odyssey* have posed many problems for modern scholars. The dramatic date of both poems is in the Mycenaean age, and many of Homer's descriptions fit the archaeological remains of that time with amazing accuracy. But there are other passages which reflect a much later period. It seems most probable that the poems of Homer drew upon a tradition of heroic verse, recited by professional bards for the entertainment of kings and nobles, perhaps without break from the time of Agamemnon. As time went on, elaborate conventions arose—the Homeric "fixed epithet," for example, which made the dawn always "rosy fingered" and the seas "wine dark"—and what may once have been separate stories coalesced around particular heroes: Achilles in the *Iliad*, and Odysseus in the *Odyssey*. Whether the poems are the work of one man, Homer; whether the *Iliad* was composed by one poet and the *Odyssey* by another; or whether both are the work of compilers has never been agreed upon by modern critics. But peculiarities of dialect seem to indicate that the Homeric poems were reduced to their final form sometime in the eighth century B.C. in Ionia.

The artistic power of the poems can be felt even in translation and after the lapse of nearly three millennia. Homer's poems have entered deeply into our cultural tradition. They provided a model for all subsequent epic poetry, and their impact on later Greek culture was tremendous. Not only did study and memorization of Homer's poems constitute an important part of classical Greek education, but the religious conceptions embodied in the *Iliad* and *Odyssey* became something of a standard for Greek religion, poetry, and art.

Homer's gods were men writ large, endowed with immortality and with miraculous but limited powers. Their relations among themselves were an image of political relations on earth: Zeus, like Agamemnon, headed a group of unruly subordinates. The gods were willful and sometimes capricious. They might occasionally be induced by sacrifices and prayers to forward human designs, but individual gods were liable to take spite and remain implacable. Similarly one god might champion and another god oppose a particular man, so that his career on earth came to depend on a contest between the rival gods. Heinous crimes might be punished by divine wrath, but the gods could not be trusted to reward good actions and punish evildoing, being far too busy with their own caprices to be systematic about anything. Above the gods loomed a vague predestination or fate, which the gods could only partially control or even foreknow; beneath them were numberless spirits who inhabited springs and trees, mountains and streams. Men's souls were immortal, but after death they lived in a shadowy and cheerless underworld, and longed vainly for a return to the world of the living.

The Olympian religion, as these Homeric conceptions are often called, offered little comfort for the individual who found life on earth difficult or beset with injustice. It was innocent of philosophical speculation or metaphysical subtlety. It sought simply to explain the unpredictable twists of human life, as experienced in a rude, semi-barbarous age; and did so by anthropomorphic myth.

3. GREEK EXPANSION TO 510 B.C.

---

    a. Economic development
        1) Population
        2) Colonization
        3) Growth of Trade and Industry
        4) Improvement of Agriculture

    b. Social Development
        1) Classes
        2) Military Changes

    c. Political Transformations
        1) General Line of Development
        2) Sparta and the Formation of the
            Peloponnesian League

    d. Cultural Development
        1) Religion
        2) Literature
        3) Art
        4) Philosophy and Science

---

a. Economic Development

1) Population. During the centuries when the Greek city states took form, population grew, probably quite rapidly. Population growth led in time to a shortage of cultivable land. Obviously land shortage did not become a problem for each city at exactly the same time; but by 700 B.C. the difficulty was general in the regions of Greece which were to become the center of city state civilization. Pressure of population on the land was relieved in several ways: by extensive colonization; by improvement in agricultural techniques; by the development of trade and industry as a supplementary means of livelihood; and, sometimes, by conquest of neighboring territory from weaker cities. In addition, land shortage sharpened the differentiation of social classes and led to widespread struggles between rich and poor. Each of these developments requires some description.

2) Colonization. About 750 B.C. the Greeks began to send out colonists in large numbers. The founding of a colony was a collective enterprise. A city, finding its population too great for the land it possessed, organized an expedition under an *oecist* or founder. Those who chose to emigrate, or

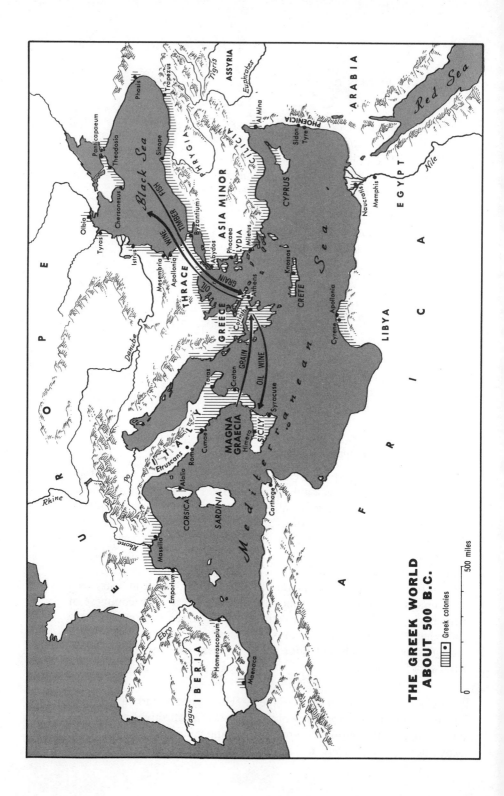

THE GREEK WORLD
ABOUT 500 B.C.

|||||| Greek colonies

0   500 miles

who were designated by the city magistrates, boarded ships and sailed off to some chosen spot, and there proceeded to set up a city state of their own. The new city was politically independent of the mother city, bound to it only by loose religious and sentimental ties. As a result, colonial empires did not arise from the movement, since the citizen body of each new colony was quite separate from that of the mother city. The cities most active in colonization were Miletus, Chalcis and Corinth; but many others followed the example of these leaders on a smaller scale.

Colonists looked mainly for two things: good agricultural land and harbors or beaching grounds for their ships. Only at a later time, when the possibilities of sea-borne commerce had been realized, did strategic trading positions come into prominence. Greek colonies clung always to the coast. As a result, in wide areas of the Mediterranean basin Greek colonial cities became transmitters of civilization to more backward natives whom they had driven inland.

Greek colonization extended in three main directions: north to the Black Sea coast, the Sea of Marmora and the north Aegean; west to southern Italy and Sicily, with offshoots in southern France and eastern Spain; and southward to Libya. One very important colony was established at Naucratis in Egypt. Through Naucratis, the Greeks came into contact with the civilization and skills of the Egyptians and learned much from them. In other areas of the Mediterranean littoral, hostile peoples shut out Greek efforts at colonization. The Phoenicians excluded them from Syria and the neighboring coast; and in the west, the Carthaginians safeguarded Algeria and part of Sicily from Greek penetration. Northern Italy was similarly closed to the Greeks by the Etruscans.

By about 550 B.C. the great period of colonization came to an end. Lack of fertile, inadequately defended land along the coast was one reason; the successful internal development of Greek cities, making absorption of surplus rural population possible at home, was a second factor.

3) Growth of Trade and Industry. Though the early colonization was principally inspired by a desire for agricultural land, from the beginning trader-pirates must have explored ahead of settlement, discovering lands where the native peoples were not well organized to resist Greek colonization, and where the soil promised good crops.

At first Greek traders acted principally as middlemen between the developed centers of Oriental civilization and the back country of the Mediterranean basin, competing with Phoenicians who had earlier monopolized that role. Miletus and other cities of the Asia Minor coast were the first to seize upon the opportunities this sort of trade afforded, although Corinth, Chalcis, and Eretria also became prominent trading centers in the eighth and seventh centuries. Lydia and Egypt exported wool and a variety of manufactured articles in return for the metals, timber, and other raw materials which Greek seamen were able to collect from the Black Sea coast and in Italian and Sicilian waters.

Greek artisans soon proceeded to imitate the products of Oriental workshops, learning how to make fine pottery, woolen cloth, metal tools, weapons and ornaments. These they not only used themselves, but exported to colonial regions and to the barbaric peoples of Europe. Trade with the Etruscans in Italy and with the Scythians in southern Russia became particularly important. Trade was facilitated by the introduction of coinage (about 650 B.C.), a device which the Greeks borrowed from the Lydians. Coins of silver came to be a measure of value not only in foreign trade but at home as well, and accelerated the development of a market economy and economic specialization within the Greek cities.

The development of trade and manufactures obviously modified the social composition of Greek cities. But farming remained the normal occupation of the citizen, and improvements in agriculture were of basic importance, sustaining both trade and industry by providing the most important export Greek cities had to offer: olive oil and wine.

4) Improvement of Agriculture. The raising of grain and the tending of livestock were the principal modes of land utilization in the Dark Age. As land became scarce, fertile grazing lands were plowed up, and rough mountain slopes alone remained as pasture. There only the hardier animals could be raised successfully. In other words, sheep, goats and donkeys became more important than horses and cattle, the animals on which primitive Greeks, like other Indo-Europeans, had mainly depended. But even when all the suitable land had been brought under cultivation, many cities found that they could not raise enough grain to supply their inhabitants. Some cities—most notably in Ionia, Athens, and the Aegean islands—solved this difficulty by specializing their agriculture. They did this by using a large proportion of available land for raising grapes and olives. Olive oil and wine could be exchanged for larger quantities of grain than could possibly be raised at home on the land devoted to olive groves and vineyards. The explanation for this advantage lay in the fact that olive trees and grapevines flourish only in regions of mild climate. Along the Black Sea coast, for example, the winters were too severe for them to grow.

In addition, the cultivation of these special crops required skill and patience; and in some areas which were climatically suited to their production, such as southern Italy and Sicily, the inhabitants for many years found it easier to concentrate on raising grain while importing their wine and olive oil. The use of wine is obvious to us; olive oil, however, played a role in the ancient economy which it is difficult to appreciate at first glance. Oil was almost the sole source of edible fat; in addition it served in place of soap as a body cleanser, and was burnt in lamps to provide light. Because of these manifold uses, olive oil became indispensable to civilized living throughout antiquity; and it remains to this day a staple of Mediterranean life.

The cultivation of olives had an additional advantage for Greece. Rocky hill slopes, which could scarcely be used as grain fields, could support olive trees quite successfully; and in effect, the potential productive acreage was greatly increased by this fact. But these crops had serious disadvantages. For one thing there was a gap of several years between the time when the trees or vines were planted and the time when the first crop could be expected; and only a man with some capital could afford such a wait. Moreover, to depend on the import of essential foodstuff was perilous in a time when navigation was dangerous and irregular. Piracy, war, or shipwreck might at any time disastrously interrupt the supply of grain from overseas.

Nevertheless, olive-vine agriculture spread as population pressure made the older self-sufficiency impossible. The Ionian cities were apparently pioneers in this development; but it was in Attica after 500 B.C. that agricultural specialization was carried to its highest pitch. In later centuries, the olive-vine type of agriculture spread over most of the Mediterranean world. The exchange between areas producing oil and wine for market, and those producing a surplus of grain always constituted the basic economic circulation of the classical world.

It is worth observing that this type of economy was different from the predominant economic pattern of Oriental civilization. Oriental cities did not normally get their food from overseas, but depended instead upon the immediately surrounding farmland. Only the Phoenician cities may have approached the characteristic Greek-classical pattern, but it is not clear that they ever imported large quantities of grain to supplement local production.

b. Social Development

1) Classes. Homeric society was thoroughly aristocratic. Warriors of noble blood constituted a superior class among whom the kings were scarcely more than the first among equals. As Greek society settled down to more peaceful ways, the claims of ancestry and personal prowess were reinforced by the economic power which came from landownership. Slaves, landless men, and tenant farmers tilled the fields of the nobles. In addition to such estates, there existed numerous small farmers who worked their own soil, but as generations passed, subdivision of such small farms among numerous children brought many families into very precarious straits. The introduction of money made their situation worse, for in a bad harvest year, small farmers might be compelled to go into debt, and could give only their land or their bodies as security. In this fashion debtors who found themselves unable to repay a loan might lose their land or even become slaves. This process tended to enlarge the estates of the noble and the rich who were in the best position to make loans. Under such circumstances, hostility between rich and poor became chronic and acute after about 800 B.C.

The appearance of artisan and merchant classes modified Greek society in some of the most important cities, but the political influence of this group was reduced by the fact that many artisans were slaves and many merchants were foreigners, native to other cities or even to non-Greek communities. Moreover, in the Greek world at large trade and industry played a relatively slight role. Only in a few favored cities did a numerous and influential artisan and merchant population arise.

2) Military Changes. The consolidation of the nobles' power through economic processes was profoundly checked by a transformation in military tactics which took place between 700 and 600 B.C. In Homeric times, fighting was done mainly by individual champions who rode to battle in chariots; later, after the Dorian invasions, cavalry played a larger role, but battles remained mêlées in which individual warriors proved their skill and strength in confused hand to hand combat. In such fighting, the nobles played the principal part, for only they were rich enough to equip themselves with the weapons and horses which effective fighting required.

About 650 B.C., however, a new and far more formidable type of battle formation developed: the infantry phalanx. The phalanx proved capable of overcoming the scattered attack of individual horsemen. As a result, cavalry formations were relegated to reconaissance, pursuit of a broken enemy, and most important, checking hostile cavalry from harassing the infantry phalanx in the rear. The main brunt of battle was borne by hoplites—heavy armed infantrymen, equipped with helmet, sword and shield, and arrayed in close order some eight ranks deep. The phalanx was trained to maneuver as a unit, keeping step by the use of a special war chant, the paean. Greek phalanxes never became adept at wheeling movements, and in particular could not operate effectively on rough or steeply sloping ground, where closed ranks could not be maintained. As a result, until the Roman conquest, Greek battles were regularly fought in plains, and it became something of a convention to permit an enemy to deploy his troops before joining battle by charging at a run. Then followed much pushing and stabbing until one or the other phalanx broke its ranks and fled. By discarding their heavy shields, it was usually possible for defeated soldiers to escape with relatively few casualties since the victors, for their own safety, had to keep their formation more or less intact. Not until the time of Philip of Macedon (d. 336 B.C.) were murderous pursuits of a broken enemy introduced into Greek warfare.

The development of the infantry phalanx made the individual skill and bravery of the nobles far less important. Instead, the discipline of the whole body of hoplites became decisive in determining the outcome of battle. Since men of moderate means could afford the equipment of a hoplite, the military balance of power in the state shifted away from the nobles and lodged in a broader (though still restricted) number of citizens.

c. Political Transformations

1) General Line of Development. Homeric society was ruled over by kings, assisted by a council of noble warriors. In special emergencies, an assembly of all the people might be called to hear advice or choose between different proposals made to them by noble leaders. From these basic elements the constitutions of all later Greek city states were derived. During the disintegration of the Dark Age, the power of high kings such as Agamemnon disappeared; but each tribal unit presumably retained in miniature something of the Homeric system of government. We must rely on inference from later constitutional practice to know what governmental changes occurred during the period before written records became available; and even with this indirect method, detailed knowledge is almost confined to the development of the Athenian state. In Athens, and probably in other cities as well, one of the tribal kings became king of the *polis* when it was formed. Heads of the constituent tribes formed the king's council, and assemblies were probably called only when emergencies suggested the need.

About 800 B.C. the Athenian kings began to lose their powers to the nobles. Kingship ceased to be hereditary, and became, in effect, an office which could be occupied only for a fixed term. Other magistrates, chosen from among the nobility, began to share the royal powers, administering justice and leading the army. In later times, the duties of the "king" were mainly religious and politically unimportant. Similar changes occurred in in other Greek cities, but we are ignorant of all details.

The nobles, when they had successfully trimmed the royal power, did not long enjoy their new position unchallenged. Wealthy newcomers were able to make their way into positions of power and influence, even when they lacked noble family connections. These newcomers were men who acquired landed estates through purchase rather than inheritance, and were recruited from among successful merchants and money lenders. Greek political theorists called such a form of government an oligarchy. Under oligarchical governments, wealth, as measured by possession of land, replaced family connection and inherited religious prerogative as the criterion for participation in public affairs.

Oligarchy was further modified after the military revolution described above. The men on whom the *polis* depended for its defense were obviously in a position to make their political wishes count. They had both arms and numbers of their side. Consequently the "hoplite franchise" became common among Greek cities, whereby the right to vote in the election of magistrates and to determine important policies was lodged in the body of moderately well-to-do citizens who were able to equip themselves with spear and shield.

But many citizens were too poor to be able to afford a hoplite's equipment. Their economic hardship, and especially the danger of falling into debt-slavery constituted potent sources of discontent. The result was unrest which repeatedly burst out in violence.

In many cities complaints of oppression at the hands of the magistrates who decided legal cases led to the writing down of the law so that all might know the principles which guided the judge. But mere definition of the law failed to solve the social conflicts which were tearing apart the city states of Greece; and in many of them, especially in those which took a leading part in the development of commerce and industry, successful revolutionary movements broke out in the course of the seventh and sixth centuries. Leaders of such movements were called tyrants. In most cases they were members of the nobility who turned against their fellow nobles, became champions of the popular cause, and established a personal government, drawing support from the industrial, trading, and impoverished agricultural classes. Tyrants regularly banished or executed political rivals, and sometimes seized the estates of noble families, and distributed the land among the poor. Some tyrants used their power to foster trade and to facilitate the transition to olive-vine agriculture.

Few Greek tyrannies remained successful for long. Their extralegal position made them easy targets of attack, and in many instances the tyrants could not resolve the social discontents which had helped them to rise, so that popular sentiment soon turned against the usurper. By 510 B.C. all the tyrannies in mainland Greece had been overthrown; but in Asia Minor, Sicily, and southern Italy, tyrants continued to play a prominent part for many years to come.

To understand the further political development of the Greek states, it is necessary to turn attention to the rise of Sparta.

2) Sparta and the Formation of the Peloponnesian League. By 500 B.C., Sparta had a constitution and a way of life quite different from that of any other Greek *polis*. The peculiarity of Sparta was not manifest in the early seventh century, when that Dorian city, located in the valley of the Eurotas, was ruled by a wealthy aristocracy and lived much as did its neighbors. When population began to press on the cultivable soil, the Spartans turned

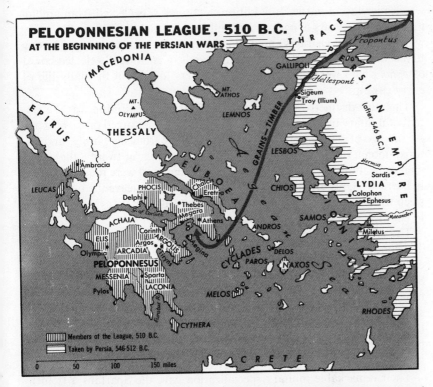

rather toward conquest of neighboring territory than to the more usual Greek solutions of colonization and intensification of economic activity. Early in the seventh century they overran the rich agricultural area of neighboring Messenia, and reduced the Messenian population to something like slavery. Then the Messenians revolted, probably about 630 B.C., and a bitter, long-fought war ensued.

This struggle had a decisive effect on Sparta's constitutional development. During the course of the war, the Spartans converted their army to phalanx form. To make the phalanx efficient and win the war, the Spartans were compelled to institute a rigid disipline which was carried over into peacetime. and even elaborated. until the Spartan *polis* became little more than a barracks and the citizen body was transformed into something like a standing army holding down a conquered territory. Undoubtedly what led the Spartans to transform their city in this drastic fashion was fear of another revolt such as the one which had nearly destroyed them towards the end of the seventh century.

As it finally crystallized. the Spartan constitution was a peculiar blend of monarchy. aristocracy. and democracy. Two hereditary royal families divided the prerogatives of kingship. most important of which was leadership in battle. In addition. a council was elected from among men over sixty years of age; and all full citizens could attend the assembly which elected magistrates and decided major questions of policy. The day to day direction of the state was in the hands of an annually elected board of *ephors* who were given very wide powers to control the daily life of every citizen.

The most distinctive thing about the Spartan constitution was the system of military training and barracks life which it enforced on all citizens. At the age of seven every boy was taken away from his family, and entered upon a rigorous program of physical training; at twenty, the young men were admitted to regular army formations, and were required to live in barracks. Only after the age of thirty could a man leave the barracks to sleep with his family; but until the age of sixty all Spartiates were required to eat their meals in an army mess.

The economic support for this garrison was provided by slave labor. The conquered Messenians and descendants of the pre-Dorian inhabitants of Sparta itself, were compelled to cultivate the land for the benefit of the Spartan citizens. They were known as *helots*. In addition, there was another group in the population, the *perioeci*, who were personally free but enjoyed no political rights. *Perioeci* might own land which they farmed themselves. They also supplied the craftsmen and traders necessary for the maintenance of the Spartan phalanx. In time of war they formed contingents of troops. Even the *helots* were used as light armed troops.

Their remarkable military specialization gave the Spartans a tremendous advantage against other Greek states in the sixth century B.C. In effect, professional soldiers were pitted against a militia; and the Spartans soon established a reputation for invincibility in the field. On the strength of their military superiority, the Spartans were able to conclude a series of alliances with nearby states in the Peloponnese, and assumed effective leadership of most of mainland Greece. They used their preponderance to overthrow tyrants and repress revolutionary movements in other Greek cities, for the constant fear of the Spartans was that such movements might encourage unrest among the helots.

The Peloponnesian League, as this system of alliances is commonly called, did not extend over the whole Peloponnese. Argos and most of the cities of Achaia never joined. But by 510 B.C. the rest of the peninsula was united into a loose federation under Sparta's leadership. It was mainly a military alliance. In time of war, each member state furnished troops which fought under a Spartan commander; but in peacetime local affairs were entirely in the hands of each city's officials, and no money payments were made to the Spartans. War between members of the league was occasionally tolerated when Sparta's interest was not directly involved. In general, the policy of the league was a conservative one: to maintain oligarchic

GREEK PALACES AND TEMPLES

We are so accustomed to classic Greek architectural forms
that it is difficult to look at the restrained simplicity
and elegance of the surviving ruins with unbiased eyes.
The columned halls of Minos and the frowning fortifications
of Agamemnon both found worthy successors in the architectural
complex of the Athenian Acropolis, for the Acropolis
was itself a fortress girded round in Pericles' age by mighty
city walls that connected Athens with the sea
whence came the city's wealth.

Palace of Minos, Knossos, Crete
Circa **1500** B.C.
(Hirmer Verlag München)

The setting of the palace of Minos among the Cretan hills emphasizes the
absence of fortifications. This openness mirrors the nature of Minoan society,
which developed through commercial rather than military contact
with various peoples and cultures of the entire Mediterranean coastland.

Lion Gate of Mycenae, Mycenae, Greece
Circa 1500 B.C.
(Hirmer Verlag München)

The walls at Mycenae, often twenty feet thick, bespeak a preoccupation with
defense and war that contrasts sharply with Minoan priestly commercialism.
This Lion Gate was the main entrance to Agamemnon's citadel. Note
how anyone approaching must expose his unshielded right side
to defenders on the wall.

The Parthenon, Acropolis, Athens
447-432 B.C.
(Alinari Art Reference Bureau)

The Parthenon, built under Pericles, is the focal point of the Athenian
Acropolis. The temple was dedicated to Athena, patron goddess of Athens,
and is an example of the Doric style. The subtlety of proportions,
balancing horizontals and verticals, was achieved without use of any
geometrically straight lines, for all surfaces are curved, sometime only
slightly. The stones of the Parthenon were fitted so carefully that mortar
was not required to hold the structure together.

The Erechtheum, Acropolis, Athens
421-406 B.C.
(Alinari Art Reference Bureau)

The Erechtheum, begun only eleven years after the completion of the Parthenon,
aimed more at opulence and elegance than at Doric simplicity. The
temple was dedicated to Erechtheus, a serpent god and mythical king of
Athens. The slender Ionic columns and decorated capitals lack the
monumental strength of the Parthenon's columns, yet the Erechtheum's
ornamental details offered models for countless later buildings
down to modern times.

governments at home, encourage them elsewhere, and refrain from foreign adventure unless the threat of attack was unmistakable.

d. Cultural Development

1) Religion. The religion of the Greeks as it took shape between 700 and 500 B.C. was strongly affected by the beliefs consecrated in the poems of Homer. Yet Homer's Olympian religion was not everything. Many local shrines, temples and rites preserved ideas that were scarcely in accord with the Homeric conception of the gods. In the course of the seventh century a religious movement called Orphism spread widely over Greece. It was a mystic cult, associated with the worship of the god of wine, Dionysos. Celebrations were often frenzied. The frenzy was interpreted as a mystic union with the god; and Orphic priests held out the hope of eternal happiness to the initiated after death. The Mysteries of Eleusis, in Attica, similarly, though in less ecstatic fashion, promised a blessed life after death to those who had participated in the rituals which celebrated the death and resurrection of Persephone. goddess of the Underworld. and the sorrowing and rejoicing of her mother, Demeter, goddess of fertility and vegetation.

Another important element in Greek religion was the pan-Hellenic oracles and celebrations. The most famous oracle was that of Delphi, where the priests of Apollo and the Pythia, or priestess, were believed to convey the answer of the god to inquiries put to him by worshippers. The Delphic oracle became important as a moderator of inter-city conflicts and as a censor of morals. The oracles, as delivered by the priests, often discouraged violence and brutality.

The quadrennial celebrations at Olympia were second only to the Delphic oracle among pan-Hellenic institutions. Gymnastic competitions and horse races as well as religious ceremonies brought the leading citizens of all the states of Greece together at the Olympics. Interstate fighting was frequently suspended for the duration of the Olympic festival. Similar but less famous celebrations were held at Corinth, Argos, and Delphi. These pan-Hellenic gatherings, coupled with the oracle of Delphi, were the only tangible institutional bond embracing all the Greek states. Yet as Greek civilization developed, the Greeks began to mark themselves off from other peoples and to consider themselves superior to the barbarians, as they called all non-Greeks. Nevertheless, this sense of cultural and linguistic unity, reinforced as it was by pan-Hellenic religious institutions, remained pale and weak in comparison with the intense bonds which tied the citizens to the *polis* of his birth.

2) Literature. Greeks learned to write after 700 B.C. They borrowed their alphabet from the Phoenicians, but in doing so made important innovations. The shape of the letters was altered. but, more important, the

Greeks adapted letters (denoting sounds in the Phoenician language which had no analogue in Greek) to signify vowels. In Semitic alphabets, vowels had been omitted. The linguistic structure of these tongue made it fairly easy to supply the appropriate sounds when only consonants were written down, but the Greek language used many vowels, and written words could not be understood unless vowels were symbolized as well as consonants. When the Greeks invented vowel signs, they made alphabetic writing more easily intelligible, and it became a relatively simple matter to adapt the improved system to other languages. Modern European alphabets are in fact all descended from the Greek.

With the dissemination of writing, literature could be written down and no longer depended on memorization for its preservation. This opened the field for prose as well as for a wider variety of poetic forms. The Greeks were not slow to exploit the new possibilities. Hesiod (eighth century) composed long didactic poems describing the routine of farming (*Works and Days*) and systematizing the confused mythology which the Greeks had inherited (*Theogony*). In the seventh century, a number of poets developed lyric and elegiac verse forms, among whom the most famous names are Archilochus, Alcaeus, and the poetess, Sappho. Only fragments of their verses have survived. They exhibit both a wide variety of form and intense personal feeling.

3) Art. After 700 B.C. the Greeks began to learn how to use stone in building and for sculpture. They probably acquired the rudiments of stoneworking from the Egyptians; but the Greeks quickly emancipated themselves from foreign examples, and, with ever-increasing mastery of the medium, developed styles of their own.

Monumental architecture was confined to temples. The style of Greek temples was developed from the simple house-form which their ancestors had brought with them from the north: four walls and a sloping roof. By degrees the ground plan was elaborated by the addition of a porch with pillars. Then a colonnade was extended completely around the building to produce the mature Greek form. The temples were further decorated with sculptured friezes and with carved ornaments on the roofs, door jambs, and elsewhere. Three distinct styles of decoration evolved: the Doric, Ionic, and Corinthian. More remarkable was the development of an extraordinary refinement in proportion and detail which has made the Greek temples a model and source of artistic pleasure to generation after generation. The full harmony of Greek architecture was not achieved until after 500 B.C., but its distinctive conventions were firmly established earlier, and by the end of the sixth century several very large temples had been constructed, not only in Greece proper but in Italy and Sicily as well.

The qualities which were to distinguish Greek sculpture began to emerge during the same period. The earliest examples of Greek statues which have been discovered show unmistakable influence of Egyptian models; but as the sixth century progressed a distinct Greek style emerged, known to art historians as the archaic. Perhaps the most notable series of archaic statues are those recovered from the Athenian acropolis where they had been thrown down by the Persian invaders in 480 B.C. Despite conventions, such as the "archaic smile," which are unfamiliar to our eyes, these statues have an extraordinary freshness and charm. The portrayal of nude figures was an early characteristic of Greek sculpture. The custom may have arisen from the glorification of successful athletes, which led Greek cities to raise statues to their sons who won victories in the Olympic games or elsewhere. Since athletes performed in the nude, their statues were likewise nude.

Another art in which the Greeks made great strides was the decoration of pottery. During the Dark Age a geometric style had become general in Greece. With the revival of civilization workmanship improved and highly conventionalized representations of men and animals were sometimes made. This line of development was interrupted by contact with Oriental, polychrome, curvilinear styles. The Oriental example led Ionian and Corinthian potters to subordinate geometrical motifs and to substitute animal and human scenes on their vases and jars. As in the case of sculpture, Oriental models were soon abandoned and distinctive Greek styles arose. The potters usually portrayed scenes from mythology. Their drawing and composition is often both skillful and effective; though, again, the most perfect examples of painted pottery come from after 500 B.C. By a curious accident, we know the names of many Greek potters from the habit they had of signing their work; and scholars are able to distinguish the work of various shops according to the style developed in each. In the course of the sixth century, Athenian potters became the finest of Greece, and their product displaced Corinthian and Ionian ware in most of the export markets.

4) Philosophy and Science. As with so many other elements of the Greek civilization, the original stimulus to speculative thought came to the Greeks from their contact with the Orient. By the seventh century Greeks had learned the geometry of the Egyptians and some of the astronomical lore of the Babylonians. But in the Hellenic city state, the religious myths and ideas in which the scientific knowledge of the Oriental peoples was embedded (and indeed almost smothered) could not be accepted. At the same time, the inherited religion of the Greek people did not offer coherent explanations of the world. The various myths which had been inherited (in part from Mycenaean times) and the new ideas introduced by Orphism and by the Eleusinian mystery cult were not consistent with one another, nor did any authoritative priesthood exist to interpret and weld them into a coherent whole. As a result, individual minds were free to wonder and to try to put things together according to rational principles. From the beginning, Greek thinkers could operate independently of any authoritative religious tradition like those of the ancient Near East.

Early speculation took a number of forms. In Ionia a school of prose writers, the logographers or story tellers, arose, who devoted themselves to harmonization and rationalization of the myths about the past. In addition they began the study of geography and history by writing accounts of the wonders of foreign lands. Hecateus of Miletus (*c.* 500 B.C.), the most prominent of Herodotus' predecessors, put the method of this school in a sentence: "I write here what I think is true, for the Greeks have many stories which in my opinion are ridiculous."

A similarly rationalistic outlook was characteristic of the thinkers who devoted themselves to explaining the phenomena of the physical universe. Thales of Miletus (*c.* 636–546 B.C.) was by tradition the first man who made such an attempt. An engineer, mathematician, and astronomer, he tried to account for the natural world by assuming that all things had formed from primeval water. Other lovers of wisdom (*philosophoi*, as the Greeks came to call such thinkers), advanced variant hypotheses as to the genesis, structure and destiny of the earth and the skies. The famous names are Anaximander and Anaximines of Miletus, Heracleitus of Ephesus, Xenophanes of Colophon and Pythagoras of Samos. These men were all natives of Ionia, although Pythagoras emigrated to southern Italy, where philosophy was to center in the generation immediately after 500 B.C.

The thoughts of these men have been preserved only in fragments and paraphrases. But it seems clear that their methods were rationalistic, their theories daring. Xenophanes, for example, rejected the myths about the gods *in toto*, calling them false inventions of the poets who had simply made the gods in the image of men.

Pythagoreanism stood rather apart. Pythagoras founded a secret society in his adopted city of Croton which taught and elaborated a semireligious doctrine which was perhaps related to Orphism. Mathematical study was especially emphasized by the Pythagoreans, and numbers were assigned mystic qualities and regarded as a basic constituent of all things.

4. THE FIFTH CENTURY: THE RISE AND OVERTHROW OF THE ATHENIAN EMPIRE (510–404 B.C.)

---

a. Early Development of the Athenian Polis

b. The Persian Wars

    1) Preliminary Campaigns

    2) The Great Invasion

c. The Rise of Athens to Imperial Leadership
   1) The Delian League and the Athenian Empire
   2) Internal Development of Athens

d. Sparta and Other Greek States (479–431 B.C.)
e. The Peloponnesian War (433–404 B.C.)
   1) Preliminaries (433–431 B.C.)
   2) First phase (431–421 B.C.)
   3) Second phase (421–416 B.C.)
   4) Final phase and Defeat of Athens
      (416–404 B.C.)

f. Greek Culture in the Fifth Century
   1) Religion
   2) Art
   3) Literature
   4) Philosophy
   5) Science

---

a. The Early Development of the Athenian Polis

The earliest date in Athenian history which can be fixed with even approximate accuracy is 632 B.C., when an Athenian nobleman, Cylon, tried unsuccessfully to establish himself as tyrant of Athens. Before that time a number of magistracies had been established, and the ancestral kingship had been converted into one of the magistracies, charged primarily with religious functions. The council of the Areopagus, recruited from among ex-magistrates, exercised vague but effective power over the general conduct of government.

Cylon's conspiracy no doubt reflected social strains in Athenian society; but we can only guess as to details. About eleven years after this abortive *coup d'état*, Draco codified the laws by which magistrates judged law suits, thus reducing the power of arbitrary interpretation which the noble judges had previously enjoyed. But this measure did not bring social conflict to an end. A generation later, revolution threatened the Athenian state. Debt-ridden farmers and others who had lost their land wanted a complete redistribution of landed property and cancellation of debts. Another serious problem was military: as small farmers lost their land from failure to repay their debts, the number of hoplites available for the Athenian phalanx was reduced and Athens' military power was thereby undermined. These problems led the Athenians in 594 B.C. to appoint Solon as an extraordinary magistrate with power to revise the laws.

Solon's reforms were directed toward moderating social conflict. He

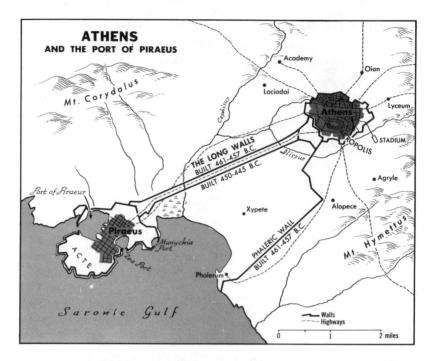

cancelled all debts and forbade enslavement for debt in the future, thus mitigating the hardships of the small farmers and tenants of Attica. The currency was reformed, sumptuary legislation enacted, the export of grain forbidden, and that of olive oil encouraged. These economic measures were supplemented by political changes. The citizen body was classified in terms of income in kind derived from land, and the political rights and military duties of each class were defined. High offices were limited to the two upper classes, but all citizens were admitted to the assembly, and had the right to sit as jurymen to hear and decide cases appealed from the decision of magistrates. This latter change worked a fundamental shift in the balance of power in the Athenian state, for after Solon's time noble magistrates no longer had the power to give judgment without appeal. Very soon the custom of appeal to the popular courts became so general that the magisterial judges lost all importance, and simply supervised the preparation of a case before it came to a citizen jury. The popular juries had an additional important function: at the close of his term of office each magistrate was compelled to appear before a special jury which audited his accounts. The council of the Areopagus continued to exist, however, and had judicial powers over capital cases. In addition, Solon established a council with 400 members. Its functions was to preside over and prepare an agenda for the assembly.

Obviously the new rights which Solon vested in the popular courts and the democratic composition of the assembly gave much greater power to the common citizens than they had enjoyed when the judges were exclusively chosen from among the rich and well-born. Thus Solon's constitutional reforms mark a decisive step in the direction of democracy.

But Solon did not succeed in bringing peace to the city. The poor were disappointed, for they had hoped for a redistribution of land, while the rich and the nobles resented the restrictions which had been put on their former powers. During the next thirty years discontent and occasional disorders continued to rack the state; and rival parties of "hill," "plain," and "shore" were formed. A long drawn out war with Megara over the possession of the island of Salamis ended in the victory of Athens, and permitted Peisistratus, the most effective military leader, to take advantage of his prestige and establish a tyranny about 560 B.C. He was twice expelled, but each time succeeded in returning, the second time with the help of mercenary soldiers.

Peisistratus preserved the forms of the Solonian constitution, but ruled from behind the scenes somewhat after the manner of a modern political boss. He banished many of his noble opponents, confiscated some of their land, and distributed it to the poorer groups in the population. He also made loans to farmers who planted olive groves or vineyards to help them over the unproductive years between the planting and the first harvest. These measures helped to transform Athenian agriculture. Under Peisistratus Attica became predominantly a land of small farms (probably the average was from 15–25 acres) whose owners worked the land themselves with the help of their family and perhaps of a few slaves or of an occasional free man who was hired. Moreover, the new crops—olives and grapes—proved well suited to the soil and climate of Attica; so that a large surplus of oil and some wine became available for export. The food deficit, which had plagued Attica in earlier generations, was at least partially relieved by import of grain from Thrace and the Black Sea coast, in which regions Peisistratus established a network of diplomatic alliances.

In Peisistratus' time, an Athenian nobleman, Miltiades, went to the Gallipoli peninsula where he became head of a mixed Greek and Thracian state. An Athenian colony was set up on the Asiatic side of the Hellespont at Sigeum. It seems probable that by these means Peisistratus sought to gain strategic control of the straits, for it was through the narrow waters of the Hellespont that much of the grain for the Athenians now began to come.

Athens became the foremost center of pottery manufacture under Peisistratus and his son, Hippias, a development closely connected with the export of wine and oil, since the pottery served as containers for these products. Under the patronage of the Athenian tyrant, the city became for the first time a leading center of the arts. The construction of large temples was begun, many statues were erected on the Acropolis, and the text of Homer was reduced to an authoritative canon which was accepted by all Greeks thereafter as standard. In addition, civic festivals such as the Panathenea and the Greater Dionysia were either founded or much elaborated by Peisistratus.

The measures taken by Peisistratus, and the economic development of Athens under his rule, did something to relieve the population problem and to reduce the social conflicts which had been so prominent in the early sixth century. Nevertheless, the tyranny had powerful enemies, especially among the exiled nobles. After the death of Peisistratus, his eldest son, Hippias, carried on the system of one man rule from behind the scenes, but he lacked his father's finesse. When malcontents plotted to assassinate the members of the Peisistratid house, and succeeded in killing one of Hippias' brothers, he reacted by harsh repression of all the suspected instigators of the deed. These punitive measures alienated many of the citizens, however, and when in 510 B.C. the Spartans were persuaded to attack Athens with the declared intention of overthrowing the tyranny, they were easily successful. Hippias fled to Sigeum, where he acknowledged the overlordship of Persia, and Athens became a member of Sparta's Peloponnesian League.

The aristocratic families flocked back to Athens, but soon quarreled among themselves. One of their number, Cleisthenes, of the Alemaeonid family, found himself in danger of being shouldered out of power. He retrieved his position by becoming champion of the popular cause. With the support of the common citizens, he was able to reorganize the constitution in 508 B.C. He systematically undermined the political position of his fellow nobles; and by so doing gave the Athenian constitution the basic form that was to persist through the fifth century.

The fundamental change Cleisthenes made was to break up the ancestral tribal system. Aristocratic families' political leadership had rested largely on their privileged position as religious-political leaders of the tribes. Cleisthenes took the radical step of depriving the old tribes of all political functions. Instead, new local units called *demes* were established which took over functions of local government, kept the roll of citizens, and checked on their military training and equipment. Groups of contiguous *demes* formed a *trittys* (i.e., a "third") and three *trittyes*, selected from different regions of Attica, formed one of the new "tribes" into which Cleisthenes divided the Athenian citizen body. There were ten such new tribes, and after Cleisthenes' time, political matters were handled through these artificial units.

The effect of Cleisthenes' gerrymandering was to dissociate religious and kinship ties from political organization. Political leadership came to depend not on noble birth so much as on persuasiveness in speaking before the assembly and on military skill in the field. The parties of "hill," "shore," and "plain," which had dominated politics in the sixth century, were effectively broken up by the device of locating each *trittys* of each new tribe in different geographic regions of Attica.

A second important change in the Athenian constitution made by Cleisthenes was the reorganization of the council. Its membership was increased to 500, fifty from each of the ten new tribes; and day to day administration of the state was placed in the hands of subcommittees of the council, called *prytaneis.* The year was divided into ten equal parts, and during each such period fifty members of the council, i.e., the representative from one tribe, presided over affairs of state, and lived at public expense in a building called the Prytaneion. The entire membership of the council might be summoned on important occasions, but major decisions were always ratified by the assembly, which met at the call of the council and deliberated on matters which the council brought before it.

The changes made by Solon and Cleisthenes deprived the magistrates of much of their practical power. When the magistrates ceased to be elected but were instead chosen by lot (probably in 487 B.C.) their influence was further undermined, since lots insured an average level of mediocrity. Military matters could not be entrusted to such officials, nor to an unwieldy committee. Accordingly, a new board of generals was instituted. The board had ten members, one for each of the tribes; and generals were elected annually by the assembly. This new office quickly became the most powerful in the Athenian state, both in war and peace; and since a man could be reelected general an indefinite number of times, continuity of policy could be maintained through this office.

Ostracism was introduced either by Cleisthenes or soon after his time. By law, the assembly was asked once a year to vote whether there was any man in the city who should be exiled; if the vote turned out affirmative, then the names of candidates for exile were written on potsherds, and the individual against whom the largest number of votes had been cast was required to leave the city for ten years. Since it was usually a political leader of the minority party who was ostracized, the device came to serve much the same function that a general election does in modern democratic states, with the difference that it was not an election to office but an election that excluded the least popular candidate from political life for ten years.

Cleisthenes' innovations confirmed the democratic character of the Athenian constitution which had already been evident after Solon. It was a direct democracy; important decisions were entrusted not to a body of elected representatives but to the people themselves—or rather to that fraction of the citizen body that had the leisure and inclination to attend the meetings of the assembly and law courts. In practice, the farmers who necessarily lived at some distance from the city can not have attended regularly. As a result, the inhabitants of the town had a disproportionate weight, while the more conservative countrymen could seldom make their wishes felt.

b. The Persian Wars

1) Preliminary Campaigns. Cyrus the Great, King of Persia, overthrew Croesus, King of Lydia, in 546 B.C. and annexed all of western Asia Minor to his empire. The Greek cities of the coast had already recognized the suzerainty of the Lydian king. They were now incorporated into the Persian empire. The Persians generally installed individual Greeks as rulers of each city and left local affairs almost entirely to them. From the Greek point of view such rulers were of course tyrants. and they were seldom popular.

In 512 B.C. Darius the Great crossed into Europe with his army and campaigned in Thrace and north of the Danube against the Scythians. As a result of this expedition, Greek cities around the Sea of Marmora and astride the Bosphorus and Dardanelles acknowledged Persian overlordship, including the two Athenian settlements which Peisistratus had helped establish in that region. The spread of Persian power to Thrace presented a serious problem to the Athenians, since their grain supply depended, in part, on free navigation of the Straits. Cleisthenes, for one, favored a policy of coming to a peaceable agreement with Persia, but other counsels prevailed.

When Miletus and other Greek cities of Ionia revolted against the Persians in 499 B.C., Athens was persuaded to send an expeditionary force in support of the rebels. The Persians were caught off guard, and the Ionians succeeded in besieging and capturing Sardis, the former capital of the Lydian empire. Thrace joined the revolt, but in Greece proper, the Ionians got little support. Eretria, on the island of Euboea, was the only city beside Athens which sent help; and both the Athenian and Eretrian forces soon withdrew. The early success was checked when the Persians brought up their main forces, which were able to subdue the rebel cities one by one. Miletus held out longest, and when captured (494 B.C.) was thoroughly plundered. The Ionian cities, which had been the leaders of Greek civilization between 700 and 500 B.C., never fully recovered from this blow. The center of Greek culture migrated westward, first to Italy and Sicily, then back again eastward to Athens.

Even after the recapture of Miletus, King Darius had some scores to settle with the Greeks. Accordingly, in 492 B.C. he sent an expedition into Thrace to bring the Thracian tribes and the Greek cities of the coast back to obedience. Although the Persians lost some ships in a storm when rounding Mt. Athos, the expedition was successful. Two years later a second expedition was fitted out to deal with the two remaining cities, Eretria and Athens, which had dared to send help to the Ionians. When they reached Greece, the Persians split their forces. One detachment besieged and captured Eretria, sacked the town and deported the surviving inhabitants tô Asia. The rest of the Persian army landed at Marathon, on the north coast of Attica, presumably to prevent the Athenians from sending help to Eretria.

In Athens, meanwhile, rival political leaders intrigued busily against one another. One group favored yielding to the Persians; but the war party, led by Miltiades, won the upper hand. Miltiades was the nephew, namesake, and successor of the Athenian who had established himself as ruler of the Gallipoli peninsula in the time of Peisistratus. He had been implicated in the Ionian revolt, and fled to Athens for safety in 492 B.C. In 490 B.C. he was elected to the board of generals, in which capacity he played the leading role in the battle of Marathon.

When the Persians began to land at Marathon, the Athenian hoplites marched out to meet them. As long as Eretria held out, the two armies simply watched one another, since the Persian plan was to wait until all their forces could be concentrated against Athens, while the Athenians wished to wait until Spartan help arrived to reinforce their strength. As soon as Eretria fell, however, the Athenians were forced to risk battle, since the city lay unprotected in their rear, helpless if the Persian force which had overcome Eretria should attack it from the sea. Accordingly, the Athenians decided to attack. Although outnumbered, the heavy-armed Athenians were able to overpower the Persians and drove them back to their ships. The Persian fleet then sailed around Cape Sunium, but finding that the Athenian army had marched over the hills and arrived in the city before them, the Persians sailed back to Asia Minor without risking a second battle.

2) The Great Invasion. It was ten years before the Persians returned to the attack. In 486 B.C. the Egyptians revolted. Before they were reconquered, Darius died. His son Xerxes, as soon as he was able, decided to enlarge Darius' projects against Greece. He undertook to conquer the whole country. Accordingly, after spending several years in perfecting his preparations—building a bridge of boats across the Hellespont, digging a canal across the peninsula of Mount Athos where the expedition of 492 B.C. had suffered shipwreck, collecting supplies, and mustering a great army—the Persians invaded Greece in full force in the year 480 B.C.

Persian plans and preparations were known to the Greeks. When Xerxes' envoys demanded the submission of the Greek cities, many of them yielded to what seemed irresistible force. Even the Delphic priests began to issue oracles that discouraged resistance. But Athens, Sparta, and the

PERSIAN WARS, 494–479 B.C.

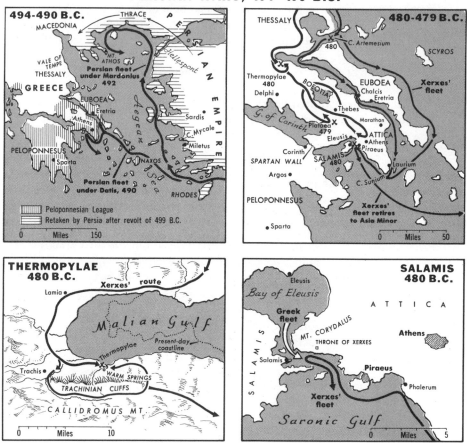

other cities of the Peloponnesian League refused to yield. At a congress called in 481 B.C. they laid plans to resist and invited other Greek cities to join them. Few dared to do so.

Athens made special preparations for the Persian attack. On the advice of Themistocles, a newly risen leader, the income which came to the state from the exploitation of rich veins of silver ore, discovered at Laurium in 483 B.C., was devoted to the building of a large fleet of warships. This fleet proved of decisive value in defeating the Persian invasion; indeed it has been said that the silver of Laurium won the war for the Greeks.

The Greeks' first plan was to send an army to the Vale of Tempe in Thessaly. but the lack of safe anchorage there for the fleet (needed to prevent the Persians from using their ships to turn the Greek flank) made that scheme impractical. Instead, the pass of Thermopylae and the roadstead of Artemisium were chosen. But when the Persian army arrived at Thermopylae (480 B.C.) only a handful of Spartans and their allies, commanded by the Spartan King, Leonidas, were on hand to resist them. After several costly and vain attempts at frontal attack, the Persians discovered a mountain path which took them around the Greek position, and, attacking both front and rear, they were then able to overcome the Greeks. Meanwhile the fleet had fought a series of inconclusive engagements with the Persians; but with the loss of the pass, further defense of the straits between Euboea and the mainland became useless. The fleet therefore withdrew to the Bay of Eleusis, behind the island of Salamis.

The Persians were thus able to march unopposed into Attica. The Athenian population was hastily evacuated to various islands and to the Peloponnese, while the Spartan army set about building a wall across the isthmus of Corinth to prevent the Persians from invading their homeland. Xerxes probably found himself in a difficult position, for the land of Attica was not fertile enough to provide support for his large army, and home bases were far distant. As a result the Persians were eager for a decisive battle, and when Themistocles secretly sent word that the Greek fleet intended to slip away to the south, the Persians decided upon attack by sea.

The result is one of the world's epic stories. The Persian fleet crowded together as it tried to sail through the straits of Salamis, and the Greeks, thanks to the superior maneuverability of their ships, were able to inflict a crushing defeat upon them. The season was already late (September) and Xerxes decided to withdraw his forces to the more fertile lands of Boeotia and Thessaly for the winter. The Persian army was divided in two, part remaining for a second campaign, and the rest returning to Asia with the King. It is likely that this move was dictated by shortage of supplies, for the relatively poor land of Greece could not long sustain an army as large as the Persian invading force.

The following spring (479 B.C.) the Persians again invaded Attica, devastated the countryside and made efforts to detach the Athenians from the Greek alliance. The Spartans would have liked to wait behind their wall at the isthmus of Corinth; but the urgent appeals of the Athenians, coupled with threats that they might sail off with their fleet and leave the sea open to the Persians (which would make the Spartan wall almost useless, since the Persians could then sail around it and land anywhere in the Peloponnese) persuaded the Spartans and their Peloponnesian allies to march northward in full force.

The Persians withdrew to Boeotia, and the united Greek army met them near the little town of Plataea, on the slopes of the mountain which divides Attica from Boeotia. Since neither side wanted to risk a frontal attack, the two armies remained facing one another for several days. But superior Persian cavalry inflicted considerable damage on the Greeks, so the Greek commander, King Pausanias of Sparta, decided to withdraw higher up the slope. The Persians mistook this movement for retreat and proceeded to make a full-scale attack. Once again the heavy-armed Greek soldiers proved more than a match for the Persians, and scattered their enemy so that only a remnant of the great host which had invaded Greece succeeded in reaching Asia again.

In the same summer (479 B.C.) the Greek fleet ventured across the Aegean at the invitation of some of the Ionians. At the approach of the Greeks, the Persian admirals beached their ships on Cape Mycale, since they did not trust the loyalty of the Ionians, who constituted a large part of their command. The Greeks followed them ashore and stormed the Persian defenses successfully. This victory led to a general revolt on the part of the Ionians.

The great and unexpected victories which the Greeks had won against their colossal enemy had enormous psychological repercussions. Previously the wonders, wealth, and wisdom of the Orient had deeply impressed the Greeks, and many elements of Greek culture had come from imitation of Oriental examples. Their victory, however, confirmed in the Greeks a sense of their superiority—a superiority not merely in military matters, but in the entire way of life which they had built up within the framework of the *polis*. The war came to be looked upon as a conflict between free men and slaves, between liberty and despotism. This constituted Herodotus' central theme, when, in the generation immediately after the wars, he set out to record the "great deeds of the Greeks and the barbarians so that each might not lose his due meed of glory."

c. The Rise of Athens to Imperial Leadership (479–431 B.C.)

1) The Delian League and the Athenian Empire

---

a) Sparta's Abdication
b) Athenian Leadership against Persia
c) The Athenian Empire
d) First "Peloponnesian" War

---

a) Sparta's Abdication (479–477 B.C.). As the Ionian cities revolted from Persia they were admitted to the loose association of states which had fought off the great invasion under the leadership of Sparta. But the Spartans were unwilling to embark on distant enterprises, fearing both helot revolt at home and the corruption of their own citizens from too extended a contact with the outside world. The Spartan King, Pausanias, who had commanded at the battle of Plataea, continued active warfare against the

Persians for two years. But his hauteur and intrigues with the Persians soon made him enemies among the Spartans and in the other Greek cities. As a result, Pausanias was recalled, and the Spartan home government withdrew from further active participation in the war against Persia. The Athenians unhesitatingly took over the vacated leadership by proceeding to organize a league, known from its meeting place on the island of Delos as the Delian League.

b) Athenian Leadership against Persia (477–466 B.C.). The Delian League was much like the Peloponnesian League which Sparta had created in the course of the sixth century. The cities of the Aegean coast and many of the islands made alliances with Athens; and representatives of each state attended periodical meetings in Delos to consider matters of common interest. For the first few years, the common interest was clear enough: to secure themselves against possible Persian counterattack the cities annually outfitted a fleet which systematically subdued adjacent regions remaining under Persian control. The fleet was always commanded by an Athenian; and the Athenians soon discovered a capable military leader in Cimon, son of Miltiades, the victor of Marathon. Under Cimon's leadership, the Delian League went from one success to another. By degrees all the cities along the Aegean seaboard were reconquered from the Persians, but not until 468 B.C. did the district of southwestern Asia Minor known as Caria come under Greek control after a great victory near the mouth of the Eurymedon river. The last Persian garrison was expelled from Europe only in 466 B.C.

Many cities, willing enough to send ships and men while the danger of a Persian counterattack seemed great, got tired of annual campaigning, and preferred to make money payments instead. The Athenians used the money so paid into the League treasury to build warships, which they manned with Athenian crews. Thus the naval power of Athens grew ever greater and soon far eclipsed that of any other Greek state. The tendency to convert contributions in men and ships into money payments was reinforced by the addition to the League of cities newly liberated from the Persians. These cities were accustomed to paying a tribute to the Persians, and found it natural to continue the practice, paying to new masters, the Athenians.

c) The Athenian Empire (466–448 B.C.). The other members of the Delian League were not unaware of the rise of Athenian power, and some of the larger cities became restive. Probably *c.* 467 B.C. the island of Naxos attempted to withdraw, and refused to send its usual contingent of ships. The Athenians and their loyal allies thereupon attacked Naxos, and compelled its inhabitants to remain members of the League. The Naxians, however, were no longer asked for ships and men, but were required to

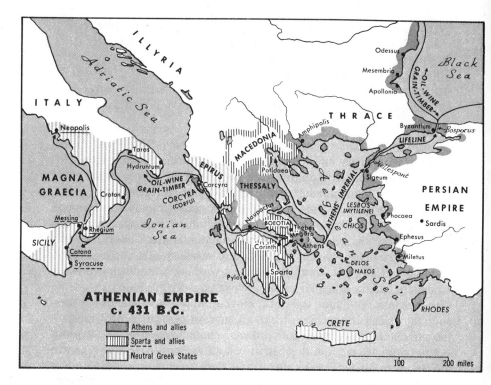

ATHENIAN EMPIRE
c. 431 B.C.

Athens and allies
Sparta and allies
Neutral Greek States

0   100   200 miles

make money payments instead. Other revolts followed, and were dealt with in the same fashion. Each such revolt added to the Athenian preponderance, and before many decades had passed only a few cities continued to contribute ships and men to the League's resources. The rest paid money, nominally to the League, practically to Athens.

The war with Persia continued spasmodically. In 460 B.C. a revolt broke out in Egypt and the Athenians dispatched a large expeditionary force to assist the rebels. For about five years the struggle in Egypt continued, but eventually the Persians overcame resistance and almost all of the Athenian expeditionary force was lost. This setback to the Greeks became the pretext for transferring the treasury of the League from Delos to the greater safety of the Athenian acropolis (454 B.C.). Thereafter the custom of holding periodic meetings of the League members gradually lapsed, and Athens became not so much the leader of a league as the ruler of an empire, using the funds which came in from the allies for general state purposes.

After an interlude when Athenian strength was turned mainly against other Greek states (see below), the Athenians and their allies once more sailed in full force against the Persians in 449 B.C. and won a victory on the island of Cyprus which led the Persians to conclude a peace by the terms of which the independence of the Asiatic Greeks was recognized (Peace of

Callias, 448 B.C.). Thus more than half a century after the beginning of the Ionian revolt, the war between Persians and Greeks came to an end.

d) First "Peloponnesian" War (461-445 B.C.). The rapid rise of Athenian power between 477 and 462 B.C. stirred uneasiness among the Spartans, but a revolt on the part of the helots (which broke out in 464 B.C. and was not entirely stamped out until 456 B.C.), temporarily paralyzed them. In 462 B.C. the Spartans were constrained to ask for help from their allies of the Peloponnesian League. Athens probably still retained a nominal membership in that league; in any case, persuaded by Cimon, the Athenians sent a small force of hoplites to the assistance of the Spartans.

When the Athenian detachment arrived, however, the Spartans evinced a deep distrust, and when the Athenians failed to capture one of the strongholds where the helots were entrenched, the Spartans curtly sent the Athenians back home. This seemed an insult to the Athenian public. The assembly reacted by voting for the ostracism of Cimon and by embarking on an active imperialist and anti-Spartan policy in mainland Greece. A series of wars with other Greek states ensued. The island of Aegina was compelled to join the Athenian league after a long naval siege, and in 459 B.C. the isthmus city of Megara (as a result of an internal revolution which brought democratic groups to power) elected to secede from the Peloponnesian league and ally itself with Athens. These successes, at a time when a major part of the Athenian armament was committed in Egypt, were amazing enough, and seriously alarmed the Spartans and their Peloponnesian allies.

In 457 B.C. the Spartans sent an army north which won a victory over the Athenians and then returned home. But later in the same year the Athenians invaded Boeotia and successfully added the Boeotian cities to their growing empire. Still other successes followed. Naupactus, on the north shore of the Gulf of Corinth, was captured by an Athenian fleet about 456 B.C. and the rebellious Spartan helots (who had been allowed to leave Spartan territory when the Spartans found themselves unable to subdue them) were later settled in that city. Friendship and alliance with both Megara and Naupactus gave the Athenians a string of naval stations connecting Athens with the Greek cities of Sicily and southern Italy by a shorter and safer route than that around the Peloponnese. The Athenians found themselves in a position to strangle the western trade of their commercial rival, Corinth, if they so willed.

These successes depended not so much on the inherent strength of Athens as on internal revolutions which took place within the cities which joined the Athenian system of alliances. Athens had become identified as the champion of the democratic parties everywhere in Greece; and when such a party gained power, it normally tended to form an alliance with

Athens. Thus the expansion of Athenian power on the Greek mainland was no more secure than were the various democratic governments in the cities of Boeotia, Megara, and elsewhere.

Nevertheless, the successes seemed overwhelming at the time, and Sparta, weakened by the helot revolt, was constrained to make a Five Years' peace in 451 B.C. Three years later, however, the Athenian power began to crumble. Revolutions in some of the Boeotian cities restored oligarchic parties to power, and when the Athenian army made ready to intervene, it was defeated (447 B.C.). This setback encouraged Megara and the island of Euboea to revolt, and the Spartans sent an army to invade Attica itself.

The Spartans soon withdrew, however, and Athenian strength was concentrated against Euboea where the rebellious cities were reduced. In some cases, the inhabitants were banished and replaced by Athenian settlers.

But Athens had been weakened by losses in Egypt and elsewhere, and could scarcely hope to overcome the enemies which surrounded her. The effort to recover Megara and Boeotia was therefore abandoned, and in 445 B.C. a Thirty Years' peace settlement was negotiated. Athens recognized the independence of Megara and Boeotia; Sparta admitted the legitimacy of the Athenian empire, and each agreed to leave the allies of the other alone and to settle any future disputes by arbitration.

2) Internal Development of Athens (479–433 B.C.)

---

    a) Economic
    b) Social
    c) Political

---

a) Economic. The damages of the Persian invasions of 480 B.C. and 479 B.C. were quickly repaired, and during the ensuing fifty years Athens entered upon a period of economic prosperity. Her imperial position increased the wealth which lay at the government's disposal; and the silver mines of Laurium continued to produce abundantly. These mines provided the metal for the Athenian coinage, which became a more or less international currency on the strength of its uniform purity and full weight. Athens established a near monopoly of the lucrative trade with barbarian states and Greek cities of the Black Sea region; and precautions were taken to assure the regular import of grain on which the city became more and more dependent. Even in the west, where Corinth had a traditional preeminence and a geographical advantage, Athenian products found a ready market. Egypt, too, came within the circle of Athenian economic influence to a slight degree.

Population continued to grow despite the heavy losses in war. Expanding trade and industry, and the administrative and military posts which imperial power opened to Athenian citizens, provided a livelihood to many. Colonies in Euboea and elsewhere took care of the surplus population which remained. As a result, the oppressive poverty and bitter social conflicts which had been characteristic of Attica in the sixth century largely disappeared.

b) Social. The number of slaves and foreigners in Athens undoubtedly increased. On the eve of the Peloponnesian war, the total population of Attica was probably between 300,000 and 400,000. Of these, perhaps 100,000 were slaves, about 150,000 citizens, and the balance were foreigners. Slaves who worked in the silver mines were kept in chains and were treated inhumanly. Those who worked as servants or artisans, on the other hand, dressed and lived not very differently from ordinary citizens. Some slaves were allowed to set up in business for themselves and could hope to accumulate money enough to purchase their freedom.

Foreigners resident in Athens engaged mainly in trade and industry, and it is probable that most of the industrial workmen of Athens were non-citizens. Some of them attained riches, and associated on friendly terms with the aristocratic families of Athens. They were without political rights, for only in very exceptional cases could foreigners become Athenian citizens.

The citizen body itself was sharply divided between the relatively conservative farming population and the restless inhabitants of the city. Many of the latter came to depend on the state for their living, drawing wages as rowers in the fleet, as workmen on public projects such as the Parthenon, or as minor officials and functionaries of the government. About the middle of the century the government introduced the practice of paying jurors who sat as judges in legal disputes. During the following decades jury pay came to serve as a sort of old age pension for citizens who could no longer row in the fleet.

c) Political. Throughout the fifth century Athenian politics revolved around two "parties" which had emerged from the overthrow of the Peisistratid tyranny. On the one hand, the "good and wellborn" aspired toward a state in which the wealthier and more gentlemanly citizens would have control. This, the oligarchic party, resisted democratic changes in the constitution, and generally proclaimed a reverent adherence to ancestral ways. Its support came from among the wealthier classes and, probably, from the farmers.

The democratic party opposed the oligarchs, and on the whole preponderated through the fifth century. As a result, the Athenian constitution was several times altered to give more power to the ordinary citizen. The wishes of the poorer classes among the urban population came to be especially effective, since they found it easy to attend meetings of the assembly or to serve as jurors in the law courts. Nevertheless, until 429 B.C., the leaders of the democratic party seem to have been men of aristocratic birth.

An important factor in maintaining the influence of the democrats in the Athenian state was the fact that it was from among the poorer classes that the rowers for the fleet were recruited; and everyone knew that the power and wealth of Athens depended on command of the sea. The fleet became a democratic stronghold; in contrast, the hoplites of the army generally leaned toward moderate oligarchy.

During the first years of the Delian League's existence, both parties united in supporting overseas operations. Later, when the need for protection against the Persians became less pressing and the connection between sea power and democracy became clear, the oligarchic party began to oppose imperial adventures. The democrats, on the other hand, became identified with an imperialist, expansionist policy, for only thus could the poorer citizens be sure of constant employment, pay, and booty.

The major changes in Athenian politics can be listed as follows:

1. During the crisis of the Persian invasion of 480–479 B.C., party strife in Athens was temporarily suspended. Themistocles and his rival, Aristides, worked together to repel the Persians. This cooperation continued for a few years after the war. While Themistocles busied himself with home affairs, Aristides established the Delian League.

2. About 471 B.C. Themistocles was ostracized and the oligarchic party, under Cimon's leadership and supported by the prestige of his victories over the Persians, entered into a period of dominance.

3. In 462–461 B.C. the democrats, headed by Ephialtes and Pericles, reduced the power of the conservative stronghold, the council of the Areopagus, by depriving it of most of its judicial powers, and succeeded in ostracizing Cimon. This ostracism was connected with Cimon's rebuff by the Spartans when he marched to help them subdue the revolting helots. (See above.) In the next few years, pay for jurors was introduced and the magistracies were opened to all but the lowest property class of citizens. These changes installed a full-blown democracy, in which the assembly was supreme and the wishes of the ordinary citizen prevailed in state policy. Under Pericles' guidance, the Athenians launched upon an aggressive imperial policy which resulted in war with Sparta, and the temporary establishment of a land empire in Boeotia (457–447 B.C.).

4. After the disruption of the land empire, the oligarchic party, led by Thucydides, son of Melesias (*not* the historian), attempted to overthrow Pericles; but the effort failed and led only to the ostracism of Thucydides sometime between 445 and 442 B.C.

5. In the years just before the outbreak of the Peloponnesian war it seems probable that a radical wing of the democratic party began to form which demanded more vigorous foreign expansion than Pericles approved. At any rate, Pericles had to face serious opposition in the assembly, and was accused by his conservative enemies of having precipitated the Peloponnesian war in order to consolidate his control of the state and appease the unruly wing of the democratic party.

d. Sparta and Other Greek States (479–431 B.C.)

The rigid conservatism of their constitution and way of life, combined with the constant fear of helot revolt, led the Spartans to abandon leadership against the Persians when the Greeks took the offensive. During the next few decades the Peloponnesian League ceased to play an active part in Greek politics. The great helot revolt of 464–456 B.C. seriously weakened Sparta, and the Athenian successes in the war which broke out in 457 B.C. damaged Spartan prestige still more.

The very fact of Athens' power, however, had the effect of bringing the Greek states which had not yet fallen under Athenian influence closer together. Corinth in particular became the bitter foe of the Athenians, for that city depended in good measure on trade with Italy and Sicily, trade which the Athenians, with their naval station at Naupactus, seriously threatened. The overthrow of pro-Athenian democracies in Boeotia by oligarchic groups in 447 B.C. added Boeotia to the circle of Athenian enemies, for the new governments could never feel secure as long as Athenian power was so great and so near to their border.

The result was the division of Greece into two hostile camps. On the one hand were the Athenians and their subject-allies, champions of democratic government and popular parties everywhere in the Greek world. Arrayed against them was the Peloponnesian League, headed by Sparta, the friend of oligarchic government and oligarchic parties in every Greek city. Under such circumstances, the Thirty Years' peace (signed 445 B.C.) was uneasy at best. It was guaranteed mainly by Athenian exhaustion and by the inability of Sparta and her allies to cope with the superior Athenian sea power.

e. The Peloponnesian War

1) Preliminaries (433–431 B.C.). As Athenian strength, both in men and money, began to recover from the severe drain of the wars between 460 and 445 B.C. the assembly began to adopt more aggressive policies. In 433 B.C.

THE PELOPONNESIAN WAR

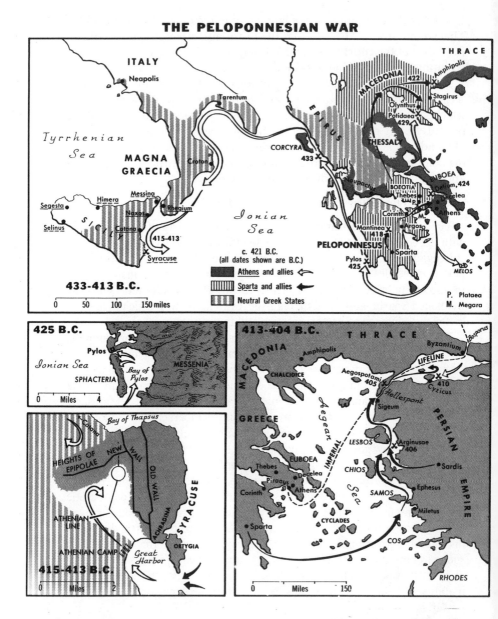

the Athenians made an alliance with the Corinthian colony of Corcyra. This island constituted an important way station on the route to the west. Possession of a naval station there made Athens' threat to Corinth's commercial "life line" so much the more dangerous.

The following year, the Athenian assembly voted to exclude Megarian ships and goods from all ports controlled by Athens, thus instituting an economic blockade. The measure may have been stimulated by border disputes; but probably it was also aimed at bringing Megara again into alliance with Athens, as had been the case between 459 and 447 B.C. Such an alliance would have given the Athenians an uninterrupted series of naval stations—Megara's port on the Corinthian gulf, Naupactus, and Corcyra—on the way to the west, and would have made it unnecessary for Athenian ships to go round the Peloponnese, skirting unfriendly shores, in order to trade or fight in Italy and Sicily.

In the northeast, too, friction between Corinth and Athens came to a head. The Corinthian colony of Potidaea had long been a member of the Athenian empire, but had nevertheless customarily received certain magistrates sent out annually from Corinth. When these officials began to lay schemes for a general revolt in the north Aegean, the Athenians demanded that no more Corinthians come to Potidaea, and that the city's walls be pulled down. The Potidaeans refused to accept these demands, and accordingly in 432 B.C. an Athenian army laid siege to the city.

In the fall of the same year Corinth took the initiative in summoning a meeting of the Peloponnesian League, and urged Sparta to declare war on Athens. Diplomatic negotiations ensued, the Spartans demanding that Pericles be banished, the Megarian decree be withdrawn, the siege of Potidaea be lifted, and the freedom of all Greek cities be respected. The Athenians refused to yield, and full-scale war broke out in the following spring, 431 B.C.

The Peloponnesian war, as it is always called after the example of its Athenian historian, Thucydides, was in one sense a renewal of the struggle between Athens and Sparta for supremacy in Greece. But the long wars between 431 and 404 B.C. eclipsed the earlier fighting in scale and duration, and in its course great changes came to Greek society. The effective independence of each *polis* came to an end as great alliances made neutrality practically impossible for most states; and, even more important, within each *polis* party struggles became so bitter that they often broke up the sense of community. Loyalty to party tended to eclipse the collective patriotism which had distinguished the city states of the early fifth century. Thus the "second round" between Athens and Sparta developed new dimensions which had been absent or only incipient in the earlier war of 457–447 B.C.

It is convenient to divide the Peloponnesian war into three phases. The first, from 431 to 421 B.C., was more or less a draw; the second, 421–416 B.C., was a period of uneasy peace, punctuated by military and diplomatic skirmishes; the third, 416–404 B.C., was marked by the renewal of full-scale war, the Athenian attack on Syracuse, the intervention of Persia, and the final overthrow of Athenian naval power and empire.

2) First phase (431–421 B.C.). The strategy which Pericles persuaded the Athenians to adopt at the beginning of the war recognized the inferiority of the Athenian army, and put entire reliance on the supremacy of the fleet. No attempt was made to defend Attica from Peloponnesian invasion. Instead, the farm population was withdrawn inside the city walls, while the fleet sailed out to raid the Peloponnese. A naval contingent was stationed at Naupactus to harass Corinth's trade with the west; and in addition it supported minor military enterprises on the mainland north of the Gulf of Corinth.

The Peloponnesians were relatively helpless in the face of this strategy. Greek armies lacked the siege engines necessary to batter down stone walls; and there was no hope of starving Athens into surrender. The city was connected with the sea by long walls so that food and supplies could come into Athens from overseas under the very eyes of a superior army. To be sure, the Peloponnesian army could and did ravage the countryside of Attica, but lack of a system of organized supply, and the fact that many of the Peloponnesian soldiers had to return to their own fields to till their farms, made it impossible for their armies to remain in Attica for more than a few weeks of each summer.

An unforeseen disaster struck Athens a heavy blow in 430 B.C. Plague from the Orient ravaged the city. Pericles himself died of the disease the following year. His place as leader of the democratic party in Athens was taken by Cleon, who was a wealthy tanner turned politician, a capable and violent man who roused the bitter enmity of his oligarchic opponents. His policy was to prosecute the war vigorously, and he was able to persuade the Athenians to abandon the cautious policy of Pericles, and to attempt large-scale offensive action. In 426 B.C. a plan was made to invade Boeotia simultaneously from the west (Acarnania) and from Attica. The plan miscarried, but a general named Demosthenes succeeded in winning northwestern Greece for the Athenian alliance.

The following year brought a far greater success for the Athenians. Demosthenes landed a small detachment of soldiers on the west coast of the Peloponnese, on the peninsula of Pylos. The Spartans reacted by sending an army and their fleet to the scene, but they foolishly allowed a detachment to be marooned on a desolate little island, Sphacteria, where the Athenian fleet was able to isolate it. An armistice was temporarily concluded whereby the Spartans surrendered their ships; and when negotiations were broken off the Athenians refused to return the vessels, so that Sparta ceased to have any fleet at all for the next twelve years. Cleon arrived on the scene with reinforcements for Demosthenes; and an assault on Sphacteria was successfully launched. The surviving Spartans surrendered—292 in all—and were brought back to Athens in triumph.

This surrender was a tremendous blow to Spartan prestige. More than that, as long as the prisoners remained in Athens, the Spartans refrained from invading Attica for fear that the Athenians would slaughter their captives in retaliation for the devastation of their fields. Cleon's success at Pylos much enhanced his popularity in Athens. His policy of vigorous offense seemed to promise success.

In 424 B.C., however, Athenian schemes miscarried. Another attempt at a converging attack on Boeotia failed when the Theban army defeated the Athenians at Delium; a fleet dispatched to Sicily returned home without accomplishing anything; and an attempt to seize Megara with the help of democratic conspirators within the city failed. Megara's port did, however, fall into Athenian hands. More important than these checks was the arrival in Thrace of a Spartan contingent of soldiers, under the command of Brasidas. Brasidas encouraged the Athenians' subject-allies to revolt, and several important Thracian cities welcomed him. The historian, Thucydides, found himself in command of the Athenian fleet which was stationed in the northern Aegean; and when he failed to arrive in time to prevent the city of Amphipolis from revolting, the assembly in Athens exiled him. Thucydides did not return to Athens during the rest of the war; instead he spent his time collecting materials for his famous history.

Sparta was anxious to liberate the prisoners who had been captured at Sphacteria; and in Athens a peace party began to make itself heard. The leader of this group was Nicias, an old-fashioned politician who looked backward to the days of Pericles, and tried always to pursue a moderate policy. The peace party drew support from the oligarchs of Athens; but the majority of Nicias' followers probably came from the more conservative wing of the democratic party as it had existed under Pericles. In effect, Cleon and Nicias split the old democratic party into two parts: extremists who wanted to win the war at all costs followed Cleon; while Nicias and the moderates were willing to negotiate peace if reasonable terms could be obtained.

Athens' conduct of the war came to depend on the state of the city's internal politics. In 423 B.C. Nicias and his supporters came into office and a truce was arranged with the Spartans. The next year Cleon was elected general, and led an expedition intended to restore Athenian power in Thrace. In a battle outside the walls of Amphipolis both Brasidas and Cleon were killed—the pestle and mortar of war as Aristophanes called them—and peace parties in both Athens and Sparta came to the top. The result was a negotiated peace, signed in 421 B.C. (Peace of Nicias).

By its terms, the Spartans recovered the prisoners of Sphacteria, and each city agreed to return the places it had captured during the war. Neither Thebes nor Corinth were parties to the peace treaty, but concluded short-term truces with the Athenians. Nor were the terms of the peace observed. The Spartan prisoners were returned; but when Sparta professed to be unable to return Amphipolis to the Athenians, they in turn refused to abandon Pylos.

3) Second Phase (421–416 B.C.). Athenian policy fluctuated unpredictably during the five years which followed the Peace of Nicias. The peace party, headed by Nicias, advocated the maintenance of peace and friendship with Sparta. Nicias even concluded a short-lived defensive alliance with the Spartans aimed against Sparta's erstwhile allies, Corinth and Thebes. But Nicias and his party never gained the sure allegiance of the Athenian assembly, and as a result the continuity and stability of policy which Pericles had been able to maintain by his personal ascendency over the citizens was no longer possible. Nicias' influence was challenged by an extreme democratic party which favored further imperial adventures. Alcibiades, the nephew of Pericles and a companion of Socrates, found such a program attractive, since it would give scope to his own vaulting ambition. He thus became the principal spokesman for the imperialists, and struggled against Nicias for the support of the Athenian populace.

The confusion of Athenian domestic politics was reflected in an erratic foreign policy. In 420 B.C. Alcibiades was elected general, and proceeded to make an alliance with Argos and other cities of the Peloponnese, directed against Sparta. But the following year he was not reelected, and the new Board of Generals refused to carry through the policy which Alcibiades had initiated. The result was that when the rival armies of the Spartans and Argives met in battle at Mantinea (418 B.C.), only a few Athenian hoplites were on hand to aid the Argives and their other allies. The Spartans won the battle decisively, and restored much of their damaged reputation by the victory.

There followed a period of uneasy cooperation between Nicias and Alcibiades. Nicias led a futile campaign in Thrace to try to reconquer the cities of that region; and Alcibiades persuaded the Athenians to send an expedition against the island of Melos, thus wantonly attacking a state which had been neutral during the war years. The inhabitants were either killed or sold as slaves, and the island was resettled by Athenian colonists (416 B.C.).

4) Final Phase and Defeat of Athens (416–404 B.C.). In the same year, the Athenian assembly was invited to come to the aid of Segesta, a city of Sicily, which was at war with one of its neighbors. Nicias opposed while Alcibiades favored intervention; and the assembly sided with Alcibiades. A great expedition was equipped and set sail the following year (415 B.C.) under the joint command of Nicias, Alcibiades, and a nonpolitical soldier, Lamachus. But while the fleet was still on its way, Alcibiades' enemies at home persuaded the assembly to recall him to stand trial for blasphemy and religious profanation. Instead of returning, Alcibiades fled to Sparta where he urged the Spartans to renew the war against Athens. The Spartans did so, sending a general to Sicily to lead the fight against the Athenians, and setting up a permanent garrison in Attica at Decelea. This latter measure particularly hurt the Athenians, for slaves from the silver mines in Laurium fled to Spartan protection. Silver mining ceased, and therewith one of the major sources of Athenian state income dried up. Equally, agricultural activity could hardly be maintained under the eyes of the Spartan garrison.

In Sicily, procrastination and divided counsels led the Athenians to disaster. Nicias delayed on his first arrival; then laid siege to Syracuse, the most powerful city of the island, but was unable to cut it off completely from its hinterland. Reinforcements sent out in 413 B.C. under the command of Demosthenes failed to bring decisive victory to the Athenians, and in the fall of that year, after losing their fleet in the harbor of Syracuse, the Athenian army began a forlorn retreat, which ended with the surrender of the survivors.

This was a tremendous blow to Athenian power, for the best Athenian ships and soldiers had been committed to the Syracusan expedition. But Athens still could command the Aegean sea, and her final defeat came only after the Spartans, with Persian help, built a fleet of their own and, after several sharp reversals of fortune, destroyed the Athenian ships. As a result, fighting during the last eight years of the war was almost entirely naval.

In 412 B.C. a small Spartan fleet appeared along the Asia Minor coast, and most of the Ionian cities revolted against Athens. The Spartans concluded a treaty with the Persian satrap of northwestern Asia Minor, whereby the Persians agreed to supply money to equip the Spartan fleet in return for cession of the Greek cities of Asia Minor to the Persians. Many disputes arose over the enforcement of this treaty, but nevertheless it provided the Spartans with the means to equip a fleet that could hope to challenge the Athenians on the sea.

Alcibiades, meanwhile, had fled from Sparta (where he had seduced the wife of King Agis), and in 412 B.C. entered into a very complicated intrigue between the Persian satrap and the oligarchic party of Athens. He promised the Athenians that if they changed their form of government to an oligarchy, he would be able to win for them the support of the Persians. This hope, combined with the discontent and distrust of democracy, which failures in Sicily and elsewhere had generated, led to an oligarchic revolution in Athens in 411 B.C. The revolution occurred peaceably enough on the surface, though only after members of secret oligarchic clubs had cowed their political opponents by a series of assassinations. The successful oligarchic leaders were not of one mind. A group of extremists wished to rule unrestricted by any assembly. They were opposed by a more moderate wing—men who hoped to establish the "hoplite" franchise or something like it, and to govern through normal constitutional forms. Quarrels between the two factions soon broke out, and the extremists appear to have entered into plots with the Spartans, hoping to confirm their personal power by betraying the city to the enemy. Meanwhile the government of Athens was entrusted to an interim council of four hundred, among whose members both of the oligarchic factions were represented.

When news of the revolution reached the Athenian fleet, which was stationed in Samos, the sailors refused to recognize the new regime. They organized a government of their own and recalled Alcibiades to take over command in the hope that he could bring Persian support with him. Alcibiades accepted, but proved unable to win over the Persians. Nevertheless, under his leadership the Athenian fleet won a decisive victory in the following year (Cyzicus, 410 B.C.) and was able to sail home triumphant and restore the democracy. Sparta, with her fleet destroyed, offered peace on the basis of the status quo; but the Athenians, elated by their unexpected success, refused.

Accordingly, the alliance between the Spartans and the Persians was renewed and another fleet was built. Equally important, the Spartans appointed as admiral a capable and vigorous commander named Lysander. In 406 B.C. the new Spartan fleet won a minor success. In their disappointment, the Athenian people voted Alcibiades out of office. He withdrew from the city, taking up residence in Thrace. (After Sparta's final victory in 404 B.C. Alcibiades fled to the Persians but before he could recoup his fortunes, the brilliant adventurer was assassinated.)

Despite his first success, Lysander was compelled to relinquish his command after just one year, for the Spartans had a rule whereby no commoner could hold command in consecutive years. Without Lysander's diplomacy and military skill, the Spartan fleet quickly lost its efficiency, and in the fall of 406 B.C., at Arginusae, the Athenians succeeded in defeating their enemies once again, but only after suffering heavy losses themselves. When the generals in charge of the fleet failed to pick up survivors who were swimming in the sea, they were accused before the assembly of criminal negligence, and condemned to death. Once more Sparta offered peace, and it was refused.

Lysander returned to command of the Spartan fleet the next year, and in a final battle at Aegospotami in the Hellespont (405 B.C.) he succeeded in capturing almost the entire Athenian fleet while it was beached on the shore. With the fleet gone, Athens could no longer feed its population; and in the following year the city was compelled to surrender. By the terms of the treaty which ended the Peloponnesian war, the Athenians gave up their empire, agreed to pull down the fortifications of the city, and became allies of Sparta.

The terrible disaster which had befallen the Athenians provided the opportunity for a second *coup d'état* in Athens. With Lysander's backing, a board of thirty (the Thirty Tyrants), headed by Critias, was appointed to revise the constitution. The Thirty proceeded to govern the city by terror and made no move to broaden the basis of government. But high-handed violence soon aroused reaction. A band of Athenians seized a border fortress and held it against an attack by the Thirty. The next spring (403 B.C.) the insurgents captured the Piraeus and a short-lived civil war ensued. The Spartans were called upon to intervene, but at Sparta, Lysander's opponents had come to power, and they were not inclined to support his friends in Athens. As a result, the Spartans disowned the Thirty, and prescribed a general amnesty. Another board was appointed to revise the constitution, and after some hesitation it revived the old democracy. This restored constitution remained in force, with only minor changes, until the time of Alexander the Great.

f. Greek Culture in the Fifth Century

1) Religion. The official religion of Greece underwent small change in the fifth century B.C. State cults in Athens became more elaborate and magnificent as the city's wealth increased; but Homer's characterization of the gods continued as a basic element in every Greek's religion. Yet rationalistic criticism of the myths embodied in the works of Homer and other poets, which had been launched by Ionian thinkers in the sixth century, was not without effect, at least among the educated classes. Such a man as Herodotus was very wary of attributing any specific act to a particular god, even though he had no doubt that the gods did intervene in human affairs. A generation later, Thucydides reflected the wider and deeper penetration of religious scepticism, for he omitted all mention of the gods as causal agents in his history.

Yet one must not judge even the Athenian public by the attitudes of a few intellectual leaders whose works have survived to the present. The power of traditional piety was attested, for example, by the way Alcibiades' opponents were able to indict the popular leader before the assembly on a charge of profanation. Local cults and supersitition undoubtedly continued to flourish among the ordinary population, and great state festivals of religion remained heartfelt expressions of the patriotic solidarity of the whole Athenian populace.

2) Art. During the fifth century Greek sculpture and architecture achieved a fineness of workmanship and a balance between naturalism and convention which aroused the admiration of subsequent generations in the classical world and in our own. Only ruins, copies, and a few damaged originals have survived to the present day, but they are sufficient to show the dignity, harmony, and grace which united to make the peculiar beauty of fifth century art. Technical problems—such as the representation of drapery and musculature, or the composition of figure to fill the triangular space on temple pediments—which had challenged the ingenuity and skill of artists in the sixth century were effectively solved in the fifth. Marble was substituted for the softer and coarser limestone which had been used for earlier temples; and masons learned how to cut building blocks with marvelous accuracy. Mortar was not used. yet stones were fitted exactly together so that cracks were scarcely visible. Subtle curves in columns and horizontal surfaces were accurately constructed to correct the optical illusion which makes geometrically straight lines appear concave.

By far the most famous artistic creation was the cluster of buildings erected on the acropolis of Athens during the second half of the century. The adornment of the acropolis was an expression of the Athenians' civic pride. Temples and such semireligious structures as theaters were the only sort of monumental building the Greeks of the fifth century knew. To help finance the buildings, Pericles used the tribute money paid by the cities of the Athenian empire.

The buildings of the Acropolis still survive in mutilated form. The temple of Athena, the Parthenon, is the largest and most elaborate of them. It is a Doric temple of regular design, distinguished by the richness of its sculptural adornment and by the subtlety of its proportions. The temple was built between 447 and 438 B.C. Considerable portions of the continuous frieze that decorated the temple wall inside the colonnade now repose in the British Museum, London. The frieze portrays the Panathenaic procession, honoring Athens' patron deity. Only a few fragments of the other Parthenon sculptures have been preserved.

The other principal structures of the Athenian acropolis are the Erechtheum, an irregular temple of the Ionic style; the little temple of the Wingless Victory; and the Propyleum, which formed a monumental entrance to the sacred precinct on top of the Acropolis. The Propyleum was never completed; the other two were finished during the course of the Peloponnesian war.

The most famous sculptors of the fifth century were Myron, Polycleitus, and Phidias. Their works are known to us only through more or less imperfect copies made in later times. The first two were specially admired for their statues of athletes; Phidias for his statues of the gods. At Athens and at Olympia. Phidias erected gigantic cult statues of Athena and Zeus made of gold and ivory. Beside these sculptors whose names we know, there were many others of great skill though of lesser reputation. To this the high level of performance on the Parthenon sculptures bears witness, for, though Phidias planned and supervised the whole, the actual carving was executed by many different hands, so that modern art critics can detect variant styles in the portions which have survived.

The art of wall painting was practiced by the Greeks, but we know nothing at first hand of their work. In the later decades of the fifth century great technical progress was made through the introduction of shading to indicate depth. Vase painting, on the other hand, reached the peak of its artistic development early in the fifth century and declined thereafter.

Athens was the most active center of Greek art. Other cities, while they also built temples and erected statues, never equaled the Athenian examples.

3) Literature. The lyric tradition of earlier centuries was continued by a Theban, Pindar (518–442 B.C.), whose odes in honor of the victors in the Olympic and other games have alone survived from among his writings. They are occasional verse in the grand manner, and lack the personal note characteristic of Sappho or Alcaeus.

A new literary form, the tragic drama, was developed in Athens during the fifth century. It grew out of choral songs, sung in honor of the gods at the festival of the Greater Dionysia. Throughout the fifth century, the performance of tragedies constituted a part of public religious celebrations. All citizens were free to attend since the costs of presentation were borne by wealthy individuals who were assigned the responsibility by the state.

The religious character of the performances prescribed the tragic subjects: the deeds of gods and of men as handed down in mythology. More recent historical events—it must be remembered that for the Greeks their myths were merely ancient history—were occasionally used by dramatists; but only one such play, *The Persians* by Aeschylus, has survived.

The three great tragedians of the fifth century were Aeschylus (525–456 B.C.), Sophocles (496–406 B.C.), and Euripides (480–406 B.C.). Their plays are distinguished by poetic magnificence, and by the seriousness and greatness of the problems they consider. Each playwright developed a poetic style of his own; and there are marked differences in their respective views of human nature and of the relation of man to the gods. It would be foolish to try to reduce to a sentence the attitudes and ideas which each of the tragedians embodied in his works. This much can be said: each dramatist wrestled with the thoughts and currents of opinion which arose in Athens in his own day; and it is not merely fanciful to see in Sophocles the moral confidence and civic solidarity which characterized the Periclean age at its height, or to trace in the more sceptical and impassioned lines of Euripides a literary reflection of the breakdown of established customs, ideas, and institutions which occurred in Athens during the Peloponnesian war.

Comedy, too, arose from religious celebrations, originally connected with fertility rites. A substratum of sexual license remained throughout what scholars later called the "Old Comedy"; to it was added un restrained humorous, satiric, or ribald comment on current issues and personalities. The result has been preserved for us in the comedies of Aristophanes (*c.* 447–380 B.C.). His plays have both vigor and dash, and combine gross obscenity with lyric passages of great beauty. He was a stout conservative who mocked innovations in thought and politics by ridiculing such persons as Socrates, Euripides, and Cleon.

The achievements of the great Athenian dramatists were fully equaled in the field of history by the works of Herodotus (*c.* 484–*c.* 425 B.C.) and Thucydides (*c.* 471–*c.* 400 B.C.). Herodotus was a native of Halicarnassos, a town in Asia Minor, and it seems likely that he spent his early life traveling (perhaps as a merchant) throughout much of the Orient and the Greek world. He was a man of insatiable curiosity. Everywhere he went he inquired about local traditions, customs and past events. The Persian wars inspired him to gather all the fruits of his inquiry (the Greek word *historia* means "inquiry") together into a discursive account of the great deeds of the Greeks and of the barbarians. His book was the first book of history ever written, if by history we mean an account of human actions written with the aim of describing what took place fairly and accurately; but there were also large epic elements in Herodotus' work, both in his conception of the world and of human affairs, and in his manner of composition, for his incorporated many asides and discursive descriptions into his narrative without, however, vouching for the truth of all the tall tales he so carefully collected. The grace of Herodotus' style won his book immediate fame. Even in translation Herodotus has few rivals as a story teller in all the literature of the world.

Thucydides' history of the Peloponnesian war was written with equal but very different artistry. If Herodotus' literary kinship was with the Homeric epic, Thucydides' lay with the tragic drama; his hero was Athens, and his history recounted her inexorable fall. Yet Thucydides, despite the fact that he was an Athenian, never obtruded his personal feeling directly. Perhaps the dramatic power of his history is all the greater because of the restraint with which he reported what happened, year by year. But by inserting lengthy speeches at critical turning points, Thucydides was able to present in dramatic form the cross-currents of thought and feeling which impelled the Athenians and their enemies to each successive action in the drama. Thucydides was also distinguished by the penetration of his insight into historical causation and by the careful accuracy of his every factual detail. He died before finishing, leaving the history of the war in mid-air in the year 411 B.C.

4) Philosophy. During the fifth century, Greek philosophers enlarged upon the physical speculations of earlier generations. During the latter part of the century human society, customs, and institutions came within the scope of philosophic speculation. and new problems were raised. such as how knowledge of any sort is possible. Various impulses led to the expansion of philosophic speculation. An important stimulus was the mutual criticism of various schools. For example, philosophers of the Eleatic school (Parmenides and Zeno were the most respected figures among them) were led to concentrate attention on questions of permanence and change by criticizing Heraclitus' view that everything was in flux. Empedocles of Acragas in his turn attempted to solve the same problem by developing the theory of four elements each unchangeable in itself, but producing changeable things by mixing together earth, air, fire, and water in varying proportions.

Empedocles' views also reflected a second important stimulus to the expansion of philosophic speculation: the effort to explain additional phenomena which earlier theories had neglected or insufficiently explored. Thus he included an account of the origin and development of living things, extending the range of philosophy beyond the inanimate phenomena on which earlier thinkers had mainly concentrated attention. Anaxagoras, a friend and associate of Pericles in Athens, inherited the problems developed by the Eleatic school and by Empedocles and tried to explain them by his theory of a mind or intelligence, which, he argued, acted upon seeds of matter to make all things. The atomists, Leucippus and Democritus, propounded the theory that the world is composed of insensibly small atoms; and met the epistemological problem (which had already been raised by sophists) by arguing that knowledge arises from the impingement of atoms upon our sense organs.

Still a third stimulus to speculation manifested itself in the sophist movement: changes in Greek social and political life provoked many of their teachings.

As political leadership in Athens and other democratically governed Greek cities came to depend upon persuasiveness before the assembled populace, a demand arose for instruction in the skills required for political success. The demand was met by a group of teachers known as sophists. They undertook not only to teach men how to speak effectively, but also to instruct them in moral and political principles so that they could know what to say as well as how to say it. The first sophists appeared in Sicily, but Athens quickly became the main center of their activity. Both Gorgias of Leontini and Protagoras of Abdera spent part of their lives as teachers in Athens; and a host of lesser men imitated them.

The sophists subjected traditional customs and ethical principles to rational examination; and raised the question—so troublesome for future philosophers—of how we know anything at all. The authority of ancestral ways and inherited moral ideas fared badly under the sophists' critical eyes. Their criticism helped to weaken the concensus within the *polis* which political and social changes were independently undermining. Gorgias, for example, is reputed to have denied the possibility of attaining certain knowledge of anything; and Protagoras coined the famous phrase: "Man is the measure of all things." In the latter decades of the fifth century, scepticism as to the existence of the gods was overtly voiced by some of the sophist teachers; and the doctrine that justice is merely an agreed convention was taught to the politically ambitious youths of Athens. Against convention, some of the sophists put nature—a nature whose law, they taught, was one of tooth and claw, a nature in which might alone made right and justice was merely a disguise for the interest of the strong and powerful. The impact of such doctrines on the public life of Athens is vividly portrayed by Thucydides through the speeches he puts in the mouths of various Athenian representatives.

Sophist teachings such as these constituted the major stimulus to Socrates' thought (469–399 B.C.). Socrates was a man of picturesque and powerful personality, clever in argument and profoundly convinced of the importance of rational examination of human life. He delighted in confuting the cocksure young men and budding politicians of Athens who had been exposed to sophist doctrines, but himself wrote nothing and apparently did not develop a systematic body of doctrine. He is known to us mainly through Plato's dialogues, but it is impossible to distinguish with any certainty where the Socrates of the dialogues becomes simply a mouthpiece for Plato's own ideas. As a result it is difficult to say anything about the positive doctrines which Socrates may have taught.

He was thoroughly convinced of the existence of a divine force in the universe by his "demon"—an inner voice which warned him against any harmful act; and he strove to establish moral principles on a firm basis of certain knowledge. But Socrates did not pretend to success: indeed he steadfastly asserted that he was wise only in recognizing his own ignorance. He probably devoted himself mainly to convincing others that they too did not truly know the things they were wont to proclaim confidently. Such criticism could not be popular among the victims of Socrates' incisive tongue. Even more unpopular was his criticism of the Athenian democracy, which he believed to be conducted by ignorant men who pandered to the corrupt desires of the people. In such a state there was scant room for justice, yet Socrates believed that justice, fixed and unchangeable, was the only right basis of society. Two of the men who did most to damage Athenian democracy—Alcibiades and Critias—were closely associated with Socrates; and when the democracy was restored after the Peloponnesian war many Athenians held the actions of his two friends against Socrates himself. The result was that in 399 B.C. a democratic politician and two other citizens brought Socrates to trial, accusing him of impiety and corruption of the youth. The court convicted Socrates and condemned him to death.

5) Science. Geometry and astronomy continued to be studied and systematized during the fifth century, but little is known of the actual achievement since no writings from the period have survived. In medicine, however, Hippocrates of Cos (*c.* 460–377 B.C.) and his pupils developed a rational system of observation and treatment for disease. Hippocrates explicitly rejected supernatural explanations of illness and propounded instead the theory of "humors." Health, according to this theory, was believed to depend on the proper balance between blood, phlegm, yellow bile, and black bile. The physician's art consisted in restoring the balance when it became disturbed. This theory continued to dominate European medicine until the eighteenth century A.D. In addition, the Hippocratic school developed very considerable skill in surgery, and originated the "Hippocratic oath" which has continued to serve as a model for medical ethics to the present day.

5. THE FOURTH CENTURY: THE RISE OF MACEDON (404–336 B.C.)

    a. Economic Changes
    b. Social Changes
    c. Political Changes
    d. Cultural Development in the Fourth Century
        1) Religion
        2) Art
        3) Literature
        4) Philosophy and Science
        5) Spread of Atticism

a. Economic Changes

Athens and the other cities of Greece recovered from the damages of the Peloponnesian war with surprising rapidity; and despite the continuation of warfare throughout most of the fourth century B.C., trade and manufacture steadily expanded their scope, and banking began to develop in Athens and some other cities as an important element in economic relations. Agriculture lost ground, relatively, to specifically urban occupations, but nevertheless remained on a high level of efficiency.

b. Social Changes

Greek cultural influence spread into new areas; but expansion took place rather through the imitation of Greek ways by barbarian peoples than through new colonization. In Italy, the Romans and other Latin peoples learned much from the Greeks. The alphabet, some religious practices (the Sybil of Cumae, for example, came from a Greek city) and the military phalanx were some of the most prominent borrowings. A similar expansion of Greek institutions and ideas took place in the northern and western parts of the Balkan peninsula, which had remained barbarous through most of the fifth century. The kingdom of Macedon became hellenized in culture, and developed into a powerful state. During the middle years of the fourth century B.C. the kings of Macedon conquered neighboring territories and brought a large part of the northern Balkan peninsula under their control. In Asia Minor, too, Greek influence began to make a mark upon the age-old civilization of that peninsula. For example, Cyrus, a Persian satrap in Asia Minor, the friend and patron of Lysander, became a warm admirer of Greek civilization and military prowess. After his time the Persians made a practice of hiring Greek mercenary soldiers for their imperial armies. Along the Black Sea coast, too, native rulers became hellenized.

But while Greek influence radiated through the Mediterranean world in this fashion, the *polis*, which had carried Greek civilization to its commanding height, suffered serious decline. The voluntary consensus which had constituted the basis of Periclean Athens broke down under the pressure of the long drawn out Peloponnesian war, and was never fully restored. The sense of civic duty and self-identification with the *polis* weakened; instead, a growing individualism manifested itself in such diverse forms as the erection of spacious private homes, and the assertion of an autonomous personal ethic by Socrates, who, patriotic Athenian though he was, nevertheless looked beyond the laws of the city state for his principles of conduct.

In Attica independent small farmers suffered severely during the Peloponnesian war. After it was over, some of them sold their farms to large estate owners who had the capital necessary to replant the land with vines and olive trees (which had been cut down during the long Spartan occupation of Decelea). Small farmers seemingly suffered in other Greek cities also. Large estates became more common than previously. They were tilled mainly by slave labor. During subsequent centuries, the number of citizen farmers continued to decline gradually, and Greek civilization tended to become more and more exclusively urban in character and outlook as a result. The change is perceptible in the fourth century B.C. but was not completed until Hellenistic and Roman times. A parallel change apparently took place among the town dwellers, who came to be more sharply divided between rich and poor than had been the case in the fifth century B.C.

These changes in Greek society obviously sharpened the age-old class warfare. Violent and bloody revolutions and counter revolutions became characteristic of the fourth century. Athens remained exempt from such disturbances, but an undercurrent of mistrust between rich and poor was quite evident in the speeches of orators of that age.

The growth of population, which had been so prominent in the fifth and earlier centuries, apparently slowed, and may even have come to a stop. But the substitution of slave for free labor on the farmlands dispossessed many citizens; and recurrent political revolutions uprooted thousands of others who fled or were banished from their native place. From these groups came recruits for the mercenary armies which tended more and more to replace the citizen militias of earlier times.

The development of such a class of city-less persons obviously weakened the city state system. The steady development of long distance trade operated in a parallel direction, loosening the ties of the merchant and sailor to his place of birth. Even more, the bitter class struggles put loyalty to political party above loyalty to the *polis*, so that it became quite normal for oligarchs to ally themselves with other oligarchs against the democrats of their own city, and democratic parties did the same. Interstate wars thus took on the character of civil wars: Sparta always figuring as the champion of oligarchy, while Athens and later Thebes favored democracy. When the Macedonian king began to play a leading role in Greek affairs, he became a supporter of oligarchy.

c. Political Changes

The internal political development of Athens in the fourth century B.C. is fairly well known through the orations of Demosthenes (*not* the general of the Peloponnesian war) and others. Information about other Greek cities is almost wholly lacking, save when some sudden outburst of domestic violence won the notice of an historian. In Athens the democratic constitution of the fifth century remained in force with only slight modifications; but its practical operation was significantly altered. The board of generals lost political preeminence by degrees as fighting became an affair of professional soldiers; instead, the direction of the state came to rest mainly in the hands of professional orators and administrators, who often held no legal position in the government, or else served on one of the numerous fiscal boards which managed the collection of state revenue and its disbursement.

Athenian foreign policy was constantly hampered by shortage of funds. The Periclean tradition of utilizing state resources for the welfare of the common citizens was carried on, and the number and variety of subsidies to the poor were increased. But when the assembly was asked to choose between spending money for military campaigns and the use of the same money for payments to its members or for the elaborate festivals and shows which the state put on for their amusement, the choice normally fell against military expenditure. To be sure, Athenian imperialism partially revived after the disaster of the Peloponnesian war. In particular, the Athenians strove incessantly to gain and maintain control of the Bosphorus and Dardanelles, through which much of their wheat supply continued to come. But beyond this essential, the expansive imperialism of the Periclean age died out. Athens' part in interstate politics was erratic and on the whole ineffectual.

The tangled diplomacy and almost incessant war of the fourth century may be divided into three major periods: the Spartan hegemony (404–371 B.C.); the Theban hegemony (371–362 B.C.); and the Macedonian hegemony (after 338 B.C.).

1. Political independence for each *polis*, a principle which Sparta had claimed to uphold during a Peloponnesian war, proved quite impractical when peace came; and indeed the Spartans made no effort to restore the independence of the cities which they had liberated from Athens. The cities of Asia Minor were handed back to the Persians; those of mainland Greece were compelled to accept puppet governments at first, and Spartan garrisons were installed at strategic points. Discontent soon became acute; and when a war broke out between Sparta and Persia, the leading cities of Greece leagued together to wage war against their Spartan masters. In this struggle Athens fought side by side with such former enemies as Corinth and Thebes; and the allies depended heavily on Persian subsidies to finance their armies. A long and desultory war resulted, ended by the mediation of the Persian King in 387 B.C. The King's peace left Sparta predominant in Greece.

2. Renewed war between Sparta and Thebes broke out only eight years later in 379 B.C. The Thebans, under the military leadership of Epaminondas, eventually won a crushing victory over the Spartans at Leuctra (371 B.C.). Epaminondas thereupon invaded the Peloponnese, and, having Sparta at his mercy, was able to set up Messenia as an independent state. This act deprived the Spartans of nearly half their land and a majority of their helots. Sparta never recovered from this blow.

But Theban hegemony lasted only as long as Epaminondas commanded the Theban armies. When he was killed in 362 B.C. (battle of Mantinea), Theban power quickly collapsed and Greece fell into a state of political chaos with no one state clearly dominating the rest. This condition opened the door to Macedon, which had, under Philip II (359–336 B.C.), developed into a formidable military power.

3. Philip was able to form a standing army, paying his soldiers largely with gold which was mined near Amphipolis, a city which he early succeeded in adding to his kingdom. He improved upon standard Greek military tactics. Philip used cavalry as the main striking arm, and equipped

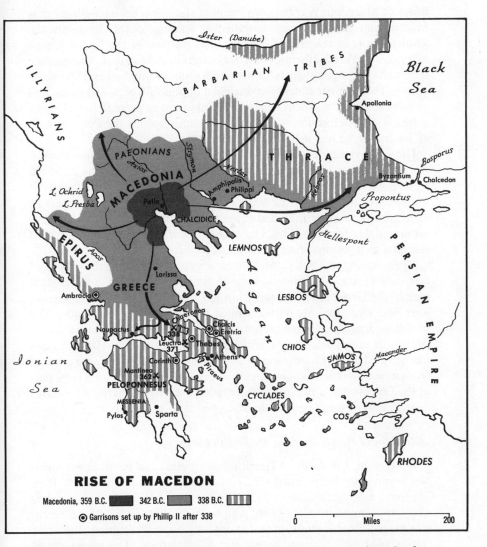

RISE OF MACEDON

Macedonia, 359 B.C. ■ 342 B.C. ■ 338 B.C. ▦

◉ Garrisons set up by Phillip II after 338

0   Miles   200

his foot soldiers with long spears whose massed points constituted a formidable defense which the ordinary Greek phalanx could not break.

With the help of his army and by virtue of his own ruthless generalship
and diplomacy, Philip extended the boundaries of his kingdom in all directions, conquering Thrace as far as the Danube and the Black Sea. In 338
B.C. he led his armies into Greece. An alliance of Thebes and Athens opposed him, but at the battle of Chaeronea the Greeks were utterly defeated,
and Philip became supreme arbiter of Greek affairs.

He used his position to found a Pan-Hellenic League under the presidency of Macedon. War between member states was declared illegal, and Macedonian garrisons were installed at strategic points to assure the loyalty of the Greek cities. The professed purpose of the league was to carry war to Persia, liberate the Greek cities of Asia Minor, and revenge the insults to the gods which Xerxes had wrought a hundred and fifty years before. The member states were assigned quotas of troops and ships, and an advance party was sent across the Hellespont to prepare for full-scale invasion. But before Philip himself could start against the Persians with all his forces, he was assassinated (336 B.C.).

His son, Alexander the Great, succeeded to the Macedonian throne. Alexander's first task was to subdue restless tribes along the northern frontier which had revolted on news of Philip's death. In Greece, the city of Thebes also revolted on the basis of a false rumor of the young king's death; but Alexander marched southward with amazing speed and captured and destroyed the city. Only the house of the poet Pindar was left standing as a gesture of respect for Greek culture.

By the spring of 334 B.C. Alexander was ready to resume the project of war with Persia. Accordingly, he mobilized the Macedonians and summoned the Greek cities to send contingents to his army. But the Greeks were reluctant and only partially filled their assigned troop quotas. The invading army numbered about 35,000 men. With this small force, Alexander succeeded in overthrowing the Persian empire. His conquests inaugurated a new phase in classical civilization. City states were eclipsed by vast new monarchies; Greek culture expanded rapidly over a large part of the Orient; and a process of interaction between the Oriental cultures and the conquering Greek civilization began to reshape both.

d. Cultural Development in the Fourth Century

1) Religion. The decay of Greek religious ideas and institutions, which had begun in the fifth century B.C., continued throughout the fourth. Public ceremonies were maintained, and the forms of religious worship underwent no significant alteration. Among the educated and intellectual groups, philosophic theory crowded out religious myths; among the lower classes, old beliefs persisted in the form of superstition. This divergence of religious outlook between the upper and lower classes was no more than an aspect of the general class division which split up the consensus of the Periclean city state.

2) Art. The styles of Greek architecture underwent no fundamental change in the fourth century. Stone theaters and some monumental buildings for secular use were constructed; and the relatively simple and regular ground plan of earlier temples was frequently altered to fit topographical or other local irregularities. Taste shifted from the Doric style and favored the more ornate Ionic and Corinthian orders, but all three continued to be employed as before. Larger and more magnificent private homes were constructed than had been customary in the fifth century; but systematic city planning and beautification was not common until Hellenistic times.

Fourth-century sculpture continued at a high level of excellence. The grandeur of the age of Phidias was succeeded by lighter, more graceful portrayals of the gods and heroes such as came from the hand of Praxiteles. Scopas, another great sculptor of the fourth century, portrayed violent action and strong emotion in contrast to the serenity which had characterized fifth-century work. Realistic portraiture became common and the earlier convention of idealizing the features of individual persons was discarded. Leucippus, the third great sculptor of the fourth century, was famous for his portraits as well as for athletic statues. All three, Praxitiles, Scopas, and Leucippus, founded schools which continued to produce sculpture in the style of one or the other master through most of the Hellenistic period.

The art of painting reached its highest classical development toward the end of the fourth century with the painter Apelles; but we know his work only through ancient literary descriptions of it.

3) Literature. New forms of literary expression rose to prominence in the fourth century, of which the most admired was oratory. The writing of speeches for plaintiff or defendant in a law suit came to be a regular profession in Athens. These speeches, prepared for other men to deliver before a citizen jury. served as models of eloquence and rhetorical skill in later classical times; and the study of rhetoric became an important part of the education of young men. In addition. as long as Athens remained independent. oratory remained one of the principal props of a political career.

The two most famous of the Athenian orators, Demosthenes (384–322 B.C.) and Isocrates (436–338 B.C.), applied themselves to both legal and political oratory. Demosthenes played a prominent role in Athenian politics as the arch-enemy of Philip of Macedon. His speeches whipped the reluctant Athenian public into unsuccessful opposition to the Macedonian king. Isocrates, on the other hand, was an advocate of pan-Hellenic unity and did not share Demosthenes' hatred of Philip. He expressed his views in a series of political pamphlets cast in the form of speeches—the nearest approach to journalism produced in the ancient world. Isocrates did not himself take an active part in Athenian politics; but he had a wide influence on later times through the school for instruction in rhetoric which he founded. It, and others like it, did much to set the standard of literary taste for the following centuries.

No important tragedies were written after Euripides' death, and toward

the end of the fourth century the Athenians adopted the practice of re-
staging classic works instead of relying on newly-written plays. Moreover,
the great Attic tragedies came to be read and appreciated as works of
literature, divorced from the actual dramatic presentation. Comedy, however, continued to develop. The so-called "Middle Comedy" abandoned
the political scurrility of earlier plays in favor of type characters—personifications of wealth, poverty, virtue, vice, etc. Only one such play has
survived, a late work by Aristophanes, the *Plutus*.

In the field of history writing the example of Thucydides was imitated
but not equalled. A few fragments are all that survive from the historians
of the fourth century, save only for the works of Xenophon (431–354 B.C.),
who wrote, in his *Hellenica*, a continuation of Thucydides' history from
411 to 362 B.C. It is, however, a far inferior work, strongly biased in favor
of Sparta despite the fact that Xenophon was an Athenian. His *Anabasis*
is a simple, vivid account of the experiences of a band of Greek mercenaries
who marched under the command of Prince Cyrus (Lysander's friend and
patron) against the Persian king, and who, after Cyrus had been killed in
battle, succeeded in fighting their way back to Greek soil. Xenophon is
probably also the author of an *Apology* for Socrates which presents a very
different picture of the philosopher from the one given us by Plato.

4) Philosophy and Science. The scientific and philosophical thought of
earlier centuries was brought together and recast by Plato (429–347 B.C.).
Socrates, the Pythagoreans, and the Eleatic philosophers had a particularly strong influence on him. No attempt to describe Plato's philosophy
can be made here; but it is perhaps worthwhile to make two observations.
First, Plato's thought was intimately connected with the social and political condition of the Athens which he knew. Far from being an ivory-tower
philosopher, he never gave up hope of effecting a reform in Greek government and society; and on one occasion seriously tried to put his plans for
a good society into operation in the city of Syracuse. Second, the influence
of Platonism on the thought of subsequent centuries has been enormous.
Ideas which derive their origin from Plato were incorporated both into
later pagan philosophy and into Christianity. More than any other single
man, Plato established the vocabulary and defined the fields of interest for
philosophy as a separate intellectual discipline. His dialogues established a
new literary form; and the Academy which he founded continued to
flourish as a center of higher learning for about nine hundred years until
it was closed by the Byzantine government in A.D. 529.

Aristotle (384–322 B.C.) of Stagira (a small town in Thrace) spent nine-
teen years as a student at the Academy, and later acted as tutor to Alexander the Great before returning in 335 B.C. to Athens, where he set up his
own school, the Lyceum. Aristotle was a professional thinker, scientist

and teacher. Problems of moral and political regeneration were less central for him than they were for Plato, and did not dominate all his thought. Perhaps for this reason, his interests were more catholic even than Plato's. Scores of treatises were written by Aristotle and his pupils on such diverse subjects as biology, constitutional history, physics, astronomy, logic, ethics, politics, and metaphysics. Only a small part of the writings of Aristotle and his pupils has survived. None of the dialogues which Aristotle wrote now exist, and in fact the Aristotelian corpus which we know (perhaps the philosophers' lecture notes, and not intended for publication) was little read for two centuries after the author's death.

Aristotle's influence in later centuries was more intermittent than Plato's. Largely neglected in later classical times, his philosophy and science rose to prominence again in the third and fourth centuries A.D. and were transmitted to the Arabs and from them to Western Europe. Only part of his *Logic* was known in the West before the thirteenth century A.D.

5) Spread of Atticism. The fourth century saw the steady weakening of the *polis* not only politically but also culturally. The cultural autonomy of each city disappeared as the predominance of Athenian literature and thought became steadily more pronounced throughout the Greek world. The Attic dialect spread as the medium both of higher education and of trade through ever larger parts of Greece. Atticism spread also into the peripheral barbarian areas where Greek culture and Athenian culture became almost synonymous, as indeed they are to us. The culture of the Greek world became more unified in this process, and by the end of the fourth century the forms of its expression were largely fixed. In the subsequent centuries, the changes were rung on the artistic, literary, and philosophical traditions which had emerged in the fifth and fourth centuries; but new departures were seldom made. As a result, the cultural supremacy of Athens was never effectively challenged; and long after Athens had lost its political and economic importance, it remained a great center of education and of the arts.

Suggestions for Further Reading for Part II, A

The Oxford Classical Dictionary. Oxford: 1948.
Cambridge Ancient History. Vols. 2–6, Cambridge: 1924–27.
Cambridge Ancient History. Volumes of Plates. Vol. 2. Cambridge: 1928.
Andrewes, Antony. *The Greeks.* New York: 1967.
Bowra, C. M. *The Greek Experience.* London: 1957.

Burnet, J. *Greek Philosophy:* Part I, *Thales to Plato.* London: 1914.

Bury, J. B. *A History of Greece to the Death of Alexander the Great.* Modern Library.

Cary, M. *The Geographic Background of Greek and Roman History.* New York: 1949.

Castigliomi, A. *A History of Medicine.* New York: 1941.

Ehrenberg, V. *The People of Aristophanes.* 2d ed. Oxford: 1951.

Farrington, B. *Greek Science.* Vol. I. *Thales to Aristotle.* Pelican Books.

Ferguson, W. F. *Greek Imperialism.* Boston: 1913.

Finley, J. H. *Thucydides.* Cambridge: 1942.

Finley, M. I. *The Ancient Greeks: An Introduction to their Life and Thought.* New York: 1963.

Freeman, K. *Greek City-States.* London: 1951.

Fustel de Coulanges, N. D. *The Ancient City.* Anchor Books.

Glotz, Gustave. *Ancient Greece at Work: An Economic History of Greece from the Homeric Period to the Roman Conquest.* New ed. New York: 1967.

Hammond, N. G. L. *A History of Greece to 322 B.C.* New York: 1959.

Hooper, Finley. *Greek Realities: Life and Thought in Ancient Greece.* New York: 1967.

Jaeger, W. W. *Paideia: The Ideals of Greek Culture.* 3 vols. New York: 1939–44.

Kitto, H. D. F. *The Greeks.* Pelican Books.

MacKendrick, Paul. *The Greek Stones Speak: The Story of Archaeology in Greek Lands.* New York: 1962.

Michell, H. *The Economics of Ancient Greece.* New York: 1940.

Murray, G. *Five Stages of Greek Religion.* Anchor Books.

Murray, G. *The Literature of Ancient Greece.* 3d ed. Chicago: Phoenix Books, 1956.

Nilsson, M. P. *Greek Piety.* Oxford: 1948.

Nilsson, M. P. *Greek Popular Religion.* New York: 1940.

Otto, W. F. *The Homeric Gods: The Spiritual Significance of Greek Religion.* New York: 1954.

Richter, G. *The Sculpture and Sculptors of the Greeks.* New Haven: 1930.

Rostovtzeff, M. *History of the Ancient World.* Vol. I. Oxford: 1926.

Samuel, Alan E. *The Mycaeneans in History.* Englewood Cliffs, N.J: 1966.

Santillana, Giorgio de. *The Origins of Scientific Thought: From Anaximander to Plotinus, 600 B.C. to A.D. 300.* Chicago: 1961.

Schroedinger, E. *Nature and the Greeks.* Cambridge: 1954.

Starr, Chester G. *The Origins of Greek Civilization, 1100–650 B.C.* New York: 1961.

Vermeule, Emily. *Greece in the Bronze Age.* Chicago: 1964.

Zimmern, A. E. *The Greek Commonwealth.* Modern Library.

Novels

Atherton, Gertrude. *The Immortal Marriage*. New York: 1938.
Buchan, John. *The Lemnian*. 1912.
Erskine, John. *The Private Life of Helen of Troy*. New York: 1925.
Landor, W. Savage. *Pericles and Aspasia*. London: 1836.
Lytton, Edward Bulwer, 1st Baron. *Pausanias, the Spartan*. London: 1873.
Renault, Mary. *The King must Die*. New York: 1958.
Renault, Mary. *The Last of the Wine*. New York: 1956.
Renault, Mary. *The Bull from the Sea*. New York: 1962.
Renault, Mary. *The Mask of Apollo*. New York: 1966.

Chronological Table for Part II, A: The Greek City States

B.C.

c. 2500–1400	Minoan civilization in Crete, the Aegean Islands, and parts of mainland Greece.
c. 1800	Greek war bands appear in Greece.
c. 1600–1100	Mycenaean civilization.
1184–1174	Traditional date for the siege of Troy.
c. 1100–800	Greek "Dark Age."
8th century	Homer.
*c. 750–550	Age of colonization.
c. 700	Introduction of alphabetic writing among the Greeks.
c. 650	Introduction of coinage among Greeks.
c. 650	Introduction of the infantry phalanx.
c. 632	Cylon's conspiracy in Athens.
c. 630	Messenian revolt against Sparta; probable occasion of the establishment of the Lycurgan constitution.
c. 621	Draco's codification of Athenian laws.
*594–593	Solon's reorganization of the Athenian constitution.
c. 560–510	Peisistratid tyranny in Athens.
546	Conquest of Lydia (Croesus) by Cyrus, King of the Persians.
546	(?) Death of Thales of Miletus.
512	Darius the Great campaigned in Thrace; extended the Persian empire into Europe.
510	Overthrow of Hippias, tyrant of Athens, by Spartans.
*508	Cleisthenes' reorganization of Athenian constitution.

499–479	*Period of Persian Wars.*
499–494	Ionian revolt against the Persians.
499	Approximate beginning of Aeschylus' dramatic career in Athens.
492	Persian expedition into Thrace.
*490	Persian expedition against Eretria and Athens; battle of Marathon.
486	Egyptian revolt against the Persians.
484	Death of Darius; accession of Xerxes to the Persian throne.
*480–479	Great Persian invasion of Greece.
480, August	Battles of Thermopylae, Artemisium.
480, September	Battle of Salamis.
479	Battles of Plataea, Mycale.
479–431	*Leadership of Athens in Greece.*
478	Organization of the Delian League.
472	Aeschylus' *Persians.*
471	Ostracism of Themistocles; oligarchic party dominant in Athens.
468	Battle of Eurymedon; Persians driven from southwestern Asia Minor.
467	Naxos revolted from the Delian League.
466	Last Persian garrison expelled from Aegean area.
464–456	Helot revolt against Spartans.
*461	Athenian expeditionary force sent home by Spartans; Ephialtes and Pericles reduce the power of Areopagus; democratic party dominant in Athens; Cimon ostracised.
460–455	Athenian expedition to Egypt.
457–450	First "Peloponnesian" war: Sparta and allies against Athens.
456	Death of Aeschylus.
454	Transfer of League treasury from Delos to Athens.
448	Peace of Callias between Persia and Athenians brings Persian wars to an end.
447–445	Boeotia, Megara and Euboea revolt from Athens; intervention of Sparta; Thirty Years' Peace concluded between Sparta and Athens in 445 B.C.
447–438	Construction of the Parthenon at Athens.

c. 443	Ostracism of Thycydides, son of Melesias; Pericles confirmed in control of Athenian politics, despite set backs of preceding years.
c. 442	Death of Pindar, the poet.
433	Corcyra granted alliance by Athenians.
432	Revolt of Potidaea; Megarian decrees.
432	(?) Death of Phidias, the sculptor.
431–404	*Peloponnesian war.*
430	Plague in Athens.
*429	Death of Pericles; Cleon succeeds to leadership of democratic party.
428	Death of Anaxagoras, the philosopher.
427	Birth of Plato.
426	Adoption of a more aggressive strategy by Athenians.
*425	Capture of Spartan hoplites at Sphacteria; Cleon's control of *ecclesia* confirmed.
425	(?) Death of Herodotus.
424	Brasidas in Thrace; banishment of Thucydides, the historian.
423	Nicias and peace party dominant in Athens; one year truce concluded.
422	Cleon and war party dominant in Athens; expedition to Thrace, death of Cleon and Brasidas.
*421	Peace of Nicias; end of first phase of the war.
420	Alcibiades elected general in Athens; concluded alliance with Argos and other cities against Sparta.
419	Nicias and peace party dominant in Athens again.
418	Battle of Mantinea reestablished Spartan prestige; ostracism of Hyperbolus in Athens as a result of compromise between Alcibiades and Nicias.
416	Conquest of Melos by Athenians.
*415–413	Expedition to Sicily; siege of Syracuse by Athenians.
415	Flight of Alcibiades to Sparta.
413	Renewal of war between Athens and Sparta; occupation of Decelea by Spartans.
412	Agreement between Sparta and Persians; subsidy to Spartan fleet in return for cession of cities of Asia Minor to Persia.

*411	Oligarchic *coup d'état* in Athens—the Four Hundred; recall of Alcibiades to command of the Athenian fleet.
411	Death of Protagoras, the sophist.
410	Athenian victory at Cyzicus; restoration of democracy in Athens.
407	Lysander in command of Spartan fleet; early in 406 won a victory and Athenians exiled Alcibiades in their disappointment.
406	Athenian victory at Arginusae.
406	Death of Sophocles and of Euripides.
405	Spartan victory at Aegospotami.
*404	Surrender of Athens; end of the war; Alcibiades assassinated.
404–371	Spartan hegemony.
*404–403	Thirty tyrants in Athens.
403	Restoration of democracy in Athens.
401–400	Cyrus attempted to overthrow his brother, King of Persia; Xenophon and the march of the Ten Thousand Greeks.
400	(?) Death of Thucydides, the historian.
*399	Execution of Socrates.
399–387	War between Sparta and Persia; Corinthian war in Greece.
387	The King's Peace in Greece.
387	(?) Foundation of Academy by Plato.
380	Death of Aristophanes, the comic poet; (?) death of Gorgias, the sophist.
377	(?) Death of Hippocrates of Cos, the doctor.
379	War between Sparta and other Greek states, headed by Thebes.
371	Battle of Leuctra; Spartans defeated in Peloponnese by Thebans; end of Spartan hegemony.
371–362	*Theban hegemony.*
362	Battle of Mantinea; death of Epaminondas, collapse of Theban power in Greece.
362–338	*Political chaos in Greece; rise of Macedon.*
359–336	Philip II, King of Macedon.
354	Death of Xenophon, the historian.

351	First Philippic delivered by Demosthenes of Athens.
347	Death of Plato.
347–335	Aristotle at the Macedonian court as tutor to Alexander the Great.
*338	Battle of Chaeronea; Macedon supreme in Greece; organization of Pan-Hellenic league.
338	Death of Isocrates, the orator.
336	Assassination of Philip of Macedon; accession of Alexander the Great.
*336–323	Alexander the Great, King of Macedon.
335	Establishment of the Lyceum by Aristotle.
334	Alexander's invasion of Persia.
322	Death of Aristotle; death of Demosthenes, the orator.

B. The Hellenistic Kingdoms (334–146 B.C.)

1. *Political Changes*
   a. *Alexander the Great*
   b. *The Successor States*

2. *Economic Development*
   a. *Population*
   b. *Technological Progress*
   c. *Economic Organization*
   d. *Growth of Trade*

3. *Social Structure*
4. *Cultural Development*
   a. *Religion*
   b. *Art*
   c. *Literature*
   d. *Science*
      1) *Astronomy*
      2) *Mathematics*
      3) *Physics and Engineering*
      4) *Geography*
      5) *Medicine and Biology*
      6) *Literary and Linguistic Scholarship*
   e. *Philosophy*

1. POLITICAL CHANGES

a. Alexander the Great

When Philip of Macedon was assassinated in 336 B.C., his son Alexander was only twenty years old. But by the time Alexander died, just thirteen years later, the political and cultural face of the civilized world had been drastically changed. More perhaps than those of any other single individual in history, Alexander's personal character, capacities and career changed the relations of civilizations and peoples, and deeply affected the subsequent development of Classical and Western civilization. To be sure, the weakness of Persia, the excellence of the Macedonian army and the capacity of the generals whom Philip had trained, all helped to make Alexander's phenomenal military success possible; but it is hard to believe that his individual genius did not play a decisive role in mobilizing the full potentialities of the fighting machine which he had inherited, or to think that without him, Greek civilization would have penetrated as deeply into the Orient as in fact it did.

Alexander's career was one of almost uninterrupted warfare. In 334 B.C. he started his invasion of Persia, the self-styled avenger of the injuries done to the Hellenes by the Persian kings. In three great battles (Granicus, 334 B.C.; Issus, 333 B.C.; and Gaugamela, 331 B.C.) he met and defeated the Persian armies, subduing most of Asia Minor, the eastern Mediterranean seaboard, Egypt, and Mesopotamia. After the battle of Gaugamela, the Persian king fled eastward but was killed by some of his own follwers. Thereupon Alexander changed roles. He now posed as the legitimate successor of the Persian kings, took on many of the outward trappings of Oriental kingship, and at least toyed with the idea of his own divinity. From 330 B.C. until his death in 323 B.C. he tried to secure his empire by melding Asiatic and Hellenic peoples and civilizations. He recruited Persians and other Oriental peoples into his army, and trained them in the Macedonian fashion. He himself married an Oriental princess, Roxane, and persuaded many of his officers and several thousand of his Macedonian soldiers to imitate his example. In the administration of the newly conquered territories, he regularly employed Persians, Macedonians and Greeks on more or less equal terms. In doing these things, Alexander definitely rejected the traditional Greek view of the inferiority of barbarian peoples, and some scholars believe that he advanced the theory that all men are essentially similar, no matter what their race or culture might be.

As successor to the Persian king, Alexander set out to conquer all the territory that had belonged to the Persian empire. For three years he fought a series of difficult campaigns in central Asia, penetrating as far eastward as the Oxus and Jaxartes rivers. Then he turned southward, invading the Indus valley. There he continued his victorious career, subdued

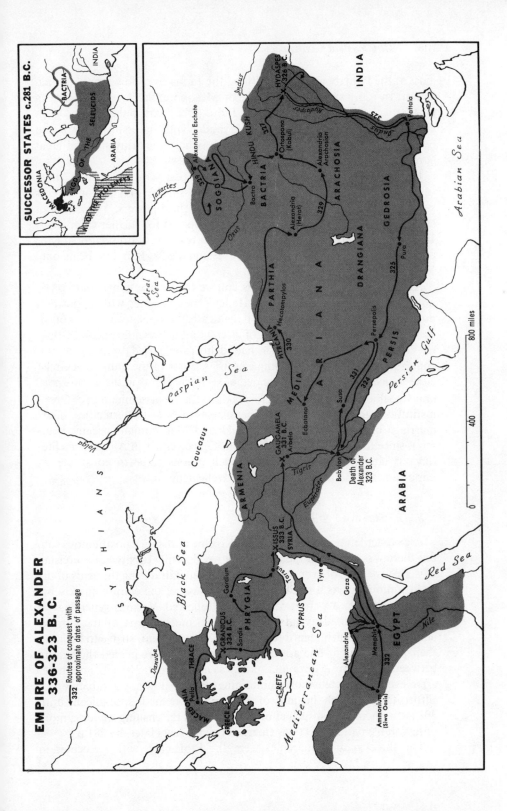

EMPIRE OF ALEXANDER 336-323 B.C.

→ 332 Routes of conquest with approximate dates of passage

SUCCESSOR STATES c.281 B.C.

BACTRIA

MACEDONIA

KGDM. OF THE SELEUCIDS

WITH THE PTOLEMIES

ARABIA

INDIA

INDIA

HYDASPES X 326 B.C.

Hydaspes

Indus

325

Pattala

Arabian Sea

Alexandria Eschate

324

Jaxartes

SOGDIAN

Bactra

Ortospana (Kabul)

327

BACTRIA

HINDU KUSH

Alexandria (Herat)

Oxus

329

Alexandria Arachosion

ARACHOSIA

ARIANA

DRANGIANA

GEDROSIA

FARTHIA

Pura

325

HYRCANIA

Hecatompylos

330

MEDIA

Ecbatana

PERSIS

Persepolis

331

Aral Sea

Caspian Sea

324

Susa

Babylon

Death of Alexander 323 B.C.

Persian Gulf

800 miles

400

GAUGAMELA X 331 B.C.

Arbela

ARMENIA

Tigris

Euphrates

Caucasus

Volga

S C Y T H I A N S

Black Sea

THRACE

Danube

MACEDONIA

Pella

GREECE

CRETE

PHRYGIA

Gordium

GRANICUS X 334 B.C.

Sardis

Tarsus

ISSUS 333 B.C.

SYRIA

CYPRUS

Tyre

Gaza

Mediterranean Sea

Alexandria

EGYPT

Memphis

332

Nile

Ammonium (Siwa Oasis)

Red Sea

ARABIA

Arabian Sea

0

most of the Punjab, and then followed the Indus river down to the Indian Ocean. In 325 B.C. he started back for Mesopotamia. A naval exploring party traveled from the mouth of the Indus river through the Indian Ocean and into the Persian Gulf, while Alexander with the main force passed overland through the desert of Gedrosia, where the army suffered great hardship from want of water and other supplies.

Upon his return, Alexander found his empire in serious disorder. Many of the satraps he had appointed, apparently assuming that he would never survive his distant enterprises, had abused their powers. He set about strenuous reform, and at the same time prepared for further campaigns. In 323 B.C., however, just as the army was ready to set out (probably to attack Arabia), Alexander caught a fever and died at Babylon, being only 33 years old.

Alexander died too soon for his empire to become consolidated. His policy of blending Oriental and Hellenic peoples met with opposition during his own lifetime, and after his death the policy was abandoned. Nevertheless, a vigorous process of interaction between Greek and Oriental culture, such as Alexander had deliberately tried to bring about, continued through the following centuries. Some of the numerous Greek cities which Alexander had founded at strategic points in the empire continued to flourish, and provided focal points for the dissemination of Greek institutions among at least the upper classes of Near Eastern cities. Intermarriage between Asiatics and Greeks and Macedonians became common, since few women emigrated from Greece either in Alexander's lifetime or later. The descendants of such unions came to constitute an important and influential class in the Hellenistic states.

b. The Successor States

Alexander left no heir at his death. Roxane bore him a posthumous son, but there was no one in the immediate royal family capable of exercising any effective control over the Macedonian generals during the years of the child's minority. As a result the central power of the empire quickly became ineffective. A period of confusion followed. Various generals who had been appointed as satraps in one or another part of the empire, acting without much regard to the central government, strove to build up their power, fought one another, and divided and redivided the empire between themselves. Alexander's son was murdered in 310 B.C., and thereafter even the pretense of maintaining central power was abandoned. Efforts to reestablish the unity of the empire were made sporadically until 301 B.C., when the last such effort failed. From the ensuing welter, a more or less stable pattern of states emerged twenty years later, by 281 B.C.

The three great monarchies were the Ptolemaic, with its center in

Egypt; the Seleucid, with centers in Mesopotamia and Syria; and Macedon, ruled by the Antigonid dynasty. Many of the peripheral areas of Alexander's empire broke away. Greek kings continued to rule in central Asia and in India for more than a century; Asia Minor came to be divided into a number of small competing states, of which the kingdom of Pergamum in the northwest became the most prominent; and Greece itself won a precarious and intermittent independence.

Wars between the successor states were frequent. One of the principal foci of strife was Greece, for the strength and security of the Hellenistic monarchies of the east depended in considerable measure on a constant supply of Greek mercenaries and administrators. In particular, Macedon and Egypt engaged in repeated struggles for influence in Greece, their policies toward the Greek cities alternating between conciliation and compulsion. Egypt and the Seleucid empire engaged in a similarly prolonged struggle for control of Palestine and southern Syria.

As playthings of great power politics, the Greek cities were in a difficult position at best. Most of them tried to maintain at least a shadow of independence by securing favorable terms of alliance with one or another of the great monarchies. A significant constitutional experiment was the development of federal leagues. The Achaean league in the northern Peloponnese and the Aetolian league in northwestern Greece became the leading powers of Greece proper. The federal government of these leagues had the right to levy taxes and to raise armies from member cities, and the representative principle was used in forming the federal deliberative bodies. Nevertheless, the inveterate particularism of the Greek city states was not overcome, and Greece as a whole never succeeded in uniting against outside powers. The "freedom of the Greeks" (i.e., the sovereignty of each city) became a political watchword for any foreign power which sought to gain support among the Greek states; but such freedom never proved practical. "Liberators" regularly turned into oppressors of Greek freedom.

Constant warfare and the potential or active hostility of the Oriental subject peoples soon weakened the Hellenistic states. When Rome began to extend her power into the Balkan peninsula after 200 B.C., the Roman legions met with only ineffective resistance. The chronic disunity of Greece helped the Romans against Macedon; and the internal weakness of the Oriental states made them relatively easy conquests. Nevertheless, the extension of Roman power was gradual, and decisive annexations were not made until 146 B.C. Only in 30 B.C. was the last area of the Hellenistic east, Egypt, added to the Roman empire; but Roman diplomacy and arms had been all powerful for more than a hundred years before that time.

2. ECONOMIC DEVELOPMENT

a. Population

Alexander's conquests opened up the whole area of the Orient to Greek commercial, military, and administrative enterprise. A large current of emigration to these relatively rich lands set in. Thousands and perhaps hundreds of thousands of Greeks left their homeland to settle in the new Greek cities which Alexander and his successors established to the number of more than two hundred. Others took service in the armies of the rival Hellenistic states or became government officials.

The slowing of population growth, which had already manifested itself in the fourth century, continued, so that emigration to the Orient probably reduced the total population of the old centers of Greek life. By the second century B.C. some land which had formerly been cultivated was turned over to pasture and literary references to abandoned villages begin to multiply. The number of slaves probably increased in relation to the free citizen population. In Macedon, however, the peasantry remained numerous until after the Roman conquest. In parts of Asia, but most notably in Egypt, the administrative and engineering skill of the Greeks extended the area of irrigation and improved the technique of farming. Presumably population rose to match the increased carrying capacity of the land, although direct information is lacking.

b. Technological Progress

Interaction between Greek and Oriental traditions led to a number of notable improvements in technology. In the field of warfare, Hellenistic armies learned how to attack walled towns, as earlier Greek armies had never been able to do. Great siege engines and catapults were invented. Elephants were introduced as animals of war, serving mainly to terrify opposing cavalry horses. Ships increased in size; harbor improvements such as moles and lighthouses were built in many ports, and the seasonal character of seafaring became less marked. City planning, the construction of aqueducts and sewers, public assembly halls, etc., added to the comforts of city life. Mechanical inventions such as the surveying level, pulleys, and cranes for lifting heavy loads were introduced or greatly improved, particularly after Archimedes reduced the principles of leverage to mathematical precision.

Social inventions such as public debts, banks, and insurance, facilitated trade and other economic activity; and the use of money certainly spread farther down the social scale than in any earlier time. Literacy, too, became common among city dwellers, perhaps for the first time, as systems of public education and endowed private schools were established. Book publication became a regular business, carried on by means of slave copyists. Writing was done on parchment or papyrus rolls, and a number of great libraries were established where scholars could command nearly all the literary heritage of the Greek world. The spread of a common language, a simplified form of the Attic dialect, over the whole Near East facilitated both trade and intellectual relations; but for the most part, works of literature were composed only in the (increasingly archaic) Attic dialect of the fifth and fourth centuries. Since the spoken language of the great Hellenistic cities continued to change and grow, the effort to freeze literary grammar and vocabulary eventually created a special literary language which only the learned could write correctly.

c. Economic Organization

Perhaps the most striking characteristic of the economy of the Hellenistic age was the thoroughgoing state control over production and distribution which was instituted in the Ptolemaic, and, to a lesser extent, in the Seleucid empire. In Egypt the administrative bureaucracy planned production; prices for many products were fixed by the government; and for some of the more valuable commodities, the government enforced a monopoly, buying from the producer at a fixed rate and selling either at home or abroad for a much higher price. This system made the Ptolemies the richest rulers of their time. Egypt became the principal granary for the Greek cities, and shipped grain (not to mention a host of manufactured goods, mainly luxuries) as far west as Rome.

In the Seleucid empire, centralization of economic control never approached Ptolemaic rigor. Rather, a conglomeration of privileged Greek cities, temple estates, royal domains, even tribal districts, pursued the divergent types of economic and political life to which long precedent had attached them. Nevertheless, the monarchy took an active part in trade. A large part of the royal income was in kind, which the government converted into money by sale or export.

Macedon and Greece remained far less wealthy than the Oriental states. Their strength lay mainly in manpower. In mainland Greece, only Corinth continued to be an active center of trade and industry. The island city of Rhodes built up an important trade, serving as entrepôt between Greece and the Orient. Later Delos replaced Rhodes as the economic center of the Aegean, and became preeminent especially as a slave mart.

d. Growth of Trade

The geographical explorations connected with Alexander's conquests established direct commercial relations between India and the Hellenistic world. Trade with China, too, attained some importance; and Hellenistic penetration of the African and European back country went farther than in earlier times.

The typical Greek trade pattern—export of olive oil, wine, and manufactured goods, in exchange for wheat and raw materials—was duplicated in the Hellenistic cities to some extent; but many of them were situated in rich grain-producing areas and so did not need to depend on long-distance transport for their food supply. The exchange of manufactured goods tended to become relatively more important than it had been in earlier centuries. Various cities established manufacturing specialities; thus Corinth became famous for its bronze work, Alexandria for its papyrus, glass, linen, and perfumes; and Antioch for its textiles.

The Hellenistic age probably witnessed the highest development of regional economic interdependence and specialization ever achieved in the ancient world. Under the Roman empire, the economic patterns of Hellenistic civilization were introduced into western Europe, but a corresponding shrinkage of the eastern margin took place, for the Romans never established their power over Mesopotamia, much less over the Iranian plateau, and trade between the Mediterranean world and these areas was probably less important than it had been in Seleucid times.

3. SOCIAL STRUCTURE

The Hellenistic world was distinguished by the sharp line drawn between the ruling Hellenized groups, mainly confined to cities, and the surrounding Oriental populations. Only in parts of Asia Minor did Greek habits and civilization spread to the countryside; elsewhere the rural population and large segments of the urban working force clung tenaciously to their old languages, customs and ways of life. Nevertheless, Hellenism never became a matter of race; individuals who acquired wealth and assimilated Greek ways found easy access to the privileged ruling class.

The gap between upper and lower classes was of course greatly widened by the cultural difference which came to prevail between them. A parallel differentiation seems to have occurred in Greece, where it appears that the level of wages failed to keep pace with rising prices. (Alexander and his immediate successors expended the Persian royal treasure which had accumulated over generations, thereby vastly increasing the amount of precious metal in circulation, with the result that the value of metal sank and prices rose correspondingly.) The fact that wages lagged meant greater hardship for the free urban working population. Echoes of revolutionary sentiment have come down to us, mainly from Asia Minor where some men dreamed of a City of the Sun where all men would be equal in property and in rights. A similar movement actually came to power in Sparta, where the concentration of landed property in a few hands precipitated social revolution during the third century B.C., but neighboring states quickly intervened to overthrow the revolutionaries.

In general, oligarchic government predominated all over the Hellenistic world. In the Orient, Greeks and Macedonians constituted a small privileged class. By degrees they shifted their activity from the crasser (and more productive) forms of economic activity to more gentlemanly pursuits. They tended to abandon trade, becoming government officials, or else retiring to live on an income drawn from landed estates or from some other form of capital. Local government of the Greek cities of the Orient was nearly always in the hands of such persons. Some cities were governed by royal appointees; others enjoyed local self-government and set up boards of magistrates, councils and, occasionally, popular assemblies on the model of the Greek *polis*. In Greece itself, the oligarchic interest was upheld first by Macedon and then by Rome, and the democratic tradition gradually faded away even in Athens.

4. CULTURAL DEVELOPMENT

a. Religion

Traditional Greek religious practices and beliefs continued to lose ground through the Hellenistic period. A more personal type of religion arose to supplement the public ceremonies of the city state; in particular, the worship of the blind goddess, Fortune, who was sometimes conceived as a sort of personal spirit which watched over each man's life, assumed a new prominence.

An important religious innovation was the worship of men, and especially of rulers, as gods. Hellenistic kings regularly styled themselves divine, and demanded that their subjects worship them. The combination of the Oriental conception of a divinely-guided kingship with the Greek custom of worshipping heroes provided the basis and outward form for these ruler-cults. It is difficult even to guess how sincere the Greeks became in their deification of the Hellenistic kings. The worship of the ruler had some of the characteristics of modern patriotism: to sacrifice before the king's statue was a gesture of political loyalty. At the same time, the absolute power of the kings raised them far above the level of ordinary life, and their acts, which might raise an individual or a whole city to heights of good fortune or the reverse, perhaps partook of an unpredictable divine nature in the eyes of ordinary men.

The emotional barrenness of Greek religion, when divorced from the city state which had given it birth, left the way open for the development of new, personal religions which drew most of their ceremony and beliefs from Oriental prototypes. Worship of Isis and Serapis, of Attis, and of the Great Mother Goddess of Asia Minor took on new forms. These cults are collectively called "mystery religions." In many respects they resembled the Orphic and Eleusinian mysteries of earlier times. A central idea in all of them was the achievement of personal salvation, sometimes conceived

as the result of a mystic or symbolic union between the god and his wor-
shipper. Orgiastic and other ceremonies were used to induce the sense of
such mystic union with the god. Once it had been achieved, the worshippers were taught to believe that the god with whom they had been
united would safeguard them in life and after death.

Such mystery religions developed an authoritative priesthood and elaborate ceremonials, but inculcated little, if any, ethical teaching. The
majority of their adherents were drawn from the lower classes of the cities.
For the educated, philosophy became, more than ever, a code of conduct
and a substitute for religion.

b. Art

Hellenistic art continued, for the most part, the traditions which had
been developed in Greece during the fourth century. The most famous
schools of sculpture were located at Rhodes and Pergamum, where such
statues as the Victory of Samothrace, Laocoon, and the Dying Gaul were
carved. Genre sculpture developed: statues of children, aged crones,
cherubs, and satyrs provided a contrast to the heroic style of earlier Greek
statuary.

The traditional Greek architectural styles were widely adapted for secular purposes. Fine porticos were built to adorn city market places; the art
of fortification developed to unprecedented levels; public assembly halls
(basilicas) and palaces were constructed. In the minor arts, mosaic work,
taken over from the Egyptians, was employed to decorate floors and walls.

c. Literature

Little has come down to us from the enormous literary production of the
Hellenistic age. Older literary forms were retained, and a new one, the
romance, became widely popular. Alexander's career became a favorite
subject of romance, and a host of marvelous deeds and adventures quickly
clustered around his name; so much so that Alexander romances became
a distinct literary form.

Prose composition was strongly colored by the study of rhetoric, which
retained preeminent interest for the Greeks long after speech-making had
ceased to play any important role in politics. Style tended to eclipse matter.
A popular amusement was to listen to set speeches, in order to savor the
elegance of diction and the manner of delivery. Literary taste was profoundly shaped by rhetorical conventions, so that histories, for example,
came to be valued mainly for their speeches and refinement of style.

Three writers deserve particular mention: Polybius, Theocritus, and
Menander. Polybius (*c.* 200–120 B.C.) was a political leader of the Achaean
league, and as a young man spent seventeen years as a hostage in Rome.

He wrote a universal history, covering the years between 264 and 146 B.C., in which he set out to describe to his fellow Greeks the causes and course of the rise of Rome. Only a part of his history has survived; in it he shows himself to be a painstakingly accurate and thoroughly self-conscious historian, but the feeling and the grace which respectively distinguish Thucydides and Herodotus are totally absent. Theocritus (*c.* 305–250 B.C.) wrote lyric poetry in which he celebrated the loves and heartbreaks of shepherds and shepherdesses. The pastoral idyll, as this form of poetry is called, was a highly artificial, but, in Theocritus' hands, an exquisitely graceful, poetic form. His poems were widely imitated in later times, both by Roman and by renaissance and early modern European poets. Menander (*c.* 340–290 B.C.) was the most famous writer of the so-called "New Comedy." In his plays, none of which has survived complete, the chorus had entirely disappeared. He portrayed a frivolous high society in a comedy of manners. Roman comedians copied the Greek "New Comedy" and through their example, many of its conventions passed into the work of early modern playwrights.

d. Science

In Hellenistic times natural science became more distinct from philosophy than it had been earlier. Partly under the stimulus of sceptic criticism of philosophical doctrines (see below), a number of men devoted their attention to careful measurement, observation, and calculation of natural phenomena. Some of their results have a startlingly contemporary ring, as for instance Eratosthenes' calculation of the circumference of the earth, or Hero's invention of a "steam engine." But with few exceptions the theories and discoveries of the scientists were not translated into technological improvements, and after about two centuries, Greek curiosity about the physical world turned largely in other directions, notably toward astrology. The major center of scientific research was the Museum of Alexandria, a state-supported institution established by the first Ptolemy for the benefit of scholars.

1) Astronomy. Two general astronomical theories were worked out by Hellenistic scientists. About 280 B.C. Aristarchus of Samos proposed the heliocentric theory—that the earth and planets revolve around the sun; but the theory did not win much support because stellar parallax could not be observed with the instruments available to the ancients. The geocentric theory, developed most notably by Hipparchus (*c.* 185–120 B.C.), was closer to common sense, and accounted successfully for the regular motions of heavenly bodies. By this theory, the earth was assumed to be at the center of the universe, while around it revolved a number of crystalline spheres in which were set the stars, sun, moon and planets. The irregular motion of the planets was explained by epicycles—that is, subordinate spheres which revolved on an axis of their own although attached to a greater sphere whose center was the earth. By postulating an appropriate number of spheres and epicycles, all the regular motions of the heavens could be accounted for mechanically, and even predicted. Comets and meteors, of course, remained inexplicable.

2) Mathematics. Euclid codified Greek geometry about 300 B.C., and his book, *Elements of Geometry*, became a classic textbook from his own day almost to the present. After Euclid's time new realms of mathematics were explored. Solid geometry and the theory of regular curves were studied by Apollonius of Perga (*c.* 247–205 B.C.) and Archimedes of Syracuse (287–212 B.C.). Trigonometry, too, was developed by the astronomer Hipparchus and others.

3) Physics and Engineering. Mathematical progress in Hellenistic times was applied, most notably by Archimedes, to mechanical theory and practice. Archimedes developed the concept of specific gravity and worked out mathematically the balance of forces involved in the age-old use of levers. He made a number of practical inventions, including the endless, or Archimedean, screw for raising liquids, the compound pulley, and a variety of war machines which were used by the Syracusans against a besieging Roman army. Another Hellenistic figure, Hero of Alexandria, who probably lived in the first century B.C., invented a mechanical toy which moved by the force of escaping steam, much as an ordinary garden sprinkler revolves from the force of escaping water. More important for his own time, Hero systematized the science of mechanics, distinguishing five simple machines from which all others were built up—the lever, wheel and axle, pulley, wedge, and screw.

4) Geography. In Hellenistic times Greek knowledge of the world was increased by voyages of discovery and by new trade connections with distant regions. Descriptive geography was as old as Hecataeus; but in Hellenistic times measurement and mathematical principles were applied to the construction of maps and the calculation of locations. The idea that the earth was spherical was generally accepted, and systems of latitude and longitude were introduced. Eratosthenes (*c.* 276–196 B.C.) calculated the circumference of the earth by making careful observations of the elevation of the noonday sun in northern and southern Egypt. He found the difference in elevation to be 7 degrees, 12 minutes, and by measuring the actual distance on the earth's surface between his points of observation, he was able to calculate the total circumference at a figure very close to that accepted today. Subsequent geographers, however, did not accept his conclusions, and reduced their estimate of the earth's size very considerably.

5) Medicine and Biology. Notable progress in detailed knowledge of anatomy and physiology was made in Hellenistic times, largely as a result of the introduction of systematic anatomical dissection. Many new drugs were likewise added to the medical pharmacopoeia. Information about animals and plants poured into the Greek world as a consequence of the great territorial expansion of Alexander's time. This information was duly recorded in learned catalogues, of which the most famous was written by Theophrastus (*c.* 372–287 B.C.), Aristotle's successor as head of the Lyceum. His book *On Plants* remained a standard authority until early modern times.

6) Literary and Linguistic Scholarship. The problem of authoritative texts arose constantly in the ancient world when books had to be reproduced by copyists. A number of Alexandrian scholars set themselves the task of editing the texts of earlier Greek authors; and all the classic Greek works which we know came down to us through their critical hands. The conventional division into books and chapters is their work. The study of grammar was likewise systematized: the parts of speech, cases, and declensions were distinguished, and standards of linguistic purity established.

e. Philosophy

During the Hellenistic period, Greek philosophy divided into fairly definite schools, of which the most important were the Cynic, Sceptic, Epicurean and Stoic. Plato's Academy and Aristotle's Lyceum continued to flourish as institutions of learning but did not retain distinctive doctrines of their own. The Academy turned to scepticism, the Lyceum to eclecticism. In all the schools, attention was centered on ethical questions, so that philosophy tended to become a way of life and a school of manners first and foremost, while more abstract, theoretical interests faded into the background.

The Cynics traced their school to Antisthenes (*c.* 450–366 B.C.), a pupil of Socrates. Like "hippies" of the 1960's, they rejected conventional standards, criticized the corruption and frauds of the society they saw around them, and held up instead an ideal of "the simple life," which, to some Cynics at least, became a sort of asceticism. Diogenes (*c.* 412–332 B.C.), who lived in a tub and went about with a lantern looking in vain for an honest man, and who, when asked by Alexander what he would most like, answered that the King might stop blocking the sunlight, epitomized the cynic attitude, whether the stories are true or not.

The Sceptics derived their school from Pyrrho (*c.* 360–270 B.C.), who denied that truth could be known by man, and recommended suspended judgment and mental calm. The Sceptics spent most of their time attacking the doctrines of other schools, trying to show their absurdity or lack of foundation.

The Epicureans took their name and philosophy from Epicurus (342–270 B.C.). He taught that pleasure was the only good, and that mental pleasures were in general superior to physical ones since they did not involve consequent pains. Epicurus adopted the atomic theory of Democritus, and used it to buttress his ethical position by disproving the active intervention of the gods in human affairs.

The most influential of all the schools was the Stoic, founded by Zeno of Citium (*c.* 336–264 B.C.), a native of Cyprus. Zeno taught that the universe was an organic whole, guided by a universal Reason; and that men, by virtue of the rationality which was in them, could discipline themselves to live in accord with the rationality of the universe, developing the virtues of courage, prudence, justice, and temperance in the face of all the ups and downs of fortune. Two especially significant doctrines were deduced from these basic tenets: the brotherhood of all mankind, and the concept of a natural moral law, to which human law should as far as possible conform. These two Stoic doctrines entered significantly into the shaping of Roman law in the time of the Roman empire, and through the Roman law entered basically into Western civilization.

The disagreements of the philosophic schools led many men to try to reconcile them, an effort known as eclecticism. The eclectic philosophers drew upon Babylonian and other learned traditions as well as upon their Greek predecessors. In particular, astrology became more and more popular as the Hellenistic age advanced. Posidonius of Rhodes (*c.* 135–51 B.C.), though often called a Stoic, reflected these eclectic tendencies in his philosophy, for he made room for demons and ghosts, the influence of the stars and the significance of dreams, omens and prophecies in his cosmological system.

With a figure like Posidonius, the Greek rationalist tradition had nearly played itself out. The change may reflect the upsurge of Oriental habits of mind, shedding a veneer of Hellenism which had been imposed after Alexander's conquest. In the west, a few of the educated Romans took over Hellenistic philosophy and resisted the mysticism of Oriental religions for another two centuries; but in the Hellenized east, philosophy and religion drew together in late Hellenistic and Roman times. This development prefigured the new synthesis which the Christian fathers were to achieve. Individual sceptics and rationalists continued to arise in the Greek world until the victory of Christianity had become complete; but the main trend of thought was against them, seeking rather an emotionally satisfactory way of life and a personal orientation to the universe—values which were found increasingly in mystic and religious doctrines.

Suggestions for Further Reading for Part II, B

The Oxford Classical Dictionary. Oxford, 1948.
Cambridge Ancient History. Vols. 7–8. Cambridge: 1928–30.
Cambridge Ancient History. Volumes of Plates. Vol. 3. Cambridge: 1930.
Cary, M. *A History of the Greek World from 323 to 146 B.C.* Rev. ed. New York: 1951.
Cary, M. *The Legacy of Alexander.* London: 1932.
Farrington, B. *Greek Science.* Vol. 2. *Theophrastus to Galen.* Pelican Books.
Jones, A. H. M. *The Greek City from Alexander to Justinian.* Oxford: 1940.
Murray, G. *Five Stages of Greek Religion.* Anchor Books.
Rostovtzeff, M. *Social and Economic History of the Hellenistic World.* 2 vols. Oxford: 1941.
Tarn, W. W. *Alexander the Great.* Cambridge: 1948.
Tarn, W. W. *Hellenistic Civilization.* 3d ed. London: 1952.
Zeller, E. *Outlines of the History of Greek Philosophy.* Meridian Books.
Zeller, E. *Stoics, Epicureans, and Sceptics.* London: 1880.

Novels

Druon, Maurice. *Alexander the God.* New York: 1960.
Fast, Howard. *My Glorious Brothers.* Boston: 1948.
Fisher, Vardis. *Island of the Innocent.* New York: 1952.
Mitchison, Naomi. *The Corn King and the Spring Queen.* New York: 1931.
Payne, Robert. *Alexander the God.* New York: 1954.

Chronological Table for Part II, B: The Hellenistic Kingdoms

B.C.

*336–323	Alexander the Great, King of Macedon.
334	Alexander's invasion of Persian empire; battle of the Granicus.
333	Battle of Issus.
332	(?) Death of Diogenes, the philosopher.
331	Battle of Gaugamela.
330	Death of Darius III; Alexander posed as legitimate successor to Persian throne.
323	Death of Alexander.
310	Murder of Alexander's son.
301	Failure of last bid to establish effective central power over Alexander's empire.
c. 300	Euclid the geometer's *Elements*.

290	(?) Death of Menander, the comic poet.
287	(?) Death of Theophrastus, the botanist and successor of Aristotle in the Lyceum.
281	Relative stabilization of successor states: Ptolemaic Empire, Seleucid Empire, Antigonids ruling in Macedonia, smaller states in Asia Minor, federal leagues and cities in Greece.
c. 280	Aristarchus of Samos, the astronomer, propounded heliocentric theory.
270	(?) Death of Pyrrho, sceptical philosopher; (?) Death of Epicurus, the philosopher.
264	(?) Death of Zeno of Citium, founder of Stoic school.
250	(?) Death of Theocritus, the poet.
212	Death of Archimedes, the mathematician and physicist.
205	(?) Death of Apollonius, the mathematician.
196	(?) Death of Eratosthenes, the geographer.
146	Most of Greece annexed by Rome.
120	(?) Death of Polybius, the historian.
51	(?) Death of Posidonius of Rhodes, eclectic philosopher.

EVOLUTION AND DEVELOPMENT OF GREEK SCULPTURE

Among the Greeks sculpture began as a means for propitiating supernatural powers. Later the art served to glorify athletes and other men whose deeds deserved to be remembered. After about 400 B.C. to surprise the beholder with some novel effect became an end in itself. In the late Roman empire, however, the celebration of the power of political rulers was the main surviving role for sculpture.

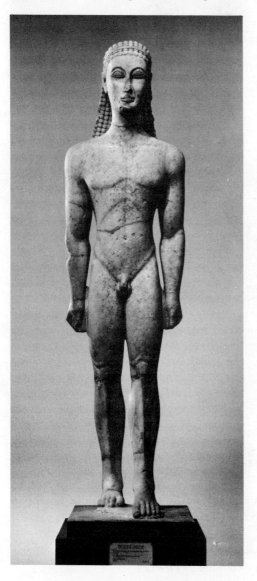

**Kouros, or Figure of a
Standing Youth
615-600** B.C.
(The Metropolitan Museum of
Art Fletcher Fund, 1932)

This naked statue is typical
of the archaic period.
The stiffness of expression and
rigidity of position indicate
the sculptor's limited
knowledge of the complexity
of the human form.
Although the sculptor fell
short of naturalistic accuracy,
he achieved an effective
representation of a man-like
god, naively yet
powerfully conceived.

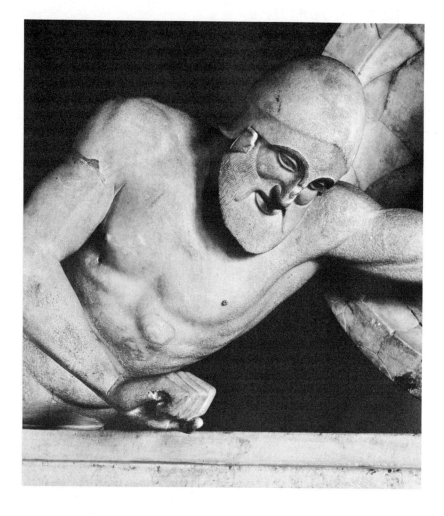

A Fallen Warrior Holding a Shield
500-480 B.C. **Glyptothek, Munich**
(Hirmer Verlag München)

The Fallen Warrior, an example of the late archaic style, once stood in the
pediment of the Temple of Aphaia in Aigina and was part of a group
probably representing an incident from the Trojan War. In comparison with
the kouros, the Fallen Warrior shows a naturalistic treatment of the
body and a more realistic rendering of the muscular surfaces. Archaic
conventions, however, persist in the handling of the face.

Poseidon or Zeus of Artemesium
460 B.C. Bronze original in National Museum, Athens
(Hirmer Verlag München)

In the Poseidon all traces of stiffness of body surfaces and rigidity in position
are now gone. In contrast to the Fallen Warrior, the face shows successful
naturalistic treatment. The surfaces of the face are carefully modelled,
while the deep furrows of the beard look like real hair. Yet despite naturalistic
details, the Poseidon represents an idealized concept of beauty, without
any real human counterpart. This statue was recovered from the sea
where it had been deposited by a shipwreck. Who made it is unknown, but
stylistic details show that it was designed and cast in Athens about the
time Pericles assumed control of the city's public life.

Hermes with the Infant Dionysos, Praxiteles
350-330 B.C. Olympia Museum
(Alinari Art Reference Bureau)

In the fourth century B.C. their growing technical virtuosity allowed Greek
sculptors to make more and more realistic statues. This is illustrated by
this work of Praxiteles, a famous sculptor in his own day, who manages to
suggest the softness of human flesh by subtle modelling of the marble
surface. Yet this extraordinary mastery of technique had its cost. Praxiteles'
Hermes lacks the majesty and awe appropriate to a god. We see instead
a handsome, slightly self-conscious young man. But in Praxiteles' time the
Greeks had already lost faith in the gods of Olympus anyway, so that
the reduction of divinity to a merely decorative level fitted the intellectual
climate of the age.

Dying Gaul
Circa 240 B.C. **Capitoline Museum, Rome**
(Alinari Art Reference Bureau)

Hellenistic sculpture continued the tradition of highly realistic treatment of
the human form. In contrast to artists of earlier periods, however, Hellenistic
sculptors often introduced a dramatic element into their works. This statue,
for instance, emphasized realistic details, but the sculptor strove for a
heightened effect by portraying a defeated barbarian warrior on the point
of death, attempting, with all his remaining strength, to rise from the ground
and regain his feet while his life's blood oozed from the wound in his side.
The sculptor thus sacrificed timelessness and monumentality for shock
value, since even a pang of sympathy for the rude invaders who briefly
frightened the security of Greek city life in the third century B.C. was sure
to startle the slightly jaded Hellenistic gentlemen for whose taste such
work was designed.

Pericles, after Kresilas
Circa **440** B.C.
(British Museum)

The bust shows Pericles as *strategos* wearing a helmet on the back of his head.
We cannot tell how much Pericles really looked like this bust. Although
it was carved during his lifetime, the sculptor may have portrayed an
idealized image of the wise and farseeing military leader and statesman
rather than the idiosyncracies of Pericles' real features.

Alexander the Great
Silver Tetradrachme, 306-281 B.C.
(Courtesy Museum of Fine Arts, Boston)

This coin aims at conveying the idea of Alexander as ruler and divinity rather
than as an individual personality. The horn visible amidst his curly hair
was a symbol of divine power and status. By issuing such a coin, Lysimachus,
one of the generals who disputed Alexander's empire after the king's
death, was laying claim to legitimate succession to the Macedonian conqueror.

Julius Caesar
(Charakterkoepfe de Weltgeschichte /
Kurt Lange Piper Verlag München)

The Roman fondness for realistic portraiture is demonstrated by this
convincing likeness of Julius Caesar.

Augustus Addressing His Troops
15 B.C. Vatican Museum, Vatican City
(Anderson Art Reference Bureau)

This statue of the Emperor Augustus addressing his troops deliberately and
consciously harked back to old times. The details on the breastplate, for
example, portray incidents from early Roman history, and the artistic style
used in making the statue imitated fifth century work (a full four hundred years
before Augustus' time) when Greek sculptors had attained a lofty idealism —
"above the battle" — in their portraits of the gods. The anonymous Greek
who made this statue was a skilful imitator indeed, and far outdid
Augustus himself, who restored a republican facade — but only a facade —
to the Roman body politic.

Caracalla
Circa A.D. 215
(Art Museum, Princeton University)

The sculptor who made this bust of the Emperor Caracalla was fully in command of Hellenistic techniques for surprising the viewer and conveying heightened, dramatic effects. The self-conscious restraint and archaizing of Augustus' day had been rejected, just as in politics Caracalla used his imperial office to give free rein to his violent and sensuous impulses.

Constantine
Circa A.D. 313 Capitoline Museum, Rome
(Hirmer Verlag München)

The disasters that struck the Roman empire in the third century A.D. are here tellingly recorded in stone. The sculptor had lost the high skills of earlier ages; realism, detail, technical mastery of the medium all have vanished. Yet the staring, strained expression so awkwardly conferred upon the Emperor Constantine manages for all its clumsiness to suggest a striving after transcendental truth — an effort to catch sight of another and better world than this. In such a climate of thought, Christianity throve.

C. The Roman Republic: Political Unification of the Mediterranean

1. PEOPLES OF WESTERN EUROPE

The western Mediterranean lands lagged far behind the eastern in the development of civilization. Neolithic settlements appear to have penetrated into Spain, Italy, and southern France by about 3000 B.C. About a thousand years later, a series of invasions from the Danubian area introduced metals and more elaborate technology into these same regions. Indo-European tribesmen began to filter into Italy probably about 1700 B.C., and about 1100 B.C. iron-using peoples followed them. As in Greece, these movements seem to have been complicated affairs, involving extensive mixture of peoples and repeated migrations and conquests. By 800 B.C., however, Indo-European languages were spoken throughout Italy. Herding took a very prominent place in the economy, and cities were non-existent.

About 800 B.C. the Etruscans landed on the west coast of Italy, coming, probably, from Asia Minor or the Aegean Islands. They spoke a non-Indo-European tongue, and although they knew how to write, modern scholars have been unable to read their few surviving inscriptions. The Etruscans brought into Italy many of the high skills of the eastern Mediterranean: stone masonry, the art of building and navigating relatively large ships, fine craftsmanship in metal working, pottery manufacture, etc. They planted a series of city states through Etruria (modern Tuscany), subduing the native population. Shortly before 500 B.C. they were able to extend their power over more than half of Italy, from Campania in the south to the Po Valley in the north.

Etruscan expansion, however, brought them into hostile contact with a people already familiar to us: the Greek colonists who had settled along the coast line of southern Italy as far north as Naples. A third element in the Italian balance of power was the Carthaginian state, which had been founded by the Phoenicians a little before 800 B.C. After the overthrow of the Phoenician cities by the Assyrians (see above, p. 20), Carthage became independent, and built up an empire in North Africa. The Carthaginians early came into conflict with the Greeks in Sicily; and since both Etruscans and Carthaginians found themselves fighting a common enemy, an alliance was concluded between them about 535 B.C. The allies were able to dominate the western Mediterranean, to check further Greek colonization and even succeeded in driving Greek colonists from the island of Corsica.

After about 500 B.C., however, the balance of power began to shift in favor of the native peoples of Italy. The Italians had learned much of the art of war from their more civilized neighbors, and were soon able to give a good account of themselves in battle against them. A decisive event was the successful rebellion of the Latin tribes against their Etruscan over-lords, which occurred in 509 B.C. if Roman traditions are to be trusted. The rebellion may have been fomented by the Greek city of Cumae, which was seriously threatened by the Etruscan-Carthaginian alliance. At any rate, a generation later, in 474 B.C., a sea battle was fought between the Greeks and their enemies near Cumae, in which the Etruscan fleet was defeated. The independence of Latium was thereby confirmed, and Etruscan control of Campania, the region south of Latium, came to an end.

Etruscan power suffered still another blow when Gallic tribesmen invaded Italy from the north, probably not long before 400 B.C., and drove them from the Po valley. These invaders were an offshoot of an Indo-European people, the Celts, who came to dominate most of Western Europe between about 1200 B.C. and 500 B.C. The Celts first appeared in what is now Austria and Bohemia early in the second millenium B.C., and from that center expanded outward in a series of waves, until they dominated France (Gaul), Britain, Ireland, northern Italy, and parts of Spain. In addition, an invading band attacked Macedon in the third century B.C. After devastating that country and many parts of Greece, they crossed over into Asia Minor and settled down on the central plateau of that peninsula, where, known as Galatians, they continued to speak their Celtic tongue as late as the second century A.D.

Far to the north, ensconced in forests and swamps, lived the Germans, located in southern Scandinavia and along the coasts of the Baltic Sea. As the Celts conquered more southerly lands, the Germans moved southward and westward in their rear, reaching the lower Rhine in the eighth century B.C., and driving the Celts from central Germany in the fourth century B.C.

Archaeologists have been able to trace a constant development in the material culture of these peoples of Northern and Western Europe. In general it seems clear that most of the important advances came from contact with and imitation of the more developed civilizations of the eastern Mediterranean regions. Trade relations existed at a very early date. Even in Minoan times, amber from the Baltic coast reached the island of Crete, and the Phoenicians traded tin from Cornwall in western England for the manufactures of the eastern Mediterranean. As Italy became civilized, the Latins borrowed much from Greek civilization; the Celts of Gaul similarly became acquainted with the goods and, to a lesser extent, with the manners of Greek life through contact with the prosperous Greek city of Massilia (Marseilles). In still later times, the Germans learned many of the arts of civilization from the peoples of the Roman empire, so that when they invaded Roman territory in the fourth and fifth centuries A.D. they were far from being the simple barbarians of a thousand years earlier.

One may think of civilization as diffusing outward through Europe, first from an Oriental, then from an Aegean, and thirdly from an Italian center, each center being somewhat different in the character of its own civilization, and each effecting a peculiar local combination with indigenous elements in the barbarian cultures of the north. Cultural influences continued to flow into Western Europe (from Arabic and Byzantine sources) until the twelfth century A.D. About 1500 A.D., cultural dominance passed to the West, and influences began to flow in the other direction, from Western Europe to the eastern Mediterranean and Orient—indeed, to all corners of the earth. If you bear this fluid analogy in mind, it may help to correct the artificial isolation and segmentation of history which the scheme of this handbook imposes upon what was in fact a living, unbroken whole.

2. THE ROMAN REPUBLIC: CONQUEST OF ITALY (509–265 B.C.)

The site of the city of <u>Rome was first occupied about 1000</u> B.C., but Rome remained only a village, or rather a group of villages, until Etruscan conquerors settled there and built a city in the seventh century B.C. About the end of the sixth century, the Etruscan kings were driven out and an aristocratic republican government, headed by two consuls, was set up instead. During the next 250 years, the Romans found themselves almost constantly at war with their neighbors; at the same time they experienced at home a prolonged struggle between aristocratic and democratic (patrician and plebeian) factions. From this turbulent period, Rome emerged supreme in Italy by 265 B.C. with a curiously mixed form of government combining aristocratic, oligarchic, and democratic elements.

a. Foreign wars

The early Roman republic was a small city state, hard pressed by hostile neighbors. Probably in 493 B.C. the Romans made an alliance with the other Latin peoples for mutual defense, and for nearly a century the Latins and Romans fought side by side to defend the fertile plains of Latium. In 396 B.C. came Rome's first important conquest: the neighboring Etruscan city of Veii was captured, its population destroyed, and its land resettled by Roman citizens. Roman prestige suffered a serious blow six years later when marauding Gallic tribesmen defeated the Roman army, devastated the city, and withdrew only upon receipt of a large sum of gold.

This setback, however, had the effect of stirring the Romans to intensified activity. The city was rebuilt and a strong wall erected to protect it from similar disasters in the future; in a series of wars the Latin allies were reduced to dependence on Rome; and, in the course of the fourth century B.C., the Roman system of alliances was extended southward to Campania. The treatment Rome accorded to defeated enemy peoples and cities was of decisive importance for the future growth of the Roman state. The particularism so characteristic of Greek political life never established itself firmly in Italy, where tribal associations and leagues between cities had existed from very early times. Thus the Romans met with less resistance to incorporation in the Roman state and were themselves more willing to extend the duties and rights of Roman citizenship to other cities than was the case, for instance, in the Athenian empire.

Relations between the Roman government and allied states varied considerably from case to case. In some instances when cities were incorporated into the Roman state, their citizens were added to the Roman citizen roll and their independent political life was thus brought to an end. This measure was sometimes taken as a punishment for rebellion or disloyalty, local autonomy being temporarily supplanted by the government of a Roman official; but after a lapse of time, to be a Roman citizen came to be counted as a privilege, and local government was restored, usually modeled after the government of Rome itself. Such communities were known as *municipia*.

In addition, the number of Roman citizens was increased by the practice of establishing colonies at strategic points in Italy. Citizens who were assigned land in such colonies sometimes retained full rights of Roman citizenship; in other cases they lost the right of voting—no great loss, since distance would usually have prevented them from coming to Rome for elections in any event.

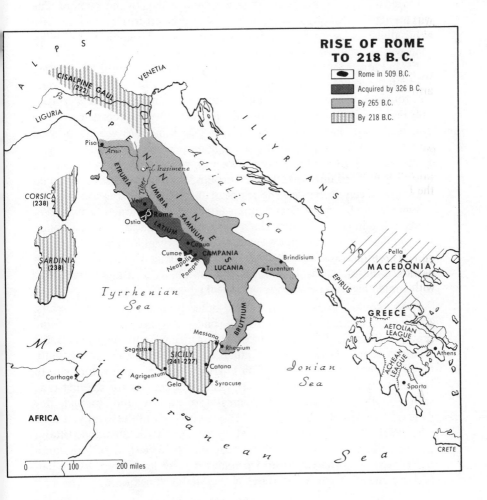

But Roman citizenship was not extended to all the towns and peoples of Italy. Some were allowed to keep their local institutions intact and were bound to Rome simply by a treaty, which regularly prescribed that they should have the "same friends and the same enemies as the Roman people," i.e., their independence in foreign affairs was abrogated. Other clauses in the treaties of alliance differed from case to case. Sometimes non-political rights of Roman citizenship—such things as the right to marry a Roman citizen and to obtain justice from Roman courts—were granted to the citizens of the allied town.

This system of alliances and colonies became an enduring element in the Roman state. No tribute was demanded from the allies, although they were expected to supply military levies for wars undertaken by the Romans. The system acted throughout Roman history to convert former enemies into loyal allies, and gave Roman power a far greater strength and stability than would otherwise have been possible.

From Latium and Campania, Roman political control rapidly extended through the rest of the peninsula. Between 326 and 290 B.C. a series of wars was fought with the Samnites, a hill people of southern Italy. It was probably in the course of these wars that the Roman army was reorganized. The phalanx, which had been imitated from Greek models, was abandoned and a new formation, the manipular legion, was introduced instead. New weapons—a short sword and the *pilum*, or javelin—were adopted, and the army was divided into small tactical groups, called maniples, which could maneuver freely in battle. The result of these changes was to make the Roman army far more flexible than Greek or Macedonian armies ever were. On flat land, the old phalanx remained superior; but on rough ground the Roman manipular legion was regularly able to break the front of enemy phalanxes. Inasmuch as most of the land around the Mediterranean is mountainous, their superior adaptability to rough terrain gave the Roman legions a tremendous tactical advantage.

In the course of the Samnite wars, other Italian peoples—Etruscans, Bruttians, Lucanians and Umbrians—had intervened against the rising power of Rome, but all had been defeated. During the following years, the Romans extended their system of alliances to the Greek cities of the south. Only Tarentum resisted, calling on Pyrrhus, King of Epirus, for help. In battles against Pyrrhus the Romans came into contact for the first time with the fully developed Macedonian style of warfare; and although they suffered two defeats, their superior staying power and the loyalty of their allies made Pyrrhus' victories nugatory. In 275 B.C. he abandoned Italy; three years later Tarentum surrendered; and by 265 B.C. all of Italy south of the Apennines had been united under Roman leadership. Rome had become one of the strongest states of the Mediterranean.

b. Internal Development

Early Roman history showed many of the constitutional features familiar in the development of Greek city states. Basic institutions—the patrilinear family, tribal organization, council, and rudimentary assembly

—came from the common Indo-European heritage; and the similarity of problems faced by a city composed predominantly of small farmers may account for other similarities. But the peculiar constitution which the Romans evolved, marked throughout by a strong conservatism and by a spirit of compromise, had no close parallel in Greek history.

The development of the Roman constitution is full of uncertainties. Modern historians have been compelled to rely very largely on inference from much later practice, and on traditional accounts heavily colored by patriotic feeling, for their picture of the internal development of Rome during the early republican period. The sketch which follows is therefore at best unsure, and rests in part on pure guesswork.

After the overthrow of the Etruscan kings, a closed group of patrician families gained control of the government. The Senate, composed of ex-magistrates and other men of aristocratic birth, exercised a strong though vague advisory power. Administration and command in war was entrusted to a pair of consuls, chosen annually, perhaps by election of the popular assembly, the *comitia curiata*. The introduction of the phalanx, probably very early in the fifth century B.C., effected a modification of aristocratic power. Property classes, not unlike those of Solon, were set up as a basis for the military levy; and the army began to meet as a second assembly, the *comitia centuriata*. Very soon this body took over electoral powers, a function which it retained throughout republican times. Thereby the basis of political power was shifted from familial-tribal relations to something like Greek oligarchy, since the richer classes had a majority in the new *comitia*, which voted not by head but by units called "centuries."

The plebeians were not content with the resulting system of government. On a number of occasions in the fifth century B.C. they "seceded." Probably what happened was that the plebeian soldiers simply refused to obey their commanders and withdrew, electing leaders of their own who defied the legal magistrates. This proto-revolutionary situation did not, however, develop into civil war. Instead, secession became institutionalized, and a third assembly, the *comitia tributa*, was grafted onto the constitution. Its membership was democratic, and it was organized by tribes based upon geographical residence. The *comitia tributa* elected special magistrates, the ten tribunes of the people, who had power to defend plebeians against arbitrary acts of the regular magistrates, especially against unjust or over-rigorous military discipline. For this purpose, the tribunes acquired the power to veto the act of any magistrate, and to call meetings of the people to air grievances or to pass resolutions. In addition, they were guaranteed personal sacrosanctity. The principal check on the tribunes' power was that all ten had to be unanimous, since any one of them could veto the acts of the others. In later times, the Senate and the aristocracy were usually able to assure themselves of at least one sympathizer among the tribunes, and his veto prevented the full utilization of the tribunes' power in favor of the plebeians.[1]

As the Roman state expanded, it became necessary to increase the number of magistrates. Financial matters were entrusted to *quaestors*; the administration of the city proper became the duty of *aediles*; and law suits were decided by *praetors*. All these magistracies were annual, and adhered to the collegiate principal, two or more men sharing office with equal powers. In extraordinary emergency, however, unified command proved desirable. Accordingly, the office of *dictator* was established, but in early times the tenure of this office was always short, rarely exceeding a few months. A second extraordinary magistracy was the censorship. At intervals of five years or so, censors were chosen to revise the citizen rolls, assigning men to their appropriate property class. They had the power to admit men or to exclude them from the Senate, although in later times that body came to be mainly recruited automatically from among ex-magistrates. In addition, the censors let major state contracts for construction of roads, aqueducts, and other public building enterprises.

Through the fourth and third centuries B.C. Rome developed in the direction of democracy. In 367 B.C. plebeians were admitted to magistracies which had previously been reserved exclusively for men of patrician family. In 287 B.C. the resolutions of the *comitia tributa* were recognized as having the force of law, even without the approval of the Senate, or the *comitia centuriata*. In theory, from this time until the end of the Republic, Rome was a democracy, with all powers derived from the people. In practice, the prestige of the Senatorial class made the influence of the aristocratic and wealthy class generally predominant. Senatorial prestige was based in part on religious and family ties, which bound individual plebeians to particular senators. This relation was known as clientage: in return for political support, the aristocrats looked after both the economic and legal interests of their clients. A second support for the aristocracy was the ready absorption of new leaders risen from plebeian ranks. After 367 B.C., plebeian magistrates, upon completion of their term of office, were normally admitted to the Senate, where they soon amalgamated with the old patrician group to form a new ruling class. The effect was to decapitate opposition to aristocratic control. Only after the Second Punic War did the Senate and magistracies once again become almost closed to new men.

Throughout the period of expansion in Italy, Rome remained basically a community of farmers. Population pressure, which played such a large

---

[1]There was still a fourth form of popular assembly in republican Rome, the *concilium plebis*. The original difference between this body and the *comitia tributa* is not fully understood by modern scholars; and in later times, the two were confused by the Romans themselves.

role in Greek history, plagued the Romans also; but military victories steadily opened up fresh lands for settlement by Roman colonists. It seems clear that peasant hunger for land constituted one of the driving motives behind Roman expansion. On several critical occasions, the plebeians precipitated wars which the more cautious Senate did not desire; and presumably it was the hope of fresh lands for settlement that lay behind the plebeian attitude.

Unlike the leading Greek cities, Rome did not become an important commercial or industrial center. A group of business men did arise; but from the beginning they depended mainly on state contracts, and prior to 200 B.C. they played only an insignificant part in Roman society and exercised little or no influence on state policy.

The Romans produced nothing in the way of literature and very little art before 265 B.C. Their religion combined Indo-European with Etruscan elements. Spirits and gods were worshipped by the father on behalf of his family, and the magistrates and special priestly colleges interceded with the gods on behalf of the whole state. Roman gods bore a general resemblance to the Olympian pantheon of the Greeks; but the myths which played such a prominent role in Greek religion were unknown to the early Romans. A peculiar element in Roman religion, derived apparently from Etruscan practice, was the taking of auspices. Before any military or political undertaking was embarked upon, the magistrates consulted the gods by observing the flight of birds and examining the entrails of sacrificial animals. The interpretation of these omens was an elaborate science, entrusted to priestly colleges of *augurs*.

3. ROMAN CONQUEST OF THE MEDITERRANEAN BASIN (265–146 B.C.)

Compared with the Hellenistic kingdoms or Carthage, Rome in the third century B.C. was a backward state. But it had unmatched military strength based upon a numerous citizenry and loyal allies; and the curious structure of Roman government was made workable by an overriding patriotism and sense of social solidarity which made Rome proof against the civil disorders which seriously weakened the Hellenistic and Carthaginian states. These qualities brought dominion throughout the Mediterranean to the Romans within little more than a century.

a. First Punic War (264–241 B.C.)

In 264 B.C. Rome intervened in Sicily and precipitated a long-drawn-out war with Carthage. In the course of it, the Romans built themselves a fleet, becoming for the first time an important sea power. They won surprising successes against the Carthaginian navy, introducing boarding tactics in place of the traditional ramming; and when after twenty-three years of fighting, Carthage at length was driven to make peace naval command of the Western Mediterranean passed definitely into Roman hands. The whole island of Sicily, too, was relinquished by the Carthaginians and came under Roman rule

The island, however, was not admitted to the system of alliances which had proved so successful on the mainland of Italy. Its government was entrusted to a Roman magistrate; and instead of supplying military contingents, Sicily was compelled to pay tribute to the Romans. This settlement, finally arranged in 227 B.C., was probably based on Syracusan and Carthaginian precedents. It established the pattern for provincial governments, which the Romans henceforth applied to their fresh conquests.

b. Second Punic War (218–201 B.C.)

Immediately after the close of the First Punic War, a serious mercenary revolt paralyzed the Carthaginian power for a number of years. Rome took advantage of this crisis to seize Sardinia from Carthage and then continued to pursue a vigorous expansive policy on the mainland, conquering Cisalpine Gaul (the Po valley), pacifying Illyria, and even extending an alliance to the Spanish city of Saguntum.

Such policies did not fail to stir Carthaginian fears and resentment; but it was necessary for Carthage to rebuild its power before a second round

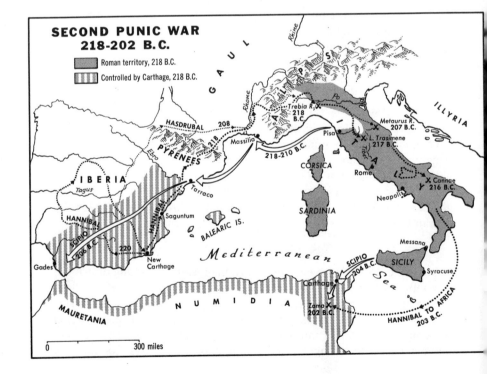

with the Romans could be contemplated. After the mercenary revolt had been brought to an end (238 B.C.), Carthage began to bring Spain under her control, hoping there to find manpower and mineral wealth that would compensate for the losses she had suffered in Sicily and Sardinia. The Carthaginian leaders in Spain were Hamilcar and his famous son Hannibal. They succeeded in building up a first-class army. It was recruited mainly from native tribesmen, maintained by income from the silver and other mines of the Iberian peninsula. Most important of all, Hannibal developed into a military commander of genius, a master of tactics, able to inspire devoted loyalty among his soldiers.

In 220 B.C. Hannibal besieged and captured Saguntum, the newly-made ally of Rome. The Romans protested, and when the Carthaginian government refused to disown Hannibal's act, war was declared. The Romans planned to invade Africa, but they were thrust back on the defensive when Hannibal appeared in Italy itself, having marched across southern Gaul and over the Alps. One Roman army after another was defeated in the field (Trebia, 218 B.C.; Trasimene, 217 B.C.; Cannae, 216 B.C.), but the Romans stubbornly refused to give up the fight. They fell back on a policy of watchful waiting, following Hannibal as he marched up and down the peninsula while always avoiding pitched battles.

The long stalemate which resulted from these tactics provided a key test of the loyalty of Rome's Italian allies; and while some cities opened their gates to Hannibal, the majority stuck firmly to Rome and helped to swell the Roman armies with their conscripts. This source of strength, coupled with Roman tenacity, eventually nullified all of Hannibal's successes.

Despite Hannibal's invincibility in the field, his army gradually wasted away, and he had difficulty in finding replacements. The Romans did not stand idle. An expedition was sent to Spain, and after several years' campaigning, the Carthaginian garrisons were driven out of that country (206 B.C.). Part of the Carthaginian force retreated northward and succeeded in marching into Italy. But there the Romans intercepted a message to Hannibal, which enabled them to concentrate their forces for a great battle (Metaurus, 207 B.C.). The Romans were victorious and the Carthaginian reinforcements scattered. After this setback, Hannibal's continued stay in Italy became only a matter of time. He could no longer hope for substantial reinforcements or for large scale defection of the allies from Rome.

Scipio, later called Africanus, the general who had won Spain for Rome, did not, however, wait for the gradual decimation of Hannibal's forces. In 204 B.C. he boldly invaded Africa, where the Romans turned the tables on Hannibal by stirring up widespread revolt among the peoples subject to Carthage in North Africa. Hannibal was hastily called home; and in a last battle (Zama, 202 B.C.) the two great generals of the war were pitted against one another. The Romans won, and Carthage surrendered. By the terms of peace, the Carthaginians gave up their empire and agreed to make war in the future only with the consent of the Romans. In Spain, Rome fell heir to the Carthaginian possessions, although it was not until the time of Augustus that all the native tribes were effectively subdued. A series of alliances and treaties of friendship bound the various peoples of North Africa and southern Gaul to the Roman state. By these means, Rome came to exercise undisputed predominance throughout the lands of the western Mediterranean.

c. Roman expansion in the East (200–133 B.C.)

Rome's victory over Carthage made the Roman state the most powerful in the entire Mediterranean world; and it was not long before quarrels among the Hellenistic states brought on Roman intervention in the east. During the Second Punic War, Philip V, king of Macedon, had made an alliance with Carthage. This left a score unsettled between Rome and Macedon; and the Roman Senate was not slow to accept alliance with some of the weaker states of the Aegean area, whose rulers feared the power of Macedon and of the Seleucid king, Antiochus III. Diplomacy drifted into war. Between 200 and 189 B.C. the Romans fought a series of campaigns in Greece and Asia Minor, in the course of which they defeated both Philip V and Antiochus III and became supreme arbiters of eastern affairs.

The Romans did not at once annex new provinces in the east. Instead they exacted heavy reparations for themselves, and rewarded friendly states with territory taken from Rome's defeated enemies. Every such settlement (and there were several) remained precarious. Roman commissioners were constantly called upon to adjudicate disputes between supposedly independent states. By this gradual and piecemeal process Roman power extended into the Hellenistic countries. Not until 146 B.C. was Macedon annexed as a province. In 133 B.C. a second eastern province—called Asia by the Romans—was added to the empire when the royal family of Pergamum in northwestern Asia Minor died out, and the last king willed his kingdom to Rome. Elsewhere in the eastern Mediterranean, client and allied kingdoms, bound to Rome by varying treaties, continued to enjoy semi-independence.

After the Second Punic War, Carthage made a remarkable economic recovery; but its very prosperity excited the fears of the Romans. In 149 B.C. the Senate intervened in a quarrel which had broken out between the Carthaginians and their neighbors in Numidia. War was declared against Carthage, and the city was captured and totally destroyed after a desperate siege and bitter street fighting (146 B.C.). The Romans carried vindictiveness to an unusual extent. They sowed the site with salt in order to prevent the renewal of Carthaginian agriculture, and solemnly cursed anyone who might dare to rebuild a city on the ruins they had made.

4. INTERNAL DEVELOPMENT OF ROME (265–133 B.C.)

a. Impact of Punic Wars on Roman Society (264–201 B.C.)

The prolonged and distant campaigning of the First Punic War, and the expense of equipping and maintaining a fleet, put a serious strain on Roman peasant society. In the postwar years there was a fresh outburst of discontent among the poorer citizens, focusing around the question of the distribution of state lands. The poor demanded that territory conquered in northern Italy be sold in small lots to themselves; the Senators, on the other hand, tried to arrogate these lands to their own use by leasing large tracts from the state. Details of the dispute cannot be reconstructed; but it is clear that the commoners in general got the better of the Senators.

Such a victory seemed to confirm the democratic tendency in Roman government and society. However, the even greater strain to which Rome was subjected during the years of the Second Punic War acted to check and reverse this line of development. Hannibal's army ravaged a large part of Italy; and Roman soldiers had to give up farming for years on end while they served in the army. The resulting damage to peasant farms was severe. Many veterans presumably lost their country habits and felt little inclined to the arduous toil of peasant life. Others went into debt after the war when it became necessary to reequip their farms, and had no way of repaying. And insolvent debtors had, by Roman law, to surrender their land or other property to their creditors.

The result was that Italy underwent an important agricultural transformation. In place of the small farms, which had predominated in earlier times, great estates became numerous. These estates were either used for grazing, or were farmed by slave gangs, using the more efficient techniques which had been developed in the Hellenistic and particularly in the Carthaginian world. On such estates, the major cash crops were oil and wine.

This agricultural transformation was promoted by two other changes: (1) Sicily and other newly won provinces paid a part of their tribute in grain, which was sold on the Roman market, thus depressing the price in the immediate vicinity of Rome and making the old style of grain farming less profitable; and (2) the development of more luxurious habits, borrowed from Hellenistic and Carthaginian society, created a demand for a great variety of imported articles which could only be purchased with money. The old subsistence farming could not support this sort of life; hence aristocrats had a strong incentive to convert their farms to cash crops, i.e., to olive trees and vines. One must, however, beware of exaggerating the rapidity of this change, or its scope. Throughout the republican age, peasant farming remained widespread in Italy, and small independent farms did not disappear at any time. The new large-scale type of commercial farming flourished mainly in the southern part of

Italy, where Hannibal's destruction had been most severe and where olive trees flourished especially well.

Since many of the great estates were owned by Senators the new agriculture provided an economic basis for the power of the increasingly exclusive Senatorial aristocracy. Moreover, events of the Second Punic War itself damaged the popular cause and strengthened the prestige of the Senate. Democratic leaders, who had been in control of the Roman state at the outbreak of the Second Punic War, went down in ignominious defeat when they tried to oppose Hannibal in the field. Roman arms were rescued by two aristocrats: Fabius Maximus and Scipio Africanus. Both were of old senatorial families, and lent the full weight of their prestige to buttress the influence of the aristocracy against the democratic tendency which had been so strong prior to the Second Punic War. As a result, the supremacy of the Senate was reestablished, nor was this supremacy challenged for more than sixty years after the close of the war.

The old constitutional forms were not overthrown. Rather, the Senator's new economic power revivified the old relation of clientage, for a rich Senator could do much to help an impoverished ex-soldier. By degrees a political machine, managed by Senators, grew up on the basis of this relationship, with the result that the various popular assemblies became passive instruments of senatorial policy. The basis of the Senator's control over the assemblies was bribery; and bribery became crushingly effective when the voting population of the city of Rome came to consist in large part of landless men who eked out a precarious living in the town. Cheap sale of the grain which was brought to Rome as tribute from the provinces attracted dispossessed farmers to the capital. Once there, many were unable or unwilling to take up productive work; and the resultant impoverished city population was easily influenced by bribes which the growing wealth of the Senators made it easy for them to offer.

A class which was to play an important part in Roman politics in the first century B.C., the *equites* or knights (so called from early times when they, the richer men, served as cavalry in the army) grew in wealth as a result of the many state contracts which came their way during and after the Punic wars. As one province after another was annexed, new areas for their business enterprise were opened up. The *equites* engaged in ordinary commerce to some extent, but busied themselves mainly with tax farming and other state contracts.

Thus from the time of the Second Punic War, Rome ceased to be a predominantly peasant state. Class divisions were accentuated; slavery assumed great importance in economic life; admission to the ruling class came to be nearly closed to men not of Senatorial family; the individual ambition of military leaders and the soldiers' eagerness for booty replaced land hunger as the predominant motive for continued military conquests.

In a sense, by these changes Roman society assimilated itself to the pattern already established in the Orient and in Greece. Yet the military virtues of the Italian peasantry did not at once decay, and, for the ensuing two hundred years, Roman armies, recruited mainly from Italy, retained a definite superiority over all rivals. This superiority made possible the continued expansion of the Roman state.

b. Provincial Administration

The administration of far-flung provinces obviously called for adjustments in the governmental system of the Roman city state. At first, the Romans solved the problem by electing extra praetors each year who served as governors in Sicily and Spain; but after 146 B.C., when the number of provinces was increased, a different system was introduced. By this system, magistrates were assigned as provincial governors after their term of office in Rome had been completed. The Senate acquired the power of making such assignments, and this became one of the main pillars of Senatorial influence. It brought the magistrates effectively under the Senate's control, since a man's future career came to depend in very large measure on which province he was assigned to govern.

Theoretically, each province was administered in accordance with a fundamental statute, compiled at the time of annexation by a Senatorial commission. This statute prescribed the status of the various communities in the province, giving some a more privileged position than others, and also defined the basis of taxation. In addition, it became customary for a governor upon entering office to issue an edict in which he proclaimed the rules and principles he would enforce during his governorship. In the course of time, these edicts became stereotyped, and constituted a body of legal precedent by which relations between cities and states subject to Rome were governed. A more or less uniform body of law thus began to emerge over all the empire. The development in the provinces was matched by a similar growth in the city of Rome itself, where Roman courts were frequently called upon to settle disputes between foreigners, or between foreigners and Roman citizens. In such cases, the written law of Rome did not always apply. A group of professional jurists arose who advised the judges in difficult cases; and they adopted the habit of falling back on principles of jurisprudence, equity, and the "law of nations" to settle cases for which no clear precedent existed. Their opinions were sometimes made into books, in which these principles were set down. Thus the foundation of rational and universal law was slowly built up.

In the provinces, the governors were not very effectively checked in the practical exercise of their power by the fundamental statute or by emerging legal principles. Every governor's primary tasks were to defend his province and keep public peace. For this purpose he commanded a garrison of Roman soldiers. In normal times, the governor's main occupation was judicial, for disputes in which a Roman citizen was involved came before him for settlement, as well as quarrels between cities or communities within his province. While in office, a governor could not himself be sued, and in practice his powers were nearly absolute. Ample opportunity for graft and extortion existed, and many governors used their office to recoup personal fortunes which had been dissipated in bribing the Roman electorate. Some rather ineffective efforts to check the rapacity of such governors were made by the central government. In 149 B.C. a special court was established to try governors after their return; but it was manned by Senators who were generally sympathetic with their fellows and little inclined to take the complaints of the provincials very seriously.

Taxes were collected by tax farmers who paid a lump sum to Roman officials in advance, and then set out to recover their money plus any profit margin they could wring from the helpless provincials. When the tax farmers were local persons, the abuses of this system were not unusually great; but when at a later time Roman citizens were given a special advantage in making bids, tax collection not infrequently deteriorated into organized robbery. The income from the provinces was substantial. After 167 B.C. all direct taxes in Italy were abolished; thenceforward the provinces supported the Roman army and administration.

The Romans usually left local government within each province very much as they found it. In areas where city states had been established, the local governments were accorded a very broad autonomy, and locally chosen magistrates attended to such matters as settling law suits, local improvements, and day to day administration. The local magistrates also paid taxes for their city to the tax farmers, or sometimes farmed their own taxes, i.e., paid them directly to the governor. How taxes were assessed or collected within local units did not concern the Romans. In more backward areas, where city states had not arisen, the Romans dealt with tribal or other established political units in a similar fashion. There was a tendency for city state organization to be extended to new territory. Some such new cities started as colonies for Roman veterans; others formed around local towns which were granted municipal status by Roman authorities. The spread of municipal organization in the west did not, however, attain large proportions until the time of Julius Caesar.

c. Culture

As the Romans came into close and prolonged contact with Hellenistic civilization, they adopted wholesale many of the trappings of Greek culture. Statues and paintings were brought back as spoils of war. Greek philosophers and writers came to the new capital of the world, and there impressed a certain circle of the Roman aristocracy with their wisdom, eloquence, and sophistication. Religious cults which had arisen in the east flooded into Rome, finding most of their adherents among the lower classes of the city; and the luxurious habits of the Greek upper classes came to be widely adopted among the Roman aristocracy.

The Romans were stirred to imitate some aspects of Greek culture themselves. A Roman literature began to develop, notably comedy. Plautus (*c.* 254–184 B.C.) and Terence (d. 159 B.C.) modelled their plays on the Greek New Comedy. Some histories, too, were written in the second century B.C., mainly in the Greek language. For art, the Romans depended almost wholly on Greek craftsmen; but Roman architecture and engineering showed a greater originality, especially in the construction of roads, aqueducts, bridges, and the like.

It would be a mistake to think that distinctively Roman traits disappeared. A group of Senators resolutely set their faces against luxurious foreign fashions, and strove to maintain the old Roman virtues and simple habits. But this movement led to no cultural achievement, since the arts came to be equated with Greek arts, of which these stout conservatives thoroughly disapproved. As a result, Roman civilization did not achieve any distinctly new expression peculiarly its own until the first century B.C.

5. Decay of Republican Government (133–30 B.C.)

a. Civil Disturbance and Party Strife (133–79 B.C.)

The rapid expansion of the Roman state and the flood of booty and tribute which brought new wealth to the city on the Tiber worked great changes in Roman society. Resultant strains in the social fabric broke out into political disorder in 133 B.C. In that year Tiberius Gracchus, a man of aristocratic birth, was elected tribune, and used his office to try to bring about a redistribution of the public lands. As tribune of the people he defied the Senate, revived the dormant democratic constitution, and passed an agrarian law which was designed to distribute the public lands of the Roman state among the poorer citizens. Since most of the public land in question had been leased to members of the Senate, this measure met with the bitter hostility of that body. Tiberius was forced into a series of illegal acts to overcome obstructionist tactics devised by individual Senators. This in turn provoked some of the Senators to organize a mob which assassinated Tiberius; and after a few years the redistribution of state lands was brought to a halt.

Tiberius' reforms were revived ten years later by his younger brother, Gaius Gracchus, who was elected tribune in 123 B.C. Gaius not only reenacted his brother's land law, but persuaded the assembly to adopt a series of other measures which were designed to create a powerful opposition party. He lowered the price of the grain sold to the urban citizenry, thus temporarily disrupting the Senatorial political machine. He wooed the support of the *equites* by making the taxes of the new province of Asia collectable in Rome itself. This meant that in bidding for the contracts for tax collection, Romans had a tremendous advantage over local persons. In effect, Gaius' law gave the Roman knights a monopoly of this lucrative business.

But his attack on Senatorial power did not succeed. He proposed an unpopular measure—the extension of Roman citizenship to the Latin allies—and the Senate set out to capitalize on this tactical blunder by out-bidding him for popular support. Gaius' adherents fell away from him, and in 121 B.C. he, too, was murdered by a mob organized by his Senatorial opponents.

Yet the Senate's apparent victory did not last long. Within a generation a new challenge to aristocratic control emerged in the person of a success-ful general named Marius. Marius was a man of low birth who associated himself with the remnants of the Gracchan party. This political faction came to be known as the *Populares*, and supporters of the Senate were called *Optimates*. Their struggle for control of the republican government eventually resulted in its overthrow.

In 108 B.C. Marius was elected consul, largely on the strength of his reputation as a soldier. He took command in a war (which had been badly mismanaged by generals of the Senatorial party) against the Numidian king, Jugurtha. In raising troops for this campaign he made a most im-portant change in Roman practice. Instead of conscripting only citizens who owned a minimum of property and requiring them, as had been the custom, to equip themselves with arms, he summoned landless men and undertook to equip and train them from state funds. This policy trans-formed Roman soldiers from draftees into long-service professional troops. The new model army soon proved itself far more effective on the battlefield. Professional soldiers did not object to long campaigns fought far from home, and submitted more readily to rigid discipline and training. The Roman army, after Marius, thus became an instrument suitable for the building and maintenance of an empire, as a citizen militia could never be.

But the army reform had other consequences for the Roman state. The new soldiers had no great personal stake in things as they were. On dis-missal from military service, they had no farm to return to, and came to depend wholly on whatever bonuses or land grants the government saw fit to award them. Since the Senate was often unwilling or unable to supply veterans with money and land, the soldiers could only pin their hopes on the general who led them. Thus a powerful, and in the end, decisive threat to Senatorial government arose. Victorious generals and their veteran troops came to have a common interest which often opposed that of the

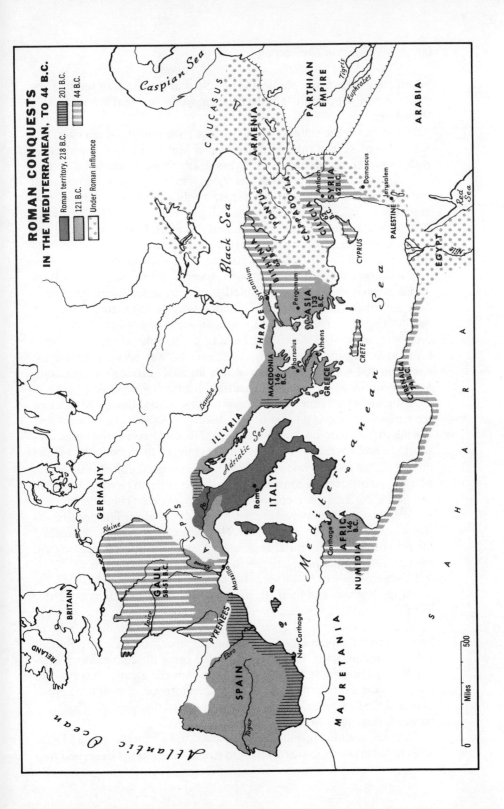

ROMAN CONQUESTS
IN THE MEDITERRANEAN, TO 44 B.C.

Roman territory, 218 B.C.
201 B.C.
121 B.C.
44 B.C.
Under Roman influence

Caspian Sea

CAUCASUS

ARMENIA

PARTHIAN EMPIRE

Tigris

Euphrates

ARABIA

PONTUS
63 B.C.

CAPPADOCIA

BITHYNIA
74 B.C.

SYRIA
62 B.C.

CILICIA
67 B.C.

Antioch

Damascus

Jerusalem

PALESTINE

Red Sea

EGYPT

Nile

Black Sea

Byzantium

THRACE

Pergamum

ASIA
133 B.C.

Pharsalus

MACEDONIA
146 B.C.

Athens

GREECE

CRETE

CYPRUS

CYRENAICA
74 B.C.

Mediterranean Sea

ILLYRIA

Adriatic Sea

Danube

ALPS

Po

Rome

ITALY

Carthage

AFRICA
146 B.C.

NUMIDIA

S A H A R A

MAURETANIA

GERMANY

Rhine

Rhône

GAUL
58-51 B.C.

Loire

Massilia

PYRENEES

Ebro

SPAIN

Tagus

New Carthage

BRITAIN

IRELAND

Atlantic Ocean

Miles

0   500

Senate; and since brute physical force rested in the hands of the soldiers, they were in a position to enforce their will when matters came to a showdown.

This threat to the stability of the Roman government did not check the expansion of Roman rule. After the time of Marius, the easiest and surest path to power and influence in the state was through successful foreign war. A general returning home victorious was in a position to realize all his ambitions, even though the Senate might oppose him. Thus a new motive came into play; and in the ensuing seventy years Sulla conquered Asia Minor, Pompey subdued Syria and Palestine, Caesar annexed Gaul as far as the Rhine, and less important campaigns extended or restored Roman control in North Africa, Thrace, Armenia, and elsewhere.

Marius was the first "new model" general. When he returned from Africa after defeating Jugurtha, another military crisis threatened Rome. German tribes, the Cimbri and Teutones, were on the march in the area beyond the Alps. They defeated a Roman army in southern France and even threatened Italy itself. Marius was the popular choice as military commander against these barbarians; and he was accordingly elected consul in 104 B.C. Despite a law which forbade successive consulships, Marius continued to hold the consulship for the following four years, in the course of which time he raised new armies, trained them, and defeated the barbarians in two pitched battles, taking thousands of prisoners, and driving the remnant back into Germany. His successive consulships constituted a gross breach of the constitution; but still more ominous was the conduct of his soldiers upon their return. The veterans united with leaders of the *Populares*, seized control of the government, and passed laws which assigned them lands in recompense for their services. The *Populares* did not long maintain themselves in power, and Marius himself helped to overthrow their principal political leader. Nevertheless, Marius' career marked the breakdown of Senatorial supremacy and of legality. Thenceforward, military force, often thinly disguised, controlled Roman politics.

This breakdown of legality was further complicated: (1) by disputes between the Romans and their Italian allies, which led to a short but bitter war (91–88 B.C.); (2) by slave revolts in Sicily (103–01 B.C.); and (3) by the revolt of the province of Asia (88–84 B.C.) when Mithridates, king of Pontus, gave the population some hope of liberation from the Roman yoke. Such dangers to Roman rule did not bring the contending parties together; rather, the struggle for military command against the revolting peoples became a turning point of the political struggle between the *Populares* and the *Optimates*, for both sides recognized that control of an army offered a clear path to control of the state.

From the resulting turmoil, Sulla emerged to supreme power in 83 B.C., when he led his victorious army back to Rome from war in Greece and Asia

Minor against Mithridates. He was thoroughly in sympathy with Senatorial policy and used his position as military commander to overthrow the *Populares*. He proscribed (i.e., executed) over four thousand of his political enemies, confiscated their property, and used some of the land so acquired to resettle his veterans. Sulla himself assumed the dictatorship with special powers to reorganize the constitution, a position which he held for three consecutive years. During this time he did his best to root out all opposition. In reorganizing the constitution, his guiding principle was to increase the power of the Senate and devise laws which would prevent any single man from again gaining supreme power such as he himself enjoyed. In 79 B.C. Sulla abdicated, and died a few months thereafter. Once more the Senate seemed to have won a victory; but events showed that the victory was merely temporary. The violence and civil war which Marius and Sulla had freely resorted to destroyed respect for law; but the path to power, which command of proletarian armies opened to ambitious generals, could not be closed by Sulla's arbitrary enactments.

b. Overthrow of the Republic (79–30 B.C.)

Sulla's constitutional settlement did not long withstand the ambition of younger men. In 70 B.C. Pompey and Crassus were elected consuls despite the opposition of the Senate, and proceded to repeal many details of Sulla's legislation. Pompey was a capable military commander who had risen to prominence through a campaign in Spain. Crassus depended for his political influence mainly on great personal wealth, but he had also won a share of military glory through suppressing a serious slave revolt which broke out in southern Italy under the leadership of a Thracian gladiator named Spartacus. Neither Pompey nor Crassus wished to overthrow the republican regime; but each was ambitious and had no scruple in brushing aside Senatorial opinion or legal obstacles that seemed to block his ambition.

During the next ten years, Pompey dominated Roman politics. He was given a sweeping military command against the pirates who were seriously hindering Mediterranean shipping, and succeeded in suppressing that nuisance in short order. Then he took over a campaign in the east, and spent several years away from Rome, during which time he led his army through Syria and Palestine, reorganized the Roman provinces of the eastern Mediterranean, and annexed new areas in Asia Minor. During these campaigns, Roman power first came into intimate contact with the Parthian empire, a state which had arisen about 250 B.C. in Iran, and from that center had expanded through Mesopotamia at the expense of the decrepit Seleucid kingdom. For nearly three hundred years after Pompey's time relations with Parthia remained a standing problem for the Roman government.

While Pompey was away in the east, street rioting and revolutionary plots were rife in Rome. Crassus and a number of his confederates, among whom was Julius Caesar, intrigued busily against Pompey. Street gangs were organized which engaged in all sorts of violence. Cicero, a "new man" (i.e., not of Senatorial family) and a successful orator, tried to weld an alliance between the Senate and the *equites*, and so bring the disastrous party strife to an end. He succeeded in winning the consulship in 64 B.C. and distinguished himself by suppressing a revolutionary plot which a dissolute Roman noble, Catiline, headed; but he could not end the struggle between *Populares* and *Optimates*.

When Pompey returned to Rome in 62 B.C. the Senate refused to ratify his acts or reward his soldiers. Pompey was thus driven to conclude an agreement with two men who had done their best to undermine his position in Rome while he had been away: Crassus and Caesar. In 60 B.C. these three formed what is known as the First Triumvirate, agreeing to support one another's plans despite the opposition of the Senate. Pompey's veterans provided the military core of the Triumvirate's strength; but both Crassus and Caesar were not slow to acquire commands for themselves: Caesar in Gaul, Crassus in the east. Pompey remained in Italy, exercising general control over the Roman state; but at the same time he governed the Spanish provinces *in absentia*, thus keeping a personal army at his command.

Despite the jealousies of the three men, the Triumvirate lasted until 53 B.C., when Crassus met his death in war against the Parthians. Thereafter Pompey and Caesar divided power between them; but mutual suspicion and hostility mounted, and in 49 B.C. open war broke out. Caesar invaded Italy with a veteran army, fresh from the conquest of Gaul (58–51 B.C.), and was easily able to drive Pompey and his supporters out of the peninsula. The following year Caesar crossed to Greece and there defeated Pompey's troops at Pharsalus. After further campaigns in Egypt, North Africa, and Spain, Caesar emerged triumphant, with unquestioned personal power over the entire Roman state (45 B.C.).

During the short time before his assassination, Caesar initiated a vast reorganization of Roman society and government. He arrogated to himself dictatorial powers, and his enemies accused him of wishing to be king. Some of his measures, too, were not popular, for example his lavish extension of Roman citizenship to provincials. It seems that Caesar deliberately tried to reduce the sharp distinction between Italy and the provinces, hoping perhaps to raise the provinces to fuller partnership in the Roman state. Caesar tried to face up to some of the fundamental ills of Roman society. Free grain distribution was curtailed, and Caesar began to resettle part of the urban proletariat in colonies; others he put to work on public building enterprises. He settled most of his veterans on land confiscated from his opponents in Italy; but some were established in colonies located in the provinces. Proposals for more uniform local government in Italy were made; the calendar was reformed; and Caesar laid plans for the conquest of the Parthians in the east.

Such policies did not fail to create enemies, and a few Senators, of whom Brutus and Cassius were the most active, entered into a conspiracy to murder Caesar. On the 15th of March, 44 B.C., the conspirators assassinated him in the Senate house. They apparently expected the machinery of republican government to resume operation as though nothing had happened. But the fabric of the state had decayed too far. Rival claimants to Caesar's position appeared in the persons of his lieutenant, Antony, and his nephew and adopted son, Octavian, later titled Augustus. Octavian, though only 18 years of age, raised a private army by appealing to Caesar's veterans who had been settled in large numbers through the Italian countryside; and with this force he challenged both Antony and the Senate.

After some complicated negotiations, Antony and Octavian, each claiming to be the true political heir to Caesar, combined their forces with those of a third Caesarian general, Lepidus, to form the Second Triumvirate. At Philippi in 42 B.C. they defeated armies that had been raised by Brutus and Cassius. After this victory they proceeded to divide the control of the Roman world among themselves. Octavian was assigned the direction of affairs in Italy where pressing problems made the task unattractive. Veterans had to be settled on lands confiscated from all and sundry, and the bitter discontent of the Roman and Italian people had to be calmed. Antony took for himself the provinces of the east, and governed Gaul through a subordinate. He took up Caesar's plans for a great campaign against the Parthians, expecting, probably, to build up a personal prestige such as Caesar had acquired through his victories in Gaul, and so rise to unchallenged primacy in the Roman state. Lepidus lacked the capacity or personal prestige to compete on equal terms with Antony and Octavian. His power was gradually eclipsed, and he lived out his life occupying honorific offices which carried with them no important political power.

Antony's plans miscarried. He was not successful in organizing his Parthian campaign; and Octavian, despite many difficulties and initial unpopularity, gradually consolidated his personal hold on Italy. When Antony's governor of Gaul died, Octavian quietly added that province to his sphere of influence. Octavian disseminated a skillful propaganda, by which he portrayed himself as defender of Roman ways and traditions against Antony's monarchical ambitions. Antony lent himself to this propaganda by falling into the toils of Cleopatra, Queen of Egypt, who fascinated him both with her beauty and with dreams of an absolute Oriental monarchy.

As a result, when the mutual distrust between Antony and Octavian flared into war, Octavian was able to mobilize the hopes and loyalty of the Italians. At Actium, on the west coast of Greece, Antony was defeated (31 B.C.), and fled to Egypt with Cleopatra. Octavian proceeded methodically to occupy the eastern provinces, and when he reached Egypt in 30 B.C. he formally annexed that country. Antony and Cleopatra committed suicide, and the Roman world once again had a single master.

6. ROMAN SOCIETY (133–30 B.C.)

a. Economy

As Rome acquired political supremacy in the entire Mediterranean region, the city gathered to itself enormous wealth in the form of tribute and booty. Conspicuous consumption on a lavish scale became characteristic of the aristocracy and knights; and Rome became an economic parasite. The provinces provided the food and manufactures consumed in Rome, while the Romans paid for what they consumed from taxes and loot. Italy, however, did not enjoy the imperial advantages of the city of Rome; and in some of the local towns industry and commerce flourished, despite the disorders of the age.

The east survived the depredations of the Roman armies and tax collectors with surprising success. In Greece, depopulation and economic decay, which had begun in the Hellenistic age, continued to weaken the original center of classical culture; but prosperous Hellenistic cities of Asia Minor, Syria and Egypt maintained the traditions of Greek life.

b. Social Classes and Groups

New wealth and contact with more civilized peoples weakened and almost destroyed the old Roman pattern of family and civil life. Women became almost completely emancipated from the control of father and husband; divorce became easy and common. Sexual immorality spread; and in the last years of the Republic the aristocracy failed to reproduce itself, so that many old Senatorial families died out and were replaced by newcomers, recruited from the ranks of the knights.

The poor of Rome grew steadily in number, and became dependent on the bounty of the state. Grain distribution to citizens living in Rome was made free of all charge in 58 B.C.; bribery continued to play a prominent political role and provided an important source of income for the urban proletarians; and to court their favor, magistrates adopted the custom of staging lavish spectacles. Hence the famous formula for winning the popular support: *panem et circenses*, bread and circuses.

Constant wars swelled the supply of slaves. The aristocrats accumulated enormous slave households to minister to their luxuries; and slave plantations became increasingly common, especially in southern Italy.

Perhaps the most important social change was the result of the wide extension of Roman citizenship. After the revolt of 90–88 B.C., nearly all Italians were admitted to Roman citizenship, and by degrees they came to share Roman patriotism. A simpler and sounder society existed in the local towns of Italy, and it was largely upon the support of the Italian townsmen that Augustus was able to found his government after 30 B.C. Throughout the early imperial period, the city of Rome remained a festering sore in the body politic.

c. Culture

Roman official religion decayed rapidly in the first century B.C. Among the lower classes, various savior cults took root, coming from the Hellenistic east. A small but growing number of wealthy Romans turned to one or another school of Hellenistic philosophy for moral, personal guidance; but in the declining days of the republic the majority of the Roman aristocrats and knights cultivated a contempt for Greek talk, and guided their conduct by unmitigated greed, selfishness, and ambition. Only under the early empire did philosophic education become general among the ruling classes, and with it came a modification of the shameless rapacity and callousness of the late republican days.

The most significant cultural activity of the Romans was in the field of literature. During the first century B.C. the Latin language was adapted to the full range of literary expression which had established itself in the Greek world. No new literary forms were developed by the Romans, yet the Latin tongue and, in some measure, the Roman national character, did put a distinct stamp on literary production, making it more than a mere copy of Greek models.

Oratory was dignified to an art by men such as Cicero (106–43 B.C.), who made use of his eloquence to sway the Senate and to conduct cases in law courts. Cicero published many of his speeches, so that some of them played the role of political pamphlets. In addition, Cicero was a prolific letter writer. Over 800 of his letters were published after his death. They permit a unique insight into the attitudes of mind of an educated and patriotic Roman. In particular, one can glimpse through them the uncertainty, distress, and confusion that a moderate man felt in the face of the party strife and civil war which tore the Roman state apart during Cicero's lifetime.

Cicero achieved preeminence in still another field of letters. During periods of political retirement he composed a number of philosophical treatises, cast in dialogue form. Most of them were adaptations of Greek originals; but through them Cicero expanded the Latin language to accommodate Greek philosophic ideas. The new vocabulary was transmitted to later times, and continued to provide Europeans with a medium of intellectual discourse in medieval and early modern times.

Other important literary figures were Lucretius (*c.* 99–55 B.C.), who wrote an epic poem, *De Rerum Natura*, in which he set forth the tenets of Epicurean philosophy with a glowing emotional force; and Catullus (*c.* 87–54 B.C.), a profligate young Roman who wrote impassioned lyric poems. History and antiquarianism were cultivated by Varro (116–27 B.C.), and Caesar found time to write histories of his campaigns in Gaul and of his war with Pompey and the Senate. Caesar's histories have in them more than a touch of party propaganda; the same is true of Sallust's (86–35 B.C.) accounts of the Jugurthine War and of Catiline's conspiracy.

Suggestions for Further Reading for Part II, C

The Oxford Classical Dictionary. Oxford: 1948.
Cambridge Ancient History. Vols. 7–10. Cambridge: 1928–34.
Cambridge Ancient History, Volumes of Plates. Vol. 4. Cambridge: 1934.
Adcock, F. E. *The Roman Art of War under the Republic.* Cambridge, Mass.: 1940.
Altheim, F. *A History of Roman Religion.* London: 1938.
Boak, A. E. R. *A History of Rome to 565 A.D.,* 4th ed. New York: 1955.
Carcopino, D. *Daily Life in Ancient Rome.* New Haven: 1940.
Cary, M. *The Geographic Background of Greek and Roman History.* New York: 1949.
Cary, M. *A History of Rome.* 2d ed. London: 1954.
Fowler, H. N. *History of Roman Literature.* New York: 1928.
Frank, T. *Economic History of Rome.* 2d ed. Baltimore: 1927.
Frank, T. *An Economic Survey of Ancient Rome,* Vol. 1, *Rome and Italy of the Republic.* Baltimore: 1933.
Heitland, W. E. *Agricola: a Study of Agriculture and Rustic Life in the Graeco-Roman World.* Cambridge: 1921.
Lewis, N., and Reinhold, M. *Roman Civilization, Selected Readings,* Vol. 1, *The Republic.* New York: 1951.
Mommsen, T. *History of Rome.* 4 vols. New York: 1869–70.
Marsh, F. B. *History of the Roman World from 146 to 30 B.C.* 2d ed. London: 1953.
Pallotino, M. *The Etruscans.* Pelican Books.
Rostovtzeff, M. *A History of the Ancient World,* Vol. 2. Oxford: 1926.
Schulz, F. *Principles of Roman Law.* Oxford: 1936.
Syme, R. *The Roman Revolution.* Oxford: 1939.
Wheeler, M. *Rome Beyond the Imperial Frontiers.* Pelican Books.

Novels

Duggan, Alfred. *Winter Quarters.* New York: 1956.
Duggan, Alfred. *Three's Company.* New York: 1958.

Duggan, Alfred. *Children of the Wolf.* New York: 1959.
Radin, Max. *Epicuras My Master.* Chapel Hill, N.C.: 1949.
Warner, Rex. *The Young Caesar.* Boston: 1958.
Warner, Rex. *Imperial Caesar.* Boston: 1960.
Wilder, Thornton. *The Ides of March.* New York: 1948.

Chronological Table for Part II, C: The Roman Republic

B.C.

c. 814	Founding of Carthage.
*753	Traditional date of the founding of Rome.
c. 535	Alliance between Etruscans and Carthaginians directed against Greek cities of Italy and Sicily.
*509	Traditional date of the establishment of the Republic by expulsion of Etruscan kings from Rome.
493	(?) Formation of League of Latin cities.
474	(?) Sea battle near Cumae between Greek and Etruscan-Carthaginian fleet.
396	Capture of Veii by Romans.
390	Sack of Rome by the Gauls.
367	Licinian laws: plebeians admitted to magistracies.
326–304	War with Samnites in south-central Italy.
298–290	War with Samnites and coalition of other peoples of Italy: Roman victory.
287	Hortensian law: law-making power of plebeian assembly recognized.
280–272	War with Tarentum and Pyrrhus of Epirus: Roman victory.
*by 265	All of Italy south of the Appennines united into the Roman alliance.
264–241	First Punic War.
c. 250	Beginning of Parthian Empire in Iran.
241	Carthage ceded Sicily to Romans.
238	Rome seized Sardinia from Carthaginians during mercenary revolt at Carthage.
237–219	Carthaginian conquest of Spain by Hamilcar and Hannibal.
227	Organization of Sicily as first Roman province.

222	Roman conquest of Po valley.
220	Hannibal's attack on Saguntum.
*218–201	Second Punic War: invasion of Italy by Hannibal.
218	Roman defeat at Trebia.
217	Roman defeat at Lake Trasimene.
216	Roman defeat at Cannae.
215–205	Philip V of Macedon in alliance with Carthage: First Macedonian war.
210–206	Scipio Africanus conquered Spain from Carthaginians.
207	Battle of the Metaurus: Hasdrubal defeated.
204	Scipio invaded Africa; Hannibal called home to defend Carthage.
202	Hannibal defeated at Zama by Scipio.
201	Carthage surrendered her empire to Rome.
200–197	Second Macedonian war; Macedonian territory curtailed.
197	Spain organized into two provinces.
192–189	War with Antiochus III, the Seleucid king; Roman armies penetrated into Asia Minor for the first time.
184	(?) Death of Plautus, comic poet.
171–168	Third Macedonian war: Macedon partitioned into four republics.
159	(?) Death of Terence, comic poet.
149–146	Third Punic War: destruction of Carthage.
*146	War in Greece; destruction of Corinth; Macedon made a province.
*133	Tiberius Gracchus tribune.
133	Pergamum willed to Rome.
123–122	Gaius Gracchus tribune; organization of *Populares*.
121	Death of Gaius Gracchus.
112–105	Jurgurthine war in Africa.
108	First consulship of Marius.
104–100	Marius holds consulship successively, repels Cimbri and Teutones.
103–101	Slave uprising in Sicily.
91–88	War against allies in Italy: grant of Roman citizenship to Italians.
88–84	First Mithradatic war: revolt in province of Asia put down by Sulla.
86	Death of Marius; disorders in Rome.

82–79	Sulla's dictatorship; reorganization of constitution.
73–71	Slave revolt in southern Italy: Spartacus.
70	Pompey and Crassus consuls; repeal of much of Sulla's legislation.
67–62	Pompey's campaigns against pirates; against Mithradates; annexation of provinces in Asia Minor; establishment of client kingdoms in Syria and Palestine.
63	Cicero consul: Catilinarian conspiracy.
62	Pompey's return to Rome: Senate failed to ratify his acts in the East.
*60	First Triumvirate; Pompey, Caesar and Crassus took effective control of the state despite Senatorial opposition.
59	Caesar and Crassus consuls.
58–51	Caesar's conquest of Gaul.
58	Grain distribution made free of charge in Rome.
53	Crassus defeated and killed in war against Parthians.
55	(?) Death of Lucretius, philosophical poet.
54	(?) Death of Catullus, lyric poet.
49	War between Pompey and Caesar: Caesar crossed the Rubicon, drove Pompey from Italy.
48	Battle of Pharsalus: Caesar defeated Pompey, who fled to Egypt and was murdered there.
47	Caesar in Egypt; made Cleopatra co-regent of Egypt.
46	Caesar campaigned in North Africa against adherents of Pompey.
45	Caesar campaigned in Spain against Pompeians; emerged as undisputed master of Roman world.
*44	Assassination of Caesar.
43	Second Triumvirate: Antony, Octavian and Lepidus opposed Caesar's assassins; sweeping proscriptions; Cicero killed by agents of the triumvirate.
42	Battle of Philippi: Antony and Octavian victorious over Brutus and Cassius; triumvirate divided Roman world.
*31	War between Octavian and Antony; Battle of Actium; Octavian supreme.
30	Annexation of Egypt.

D. The Roman Empire (30 B.C.–A.D. 410)

1. THE AUGUSTAN AGE (30 B.C.–A.D. 14)

---

a. *The Political Settlement*
b. *Augustus' Social and Administrative Reforms*
c. *Financial Reorganization*
d. *Military Reforms*
e. *Foreign Policy*
f. *Geographical and Social Survey of the*
      Roman Empire
g. *Culture of the Augustan Age*

---

a. *The Political Settlement*

When Octavian overthrew Antony he acquired unchallenged power over the whole Roman Empire. The fate of the Roman world rested largely on his decisions. Peace, stability, and an end to the incessant civil war were almost universally desired; at the same time, Roman sentiment was profoundly attached to the republican form of government which had raised Rome so high among the nations of the earth. Octavian was able to satisfy both aspirations: he brought internal peace to the Roman state and he "restored the Republic."

Peace depended on one-man control over generals and armies, which Octavian reserved for himself; the restoration of the Republic meant a return to old forms of government. But Octavian modified the republican institutions of Rome in numerous details; and the net effect of his changes was to make a single will preeminent in all matters of state policy. Thus the restoration of the Republic did not create chaos again. The revived republican institutions were weak from the beginning, and the future was to show that in restoring the republic Octavian was in fact founding the Roman empire.

In 27 B.C., after his victorious return from the war with Antony, Octavian formally relinquished his extraordinary powers to the Senate. Thus the Republic was officially reestablished. In gratitude the Senate bestowed on him the honorific appellation "Augustus" by which Octavian was afterwards generally known. More than this, the Senate gave him pro-consular power in Syria, Spain, and Gaul for a period of ten years, thereby assuring Augustus' continued control of nearly all of the Roman army. Two legions—one in Macedon, the other in Africa—were exempted from Augustus' control by this settlement; but in 23 B.C. he was granted an overriding military authority even in these cases—the so-called *imperium proconsulare maius*. Thus, control of the Roman armies was effectively concentrated in the hands of one man, and the danger of civil war between rival armies and generals was correspondingly reduced.

Until 23 B.C. Augustus himself held successive consulships; after that year he declined reelection to this office save on exceptional occasions. His legal power thereafter rested on two extraordinary prerogatives: the power of a tribune and command of the armies. He filled the supreme religious office of *pontifex maximus* after 13 B.C. when Lepidus, his former colleague in the Second Triumvirate, died. In addition, Augustus was *princeps* of the Senate and first citizen of the Republic. These positions carried no definite powers, but from his position as *princeps* derives the name by which Augustus' government is usually called: the principate.

The principate lasted for more than two centuries, and during that long period wars were on the whole unimportant, and most of them were fought by professional soldiers on the distant frontiers of the Empire where they hardly affected the lives of the ordinary inhabitants of the Roman world. The success of the Augustan political settlement must be measured against the incessant disorder that preceded and the destructive wars that came after the relative peace which the principate brought to the Roman world.

b. Augustus' Social and Administrative Reforms

Augustus based his campaign against Antony on an appeal to Roman and Italian sentiment; and in the reorganization of society and government which he carried through after his victory, he continued to rely mainly on the support and cooperation of the Italian population. The provinces were not taken into any sort of active partnership with Italy, except insofar as some provincials enjoyed Roman citizenship by virtue of earlier grants or through descent from Roman colonists.

The wholesale proscriptions of the civil wars largely destroyed the Senatorial class of the late Republic. Augustus reconstituted the Senate, limiting its membership to 600, and establishing strict property and moral qualifications for membership. In theory the Senate retained all its earlier rights. However, in those provinces where Augustus exercised pro-consular power, the Senate's practical control became nil. Yet some provinces remained under the old system of government. These are often called "Senatorial" provinces to distinguish them from the "imperial" provinces which were under Augustus' personal control. In general, the Senatorial provinces were those where no important army garrison was needed. Particular provinces were shifted from imperial to Senatorial control as they became pacified and the legionary garrisons could be withdrawn. Conversely, if war threatened in a Senatorial province, it was usually transferred to (or a portion of it split off and put under) imperial control. The old republican magistracies of Rome continued to be filled by annual election. Yet Augustus adopted the practice of recommending particular candidates, and his recommendation became nearly equivalent to election, since no one cared or perhaps dared to flout his will. In addition, Augustus regularly appointed members of the Senate to the principal military commands and provincial governorships which lay within his personal gift. He adopted the policy of entrusting command in active campaigns mainly to members of his own family, thus minimizing the danger of revolt by a successful general.

The equestrians, too, were drawn into the service of the government. Lesser military commands were offered to them and imperial procurators were recruited from their ranks. Procurators administered the various governmental functions which were entrusted to Augustus by the Senate. Most of them attended to the collection of taxes in the imperial provinces, and were under the supervision of a governor of Senatorial rank. In some of the smaller provinces, however, equestrian procurators were in supreme control, responsible directly to Augustus. Special tasks, such as the administration of the grain supply for the city of Rome, the command of the Praetorian guard (a privileged force stationed in Italy), and of the city police (which Augustus organized for the first time) were also in the hands of equestrians.

The administrative jobs thus opened up to members of the equestrian class proved so attractive that few of them preferred to continue banking, trading, or other business careers. Tax farming became far less lucrative because Augustus would not allow extreme, violent extortion such as had been common before. The social role of the equestrian class consequently underwent a rapid change: equestrians had been rivals of the Senate and supported an opposition political party; they now became predominantly a group of government officials and landowners. The political conflict, which had been so acute in the later years of the Roman republic, thereupon disappeared. Trade and industry were largely relinquished to foreigners, especially to immigrants from the eastern part of the Empire.

The city of Rome continued to support a large proletariat; and how to secure the supply of grain for free distribution to the swarm of impoverished citizens in the capital remained a problem. Augustus undertook this task at the request of the Senate, and succeeded in organizing it more systematically, so that shortages seldom occurred, and occasions for rioting were thereby reduced. The popular assemblies continued to function throughout Augustus' lifetime, but as vestigial forms. His successor, Tiberius, transferred the right to elect magistrates from the people to the Senate. Elections had become so much a mere formality that there was no perceptible opposition to this move.

The new senatorial and equestrian classes were recruited not merely from the city of Rome but from all of Italy. In the late days of the Republic nearly all of the local townsmen of Italy had been granted full Roman citizenship; hence, any man of sufficient property, native to an Italian town, became eligible for a Senatorial or equestrian career. In point of fact, most of Augustus' Senators and equestrians came from just such towns. Italy also provided a main recruiting ground for the army, since Roman citizenship was a prerequisite for military service in the legions. An ordinary soldier who rose through the ranks to the position of centurion (about equivalent to master sergeant in our army) could usually establish himself in his native town or elsewhere as a member of the equestrian order when his army service was finished; and his sons might then enter upon higher offices, and rise to the Senate itself, given luck and capacity.

The classes, although rigidly defined according to wealth, were in no sense closed castes; and the continued failure of the upper classes to reproduce themselves meant that there was always room at the top. Thus the system worked to draft the most active and ambitious men from the Italian towns into the service of the government; and it was on their loyalty and contentment that the government mainly depended. Insofar as Roman citizenship had been extended to the provincials, they too shared in this ladder of promotion, but it was not until the second century A.D. that the provinces came into full partnership with Italy.

c. Financial Reorganization

The wealth of the provinces and of Italy had been damaged by the civil wars; and economic recovery came only by degrees. After 30 B.C. Augustus' wars did not bring in large windfalls of treasure and booty as the wars of the late Republic had sometimes done, so this extraordinary source of income was cut off. As a result, the government found itself chronically short of funds, and Augustus on several occasions found it necessary to replenish the treasury with gifts from his personal resources. In fact, Augustus accumulated tremendous personal wealth so that his private income began to take on some of the characteristics of public moneys. He kept the whole province of Egypt as a personal possession, and in other parts of the Empire he acquired vast estates by legacy and by confiscation (mainly from Antony in the east).

The central problem of Augustus' financial administration was to get enough ready cash to pay the wages of the soldiers and, in particular, to accumulate sufficient money to pay discharge bonuses to veterans. The ordinary income of the state was not sufficient to meet this need; and toward the end of his life Augustus established new taxes, with the approval of the Senate. Proceeds from a sales tax applicable to Italy, an inheritance tax payable by all Roman citizens, and a tax on the manumission of slaves were paid into a special military treasury from which veterans' bonuses were thereafter paid.

In the provinces, Augustus greatly restricted the abuses of tax collection which had flourished under the Republic. In provinces assigned to his direct control by the Senate, equestrian procurators were put in charge of taxes; in Senatorial provinces the old system of tax farming persisted, but new regulations, and the fact that governors were paid handsome salaries, reduced graft and extortion. Under the principate, tax farming ceased to be an important source of wealth for Roman citizens; and tax contracts were usually let locally. A census of some or perhaps of all the provinces was undertaken in order to adjust the tax burden more equitably; and after A.D. 6 imperial procurators were assigned even to Senatorial provinces where they collected the taxes for the military treasury and administered those estates which belonged personally to the emperor. Within a few decades, the duties of these procurators were extended, until the old tax farming system came completely to an end.

The total population of the Empire under Augustus probably numbered between 70 and 100 million, not more than a third of what the same area supports today. Of the total, nearly five million were Roman citizens. Population growth came nearly to an end after Augustus' time, for gains in some provinces such as Gaul and Africa were offset by decline in other areas, such as Italy and Greece. It seems likely that by A.D. 200 the total population of the Western provinces had declined seriously, due largely to a series of severe epidemic diseases that became especially serious in the second century A.D. But really reliable numerical estimates can not be made.

d. Military Reforms

One of Augustus' main tasks was to reorganize the army so as to assure that it would not again rise in support of some successful general to challenge the central authority of the Roman state. His first concern after the end of the civil war was to reduce the size of the army to manageable proportions. Nearly half of the soldiers were discharged in the years immediately after Actium, and all of them were given either land or cash bonuses which Augustus personally supplied. The army which he retained numbered about 250,000 men, of whom about half were legionaries, half auxiliaries. The legionaries were Roman citizens mainly recruited from Italy, as we have seen. The auxiliaries, on the other hand, were recruited among the more warlike provincials, and usually kept their native arms and tactical formations. They were, however, placed under the command of Roman officers. Both legionaries and auxiliaries were voluntarily recruited. For a poor Roman citizen, service in the army offered an avenue to social advancement, and the prospect of a liberal bonus upon discharge. The auxiliaries could look forward to gaining Roman citizenship when their term of service was up. Legionaries served twenty years;

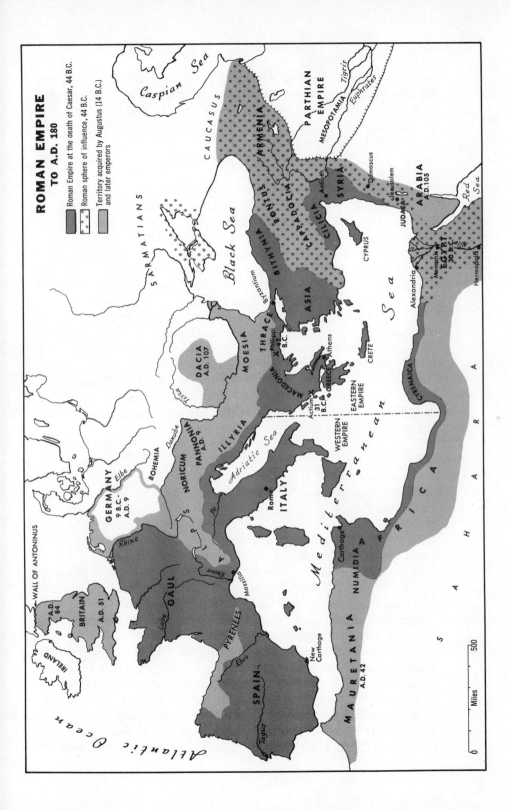

ROMAN EMPIRE
TO A.D. 180

Roman Empire at the death of Caesar, 44 B.C.

Roman sphere of influence, 44 B.C.

Territory acquired by Augustus (14 B.C.) and later emperors

Atlantic Ocean

IRELAND

BRITAIN
A.D. 51

A.D. 84

WALL OF ANTONINUS

GERMANY
9 B.C.-
A.D. 9

Elbe

BOHEMIA

Danube

Rhine

Tisza

NORICUM

PANNONIA
A.D. 9

DACIA
A.D. 107

SARMATIANS

Caspian Sea

Black Sea

CAUCASUS

ARMENIA

PARTHIAN
EMPIRE

Tigris

MESOPOTAMIA

Euphrates

GAUL

Loire

Rhône

PYRENEES

Marseilles

ALPS

Po

ILLYRIA

Adriatic Sea

MOESIA

THRACE

Byzantium

BITHYNIA

PONTUS

CAPPADOCIA

CILICIA

SYRIA

Antioch

Damascus

Jerusalem

JUDAEA

ARABIA
A.D. 105

Red Sea

SPAIN

Ebro

Tagus

New Carthage

MAURETANIA
A.D. 42

NUMIDIA

Carthage

ITALY

Rome

MACEDONIA

Philippi
X 42
B.C.

Actium
X
31
B.C.

GREECE

Athens

ASIA

CRETE

CYPRUS

Mediterranean Sea

EASTERN EMPIRE

WESTERN EMPIRE

A F R I C A

CYRENAICA

Alexandria

Memphis

EGYPT
30 B.C.

Hermopolis

S A H A R A

0   500
Miles

auxiliaries, twenty-five; but, despite Augustus' special taxes, funds were not always available to pay bonuses to time-expired veterans, and they were often kept in service for a number of years beyond their term. This practice naturally led to discontent, and immediately after Augustus' death provoked a short-lived mutiny.

e. Foreign Policy

Augustus did not allow the army to remain idle. A long series of campaigns extended the boundaries of the Empire north to the Danube. In addition, Augustus subdued the Alpine tribes for the first time, and pacified northwestern Spain. In the east, he abandoned the plans nurtured by Crassus, Caesar, and Antony for conquest of the Parthian empire, and instead made a diplomatic settlement by which the northern Euphrates and the Arabian desert became the Roman boundary. Between 12 and 6 B.C. the territory between the Rhine and the Elbe rivers was conquered; and in A.D. 6 Augustus' stepson, Tiberius, started on a campaign designed to subdue the only remaining important German kingdom, located in what is today Bohemia. However, a revolt in his rear, in Pannonia, south of the Danube, made it necessary to withdraw. Three years later, a German confederacy under Arminius inflicted a serious defeat on a Roman army, and the land between the Rhine and Elbe was abandoned. Thereafter Augustus gave up plans for further conquests, and rapid expansion of the Roman empire came to an end.

f. Geographical and Social Survey of the Roman Empire

The Roman empire as it had taken shape by the end of Augustus' life ringed the Mediterranean Sea, and in the north extended well into western and central Europe. In the east it included only a part of the ancient center of Oriental civilization: Asia Minor, Syria, Palestine, and Egypt. In these areas the age-old social patterns, combining Hellenistic with Oriental elements, persisted. City life was firmly established, and trade and manufacturing were carried on actively. The Greek language was a universal medium of trade and culture in the east, although a wide variety of native languages continued to exist among the common people, especially in country districts. Peculiarly Roman attitudes or culture never penetrated these regions to any significant degree.

In Africa, the Sahara provided an effective natural boundary to the south. Roman possessions extended along the Mediterranean coast, and penetrated inland as far as skillful water engineering permitted. The province of Africa, lying around Carthage, became Romanized to a considerable extent, although the Punic language continued to be spoken until the fifth century A.D. and even later. Municipal organization took root save in the far west (Mauretania), where tribal government persisted throughout Roman times. The province of Africa became an important source of grain for the city of Rome, surpassing Sicily and rivaling the other granary of the Empire, Egypt. Egypt remained always a land apart. Its administration continued the patterns of Ptolemaic government, and the whole land was counted as the private property of the emperor. The prosperity of Egypt steadily declined under the Roman administration for reasons that are far from clear.

In Europe, the Roman empire embraced two distinct geographical regions: (1) a Mediterranean zone and (2) a continental zone.

1. Spain (except the central plateau), Italy and Greece, southern France and the eastern shores of the Adriatic all lie within the Mediterranean climatic zone. It was in this region that classical civilization first arose; and between 200 B.C. and A.D. 200 the characteristic social patterns of classical civilization established themselves throughout the Mediterranean belt of Europe. Economic life and political administration came to be organized around urban centers. In the western regions, Roman civilization and the Latin language predominated; east of the Adriatic in the Mediterranean zone, Greek language and Greek culture remained supreme. Thus the Roman empire was culturally divided into two great halves: in the west, Roman; in the east, Hellenistic.

Under Augustus and his successors, the western, Romanized half of the Empire dominated the east as far as politics was concerned, for the imperial civil service and army were mainly recruited from Italy and the Romanized provinces. Economically, however, the East, particularly the Oriental East, was more active. Trade and manufactures never flourished on the same scale in the western cities as in the eastern ones. The urban ruling class of Spain, southern France, and Italy were usually landowners, not merchants or manufacturers. In the third century A.D. the superior economic organization of the east provided the basis for the reassertion of its political autonomy; and in the following century the split between the two halves became irreparable.

2. The conquests of Caesar north of the Loire in Gaul and of Augustus' generals in the Danubian area advanced the Roman frontiers into a different climatic and geographical zone: continental and western Europe. In these regions rain is more abundant and falls the year round. Soil is deeper and richer. The agricultural techniques which suited the Mediterranean lands were ill-adapted to the conditions of the north. Forests and swamps made land clearance difficult, and some of the crops which were characteristic of the Mediterranean zone could not grow in the north where winters were more severe and the weather more cloudy.

During Roman times the rich plain and valley soils of the north were never fully exploited. Regions which were later to be the center of Western civilization remained largely forest and swamp. Only hill slopes and chalk or loess soils (on which the natural drainage was unusually good, and where heavy forests did not grow naturally), were broken to the plow. Population remained scanty, and cities were comparatively scarce, save where permanent Roman garrisons established themselves along the frontiers. These regions remained frontier districts, only imperfectly incorporated into Mediterranean society and civilization.

Nevertheless, Latin spread widely, especially among the upper classes both in Gaul and in the Danube regions; and with the Latin language spread a familiarity with the civilized ways of the Roman world. Municipalities were organized, often following older tribal lines of demarcation; and the presence of Roman armies acted as a powerful agent of Romanization. Greek language and culture did not penetrate far into the continental zone, even in the Balkan peninsula. Urban life, on which classical civilization was profoundly based, remained comparatively weak and tenuous in the north; and when the Mediterranean center weakened in the third century A.D. and barbarian invasions began, the facade of urban, classical civilization in these regions soon crumbled away.

g. Culture of the Augustan Age.

During the years of Augustus' rule, he made a conscious effort to revive and restore old Roman ways in religion and morals. In the field of literature and art, Greek examples were not rejected; but in the hands of such men as Vergil, Horace, Livy, and the Augustan architects and sculptors, a definite Roman spirit found expression through Greek forms.

Augustus looked upon religion as one of the bulwarks of the Roman state, and he used his political power to revive ceremonies and rebuild temples which had fallen into decay during late republican times. He tolerated, though he did not encourage, the worship of himself as a god in the eastern provinces, but insisted that such worship always be united with the cult of Rome. In Italy itself Augustus did not permit emperor worship, for such customs were felt to be un-Roman.

The Augustan age was one of great building activity. Augustus is said to have boasted that he found Rome a city of brick and left it a city of marble. Numerous temples, baths, public buildings, arcades, and aqueducts were erected, making Rome as magnificent as any city of the Hellenistic east. Sculpture combined realistic portraiture (of the sort developed in the time of the Republic) with the use of allegorical figures, and served sometimes as a vehicle for propaganda–for example, the account of Augustus' achievements carved on the breastplate of his statue of Prima Porta.

Literature, too, served Augustus' policy of promoting a Roman patriotic revival. Maecenas, a wealthy friend of Augustus, formed a brilliant literary circle, whose most famous members were Vergil and Horace. Vergil (70–19 B.C.) was a native of Cisalpine Gaul. His estate was confiscated after the battle of Philippi, but through the patronage of Maecenas another one was granted to him. Vergil repaid his benefactor by embodying the ideals and hopes of Augustus in his poetry, not because he wrote to order, but because Vergil personally shared the ideals and Roman patriotism for which Augustus had come to stand. His earliest poems, the *Eclogues*, were modelled on the idylls of Theocritus; the *Georgics* describe the life and work of the small farmer in Italy, and bear a certain likeness to Hesiod's *Works and Days*; his greatest work, the *Aeneid*, is an epic poem describing the career of the mythical founder of the Roman race, and is consciously modelled on Homer. Yet despite the Greek influence on all of Vergil's poetry, he is distinguished by a stubbornly Italian sentiment and proud Roman patriotism. His poems, particularly the *Aeneid*, became enormously popular and played a significant part in shaping Roman attitudes in later centuries. His portrayal of Aeneas, directed and dominated by a sense of *pietas*—perhaps best translated by the words "reverent dutifulness"—became something of a standard ideal for Roman character. Strangely enough, the Fourth Eclogue, in which Vergil predicted the birth of a child who would bring back the Golden Age, came to be interpreted by Christians as a prediction of the birth of Christ. They therefore counted Vergil as a pagan prophet, and his poems remained well known in medieval times.

Horace (65–8 B.C.) was the son of a freedman, and fought for a while against Augustus and Antony immediately after Caesar's assassination. He too acquired an estate through Maecenas' patronage, and after Vergil's death succeeded to something like an official poet laureateship. He wrote lyric and didactic poetry in a variety of forms—odes, epodes, satires, and epistles. His style was more self-conscious and formal than that of Catullus, his principal rival as a Latin lyric poet.

A quite different spirit breathed in the works of Ovid (43 B.C.–A.D. 17). He catered to the frivolous aristocracy of Rome with poems such as the *Art of Love*, and versified some of the Greek myths in his *Metamorphoses*. Such poems did not endear Ovid to Augustus, who strove to reform the morals of Rome; and in A.D. 8 Ovid was banished (for what exact reason is not known) to a remote corner of the Empire where he died.

The great prose work of the Augustan age was Livy's *History of Rome*. Livy (59 B.C.–A.D. 17) was, like Vergil, a native of Cisalpine Gaul. His book covered the whole expanse of Roman history from the foundation of the city to his own time, but only a small part of it has survived in full, the rest being preserved in epitome. His history was inspired by a profound admiration for the great days of the Republic and for the personal and public virtues which had made Rome great. His view of history put great emphasis upon individual character, and some of Livy's heroes—Cincinnatus, Regulus, Scipio Africanus—come alive like figures of epic poetry. But Livy's general mood was one of stern nostalgia for the glories and virtues of a vanished past, since his stout republicanism did not permit him to see in the Augustan principate any hope of real revival.

Nostalgia, indeed, became under the principate a pervasive element in Roman literature—it is surely significant that the greatest Latin poet, Vergil, found his principal subject in Rome's earliest days. A parallel movement in the plastic arts took the form of deliberate imitation of archaic styles; and the Augustan attempt to revive old religious forms smacks of the same backward-looking spirit. The peace which Augustus brought to the wracked body politic certainly stirred new hope in many hearts, but it failed to bring fresh new life to the culture of the Classical world.

2. THE PRINCIPATE AFTER AUGUSTUS (A.D. 14–180)

a. The Julio-Claudian Emperors (A.D. 14-68)
b. The Flavian Emperors (A.D. 69-96)
c. The Adoptive Emperors (A.D. 96-180)
d. Social and Economic
  1) Provincial municipia
  2) Decline of Slavery
  3) Changes in the Composition of the Army
  4) The Economy
e. Culture
f. Religion
  1) Paganism
  2) Judaism
  3) Christianity

a. The Julio-Claudian Emperors (A.D. 14-68)

Tiberius	A.D. 14–37
Caligula	A.D. 37–41
Claudius	A.D. 41–54
Nero	A.D. 54–68

Though Augustus always preferred to regard himself as a magistrate of the Republic, in fact his power verged on monarchy, and he made arrangements during his lifetime for the succession. Augustus outlived nearly all his blood relatives, so that imperial power devolved upon his step-son, Tiberius. Members of Tiberius' family—the Julio-Claudian house—

continued as emperors until A.D. 68 when Nero was overthrown by a military revolt. During these years, the provinces enjoyed a fairly equitable government; but in Rome itself recurrent friction and distrust marred relations between the emperors and the Senate, some of whose members still clung to republican ideals. Much depended on the individual character of the emperor. Tiberius, Caligula, and Nero all quarreled with the Senate, and resorted freely to trial and execution of their opponents. The imperial family itself was rent by intrigue; and of Augustus' four immediate successors, only Tiberius (probably) and Claudius (possibly) died natural deaths.

The reign of Claudius is notable for his policy of extending citizenship to the inhabitants of the Romanized western provinces. Claudius even co-opted Gauls into the Senate, seeking, perhaps, to bring the provinces into active partnership in the government of the Empire. During his reign, too, the imperial bureaucracy underwent a vast expansion, as one function after another was transferred from the Senate to the emperor's sphere of action. Claudius also began the conquest of Britain, and made Mauretania and Thrace into Roman provinces by annexing former client kingdoms.

b. The Flavian Emperors (A.D. 69-96)

Vespasian	A.D. 69-79
Titus	A.D. 79-81
Domitian	A.D. 81-96

Nero committed suicide when the Praetorians and other army units revolted against his capricious government. A period of civil war and confusion followed. Three emperors were proclaimed within a year, but the candidate who eventually secured power was T. Flavius Vespasianus, a man who had risen through the imperial bureaucracy from relatively humble origins in an Italian town. He managed to restore peace and military discipline, and administered the government with care and parsimony.

Under his second son, Domitian, a serious economic crisis manifested itself in Italy. The price of wine fell disastrously. The cause was probably the disappearance of an export market for Italian wine resulting from the spread of viticulture to the western provinces, and especially to Gaul. Thus while the prosperity of the western provinces—or at least of the landowning classes in those provinces—increased, economic decay manifested itself in Italy. Domitian tried to meet the crisis by forbidding the planting of more vines in Italy, and by ordering that half the vineyards of the provinces should be uprooted; but the decree does not appear to have been enforced. In any case prosperity did not return to Italy. Italian population seemingly fell off, or at least ceased to grow. Italian recruits for the army could no longer be found in sufficient numbers; more and more

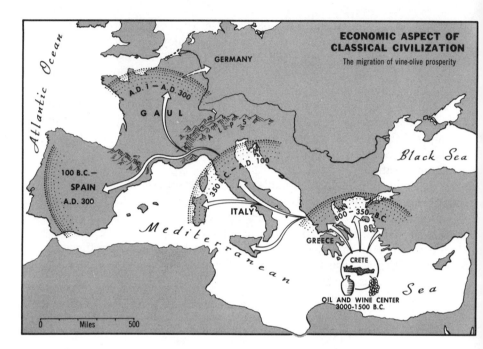

soldiers and officials were recruited instead from the more Romanized of the western provinces. As a result, Italy tended to lose the peculiar and privileged position it had enjoyed under Augustus and the early emperors.

Serious foreign wars troubled the Flavian emperors. In Judea, a Jewish revolt was suppressed only after hard fighting (A.D. 66–70); the triangle between the upper Rhine and the upper Danube was annexed and Roman power in Britain extended in a series of campaigns; but along the lower Danube, Domitian met a serious check from the Dacians, a people inhabiting what is today part of Rumania. He also engaged in a number of inconclusive campaigns against barbarian tribes who were living in the plain of Hungary.

Opposition to the emperors continued to smoulder among the members of the Senate. Some of them, stimulated by Stoic philosophers, developed a theory of government which asserted that hereditary power was fundamentally wrong. They proposed instead that each emperor should choose the best man from among the Senators as his successor. Vespasian defied this theory by handing his power down to his son, Titus; and when Titus died, his younger brother Domitian made good his claim to supreme power. But the opposition in the Senate became embittered by Domitian's "usurpation" (it was perhaps also influenced by the economic difficulties which faced Italian landowners); and Domitian resorted freely to execution of recalcitrant Senators. Yet in some sense the Senatorial opposition

won a victory, for after Domitian had been assassinated in A.D. 96, the
Roman empire was governed by a series of "adoptive" emperors, and the
hereditary principle of succession was not brought into play. The fact that
until the time of Marcus Aurelius, none of the "adoptive" emperors hap-
paned to have a son undoubtedly helped the translation of the theory into
practice.

c. The Adoptive Emperors, A.D. 96–180

Nerva	A.D. 96– 98
Trajan	A.D. 98–117
Hadrian	A.D. 117–138
Antoninus Pius	A.D. 138–161
Marcus Aurelius	A.D. 161–180

Domitian's assassination aroused unrest in many quarters, and Nerva,
an aged Senator who succeeded to the throne, stilled discontent only by
adopting Trajan, a successful military commander, as his son and successor. Trajan was of Spanish birth, and his accession to the throne of the
Caesars reflected the transformation which had come over the Roman
government. It rested no longer on Italians alone, but on the loyalty of the
landowners of all the western provinces.

Trajan embarked on a series of wars. He conquered Dacia after two
hard-fought campaigns, and made it a Roman province. It was settled
principally by Roman veterans, and the modern Rumanians claim descent
from them. In the east, war with Parthia resulted in the annexation of
Mesopotamia; but Hadrian, Trajan's successor, abandoned this province
at once so that it came within the sphere of Roman power for only two or
three years. After the time of Trajan, Roman armies generally fell back on
the defensive. Walls were built in Britain and parts of Germany to mark
the frontier and to make it easier to intercept raiders from the barbarian
lands. Campaigns occasionally took Roman soldiers outside these fortifications, but the days of Roman expansion had come to an end.

The long-standing friction between emperor and Senate ceased with
the reigns of Nerva and Trajan. The immediate issue at stake—hereditary
succession—did not arise, since Trajan had no children; and the individual
characters of succeeding emperors were such as to give the Senate no cause
for discontent.

Measures to check the economic decay of Italy were undertaken by
Nerva and carried through by Trajan. A loan fund for the relief of impoverished small landowners was established; and repayments were
assigned to the municipalities of Italy, where the money was supposed to
be used to reward parents of large families. But these measures did not
succeed in checking the decline of Italian population nor in arresting the

decay of Italian agriculture. In the second century A.D., Italy became what Greece had been in the third century B.C., a land oppressed by poverty and plagued by depopulation.

Under Hadrian and his successor, Antoninus Pius, the Empire remained at peace except for a few border skirmishes and a second Jewish revolt (A.D. 132–35). The Jewish revolt, which was put down ruthlessly, resulted in the near extermination of the Jewish population of Palestine. Hadrian was distinguished by his active concern for the welfare of the provinces, spending much of his time traveling through the Empire. He was a warm admirer of Greek culture.

Marcus Aurelius (A.D. 161–80), himself a Stoic philosopher, was the last of the adoptive emperors. During his reign, serious wars broke out in the east and also along the middle Danube, and the economy of the empire manifested an ominous weakness. In order to get money for his campaigns, Marcus resorted to sale of the crown jewels. Moreover, during his reign a plague swept the Empire that may have killed as much as a quarter of the population.

It is obvious that behind the facade of peace and prosperity, the Roman empire was suffering from serious ills. A vigorous, growing society might have quickly recovered from the shocks of war and disease which struck in the time of Marcus Aurelius. But this failed to happen in the Roman empire. Instead, population declined, and, in particular, the landowning class of the western provinces, on which the Empire had come to depend, kept on growing smaller and less willing or perhaps less able to protect the Empire. Whatever the cause, the fabric of Roman society proved itself fragile in the test which came during the next century.

d. Social and Economic

1) Provincial Municipia. As familiarity with Roman civilization spread through the western provinces, local municipalities were organized on the pattern of Rome itself, so that by the second century A.D. the Roman empire can be described as an agglomeration of cities, each surrounded by a dependent country area. There were, of course, many local variations, but a definite tendency toward uniformity in government and social structure was manifest. An ordinary provincial municipality was governed by elected magistrates who served without pay, and indeed normally paid for the privilege of holding office. Most of the fine buildings which came to decorate provincial towns were constructed by private persons as gifts to their native town. The magistrates were regularly assisted by a Senate, whose members in the West were known as *decuriones*, or *curiales*. The *curiales* were normally local landowners. Popular assemblies existed in some towns, but, as in Rome itself, they generally sank into insignificance or disappeared entirely under the principate.

From the point of view of the central authorities, the most important function of municipal governments was the collection of taxes. In addition, the municipalities administered justice within the territory assigned to them, and were responsible for maintenance of roads, and for the transport of imperial officials and messages.

In the eastern parts of the Roman empire, where city life was much older, the variety in municipal organization was greater than in the West. Trading and industrial groups in the population were more numerous and influential, and in some cases these classes continued to meet in popular assemblies and played an active part in local government.

2) Decline of Slavery. With the cessation of large scale warfare, the supply of slaves shrank. Their price rose as a result, and it became necessary for owners to make arrangements which would permit slaves to reproduce themselves, i.e., permit slaves to marry and raise families. Furthermore, the agricultural crisis in Italy, at the end of the first and throughout the second century, made slave plantations generally unprofitable, since the Italian market for wine and oil was glutted. Landowners met the difficulty by abandoning large-scale production for the market, and broke up their estates into small holdings, which they let out to slaves or to free men in return for payments in kind, labor service, and small money rents. The result of such a shift was to raise the status of agricultural slaves so that they became scarcely different from ordinary peasants; but, at the same time, free and independent farmers (insofar as any had survived in Italy or had ever existed in the western provinces) sank to dependence on the great landlords. In the western provinces, tenant farmers were known as *coloni*, whether they originated slave or free. The change was gradual. It only began in some areas during the second century A.D., but was to spread widely in later times.

3) Changes in the Composition of the Army. During the peaceful years of the second century, the Roman armies lost much of their mobility. Permanent garrison posts were established at strategic points along the frontier, and towns tended to grow up around such camps. Recruitment from Italy became unimportant after the first century; and in the second century, provincial townsmen, too, ceased to flow into the ranks of the legions. In their places there came sons of *coloni*; and more and more commonly, recruits were gathered from the immediate locality of each legionary camp. Soldiers were not legally permitted to marry, but many of them did contract irregular unions, and their sons became an important source of new recruits. The size of the army remained nearly constant, but its military efficiency undoubtedly declined. Even more important, the psychological ties between the soldiers and the ruling class of urban landowners, and between the various frontier armies and the central government, were weakened. Soldiers who were born in the camp, who were recruited locally, and who seldom traveled beyond the immediate frontier district which they guarded, inevitably came to have a different point of view from the soldiers of the Republic and early Empire who had come from Italy and expected usually to return there and set themselves up as farmers or small landowners in civilian society after their discharge. It was this transformation in military psychology, more than any other single factor, that precipitated the civil convulsions which came to the Roman empire in the third century.

4) The Economy. Very little is known of the life of the dependent peasantry (*coloni*) who constituted the overwhelming majority of the population of the Empire. Undoubtedly their life was a hard and laborious one. In the towns, an urban proletariat existed, few in number in the West, more numerous in the East. They produced goods for local sale; and, mainly in the East, continued to supply a luxury market and to manufacture articles for long distance trade. But as estates in the West tended to convert from large-scale market production to a more self-sufficient economy, the demand for luxuries inevitably shrank. Even the great landlords had a lessened money income, and could no longer afford large-scale purchases of the precious goods produced by the skilled artisans of the eastern cities. Thus the quantity of long distance trade tended to diminish; and local trade in the West failed to expand, or even began to contract, as estates became more self-sufficient. In other words, artisans migrated from the town centers to the great estates, where they worked in large part for payments in kind.

It is difficult to assess how far this devolution of the money economy went during the second century. Different areas had a different development. Thus when Italy was already in the throes of economic decay, the provinces of Gaul and Spain were still developing toward a market economy, largely oriented around the sale of goods to the army; and the reversion toward local self-sufficiency did not begin in the western provinces until after the end of the second century. It is worth emphasizing that throughout Roman times, local trade between urban centers and the surrounding countryside continued to flourish on a far larger scale in the East than it did in the West. City life and artisan skills were far more firmly established in the ancient areas of civilization; and the land-owning aristocracy enjoyed a less favorable political and social position as against other groups of society. In particular, the imperial bureaucracy was not recruited in any significant numbers from among the eastern landowners; governmental and public activity took less of their attention, and they were not raised so high above their fellow citizens as to be able to reduce them to economic and social dependence as happened in the West.

e. Culture

The cultural efflorescence of the Augustan age was not continued through the later principate. Yet monumental building, usually conforming to established styles, made an impressive show. Especially in the provinces of the west, municipalities imitated the buildings and urban conveniences of Rome so far as their resources permitted. Aqueducts, baths, amphitheaters, public buildings, and temples were erected in hundreds of towns. Rome, too, was decorated with many new and imposing structures. The Colosseum was built under the Flavian emperors; Trajan erected an enormous forum, and placed in its center a sculptured column on which his Dacian victories were recorded in a spiral frieze; triumphal arches of stone were built to commemorate the military successes of various emperors; a number of luxurious public baths were constructed. Rome became a city of magnificence and slums.

No great poets arose to continue the tradition of Vergil and Horace. Martial (A.D. 40–104) composed bitter epigrams; Juvenal (*c.* A.D. 55–138) wrote satires in which he attacked the pretenses and vices of Roman society. Among prose writers, Seneca (A.D. 1–65) wrote a number of philosophic works in which he set forth Stoic moral principles. He also tried his hand at tragedy. Pliny the Elder (A.D. 23–79) compiled a *Natural History*, into which he incorporated odd scraps of miscellaneous information; his nephew, Pliny the Younger (*c.* A.D. 61–113), composed speeches and letters. Pliny's letters provide one of the few pagan accounts of the early Christians, with whom he came in contact while governing a province in Asia Minor. Tacitus (*c.* A.D. 54–120) is perhaps the most interesting of the later Roman authors for modern readers. He wrote an account of the history of the early Empire in two books, the *Annals*, covering the period from the death of Augustus to the overthrow of Nero, and the *Histories*, which continued the account to the death of Domitian. Only parts of these works have survived. In addition, he was the author of the *Germania*, a sketch of the customs and peoples of Germany, and of a biography of his father-in-law, Agricola, who played a prominent part in conquering Britain for the Romans. Tacitus wrote from the point of view of the Senatorial opposition, and painted a sombre picture of the imperial families. His style is epigrammatic and sometimes tortuous; but he was the last great master of classical Latin.

Greek literature, which had undergone somewhat of an eclipse in the first century B.C., revived under the early empire—or perhaps it would be more accurate to say that several notable works have survived from that period as they have not from the earlier one. About the beginning of the second century A.D., Plutarch (*c.* A.D. 46–120) wrote his famous and ever popular *Parallel Lives of the Greeks and the Romans*. Somewhat earlier,

Josephus (A.D. 37–100), a Jew, used Greek for his account of Jewish history. In the second century Arrian (*c.* A.D. 96–180) wrote a biography of Alexander the Great which is the principal surviving source for Alexander's career, and Lucian (*c.* A.D. 120–after 180) wrote a number of satirical dialogues and novelettes in which he exhibited a sceptical, mocking mind. The achievements of Hellenistic medicine and astronomy were, so to speak, codified in the works of Galen (*c.* A.D. 130–200) and Ptolemy (second century A.D.). The former wrote a number of medical treatises which became standard for subsequent ages in both the Arab and Western worlds; and Ptolemy set forth the geocentric theory of astronomy in a book which we know by its Arabic title, the *Almagest*. Epictetus (*c.* A.D. 60–140), the slave, and Marcus Aurelius (A.D. 121–80), the Roman emperor, continued the Greek philosophic tradition. Both were Stoics; and Marcus, Roman of Romans though he was, preferred to use the Greek language for his *Meditations*.

f. Religion

1) Paganism. The Augustan revival of Roman religion may have had some effect in consolidating Roman society and government. The official cult of Rome and the emperor became a focus and symbol for the expression of loyalty to the Roman state, analogous to modern patriotic ceremonies. But official religion lacked emotional appeal, and quite failed to assuage the sense of personal frustration and futility which spread widely in the Empire, even among the upper classes. Hence it is not surprising that Hellenistic mystery religions, offering salvation and eternal life to their initiates, continued to spread. New cults, most notably the worship of Mithra, penetrated the Empire. Mithraism derived some of its elements from Zoroastrianism, the religion of the ancient Persians. Mithra won followers especially among the soldiers of the Roman Empire—so much so that Mithraism became almost an official military religion.

2) Judaism. Jewish communities had been established in all the major Hellenistic cities long before the Romans conquered the eastern Mediterranean lands, and during the Roman principate Jews established themselves in the principal cities of the West as well. In addition, important Jewish communities existed outside the boundaries of the Roman Empire, especially in Babylonia.

Constant friction arose between these communities and their pagan neighbors. There were occasional outbreaks of anti-Jewish riots, especially in the East. In Palestine itself, a revolt against Roman rule led to the destruction of the Temple when Jerusalem was sacked in A.D. 70. Continued friction culminated in a bitter war, A.D. 132–35, which destroyed the Jewish peasant population of Judea. These events drastically transformed

Judaism. With the destruction of the Temple and of the Judean peasantry, the territorial and priestly organization of the religion, as set up by Ezra and Nehemiah in the fifth century B.C., disappeared. What remained were the Jewish communities of the cities of the Roman and Persian Empires whose religious life centered around synagogues, presided over by rabbis (i.e., teachers). From the second century A.D., therefore, Judaism became the religion of an almost exclusively urban group, active in trade and industry, marked off from the surrounding population by the ceremonial prescriptions of the Mosaic Law and by a categorical refusal to worship pagan gods.

The destruction of the Temple and of the priestly college which had administered its rites and interpreted the Sacred Books involved a shift in the basis of authority within Judaism. Individual rabbis and rabbinical schools—the most important of them located outside the Roman Empire in Babylonia—devoted themselves to commenting upon the Torah (i.e., the first five books of what Christians call the Old Testament). Rabbinical interpretations were gradually consolidated into the *Talmud*, authoritative editions of which were produced in the fifth century A.D. by rabbis of Babylon. The learned rabbis sought to discover God's will as applied to matters of everyday conduct, as well as to religious ritual and practices. The result of their labours was therefore a very detailed system of law, whose observance marked the Jewish communities off from the rest of mankind.

3) Christianity. During the reign of Tiberius the religion which was destined drastically to reshape Classical civilization came into being. Jesus of Nazareth (*c.* 6 B.C.–A.D. 30) was one of many Jewish teachers and preachers; but his career and personality launched a movement which spread from very humble beginnings among the peasants and fishermen of his native Galilee, first to the Greek-speaking urban proletariat of the Eastern Mediterranean, and then by degrees into the West and up the social scale, until by the fifth century A.D. nearly the whole of Roman society was at least nominally Christian, while other Christian churches had come into existence beyond the Roman borders, east, south, and north.

The teachings of Jesus and the early development of Christianity are recorded in the New Testament; but the interpretation of these books is difficult, and many divergent views have been expressed by ancient, medieval and modern writers. What alone is indisputable is that a tremendous energy born of deep conviction was generated among the immediate followers of Jesus, who recognized him as the Messiah promised by the prophets of old. Converts to the new religion were first found among the Jews of Palestine; but very soon the movement spread to Jews living in the cities of the Hellenistic east, and pagans, too, became converted. Speaking

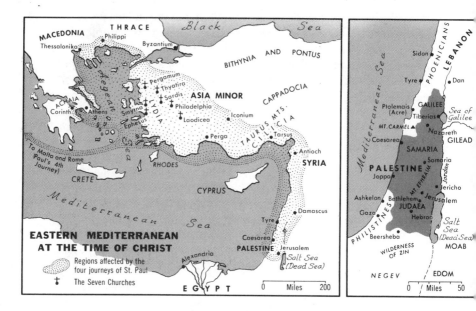

EASTERN MEDITERRANEAN
AT THE TIME OF CHRIST

Regions affected by the
four journeys of St. Paul

The Seven Churches

Greek, these converts used the Greek term "Christ," that is, "the anointed one" in place of the Hebrew word "Messiah" to describe Jesus' office and role. As the number of pagan converts increased, a crucial question as to the relationship between Judaism and the followers of Christ arose. Some argued that the prescriptions of the Mosaic law were binding among Christians, but others (chief among whom was Paul) believed that the old law had been superseded by a new revelation of God's will, and that pagan converts should not be compelled to observe Jewish ceremonials. It was this second view that prevailed.

St. Paul (*c.* A.D. 3–64) was a key figure in the development of early Christianity. He was a highly educated Jew from the Hellenistic city of Tarsus in Asia Minor. As a young man he persecuted the new sect; but he experienced a sudden conversion on the road to Damascus, and thereafter became a tireless missionary of the new religion. Paul's letters are the earliest of the writings which were later gathered together in the New Testament. They were addressed to various Christian communities of Asia Minor and Greece which Paul had founded; and one letter was sent to the Christians of Rome. The letters were apparently written to meet specific problems which arose among the new "brethren in Christ"; but in answering their appeals or admonishing them against un-Christian behavior, Paul was compelled to write down Christian doctrine as he understood and taught it. He emphasized the Divine nature of Jesus, who had come to earth as the Son of God in order to open a new path to salvation and eternal life for sin-burdened men. Faith in Christ, Paul taught, could transform men's souls and bring them salvation. His doctrine won many converts among the pagans, but among Jews Christian missionaries had little success, and indeed aroused hostility. Thus the two religions diverged—the Jews looking upon Christianity as a heretical sect, and Christians regarding Judaism as a religion which had been superseded by the new divine revelation of Jesus Christ.

By the beginning of the second century, if not earlier, it was usual for the Christian church of a particular city to be under the guidance and direction of a single bishop, who was assisted by various other officials—presbyters, deacons, and the like. The early Christians met weekly for prayer, singing, and recitation of the deeds and teachings of Jesus. They also partook of a common meal in commemoration of the Last Supper which Jesus had had with his disciples. Christian communities were very active in charitable service among their own members, and to a lesser extent among pagans too; and missionary activity never ceased.

As Christian communities spread around the Mediterranean world, questions of correct doctrine inevitably arose. In meeting these questions the first step was to reduce oral tradition to written and authoritative form. Accordingly, soon after A.D. 70 the deeds and sayings of Jesus were written down in the Gospel of Mark. Within the next thirty or forty years the other Gospels according to Luke, Matthew, and John were written. The four Gospels, together with the letters of Paul and some other writings, became, with the Old Testament, the sacred Scriptures of the new religion. The canon of the New Testament was finally fixed and generally accepted among Christians by about A.D. 200.

But agreement upon the text of the New Testament did not eliminate differences of interpretation and doctrine. One group, the Gnostics, denied the sacred character of the Old Testament and strove to interpret the teachings of the New Testament in allegorical and philosophical terms. Debates raised by such innovations began to create an orthodox theology. The main center of early theological discussion was Alexandria in Egypt, where a school for the training of teachers and priests was established toward the end of the second century. But as might be expected, the foundation of a center of higher Christian education did not bring doctrinal disputes to an end. Orthodoxy had steadily to be defined more exactly as fresh sects and heresies appeared.

A third great problem arose among the early Christians as they became more numerous: namely, the relation of their religion and churches to the Roman state. From the beginning, Christians refused to worship idols. This of course meant that they refused to worship at the shrines of Rome and the emperor, a refusal which seemed in pagan eyes an indication of treasonable intention against the state. As long as Christians were relatively few, and were drawn almost exclusively from among the poorest classes of the great cities, they attracted little or no attention from the Roman government. Under Nero, the Christians were persecuted for a short time in the city of Rome, being made scapegoats for a great fire which destroyed a large part of the city. But systematic persecutions throughout the whole Empire were not launched until the third century A.D. Nevertheless, the pagans circulated many rumors about immoral and secret acts which they accused the Christians of performing at their religious services; and occasional outbursts of mob violence took place.

Inasmuch as the Church was a semisecret organization, and its members refused to sacrifice to the emperor, it was illegal, and individual Christians could be prosecuted for membership in such an organization. Early in the second century, Pliny the Younger, as governor of a province in Asia Minor, wrote to the emperor Trajan to ask what policy he should follow in dealing with Christians who were brought before him for trial by private accusers. Trajan answered him, saying that Christians should be asked to sacrifice to the gods, and if they refused to do so, should be punished; but that no systematic effort should be made to search them out. The result of such a policy probably was that Christians were accused only when some private grudge could be settled by involving a Christian in the toils of the law.

The important fact about early Christianity was that in a society shot through with indifference and vague pessimism, the new religion stirred men's minds and hearts with a bright and burning hope for a happy and blessed life after death; and on earth, Christian hope welded believers into tightly-knit communities whose members helped one another and were willing to make great sacrifices for their religion. The élan and vitality of the Christian churches exceeded that of other social organizations in the Roman empire; and as a result the churches continued to grow and make fresh converts. Against such conviction and cohesion, the power of the state was, in the end, ineffectual.

3. Military Despotism and Anarchy (a.d. 180–285)

a. Political
b. Social and Economic
c. Cultural

a. Political

When misgovernment of Marcus Aurelius' son, Commodus (A.D. 180–193), led to his assassination, an attempt was made to revert to the principle of adoptive succession. But the soldiers were not any longer of a temper to accept a Senatorial appointee as emperor without demanding special privileges for themselves. Accordingly, the Praetorian Guard murdered Commodus' successor when he tried to discipline them, and went so far as to auction off the imperial office to the highest bidder. This action stirred the provincial armies to revolt. Each of three generals was proclaimed emperor by the troops under his command. Civil war between Roman armies ensued, from which L. Septimius Severus emerged victorious in A.D. 197.

Severus (A.D. 197–211) was a native of Africa, and shared only slightly the culture of the Roman world. He even spoke Latin with a Punic accent. But he was a successful general, and by choice—perhaps also by necessity —rested his rule solely on the soldiers who had first proclaimed him emperor. He systematically slighted the Senate, favored the soldiers by raising their pay and legalizing their marriages, and assumed the right of making law simply by his own proclamations, without the formality of first securing the agreement of the Senate. To support the army, he increased taxes. The *curiales* suffered most immediately, for they were responsible for tax collection, and if the emperor demanded more money than they could wring from their city by ordinary means, the *curiales* themselves had to make good the deficit by paying funds from their personal resources. A rapid impoverishment of the *curiales* took place as a result; and instead of seeking local magistracies as an honor, men began to resort to every means within their power to avoid being appointed to that uncomfortable and ruinous position.

Until A.D. 235, most of the emperors were members of Severus' family. During these years the discipline of the armies steadily deteriorated, every emperor after Severus being killed by mutinous troops. Owing to increasing difficulty in the collection of money taxes, soldiers were granted plots of land which they were expected to cultivate themselves when not campaigning actively. This change made the legions little more than border militia forces. For mobile campaigning new formations were created, partly from special legionary detachments, partly by fresh recruitment both within and without the Roman boundaries.

Roman law underwent a significant development under the Severi. A series of jurists compiled books in which the legal precedents established in Roman courts were gathered together and classified according to types of cases. General principles underlying the legal decisions were expounded at the same time. Largely on the basis of the writings of these jurists, Roman law was later codified by Justinian in the sixth century A.D.

The practical importance of Roman law was enlarged by a proclamation issued in A.D. 212 by which all free men of the Empire were declared to be Roman citizens. The motive behind this proclamation was probably fiscal—to make more persons liable to the inheritance tax assessed on

Roman citizens; but its effect in standardizing legal procedures and relationships was nonetheless important. It also had the effect of bringing the eastern provinces onto a legally equal plane with those of the West, where earlier emperors had widely extended Roman citizenship in the first and second centuries A.D. The wholesale extension of Roman citizenship to natives of the eastern provinces thus cleared the way for the emancipation of those provinces from the control of men native to the West; and this, in turn, made for the revival of political autonomy in the richer, Greek-speaking half of the Empire.

Between A.D. 235 and 285 the Roman world passed through a period of internal anarchy. Provinces were pillaged, towns destroyed, Roman armies fought one another, barbarian invaders ravaged the countryside, and the central power seemed about to disintegrate. For more than a dozen years, a separate state existed in the western provinces; and a similarly independent kingdom grew up in the eastern provinces under a dynasty native to the desert city of Palmyra. The emperors at Rome were constantly threatened by revolt or mutiny on the part of troops nominally loyal to them. In addition they had to meet invasions of German barbarian war bands and the attack of a new and vigorous Persian empire (established in A.D. 227 by revolt against the Parthian state, which thenceforth disappeared). Only Africa escaped from serious ravages of war, and that province remained conspicuously more prosperous than the rest of the Roman empire throughout the following century.

The rise of a series of skillful and resolute generals to the imperial throne saved the Roman empire from dissolution. Aurelian (A.D. 270–75), building on the work of his predecessors, reunited the entire empire under his single control; ten years later Diocletian ascended the throne, and during a reign of twenty years (A.D. 285–305) reestablished a modicum of peace and order in the Empire.

b. Social and Economic

The anarchy and invasions of the third century impoverished Roman society and altered its structure profoundly. The landowners who had staffed the imperial bureaucracy, commanded the Roman armies, and dominated provincial municipalities were crushed down by the weight of taxation. In their place, government officials were more and more recruited from the ranks of the army; and that meant from among men who had little or no understanding of, or respect for, the old traditions of classical culture. Money taxes became steadily more difficult to collect; and levies in kind, exacted in accordance with no sort of law, came to form the principal support of the army and of the state. Tax collection amounted to little more than organized robbery—the soldiers taking what they could find, and dividing it among themselves and their higher officers as they saw fit. The Senatorial class of the second century was largely destroyed; and with it perished the civilian, constitutional, peculiarly Roman, conception of government. In its place soldier-emperors were able to substitute little but naked force; it remained for Diocletian and Constantine to try to clothe the imperial office with a more effective religious sanction and authority.

Peasants and townsmen suffered from the ravages of hostile armies almost as much as the upper class. Famine and pestilence decimated the population, and manpower became increasingly scarce. The shortage was met in part by incorporating barbarians, especially Germans, into the army, and by allowing others to settle as farmers on empty lands inside the Roman borders.

c. Cultural

Classical culture as it had been shaped by the Greek city states came virtually to an end during the third century A.D. A new philosophy, Neo-Platonism, adapted Platonic terms to a mystical and semireligious doctrine which had an important impact upon Christian theology. Plotinus (c. A.D. 205–70) was the most famous of the Neo-Platonists. This, the last important pagan school of philosophy, reflected the changes which had come over classical society: despair of unaided reason and of this world and a strong desire for mystical union with God. Technical skill in the plastic arts lessened, and public building concentrated largely upon the construction of fortifications to protect the cities of the Empire.

Christian culture, however, expanded and enriched itself during the social disintegration of the third century. Writers like Origen (c. A.D. 182–251) in the East and Tertullian (c. A.D. 150–225) in the West carried on vigorous controversy with pagan critics of Christianity. In his defense of Christianity against philosophical attacks, Origen grafted onto Christian tradition much of the vocabulary and some of the concepts of pagan philosophy. A distinct tradition of Christian art began to arise—a tradition which fused classical art forms (especially the architecture of the Roman basilica) with more naive and informal styles within reach of the urban lower classes.

The hardships undergone by Roman society in the third century helped to focus pagan indignation upon the growing body of Christians, who not only refused to make sacrifices before statues of the emperors, but also declined military service and refused to take public office. Systematic persecutions of the Christians were organized by the imperial government in an effort to stamp out the rising religion. Persecution was not constant, however, for the government seldom had power or leisure to pursue a consistent and vigorous religious policy. The persecutions certainly shook the Church, for many Christians recanted under threat of torture. But other thousands deliberately courted martyrdom, believing that such a death assured them a favored place in heaven. Martyrs came to be highly honored among the Christians, and many of them were recognized as saints. On balance, it seems probable that the persecutions helped rather than hindered the growth of Christianity, heightening the fires of conviction among the faithful, and advertising the Christian religion widely among pagans, who could not but be impressed by the martyrs' confidence and courage.

4. THE AUTOCRATIC EMPIRE (A.D. 285–410)

a. Diocletian and Constantine (A.D. 285–337)
*b. The Division of the Empire and its Disintegration
    in the West (A.D. 337–410)*
c. The Christian Church (A.D. 285–410)
d. Culture

a. Diocletian and Constantine (A.D. 285–337)

Diocletian came to the throne in A.D. 285. He was of peasant origin, a native of Dalmatia who had risen through the ranks of the army. He faced the problem of how to organize the Roman administration on a basis which could halt the disastrous civil wars. His problem resolved itself to an old one in Roman history: the need of securing the soldiers' loyalty. Diocletian tried to assure their obedience by surrounding himself with Oriental pomp and by styling himself divine. In addition, he sought to assure smooth succession from one reign to another by an elaborate system of cooption. Thus he associated with himself another "Augustus," with whom he divided the administration of the Empire, entrusting the western provinces to his colleague. Each Augustus had as an assistant a "Caesar," who was intended to succeed in due course to the rank of Augustus and select another Caesar to carry on the succession. In practice this artificial system broke down as soon as Diocletian ceased to rule.

To make successful revolt more difficult, Diocletian separated military from civil power, in effect erecting two parallel bureaucracies in every part of the Empire, the one military and the other civilian. Provinces were subdivided until a total of one hundred and one existed; these were grouped into twelve dioceses, and the dioceses in turn into four prefectures. The Senate's power in the provinces had disappeared under the Severi, and that august body persisted only as a municipal council for the city of Rome. Senatorial rank remained, however, a high privilege accorded to the top members of the imperial bureaucracy.

The army was divided into two distinct forces. On the frontiers, militia under the command of *duces*—from whence the medieval dukes—guarded against small-scale raids from barbarian neighbors; but serious campaigning was reserved for mobile and more highly trained forces maintained at strategic centers near the persons of the two Augusti. The emperors' companions, the *comites* (i.e., counts) supplied leaders for this force.

Diocletian's tax reforms amounted to little more than a legalization of the forced exactions which had become common during the anarchy of the preceding fifty years. Taxes were assessed in kind; and a very elaborate and highly centralized bureaucracy was organized to assure collection and distribution of the materials which were collected. Money taxes did not disappear, but the decay of exchange economy and a general impoverishment of the Empire meant that tax monies became harder and harder to find. Tax collection remained a very oppressive and often violent proceeding, despite Diocletian's efforts to the contrary.

In A.D. 305 Diocletian retired "to raise cabbages." He steadfastly refused to resume the imperial office during the remaining years of his life, despite appeals that he should intervene to settle the disputes and rivalries which soon broke out among the Augusti and Caesars who succeeded to the imperial power. Within a few years civil war broke out once again. From these struggles Constantine emerged supreme by A.D. 324. He retained control of the whole Empire until his death in A.D. 337.

Constantine made some important changes in Roman government, and his laws gave the shape to late Roman society which was to last in the East through the Byzantine period. Undoubtedly his most important act was to make Christianity a legal and favored religion. Constantine convinced himself that he owed his success in the civil wars to the God of the Christians. He therefore became a Christian and used his imperial power to favor Christianity in every way he could.

Though it seems improbable that Constantine was much influenced by narrowly political considerations in his espousal of Christianity, it was nevertheless true that by favoring the Christian religion he enlisted a new, and, as it proved, a very active and vigorous force in support of the Empire. The imperial power which Constantine and other Christians believed had been conferred upon him by Almighty God was made more secure by that very belief. His immediate predecessors on the imperial throne had rested their power on undisguised force; and what the soldiers had given, they could always take away. After Constantine's time the idea that the imperial power was supported and maintained by Divine Will gained an ever wider acceptance. The practical power of the soldiery to raise and overthrow emperors remained as before; but by slow degrees the armies' resort to insurrection became less frequent, and government slowly became more stable, at least in the eastern provinces. The teachings of

Christian leaders and the powerful hold which Christianity was able to exercise over men's minds undoubtedly helped to bring about this stabilization.

Thus the naked power of secular government gradually came to be clothed, after Constantine's time, with the sanctions of a living and powerful religion. Church and state came into intimate connection and lent mutual support to each other. This change was to have tremendous repercussions through later centuries, and has been taken by many historians to mark the end of the classical and the beginning of the medieval age.

Constantine also promulgated some important laws legalizing changes which had come gradually into Roman society. He made it illegal for a man to run away from the obligations which he owed to the state by virtue of his station in life. Thus the *coloni* were bound to the soil, and forbidden to leave the estate onto which they were born. Similarly, the *curiales*, responsible as ever for tax collection, were required to stay in their native town and produce the taxes demanded of them. It was even made illegal for *coloni* or *curiales* to join the army, or to become members of the Christian clergy, both of which groups enjoyed a privileged status in the new order of society. Something resembling an hereditary caste system was thus imposed on Roman society. The motive behind such legislation was fiscal: the state needed taxes, and tried to assure a regular income by pinning down tax-paying individuals where the long arm of the law could regularly find them.

Two lines of development were already evident in Constantine's time, which were eventually to destroy the Roman empire in the West. One was the progressive barbarization of the army and government bureaucracy through the admission of Germans and others to the imperial service; the second was the difficulty which the central government had in maintaining control over its local officials.

The practice of allowing barbarians to settle inside the Roman frontiers in return for military service was not new. Even in the time of Augustus such measures had been resorted to occasionally. But in the third and fourth centuries, as depopulation continued to weaken the Empire and great tracts of land fell vacant, the number of such grants increased greatly. Among the newly settled barbarians, the old classical culture made little progress. Yet barbarian volunteers were freely incorporated into the regular Roman army, and many individual Germans were able to rise to high military posts. The emperor-makers of the fifth century A.D. were almost all such barbarian adventurers. A growing dependence on barbarian soldiers and military leaders obviously augured ill for the indefinite continuance of the Roman state.

A second danger to the stability of the imperial government arose from the difficulty Constantine and his successors found in controlling the

officials, and particularly the high officials, under them. Since money was
scarce, officials were remunerated in large part through payments in kind.
Sometimes they were granted land, the income from which served in lieu
of other salary. The physical difficulties of accounting for and controlling
payments in kind were very great, so that in practice high officials were
generally free to make requisitions on public stocks for their private uses
without much regard for the policies or wishes of the central government.
Thus the whole distinction between private and public tended to become
blurred. The emperor's best efforts to prevent abuses were not successful,
for while individual malefactors could be replaced, the system corrupted
their successors as rapidly as they could be appointed. As a result, the income of the central government was never secure, and the emperors were
constantly hard put to it to lay their hands on sufficient cash and goods to
maintain their own personal, mobile army. Yet the effective preservation
of the central power depended on the existence of such an army.

Another development which had begun in Constantine's time and
steadily weakened the central government in subsequent decades was the
practice of granting immunity from regular taxes to estates owned or
occupied by high state officials, or by individuals who won or bought special imperial favor. Insofar as estates were granted to officials in lieu of
salary, such exemption from taxation seemed sensible enough. But the
precedent proved dangerous. Immune estates tended to grow in size at the
expense of ordinary tax-paying land. The growth of such estates depended
in part on their owners' use of force and fraud; but it was greatly facilitated
by the fact that many small landowners and farmers found it worthwhile
to transfer the legal title to the land they possessed to such a "lord"
("commend" it to him) on the understanding that they would continue to
occupy what had formerly been their own property. The "lord" could protect the small man from the rapacity of imperial tax collectors; in return
he collected payment from the tenant—legally a rent, but in actuality more
like protection money. Owners of immune estates did not escape taxation
completely. Constantine devised special taxes applicable to their lands;
but it seems certain that the tax burden on these great estates was proportionately less than on the ordinary land attached to municipalities according to the old Roman system.

The full development of the system of immunity and commendation
did not come until after the collapse of the central Roman administration
in the West. Only germs of the later development were present in the time
of Constantine. Under his successors, however, the power of great landlords steadily increased, and the municipal organization through which
regular taxes were collected decayed in proportion as lands were withdrawn from the sphere of municipal tax officials. Thus in a very real sense
the Roman empire in the West was destroyed by its own high officials, who

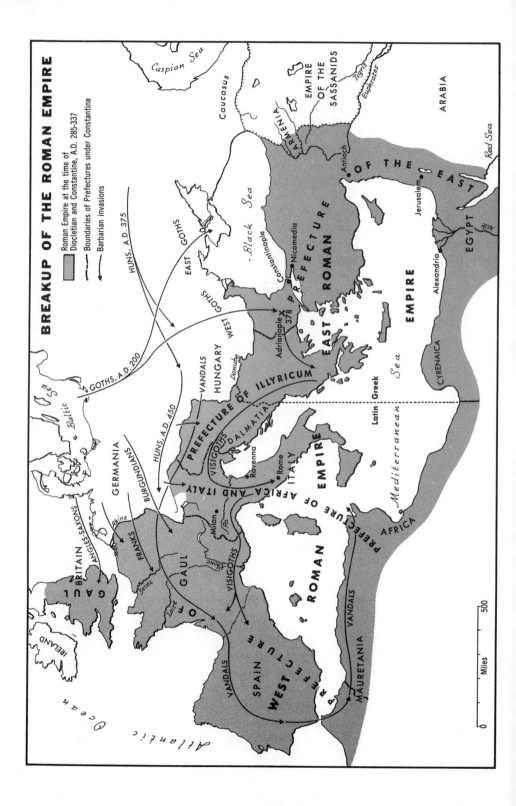

BREAKUP OF THE ROMAN EMPIRE

Roman Empire at the time of
Diocletian and Constantine, A.D. 285-337

Boundaries of Prefectures under Constantine

Barbarian invasions

Caspian Sea

Caucasus

EMPIRE OF THE SASSANIDS

Tigris

Euphrates

ARABIA

ARMENIA

Red Sea

Antioch

PREFECTURE OF THE EAST

Jerusalem

EAST ROMAN

Nicomedia

Constantinople

Black Sea

EMPIRE

Alexandria

EGYPT

EAST GOTHS

HUNS, A.D. 375

WEST GOTHS

Adrianople X 378

CYRENAICA

GOTHS, A.D. 200

VANDALS

HUNGARY

Mediterranean Sea

PREFECTURE OF ILLYRICUM

Danube

Latin Greek

Baltic Sea

HUNS, A.D. 450

DALMATIA

VISIGOTHS

GERMANIA

Ravenna

Rome

ITALY

BURGUNDIANS

Rhine

PREFECTURE OF AFRICA AND ITALY

BRITAIN

ANGLES-SAXONS

Milan

Po

AFRICA

GAUL

FRANKS

ROMAN EMPIRE

Seine

PREFECTURE OF GAUL

Rhône

VISIGOTHS

Loire

IRELAND

VANDALS

WEST PREFECTURE

SPAIN

Atlantic Ocean

VANDALS

MAURETANIA

500

Miles

0

so abused their position as to destroy the tax income and hence the military power of the central government.

b. The Division of the Empire and its Disintegration in the West (A.D. 337–410)

During the third century A.D. the division between the Greek-speaking East and the Latin-speaking West became increasingly apparent; and the system of prefectures, which Diocletian set up, gave the two great segments of the Empire a distinct political organization. The western provinces suffered more severely from civil wars and invasions, and the center of gravity of the Empire shifted perceptibly eastward. Diocletian reserved for himself the eastern portion of the empire, assigning the west to his fellow-Augustus; and Constantine built himself a new capital on the ancient site of Byzantium, which he renamed Constantinople (A.D. 330). Rome ceased to be the functioning capital even of the western part of the Empire, when more strategically located cities in northern Italy, first Milan and later Ravenna, became the usual residence of the western emperor. Yet the imperial idea remained strong in men's minds and Rome remained a symbol and, so to speak, a sentimental capital long after the actual business of government had been transferred from the banks of the Tiber.

Constantine divided the Empire among his sons, who soon fell to quarreling with each other. Nevertheless, members of Constantine's family ruled over the Empire until A.D. 363. The last of the line, Constantine's nephew Julian (A.D. 361–63), was a pagan, and tried to establish a pagan church which would inculcate the virtues of patriotism. His attempt was short-lived and a failure.

During the later fourth century, Roman government weakened, especially in the West. The central power was often unable to make its will felt in some of the provinces; and the practice of establishing two or more co-rulers sometimes resulted in the pursuit of differing policies. Wars with the Persians in the east and with German tribes in the north were chronic, and the Roman armies were seldom able to do more than hold their own against these enemies. Warfare against pretenders to the throne, or between colleagues in the imperial dignity, were frequent; and beneath the surface of political and military disorder we can glimpse progressive impoverishment, sporadic outbreaks of brigandage, and desperate revolts against rapacious tax collectors.

During the second half of the fourth century the pressure of the barbarians along the northern frontier increased. Social and political changes among the German tribes made them more formidable enemies than those Roman armies had faced at the beginning of the Christian era. Population apparently increased and agriculture became more important among the Germans. Larger political units were formed through federation of older tribes. The names of some of the historic German peoples betray their origin from federations: e.g., the Franks means the "free" men, and the Alemanni means literally "all men." Rising population and larger political units supplied motive and means for a substantial expansion of the area occupied by German peoples. A general movement southward and eastward occurred. The Goths played a particularly prominent role in this expansion. Starting from southern Sweden, or perhaps from the Baltic coast, they conquered what is now southern Russia and modern Rumania in the course of the second and third centuries A.D.

Against the rising power of the German peoples, the Romans could oppose only a weakening army and a decaying society. The precarious balance was tilted rather abruptly by the appearance of a nomadic people from Central Asia, the Huns. The Huns burst upon the Gothic kingdom of southern Russia in the third quarter of the fourth century A.D. and conquered the eastern branch of the tribe, known to history as the Ostrogoths. To escape a similar fate, the western branch, the Visigoths, sought and obtained permission to cross the Danube and settle in the Roman empire. But a quarrel broke out between Roman officials and the Gothic chieftains. Hostilities ensued, and in A.D. 378 the Visigoths were able to defeat a Roman army near the city of Adrianople and killed the co-emperor, Valens. This battle marks an important stage in the breakup of the Roman empire, for the Goths were never effectively subdued nor driven from Roman soil. Instead, peace was patched up in A.D. 382 (after the Goths had ravaged almost the whole Balkan peninsula). By its terms, the emperor agreed to pay a subsidy to the Gothic chieftains in return for a supply of Gothic soldiers for the imperial army.

The emperor who made this settlement was Theodosius, sometimes called the Great. He reigned in the east from A.D. 379 until his death in A.D. 395, and during the last year of his life he succeeded in reuniting the whole Roman empire under his personal power. He was the last emperor ever to do so. Upon his death, the Empire was divided between his two sons, Honorius in the west and Arcadius in the east. Thereafter the two segments of the Empire traveled different and divergent paths, and although the theory of a united Roman empire was not abandoned for centuries to come, the reality of Roman unity disappeared forever.

Honorius (A.D. 395-423) was an incapable man, and the effective administration and defense of the western part of the empire fell into the hands of the commander of the army, a German named Stilicho. Stilicho tried vainly to stem fresh invasions. In A.D. 406 bands of Franks, Sueves, Vandals, and Alans crossed the Rhine frontier and ravaged Gaul. The Visigothic king, Alaric, made several attacks on Italy also. When Stilicho agreed to pay him a large ransom and take him into Honorius' service, the emperor refused to accept the terms and assassinated Stilicho. Alaric thereupon marched unopposed through Italy and in A.D. 410 captured and sacked the city of Rome. This event has sometimes been taken to mark the fall of Rome. Another date, A.D. 476, when a barbarian soldier, Odoacer, deposed the last Roman emperor of the West and sent the imperial insignia to Constantinople, is also sometimes taken as marking the final end of Roman power in the west.

Yet the German invaders did not deliberately strive to overthrow the Roman empire. They came to enjoy, not to destroy, the riches and comforts of Roman society. As barbarian kingdoms arose on Roman soil, the German kings attached Roman titles to their names, frequently posed as legitimate Roman officials ruling Roman provinces, and often strove to win recognition from the emperor in Constantinople. In theory, the emperor in Constantinople continued to rule over an undivided empire, and the transfer of insignia in A.D. 476 marked not the end of the Roman empire but its reunion under a single head.

But the facts were of course otherwise. German kings and tribesmen injected a new element into Roman society in the West, and under the impact of their invasions and the subsequent disorders which perennially plagued the public peace, Classical civilization as well as the amenities of Roman life gradually disappeared. No particular date can be attached to such a transformation. The weakening of Roman society was perceptible even in the first century A.D., in Italy at least; and traces of Roman culture and social organization never disappeared, being constitutive elements of our own civilization today. One can only say that the first decade of the fifth century witnessed the irruption of German tribes into the heart of the western Roman empire; and Alaric's sack of Rome in A.D. 410 stands as a milepost in the process.

c. The Christian Church (A.D. 285–410)

Diocletian directed a severe and systematic persecution against the Church during his tenure of imperial power. But it survived this last great trial, and in A.D. 313 Constantine made Christianity legal and himself became a Christian. Nearly all succeeding emperors were Christians also; then in A.D. 393 Theodosius declared paganism illegal and made Christianity the official religion of the Empire. At the time of Constantine's conversion, only a minority of the Roman population was Christian. During his reign the number of converts increased enormously; yet for many decades and even centuries paganism remained common at the extremes of the social scale, among the upper classes on the one hand, and among simple country people on the other.

During and after the time of Constantine the Christian Church underwent rapid change. First of all, worldly advantages were heaped upon the

clergy. Constantine assigned state funds for the erection of church buildings, exempted the clergy from ordinary taxes, and allowed them free use
of the imperial post service when traveling on ecclesiastical business. He
recognized the Church as a legal corporation; or perhaps it would be more
accurate to say that he recognized the right of individual churches to own
property acquired by gift or legacy. As a result the Church very rapidly
became an important property owner in the Roman world.

As long as the state had remained hostile, divisions and differences
among Christians tended to be minimized by the need for presenting a
common front to an unfriendly world. But when the pressure of persecution was removed, it was not long before serious quarrels over theological
and other matters split the Church into factions. Constantine repeatedly
intervened in an effort to bring about peace and unity among all Christians,
but his endeavors met with small success. In Africa, the power of the state
failed to suppress the Donatist heresy; and in the East a great controversy
over the relation of Father and Son in the Trinity split the Church. Bitter
disagreement was not ended even when Constantine called a general
council of Christian bishops at Nicaea (A.D. 325) to settle the issue. In this
controversy the view which eventually was accepted as orthodox was
championed by Athanasius; while the opposed and eventually heretical
view was proclaimed by Arius (hence the Arian heresy). Throughout the
fourth century this dispute divided the Christian Church into rival camps.
Some of Constantine's successors were Arian Christians, and used the
power of the state to persecute the Athanasians; when the Athanasians
were in power they retaliated against the Arians in similar fashion.

As the number of Christians rose, the complexity and size of the church
organization grew correspondingly. Ecclesiastical administration tended
to parallel the political organization of the state. Thus it became a rule that
every *municipium* should have a bishop, and that in every province there
should be a prelate of superior rank—called metropolitan or archbishop—
who had general disciplinary powers over the other bishops of his province. Moreover, bishops of especially important cities, such as Milan and
Constantinople, were able to assert a much wider leadership in the Church,
largely through their nearness to the seats of imperial power. Other cities
claimed an especially important part in settling questions of doctrine and
discipline on the ground that they were apostolic foundations, and so
preserved in purer and more authoritative form the original teachings of
the apostles. By the early fifth century five bishoprics (or patriarchates)
were recognized as preeminent: Rome, Constantinople, Antioch, Jerusalem, and Alexandria. But the practical influence of these patriarchates
depended largely on the individual character of the bishop who happened
to occupy the see. Issues of great moment were regularly settled by councils summoned by the emperor, to which all bishops were invited.

Another problem which Christians had to face was that of the relation between Church and State. As long as Christianity was a persecuted and minority religion theoretical difficulties were not serious, though the practice of Christian principles was sometimes fraught with danger since Christians could not conscientiously take part in pagan government nor obey idolatrous laws. But when the government itself became Christian, a new relation had to be found. Constantine tried at the beginning of his reign to allow the bishops to manage Church affairs and settle disputes among themselves; but he quickly discovered that the defeated party would not abide by the judgment of the majority and insisted on appealing to him. Thus Constantine found himself irresistibly drawn into ecclesiastical disputes. During the latter years of his reign he took active part in formulating creeds and used the power of the state to repress heresies.

But secular interference in Church affairs was not everywhere and always accepted. Inasmuch as the emperor was himself a Christian, it could be argued that he, like any other member of the Church, was subject to the moral and other laws of God as they were set forth in Scripture and interpreted by priests. Toward the end of the fourth century, St. Ambrose, bishop of Milan strenuously asserted this position, and succeeded in compelling the emperor Theodosius to do public penance for a massacre which he had authorized. As in questions of Church organization, much depended on the personalities of individual emperors and prelates; and few bishops dared to imitate Ambrose's example. The question of the relation between Church and State was not clearly settled at any time, and passed down to the Middle Ages as one of the central issues of politics.

d. Culture

The destruction of the classes in Roman society which had been the carriers of the classical tradition took place in the third century. The impoverishment and disorder of the fourth century were obviously not favorable to revival of the ancient culture, nor to cultural achievement of any sort. Yet the Christian Church produced several notable writers and thinkers. The vigorous theological debate between Arius and Athanasius has been mentioned already; it and other doctrinal disputes precipitated much polemical writing, mainly in the eastern part of the Empire. The greatest preachers and teachers of the Eastern Church were St. Basil (A.D. 330–79) and St. John Chrysostom (c. A.D. 347–407). Christian history was initiated by Eusebius of Caesarea (c. A.D. 264–340), a friend and adviser of Constantine's. He wrote a book of *Church History* recounting the growth of Christianity. In another work, the *Chronicle*, he tried to bring the historical tradition of the pagan classical world into harmony with the sacred history preserved in the Old Testament.

In the West, the fourth century saw a profound change in the character of Christianity. The early Christian communities of the West had been mainly limited to Greek-speaking immigrant groups, except in Africa where Latin Christianity took root very early. Only by degrees did Christianity extend beyond the immigrant and slave population to embrace persons whose native tongue was Latin. Constantine's conversion changed this situation radically. Thousands took up Christianity, and persons of all social classes began to gather in the Church. Toward the end of the century the change in status of the Church bore fruit in the development of a distinctly Latin type of Christianity. Three great names are associated with this development, the so-called Latin Doctors (i.e., teachers) of the Church: St. Ambrose, St. Jerome and St. Augustine.

Ambrose (c. A.D. 340–97) was a high official of the Roman government, thoroughly educated in the Latin classical tradition, before he became Bishop of Milan. He was important not only as an ecclesiastical statesman, able to humble even the emperor Theodosius, but also as an intellectual leader. Ambrose and Augustine bear a relation to the Latin Church not unlike that of Origen to the Greek Church: they made Christianity intellectually the equal or superior of any pagan creed. Before their time, the Christians in the West had been far more suspicious of, and hostile to, philosophy than were the Christians of the Greek East; and the expectation of an imminent end of the world had remained much more important in their teaching than it was in the East. Ambrose and Augustine enriched and enlarged the doctrines of the Western Church, partly through borrowings from Greek theologians, partly through independent intellectual development. Ambrose incorporated many of the details of ritual which had grown up in the East into the Church services he presided over in Milan, and introduced the allegorical interpretation of the Bible to the Latin-speaking world. This mode of interpretation became basic for all Medieval Christianity. It permitted the incorporation of much of the wisdom and learning of pagan philosophers into the Christian tradition, for the words of the Bible were treated as symbols and signs of philosophic and religious truths at which the superficial meaning of the texts only hinted.

St. Augustine (A.D. 354–430), a native of Africa, began a brilliant career as a teacher of rhetoric before becoming a convert to Christianity. He was, significantly, baptised by Ambrose himself; and in a real sense Augustine fulfilled the task which Ambrose had begun, adapting Christian theology to the peculiar temperament of the Latin world. He wrote many polemical works and theological treatises in which Christian doctrines were eloquently set forth. The most famous and influential of his works were the *Confessions*, in which he tells the story of his conversion to Christianity, and the *City of God*. Augustine undertook the writing of the *City of God* in order to refute pagans who interpreted Alaric's sack of Rome as a punishment for the abandonment of the pagan deities by the Roman state. In this book he developed a Christian philosophy of history, extending from creation to the last judgment, in the light of which the sack of Rome became nothing but a petty incident in God's providential plan for the universe and for man. For more than a thousand years, Augustine's *City of God* provided Latin Christendom with a seldom questioned picture of the destiny of human life.

The third Doctor of the Latin Church, St. Jerome (*c.* A.D. 340–420), was preeminently a scholar. His great work was a translation of the Bible into Latin, for which purpose he acquired a knowledge of Hebrew as well as of Greek, and carefully gathered the best manuscripts he could lay hands on. His translation, known as the *Vulgate*, is still used by the Roman Catholic Church.

Suggestions for Further Reading for Part II, D

The Oxford Classical Dictionary. Oxford: 1948.
Cambridge Ancient History. Vols. 9–12. Cambridge: 1932–39.
Cambridge Ancient History, Volumes of Plates. Vol. 5. Cambridge: 1939.
Baynes, N. H. *Constantine the Great and the Christian Church.* London: 1931.
Bettenson, H. S. ed. *Documents of the Christian Church.* The World's Classics. 2d ed. Oxford: 1947.
Blair, Peter J. *Roman Britain and Early England 55 B.C.-A.D. 871.* Camden, N.J: 1963.
Boak, A. E. R. *A History of Rome to 565 A.D.* 4th ed. New York: 1955.
Bultmann, R. *Primitive Christianity in Its Contemporary Setting.* Living Age Books.
Burckhardt, J. *The Age of Constantine the Great.* Anchor Books.
Carcopino, D. *Daily Life in Ancient Rome.* New Haven: 1940.
Cary, M. *A History of Rome.* 2d ed. London: 1954.
Charlesworth, M. P. *The Roman Empire.* Oxford: 1951.
Cochrane, C. N. *Christianity and Classical Culture.* Galaxy Books.
Cumont, F. *Oriental Religions in Roman Paganism.* London: 1912.
Dill, S. *Roman Society from Nero to Marcus Aurelius.* Meridian Books.
Fowler, H. N. *History of Roman Literature.* New York: 1928.
Frank, T. ed. *An Economic Survey of Ancient Rome.* Vols. 2–5. Baltimore: 1936–40.
Gibbon, E. *Decline and Fall of the Roman Empire.* Vol. 1. Modern Library.
Glover, T. R. *Paul of Tarsus.* New York: 1925.
Goguel, M. *The Life of Jesus.* New York: 1933.

Goodspeed, Edgar J. *History of Early Christian Literature.* Rev. and enlarged by Robert M. Grant. Chicago: 1966.

Grant, M. *Roman History from Coins.* Cambridge: 1958.

Harnack, A. *The Expansion of Christianity in the First Three Centuries.* 2 vols. New York: 1904–5.

Lewis, N. and Reinhold, M. *Roman Civilization: Selected Readings.* Vol. 2. *The Empire.* New York: 1955.

Lietzman, H. *The Era of the Church Fathers.* London: 1951.

Lot, F. *The End of the Ancient World.* New York: 1931.

Mattingly, H. *The Man in the Roman Street.* New York: 1947.

Mattingly, H. *Roman Imperial Civilization.* London: 1957.

McGiffert, A. C. *History of Christianity in the Apostolic Age.* Rev. ed. New York: 1906.

Mommsen, T. *Provinces of the Roman Empire.* New ed. Chicago: 1968.

Mowry, Lucetta. *The Dead Sea Scrolls and the Early Church.* Chicago: 1962.

Pfeiffer, R. H. *History of New Testament Times.* New York: 1949.

Richmond, I. R. *Roman Britain (The Pelican History of England,* Vol. 1).

Rostovtzeff, M. *History of the Ancient World.* Vol. 2. Oxford: 1930.

Rostovtzeff, M. *Social and Economic History of the Roman Empire.* 2d ed. Oxford: 1957.

Salmon, E. T. *History of the Roman World from 30 B.C. to A.D. 138.* 3d ed. New York: 1957.

Walbank, F. W. *The Decline of the Roman Empire in the West.* London: 1946.

Novels

Asch, Shalom. *The Apostle.* New York: 1943.

Asch, Shalom. *Mary.* New York: 1949.

Asch, Shalom. *The Nazarene.* New York: 1949.

Byrne, Don. *Brother Saul.* New York: 1927.

Duggan, Alfred. *Family Favorites.* New York: 1961.

Fast, Howard. *Spartacus.* New York: 1952.

Feuchtwanger, Lion. *Josephus.* New York: 1932.

Feuchtwanger, Lion. *Jew of Rome.* New York: 1936.

Feuchtwanger, Lion. *Josephus and the Emperor.* New York: 1942.

France, Anatole. *Thais.* London: 1891.

France, Anatole. *The Procurator of Judaea.* London: 1908.

Graves, Robert. *I, Claudius.* New York.

Lagerkvist, Par. *Barabas.* New York: 1951.

Lytton, Edward B., 1st Baron. *The Last Days of Pompeii.* London: 1834.

Macpherson, Annie W. *Roman Wall.* New York: 1954.

Pater, Walter. *Marius the Epicureau.* New York: 1885.

Schmitt, Gladys. *Confessors of the Name.* New York: 1952.
Sienkiewicz, Henry K. *Quo Vadis?* Boston: 1896.
Treece, Henry. *The Dark Land.* New York: 1952.
Treece, Henry. *Red Queen, White Queen.* New York: 1952.
Wallace, Lew. *Ben Hur.* New York: 1880.
Waugh, Evelyn. *Helena.* Boston: 1950.
Yourcenar, Marguerite. *Memoirs of Hadrian.* New York: 1954.

Chronological Table for Part II, D: The Roman Empire

B.C.

*27 B.C.–A.D. 180	*The Principate*
*27	Augustus relinquished his extraordinary powers to the Senate, thus "restoring the Republic."
23	Augustus changed the basis of his power; abandoned annual consulship.
19	Death of Virgil, the poet.
12–6	Conquest of Germany to the Elbe.
8	Death of Horace, the poet.
6	(?) Birth of Jesus.

A.D.

6	Failure of campaign against German tribes in Bohemia; Augustus adopted a nonaggressive policy; cessation of rapid expansion of Roman empire.
9	Revolt of German tribes between Rhine and Elbe; Romans accepted Rhine as frontier.
*14	Death of Augustus; his step-son, Tiberius, succeeded.
14–37	Tiberius, Roman emperor.
17	Death of Livy, the historian; of Ovid, the poet.
*c. 30	The Crucifixion.
37–41	Caligula, Roman emperor.
41–54	Claudius, Roman emperor.
43	Invasion of Britain by Roman armies.
54–68	Nero, Roman emperor.
64	Great fire in Rome; first persecution of the Christians; probable deaths of St. Peter and St. Paul in Rome.
65	Death of Seneca, the philosopher and litterateur.
66–70	Jewish revolt in Palestine; destruction of the Temple.

69–70	Year of the three emperors: Galba, Otho and Vitellius.
69–79	Vespasian, Roman emperor.
c. 70	Gospel according to St. Mark, the earliest of the Gospels, written down.
79–81	Titus, Roman emperor.
79	Eruption of Vesuvius; Pompeii and Herculaneum buried; death of Pliny the Elder.
81–96	Domitian, Roman emperor; wars on the Danube; economic crisis in Italy.
96–98	Nerva, Roman emperor.
98–117	Trajan, Roman emperor.
c. 100	Death of Josephus, the historian.
c. 104	Death of Martial, the poet.
106	Dacia annexed as Roman Province.
c. 113	Death of Pliny the Younger.
113–117	Campaign against the Parthians; temporary annexation of Mesopotamia; Roman empire attained its largest extent.
117–38	Hadrian, Roman emperor.
c. 120	Death of Tacitus, the historian; of Plutarch, the biographer.
c. 138	Death of Juvenal, the poet.
132–135	Jewish revolt; destruction of the Jewish community in Palestine.
138–161	Antoninus Pius, Roman emperor.
161–180	Marcus Aurelius, Roman emperor.
c. 180	Death of Arrian, litterateur and historian.
*180–285	*Military Despotism and Anarchy*
180–193	Commodus, Roman emperor.
193–197	Civil war between Severus, Clodius Albinus and Pescennius Niger for the imperial power.
197–211	Severus, Roman emperor.
c. 200	Death of Galen, the medical writer.
*by 200	Canon of the New Testament fixed and generally accepted among Christians.
212	Edict making all free men of the Empire Roman citizens.
c. 225	Death of Tertullian, Latin Church father.
227	New Persian Empire established by revolt against Parthian state.

235–285	Anarchy in Roman empire; temporary breakdown of imperial unity, barbarian invasions, plague, civil war.
c. 251	Death of Origen, the theologian.
c. 270	Death of Plotinus, the philosopher.
270–75	Aurelian, Roman emperor; restored effective central control of the empire.
285–410	*The Autocratic empire*
*285–305	Diocletian, Roman emperor; established absolutism, reorganized bureaucracy, persecuted Christians.
305–324	Conflict and frequent civil wars between "Augusti" and "Caesars."
312	Battle of the Milvian bridge; Constantine gained control of western part of the Empire.
*313	Edict of Milan; Christianity made a legal religion, and Constantine favored it in the part of the empire he controlled.
324	Constantine won control of the entire Empire.
*325	Council of Nicaea called by Constantine to settle doctrinal disputes among Christians.
330	Constantinople made capital of Roman empire.
337	Death of Constantine.
c. 340	Death of Eusibius, bishop of Caesarea, Christian historian; birth of St. Ambrose and St. Jerome.
354	Birth of St. Augustine.
361–363	Julian the Apostate, Roman emperor; tried to restore paganism as official religion.
376	Visigoths settled within Roman borders as *foederati*.
*378	Battle of Adrianople; Visigoths defeated Roman army and killed co-emperor.
379–95	Theodosius, emperor in the East; reunited the whole empire under his control, 394–395; after his death the division between Eastern and Western halves became permanent.
393	Theodosius made paganism illegal; Christianity became the official religion of the empire.
395–423	Honorius, Roman emperor in the West.
397	Death of St. Ambrose, bishop of Milan.
406	Germanic invasion of Rhine frontier.
*410	Visigoths under Alaric sacked Rome.

420	Death of St. Jerome, the translator of the Bible into Latin.
*430	Death of St. Augustine, bishop of Hippo.
*476	Deposition of Romulus Augustulus by Odoacer; disappearance of western emperor.

E. The Byzantine Empire and Civilization (A.D. 410–1453)

1. *Introductory*
2. *Political Survival*
3. *Social and Economic*
4. *Cultural*
5. *Influence of Byzantine Civilization*
6. *Decay and Overthrow*

1. INTRODUCTORY

While the Roman empire in the West broke down in the course of the fifth century A.D., in the East Roman government survived without a break until A.D. 1204; and not until the conquest of Constantinople by the Ottoman Turks in A.D. 1453 did self-styled successors to Caesar and Augustus permanently disappear from Constantine's capital. Sweeping changes came over society and government during these long centuries, and it is customary to speak of Byzantine civilization and of the Byzantine empire to distinguish this long period from Roman classical antiquity. The name Byzantine is, of course, derived from the old Greek name for the capital city which Constantine had refounded as Constantinople; and the name is well chosen inasmuch as it reflects the essentially Greek character of Byzantine society and culture. It is well to bear in mind that for about 800 years the Byzantine East supported a far more complex and civilized society than was known in the West, and that it was from Byzantium that all of eastern Europe learned the arts of civilization. It is sobering to reflect that the division between East and West, which so plagues our own time, has one of its roots in this ancient bifurcation of the Roman world.

2. POLITICAL SURVIVAL

The eastern provinces of the Roman empire were subjected to a long series of attacks from both the east and north, and Constantinople itself was more than once besieged by Oriental or barbarian enemies. Certainly one of the reasons for the survival of the Byzantine state was the eminently defensible location of the capital, which could only be taken by a combined land and sea attack such as few enemies were capable of organizing. Another factor which promoted Byzantine survival was the existence of a reservoir of military manpower in Asia Minor. But what was perhaps

most decisive of all was the persistence of a money economy, which made it possible for the government to gather taxes in coin and so pay soldiers and officials in money rather than in kind or by giving them grants of land. This made it possible for the eastern emperors to keep at least a core of loyal and obedient soldiers directly under their command; whereas in the West no such force could be successfully maintained.

The political history of the Byzantine empire is one of many vicissitudes, and time and again it seemed that foreign attack would overthrow the state. But each time the empire rallied its forces, elevated a capable general to the imperial throne, and beat off the enemy. Several times Byzantine rulers were able to extend their control outward from the enduring base of Byzantine power in the eastern Balkan peninsula and western Asia Minor. In the fifth century A.D. a combination of ruse, subsidy, and force diverted the major German attack to the western provinces. In the sixth century, under the emperor Justinian (A.D. 527–65), the Byzantine government succeeded in reconquering Italy, parts of North Africa, and southeastern Spain. But this expansion westward was not permanent. Even during Justinian's reign new and formidable enemies appeared to the north, where the Avars, a Turkish-speaking nomadic people, invaded the Hungarian plain and repeatedly raided the Balkan peninsula. It was as subjects and slaves of the Avar khans that Slavic peasants began to filter into the Balkan peninsula, and settled in what is now Yugoslavia and Bulgaria. Long after the Avar power had disappeared, Slavic peoples continued to live in the northern Balkan peninsula, sometimes independently, sometimes as subjects of the Byzantine or of some other alien government. But from the sixth century onward Slavic-speaking peoples predominated in the northern Balkan peninsula, and the Latin culture and language which had impressed itself on the Danubian districts under the Roman empire went into retreat.

In A.D. 634 a new danger to Byzantine power emerged: the Arabs, stimulated by the teachings of Mohammed, began large-scale raids from their homeland in Arabia, and in the course of the following ten years were able to seize Syria, Palestine, Egypt, and part of Asia Minor from Byzantine control. Thereafter the Byzantine Empire was restricted to western Asia Minor and the Balkan peninsula.

During the centuries that followed, new attacks were launched by the Bulgars and Hungarians (or Magyars), Asiatic nomad peoples from Central Asia; and by the Rus, who set up a capital at Kiev in the late ninth century. The Rus were Scandinavian freebooters who penetrated the Russian river system, imposed their political control on the Slavic populations, and thus founded the first Russian state. In the eleventh century, still another people from Central Asia, the Seljuk Turks, attacked the Byzantine frontier in Asia Minor and succeeded in winning control of nearly all that peninsula. After this time, the Byzantine state was left standing on one leg, so to speak, having lost one-half of its base area. Crusaders from the West came to the assistance of the Byzantines against the Turks, and succeeded for a while in freeing Palestine and part of Syria from Moslem control; but the westerners were dangerous allies and in the long run contributed to the overthrow of the Byzantine state.

3. SOCIAL AND ECONOMIC

Byzantine society was in many respects a continuation of the elaborately organized semicaste society of the late Roman empire. To be sure, some of the regulations which fixed men to their occupations and place of birth were removed in the early sixth century; and the continued existence of city life, with an essentially mobile population, mitigated these regulations from the beginning. Indeed the most significant fact about Byzantine society was the survival of cities, with their industrial and mercantile populations. It was from these classes that the government was able to draw money taxes, with the far-reaching consequences already mentioned; and it was in large part through trading connections that Byzantine culture, ideas, and attitudes penetrated into south-central and eastern Europe.

Serf cultivation of great estates was the predominant form of agriculture; and something rather like the feudal system of western Europe grew up, for the great landlords were expected to come with armed retainers to fight in the imperial armies when summoned to do so. But the feudal army was always supplemented by a standing mercenary force directly under the emperor's control, and his power consequently remained independent of the feudality. The absolutism of late Roman government remained unchallenged in theory, powerfully supported as it was by the Orthodox Church, which became subservient to the state in most matters.

Economic life of the Byzantine empire has not been carefully studied by modern scholars. Nevertheless, it is clear that trade and industry on a substantial scale continued to flourish. Two notable technological improvements deserve mention: silk worms were smuggled from China in the time of Justinian, and a famous silk manufacture and export trade grew up in succeeding centuries; also, a chemical preparation known as Greek fire was discovered which was used with great effect as an incendiary agent in warfare to burn enemy ships and terrify hostile armies.

4. CULTURAL

No great cultural innovations were made by the Byzantines. Classic Greek remained a literary language, supplemented by a somewhat different language, ecclesiastical Greek. The common tongue of the streets was different from either of these literary vehicles, so that education consisted in no small part in acquiring the languages of learning, which, when they had been acquired, were used mainly for writing commentaries on ancient texts.

In theology, the Greek penchant for abstract argument continued to produce bitter controversies, and a series of new heresies arose—Nestorian, monophysite, iconoclastic, and others. Opposition to the government often tended to take religious form, so that theological and political issues were inextricably tangled. Feeling ran high over abstruse points of theology and led to many riots, persecutions, and rebellions.

The Byzantines evolved a distinctive style of art. Justinian's great church, Hagia Sophia, in Constantinople, established the style which most Orthodox Church buildings afterward imitated. The central feature was a great dome supported by pendentives and heavily buttressed walls. The exterior was not particularly impressive, since the buttresses broke the surfaces into an apparently disorganized mass; but the interior, with the great central dome and walls richly decorated with mosaics, was and remains a triumph of ecclesiastical architecture. Schools of painting, which confined their efforts almost entire to holy subjects (iconography), developed; but sculpture fell under religious ban as being perilously close to idolatry, and so disappeared.

Justinian ordered the codification of the Roman law, and from his time to the present Roman law has meant the code which was then drawn up, titled *Corpus Iuris Civilis*. The *Corpus* had four parts; the principles of law which had gradually evolved over the long history of the Roman state were reduced to a convenient *Digest*, supplemented by the *Institutes*, a text book in which legal classifications and first principles of jurisprudence were set down. In addition, the decrees of the emperors were compiled into the *Codex*, and subsequent decrees were added as the *Novellae*. These four books, of which the first two were the more general in application and thus the more important, have played a powerful part in subsequent history. The Canon law of the medieval Church was modeled in great measure on the Roman law as preserved in Justinian's code; and in early modern times the study of the Roman law resulted in a wholesale remodeling of the legal structure of most European states. Only in England did an independent legal system hold its own against the Roman law.

5. INFLUENCE OF BYZANTINE CIVILIZATION

Byzantine cultural influence on western Europe was constant, but the most significant borrowings came only after about A.D. 1200 when the West's own development made westerners more receptive to the classical heritage which had been preserved by Byzantine scholars. Byzantine models played a part in stimulating Italian Renaissance painting; and the rediscovery of the Greek classics, through Byzantine and Arab intermediaries between the thirteenth and fifteenth centuries, played an important part in stimulating both the high medieval and the Renaissance cultural development of the West. Similarly, the Italian cities which provided the social milieu for the Italian Renaissance owed much of their industrial and commercial techniques to Byzantine and Arab forerunners.

Equally important for subsequent history was the extension of Byzantine influence northward into Russia and eastern Europe. Trade with these regions was followed by missionary enterprise. Most of the Slavic peoples of the Balkan peninsula were converted to Greek Orthodox Christianity in the course of the ninth century. Two brothers, Cyril and Methodius, extended missionary enterprise into Moravia, and initiated the literary culture of the Slavic peoples by translating liturgical and other works from Greek into what is called "Old Slavonic." A modification of the Greek alphabet, known as Cyrillic, was devised to fit the Slavic tongues. It remains in use to the present day, with some modifications, in Russia, Bulgaria, and parts of Yugoslavia.

In central Europe, Byzantine Christianity and political influence came into conflict with Latin Christianity and the political power of the German kingdoms; but farther east, in Russia, Byzantine influence was almost unchallenged. In the tenth century the Russian princes were converted to Christianity; in succeeding generations Byzantine political ideas and artistic traditions followed in the wake of religion, and made early Russian culture a barbarian adaptation of Byzantine civilization.

6. DECAY AND OVERTHROW

In A.D. 1204 Crusaders from the West attacked Constantinople. After complicated diplomatic negotiations, they besieged and captured the city. Several Latin states were thereupon erected on Byzantine soil; but they did not last for long, and by A.D. 1261 a Greek emperor once more ruled in Constantinople. Nonetheless, the Byzantine empire never recovered from this blow. Only part of its former territory was reconquered; and, what was equally important, the commercial activity of the empire fell more and more into the hands of Italian cities, chiefly Venice and Genoa. Their fleets came to dominate the seas, and the Byzantine empire dragged out a precarious existence as a pawn of the commercial imperialism of the Italian cities.

In the fourteenth century a new people, the Ottoman Turks, began to extend their power, starting from a small principality in northwestern Asia Minor. They subdued most of the Balkan peninsula before besieging Constantinople itself. After stout resistance, the city was captured in A.D. 1453. With its capture, the Byzantine state came to an end.

Suggestions for Further Reading for Part II, E

The Cambridge Medieval History. Vol. 4. The Byzantine Empire. New York: 1966.
Barker, John W. *Justinian and the Later Roman Empire*. Madison, Wis.: 1966.
Baynes, N. H. *The Byzantine Empire*. London: 1926.

Baynes N. H. and Moss, M. St. L. B. eds. *Byzantium, An Introduction to East Roman Civilization.* Oxford: 1948.

Bury, J. B. *History of the Later Roman Empire.* 2 vols. London: 1923.

Diehl, C. *Byzantium.* New Brunswick, N.J.: 1957.

Holmes, W. G. *The Age of Justinian and Theodora.* 2 vols. London: 1905–7.

Hussey, J. M. *The Byzantine World.* New York: 1957.

Jackson, T. G. *Byzantine and Romanesque Architecture.* Chicago: 1913.

Jenkins, Romilly. *Byzantium: The Imperial Centuries A.D. 610–1071.* New York: 1966.

Ostrogorsky, G. *History of the Byzantine State.* Oxford: 1956.

Runciman, S. *Byzantine Civilization.* Meridian Books.

Vasiliev, A. A. *History of the Byzantine Empire, 324–1453.* Oxford: 1953.

Vryonis, Speros. *Byzantium.* London: 1968.

Novels

Duggan, Alfred. *The Lady for Ransom.* New York: 1953.

Kingsley, Charles. *Hypatia.* New York: 1853.

Lamb, Harold. *Theodora and the Emperor: The Drama of Justinian.* New York: 1952.

Masefield, John. *Basilisea.* New York. 1940.

Masefield, John. *Conquer.* New York: 1941.

Phillpotts, Eden. *Eudocia.* New York. 1921.

Chronological Table for Part II, E: The Byzantine Empire

A.D.	
330	Constantinople refounded on ancient site of Byzantium as capital of Eastern Roman Empire.
395	Division of Roman empire between eastern and western emperors; unity of central control never effectively reestablished.
527–565	Justinian, east Roman emperor; reconquest of Italy, Africa, and part of Spain from barbarians; codification of Roman law.
634–711	Arab attack on eastern provinces; loss of Palestine, Syria, Egypt, Africa and Spain.
1054	Final schism between Roman Catholic and Greek Orthodox churches.
1071	Battle of Manzikert; loss of most of Asia Minor to Seljuk Turks.

*1204	Fourth Crusade; westerners captured Constantinople, established Latin states in the Levant.
1261	Greek emperor restored to Byzantine throne.
*1453	Capture of Constantinople by Ottoman Turks; final destruction of Byzantine empire.

F. Successor Kingdoms in the West

1. INTRODUCTION

In the five centuries which followed Alaric's sack of Rome in A.D. 410 a series of Hunnic, German, Arab, Hungarian, and Viking raiders, conquerors, and settlers overran the area which had once been Roman in Western Europe. Movement of peoples and mixture of variant stocks took place on a considerable scale; kingdoms rose and fell with confusing rapidity; Roman civilization flickered and came close to extinction in what is traditionally called the Dark Ages. One can think of the confused particular movements as constituting three great waves of invasion: (1) the German invasion of the Roman provinces in the fifth and sixth centuries A.D.; (2) the Arab and Austrasian invasions of the more Romanized German kingdoms in the eighth century A.D.; (3) the Hungarian and Viking invasions of the Carolingian empire in the ninth and tenth centuries A.D.

With each wave of assault, the economic prosperity and cultural level of the peoples of the western provinces sank further toward local self-sufficiency and barbarism; but after each invasion there was a rally of sorts as the conquering tribes or groups set up relatively strong governments and assimilated or added to the culture of the conquered population. The rally which followed the Arab conquest of Spain brought that country within the pale of Arab civilization for a period of several centuries; the rally which followed the Hungarian and Viking invasions in northwestern Europe proved to be the genesis of a new and extremely successful style of European or Western civilization which has endured to the present.

Thus the period from the fifth to the tenth centuries A.D. was a time of death and rebirth. Where one draws the line between Classical and European or Western civilization must depend on personal choice. The year A.D. 900 has been chosen here largely because it approximately marks the low point in political orderliness and economic interdependence which immediately preceded the rally which gave birth to European civilization. From other points of view, different dates would be more appropriate, ranging from A.D. 313 when Constantine initiated alliance between state and Church, to the date chosen here.

2. THE FIRST WAVE OF INVASION (A.D. 410–687)

---

a. New peoples and States
b. The Church
  1) Ecclesiastical organization: the Rise of the
       Papacy
  2) Monasticism
  3) Irish Christianity
  4) Barbarization of the Church

c. Government, Society and Economy
d. Culture

---

a. New peoples and States

During the fifth century A.D. a number of other German peoples followed the examples of the Visigoths by invading the western provinces of the Roman empire. Booty and better land attracted invaders who came from across the Rhine; others who came from the Danubian area of central Europe were also impelled by fear of the Huns.

During the early part of the fifth century A.D., the Huns established an extensive empire, centering in the grasslands of the Hungarian plain.[1] About the middle of the century marauding bands of Huns, led by their khan, Attila, ravaged central Gaul and northern Italy. But after Attila's death in A.D. 453 the Hunnic power disintegrated rapidly. German and Slavic tribes which had been subjugated by the Huns revolted and drove their former masters eastward to the Volga.

The disappearance of the Huns from central Europe removed one of the main impulses to the migration of peoples which had assumed a massive scale during the late fourth and early fifth centuries A.D.; and by degrees a more stable political pattern emerged as new Germanic kingdoms took root in what had been the western provinces of the Roman Empire.

Spain and southern France fell to the Visigoths. After their famous sack of Rome in A.D. 410 Visigothic chieftains once again came to terms with

---

[2]This plain on the middle Danube was the westernmost extension of the steppe zone of Asia; and both before and after the time of the Huns, steppe peoples invading Europe on horseback penetrated to that plain, and there stopped. Forest and mountain blocked further passage westward; for in such regions they could not easily find year round forage for their horses. This geographical limit to the encroachment of horse-nomads from Central Asia played an important part in determining the course of European history; for while wave after wave of Asiatic invaders appeared in Hungary and raided further west, they never tried to settle permanently in the forested country of Western Europe, despite the military superiority which they frequently enjoyed.

Roman authorities, and accepted a commission from the Roman Government of the West to drive the Vandals and other Germanic marauders from Spain. They were successful in this enterprise, and set up their own kingdom which maintained an official though merely nominal subordination to the Roman Government until the time of Justinian. The Visigothic kingdom was finally overthrown by Arab and Moorish invaders between A.D. 711 and 718.

The Vandals, however, had not been destroyed by the Visigoths. Driven from Spain, they crossed to North Africa, and set themselves up in the old Roman province of Africa. They also built a piratical fleet with which they ravaged the shores of the Western Mediterranean and acquired the reputation still preserved in the English word "vandalism." Justinian destroyed the Vandal kingdom in 533-34. Thereafter, Byzantine rule lasted in Africa until the Arab assault at the end of the seventh century A.D.

In Italy a series of Germanic adventurers manipulated successive emperors as their puppets until A.D. 476. In that year the farce was brought to an end by Odoacer, who set out to rule Italy in his own name as "patricius" of the Emperor of the East. He was in turn overthrown in A.D. 493 by Theodoric, King of the Ostrogoths, who had been commissioned by the eastern emperor to destroy Odoacer. Theodoric (A.D. 493-526) proceeded to set up one of the strongest and best governed of the barbarian kingdoms. But the Ostrogothic kingdom did not long outlast its founder, for Justinian reconquered most of Italy in a series of long drawn-out campaigns between A.D. 535 and 554. These wars were very destructive and did more to break up Roman civilization in Italy than any earlier disorders. The woes of Italy were deepened by the appearance of another Germanic people, the Lombards, who invaded from the Danubian area in A.D. 568. Thereafter a long series of wars between the Lombards and Byzantines led to the division of Italy into a number of rival provinces, some Byzantine, some Lombard.

In Britain, Roman government came to an end about A.D. 420, when the last Roman armies withdrew and left the Britons to defend themselves as best they might against the raids of barbarous neighbors. It is in this period that the stories of King Arthur and his knights originated, stories which were to have a distinguished literary career in medieval times. The Britons were not long able to defend their land, however; and after about the middle of the fifth century, Jutes and Anglo-Saxons, sailing across the North Sea from what is now Holland, northwestern Germany and the Danish coast, began to settle in growing numbers. The invaders did not come at one time, nor in large groups. They set up several independent kingdoms, gradually driving the Britons westward into Cornwall and Wales.

The largest and richest area of the western empire was Gaul, reaching from the Pyrenees and the Mediterranean northward to the Rhine. Until

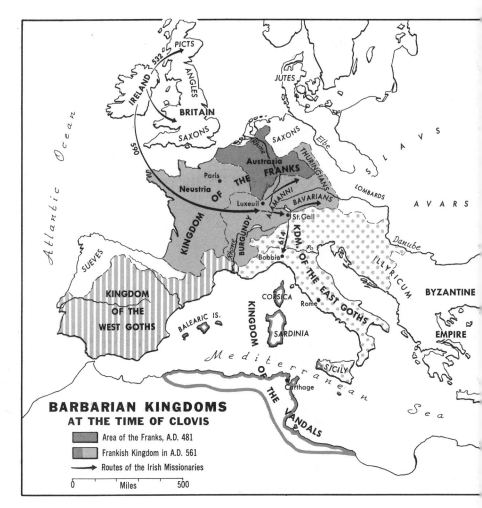

BARBARIAN KINGDOMS
AT THE TIME OF CLOVIS

- Area of the Franks, A.D. 481
- Frankish Kingdom in A.D. 561
- → Routes of the Irish Missionaries

0 ———— Miles ———— 500

the fifth century was well advanced the central part of Gaul remained under a Roman ruler; but in A.D. 486 Clovis, King of the Salian Franks, defeated the surviving Roman forces and proceeded to incorporate what is now northern France into his kingdom. The Franks were a numerous but comparatively backward people until the time of Clovis. They had remained pagan while the other Germanic tribes which had invaded the Roman empire (except for the Anglo-Saxons) were already converts to Christianity. Furthermore, the Franks had not succeeded in organizing a unified state, but remained separated into a number of relatively small tribes, loosely associated into two great groups, the Salians (along the sea coast in modern Belgium and southern Holland) and the Ripuarians (along the middle Rhine). Clovis, by dint of personal ruthlessness and military successes, united the Frankish tribes into a single kingdom. During his reign and that of his sons (A.D. 481–561), Frankish power was extended over nearly all of Gaul and far into Germany as well. Lesser Germanic kingdoms which had been set up on Roman soil by the Burgundians and Alemanni were incorporated into the Frankish state, while wars and astute diplomacy drove the Visigoths out of southern Gaul. In Germany, Frankish power extended far beyond the old Roman boundaries. To the east, the Thuringians and Bavarians were reduced to semi-dependent status. Only the Saxon tribes, to the northeast, remained wholly independent.

Thus by the middle of the sixth century the Frankish kingdom had become by far the strongest and most extensive of the Germanic successor states. It was also the only one which long survived, for from it are descended the modern states of both Germany and France.

An important factor in the Frankish success was the conversion of Clovis and his people to Catholic Christianity (A.D. 496). Other German peoples on Roman soil were mostly Arians (except the pagan Anglo-Saxons) owing to the fact that the German tribes of the Danube area had been converted to Christianity by Arian missionaries in the fourth century A.D. As a result, in the eyes of the Roman population of the western empire, their Germanic rulers were foul heretics; and many of them welcomed the Catholic Franks as deliverers from an heretical yoke. The Frankish state was thus able to muster support from both Germans and Romans; and its power was never based wholly on a small conquering group, as was true of the other Germanic kingdoms of the West.

Frankish custom and law did not distinguish between private and public inheritance. Clovis and his successors therefore divided and redivided the kingdom among their male heirs. As a result, the unity of the Frankish state was very loosely maintained, and wars between rival brothers and cousins broke out frequently. After the last of Clovis' sons had died, in A.D. 561, the kingdom fell into two fairly distinct parts: Neustria (the "new land," roughly corresponding to northern France) and Austrasia (the "eastland," situated along the banks of the Rhine). Austrasia remained almost wholly Germanic in population and more backward in culture than Neustria, where Roman population and customs survived and where Latin retained a predominant position as the everyday speech of the population.

b. The Church (A.D. 410–687)

1) Ecclesiastical organization: the Rise of the papacy. The breakup of bureaucratic administration in the western provinces allowed the Church to take over many of the functions of government. As leaders of the

Roman population, bishops became important political figures. More-over, the barbarian kings often depended on members of the clergy for the performance of tasks which required a knowledge of reading and writing, without which even barbarian government was difficult to carry on.

The organization of the Church itself was gradually adjusted to the changed conditions of social life. The original Christian communities had been concentrated in towns; but as town life decayed and the rural population was converted to Christianity, country parishes were organized under the authority of bishops who remained, generally, in towns, or where towns once had been. Moreover the practice of electing bishops by acclamation of the people fell into decay. Choice was legally entrusted to the clergy of the diocese (as the bishop's area of jurisdiction came to be called). In fact, however, local magnates or barbarian kings were frequently able to control episcopal elections.

The fact that the later Roman emperors seldom visited Rome and never resided there for any length of time gave wide scope to the bishops of that city. Rome's enormous prestige as the ancient center of the Empire was reinforced by the fact that, according to an early tradition, the Roman Church had been established by Peter, Prince of the Apostles.

By the fourth century, if not earlier, the theory of "Petrine supremacy" had been promulgated by the bishops of Rome, or, as they are more usually called, by the popes. This theory asserts that the Pope, as the direct successor of St. Peter, is the rightful head of the Christian Church in all its branches and parts. The claim is based on a passage in the Gospel according to St. Matthew in which Christ says: "Thou art Peter and on this rock I will build my church; and the gates of hell shall not prevail against it. And I will give unto thee the keys of the Kingdom of Heaven; and whatsoever thou shalt bind on earth shall be bound in heaven; and whatsoever thou shalt loose on earth shall be loosed in heaven." (Matthew 16:18–19).

On the basis of their interpretation of this passage the popes of the fourth and fifth centuries repeatedly intervened in ecclesiastical disputes and questions which arose in other dioceses. The primacy of Rome was generally admitted among bishops of the West, though the extent of papal power was not defined. In the East, on the other hand, papal claims were never widely accepted. Disputes over the power of the pope became one of the issues which divided the Greek Orthodox from the Roman Catholic Church.

Two great popes deserve mention for the part they played in organizing the papal monarchy and shaping the tradition of Roman Catholicism. Leo the Great (A.D. 440–61) strenuously asserted the sovereignty of the pope in questions of dogma, and succeeded in getting a council of the Church (Chalcedon, A.D. 451) to accept his formulation of doctrine as to the divine and human natures of Christ. This was a great moral victory for the papacy. Leo's prestige was enhanced when he headed a deputation which dissuaded Attila from attacking Rome in A.D. 452. But Leo's formulation of Christological doctrine did not satisfy the Greeks; and a generation later, when the Emperor of Byzantium tried to alter Leo's definition, the first open schism between eastern and western Churches took place.

The schism was not permanent; but from the fifth century onward the two Churches developed independently. Papal power was restricted to Latin Christendom; in the East the Byzantine emperor effectively controlled the Church organization, and the Greek Orthodox Church became, on most questions, a passive tool of state policy. After the time of Justinian, when the Byzantine emperors had regained control of the city of Rome and its immediate environs, the emperors tried to reduce the papacy to a similarly dependent status, but many popes resisted the attempt. The popes, as a result of these quarrels, became champions of the claims of the Church to independence from all secular control.

The work of Gregory the Great, pope from A.D. 590 to 604, confirmed the independence of the papacy. During his lifetime Italy was torn between Lombard and Byzantine armies. Gregory steered a discreet course between the two secular powers, playing one off against the other. He became *de facto* the ruler of the city of Rome, organizing its defense against all comers despite a nominal subordination to Byzantium. His activity thus marks a stage in the development of the Papal States which later came into existence in central Italy.

Gregory was able to exercise effective headship over the western bishops, and he initiated a missionary enterprise among the Anglo-Saxons of England, as a result of which England was brought within the pale of Latin Christendom during the seventh century.

2) Monasticism. From early Christian times individuals who sought an especially holy life were accustomed to retire to the Palestinian, Syrian, or Egyptian deserts, where they lived as solitary ascetics or hermits. It became customary in the fourth century for colonies of Egyptian hermits to hold common worship services and to follow a fixed routine of Scriptural reading and other devotional exercises. From Egypt the practice spread first to other eastern lands, then to the West. In the harsher climate of Europe the extreme ascetic practices of Egyptian monks were impossible. Instead of living in caves or isolated cells, it became usual for such groups to live together in specially constructed buildings known as monasteries.

Until the sixth century monastic practices varied widely in the West; but about A.D. 529 St. Benedict of Nursia devised a rule for a group of monks who had gathered around him at Monte Cassino in Italy. The Benedictine rule was gradually adopted by other monasteries. Gregory the Great was especially prominent in spreading Benedictine monasticism, and used the prestige of the papacy to secure its adoption through most of the West. Because monks lived according to a rule (Latin: *regula*), they were known as regular clergy in contrast to the secular clergy—bishops, priests, deacons, etc.

The central aim of the monastic life was to assure the salvation of the monks' own souls. To this end, the Benedictine Rule prescribed in detail the daily life, dress, and behavior of the monks, and the organization of the monastery. The monks' principal activity was prayer and worship, but time was also set aside for manual work and for study. Monasteries came to be looked upon as peculiarly holy, and monastic lands and buildings were comparatively immune from the constant warfare and petty violence which characterized the normal life of the age. As a result, monasteries became havens in a barbaric world, and we owe the survival of many books of Christian and pagan authorship to the preservation of manuscripts in monastic libraries. Learning as such was not encouraged among the monks, since erudition smacked too much of pride; yet what learning there was during the Dark Ages usually centered in monastic schools. The government of each monastery rested in the hands of an abbot who was supposed to be chosen by the monks themselves. In practice, however, abbots were often chosen by secular magnates and rulers, just as were bishops.

3) Irish Christianity. In A.D. 432 St. Patrick, a native of Britain, began the conversion of Ireland. Within a few years Ireland became Christian, but the Irish Church which Patrick established had many peculiarities not matched elsewhere in Christendom. Monasteries of the Egyptian rather than the Benedictine type were the principal religious institutions; and nothing which quite corresponded to the hierarchy of the secular clergy of the Roman Catholic Church existed.

The Irish monks were remarkable for two things: their devotion to learning and their missionary enthusiasm. Strangely enough, Irish monks knew Greek at a time when knowledge of that language had disappeared from the rest of Western Europe, and their Latin learning far exceeded that of the mainland. Irish missionaries traveled forth first to Scotland and Wales, then to England and the continent. St. Columban (d. A.D. 615) founded no less than three famous monasteries on the continent of Europe: Luxeuil in France, St. Gall in Switzerland, and Bobbio in Italy. These monasteries and their numerous daughter institutions played an important role in raising the intellectual level of the western Church in Carolingian times.

The Irish Church made another significant contribution to Roman Catholicism, for the sacrament of private penance was first developed by Irish monks. Its adoption completed the sacramental system as established in the medieval Church. The seven sacraments—baptism, confirmation, marriage, extreme unction, mass, penance, and ordination (the last for clergy alone)— were "outward signs of inward grace." The administration of the sacraments by duly ordained members of the clergy opened the path of salvation to individual Christians; and the Church itself was conceived as the channel through which God's redeeming grace was transmitted to sinful men. The growth of the sacramental system has been a subject of much debate between Protestant and Roman Catholic scholars. Some of its elements were present in very early Christianity—e.g., baptism; but authoritative definition of the complete system was not achieved until the thirteenth century A.D.

4) Barbarization of the Church. Despite the efforts of individual popes, of monks and of Irish missionaries, the Church of Western Europe underwent a profound intellectual and moral decay during the sixth and seventh centuries. Among the Franks and other German peoples many pagan ideas and practices survived; and the educated Roman population almost wholly disappeared. Under such circumstances many superstitious practices penetrated Christian rituals, and pagan deities not infrequently reappeared as Christian saints.

An important factor in promoting the decay of the Church was its acquisition of extensive lands and other wealth, largely through bequest. As the wealth of the Church increased, high ecclesiastical positions became attractive to the turbulent nobility, and it became common for younger sons of noble families to take Holy Orders in order to enjoy the perquisites of some bishopric or abbacy. Many such prelates continued to live lives of violence and debauchery, and their conduct was often indistinguishable from that of the lay nobility. Piety and missionary enterprise inevitably suffered when the Church was headed by such men.

Indeed, the papacy itself became an object of feud and faction among local Roman nobles, and many popes were little if at all superior to other bishops in their moral or intellectual stature. Men like Leo and Gregory stood out the more brilliantly by contrast.

c. Government, Society, and Economy

The Germanic peoples who invaded the Roman empire had a variety of institutions, and they had reached different levels of culture prior to their appearance on Roman soil. In general, the peoples who came from the Danube region were more deeply tinctured by civilization than those who crossed the Rhine. Thus Gothic society was more differentiated within itself and the Goths had a more definite system of government than had the Franks at the time they first settled on Roman lands.

Primitive German institutions were not unlike those of other Indo-European peoples. The basic elements of patriarchal family, tribal organization, chieftainship in war (more or less elective), council of notables, and assembly of free warriors probably existed among all Germanic peoples. These basic elements underwent various changes as the Germans came into intimate contact with Roman society. Usually, the assembly weakened or disappeared entirely, and the power of the chieftain increased and became royal—valid in peace as well as in war, and hereditary. Thus Clovis and his successors in Gaul claimed and were able to exercise irresponsible power, checked only by the unruliness of their followers.

The government of the Frankish kingdom was constantly beset with internal disorders. Private feuds were regularly settled by resort to violence; and the bands of armed men who marched to and fro through the countryside, ravaging and looting as they passed, made small distinction between friend and foe. The Ostrogothic kingdom in Italy was comparatively well governed and the central power was more effective in keeping peace in the countryside; but Justinian's conquest, and the long wars which accompanied and followed it, brought Italy to the level of Gaul as far as public order was concerned.

A number of law codes, written down by order of the German kings, have been preserved. They deal mainly with criminal matters, prescribing the sum of money (wergild) to be paid by men found quilty of various crimes against their fellows. From variations in the wergilds it is possible to discern the existence of social classes among the Germans, but the meaning of terms is seldom clear and disputes over their interpretation have been endless. It seems certain that not all Germans were free; and it is probable that the essential qualification for full participation in the tribal group was the possession of arms. In addition there were chiefs or "nobles" who specialized in warfare. They lived on booty, on income from land tilled by dependents, and on gifts given by humbler tribesmen in return for protection which the nobles afforded them. Such nobles regarded the king as first among equals rather than as a sovereign of the Roman or Oriental sort; and from their number were drawn the council or court which advised the king.

When the German tribesmen took up residence in the Roman provinces, they did not abandon their ancestral customs. Neither did they take the Romans into their tribal organization. Rather the kings led their German followers as before, and ruled over the Roman population in accordance with Roman law and precedent. The Germans simply appropriated for themselves a part of the land. Their chiefs set themselves up as landlords in place of dispossessed Romans, and supported a group of retainers on income from the land so acquired. In effect, two systems of law and two societies existed side by side with the king as the only legal connecting link between them. In practice, of course, the Germans were an armed and dominant minority—and a turbulent and lawless one at that, among whom private feuds frequently led to bloodshed and excused attacks upon the more or less helpless Roman population.

Separation between Roman and German populations was less marked in the Frankish state than in other barbarian kingdoms, partly because the barrier of religious difference was absent. Romans as well as Franks were appointed to official positions and intermarriage must frequently have occurred. The government tried to continue Roman forms of administration as applied to the Roman population. But the taxation system quickly broke down, and, by the end of the period, the kings came to depend mainly on income from the royal domain, i.e., on rents paid by cultivators of estates owned personally by the king.

Officials known as counts supervised the administration of justice within a given area (county), and were supposed to give to the king a part of the fines which were assessed by their courts. But this system, too, tended to break down through the sale of immunities to various local landholders, who were thereby exempted from all royal jurisdiction. Bishops, especially, bought or were granted such immunity. Local courts, presided over by bishops or other local magnates, thus tended to acquire full sovereign jurisdiction. Under these conditions, public functions and rights were steadily confused with private property rights. In other words, private estates tended to become political units also, ruled over by the "lord." Law remained personal; that is, a Frank was tried by Frankish law, a Roman by Roman law, a Burgundian by Burgundian law, etc. At the same time, local customs, varying from estate to estate, gradually came to have the force of law, so that uniformity of legal institutions and procedure vanished.

In the purely Germanic parts of the Frankish kingdom, and in England, the fifth, sixth and seventh centuries apparently saw a steady differentiation of social classes and the gradual development of a landed aristocracy. But armed free men, who tilled their own soil and took arms when summoned by the king to repel invaders or go on raiding expeditions, remained numerous and influential in Austrasia and in England long after they had disappeared in the more Romanized German kingdoms to the south.

In late Roman times great estates cultivated by serfs had become the usual form of agrarian organization. The German invasions made no change in this system. Some villas which had previously been owned by Romans were taken over intact by German warrior-nobles and run much as before. Others were left in the undisturbed possession of their Roman owners. Similar estates began to grow up in the purely German areas, though the process by which they were formed cannot be discerned from surviving records and causes of the development can only be surmised.

Wars, famine, and disease continued to depopulate former Roman areas. Great stretches of land, which had once been cultivated, returned to forest. In the purely German districts, however, population probably continued to grow, fresh fields were brought under tillage, and agricultural skill improved, especially after the adoption of the mouldboard plow. On the other hand, the level of agricultural skill declined in Roman districts: only on lands owned by the Church, particularly monastic lands, did some of the old Roman agricultural methods survive. In Gaul, for example, the cultivation of vines became mainly a speciality of monastic properties; and some monasteries exported their wine as far afield as Britain and even Byzantium.

But such trade was unusual and its volume small. The constant disorders within the barbarian kingdoms and the autarkic organization of each estate discouraged trade and urban industry. The few towns which had survived late Roman times continued to decay; and such long distance trade as persisted fell largely into the hands of peddlers, many of whom were Syrians or Jews.

Society thus tended to divide into three major groups: at the bottom a large mass of peasant serfs who tilled the soil; and over them two sorts of lords, Church prelates and warriors.

d. Culture

Despite the chaotic conditions of life which prevailed in the barbarian kingdoms, the cultivation of learning and letters did not entirely disappear. A series of textbook writers collected fragments of pagan learning into primers, which were used through succeeding centuries in the monastic and episcopal schools. Secular learning was classified into the seven liberal arts: grammar, rhetoric, logic, arithmetic, geometry, astronomy, and music; but only scraps and pieces of the learning of the pagan world survived under these rubrics.

Education in practice usually amounted to acquiring an imperfect mastery of Latin, with the addition of the merest smattering of higher learning. The popular speech changed and simplified itself, so that literary Latin became a learned tongue, unintelligible to ordinary men even in the old Roman provinces. From the popular (or vulgar) Latin emerged in time the various romance languages: French, Spanish, Italian and others. Many local variations arose, and the new languages did not achieve literary definition until much later.

Despite the general decline of intellectual and artistic life, a few writers arose who exercised an important influence on later generations. Boethius (d. A.D. 524), a high official at the court of Theodoric the Ostrogoth, translated part of Aristotle's *Organon* into Latin and wrote his *Consolations of Philosophy* while in prison awaiting death. The latter is a remarkable work which seems to breathe much of the spirit of ancient pagan philosophy.

Far more important in subsequent times were the writings of Pope Gregory the Great (*c.* A.D. 540–604). He wrote *Pastoral Care*, describing the duties of a bishop, published a collection of sermons, and one of pious tales, the *Moralia*, cast in the form of a commentary on the Book of Job. These books attained a wide popularity in the Middle Ages. They were particularly influential in fixing the style and supplying much of the matter for preaching in the churches. Gregory's sermons were built around the exposition of Biblical texts and he frequently resorted to anecdotes for illustration. His theology reflected many popular practices and beliefs of his time. Purgatory, a place where souls go immediately after death to suffer for sins committed on earth, appeared in his writings as it had not done in the writings of earlier Church fathers. He likewise taught the efficacy of prayers addressed to saints, and believed in the constant intervention of angels and devils in daily life. His influence was so commanding in later centuries that Gregory has been traditionally associated with Ambrose, Jerome, and Augustine as one of the four Latin Doctors of the Church.

An interesting and vivid portrayal of life in fifth and sixth-century Gaul is preserved in the *History of the Franks*, written by Gregory of Tours (*c.* A.D. 540–594). It is a barbarous, brutal, and superstitious society that emerges from his pages. Gregory himself, although well-educated for his day, could not write correct classical Latin; but his style was perhaps the more vigorous and fresh from the fact that he was at least partially emancipated from the strict grammatical rules of Cicero's language.

Little was produced in the realm of the fine arts. Building in stone almost ceased, save for a few churches erected in Italy by Byzantine workmen in the Byzantine style. Painting, in the form of illumination of manuscripts, was executed with great skill by Irish monks, and was practiced with indifferent success on the continent as well. The use of music in church services was expanded through the practice of chanting passages from Scripture, hymns, and prayers. Definite musical modes were established for such singing, and for reasons unknown, Pope Gregory the Great's name came to be attached to this form of choral music—the Gregorian chant.

3. THE EARLY CAROLINGIAN PERIOD (A.D. 687–814)

---

a. The second wave: Arab and Austrasian
    Invasions
b. The Carolingian Monarchy and Empire
    (A.D. 751–814)
c. Carolingian Government
d. The Church
e. Society and Economy
f. Culture
g. English Development

---

a. The Second Wave: Arab and Austrasian Invasions

In A.D. 711 Arab and Moorish invaders crossed from Africa into Spain, and during the next seven years overthrew the Visigothic kingdom. In A.D. 720 they crossed the Pyrenees and proceeded to occupy part of southern France and to raid far and wide. Thirteen years later, near Tours, the Frankish army under Charles Martel met and defeated an Arab army, and from that time the Arab dominion gradually shrank back southward. Perhaps more important than their victories on land were the Arab successes on the sea, for they won domination of the western Mediterranean and for some three centuries raided the Christian coastal districts at will. Their sea power cut off the Frankish state from easy communication with Byzantium, and the small trickle of long distance trade between the Frankish lands and the eastern Mediterranean, which had persisted through the preceding centuries, came almost to an end.

Almost simultaneously with the Arab invasion of Europe, the Romanized provinces of the Frankish state were subjected to another invasion from the Germanic lands of the east. Clovis' grandsons and their successors did not retain the vigor or brutality of the founder of the Frankish kingdom. Instead, they became mere puppets and figureheads, while real power came into the hands of officials known as Mayors of the Palace. In A.D. 687 Pepin, the Austrasian Mayor of the Palace, defeated his Neustrian rival in battle, and added Neustria to his dominions. Kings of Clovis' house (called Merovingians) remained as figureheads, but from this time properly dates the Carolingian period. (Pepin's family is called Carolingian from the name of its most famous member, Charles the Great or Charlemagne.) Pepin was succeeded by his son, Charles Martel (i.e., the Hammer), under whose rule (A.D. 714–41) a second German invasion of Neustria took place. Charles set out to restore the Frankish state which had broken into a number of practically independent parts since the time of Clovis. To secure himself an army and loyal followers, he expropriated large tracts of land in Neustria and granted them to Austrasian warriors in exchange for their promise of military service. Much property was taken from the Church, although not by outright confiscation; it was accomplished rather through the legal device known as *beneficium*, or benefice, whereby the owner (in this case a church or monastery) granted land to a tenant in return for services (in this case protection). Such benefices were only a thinly disguised form of confiscation, for Charles expected and secured the regular service of benefice-holders in his army.

An important change in military tactics is associated with the activity of Charles Martel. Before his time the Austrasian army was mainly composed of freemen, who fought on foot with sword and shield. Charles demanded that the men whom he had enriched by the gift of estates or benefices should provide themselves with horses and serve in the army as heavy armed cavalry. It was with such a force that he defeated the Arabs near Tours in A.D. 733; and with its help he proceeded to reassert authority over the Bavarians and Alemanni who had broken loose from the Frankish state. He was thus able to reunite the entire Frankish kingdom under a far more powerful government than it had known since the time of Clovis. The decentralization of power, which had become so pronounced in late Merovingian times, was checked for a while by the political and military changes made by Charles Martel, and the Frankish kingdom entered upon a second period of rapid expansion and military success.

b. The Carolingian Monarchy and Empire (A.D. 751–814)

Charles's son, Pepin the Short, succeeded to his father's position as Mayor of the Palace and *de facto* ruler of the Frankish kingdom. In A.D. 751 he became, with the approval of the pope and the consecration of the Frankish bishops, King of the Franks in his own right. The last of the Merovingian kings was deposed and sent off to end his days in a monastery.

The fact that Pepin's title to the throne was legally faulty encouraged him to cultivate the good graces of the Pope, for papal sanction could do much to dignify and justify his usurpation. The popes, too, badly needed help from Pepin. The city of Rome and its environs were still nominally a part of the Byzantine Empire, but the popes had quarreled with Byzantine authorities over the question of the proper use of images in church worship, and so could not desire to see effective Byzantine military control of Rome. Yet the Lombards, who were engaged in a strenuous effort to conquer all Italy, seriously threatened the old capital of the Roman Empire.

Under the circumstances, both Pepin and the pope had much to gain from mutual support. Accordingly, in A.D. 754 the pope made a trip to Gaul and there formally consecrated Pepin according to the rites of the ancient Hebrew kingship, and declared him *patricius* of the Romans. In return, Pepin led a Frankish army into Italy, where he defeated the Lombards. Two years later the Franks invaded Italy a second time, and formally transferred a substantial area of central Italy to the secular rule of the pope (A.D. 756). Thereby the Papal States, which endured as one of the principalities of Italy until A.D. 1870, were established.

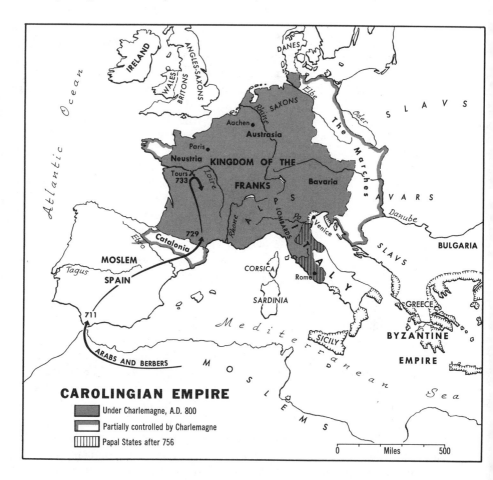

CAROLINGIAN EMPIRE

Under Charlemagne, A.D. 800
Partially controlled by Charlemagne
Papal States after 756

0   Miles   500

Upon Pepin's death (A.D. 768) the kingdom was divided between his two sons, but three years later the younger died, and Charles the Great, or Charlemagne, reunited the whole kingdom under his own rule. Charlemagne continued the policies of his father and grandfather. In a series of campaigns he subdued the Lombards and himself assumed the Iron crown of Lombardy (A.D. 774). Then he turned attention eastward where the Saxons still lived, independent and pagan, in the Weser and Elbe valleys.

Long and bitter fighting reduced the Saxon tribes to obedience and compelled them to accept Christianity. Further wars consolidated Charlemagne's power over the Bavarians, who had previously enjoyed a semiautonomy within the Frankish state. These campaigns united the Romano-German world (except for the Anglo-Saxons of England and the Scandinavians) under one king; and on his eastern border, which ran roughly along the Elbe river, Charlemagne set up a series of marches which extended German power far eastward into Slavic lands. The Avars (who, like the Huns before them, had set up their khanate in the Hungarian plain), were destroyed in A.D. 796; and in the south, Frankish power pushed across the Pyrenees into Catalonia.

Thus by A.D. 800 the kingdom of the Franks was an imposing structure, at least in terms of size. Nearly all the area which was to be the center of Western civilization was united into a single state. In that year Charlemagne visited Rome. On Christmas Day, A.D. 800, he attended mass in St. Peter's church, and as he knelt in worship Pope Leo III crowned him Emperor of the Romans, while the assembled multitude hailed him as the successor to Caesar, Augustus and Constantine. During the rest of his life, Charlemagne addressed himself to the task of securing recognition of his new imperial title from Byzantium. Shortly before his death in A.D. 814 the Byzantine emperor agreed to authenticate the pope's act in return for the cession of some territory along the upper Adriatic.

c. Carolingian Government

The government of Charlemagne's extensive empire was carried on in much the same fashion as before. Counts were entrusted with the exercise of royal functions in local districts (counties), and along the frontiers, special officials (called *margraves*, i.e., mark grafs, or counts of the marchlands in German and *duces*, i.e., dukes in Latin) were appointed with a larger jurisdiction and greater powers to defend the kingdom against invasion. But the power and vigor of the Carolingian rulers was such as to secure much more careful obedience from their counts than later Merovingian rulers had been able to exact. Special traveling envoys of the royal court were appointed to check up on the conduct of the counts, and in cases of malfeasance counts were deprived of their powers. Judicial reforms were made whereby decisions were rendered by panels of local landowners—the germ of the jury system of later times.

The army was drawn from two sources: the levy of free men, and the mounted warriors who had been given special grants of land by the king. The military effectiveness of the mounted cavalry was greatly superior to that of the raw levy of untrained farmers; and, for the distant campaigns which Charlemagne constantly carried on, such professional soldiers became more and more necessary. The development presaged what is called the feudal system; but it was not until after the time of Charlemagne that the mounted warriors usurped royal rights on a widespread scale and established what historians call feudalism.

The king himself depended on income from his estates. Between campaigns, Charlemagne spent his time traveling from one estate to another with his retinue, since no single spot could long support the economic demands of his court. Royal income was supplemented by booty (most notably from the Avars, who had accumulated a great hoard as a result of their many raids) and by a share of the income from judicial fines.

d. The Church

The alliance between the papacy and the Carolingians was accompanied by a notable revival in Church discipline. The principal agents of the revival were missionaries who came from England, where the Irish example had raised the level of learning and piety far above that of the continent. St. Boniface (A.D. 680–753), a native of England, spent his life converting the Bavarians and Thuringians in central Germany, where he set up an ecclesiastical organization, and reformed or founded monasteries which became important centers of piety and learning. Charlemagne continued Christian missionary work by forcibly converting the Saxons.

Throughout his reign he paid careful attention to ecclesiastical matters. He appointed bishops and controlled the elections of abbots; even the pope submissively accepted Charlemagne's dictates on several occasions. His government depended heavily on bishops, who often were drawn into government service as traveling inspectors. Moreover, bishops were granted extensive regalian rights, especially in the newly Christianized areas of Germany. The bishops of Germany thus became minor princes ruling over extensive domains, where they held court and otherwise acted as agents of the central government.

e. Society and Economy

The Carolingian age was not one of economic revival. The Arabs effectively cut off trade with the more civilized East; and town life made no recovery. The economy was thoroughly agrarian. On the large estates, or, as we may now call them, on manors, serfs worked the land, and surrendered to the lord of the manor a portion of the produce of their labor. In addition, serfs were compelled to work on land kept in demesne, i.e., kept directly under the control and management of the lord.

The small freeholders suffered from the constant military demands made upon them by the Carolingian government. Some of them rose to the level of professional fighters, and became lords themselves; others sank to a status of dependency, owing rents and services to some lord. Thus Germany was progressively assimilated to the society which had grown up in

EARLY CHRISTIAN ART

Christian art undertook the function of teaching religious doctrine to illiterate members of the Christian community. In addition, art bodied forth for the entire church the glory of Christ and the Apostles and the holiness of saints. When rulers became Christian, their power and glory also became an appropriate theme for Christian art.

Christian Apostles, Domitilla Catacomb, Rome
Mid fourth century
(Hirmer Verlag München)

The early Christians expected the Second Coming of Christ at any moment. This fresco depicts the Apostles waiting the return of their master to judge the living and the dead.

Emperor Justinan and Attendants, Mosaic from the Apse of the Church of San Vitale, Ravenna.
Circa **547**
(Hirmer Verlag München)

Two hundred years later, however, the triumphant Christ has not yet returned and through default, Justinian fills the void. Here is man judging man but with eyes firmly fastened upon a supernal goal and transcendant reality. The mosaic technique became characteristic of Byzantine art but never took firm root in the Latin West.

Emperor Charles the Bald Enthroned, Detail from *Codex Aureus* of St. Emmeran of Ratisbon
Finished 870. Staatsbibliothek, Munich
(Hirmer Verlag München)

In this Carolingian manuscript illumination, the hand of God appears over the head of Charles the Bald, seated in imperial state. His two earthly supporters at either side are matched by two angelic protectors, poised above the arch of the sky. The composition thus offers a clear and simple visual statement of medieval political theory and cosmology.

Initial Page "XPI." *Book of Kells*
Late Eighth Century. Trinity College Library, Dublin
(The Board of Trinity College, Dublin)

These illuminated initial letters from the *Book of Kells* were painted in an
Irish monastery. The curvilinear patterns elaborate a geometrical style of
decoration that extended widely through Europe and Asia among steppe peoples
and their descendants; but the precision and complexity of a page like
this was unequalled elsewhere. As such it aptly symbolizes the precocious
elaboration of Irish Christian culture building upon barbarian Celtic roots.

Roman areas; but in the more backward and peripheral districts, especially in the marchlands (where freemen were seldom called away on distant campaigns, since they were needed to defend their own district against foreign attack) the older type of German society persisted until after the Carolingian period.

f. Culture

The Carolingian reform of the Church involved an improvement in the level of literacy and encouragement of learning among the clergy. Charlemagne organized a palace school, headed by an Englishman named Alcuin (d. 804), whose members busily set about teaching, collecting, and copying manuscripts, and writing books of their own. Most of these books are by no means distinguished: commentaries on scripture, dialogues on the seven liberal arts, encyclopedias of miscellaneous learning, etc. Paul the Deacon (d. *c.* 797) wrote a *History of the Lombards* which is full of edifying and miraculous tales; and Einhard (d. A.D. 840), a personal friend of Charlemagne and of his son, wrote a biography of Charlemagne which was modeled on the classical pattern of Suetonius' *Lives of the Caesars.* In the field of philosophy, one remarkable figure arose: John the Scot (Scotus Erigena d. *c.* 877), whose book, *On the Division of Nature,* is an attempt to reconcile Christian with Neo-Platonic doctrine. John was an Irishman by birth who came to Gaul shortly after Charlemagne's death. He was especially remarkable for his fluent command of Greek. His learning was not transmitted to later generations however, and with the destruction of the Irish monasteries in the ninth and tenth centuries by Viking raiders, knowledge of Greek disappeared from Western Europe until the renaissance.

The Carolingian "renaissance," as this revival of learning has sometimes been called, was remarkable for one more thing: the development of the style of lettering which we use today. Roman books had been written in what we know as capital letters; but in late Roman times a variety of smaller forms of lettering were introduced. In the time of the Carolingians a particularly legible style of lettering was invented and widely adopted. Modern typefaces are all descended from this "Carolingian miniscule."

g. English Development

The Anglo-Saxon kingdoms, which had arisen after the invasions of the fifth century, stand apart from the general evolution on the continent. At the end of the sixth century Christianity and a modicum of civilization came to the Anglo-Saxons from Ireland, and, almost simultaneously, from Italy, for Gregory the Great despatched missionaries from Rome who landed in Kent in A.D. 597. The Irish stronghold was in the north, in the Kingdom of Northumbria, and the Roman Catholic in the south. For several decades the two were in frequent conflict, until in A.D. 664 a synod met at Whitby to choose between the two rival types of Christianity. The synod decided in favor of Roman Catholicism, and thereafter the Irish withdrew to Scotland and Ireland.

But Irish influence made a lasting impression on the English Church. The learning of the English clergy remained far superior to that of their counterparts in Merovingian Gaul. Accordingly, the missionaries and scholars who carried through the reform of the Church in Carolingian times came mainly from England. One of the most notable figures of the English Church was Bede (d. A.D. 735), a learned monk who wrote many books of scriptural commentary, a work on chronology which popularized for the first time the system of dating from the Christian era which we use today, as well as numerous treatises on elementary education, astronomy, and other subjects. He is most famous for his *Ecclesiastical History of the English*, an admirably careful book, written in more correct and classical Latin than anyone else could command until the twelfth century.

4. RENEWED INVASIONS AND COLLAPSE OF THE CAROLINGIAN EMPIRE (A.D. 814–900)

Even before Charlemagne's death a new barbarian attack, coming from Scandinavia, began to threaten the security of western Christendom. The Vikings, as these Scandinavian raiders are usually called, were closely related in language and racial stock to the German tribes. Remote in the north, they had remained untouched by Christianity; but in the course of the seventh and eighth centuries obscure changes took place in Scandinavian society which led to a great outpouring of peoples in the following centuries. Overpopulation may have been a factor in stimulating the Viking expansion. Another factor undoubtedly was the acquisition of ship-building skill which led to the development of seaworthy vessels in which raiders were able to travel boldly over the northern seas, along the Russian rivers, and even into the Mediterranean. The mobility which their vessels assured them made the Viking attack a fearful one for the peoples of Europe to withstand. The raiders could easily gather an overwhelming force at any given point, land there, and ravage the surrounding country— only to withdraw when a defending army drew near. Against such tactics the military system of the Carolingian state was nearly helpless; Viking raiders were able to attack almost with impunity, destroying with fire and sword wherever they went.

The effect of Viking raids on Ireland was disastrous to the civilization which had grown up there. The great Irish monasteries were all destroyed, and the Irish tradition of learning and piety was uprooted. Considerable numbers of Scandinavians settled in Ireland and in Scotland, where they

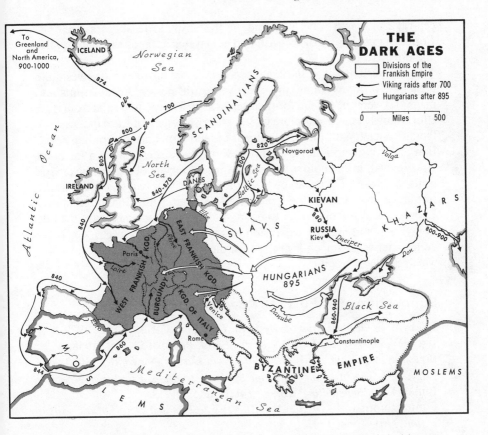

THE
DARK AGES

Divisions of the
Frankish Empire
Viking raids after 700
Hungarians after 895

0   Miles   500

soon were assimilated into the clans existing among the Celtic inhabitants
of those countries.

In England, the Viking assault had similar consequences. Northumbria,
where Bede and his fellow-scholars had lived, was overrun; but in the
south, the kingdom of Wessex survived the attack, and under Alfred (A.D.
871–99) was able to organize effective military resistance. In the following
century the kingdom of Wessex succeeded in uniting all of England into
one state.

On the mainland, the imposing structure of the Carolingian empire
proved quite incapable of withstanding the Viking attack. Under Charlemagne's successors the unity of the empire was broken, for his son, Louis
the Pious (A.D. 814–40), followed the old Frankish practice of dividing the
empire among his sons. Internecine wars distracted attention from the
foreign threat, and toward the end of the ninth century still another danger
arose from the raids of the Hungarian horsemen who succeeded the Avars
as rulers of the plain in the middle Danube. The Hungarians, like the Huns
and Avars, came from the steppes of central Asia. They first appeared in

central Europe in A.D. 899, and in the ensuing decades ravaged the Frankish marchlands of the east, and penetrated as far as the Rhine valley and northern Italy.

Under such attack, Charlemagne's successors proved themselves quite incapable of maintaining any effective central power. Local counts and magnates were left to fend for themselves as best they could; and from their efforts slowly emerged a more or less effective system of local defense, the feudal system. With the development of feudalism and the gradual cessation of Viking and Hungarian raids, European society began a long and slow revival, in the course of which appeared some of the characteristic traits of modern European civilization. No one year can be chosen as the turning point. But by the year A.D. 1000 the civilization of Medieval Europe had definitely begun to form; and in the eleventh century the tide of invasion and military expansion was reversed when Western Christendom went over to the offensive against the Arab, Greek, and Slavic worlds which bordered upon it.

Suggestions for Further Reading for Part II, F

Baldwin, S. *Organization of Medieval Christianity.* New York: 1929.

Bark, W. C. *Origins of the Medieval World.* Palo Alto, Calif: 1958.

Boissonade, P. *Life and Work in Medieval Europe.* New York: 1927.

Bury, J. B. *The Invasion of Europe by the Barbarians.* London: 1928.

Butler, E. C. *Benedictine Monachism.* London: 1919.

Cantor, Norman F. *Medieval History: The Life and Death of a Civilization.* New York: 1963.

Cantor, Norman F. *The Medieval World 300–1300.* New York: 1968.

Dawson, C. *The Making of Europe.* Meridian Books.

Dill, S. *Roman Society in Gaul in the Merovingian Age.* London: 1926.

Duckett, E. S. *The Gateway to the Middle Ages.* New York: 1938.

Dudden, F. H. *Gregory the Great.* 2 vols. New York: 1905.

Haskins, C. H. *The Normans in European History.* Boston: 1915.

Hay, D. *Europe: The Emergence of an Idea.* New York: 1957.

Hodgkin, R. H. *A History of the Anglo-Saxons.* 2 vols. Oxford: 1935.

Katz, S. *The Decline of Rome and the Rise of Medieval Europe.* Ithaca, New York: 1955.

Kendrick, T. D. *History of the Vikings.* New York: 1930.

Laistner, M. *Thought and Letters in Western Europe, A.D. 500–900.* Rev. ed. Ithaca, New York: 1957.

Lewis, Archibald. *Emerging Medieval Europe A.D. 400–1000.* New York: 1967.

Lewis, Archibald. *Naval Power and Trade in the Mediterranean 500–1100.* Princeton: 1951.

Lot, F. *The End of the Ancient World and the Beginnings of the Middle Ages.* London: 1931.

Loyn, H. R. *Anglo-Saxon England and the Norman Conquest.* New York: 1962.

Olrik, A. *Viking Civilization.* London: 1931.

Painter, S. *A History of the Middle Ages, 284–1500.* New York: 1953.

Pirenne, H. *Economic and Social History of Medieval Europe.* Harvest Books.

Stenton, F. M. *Anglo-Saxon England.* 2d ed. Oxford: 1947.

Taylor, H. O. *The Medieval Mind.* 2 vols. London: 1911.

Trevor-Roper, Hugh. *The Rise of Christian Europe.* New York: 1965.

Ullmann, Walter. *The Individual and Society in the Middle Ages.* Baltimore: 1966.

Whitelock, D. *The Beginnings of English Society.* Penguin Books.

Winston, R. *Charlemagne: From the Hammer to the Cross.* New York: 1954.

Zimmer, H. *The Irish Element in Modern Culture.* London: 1913.

Novels

Carberry, Mary. *Children of the Dawn.* London: 1923.

DuBois, Theodora M. *Emerald Crown.* New York: 1955.

Duggan, Alfred. *Conscience of the King.* New York: 1952.

Duggan, Alfred. *The Little Emperors.* New York: 1953.

Fisher, Vardis. *Darkness and the Deep.* New York: 1943.

Jensen, Johannes V. *Fire and Ice.* New York: 1923.

Kipling, Rudyard. *Puck of Pook's Hill.* New York: 1906.

Kipling, Rudyard. *Rewards and Fairies.* New York: 1910.

Macpherson, Annie W. *Ruan.* New York: 1960.

Treece, Henry. *The Great Captains.* New York: 1956.

White, Terence H. *The Sword in the Stone.* New York: 1939.

Chronological Table for Part II, F: The Successor Kingdoms of the West

A.D.	
406	Invasian of Gaul by German raiders.
*410	Sack of Rome by the Visigoths under Alaric.
411–532	Burgundian kingdom in upper Rhone valley.
412–415	Visigoths in southern Gaul.
415–419	Visigoths invade Spain, drive Vandals out and establish kingdom in Spain and southern Gaul.
c. 420	End of Roman government in Britain.

429–439	Vandal conquest of North Africa.
430	Death of St. Augustine.
432	Mission of St. Patrick to Ireland.
440–461	Pope Leo I, the Great.
c. 450	Anglo-Saxon invasion of England began.
451	Council of Chalcedon; Leo the Great secured the acceptance of his definition of Christological doctrine.
451	Defeat of Attila the Hun by Roman and Visigothic forces in Gaul—Battle of the Catalaunian field.
452	Huns invaded Italy; retreated from Rome after Pope Leo's embassy.
453	Death of Attila; breakup of Hunnic empire.
455	Vandal sack of Rome.
461	Death of St. Patrick.
*476	Deposition of Romulus Augustulus, last Roman emperor of the West.
*481–511	Clovis, King of the Franks, established the Merovingian dynasty.
486	Clovis defeated the Roman ruler of northern Gaul; annexed area to Frankish kingdom.
493–526	Theodoric the Ostrogoth established Ostrogothic kingdom in Italy.
496	Clovis and Franks converted to Catholic Christianity after successful battle against Alemanni.
500	Clovis defeated the Burgundians, made their kingdom tributary.
507	Clovis defeated the Visigoths, annexed part of southern Gaul.
524	Death of Boethius, the philosopher.
527–565	Justinian, Roman emperor in the East.
c. 529	St. Benedict wrote his monastic *Rule*.
533–534	Justinian reconquered Africa; destroyed Vandal kingdom.
535–554	Long wars in Italy between Byzantines and Ostrogoths; destruction of Ostrogothic kingdom, annexation of most of Italy to East Roman empire.
561	Death of last of Clovis' sons; division of Frankish kingdom into Neustria and Austrasia, break-away of marginal areas.

568	Lombard invasion of Italy; prolonged fighting with Byzantine forces.
*590–604	Pope Gregory the Great.
594	Death of Gregory of Tours, historian of the Franks.
597	Mission of St. Augustine (not of Hippo) to England.
615	Death of St. Columban, Irish missionary to the European continent.
632	Death of Mohammed; beginning of rapid Arab expansion.
664	Synod of Whitby in England decided in favor of Roman as against Irish Christianity.
687	Pepin of Heristal, Mayor of the Palace in Austrasia, defeated Neustrian forces, and began to reunite Frankish kingdom.
711–718	Arab conquest of Spain; destruction of Visigothic kingdom.
714–741	Charles Martel, Frankish Mayor of the Palace, reestablished single control over all the Frankish kingdom: the Austrasian invasion.
*733	Battle of Tours: defeat of Arabs by Charles Martel.
735	Death of Bede, the scholar.
741	Pepin the Short succeeded his father, Charles Martel, as Mayor of the Palace.
751	Pepin crowned King of the Franks; Merovingian king deposed.
753	Death of St. Boniface, "apostle to the Germans."
*754	Pepin consecrated King by the Pope; alliance between papacy and Frankish kingdom
756	Pepin established Papal states in central Italy after two campaigns against Lombards.
768	Death of Pepin; accession of Charlemagne.
772–804	Charlemagne campaigned against Saxons; conquered and Christianized them after hard fighting.
774	Charlemagne conquered Lombards; assumed Iron crown of Lombardy.
796	Destruction of Avar power by Frankish army.
*800	Charlemagne crowned Emperor by Pope Leo III; in theory a revival of Roman empire in the West.

804	Death of Alcuin, scholar and head of Charlemagne's palace school.
*814	Death of Charlemagne.
814–840	Louis the Pious, Emperor.
840	Death of Einhard, Charlemagne's biographer.
843	Treaty of Verdun: division of Carolingian empire into three parts, Lotharingia, France and Germany.
871–899	Alfred the Great, King of Wessex.
899	First appearance of Hungarian raiders in central Europe.

G. The Arab World

1. *Introductory*
2. *Islam*
3. *Political Expansion*
4. *Social and Economic*
5. *Culture*
6. *Later History of the Arab World*

1. INTRODUCTORY

In the hundred years between A.D. 632 and 732 the Arabs succeeded in conquering a tremendous area of the world's surface. The Arab empire extended from southern France and Spain eastward along the shore of North Africa to the Near East, and beyond to Central Asia and the Indus river. Fully half of the old Roman empire fell under Arab control, and the entire area of the ancient Near Eastern civilization was united once again. The Arabs did not destroy nor significantly damage the society and culture which they found in these regions, but they did transform both. The Arabic language became a medium of literary communication throughout the area which the Arabs conquered, and in a relatively short time Arabic displaced other tongues as the everyday speech of the population over most of North Africa and the Near East. Thought and learning flourished; trade and industry prospered; a brilliant and graceful civilization arose beside which Western Europe seemed barbarous and even Byzantium paled. Contact with the Arabs in Spain and Sicily provided one of the important stimuli to the West when civilization began to revive after about A.D. 1000. It is, however, not possible to do justice to the achievements of the Arabs here; a few generalizations must suffice.

2. ISLAM

The immediate stimulus to the Arab expansion was the appearance of a new religion. Mohammed (*c.* A.D. 570–632) was a native of the city of Mecca, who, when a young man, made his living as a camel driver and petty trader. On his travels he picked up a smattering of Jewish and Christian religious ideas. He arrived at the conviction that the polytheism of his fellow Arabs was false; that there was only one God, the God Jews and Christians worshipped. He acknowledged the prophets of the Old Testament and Jesus of Nazareth as worthy predecessors of his own prophetic mission. They had revealed the Divine plan for men but with time misunderstandings and corruptions crept in. Mohammed claimed simply to correct and restore God's revelation. His teachings were set forth in oral messages, cast in poetic form. Just after Mohammed's death they were written down and became the *Koran*, the sacred book of the Moslem religion.

Mohammed's central message was summed up in the phrase: "There is no God but Allah, and Mohammed is His prophet." Hopes of a blissful paradise, reserved for true believers, and a vigorously missionary attitude were also important elements in the new religion. No Moslem church ever came into existence, nor did anything strictly comparable to the Christian clergy develop among the Moslems. Mosques became places of worship and instruction, and they had caretakers, teachers, and leaders of public prayers attached to them; but no hierarchical clergy or independent ecclesiastical organization was formed. Generations of Moslems after Mohammed set out vigorously to use the *Koran*—God's word—as a guide to everyday conduct. Elaborate legal systems were formed on this basis, deriving rules for most of the circumstances a pious man could encounter in his whole lifetime from the *Koran* and traditions about the way the Prophet had himself behaved. As a result Islam (meaning "obedience") became a religion of personal piety and legal scholarship without the political and organizational aspects which distinguish Christianity. The sovereignty of the state was seldom challenged by Moslem religious officials; indeed for orthodox Moslems the secular ruler was also supreme religious head.

3. POLITICAL EXPANSION

Mohammed's preaching won few converts at first. In A.D. 622, however, a neighboring city, Medina, invited him and his followers to come. This, the *Hegira*, marked the beginning of a rapid success for the new religion, and from that year is counted the Mohammedan era. Within a short time, Mohammed had become the effective ruler of Medina; by the time of his death he had won control of his native city, Mecca, and had united almost all of Arabia under the banner of the new religion.

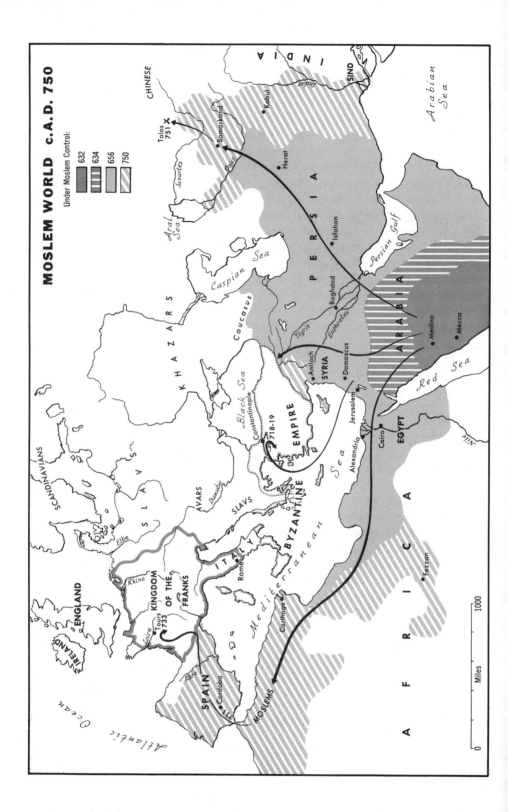

MOSLEM WORLD c.A.D. 750

Under Moslem Control:

632
634
656
750

CHINESE

INDIA

SIND

Indus

Kabul

Samarkand

Talas
751 ✕

Jaxartes

Herat

Aral Sea

Oxus

PERSIA

Isfahan

Arabian Sea

Caspian Sea

Persian Gulf

ARABIA

Baghdad

Tigris *Euphrates*

Medina

Mecca

KHAZARS

Caucasus

Antioch
SYRIA
Damascus

Red Sea

Black Sea

Constantinople

EMPIRE

Jerusalem

718-19

SCANDINAVIANS

SLAVS

AVARS

Danube

SLAVS

Alexandria

Cairo

EGYPT

Nile

BYZANTINE

Elbe

ENGLAND

IRELAND

Rhine

KINGDOM
OF THE
FRANKS

ITALY

Rome

Mediterranean Sea

Fezzan

A F R I C A

Loire
Tours
733

Ebro

SPAIN

Cordoba

Carthage

MOSLEMS

Atlantic Ocean

Miles

0   1000

Following his death (A.D. 632), expansion continued at a very rapid rate. A series of Caliphs (i.e., successors to the Prophet) united the Arab tribesmen for great raids into Syria and Mesopotamia. Within an amazingly short time, they stripped the Byzantine empire of its eastern provinces and completely conquered the Persian empire. During the following generations, Arab armies, reinforced by local converts, reached the Atlantic coast of Africa and crossed into Spain, penetrating as far as central France before suffering defeat at the hands of the Franks under Charles Martel in A.D. 733. In the east, Arab expansion continued at a similarly rapid rate, extending into India and the oases of Central Asia. After A.D. 750 the capital was fixed at Bagdad in Mesopotamia; but very soon sectarian differences became acute, outlying districts began to break loose from central control, and a series of independent and often warring states, sometimes divided by hard-fought religious differences, gradually arose throughout the Arab world.

4. Social and Economic

The rapidity of Arab conquest was made possible by the fact that they displaced only a small ruling class. Their liberal policy toward the conquered population actually made the Arabs welcome to the vast majority of the inhabitants of the Near East. In general, the Arabs maintained the social and governmental system which existed before their advent. City life flourished. Trade extended a net from India and China all the way to Spain, and southward far into Africa. Renewed trade allowed a number of important inventions to spread westward, where they were in due course taken over by Europeans. Chief among these were Arabic numerals— derived from India. In addition, the compass, block printing, and fireworks were all known to the Arabs, probably as borrowings from the Chinese. The industrial traditions of the ancient world were preserved and elaborated by Arab craftsmen. Things as diverse as muslin, damascene steel, apricots, tariffs, and algebra betray their Arabic derivation in our English names for them.

5. Culture

Works of philosophy and science were translated into Arabic from Greek, Persian, and Sanscrit in the ninth century; and during the succeeding two hundred years a series of Arabic doctors, astronomers, mathematicians, and philosophers added to the learning of their predecessors and digested it into the forms which first penetrated into Western Europe. Avicenna (d. 1037, more properly Ibn Sina), a medical writer, and Averroes (d. 1198, more properly Ibn Rushd), a philosopher who tried to reconcile Aristotelianism with the tenets of Islam, were among the most influential in the West.

Literature, especially poetry, flourished and was highly esteemed. A collection of Arab tales, the *Thousand and One Nights*, became familiar to Westerners; but this was only a tiny part of the entire bulk of Arabic literature.

Art forms were limited by the religious prohibition against representation of human or animal form. As a result, Arab decorative art specialized in intricate geometric and floral designs. Architecturally, the Arabs combined Byzantine and Persian elements to produce a style of their own, marked by cusped and horseshoe arches, domes and minarets.

6. LATER HISTORY OF THE ARAB WORLD

The height of Arab political power passed with the tenth century. Thereafter Arab states fell prey to internal disorders, and to encroachments of nomadic peoples from the steppes of Central Asia, most prominent of whom were the Turks and the Mongols. In the sixteenth century, the Ottoman Turks succeeded in uniting nearly all the former Arabic lands into a single state, and for a while seriously threatened central Europe. But the Ottoman empire in its turn decayed, and during the nineteenth and twentieth centuries it broke up under European pressure into the states of the Near East as they exist today.

Suggestions for Further Reading for Part II, G

Andrae, Tor. *Mohammed: The Man and His Faith*. New York: 1960.
Arnold, T. W., and Guillaume, A. eds. *The Legacy of Islam*. Oxford: 1931.
Gibb, H. A. R. *Mohammedanism: An Historical Survey*. New York: 1953.
Gibb, H. A. R., and Bowen, H. *Islamic Society and the West*. New York: 1951 and 1957.
Lewis, B. *Arabs in History*. New York: 1957.
Margoliouth, D. S. *The Early Development of Mohammedanism*. London: 1912.
Margoliouth, D. S. *Mohammed and the Rise of Islam*. New York: 1905.
Pickthall, M. *The Meaning of the Glorious Koran*. New York: 1930.
Pirenne, Henri. *Mohammed and Charlemagne*. New York: 1955.
Von Grunebaum, G. E. *Medieval Islam*. Chicago: 1946.
Watt, W. M. *Muhammad at Mecca*. New York: 1953.
Watt, W. M. *Muhammad at Medina*. New York: 1956.

Chronological Table for Part II, G: The Arab World

A.D.

c. 570	Birth of Mohammed.
*622	The *Hegira* to Medina.

632	Death of Mohammed.
636	Conquest of Palestine and Syria from Byzantine empire.
640–642	Conquest of Egypt from Byzantine empire.
641	Overthrow of New Persian Empire.
661–750	Ommiad caliphate: Damascus the capital; expansion into India and across North Africa into Spain.
711–718	Arab invasion of Spain; destruction of Visigothic kingdom.
717–718	Arab siege of Constantinople: first important Moslem set-back.
733	Battle of Tours: Franks defeated Arab raiders in central Gaul.
750	Establishment of Abbasid caliphate; Bagdad the capital.
1037	Death of Avicenna.
1198	Death of Averroes.
1258	Capture of Bagdad by Mongols; destruction of the caliphate.

PART III

European
Civilization
(c. A.D. 900–Present)

The history of our own civilization is in many respects more difficult to study than that of an age more remote about which less is known or knowable. Through the formation of a number of national states, European society came to be divided into rival groupings, and changes in one nation did not exactly parallel those of another. Moreover the problem of periodization presents many difficulties, since intellectual, political and economic changes do not always parallel one another. Consequently a division based upon one field of human activity will not fit development in another, and it is often difficult to describe European civilization as a whole. The historian's problem arises in large part from the fact that so much is known about the history of European civilization. The comparative simplicity of classical history is mostly fictitious, for the preeminence of Athens and Rome in our eyes is a consequence of our ignorance of the history of the many other states which existed in the classical world.

Another major difficulty troubles any student of recent and contemporary history—a lack of time perspective. Knowledge of what comes after always makes the task of the historian easier, for he can then focus his attention on the aspects of an age which relate to developments of the succeeding period. Such a practice of course simplifies and distorts the complex and disparate reality of past ages; but without such a guide, attention tends to be sadly dissipated and the cohesion of any historical narrative is likely to be impaired.

It follows that the arbitrary nature of the organization and emphasis in this, the concluding part of this *Handbook*, is more obvious than before. On the other hand, the history of the West has an immediacy and vitality which more ancient history cannot share. It deals, however imperfectly, with institutions, ideas, and attitudes which still exist among us, and describes personalities and events which influence our lives both intimately and profoundly.

It should already be clear that the beginnings of European history reach backward to the ancient Greeks, Hebrews and beyond. The Classical and Judeo-Christian traditions have been of incalculable importance in shaping the history of European civilization; and the political institutions of the Roman empire, the legal relationships embodied in Roman law, the social attitudes established by Germanic custom, all have entered fundamentally into the European tradition. There was in fact no break in continuity between the Classical and the Modern world. More than that, the wisdom of the ancient world has in every generation been a living force acting upon those who perused the pages of the Bible or of the Greek and Latin classics.

Yet it is convenient to distinguish phases of history and call distinct styles of life "civilizations." At what date one chooses to draw the line between one civilization and another, and by what criteria the line is drawn, must perforce be a matter of taste. In this *Handbook* the year A.D. 900 has been taken as a dividing line, and the criterion has been largely economic and political. From that date to the present the economic organization of Western Europe has become more and more complex, though there have been numerous local and temporary reversals. Equally, during the past thousand years European states (and since the sixteenth century extra-European states of European type) have tended to develop into larger, more closely integrated, and more powerful units; though, again, so general a development has not been without numerous setbacks and breakdowns.

From other points of view, the year A.D. 900 may not seem so well chosen. The intellectual and artistic life of Europe underwent two profound changes: one in the fourth century A.D. when Christianity became the dominant religion; and a second in the fourteenth and fifteenth centuries when a new knowledge of and admiration for pagan antiquity spread widely among educated men. These dates have often been used by historians to mark off a period called the Middle Ages. Yet within the thousand years A.D. 400–1400 intellectual and artistic history, too, fell into two contrasting segments: a period of decline, and a period of revival. The unmistakable revival of intellectual and artistic life, to be sure, came about a century after economic and political revival, but the existence of such a lag is perhaps to be expected.

Thus, recognizing the artificiality of any such dividing line, it still seems possible to speak of a new patterning of human experience which began in Western Europe about A.D. 900; a patterning that has developed in many devious and unexpected ways to the present and which we may conveniently call European civilization.

A. Geographical Setting of European Civilization

1. Transfer of the Center of Civilization

Near Eastern civilization originated and reached its fullest development in the river valleys of Mesopotamia and Egypt together with adjacent zones of agriculturally fertile land. It penetrated into a part of the Mediterranean basin, and touched such outlying regions as Greece, North Africa and even Italy (the Etruscans); but in those regions it never took deep root. Classical civilization originated and flourished principally in the Mediterranean coast lands. It penetrated into continental Europe—southern Britain, northern France, southern Germany and the Danubian lands were all parts of the Roman empire for centuries. Yet these regions, where European civilization was to have its focus, remained rude and backward in Roman times. It is noteworthy how the transitions from Oriental to Classical and from Classical to European civilizations each time involved a shift toward the periphery of the older society.

The territory which had been united into the Roman empire came to be divided among three distinct civilizations after the seventh century A.D.: in Spain, North Africa and the eastern Mediterranean, the Arabs; in Asia Minor, the Balkan peninsula, and southern Italy, the Byzantines; and in western Europe, the Latin and Germanic peoples. For practical purposes one may draw the distinction in terms of religion: Islam defined the Arab world, Orthodox Christianity defined the Byzantine world, and Latin Christianity defined the West.

The geographical extent of European civilization altered markedly through the centuries. In the tenth century Latin Christendom did not extend east of the Elbe river in Germany; it was circumscribed on the south by Byzantine possessions in southern Italy and by the Arab lands in Spain. Remote parts such as Ireland and Scotland, where independent Celtic traditions persisted, were not yet incorporated into the body of Latin Christendom. Likewise, pagan Scandinavia was still a world apart. One of the enduring characteristics of subsequent history was the expansion of these frontiers in all directions, until European influence became literally world wide after the sixteenth century.

Within the original homeland of European civilization there was considerable geographical diversity. To the north lies a wide coastal plain, extending from the Pyrenees along the Atlantic and Baltic coasts into Russia. Inland from the plain rise a series of hills and mountains which form an irregular barrier between the north and the Mediterranean lands of the south. The mountain barrier, combined with important differences in climate between northern and Mediterranean Europe, divided the homeland of European civilization into two contrasting geographical parts. As one would expect, Roman institutions, agricultural methods, and forms of social organization persisted more strongly and underwent less drastic modification in the Mediterranean zone than in the north where the influence of the Germans was far more pervasive and where a different geographical base compelled or encouraged departures from Mediterranean patterns of land use. These geographical and social differences have made possible a constant and frequently fruitful interaction between the peoples who inhabited northern and those who lived in southern Europe.

2. TRANSPORT AND COMMUNICATION

The plains of the north are wide, penetrated by a number of rivers which flow relatively slowly to the sea. Most of these rivers are navigable for considerable portions of their length; consequently they became important channels for the transport of heavy goods. The cluster of riverways which forms at the mouth of the Rhine was particularly important. The economic prominence of the Low Countries, which lie on either side of the Rhine mouth, has been a striking fact in European history; and their wealth has always been fostered by the easy transport to an extensive hinterland offered by the branching waterways.

The coast line of northwestern Europe is deeply indented as a result of geologic subsidence. Numerous harbors result. The continental shelf extends far out into the Atlantic; and, in the relatively shallow water which is thus formed. fish proliferate and constitute a valuable source of food. Geography thus encouraged seafaring. But the storminess of northern seas and the fact that tides run high along many parts of the European coast constituted formidable obstacles to early mariners, especially to those who were accustomed to the relatively calm and tideless waters of the Mediterranean. Thus the Romans were never able to traverse the northern seas with ease; and it was only after a number of technical improvements had been made in ship construction—the development of a sternpost rudder (thirteenth century) in place of the steering oar, for example—that ships became able to navigate with confidence. The Viking raiders greatly improved shipbuilding design, and when their warlike raids came to an end, trading and fishing ships continued to ply the seas which they had first made familiar.

The mountains which divide northern from southern Europe—the Pyrenees, Cevennes and Alps—are not difficult to traverse. The highest range, the Alps, is penetrated by a number of passes which medieval pack trains and armies could negotiate easily enough. The Rhone valley constituted another avenue of access to the Mediterranean, though the speed and strength of the Rhone current made the river itself of relatively little use for transport. Further to the west, a broad gap between the Cevennes and the Pyrenees helped to make the fortune of the medieval county of

Toulouse. The remains of Roman roads facilitated overland transport and helped to keep northern Europe in contact with the Mediterranean.

3. CLIMATE AND VEGETATION

The climate of northwestern Europe is far moister than that of the Mediterranean basin. Rain falls the year round, owing to the fact that the land lies in the zone of prevailing westerlies which sweep in from the Atlantic both summer and winter. This fact also moderates extremes of temperature, since the ocean is cooler in summer and warmer in winter than the land. The Gulf Stream, which sweeps across the North Atlantic and bathes the European coast, reinforces the ocean's moderating effect, and makes corresponding latitudes in Europe far warmer than along the North American coast opposite. (Labrador and the British Isles are on the same parallels of latitude, for example.)

As one travels eastward, the effect of the Atlantic weakens. Winters become colder, summers hotter, and rainfall decreases until the steppe conditions of the lower Danube valley and southern Russia result. Germany east of the Elbe is a transitional zone between the moderate western and the severe eastern European climates. The fact that the soils of eastern Germany are predominantly sandy and not so fertile as the loam and clay soils to the west acted in combination with the more severe climate to restrict medieval exploitation of the trans-Elban regions. Only in later centuries, with the development of more efficient agricultural methods and new crops, could these regions come more nearly abreast of the better favored western districts.

Climate and topography combined to clothe most of northwestern Europe in heavy forest before men transformed the face of the land. The fact that large areas of the coastal plain are nearly flat resulted in numerous swamps and swampy places. Indeed without some sort of artificially improved drainage, great areas of the plain did not dry off early enough in the spring to permit the raising of crops before autumn rains and frosts came to kill them.

These conditions constituted serious obstacles to the agricultural exploitation of the rich soils of the north in Roman and earlier times. In general, agriculture was confined to specially favored localities where drainage was unusually good (e.g., hill tops, chalk or loess soils) and where heavy forests did not grow naturally. The reclamation of the plain lands was a long and slow process which took centuries. The great lowland forests had been cut into fragments by the end of the fourteenth century in most of western Europe; but the process of reclamation has never entirely ended.

Climatic conditions of northern Europe resulted in several significant differences in the agricultural system medieval farmers established there, as compared with the far older system of the Mediterranean. Relatively abundant rains supported succulent herbiage through large parts of the year, so that horses and cattle played a primary role among the domestic animals, instead of the donkeys, sheep and goats which are characteristic of Mediterranean regions. Acorns from the extensive oak forests provided nourishment for pigs so that herds of swine became important as was not the case in southern Europe where forests had largely been destroyed during classical times.

The olive, of course, cannot withstand the winter cold of northern Europe so that other sources of edible fat—butter and animal fat—replaced that staple of Mediterranean life. Vines were successfully acclimated in many parts of northern Europe, notably in the upper Rhine valley, but wine growing never had the basic importance for the West that it had in Mediterranean areas; and indeed a staple of early trade was the exchange of southern wines for various northern products. Among the cereal crops, wheat remained of great importance in northern Europe. In some regions, however, wheat could not be depended on since the moisture and coolness of the climate caused partial crop failures. In such places hardier cereals such as rye and oats were grown instead of wheat, despite the fact that they yielded less food per acre.

4. Mineral Resources

Northern Europe has abundant and varied mineral deposits. The recent industrial phase of European development, for example, was made possible by the exploitation of iron and coal. The principal deposits of these two prime minerals are located in a belt which runs from the central part of the British Isles eastward through Belgium, northern France and the middle Rhinelands. There are also numerous secondary deposits in Silesia and elsewhere. The existence of this belt of minerals has gone far toward dictating the course of European economic development in the past two hundred years. But long before the industrial revolution, mining and metallurgy were important economic activities, and supplied most of the weapons and some of tools with which Europeans fought and worked.

B. Western Christendom, 900–1500

1. Revival of Civilization, 900–1050

---

    a. The Economic base: Manorial Agriculture
      1) Agricultural Technique
      2) Social Adjustment to the New Agricultural
         Technique
      3) Social Classes within the Manor

---

a. The Economic Base: Manorial Agriculture

1) Agricultural Technique. In Near Eastern and Mediterranean climates grain had to be sown in the fall and was harvested in the spring at the beginning of the summer drought. In northern Europe, however, there was no prolonged dryness in summer, and it was therefore possible to sow grain both in the fall and in the spring, and to harvest the resulting crops successively in summer and early fall. This had the effect of spreading agricultural work more evenly over the year so that a man's labor power could be applied to a larger area of land. In medieval England, for example, thirty acres was counted as the normal size for a single peasant's arable land, whereas in ancient Greece the average farm which a single Athenian family could work was probably about a third as large. The reason for such a difference is that in Greece the seasons for plowing and harvest were definite and short, while specialized crops such as olives and grapes required prolonged and laborious hoe cultivation. The fact that both winter and spring crops could be raised successfully under the climatic conditions of northern Europe helped, therefore, to counterbalance the lower yield of rye and oats as compared with the Mediterranean staples, wheat and barley.

But land which did not dry off rapidly in the spring could not be used either for winter or spring grains. Before the north European plain could become agriculturally productive on a wide scale it was therefore necessary to invent means of improving the natural drainage. This need was met by the use of a type of heavy "mouldboard" plow which turned the soil over in furrows, and created a series of artificial rounded humps (ridges) separated by shallow ditches (baulks) that ran parallel through the length of the field. Such ditches helped to drain off standing water in the spring and permitted earlier planting then would otherwise have been possible.

The mouldboard plow was invented in Germany, probably a considerable time before the period of the great migrations of the fourth and fifth centuries A.D. But the seminomadic habits of the Germans and the low repute in which they held the work of the farmer probably operated to minimize the importance of the new invention and slowed the process of clearing the forests for agriculture. Yet differences between the descriptions of Germany by Caesar and by Tacitus suggest that the Germans had made considerable progress toward settled agriculture between 50 B.C. and A.D. 100; and throughout Merovingian and Carolingian times a slow process of clearing fields and breaking them to the plow continued in the purely German districts between the Rhine and the Elbe.

In Romanized areas social obstacles to the adoption of the mouldboard plow were initially insurmountable. Roman conceptions of private property in land and chattels accorded ill with the demands of the mouldboard plow. The principal difficulty lay in this: few individual farmers could own the necessary number of draught animals with which to pull so heavy a plow. The mouldboard plow required considerable force to drive it through the ground, and in medieval times several teams of animals were usually hitched together for plowing. One consequence was to make it a clumsy matter for the plow and team to turn around; from this arose the habit of plowing fields into elongated patterns—the so-called strip or long-acre field. Indeed, for efficient use the squarish field patterns which Roman agriculturalists everywhere set up had to be altered in order to allow for the difficulty of turning the plow. As a result, it was not until after the barbarian invasions that agriculture based upon the mouldboard plow came to be widely established in northern France, in the Po valley of Italy and in England. South of the Loire the new type of agriculture never established itself generally; and in some outlying regions—e.g., Ireland—the mouldboard plow did not penetrate until much later. In mountainous districts the lie of the land made it impossible to use the heavy plow. But in the regions of the north European plain mouldboard agriculture had become general by the tenth century.

No comparable change in agricultural technique took place in the south of Europe, where Roman methods and crops remained in use, although the skill and care with which the land was tilled retrogressed very much from, say, the first century B.C.

2) Social Adjustment to the New Agricultural Technique. It required from six to eight of the small oxen of medieval times to pull an ordinary mouldboard plow. To assemble such a plow team European farmers hit upon the device of pooling their resources and cultivating cooperatively. Some of the most distinctive characteristics of medieval farming arose from this need to pool resources in order to create plow teams.

By the tenth century most of northern Europe was divided into farming units known as manors. Some manors descended from villa estates, which had existed in Roman times; others were derived from German villages. Roman and German customs intermingled to create the manors of the Middle Ages, and scholars have carried on learned disputes as to the exact contributions of each. However that may be, the adoption of new

SCHEMATIC DRAWING OF A MEDIEVAL MANOR

RECTANGLES REPRESENT ONE FAMILY'S HOLDINGS

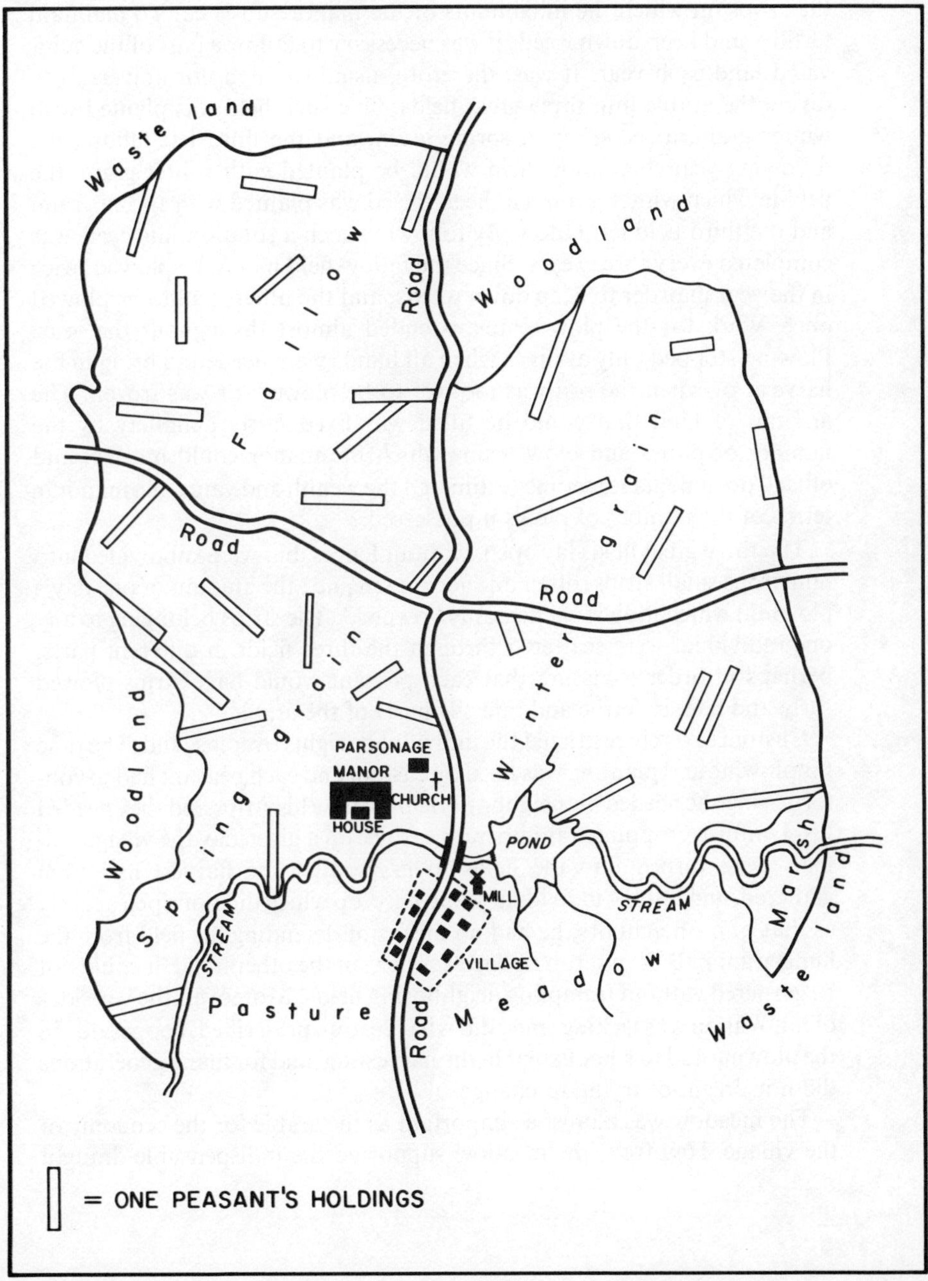

Waste land

Woodland

Fallow

Road

Winter grain

Road

Road

Woodland

Spring grain

PARSONAGE

MANOR
HOUSE

CHURCH

POND

STREAM

MILL

Marsh

VILLAGE

Pasture

Road

Meadow

Waste land

▯ = ONE PEASANT'S HOLDINGS

agricultural technique during the long period of the migrations, and the rise of a military aristocratic class—the knight who was also lord of a manor, or of several manors—tended to establish a measure of uniformity in the region where the mouldboard plow came into use.

Almost always a manor comprised four parts: arable, meadow, waste and the village area itself. The arable was of course the land which grew the crops on which the inhabitants of the manor subsisted. To maintain fertility and keep down weeds it was necessary to fallow a part of the cultivated land each year. It was, therefore, usual (though not universal) to divide the arable into three great fields. One such field was planted with winter grain, a second with spring grain, and the third left fallow; the following year, the fallow field would be planted with winter grain, the field in which winter grain had been raised was planted with spring grain, and the third field left fallow. By following such a rotation, the cycle was completed every three years. Since the fallow field had to be plowed twice in the year in order to keep down weeds, and the others had to be plowed once, work for the plow teams extended almost throughout the year. Plowing stopped only at times when all hands were needed to bring in the harvest, or when the soil was too wet to be plowed, or was frozen. The amount of land that could be tilled was fixed fairly definitely by the number of plows and plow teams which the manor could muster; and official documents sometimes estimated the wealth and value of a manor in terms of the number of plows it possessed.

The three great fields lay open, without fences, but were subdivided into numerous small strips (often one acre in size, i.e., the amount of one day's plowing) which individual peasants "owned." The strips belonging to any one individual were scattered through the three fields in different parts, perhaps in order to assure that each peasant would have strips plowed early and late, in fertile and infertile parts of the arable.

Custom severely restricted the individual's rights over his land. The time for plowing and planting was fixed by custom and each peasant had to conform, since he needed his neighbor's help to plow his strips and they needed his. Uniform cropping was imperative, since on a given day the village animals were turned into the fields to graze after the harvest had been gathered, and if some individual planted a crop which did not ripen as early as that of his neighbors, he had no means of defending his field from the hungry animals. If his crop ripened sooner, on the other hand, it could not be garnered without trampling neighboring fields. Moreover, the very idea of innovation was lacking: men did what custom prescribed, cooperated in the plowing and to some extent in the harvesting, and for many generations did not dream of trying to change.

The meadow was almost as important as the arable for the economy of the village. Hay from the meadow supported the indispensable draught animals through the winter. The idea that hay might be sown did not occur to men in medieval times; consequently they were compelled to rely on natural meadows alone. One result was that in many manors shortage of winter fodder for the plow teams was a constant danger. It was common practice to feed oxen on leaves picked from trees, and on straw from the grain harvest; but despite such supplements the draught animals often nearly starved in winter. In some cases oxen actually had to be carried out from their winter stalls to spring pastures until some of their strength was recovered and plowing could begin. Thus on many manors meadow land was even more valuable than the arable, and was divided into much smaller strips (often the width of a scythe stroke).[1]

The waste provided summer pasture for the various animals of the manor—pigs, geese, cattle and sheep. The animals of the whole manor normally grazed together under the watchful eyes of some young children or other attendants who could keep them from wandering too far afield, and bring them back to the village at night. The waste also was the source of wood for fuel and for building purposes, and helped to supplement the food supply with such things as nuts, berries, honey and rabbits. In early medieval times, manors usually adjoined wide stretches of forest and waste. A bird's eye view of western Europe in the tenth century would have shown great stretches of forest with clearings at various places, such as along rivers. Three or four hundred years later, the aspect had been changed. By 1400, forests and wastes would have appeared as a comparatively slight reticulation around and between tilled areas. As new manors were established and old clearings enlarged, more or less definite boundaries had to be drawn to define the waste land belonging to each manor.

The fourth segment of the manor was the village itself, usually located in the center of the arable near a source of drinking water, and perhaps along a road or footpath leading to the outside world. The cottages of medieval peasants were extremely humble, usually consisting of a single room, with earthen floor and thatched roof. Around each cottage normally lay a small garden in which various vegetables and sometimes fruit trees were planted. In the village streets chickens, ducks and dogs picked up a precarious living.

It is worth emphasizing the importance of manorial agriculture in European history. The vast majority of the population of Europe down to the nineteenth century lived on the land, and farmed cooperatively. Until

---

[1] An interesting survival of manorial agriculture is the nursery song:

> Little Boy Blue come blow your horn
> The sheep's in the meadow, the cow's in the corn.

The meadow would seem, to the uninitiated, to be exactly the place where sheep belonged; but not so in the medieval manor, where the corn (i.e., grain) of the arable and the hay of the meadow had both to be guarded for winter use of man and beast respectively.

about a hundred years ago nearly all the food of the entire population of Europe came from fields tilled by peasants. To be sure, the methods of manorial agriculture changed as time passed; and in some areas of Europe—most notably in Holland and England—the pattern of cooperative tillage broke down in the sixteenth to eighteenth centuries. But for most of northern Europe cooperative agriculture remained the usual form of tillage until after the middle of the nineteenth century.

Thus cooperative agriculture based on the mouldboard plow became for northern Europe what the grape-olive-grain complex was for the Mediterranean lands: a fundamental and distinctive agricultural adjustment to peculiar geographical conditions. It was this adjustment which transformed the north European plain from the sparsely settled, frontier region, which it had been in Roman times, into a center of agricultural production which rivaled and eventually surpassed the wealth of Mediterranean lands.

3) Social Classes within the Manor. From the earliest times for which records exist there were elaborate and somewhat confusing social and legal distinctions among persons living on the land. As will be described more at length below (see p. 256) an aristocratic class rose in western Europe during the eighth, ninth and tenth centuries which drew its economic support from manors by preempting rents and services from the peasants. A member of the aristocratic class might possess many manors, or only one; in some cases a single operating agricultural unit was divided between two or more "lords," although such subdivision probably became less common as feudal institutions solidified. The most fundamental social distinction consequently came to be that between the men who tilled the soil and the "lord of the manor," who by virtue of his position was entitled to a wide variety of income. Indeed the social status of the various members of a manorial community was usually defined by the obligations they bore toward the lord of the manor. It is impossible to describe accurately in general terms what such obligations were. They varied endlessly according to the custom of the manor, and often each individual and even each piece of land carried peculiar obligations of its own.

It was usual in early medieval times for the lord of the manor to retain a right to the produce of some part of the arable land. Sometimes the lord's land was located in one place (a "close"), sometimes his land was scattered among the peasants' strips. In either case the labor of cultivation was performed by humbler members of the community as a part of their obligation toward the lord. Land thus directly exploited by the lord was called the "demesne farm," and was frequently managed by a bailiff appointed by the lord to look after his interests and enforce the labor service owed to him by the peasants.

In addition to income from the demesne farm, the lord of a manor almost always collected income directly from the peasants. Thus dues had to be paid at specific times of the year—in the form of such things as a sheaf of the best grain, a chicken, a suckling pig or other delicacy. The exact dues owed by each family varied greatly but were fixed by custom. An especially burdensome right which the lords sometimes enjoyed was the power to take possession of the best animal of the peasant family whenever the head of the house died. Sometimes money payments were likewise demanded by the lord, though this became common only after the revival of town life in the late eleventh and twelfth centuries. Two more sources of income were important for the lord: fees for the use of mills, wine-presses, bake ovens, etc., and income from fines assessed by his manor court.

The lord's relation to the peasants on his manor was not simply that of a landlord. He was also a political ruler over them, and their defender against outside attack. Thus the lord usually held a court at which local disputes and transgressions against custom were brought up for settlement and punishment. Fines whether in kind or in money were paid to the lord, and from his decision, or the decision of his bailiff, there was no appeal.

Official records, such as William the Conqueror's *Domesday Book* which surveyed the manors of England, list a confusing number of different statuses among the inhabitants of manors. Some were classified as free men, whose obligations to the lord of the manor were limited to certain fixed dues. Others were counted as villeins or serfs and owed not only payments in kind but labor service as well. A third class, cotters or bordars, were apparently squatters who had no right to any of the manor's arable, but lived in small cottages and presumably survived by working for wages. But these general distinctions had many degrees and easily shaded off into one another. Especially in later times a serf might hold "free" land, or a free man might occupy "servile" land for which he owed labor service. In other words particular obligations or rights came to rest on possession of a particular strip of land regardless of the personal status of the possessor. The result came to be confusion that only a lawyer can appreciate.

A third element in the manorial community was the Church. Not every manor had a priest resident on it or a church building; but peasants usually had to pay a tithe (i.e., a tenth) of their harvest for the support of the Church. Sometimes the tithe was paid directly to a priest or to a bishop's agent; sometimes it was paid to the lord of the manor who might or might not pass it on to the Church.

The poverty and hardships of peasant life in medieval times were very great. Famine and disease were constant dangers; and in time of war, the peasant population almost inevitably suffered most immediately and severely from requisition, ravage, and forced labor. Yet while the dues paid to the lord of the manor and his power over the peasants may seem excessive, it must be realized that the lord did have a common interest with his peasants: without them his land was worthless. Consequently the lord of the manor did not want so to oppress his peasants as to make them starve or cause them to run away in despair. The custom of the manor came to have a strong and even a binding effect on both lord and peasant; and the law administered in the lord's court came to be based on such custom. In time of famine, the lord might help his peasants to survive by distributing grain or seed to them. Lords, too, frequently organized the clearance of new land as individual peasants could not have done unaided; and in some cases improved agricultural methods were introduced by the lord or his bailiff, especially in the case of lands owned by monasteries.

From the point of view of the peasants, the protection which the lord was able to afford them was vastly worth while, for with the development of military technique, ordinary farmers found themselves altogether unable to defend themselves effectively. The manor, thus, was an institution from which both lord and peasants benefited, though perhaps in different degrees. Manorial custom came to embody a very stable way of life which proved able to survive manifold changes and shocks throughout medieval and far into modern times.

b. Political Reorganization

1) Local Self defense: The Growth of Feudalism. Charlemagne's army was composed predominantly of foot soldiers, equipped with sword and shield, who spent most of their time as farmers or herdsmen and made warfare an avocation. But this force was stiffened by mounted men, more elaborately equipped. who made warfare and related pursuits into a full-time occupation. It will be recalled that Charles Martel, the grandfather of Charlemagne, had introduced or greatly extended the practice of granting estates to such men in return for their military service. By the extension of this principle a formidable military aristocracy—the medieval knightly class—came into existence. A knight was a professional fighting man who rode into battle on horseback, armed with spear, sword, and battle-axe, protected by a shield and by armor. It was not easy to manage such ponderous equipment, and long years of training and constant exercise were required to produce a truly efficient knight. But such men, when fully trained and equipped, proved themselves far superior as a fighting force to raw infantry levies, and were able to meet and repulse the dreaded attack of Viking and Hungarian raiders, who had done so much to bring down the centralized structure of the Carolingian state.

Knights were by necessity few in number, since any one locality could not support many of them. Consequently, to guard against the sudden

assault of Saracens, Vikings, or Hungarians, it was needful to build fortified places where a handful of knights, perhaps assisted by the local
peasantry, could stand off their assault, at least long enough for a more
considerable force of knights to assemble and ride to the counterattack.
Thus in the latter part of the ninth century and through the tenth century
numerous fortified places were erected in nearly all parts of the old Carolingian state. Such fortifications were at first very simple affairs—little more
than an earthen mound surmounted by a palisade, with perhaps a wooden
tower in the center to serve as a lookout, storage place, and last defense if
the outer wall were breached. From such simple beginnings the medieval
castle developed in the course of the following three centuries.

The relationship between knights and peasants has already been indicated in the discussion of manorial agriculture, for the lord of the manor
was usually a member of the knightly class. Relationships among knights,
on the other hand, constituted what is usually called the feudal system or
feudalism.

According to theory developed in later generations by ingenious lawyers, feudal relationships conformed to a relatively simple and neat system.
At the top stood a sovereign, invested by God with possession of all the
land of his kingdom. The sovereign then divided his land into segments
known as fiefs, which he entrusted to various of his faithful followers or
vassals. These vassals-in-chief in their turn divided the land they had received from the sovereign into smaller fiefs which they entrusted to vassals
of their own. Sub-infeudation extended downward in this fashion to the
ultimate link—the simple knight who had no vassals under him and a
graded series of overlords or seigneurs over him. The whole series of relationships may be thought of as a pyramid, with the sovereign at the apex.
The various levels of the feudal pyramid were distinguished by titles: duke,
count, viscount, baron, earl, graf, margrave, and others, varying from
country to country.

The granting and receiving of a fief involved a contract between seigneur
and vassal which defined the rights and duties of each toward the other.
Oaths of homage and fealty offered by the vassal to his seigneur solemnized and sealed the contract; and whenever either party died, the oaths
had to be renewed by the heir. The basic element of the feudal contract was
an exchange of rights over land (given by the seigneur) for military and
other honorable services (given by the vassal). Depending on the size of the
fief which he received, the vassal promised to provide his seigneur with a
larger or smaller number of knights, fully equipped for battle, whenever
called upon to do so. (Sometimes limitations were placed on the length of
time the vassal and his knights had to serve in the field, as well as on the
place in which they could be required to fight.) Since the exact terms of the
contract between seigneur and vassal were seldom reduced to writing,

there were frequent quarrels over the exact duties owed by each to the other.

The vassal's obligations to his seigneur were not confined strictly to military service. The vassal swore to be the seigneur's "man"; that is, to be loyal to him and to support him in any quarrels that might arise. The seigneur, for his part, undertook to champion his vassal's cause and to protect him from unlawful molestation. Normally, too, a vassal was expected to make certain money payments to his seigneur on special occasions, such as when the seigneur's eldest daughter was married or when his eldest son was knighted, etc. Another important tie between lord and vassal was the vassal's obligation to attend his seigneur's court at specified times of the year. At such gatherings, feasting and jollification were combined with consultation and judicial processes. If two of the seigneur's vassals quarreled, their dispute could be settled by the seigneur in consultation with the other vassals. Similarly, in case of dispute between the seigneur and a vassal, the mediation of the whole body of vassals assembled together at the seigneur's court was supposed to bring a settlement. Methods of judicial process were simple and crude: often quarrels were settled simply through trial by combat; more often still, a vassal who knew himself to be in the wrong or to have only small support at the seigneur's court, simply refused to attend. In such cases, only force and private warfare could bring a dispute to a close.

Fiefs, particularly the larger ones, frequently originated as official government positions. The idea that the fief was also an office never entirely disappeared. One consequence of this idea was the general establishment of primogeniture as the mode of inheritance, for while private property can easily enough be divided, an office by its very nature cannot. It became a general characteristic of feudal custom to pass the fief on to the eldest son undivided; and he could make what provision he saw fit for enfeoffing his younger brothers. As may be imagined, this was a fertile source of discontent and led to many intestine family struggles.

It would however be a mistake to dwell exclusively on the theory of feudal relationships. In actual practice the feudal hierarchy arose as a makeshift means of local self defense against the raids of Saracens, Vikings and Hungarians, and in the face of near anarchy at home. In the general political chaos of the ninth and tenth centuries, a strong right arm, pugnacious character and lack of scruple often counted for more than legal rights. Sometimes officials who had been appointed by Charlemagne or his successors simply took matters into their own hands, and made what local arrangements for defense they could, hiring, equipping or enfeoffing as many competent knights as they could attract and support. Such feudal principalities as the county of Flanders or the duchy of Aquitaine arose in this manner. In other cases obscure adventurers first established themselves as master of a district, and afterward secured some sort of legal recognition of their power. The most famous such case was the foundation of the duchy of Normandy along the lower Seine. Hrolf, a Viking chief, was granted the fief of Normandy by the king of France in A.D. 911 after his power had been firmly established there already. This grant amounted to a peace treaty between former enemies, and, despite legal form, gave the King of France no effective power over the duke of Normandy.

The power of the central government and of public authority all but disappeared in the century after Charlemagne's death. Feudalism, through oaths of fealty and homage, maintained a faint fiction of central power, but did nothing to restore the reality. The actual locus of effective sovereignty varied considerably. In Normandy, for instance, the dukes

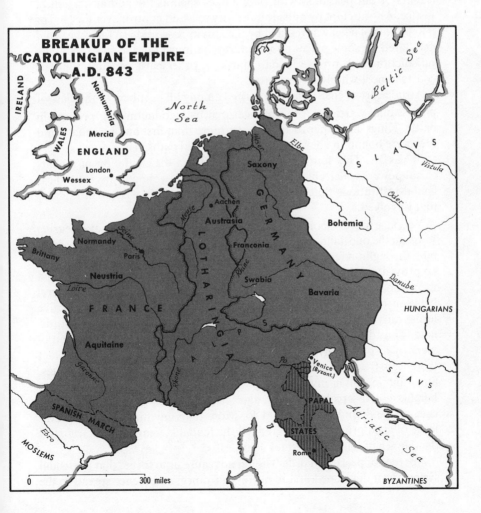

BREAKUP OF THE CAROLINGIAN EMPIRE A.D. 843

were able to control all castles built in the duchy, and even maintained a sort of rudimentary public administration. As a result, within the confines of Normandy the will of the duke was supreme. In other places, the devolution of power went much further. In the Ile de France, for instance, petty fief holders were regularly able to defy the will of their feudal superior, the King of France, and made the roads unsafe by their robberies until after the beginning of the twelfth century. A consequence was that the duke of Normandy (and half a dozen other feudal princes) were far more powerful than was their nominal sovereign, the King of France.

The distinction made both in Roman and in more recent times between private property and public rights collapsed under feudalism. Within his fief, the feudal lord combined in himself private rights of possession ("rents" from peasants) with public ones such as the administration of justice. Any attempt by outside authority to assert control over the land or inhabitants of a fief was resisted by the lord in possession so far as he could and dared. In some places public courts continued to have an overlapping jurisdiction with private feudal courts; in other parts of Europe public courts almost wholly disappeared.

A rude sort of egalitarianism existed among all members of the class of professional warriors. All were measured by a common test: prowess in battle. Kings and other rulers were no more than first among equals, and they were bound to obey the terms of the feudal oaths just as much as were their vassals. This spirit was far removed from the exaltation of monarchical powers which characterized late Roman law; and it was from these feudal institutions that the forms of representative government familiar today evolved.

Yet once more, theory and practice differed widely. Harsh, overbearing lords on the one hand, and violent, lawless vassals on the other, were common throughout feudal times. Moreover, the feudal system of justice made no provision for prompt settlement of disputes which might arise between men who were vassals of two different lords; and indeed a petty quarrel between two such vassals might easily come to involve their respective lords, each of whom was bound, at least in theory, to defend his subordinate. Thus despite the existence of a series of feudal courts for the settlement of disputes between the members of the feudal aristocracy, in fact there were frequent outbreaks of small-scale war between local magnates. Such fighting often involved only a handful of armed men, but a dozen knights could wreak great damage on the peasant population of their enemy's land, and regularly did so. More than anything else, the prevalence of such private war discredited the feudal system, particularly after the danger of barbarian attack had passed.

Absence of peace and order should not cause us to forget that the feudal system, as it developed first in northern France, and thence spread to the adjacent parts of Europe, did create a formidable military force, well equipped and professionally trained, available at a moment's notice for any sort of local affray. The knights of Western Europe repelled the barbarian attacks which had threatened to engulf Latin Christendom entirely, and within an amazingly short time proved themselves capable of taking successful offensive action against all their neighbors.

2) Revival of the Empire. The development of feudalism and knighthood was peculiarly the work of the French. In Germany a somewhat different evolution occurred. The old German tribes which had been incorporated into Charlemagne's empire succeeded in maintaining some sense of their corporate existence under the rule of the rudimentary Carolingian bureaucracy; and as the strength and efficiency of the central government decreased under Charlemagne's successors, new political units began to form along the old tribal lines. Thus arose four stem (German: Stämme) or tribal duchies: Saxony, Franconia, Swabia (the land of the Alemanni) and Bavaria.

The last Carolingian ruler of Germany died in A.D. 911, whereupon legal as well as actual power passed to the dukes of the tribal duchies. They chose one of their number to be king of Germany, but yielded only nominal obedience to the sovereign so selected. This situation was changed when Otto the Great (936–73). duke of Saxony, succeeded his father Henry as king. Otto was not content to remain merely titular ruler of Germany while leaving effective power outside his own duchy to other dukes. After a series of struggles, he was able to reassert the old Carolingian principle that dukes were royal officials, subject to the control of the king. Otto tried to consolidate his authority by putting his own kinsmen into ducal positions, but even so they did not always prove loyal to him and revolts were frequent throughout his reign. Nevertheless, Otto was able to take the offensive against Slavic tribes to the east, and extended German power beyond the Elbe river as far as the Oder. Bohemia was reduced to a state of dependence, and forced to recognize Otto's overlordship; and in A.D. 955 a great and decisive victory over the Hungarians turned back the last great raid that still barbarian people made into Germany. Simultaneously. a series of blockhouses, erected by Otto and his father along the North Sea coast. checked the Viking raids effectively, and Otto actually turned the tables by ravaging part of southern Denmark. Following the example of Charlemagne. he invaded Italy, assumed the title of King of that country. and in A.D. 962 was crowned Emperor at Rome.

Thus once again the ghost of the Roman empire was called upon to sanction the successful state building of a semibarbarian king. The imperial title which Otto revived in 962 was to persist until 1806. It was associated almost invariably with the political leadership of Germany, and also implied a rather vague claim to political headship of all Latin Christendom. But, the kingdoms of France and England never admitted any dependence on the German emperor; and his real powers, even in Germany, were always uncertain. For several centuries it was customary for the king of Germany to assume the imperial title only after being crowned by the pope. This custom was based on the precedent of Charlemagne and Otto the Great, and it was not until the fourteenth century that papal coronation was dispensed with.

Within Germany and Italy, imperial claims based on Roman precedent were largely nullified by the difficulty successive emperors found in securing the loyal and obedient service of subordinates. As compared with France, however, in the tenth and eleventh centuries the German state retained a much more effective central power; and among the rulers of Western Europe, Otto and his immediate successors towered preeminent.

Otto's reign marks a decisive turning point in the relationship between Western Christendom and its barbarous neighbors to the east and north. His military successes against them prepared the way for cultural penetration which in the course of the ensuing two hundred years brought Slavs, Scandinavians and Hungarians within the pale of European civilization. Otto's achievement can be compared with the development of feudal institutions in France, for the two acted along parallel lines in repulsing barbarian attack and initiating European expansion.

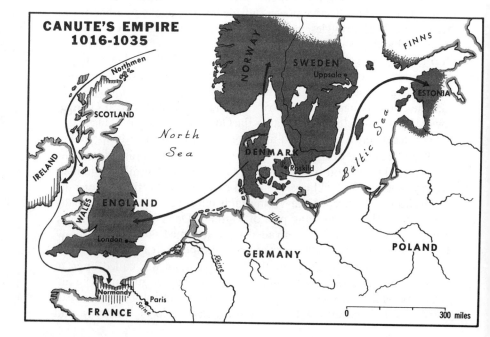

3) England. From the time of the Anglo-Saxon invasion in the mid-fifth century, England had followed a distinct line of social development. Only one of the Anglo-Saxon kingdoms, Wessex, proved strong enough to resist the Viking raiders successfully, and its survival often seemed precarious. For a few years, indeed, England was ruled by Canute, King of Denmark (1016–35), who succeeded in erecting a veritable northern empire, uniting Norway, part of Sweden and Esthonia, as well as Denmark and England under a single rule. His death, however, led to the disintegration of this empire. The English established a native, Edward the Confessor, as king.

The force of feudal institutions was well illustrated in the gradual process by which the late Anglo-Saxon kings began to graft French modifications onto native English practices. However, the feudalization of England had only begun when the Norman conquest (1066) interrupted English development and imposed a full-blown feudal system upon the country.

4) The Church and Feudal Society. The breakdown of central government was paralleled by a disruption of centralized control over the Church. The papacy became a prize for noble factions in Rome and Italy, and battles between rival claimants were not infrequent. Popes so appointed had neither the prestige nor the means to control religious affairs in the wide territory of Western Christendom.

Extensive and rich lands were possessed by monasteries and bishoprics. Under the chaotic conditions of the ninth and tenth centuries, such lands were tempting prey for the strong and rapacious, and in the absence of effective public enforcement of peace and order, it became necessary for the abbots and bishops to do what they could to safeguard their possessions. This meant, of course, finding knights and granting them fiefs in return for their service as defenders of the Church lands. Thus the Church became thoroughly feudalized, and in fact the abbots and bishops themselves came very generally to be recruited from among the younger sons of the feudal aristocracy. As abbot or bishop a younger son of a duke or count could come into possession of broad lands and an income commensurate with his rank; and not infrequently such ecclesiastics found opportunity to employ their knightly education by leading their men to battle against some neighboring lord with whom they had quarreled. It is true, however, that traditions of Roman law and administration were never entirely forgotten, and persisted most strongly among churchmen.

Since ecclesiastics could not legally marry, their positions could not easily become hereditary. Thus the power of appointing bishops and abbots was an important one. Whoever could assert control over ecclesiastical elections could expect political and military support from his appointees, and might be able in addition to secure a handsome increase to his revenues, since an eager candidate could be expected to pay something for his office.

In Germany, Otto and his successors asserted the power of ecclesiastical appointment, and indeed came to rely mainly on churchmen for the administration of the Empire, since they alone of all the great landholders were fully dependent on the Emperor for their positions. The fact that churchmen were at least sometimes acquainted with Roman conceptions of the dignity of sovereign authority and of public administration made them especially valuable to the Emperor, since precedent for any assertion of imperial power could readily be found in Roman law. Churchmen also had a near monopoly of literacy, and even semibarbarian governments required the services of men who could read and write.

In France practice varied widely. The duke of Normandy controlled ecclesiastical appointments in his duchy, and other feudal princes exercised similar powers within their own territories. However, some bishoprics and abbeys remained fair game for dispute between ambitious noble families of the neighborhood, and some, notably the archbishopric of Reims, were under royal influence.

Local religious duties were of course entrusted to parish priests. These were usually appointed by the lord of the manor on which they officiated, and were frequently men of little or no education. Nonetheless, the Church continued to make steady progress in extending the number of parishes, and in combating pagan practices among the peasantry during the tenth and eleventh centuries.

As may readily be imagined, the Church was not infrequently demoralized under feudal conditions. Many bishops and abbots could scarcely be distinguished from their fellow nobles as far as their conduct was concerned. Most parish priests were married despite the prohibitions of Church law. Pious men were troubled by these and other shortcomings, and efforts were made to correct them. The most important such effort dates from 910, when the duke of Aquitaine in southern France founded a monastery at Cluny. By the provisions of its charter the monastery of Cluny was expressly exempted from all secular control. The monks were to choose their abbot according to the Rule of St. Benedict, without external interference, and were subject only to the pope in Rome. This monastery soon became the center of a movement for Church reform. Other monasteries associated themselves with Cluny, adopted its rules, and accepted priors, appointed by the abbot of Cluny, as their heads. Eventually more than three hundred Cluniac monasteries came into existence, scattered widely through Western Europe; and since the Cluniac monks quickly established a reputation for piety and holiness, the reformed monasteries speedily attracted the gifts of pious or repentant men who felt the need of the monks' prayers on their behalf. Thus the congregation of Cluny, as the association of monasteries was called, came to enjoy great wealth and wide influence.

The Cluniac monks used their position to criticize the abuses of the feudalized Church, attacking at every opportunity the twin evils of simony and lay investiture. (Simony was the name given to the purchase of Church offices in contravention of canon law; lay investiture meant the installation of an ecclesiastic in his office and lands by a layman.) Celibacy of the clergy was also strenuously advocated by the reformers of Cluny.

As long as the papacy itself remained the plaything of petty nobles of the city of Rome, the Cluniac reform movement was mainly limited to monastic affairs. Some monks trained in the Cluniac monasteries became bishops and tried to apply their principles to the secular branch of the Church; but their efforts were not very successful, since only unusually pious laymen were willing to renounce the powers and perquisites that came to them through the control of ecclesiastical appointments. Thus the Cluniac reform made little progress outside monastic walls until after the reorganization and revival of the papacy which occurred in the second half of the eleventh century.

The beginning of papal revival came largely as a consequence of the intervention of the German Emperors. Otto the Great, like Charlemagne before him, had constituted himself judge over a pope accused of malfeasance. In fact, he actually deposed one pope and installed his own secretary instead. On several occasions succeeding German emperors did likewise, but their control over the papacy, like their control over Italy in general, was sporadic, enforced only by occasional armed expeditions from the north. Nevertheless, it remains true that the popes appointed by the German emperors were in most instances men of some moral and personal worth. The most famous of them was Silvester II (999–1003) who, as Gerbert of Aurillac, had won fame as a scholar before becoming pope. The papacy, however, remained enmeshed in the degrading quarrels of Italian and Roman politics; and until after the middle of the eleventh century the efforts of individual reforming popes were largely nullified by the behavior of others who, as nominees of one or another noble faction in Rome, used their office mainly for the benefit of the unscrupulous men who had won it for them.

c. Beginnings of Cultural Revival

Definite signs of cultural revival in Western Europe prior to A.D. 1000 were not numerous, but in the first half of the eleventh century new interest and activity in education, architecture and music foreshadowed the much fuller growth of the succeeding two centuries.

The tenth century was not completely barren, however. By A.D. 1000 missionaries had succeeded in converting the Scandinavian rulers to

Christianity, and similar success met missionary efforts in Hungary. The Church also maintained educational institutions preserving a trickle of classical learning. Monastic schools, prominent in earlier times, tended to give way to schools organized by bishops, known as cathedral schools. Gerbert of Aurillac (later Pope Silvester II) presided over the cathedral school of Reims from 972 to 982 and made it one of the most advanced centers of study in Western Christendom. As a young man Gerbert had studied in Spain, where he had come into contact with Arabic learning. Some of it he mastered and brought with him to Reims, where his knowledge of the abacus and possession of an armillary sphere (i.e., a model of the Ptolemaic universe) sufficed to give him a reputation as a magician.

One of the earliest expressions of cultural revival was the reappearance of building in stone. Skill in stone working was developed first of all for the construction of more elaborate and secure fortifications. During the eleventh century mounds and stockades were quite generally replaced by stout towers of stone, sometimes surrounded by a ditch which might be filled with water if a stream could be diverted for the purpose. Since the power and security of a feudal noble frequently depended on his ability to retire to such a castle when attacked by superior forces, every member of the feudal aristocracy was eager to construct for himself as impregnable a refuge as possible. As a result, hundreds of stone castles were built in the early eleventh century.

Stone building was also used for the construction of monumental churches. Shortly before 1050 a new style, called romanesque, began to develop. As the name implies, romanesque building used methods of construction derived from Roman architecture, in particular the semicircular arch. In early romanesque churches arches were round, and the roof (when not of wood) was constructed by the simple method of broadening an arch to make what is called a barrel vault. The ground plan of romanesque churches was derived from the Roman basilica, with the addition of a transept to make it cruciform. The full elaboration of the romanesque style, it should be emphasized, did not come until several decades after the period here under consideration.

Another activity in which monasteries and churches took a leading part was the development of polyphonic, measured music. Chants and singing, of course, constituted an important part of the Church services. In earlier centuries the voices sang in unison. Polyphony started as a separation of the voices by fixed intervals (a fifth, fourth or octave); then innovators began to vary the melodies sung by the different voices to produce a variable series of chords. To keep the voices together required some sort of system for measuring notes, and the development of musical notation. Polyphonic music of this kind began to develop in the tenth century, although it reached a wider and fuller variety later.

Literary activity was at a low ebb between 900 and 1050. Yet many pious stories of the lives of saints and a number of historical chronicles from the period have survived. Undoubtedly a vigorous oral tradition of epic poetry flourished in the courts of feudal nobles and among the Vikings' descendants, but written examples of such poetry all date from the twelfth century or later.

2. THE HIGH MIDDLE AGES, 1050–1270

---

a. Introductory
b. Economic Changes
   1) Revival of Town Life
   2) Impact of Towns on Medieval Society
c. New Political Forms
   1) Expansion of Europe
   2) Rise of the Papacy to Political Preeminence
      a) The Papacy and Empire
      b) The Rise of the Kingdoms of France and England
      c) The Papacy as Head of an International Government
d. Cultural Growth
   1) Religion
   2) Art
   3) Literature
   4) Music
   5) Education
   6) Philosophy and Theology
   7) Natural Science

---

a. Introductory

During the eleventh, twelfth, and thirteenth centuries a new and brilliant civilization arose in western Europe, emerging from the crudity, ignorance and poverty of the preceding age. The most distinctive characteristic of that civilization was the prominence of the Church in nearly every aspect of life. Political developments in the various states of Europe were all powerfully affected by the policies of the rulers of the Church. Indeed the Church became a government in its own right, centrally controlled by the popes. Cultural expression, too, was dominated by the Church and by religion. The cathedrals, education, and scholastic theology all reflect the dominion which the Church and religion exercised over men's minds and hearts. Economic life was distinguished by the rapid growth of trading and manufacturing towns, which injected a new and powerful leaven into the earlier agrarian society. Indeed, the history of the High Middle Ages may be studied as the interaction of the influence of towns and townsmen on the one hand, and of the Church, particularly of the papacy, on the other. Between them, these two elements—the one economic, the other religious—transformed medieval society, raising it from semibarbarism to the plane of a flourishing civilization.

b. Economic Changes

1) Revival of Town Life. Beginning about 1050, western Europe became the scene of a rapid development of towns, inhabited and governed by merchants and artisans. The connection between the towns of Roman and

those of medieval times has been much debated by scholars, and valid generalizations are difficult. Many medieval towns arose on old Roman sites, and some sort of settlement undoubtedly persisted unbrokenly in several such towns. Roman fortifications were used continuously as places of refuge or as administrative centers for a bishop or count. But such "towns" did not perform the economic functions which we associate with the word. They did not serve as places of exchange and manufacture, save when some band of traveling peddlers, traders or artisans happened to stop there briefly for the protection which walls and established authority might afford them. The mercantile and artisan populations which came to live in medieval towns during the eleventh century probably originated (in northern Europe at least) when itinerant traders and workmen settled down. As business picked up, they found it possible to establish permanent headquarters at some favorable spot where communication, a market, and the security of walls were available.

Trade never disappeared in western Europe. It had existed from neolithic times; and the manor of early western history was never completely self-sufficient. Iron for plowshares and tools, salt, and mill stones were necessities which usually had to come from outside. The knightly class had need of arms and armor which could only be manufactured by skilled craftsmen; and luxuries such as wine, jewelry and fine cloth, hunting dogs, falcons and strong warhorses were always in demand through Europe's most stormy and poverty-stricken days. And when other exports failed, Europeans offered slaves captured in war in return for such goods.

Thus after 1050 there was not so much a revival as a rapid expansion of trade. The rapidity with which towns grew can be partly attributed to the settling down of artisans—smiths and metalworkers especially—and of merchants who had previously led a semivagrant life, moving from one noble household to another, or from fair to fair. Once towns had begun to function as centers of exchange, other kinds of artisans found purchasers who preferred the more expert product of professional weavers, carpenters, shoemakers, etc., to the rough handicraft of some manorial jack-of-all-trades. Thus towns came to serve as a focus for local exchanges of goods and services, and in proportion, manors became less and less self-sufficient.

But equally important, and probably more profitable, was the long-distance exchange of commodities. This sort of trade, which had shrunk to a small trickle during the eighth and ninth centuries, underwent a very rapid expansion in the eleventh. Western Europe began to import a variety of finely manufactured goods from Byzantium and the Arab lands, and in exchange exported raw and semifinished goods such as timber, furs, fish, woolen cloth, iron and other metals.

Obviously Italy occupied a strategic middleman's position for such trade. Town life survived more strongly in Italy than in other parts of western Europe, and as early as the tenth century, Venice, at the head of the Adriatic Sea, took a leading part in commerce with Byzantium. About the beginning of the eleventh century Genoa, Pisa and Amalfi, on the west coast of Italy, successfully challenged Arab sea power and soon began to rival the Venetians. The Italians were mainly middlemen at first. It was not long, however, before Italian workmen began to imitate the fine products of the east. Venice, for example, became famous for its glass during the twelfth century; and Florence became a center for the manufacture of fine cloth almost as early. Thus many of the artisan skills of the east were brought into western Europe and by degrees diffused northward from Italy.

Flanders was second only to Italy as an economic center. It lay at the point where the overland trade routes from Italy met the coastal commerce of the North Sea and Baltic coasts. This commerce was fed by numerous rivers: the Seine, Meuse, Thames, Humber, Rhine, Weser, Elbe and others, whose navigable portions tapped a very considerable part of western Europe. Consequently the juncture between Italian and northern trade routes in Flanders became the scene of extensive exchange. Flemish towns became great entrepôts; but their prosperity was due equally to the development of the cloth trade. Wool from England and elsewhere was woven into cloth by Flemish weavers who then exported their handiwork to all of Europe. Some of it was taken to Italy by Italian merchants to be "finished." In addition to their cloth manufacturing specialty, Flemish towns boasted numerous other industries, one of the most important of which was the curing of fish, caught in great numbers in the shallow waters of the North Sea.

The great towns of Flanders were Bruges, Ghent, Ypres, and Cambrai. Elsewhere in northern Europe large towns were relatively rare, but towns such as London, Paris, Rouen and Cologne became important mercantile and manufacturing centers in the course of the twelfth century; and there were hundreds of smaller ones. One must guard against exaggerating the size of medieval towns; an urban population as great as 25,000 was very exceptional in twelfth century Europe.

2) Impact of Towns on Medieval Society. Though the total number and population of the towns was not great, they were able to exercise important influence on the social relationships which had existed earlier. One obvious consequence was the spread of a money economy over a much wider area of human relationships. Peasants from manors near to the new towns could find a market for their surplus crops, and could buy such articles as cloth, iron, and salt in exchange. In some parts of Europe commercial farming made a beginning—for instance, great sheep runs arose in

northern England to supply the busy looms of Flanders. The feudal aristocracy came to desire the fine products of the East, and began to feel the need
for a money income in order to be able to buy such commodities. It became not uncommon for a feudal lord to commute some or even all of the
dues and services which manorial serfs owed him into money payments,
and to rent out the demesne land instead of farming it for his own consumption. Such an arrangement assured a money income to the lord and
freed the serfs from onerous burdens.

The rise of towns opened up a new way of making a living to any enterprising or discontented peasant. By running away from the manor on
which he was born and taking up residence in a town, it was possible to
escape from the lord's control: and since the towns were in the beginning
populated in considerable part by just such run-aways, the townspeople
protected such men as best they could. It became a general rule that residence in any town for a year and a day made a man free, and that no claim
by any feudal lord could even be considered after a lapse of such time.
Consequently, it became more necessary for a manorial lord to keep his
peasants as well content as possible. The result in the economically more
active parts of Europe was that the personal services of serfdom were
largely abolished or commuted to money payments by A.D. 1300.

The most immediate consequence of the rise of towns in the sphere of
politics was the appearance of a new, non-feudal type of government
within the towns themselves. Even itinerant merchants banded together
for mutual support and protection; and as permanent settlements arose
such associations began to take on the characteristics of a local government. The rules of a manorial court obviously were not suited to the life of
the merchants; and new forms of commercial law for the settlement of disputed contracts developed. Some sort of agreement had to be reached with
the feudal lord who happened to control the district in which the town
arose. In northern Europe the towns were seldom able to win complete independence of feudal superiors. A compromise was more usual, whereby
the lord agreed to respect certain special liberties of the townsmen in
return for which he was entitled to various forms of income—rents, a
proportion of the market tolls, a share in fines levied in the town courts,
etc. Indeed it soon dawned on feudal nobles that a town was a very valuable asset, and new towns were frequently founded by enterprising feudal
rulers, in the hope and expectation that a thriving community of merchants and artisans would bring them additional revenue. Such new towns
were granted charters in which the liberties of the burghers were set forth.
Other towns which had grown up by themselves generally acquired similar
charters by purchase or agreement with the feudal possessor of the land
on which they had formed.

The special liberties granted to the burghers by such charters varied from case to case. In general the townsmen were guaranteed personal freedom from manorial exactions, were allowed to buy, sell or bequeath land freely within the town limits (subject only to a quitrent payable to the lord), and were assured a commercial monopoly within some definite region round about. In France and England, the king early became a guarantor of many town privileges, and what amounted to an alliance between the royal power and the burghers came into existence, since the interests of each in general opposed the feudal nobility. This alliance became one of the essential elements in the consolidation of the national monarchies of France and England, and constituted an indirect political consequence of the rise of towns which was of fundamental importance.

In Germany and Italy, however, the economic and military strength of towns did not play an analogous role in support of the central imperial government. Instead, some towns were able to set up what were in effect sovereign governments of their own; in other cases towns remained subject to a local feudal prince. The towns of Italy are to be distinguished from those of other parts of Europe by the fact that the noble landowners quite generally came to live in the towns and became citizens themselves. The result was not always happy, for long standing family feuds were frequently transplanted within the city walls, and control of the town's government regularly became an object of rivalry among nobles. In northern Europe, by way of contrast, the feudal nobility remained aloof from the new bourgeois class and continued to live in the countryside.

As towns became more populous, internal affairs required the elaboration of town governments and gild associations. The forms which such governments and associations took were various, as would be expected. The earliest records show a single organization, the gild merchant, which concerned itself with all of the common affairs of townsmen. By degrees various crafts—shoemakers, weavers, costermongers, etc.—organized separately. The purpose was to protect their special occupational interests. Town government was at first scarcely differentiated from the gild merchant; at a later time, when the gild merchant had split into craft gilds, general concerns of all the townsmen were entrusted to elected officials. These magistrates administered justice among the townspeople, collected market tolls, looked after the walls, streets, and other public works, and represented the town in its dealings with outsiders, including the feudal lord and king. It must not be supposed, however, that medieval town government was democratic. Only some of the inhabitants took part in the selection of town officials, and in most instances a rather small oligarchy came to control the government.

Gilds were created to protect their members against the various dangers and vicissitudes which threatened them. Rules designed to prevent competition by non-members were almost universal; regulations as to prices and quality were also frequently imposed as a means of checking unfair practices. Protection of the consumer may sometimes have played a part in such regulations, although the ordinary gildsman was probably far more concerned with making his own living secure. Many gilds tried to keep all members as nearly as possible on an equal footing, and adopted regulations designed to prevent any one member from acquiring greater wealth than the others. But gilds were not only economic associations. A wide variety of social and religious activity was also carried on within their framework.

In the course of the thirteenth century regulations designed to assure the local monopoly of a gild quite generally resulted in the more or less permanent exclusion of certain individuals from membership, even though they might be fully skilled craftsmen. Such individuals, known as journeymen (i.e., day men) were employed by the gild members at fixed wages; and themselves sometimes formed associations designed to protect their peculiar interests. A third status in the fully developed gild system was that of apprentice. Apprentices were bound to gild members for a fixed number of years in order to learn the trade. After their apprenticeship was over, the more fortunate ones (usually those who could pay the admission fee) became members of the gild or masters; others remained journeymen throughout their lives.

Another line of distinction arose in the medieval towns between different gilds. Obviously goldsmiths, who often were bankers on the side, were normally wealthier and more influential than, for example, costermongers. The role of the various craft gilds in town government tended to reflect the wealth and prestige of the gild; but the local variations from town to town were very great and no general pattern for town government can be described.

Conflicts between members of different gilds, or between masters and journeymen of the same craft frequently arose, and sometimes led to internal troubles. These conflicts were most serious when, as in Italy, no feudal superior existed against whom all the townsmen were united by a common interest. Against outsiders the townsmen could usually unite. Contests between the feudal possessor of the ground on which a town was located and the burghers were common. Often the townsmen were able to settle disputes by purchasing new rights and exemptions thus increasing the scope of their sovereignty little by little. In France and England, however, the kings were able during the thirteenth century to encroach on some of the liberties of the towns, and began to collect taxes of various sorts from them.

The organization and attitudes of the Church were not adjusted to town conditions, and it was not until the beginning of the thirteenth century that ecclesiastics found effective answers to the problems town life offered to the older religious system. Selling a product at a marked up price was regarded by many Christian thinkers as a form of cheating; even more crucial was the fact that long-established teachings of the Church condemned usury, i.e., the taking of interest on money. Yet the commercial relations of merchants and craftsmen were based very largely on marked up prices and on lending and borrowing for interest. Moreover, diocesan and parish organization of the Church had been established when Europe was almost wholly agrarian, and the growth of new centers of population did not at once lead to a reorganization of parishes. As a result many medieval towns found themselves without an adequate number of priests. It was not until the establishment of the Franciscan and Dominican orders of friars (early thirteenth century) that this lack was remedied.

The rather unsympathetic attitude of many churchmen, and the contact with foreign regions and new ideas which the mercantile life involved, led to the appearance of a number of heresies in western Europe during the twelfth century. One may distinguish, almost from the beginning, two opposing religious attitudes which appealed to many townsmen. Some individuals developed a worldly and more or less irreligious (or at least anti-clerical) point of view; others were impatient with compromise and tried to recover a more rigorous, purer religion, and frequently tried to model themselves directly on the life of Christ and the apostles. These opposing reactions to town conditions were present throughout the High Middle Ages, and foreshadowed the later movements of the renaissance and the reformation respectively.

In the twelfth and thirteenth centuries the most important group of heretics was the Cathari or Albigenses. The movement had its strongest support in southern France. The ideas promulgated by the Cathari (the name means "the purified ones") had come from the east, and were probably descended from Manicheanism, though with many changes and alterations through the centuries. Other groups sought a return to apostolic Christianity and fell into heresy through their opposition to various practices of the Church. The Waldenses and the Humiliati (i.e., the humbled ones) were two such sects of the late twelfth century. These movements uniformly found their most receptive audience among the townspeople; but their development was arrested by vigorous countermeasures undertaken by the Church in the early thirteenth century.

The influence of towns on art and thought can be appreciated when one reflects that the gothic cathedrals and the universities of the thirteenth century were both urban products. Thus not only in economic relations, but in politics and culture too, the growth of towns introduced a new stimulus of profound importance. From the twelfth century to the present, town dwellers have been the leaders of European civilization in nearly all its aspects.

c. New Political Forms

1) Expansion of Europe. Beginning about 1050 European warriors and settlers began to encroach on neighboring peoples in all directions. In the northeast, a number of German feudal princes carried on aggressive war against the pagan Slavic tribes who lived between the Elbe and Oder. Settlers were systematically brought in from western Germany and planted on new manors. This eastward expansion of Germany was checked only in the fourteenth century, as a consequence of the development of formidable kingdoms—Poland, Bohemia—among the Slavs themselves. In order to survive these states adopted many of the characteristics of western organization. A similar process of acculturation brought Hungary within the limits of Latin Christendom during the eleventh and later centuries.

To the south in Spain a similar expansion occurred. Despite the great cultural superiority of the Moorish rulers of the Iberian peninsula, Christian knights succeeded in steadily pushing back the limits of Mohammedan control. The process was not completed until 1492 when the last Moorish stronghold was captured; but long before then most of Spain had been recovered for western Christendom.

The Normans took an especially active part in European expansion. In 1066 William, Duke of Normandy, led an army of about 5000 knights across the channel and conquered England. The Norman conquest had the effect of connecting England firmly with the rest of Western Europe, and thenceforth its cultural insularity came to an end. An even more brilliant conquest was the subjugation of southern Italy and Sicily by irregular Norman bands, under the leadership of Robert Guiscard and his brother Roger de Hauteville. The conquest took several decades and was completed by 1091. Previously, Sicily had been ruled by Moslems, and southern Italy had been divided between Lombard and Byzantine control. Under the capable Norman rulers of the de Hauteville family a strong, unified state emerged, which by virtue of its geographic position and the mixed Arab, Greek, Lombard and Italian population which inhabited it, became one of the principal channels through which acquaintance with the arts and ideas of Arab and Byzantine civilization reached western Europe. This Norman state was also to play an important role in Italian politics.

The most spectacular early step in the expansion of Europe was the conquest of the eastern Mediterranean coast as a result of the First Crusade (1096–99). The Crusade was proclaimed by Pope Urban II. A motley feudal army responded to his summons. Knights and princes from all parts of Europe, but mainly from France, participated in the Crusade. Despite much ignorance of the terrain and bad management, the knights succeeded in capturing Jerusalem, where they established a feudal state on European models. Not only Jerusalem but the entire eastern coast of the Mediterranean was taken over by a series of similar crusaders' states. It

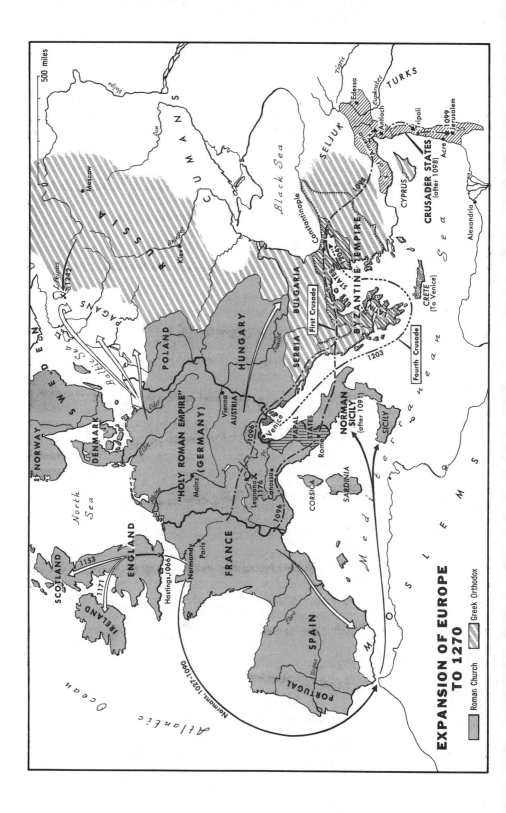

500 miles

Volga

Don

Dnieper

Tigris

Euphrates

TURKS

Edessa

Antioch

Tripoli

1099

Jerusalem

Acre

CRUSADER STATES
(after 1098)

CYPRUS

Alexandria

Moscow

RUSSIA

Kiev

CUMANS

PAGANS

Lake Peipus
1242

Black Sea

SELJUK

Constantinople

1098

BYZANTINE EMPIRE

First Crusade

SLAVS

LATIN

CRETE
(To Venice)

Fourth Crusade

1203

SERBIA

BULGARIA

HUNGARY

POLAND

Oder

Elbe

Vienna

AUSTRIA

Danube

1096

Venice

Po

PAPAL
STATES

Rome

NORMAN
SICILY
(after 109

SICILY

SWEDEN

NORWAY

DENMARK

Baltic Sea

North
Sea

"HOLY ROMAN EMPIRE"
(GERMANY)

Mainz

Legnano
1176

Canossa

1096

SARDINIA

CORSICA

Mediterranean

Sea

M U S L E M S

SCOTLAND

1153

1171

IRELAND

ENGLAND

Hastings, 1066

Normandy

Paris

Rhine

FRANCE

Ebro

Tagus

SPAIN

PORTUGAL

Atlantic Ocean

Normans, 1027-1090

EXPANSION OF EUROPE
TO 1270

▨ Roman Church

▨ Greek Orthodox

may be noted in passing that the success of the First Crusade was made possible not only by the knights of Christendom, but also by the Italian merchants who brought supplies to the crusading army at a most critical juncture, when it was besieging the city of Antioch. In return for this help, the Italian cities were granted extensive trading privileges in the regions the Crusaders captured.

The motives which impelled the Crusaders to embark on their venture were mixed. Religious enthusiasm, stirred up by the pope and by numerous preachers, played a decisive part. The aim of the Crusade was to free the Holy Land from Moslem rule, and Crusaders were promised absolution from their sins as a consequence of their service. Other motives, of course, were added to religious ones: the spirit of adventure, the hope of carving out new estates and principalities (especially attractive to younger sons of the feudal nobility who were largely disinherited by the principle of primogeniture), the diplomacy of the Byzantine emperors who needed military help against the Turks, and, to some small extent, the commercial ambitions of a few Italian towns all contributed to the First Crusade. Yet, when due allowance is made for these subsidiary motives, it still seems safe to regard the First Crusade as a striking example of the power of the Church and of Christian ideals to inspire military and political action.

It is even more difficult to assess the consequences of the First, and subsequent, Crusades. Numerous knights, pilgrims, sailors and merchants were brought into contact with the manifold wonders of the east, and doubtless brought back new tastes and ideas when they returned home. The success of the First Crusade greatly increased the prestige of the papacy in western Europe. It also may have helped to improve the peace of the countryside by drawing off the more turbulent knights. The crusades reinforced the ideal of Christian, chivalrous knighthood, an ideal which by degrees mollified the violence and brutality of European fighting men, hedging them round with an elaborate code of knightly honor. And the crusades certainly promoted the rise and increased the prosperity of Italian cities, whose ships carried supplies, pilgrims, and reinforcements to the Holy Land. But it would be an exaggeration to suppose that the Crusades alone caused these various manifestations of the growth and expansion of Europe.

The linkage of commercial, military and religious expansion is most clearly illustrated by the history of the Fourth Crusade (1202–04) which started for the Holy Land but was diverted by Venetian pressure to Constantinople instead, where the Crusaders succeeded in capturing the Byzantine capital, a feat which earlier attackers had never been able to accomplish. As in Palestine a century before, feudal states were carved out of the former Byzantine territory, and the Venetians reaped a rich reward of commercial monopolies and extraterritorial rights.

The unexpected outcome of the Fourth Crusade, which turned its arms against a Christian state instead of fighting the Moslems, marked a stage in the degeneration of the crusading ideal. In later times the popes proclaimed numerous crusades not only against infidels, but against political opponents of the papacy within Europe. The effectiveness of the crusading idea gradually declined, but it did not entirely disappear until the sense of the unity of Christendom and the acknowledgment of papal leadership of Christendom had been supplanted by the rise of national states and national patriotism.

2) The Rise of the Papacy to Political Preeminence. The relation between the Christian Church and secular rulers had been in dispute almost from the first days of Christian history. In the two hundred years between 1050 and 1250 the issue took a new form when a number of vigorous popes, supported by the piety of clergy and laymen alike, were able to assert papal control over ecclesiastical and political life in nearly all parts of Europe. Papal claims to political power took various forms, according to circumstance and the character of individual popes. Every pope strove to secure effective control of the church organization, which, in an age when bishops and abbots controlled a large proportion of the land of western Europe, carried with it enormous political and economic power. Some popes advanced even more exalted claims, arguing that the pope was the rightful sovereign of all Christians. Not all medieval popes aspired to such political eminence, and no pope was ever able to translate the ideal completely into practice; yet the hope of reducing all Europe's rulers to Christian obedience inspired the actions and fired the imaginations of the greatest and most active medieval popes. These efforts plunged the papacy directly into the maelstrom of politics and war throughout the High Middle Ages.

a) The Papacy and the Empire. From the time of Charlemagne and Otto the Great there had been emperors in the West who regarded themselves as the legitimate political heirs of the Roman emperors of antiquity. To be sure, the territory under direct imperial overlordship did not include the kingdoms of France and England to the west, the kingdoms of Denmark, Norway and Sweden to the north, nor the kingdoms of Hungary and Poland to the east; yet a great belt of territory, including not only Germany and northern and central Italy, but modern Bohemia, Austria, Switzerland, Belgium, Holland and a large slice of what is today eastern France recognized the overlordship of the Emperor in some fashion or other. Obviously, therefore, papal claims to the political leadership of western Christendom found their most immediate rival in the person of successive bearers of the imperial title.

Indeed, in the eleventh century, when papal authority was first successfully asserted against the emperors the movement had something of the nature of a revolution. In the days of Charlemagne and Otto, emperors had as a matter of course appointed, deposed or confirmed popes just as they did other powerful bishops. Yet such procedures were difficult to reconcile with canon law, which prescribed that election to vacant bishoprics should be made by the clergy of the diocese; and in the course of the tenth and eleventh centuries, many pious men, clergy and laymen alike, came to believe that the prevalent corruption and degradation of the Church could not be remedied as long as laymen had the power to appoint prelates, and especially as long as they sold such offices to unworthy candidates. Simony, as this latter practice was called, and lay investiture seemed, especially to the monks of the Cluniac monasteries, the principal obstacles to the reform and purification of the Church.

From the imperial point of view, however, such a reform was difficult to reconcile with traditional powers and methods of administration. Bishops and abbots held extensive lands, and the right to appoint men to such offices brought a substantial income and influence to the imperial court. Even more basic was the fact that the imperial government depended very largely upon the administrative services of clergymen: or put the other way round, the emperors were able to pay their loyal servants by appointing them to church offices, and had no easy or obvious substitute source of income with which to maintain a loyal body of administrative subordinates. Full accomplishment of the papal reform program might improve the spiritual quality of the Church, but it was also sure to destroy the existing basis of imperial power. The ground was thus laid for a mighty collision between papacy and Empire, Church and state.

Before the reformers could effectively challenge established practices, it was first necessary to secure the independence of the papacy itself from imperial control. Two changes made in 1059 accomplished this first step. In that year, a synod spelled out the canonical method for the election of popes. A college of Cardinals was established, whose members had the right to elect a new pope, and a majority of the new body belonged to the reformist, anti-imperial persuasion. This assured that future popes would not be imperial servants or puppets, but instead would champion the claims of the Church to become independent of lay control.

In the same year, the papacy concluded an alliance with the upstart Norman rulers of southern Italy. The Norman adventurer, Robert Guiscard, had come to southern Italy as a simple knight, but by force, fraud, personal prowess and good fortune he had, by 1059, become de-facto ruler of a powerful, compact state in southern Italy. Yet Guiscard needed legitimation and the pope needed military help. An agreement was therefore mutually advantageous, and took the form of a feudal enfeoffment: that is, the Norman adventurer formally recognized the overlordship of the pope and swore to be his good and faithful man, and the pope in turn formally granted Guiscard the right to rule what he had already won by his sword. This arrangement assured potent military support for the papacy in any future collision with the emperors; and with its newly gained prestige, the papacy was speedily able to challenge and undermine imperial authority in northern Italy, and, indeed, in Germany itself.

The conflict came to a head when in 1073 a Tuscan peasant's son, Hildebrand, became pope and assumed the name of Gregory VII. Hildebrand had been the moving spirit of papal policy for nearly twenty-five years before his elevation to the papal throne. He was a man of fiery temperament, wholly devoted to the reform program, and convinced that the pope was by right the ruler of all Christendom and the direct representative of God on earth. As pope, Gregory VII bent all his energies to make his vision of papal power come true. The first step was to bring the German prelates and the emperor, Henry IV, to obedience. Accordingly, in 1075 Gregory called a synod to consider the disordered state of Germany. At this synod lay investiture of clerics was prohibited, and a number of Henry's advisers and supporters were laid under threat of excommunication if they did not promptly make their peace with the pope and abandon their sinful ways.

The emperor was in no mood to accept the papal program and flatly refused to cooperate. Gregory responded by formally deposing Henry, and absolving all his vassals of their oaths of obedience. The result was a widespread revolt against the emperor in Germany. Henry was unable to suppress it, and in 1077 found it expedient to make his peace with the pope. Despite the winter snows, Henry crossed the Alps, and arriving at the small Italian town of Canossa, stood humbly penitent and barefoot in the snow, until after three days the pope finally condescended to receive him and grant him absolution. The scene at Canossa became a symbol of the prestige and power which the papacy had acquired. At the time, however, it was a dubious victory, for when Gregory absolved Henry and reinstated him as emperor, the feudal lords of Germany who had revolted at the pope's instigation were left to face Henry's wrath. In spite of Gregory's efforts on their behalf, Henry reasserted his authority over nearly all Germany by 1080.

This done, the emperor turned his attention to Italy. First, an assemblage of German prelates, picked by Henry for the purpose, declared Gregory to be deposed. Then in 1081 Henry invaded Italy with the intention of installing a new pope and reestablishing imperial power in the peninsula. There followed three years of fighting in Italy. The emperor occupied Rome for a few months in 1084 and drove Gregory from the city; but the arrival of Guiscard's Norman forces from the south turned the balance and compelled the emperor to withdraw, though not before the Normans had burnt and sacked the city. The inhabitants of Rome were so enraged at the behavior of these champions of the papacy that Gregory did not dare to remain in the city after the Normans departed, and instead withdrew to Salerno where he died in the next year (1085).

Although Henry IV survived his papal enemy by more than twenty years, he was not able to carry through any of his projects for strengthening the imperial power. While he was fighting in Italy fresh revolts broke out in Germany and he had to abandon his half-completed Italian conquests to hasten home. Until his death in 1106 sporadic warfare continued to torment the German state, and Henry's power in Italy nearly disappeared. Successive popes supported the German rebels, and Henry died under the excommunication of the papacy.

The dispute dragged on between papal and imperial successors until 1122, when a compromise was agreed upon in the Concordat of Worms. According to its terms, episcopal elections in Germany were to be conducted in accordance with the canon law, but were to be held in the presence of the emperor or his representative. Moreover, the emperor was accorded the right to invest the newly elected bishop with the *regalia* (i.e., the lands and temporal powers' of his office while the competent prelate of the Church invested him with the *spiritualia* (religious powers).

The net result of this round in the conflict between papacy and empire was thus a qualified victory for the papacy. The unquestioned control which earlier emperors had exercised over ecclesiastical appointments was diluted; the papacy itself as well as Italy were, at least for the time being, exempted from imperial control; and within Germany powerful assistance had been given to the various feudal lords and princes who constantly strove to extend their powers at the expense of the emperor.

Following the conclusion of the Concordat of Worms there ensued a period of comparative calm in the relations between pope and emperor. The direct imperial line died out in 1125. For several decades rival families disputed the imperial position: on the one side there was the Hohenstaufen (or Waibling) family and rivaling it were the Welfs. Germany began to divide into something resembling two rival parties, and each devised a doctrine of political legitimacy to support its cause. The Hohenstaufens claimed to be the heirs of universal imperial power, descended unbroken from the Romans, and granted directly by God without the mediation of any pope. In opposition, the Welfs took up and championed papal claims. In fact the Hohenstaufen emperors, like their predecessors, remained German kings whose claims to universal power over a "Holy Roman Empire" (as their state soon came to be called) were only dreams. But they were dreams that inspired action; and a "Roman" emperor's first goal, after securing his power at home, was control of the city of Rome and of Italy. Thus what had begun as a scramble for power between German feudal families was translated into German and Italian politics at large.

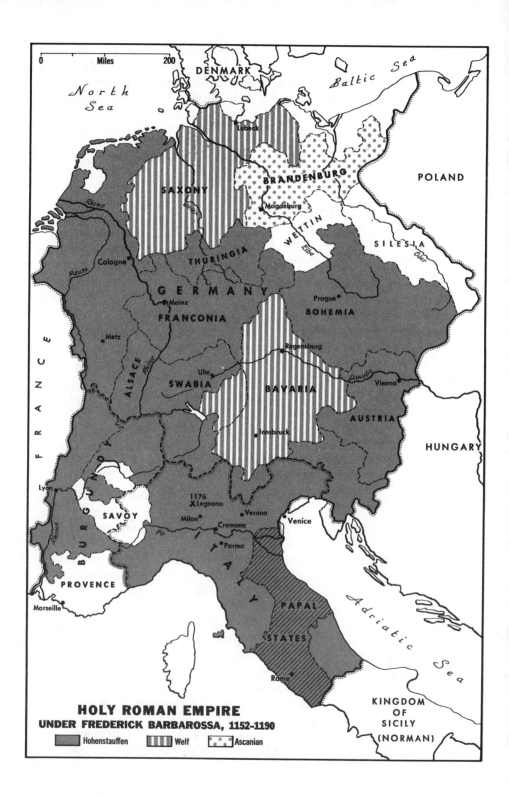

Miles
0   200

DENMARK

Baltic Sea

North
Sea

POLAND

SAXONY

Lubeck

BRANDENBURG

WETTIN

Magdeburg

SILESIA

Rhine

Cologne

THURINGIA

GERMANY

Elbe

Oder

Meuse

FRANCONIA

Mainz

BOHEMIA

Prague

Metz

ALSACE

Rhine

SWABIA

Ulm

Regensburg

BAVARIA

Danube

Vienna

FRANCE

AUSTRIA

Innsbruck

HUNGARY

BURGUNDY

Lyon

SAVOY

1176
X Legnano

Milan

Verona

Venice

Rhone

I

Cremona

Po

T

Parma

A

PROVENCE

L

Y

Marseille

PAPAL

Adriatic
Sea

STATES

Rome

KINGDOM
OF
SICILY
(NORMAN)

HOLY ROMAN EMPIRE
UNDER FREDERICK BARBAROSSA, 1152-1190

Hohenstauffen   Welf   Ascanian

In Italy Welf and Waibling were transliterated as Guelf and Ghibelline, and local factions adopted the appropriate label depending on whether they attached themselves to the papal or to the imperial side.

When the Hohenstaufen Frederick Barbarossa (Red Beard) secured election to the throne of Germany in 1152 the quarrel seemed momentarily to be ended, for he was related to the Welfs on his mother's side, and inaugurated his reign by making peace with that family. The cessation of quarrels in Germany left him free to attempt a genuine subjugation of Italy—a program which the popes were bound to resist with every means at their disposal. The popes now had two powerful allies, the Normans of the south, and the rising towns of Lombardy in the north. Many of the Lombard towns had been able to throw off the control of feudal superiors and were well on the way toward becoming sovereign city states. To the Emperor Frederick Barbarossa, such communities seemed rebellious upstarts, and in 1158 he invaded Italy in order to reduce them and the papacy to obedience.

For the next eighteen years a bitter struggle raged between Pope Alexander III and Frederick Barbarossa. The emperor won several military victories, but was never able to hold Italy securely. Moreover, Alexander was able to stir up again the embers of the Welf-Hohenstaufen quarrel in Germany, thus undermining Barbarossa's power at home. In 1176 a decisive battle was fought at Legnano, where the armies of the Lombard cities (which had formed themselves, with papal support, into a league) met and defeated the imperial German army. This battle is an important one in military history. At Legnano, disciplined infantry, equipped with pikes and cross bows, for the first time proved capable of withstanding the charge of heavy armed knights. Barbarossa's feudal cavalry vainly threw itself against the massed points of the heavy pikes, whose hafts were planted securely on the ground. Thus the battle of Legnano marks the end of the unchallenged supremacy of the mounted knight on the battlefield, although it was centuries before armies of knights were entirely discredited. Legnano also worked a decisive change in the struggle between empire and papacy. After his defeat, Frederick gave up hope of reestablishing full imperial control of Italy. He arranged a peace with the pope in 1177, and made a truce with his other Italian enemies—the Lombard League and the Normans of Sicily. In 1183 he signed a peace with the Lombard cities (Peace of Constance) which accorded the towns of northern Italy a wide autonomy. Three years later Frederick also came to terms with the Normans and seemed likely to reverse the entire balance of forces in Italy by marrying his son to the heiress of the Kingdom of Sicily (as the Norman state was now known.).

The emperor did not, however, revive the struggle in Italy, preferring perhaps to wait until his son could inherit the resources of the Norman kingdom and add them to the imperial power. Instead, in 1189 Frederick Barbarossa, as befitted the leader and would-be suzerain of Europe, put himself at the head of the Third Crusade. The Moslems, under the capable leadership of Saladin, ruler of Egypt, had overthrown the Christian states established in Palestine and neighboring regions by the First Crusade. This loss precipitated a combined operation, in which Frederick, Richard Coeur de Lion, King of England, and Philip Augustus, King of France, led crusading hosts against the infidels. Frederick himself was drowned in a small river of Asia Minor before he could reach the Holy Land (1190). Despite the magnitude of the undertaking as compared with the First Crusade and the chivalry of Richard Coeur de Lion, the fact that this time the Moslems were united and led by a capable military leader prevented the crusaders from capturing Jerusalem. In 1192 a truce was patched up by which Christians were assured free access to the Holy City, but nothing more was gained.

The rather inglorious result of the Third Crusade had little effect on the struggle between empire and papacy. Barbarossa's son, Henry VI (1190–97), succeeded in making good his claim to the Norman kingdom in spite of a widespread diplomatic and military coalition against him. For a while it seemed possible that a powerful, centralized state might arise as a result of the efforts of Barbarossa and his son; but Henry's sudden death in 1197 cut short the development of imperial strength. Henry VI left as heir a four year old child, Frederick (later Emperor Frederick II), who became king of Sicily but did not immediately succeed to the imperial title. Instead, Germany was once more torn between two rival factions, each of which elected its own emperor. The newly installed pope, Innocent III (1198–1216), found himself in the position of being able to play one emperor off against the other, exacting promises and concessions from each in turn.

During the course of the twelfth century a significant change had come over the German imperial administration. Before the outbreak of the investiture controversy in 1075, as we saw, the emperors had depended heavily on the service of bishops, abbots and other clergymen to administer the empire. After the time of Gregory VII the emperors could no longer safely rely on the obediance of the ecclesiastics of Germany, and a new basis for the administration had to be found. The Hohenstaufen emperors therefore adopted a policy of awarding small estates to commoners, mostly soldiers. These so-called *ministeriales* served the emperor directly without any feudal intermediary. In addition, the rudiments of a salaried bureaucracy began to develop, staffed partly by *ministeriales*, and partly by lawyers trained in Roman law.

As long as Frederick Barbarossa and his son Henry VI ruled, this system worked fairly well; but when Henry died, the great feudal nobles, both secular and ecclesiastical, were able to defy the rudimentary administrative machine which the Hohenstaufen emperors had begun to build up. Heirs of the *ministeriales* became "imperial knights" whose only political superior was an emperor whom they no longer always troubled to obey. Under these circumstances, the apparently impressive success of the Hohenstaufen emperors crumbled very rapidly, and Germany came to be an aggregation of states, large and small, ecclesiastical and secular. The towns, which in France and England constituted the backbone of the royal power by supplying taxes and moral support to the central government, either fell under the control of some local prince, or asserted their own effective sovereignty as free imperial cities. Thus the combination of papal opposition, imperial policy and the ambitions of local princes, landowners and cities resulted in the almost total dissipation of central power in Germany at the beginning of the thirteenth century.

The emperor Frederick II (1211–50, son of Henry VI), did not even try to pick up the broken pieces. Lords both lay and ecclesiastical were transformed into petty sovereigns by Frederick's grant of "privileges" to them in 1220 and again in 1231. This gesture simply abandoned nearly all of the regalian rights to which earlier emperors had clung. From then on Germany became, not a single state, but a collection of states bound together in name but scarcely in fact by a common fealty to the emperor.

Frederick's action in Germany was not the result of weakness or incapacity on his part. Rather he was interested in his Norman inheritance, and hoped to construct a strong and united Italian state on the basis of his power as king of Sicily. Abandoning Germany meant for him simply the relinquishment of claims which it would be difficult to enforce in any case, and which it would be impossible to enforce if he were to concentrate attention on building up his power in Italy.

But Frederick's plans for Italy once more aroused the bitter hostility of the popes. Innocent III died in 1216 before Frederick revealed (or perhaps formulated) his ambition; but the succeeding popes were all imbued with the ideal of papal supremacy over all the rulers of Christendom which Innocent III had done so much to translate into practical politics, and they vigorously resisted every move Frederick made to consolidate an Italian kingdom. The details of the long dispute cannot here be described. The most bizarre incident was the successful crusade which Frederick led while under papal excommunication (1228–29). By diplomacy and mere show of force he persuaded the Saracen ruler to cede Jerusalem, Nazareth and Bethlehem to him, thus reestablishing Christian control of the Holy Places.

The struggle between Frederick II and the popes was different from the earlier contests of empire and papacy in a number of important respects. Instead of feudal armies, Frederick relied mainly upon paid armies of mercenaries; the popes fought him with equally mercenary armies, and were driven to seek support from the rising strength of the English and French monarchies. As long as Frederick lived, he met with considerable success. His heirs, however, could not maintain themselves in the face of papal hostility. In 1266 the last of them was driven from Sicily by a French expedition; and Charles of Anjou, brother to the French king, became king of Sicily.

Thus the conflict between papacy and empire came finally to an end. The empire had been destroyed as an effective government. After an interregnum when there was no emperor even in name, a petty noble, Rudolph of Hapsburg, was elected to the imperial throne in 1273. He followed Frederick's example of abandoning attempts at central control, and instead used his imperial dignity to acquire a promising private inheritance when the holder of the Bavarian East Mark, or, as it is better known, of Austria, died without heirs.

b) The Rise of the Kingdoms of France and England. In overthrowing the Hohenstaufen emperors the papacy seemed to have gained a great victory. There was no longer any rival who challenged papal claims to the universal headship of Christendom; but just as the power of the emperors had proved fragile even when it seemed most secure, so also did the universal power of the papacy prove fragile when it came into collision with the national monarchies of France and England, which had slowly been consolidating themselves while emperor and pope were locked in mortal combat.

The kingdom of France had its origin in the division of the Carolingian empire among Charlemagne's grandsons, one of whom fell heir to the most westerly portion of the Frankish state, but continued to style himself king of Francia (i.e., land of the Franks) or, as it later came to be written, of France. The chaos of the ninth and tenth centuries eradicated the power of the French kings from all parts of the kingdom except for a family patrimony, the Île de France.

From this low ebb, the power of the French monarchy began a slow recovery about the beginning of the twelfth century. The eventual success of the French kings in creating a fairly strong central government throughout their kingdoms stands in marked contrast to the fate of Germany. A number of reasons for this opposite development may be suggested. One was the accident that the kings of France had legitimate heirs without break until 1328. In 987, when Hugh Capet was chosen as king, the elective character of the monarchy in France was neither more nor less than in Germany. However, the German kings and emperors never succeeded in firmly establishing the hereditary principle, owing in good part to the fact that one dynasty after another died out after only a few generations. The Capetians on the other hand were long-lived, and when they died they left mature men as heirs. (One may speculate that this reflects the very modesty of early Capetian ambition. A surprising number of the German kings and emperors died in Italy, where the unfamiliar climate and diseases of the south seized them in their prime, before heirs were born or had come of age.) The long succession of mature heirs in the Capetian house resulted in the firm recognition of the hereditary principle—an important fact since a king who inherited his throne by right did not have to make concessions to vassals in order to win their support for his election.

Another factor which helped the Capetian kings was their possession of a centrally located, compact territory, the Île de France. This was an irregular patch extending from Paris on the Seine to Orleans on the Loire. It lay near the center of the Kingdom, and commanded important lines of communication which, as trade developed, meant an important source of income to the king. The German emperors, in contrast, did not retain any compact block of territory under their personal rule, but granted away family inheritances in the vain hope of creating loyal political supporters.

A third weakness of the German imperial state resulted from its very size. Emperor after emperor divided his attention between unruly nobles in Germany and equally unruly cities and princes in Italy, with the result that success in one country was frequently nullified by failure in the other. Prolonged, patient and persistent efforts to establish firm control over any one region were neglected in favor of grandiose, but in the long run futile, attempts to rule the whole territory included within the imperial boundaries.

During most of the twelfth century, the French kings were content to consolidate their administration within the Île de France. In the middle of the century such modest success as the French kings had attained was threatened by the formation, as a result of marriage alliances, of what may be called the Angevin empire. By 1154, a French noble, Henry of Anjou, had inherited or acquired by marriage not only the kingdom of England, where he was known as Henry II, but also Normandy, Anjou, Touraine, Brittany and Aquitaine. In legal theory, Henry held all his French fiefs by grant from the French King; but in fact his territories, power and wealth far overshadowed those of his nominal superior.

During the reign of Philip Augustus, king of France from 1180–1223, a decisive shift in the balance of power between the Angevins (i.e., house of Anjou) and Capetians took place. In 1189 Philip Augustus accompanied Frederick Barbarossa and the English King, Richard, Coeur de Lion, on the Third Crusade. Richard was, like his father Henry, not only King of England but feudal lord of more than half of the French Kingdom; but he cared little for the labor of administration and preferred to leave his possessions to look after themselves while he sought military glory in the Holy Land. Not so Philip. After spending only a few months in Palestine he

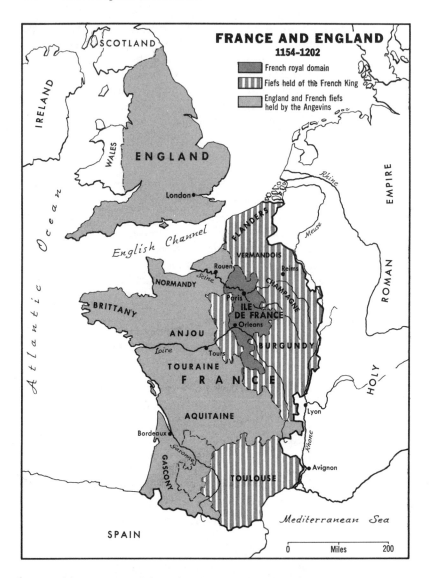

hastened home to attend to the affairs of his kingdom, and in Richard's absence he attacked Normandy. Even after the Third Crusade came to an end, Richard did not immediately come home to defend his French fiefs. Instead he suffered imprisonment in a castle belonging to the Hohenstaufen Emperor (Richard had supported the Welf faction in Germany) and was not released until after a large ransom had been paid in 1194. During the next five years Richard waged war against Philip and won a number of indecisive successes before his death in 1199.

Richard's younger brother, John, thereupon succeeded to the Angevin inheritance. But Philip was able to stir up powerful opposition among John's vassals, both in England and in France. In 1202 Philip formally summoned John to come to the French court to answer a charge which had been made against him by one of John's French vassals; and when John refused to obey this summons from his feudal superior, Philip Augustus declared all the fiefs which he held from the French King to be forfeited. Such a legal maneuver was in itself of no great moment: what mattered was that Philip was able to gather an army and occupy Brittany, Anjou, Maine and Normandy, adding these rich and valuable lands to the royal domain.

John was helpless for the moment. In 1205 he fell under the displeasure of the pope owing to a dispute over the election of the archbishop of Canterbury; in 1208 Innocent III put all England under the interdict (i.e., forbade all Church services, burials, sacraments) and formally released the English barons from their oaths of allegiance to John. Pope Innocent even authorized Philip Augustus to organize a crusade against John and recognized Philip's son as the legitimate king of England. In 1213 John had to yield. He agreed to all the demands which Innocent made concerning the freedom of the Church in England from royal interference, and formally surrendered England to the papacy and received it back as a fief from Pope Innocent. As vassal of the pope, John undertook to pay annual tribute to the papal court.

John's reconciliation with Pope Innocent abruptly changed the balance of forces in France. Philip Augustus was compelled to give up his crusade against John, and instead found himself on the defensive when John and the Welf party of Germany organized an army to march against him. The danger to the new-found power of the French monarchy was beaten back by Philip's victory at the battle of Bouvines in 1214. John's defeat on the continent, in turn, encouraged the English barons to rebel in 1215. John could not resist them with arms, and was compelled to sign the Magna Carta, in which he promised to respect the rights and privileges of the barons and to refrain from numerous practices which he and his royal predecessors had introduced into England as means of increasing the royal income.

Ironically enough, Innocent III, who a few years before had stirred up the barons against John, now came to the defense of his new vassal, and absolved John from the oath he had taken to observe the provisions of the Magna Carta. For a while the English barons and Philip Augustus tried to defy papal policy, and Philip's son, Prince Louis, actually arrived in London in 1216 and was recognized by the rebellious English nobles as their king. But John's death in the same year removed the principal target of the barons' wrath; and their insurrection collapsed when John's son,

Henry III, renewed his father's oath to observe the provisions of the Magna Carta.

Peace between the Angevin and Capetian rulers was not concluded until 1259. In that year Henry III of England and Louis IX (St. Louis) of France signed an agreement whereby Henry surrendered claim to the fiefs his father had lost to Philip Augustus. By this settlement, Aquitaine, in southern France, remained the sole French fief in the possession of the English king.

A generation earlier, the rise of the French monarchy had received fresh impetus under Louis VIII (1223–26), son and successor of Philip Augustus.

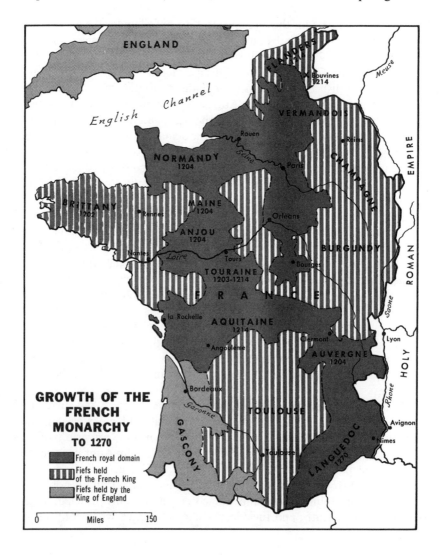

GROWTH OF THE
FRENCH
MONARCHY
TO 1270

French royal domain
Fiefs held of the French King
Fiefs held by the King of England

0   Miles   150

While Philip was busy fighting against John, the papacy had instigated a crusade against the Albigensian heretics, who were especially numerous in southern France in the county of Toulouse. In 1209 a miscellaneous group of French nobles attacked Toulouse, and a bloody and destructive war commenced. One of the crusaders, an adventurer named Simon de Montfort, was recognized by the papacy as count of Toulouse in place of the hereditary ruler; but he proved unable to maintain his power when disputes broke out among the crusading host. As a result the Albigensian heretics regained ground. With the blessing of the papacy Louis VIII seized this occasion for intervention, and succeeded in annexing most of the county of Toulouse before his death; his successor, St. Louis (reigned 1226–70), retained control of what his father had conquered, and, through a marriage alliance, the remnant of the county of Toulouse was added to the royal domain in 1272.

Thus within the space of thirty years, between 1202 when Philip Augustus declared King John's fiefs forfeit and 1229 when the count of Toulouse made peace with St. Louis, the territory directly controlled by the king of France increased by about eight times. The personality of the French kings, the support of the papacy at critical junctures, the mistakes of opponents, and the technicalities of feudal law all contributed to the startling success which changed France from a collection of independent feudal principalities into a strong kingdom, able by virtue of the prowess, wealth and culture of its inhabitants to take the leading place in medieval Europe. At the same time, the kings of England lost the larger part of their possessions on the continent, and became more truly English in their interests and outlook. Thus the result was the beginning of the development of two distinct national states, whose rulers and population came by degrees to identify themselves as French or English rather than as Christian, or Norman, or members of some manor or town or noble family.

The internal development of French and English political institutions was profoundly influenced by the different manner in which the two kingdoms were established. When William of Normandy conquered England in 1066 he found himself able to reorganize the kingdom as he saw fit. He made England a thoroughly feudal yet strongly centralized state. William officially laid claim to ownership of all the land of his new kingdom, and adopted the policy of scattering the fiefs he granted to each of his vassals over different parts of the kingdom. This prevented any of them from being able to build a territorial base for independent power. As an additional safeguard against feudal disorder, William required all rear vassals (i.e., vassals of his vassals) to swear an oath of fealty directly to himself.

The Norman conqueror retained some Anglo-Saxon institutions which promised to increase the king's power. Thus William kept the shire system of local government, which had originated in the course of the struggle against the Danes. He entrusted the shires to appointive officials, the sheriffs, who presided over shire courts, were responsible for the collection of all forms of royal revenue originating within their jurisdiction, and were supposed to maintain the public peace.

During the following two centuries English institutions underwent several significant changes. The feudal army of some 5000 knights guaranteed by William the Conqueror's enfeoffment was satisfactory only for border wars in Wales and Scotland. Enterprises in France needed long-service professional troops, and as a result the kings early began the practice of commuting military service for payments of scutage (i.e., shield money). Thus the English kings came to depend mainly on a mercenary army, although shortage of money always made it difficult for them to maintain such an army on a permanent basis.

Relationships with the Church were frequently troubled by the efforts of the papacy to assert its control over ecclesiastical personnel and wealth. Disputes over lay investiture were settled for a while by agreement between Anselm, archbishop of Canterbury, and King Henry I reached in 1107. This agreement was similar to the Concordat of Worms, for which, indeed, it provided the model. During the reign of the Angevin, Henry II (1154–89), fresh quarrels arose when Thomas a Becket, archbishop of Canterbury, refused to accept a definition of the rights of the Church which Henry had drawn up. Becket was compelled to leave England for a while, and after he returned he was murdered in Canterbury Cathedral by three of Henry's knights. Becket's murder created a great scandal and made that haughty prelate into a saint. The papacy took up Becket's cause, so that in 1170 the king felt compelled to come to terms with Pope Alexander III. By this settlement, the Church was accorded exclusive right to try members of the clergy who were accused of crime, and the right of appeal to Rome was established. King John's relationships with the papacy, as a result of which England became a papal fief, have already been sketched. The suzerainty of the pope was officially recognized by the English kings until 1365.

Perhaps the most significant development of the period was the expansion of the royal system of justice. The reign of Henry II was especially important in this respect, for he began to appoint itinerant justices who traveled around England deciding various types of legal disputes according to a body of precedent which came to be known as the common law because it was common to the whole kingdom. When disputes hinged on local information (such, for instance, as whose grandfather had owned a particular piece of land) it became customary to call together a jury (i.e., a sworn group) of local men to declare the circumstances of the case. From this custom trial by jury later evolved. The development and expansion of the system of common law and royal justice was initiated by the English kings and their officials mainly as a method of raising revenue, for they received fees from the plaintiff before a case ever came to court, and collected fines from parties adjudged guilty. Nevertheless the growth of a system of royal justice had the effect of making available to any freeman of the kingdom a fairly dependable means of redress against the aggressions of local feudal lords and other powerful enemies. Incidentally, too, the common law bound the whole country together by establishing a uniform, nation-wide body of law.

The French kingdom never achieved the same degree of uniformity in administrative institutions and law as did the English state. The manner in which the Capetians acquired their territory made any such uniformity almost impossible. Instead, whatever local institutions had grown up in the various counties or duchies before their annexation to the royal domain were retained in operation afterwards with only minor changes. The king of France simply took over the rights and income which had previously been enjoyed by the local count or duke.

However, just as in England, the royal government found itself constantly in need of money and developed practices which added to the king's income. Philip Augustus began to appoint salaried officials who were responsible for collecting the royal income within a specified district. In addition these officials had the right to settle legal disputes according to their own good judgment and local precedent. Cases appealed from any of the wide variety of local courts to the king's justice were settled before a body of professional judges known collectively as parlement. A number of such bodies arose, of which the parlement of Paris was the most important.

Feudalism had originated and became most highly developed in France. As a result, the king's efforts to limit resort to private war were far less successful than in England. Similarly the conversion of the royal army from a feudal to a mercenary basis did not proceed so rapidly in France as in England, due in part at least to the fact that French royal campaigns were fought for the most part under circumstances where the feudal army was quite efficient—that is, close at hand, not overseas.

Philip Augustus adopted a policy of granting various privileges to towns in return for money payments, and, sometimes, military service. He also policed the roads and protected merchants from feudal attack or exploitation. It was during his reign that Paris began to develop into the most important town in France, and Philip made it his usual place of residence. St. Louis followed a rather less favorable policy towards the towns, being less urgently in need of their support. He compelled them to accept royal appointees as mayors and to admit the jurisdiction of royal officials within their walls.

The relations between the papacy and the French kings have already been sketched. Before the time of Philip Augustus the monarchy was so weak that there was little occasion for friction. Philip Augustus profited greatly from the quarrel his enemy, John of England, had with the papacy; his successor benefited almost equally from the Albigensian crusade. Under St. Louis the French monarchy remained on good terms with the papacy. The popes fell back on French support in the bitter struggle with Emperor Frederick II, and it was a French prince, St. Louis' brother, who invaded Sicily in 1266 and finally brought the Hohenstaufen family to ruin.

c) The Papacy as Head of an International Government. It should already be clear from the preceding summary of the political activities of the papacy during the twelfth and thirteenth centuries that the popes had become the head of a powerful government which concerned itself not only with mens' souls but also with their bodies in all of western Christendom. This government was, of course, the Medieval Church. The growth of its organization and activities was gradual, built partly on the precedent of late Roman times, partly on new interpretations of the Bible, and on decrees and decisions of successive popes and Church councils.

Papal claims to political leadership of Christendom were justified in theory by the Donation of Constantine and the doctrine of the "Two Swords." The Donation of Constantine was a document purporting to show that when Constantine transferred his capital to Constantinople he delegated his imperial authority in the west to the popes. It was a forgery, executed in the papal chancellery in the eighth century; but its authenticity was not generally called into question until the fifteenth century. The doctrine of the Two Swords was an interpretation of the Biblical passage in the Gospel of St. Luke: "But now, he that hath a purse, let him take it, and likewise his scrip; and he that hath no sword let him sell his garment and buy one.... And they said, Lord, behold here are two swords. And He said unto them, It is enough." (22:36, 38) The two swords in the possession of the disciples were interpreted by medieval commentators as symbolizing the temporal and spiritual power; and since both were in the hands of the apostles, both, it was argued, belonged to the heirs of the apostles, that is, to the ordained bishops of the Church, and to their chief, the pope.

Such theoretical claims to temporal authority were made into practical realities by the organization of the Church. It was divided into two parts: the secular clergy who ministered to men in ordinary life, and the regular (i.e., monastic) clergy who devoted themselves to personal holiness and salvation. The secular clergy were hierarchically organized. Western Europe was divided into a series of archbishoprics; these were subdivided into bishoprics or dioceses, and the dioceses in turn were subdivided into parishes. The popes were able to exert varying but usually important in-

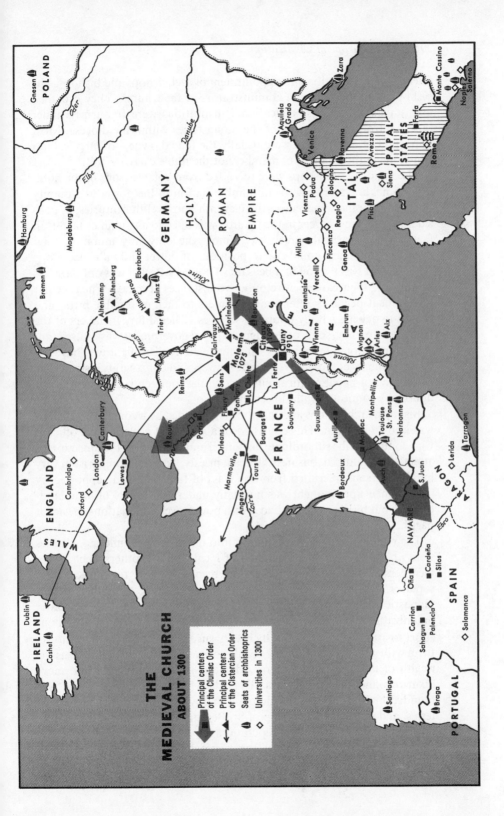

THE
MEDIEVAL CHURCH
ABOUT 1300

▪ Principal centers of the Cluniac Order
▲ Principal centers of the Cistercian Order
⚑ Seats of archbishoprics
◇ Universities in 1300

POLAND
Gnesen

Oder

Elbe

Danube

GERMANY

HOLY ROMAN EMPIRE

Hamburg
Bremen
Magdeburg
Altenkamp
Altenberg
Eberbach
Himmerod
Mainz
Trier
Meuse
Rhine

Aquileia
Grado
Venice
Zara
Ravenna
Faria
PAPAL STATES
Arezzo
Rome
Siena
Bologna
Reggio
Padua
Vicenza
Po
Placenza
Milan
Genoa
Pisa
ITALY
Monte Cassino
Naples
Salerno

Clairvaux
Morimond
Citeaux 1098
Molesme 1075
Cluny 910
Besançon
S
Vienne
Tarentaise
Embrun
Avignon
Aix
Arles
L
R
Rhône
La Ferté
La Charité

Reims
Sens
Fleury
Pontigny
Souvigny
Sauxillanges

Rouen
Seine
Paris
Orleans
Bourges
FRANCE
Marmoutier
Angers
Tours
Loire

Aurillac
Moissac
Montpellier
Toulouse
St. Pons
Narbonne
Bordeaux
Auch
S. Juan
NAVARRE
Ebro

ENGLAND
WALES
Cambridge
Oxford
London
Lewes
Canterbury

IRELAND
Dublin
Cashel

ARAGON
Lerida
Tarragon

SPAIN
Oña
Cardeña
Silos
Carrion
Sahagun
Palencia
Salamanca
Santiago

PORTUGAL
Braga

fluence on the selection and appointment of archbishops and bishops. The bishops were the principal administrators of the Church. They ordained and supervised priests; educational institutions were frequently under their control, as were some of the monasteries within the diocese. Most important of all, bishops were usually the feudal owners of large estates which made them powerful members of the noble class.

The majority of bishops were recruited from younger sons of the nobility. Some, however, rose from humble station to the power and dignity of episcopal office. Indeed, in the eleventh and twelfth centuries, in considerable degree a career in the Church was open to any man of talent. In fact, an ecclesiastical career was almost the only way ambitious and capable commoners could rise to positions of power and influence. Pope Gregory VII was the son of a peasant; Thomas à Becket was of bourgeois origin; and their careers were only two instances of many. When secular government began to offer similar careers to men of humble birth, and ceased to depend wholly upon the services of hereditary members of the feudal aristocracy, some of the vigor of papal government was infused into the rising national monarchies; and men who earlier might well have become members of the clergy, became lawyers and bureaucrats instead. The weakening of papal political influence in the fourteenth century was undoubtedly connected with this change.

Bishops, archbishops and the popes were aided by a court, or *curia* as it was known in Latin. This consisted of a variety of ecclesiastical officials who controlled the subordinate personnel and property of the diocese, and attended to judicial business. Parish priests were by comparison very humble persons, recruited from the class of free men, and supported by tithes. Their appointment was normally under the control of local landowners, but bishops usually had a veto power over nominations to vacant parishes.

The regular clergy were organized into monasteries. Some monasteries were under the general supervision of local bishops; others, such as the members of the Cluniac congregation, recognized only the pope as their superior. During the eleventh and twelfth centuries, a number of new monastic orders arose, largely in reaction against the decadence of older organizations. Monastic orders regularly began with a strict and strenuous effort to attain a holy life, but their very success caused laymen to shower them with gifts in return for the monks' prayers on their behalf; and as the wealth of the monasteries increased the monks generally fell into more luxurious and easygoing ways. Thus the Cistercians, whose order was founded in 1098, sought out desolate and waste places for their monasteries, and under the leadership of St. Bernard of Clairvaux (1090–1153), they achieved an unrivaled reputation for strictness and holiness. Yet before a century had elapsed the Cistercians had become extremely wealthy and were particularly noted for their shrewd activity as traders and commercial farmers.

The power of the papacy over the various levels of the Church hierarchy was maintained in part by legates—men appointed by the pope to carry out a particular project. Thus the First Crusade was under the supervision of a papal legate, as was the Albigensian crusade later. Another important device used by the papacy to confirm its control was calling frequent assemblies of bishops and other prelates. At such general councils or local synods the pope was able to present his wishes and instructions to the assembled prelates, and to discipline those who had failed to obey the rules of the Church. A third pillar of papal power was the right to hear appeals in cases which came before Church courts of any level. This gave the popes frequent opportunity to enforce their policy on local bishops and archbishops; and indeed for certain especially important cases, the papal *curia* was the court of first instance.

To maintain the papal *curia* and the numerous administrative officials who served the popes, a large income was necessary. In point of fact, the income which the papacy enjoyed in the thirteenth century was probably a good deal larger than that of any other government of Europe. Sources were various. The pope, as ruler of the papal states in Italy, enjoyed from them the income of a secular prince. Countries which had become papal fiefs, such as England, paid sums into the papal treasury as a token of their subordination. Bishops and other officials were expected to pay a part of the first year's income of their office to the pope in return for his confirmation of their election; and regular papal taxation of the clergy was imposed for special projects, such as financing a crusade. The gifts of pilgrims and penitents who visited Rome formed another important source of income; and the fines and fees which were paid in connection with the judicial activity of the papal court were still another. Yet like all medieval governments, the papacy was chronically short of funds, and regularly borrowed from Italian bankers, who became agents for the collection of papal revenues throughout Europe. The fortunes of numerous Italian banking families were based upon their activities on behalf of the papacy.

The rapid development of town life in the late twelfth and throughout the thirteenth century presented a serious challenge to the medieval Church. As was suggested above, the Church at first looked with scant sympathy upon the activities of the bourgeois, among whom heresies found fertile ground in the latter part of the twelfth century. In the eyes of the Church, this was a serious threat. It was met in two ways: by the fervor of new religious orders, the friars; and by the foundation of the Papal Inquisition.

The two great orders of friars were the Franciscans and the Dominicans, named after their founders, St. Francis (1182–1226) and St. Dominic

(1170–1221). St. Francis of Assisi was the son of a merchant who turned his back upon ordinary secular life, and set out to imitate the life of Christ by preaching the gospel, by living in absolute poverty, and by ministering to the needs of the poor and the sick. He remained a simple layman all his life, and always professed the greatest respect for priests, even those far less holy than he. The personality of St. Francis was a singularly attractive one, blending selflessness, gaiety, mysticism, charity and humility into an extraordinary and magnetic whole. He attracted a large number of disciples, who came to be known as friars, that is, brothers.

Pope Innocent III recognized the new association in 1210, though only after some hesitation. Very quickly problems arose, for St. Francis was an uncompromising idealist who rejected the idea of formal organization and discipline among the friars, and sought always to stimulate and pursue a mystical love of God. A particular point of friction was the question of property, for St. Francis wished his friars to give up all possessions, not only as individuals but also collectively as an order. Such a complete renunciation of the goods of this world implied a powerful rebuke to worldly and wealthy prelates of the Church. In 1220 St. Francis was persuaded to renounce his headship of the Franciscans, and a new rule was drawn up under papal supervision which formalized the organization of the new order. After St. Francis' death the prohibitions he had made against the collective ownership of property were annulled. Many of his followers felt this to be a betrayal of Francis' true ideal, and held up the example of his life, embroidered with legend, as a model. Indeed by 1266 the legend seemed so pernicious to Church officials that all earlier accounts of his life and activity were suppressed and a life of the saint, written by the head of the order, St. Bonaventura, was made official.

St. Dominic was a very different man from St. Francis. He founded his order with the intention of training eloquent and learned preachers who would be able to refute and convert the heretics who were distressingly numerous in the towns. The Dominicans consequently emphasized the importance of learning, and they became prominent as theologians and philosophers in the newly established universities. The mode of organization which St. Dominic devised for the direction of his order is of peculiar interest, for it incorporated the representative idea. Each chapter house annually chose two delegates to attend a provincial "chapter meeting"; and the delegates had the duty to elect a provincial prior and to appoint four administrators to attend to the affairs of the province until the next chapter meeting. Similarly, delegates from all the provinces constituted the chapter-general, which elected the head of the order and supervised general administration. A similar pattern of organization was imposed on the Franciscans after St. Francis' death.

The activities of the friars infused a new ardor and idealism into

Christian practice. The fast growing towns were from the start the principal scene of their work. Friars cared for the sick and the poor by establishing hospitals; in addition they preached, often on street corners, and took a leading place in education. For the first time the inhabitants of the towns of western Europe were brought into contact with the full force of Christian idealism by the Franciscans, while sceptics and heretics were exposed to the subtle and forceful argument of highly educated Dominicans. But it was soon felt that argument was not enough to deal with obstinate heretics. In 1233 the papacy authorized the organization of a Holy Office (as the Inquisition was officially termed), whose duty it was to seek out and examine persons charged with heresy, and to hand over those who refused to recant to secular authorities for punishment. The Dominicans became the principal inquisitors. Their methods were those of the day: interrogation and (after 1244) torture. In the parts of Europe where the Inquisition functioned it was on the whole quite successful in stamping out dissent. In combination with the preaching and good works of the friars, the inquisition succeeded in checking heresy and reestablished a nearly uniform Catholicism.

The Church, of course, lacked one of the usual attributes of a government: it did not dispose of military or police power directly. The fundamental basis of the Church's political might was the hold it exercised on men's minds and hearts. The Church was believed to be the channel of grace, through which sinful men might hope to achieve salvation. Excommuniation thus threatened damnation; and the tortures of hell loomed large in the imaginations of many men, particularly toward the end of their lives. In political quarrels, the papacy sometimes resorted to the interdict, by which some or all of the activities of the Church were prohibited in a given area. The interdict could often turn a ruler's subjects against him, for they saw their souls imperiled by his quarrel with the pope.

Besides attendance at Church services, the Church impinged on the day to day lives of ordinary men in two principal ways. At the Fourth Lateran Council of 1215 it was declared obligatory for all Christians to confess their sins at least once a year to a priest, to perform whatever penance the priest might assign, and then to partake of the Eucharist. The custom of private confession and penance had grown up gradually in the Church, and was common long before 1215. It became a basic element in the discipline of the laity and had the effect of bringing laymen more fully under ecclesiastical influence.[2]

[2]The Fourth Lateran Council also formulated authoritatively the doctrine of transubstantiation which had previously been a matter of dispute, and which later became a point of issue with Protestant theologians. The doctrine defined the Mass as a miracle. Upon the utterance of the words of the rite by the priest, bread and wine were held to be transformed into the substance of Christ's body and blood even though the accidents of their appearance remained unchanged.

The second principal means by which the Church touched everyday living was through the canon law. Canon law was (and is) the law administered by the Church. It was based upon the Bible, supplemented by decisions of Church councils and decretals of the popes. But it did not concern only clergymen. Heresy, apostasy, and simony were all crimes under canon law; moreover, any dispute arising from the administration of the sacraments or of an oath was brought within its scope. Thus cases touching marriage, adultery, dowries, legitimacy, wills, and contracts which had been solemnized by oaths were all subject to the jurisdiction of Church courts. Such disputes were brought before clergymen for settlement, and could always be appealed to the papal court in Rome. Thus the Church handled an enormous amount of judicial business. The exact scope of the jurisdiction of ecclesiastical courts varied from place to place in Europe, and from time to time. Secular rulers quite generally tried to restrict the activity of Church courts, and were sometimes successful, sometimes not.

Another pillar of the strength of the Church was its control of education. There were, to be sure, some secular schools designed to teach budding merchants how to write and keep accounts; but these were unimportant in comparison with ecclesiastical educational institutions. Higher education was carried on in universities. These originated as gilds of teachers or, in some cases, of students. The teachers were all members of the clergy and most of the students were clergymen also. Professors were thus under ecclesiastical discipline by virtue of their clerical status; in addition the university as a whole was usually subject to a local bishop, or in some cases to the pope directly.

Thus in various ways the Church undertook to guide men's minds and hearts, and was able to do without the military and police power customary among governments. Yet when exhortation, preaching, education, excommunication and interdict failed to secure obedience, the popes not infrequently did fall back upon coercion of the "secular arm." Within Italy, papal armies of mercenaries were a usual feature of the balance of power from the thirteenth century onward; bishops, especially in Germany, often controlled miniature armies also; and secular rulers often agreed to use the force at their command on behalf of the Church.

d. Cultural growth

The twelfth and thirteenth centuries witnessed a very rapid, rich and varied growth of European culture. Art, literature and philosophy developed new forms and reached a high level of achievement. All cultural activity was deeply pervaded by religion, which itself underwent some significant elaborations.

1) Religion. The splendor of Church services was steadily enhanced as magnificent cathedrals and churches were erected in the towns of Western Europe. Music, the graphic arts, incense and splendid robes all contributed to the impressiveness of the celebration of the mass. Modern drama originated with the reenactment of scenes from Biblical history and the lives of saints—the miracle plays. Such performances occurred in connection with the special festivals of the Church, often on the steps of a church building itself.

Popular piety was not built around the philosophic structures raised by medieval theologians so much as upon the veneration of saints and saintly relics and the cult of the Virgin Mary. In the twelfth century the papacy asserted its right to enroll new saints, and a legal procedure was established for the testing of sainthood. Relics were believed to work miracles and to have curative powers. Hence, they were eagerly sought. But the most distinctive development of popular religion was the vast expansion of the cult of the Virgin. She was regarded as an intercessor with God, more powerful than ordinary saints, and infinitely compassionate. The prayers of men were more and more directed to her attention.

A remarkable example of the power of religion in medieval times was the Christianization of knighthood. The rough and brutal warriors of the tenth century were by slow degrees transformed into "gentle, perfect knights," chivalrous defenders of the poor and weak, dedicated to the welfare of religion and to the defense of the Church. Or such was the ideal expressed in countless romances (e.g., The Holy Grail) and symbolized by ceremonies connected with the conferring of knighthood. The reality, as always, fell far short; yet one should not disparage the force of the Church and of religious sentiment in mitigating the internal warfare of Christendom. At various times Churchmen tried to reduce the pest of private war by declaring a truce of God during which no fighting among Christians would be allowed. Such pronouncements were of course not universally honored, but all the same may have contributed to an improvement in public peace in the European countryside.

2) Art. The major expression of art in the twelfth and thirteenth centuries was the construction of great cathedrals. The cathedrals were not merely architectural monuments; sculpture and painting and the minor arts were also employed to embellish them. Especially notable was the development of the art of making stained glass windows, which, in a fashion reminiscent of mosaic techniques, portrayed Biblical and other religious scenes.

The romanesque style of church construction, which had begun to develop early in the eleventh century, was elaborated and by degrees transformed into the Gothic style. A number of technical problems had to be solved before the fully developed Gothic cathedral evolved from the solid masonry construction of early romanesque building. The fundamental problem was how to support a stone roof and at the same time allow for the penetration of light. It was met by the development of groined vaulting, which carried the weight of the roof to particular points in the church wall, where piers and buttresses could transmit the weight to the ground. In the wall spaces between piers it then became possible to insert great windows. This development was accompanied by the substitution of pointed for round arches, a shift made necessary by the need of constructing groined vaults over rectangular areas. (Round arches, designed to span differing distances, would intersect at different heights, making vaulting awkward.)

The use of pointed arches and groined vaults made it possible to raise the roof high above the ground; and indeed towns began to compete with one another, each striving to build a bigger and higher cathedral than its neighbor had done. In some instances burghers, artisans and peasants joined with professional masons in the work of construction, donating their labor and using their conveyances for hauling the stones.

Medieval sculpture was distinguished from classical by the fact that almost all of it was architectural. Figures of saints and apostles were designed to occupy niches in the cathedrals; and special areas, such as semicircular tympani over the cathedral doors, were used to portray entire religious stories. Within the church structure, tombs were often adorned with effigies of the dead—the nearest approach to portrait sculpture of the period.

Painting, too, found some scope in the decoration of such parts of the cathedral as the altar screen; and artists sometimes used their skill in the decoration of plaster walls and ceilings. Most Gothic interiors, however, were of bare stone; but the large multicolored glass windows provided a most effective substitute for painting. Lesser arts, such as woodcarving, were also freely employed to decorate details of the cathedral furnishings.

The only other form of monumental building which was practiced in the twelfth and thirteenth centuries was the construction of castles. The art of fortification underwent a great elaboration, especially after the experiences of western warriors with eastern fortifications during the crusades. Castles became large and elaborate, consisting of a series of concentric rings of fortification, complete with moats, bastions, crenellations and other refinements of construction which permitted the defenders to ward off attackers in relative safety. Siege technique improved also, but in general the defenders retained the advantage they had earlier enjoyed so that, in the absence of treachery from within, the only practicable method of capturing a castle was to starve it out.

Private dwellings in the towns were usually built of timber, or of timber

MEDIEVAL ARCHITECTURE

Medieval architecture eloquently expressed the dominant position of the Christian church. The unending stylistic variations of medieval cathedrals mirrored the political diversity of Europe. Yet their effort to symbolize and body forth man's hope of coming at last into the presence of God also demonstrated the limited but real coherence of Latin Christendom.

In the period of economic hardship that followed the Carolingian era, the Church was the sole agency rich enough to erect monumental structures. These churches were built in the Romanesque style, often as parts of larger monastic complexes. The mass and bulk of Romanesque churches made them fortresses against a world that threatened the spiritual life.

The twelfth and thirteenth centuries, characterized by a growing prosperity and enriched through commercial and cultural intercourse with the Middle East, saw an increased scale of church building and a shift of patronage from the monastery to the town or secular prince. A new style of architecture, the Gothic, evolved which, with its ever growing emphasis on height and verticality, expressed the builder's spiritual aspirations.

Notre Dame La Grande, Poitiers
1135-40
(Ampliaciones y Reproducciones MAS)

This Romanesque church at Poitiers is characterized by the repeated use of semicircular arches. Despite the use of sculptural decoration, the weight and bulk of the facade remain uncompromised. The purpose of the numerous sculptures was to educate and instruct the illiterate. The twelve Apostles and Saints Martin and Hilary are shown at the middle level, while below them are scenes from the life of the Virgin.

Cathedral of Notre Dame, Amiens
Principal Facade begun 1220
(Photo James Austin)

Amiens cathedral, though not complete because the crowning spires of the
towers were never erected, is a superb example of Gothic verticality. No
horizontal line is permitted to continue unbroken for long. The vertical thrust
is reinforced by the airiness of the facade. Note, for example, how the
rows of sculptured saints appear almost in the round, whereas at Poitiers
the flat surface at the back of the niches held each figure closely pinned to
the supporting wall. The reason this facade could be so full of recesses
and air spaces was, of course, that the weight of the structure was not carried
by the walls, but by great isolated piers.

Cathedral of Notre Dame, Amiens
Buttresses of the Choir and South Transept Viewed from Above
(Clarence Ward)

Flying buttresses, here pictured from an unusual angle of vision, allowed
Gothic architects to construct the walls of their churches mainly of glass. The
weight of the roof was supported by these buttresses; and this, in turn,
made it possible to raise the roof much higher than when masonry walls had
to carry the load, for such walls had to be made thicker with every foot of
additional height to keep from toppling over.

Cathedral of Notre Dame, Amiens
South Transept Showing Detail of the Rose Window
(Photo James Austin)

Gothic windows were filled with stained glass. Sunlight streaming through such
windows created an interior atmosphere that stood in sharp and impressive
contrast to ordinary everyday experience, whether indoors or out. A
special sense of awe and religious expectation is associated in our minds
with such a scene, and the same was presumably true for medieval
Europeans who constructed these marvels.

Cathedral of Notre Dame, Amiens
Detail from the Central Portal of the West Front Showing the
Tympanum
(Photo James Austin)

This crowded scene above the main entrance door to Amiens cathedral portrays the Last Judgment. In the center, Christ enthroned judges the quick and the dead, flanked by saints and angels. In the band below, human souls are being separated into the blessed, who are headed towards the gates of Heaven (extreme left) and the damned, who are being herded by the devil towards the gaping jaws of Hell (extreme right). The scene below shows the dead arising from their coffins as the angels blow the Last Trumpet, announcing Judgment Day.

Through this simple sculpture, therefore, one of the fundamental doctrines of the Church took vivid, memorable form.

Cathedral of Notre Dame, Amiens
Interior View Showing the Choir and Apse Vaults
Completed 1269
(Clarence Ward)

The camera in this photograph both demonstrates and exaggerates the soaring height of Amiens' interior. The visual pattern made by the vaults, ribs, and piers fingering the light that floods in far above the worshippers' heads was like a foretaste of the delights of Heaven itself.

Cathedral, Ely
The Western Towers
Begun about 1081
(Harold Allen)

French Gothic architecture was admired in its own day as in ours, and peoples round about were ready and eager to take over elements of the Gothic style and make them their own. In such cases, the borrowers did not copy French models slavishly. The resulting "Gothic" structures betray mixed and mingled antecedants. In England, for example, Gothic cathedrals used arches and other French elements to achieve quite different decorative effects, as illustrated here at Ely.

Münster Church, Ulm
1377-1492
(Deutscher Kunstverlag)

The German Gothic cathedral derived directly from French prototypes. The upper part of the lofty tower and spire was completed only in the nineteenth century. In accordance with the original plans, it rises 529 feet, thus making Ulm the tallest church in Christendom.

Cathedral, Siena
Facade and Nave
Begun thirteenth century. 1226-1380
(Alinari Art Reference Bureau)

In Italy, French Gothic ran into competition from classical Roman traditions
of monumental building. The cathedral at Siena, for example, used Gothic
details for the west facade, but refrained from using flying buttresses
to open out the side walls for stained glass windows in the French fashion.
Moreover, the dome over the crossing descended directly from classical
techniques of building, and had no analogue in Gothic buildings
north of the Alps.

Cathedral, Burgos, Spain
1229-1457
(Ampliaciones y Reproducciones MAS)

The strong vertical thrust of the facade of Burgos cathedral is reminiscent of
Amiens. The exuberant use of ornament, especially in the tower and
pinnacles over the crossing, is peculiarly Spanish and is due to Moorish influence.

The White Tower, The Tower of London
Begun 1097
(National Monuments Record, London)

The Tower of London was built initially as a fortress and place of refuge in case of attack. Its design was not adapted to withstand heavy missiles, but simple knights or other lightly equipped troops were entirely unable to to do any damage even to such simple structures as this. Until the windows were let into the walls in the seventeenth century, the interior was dark and damp — so uncomfortable, indeed, that the Tower was mainly used as a prison for especially dangerous (often highborn) enemies of the King.

Carcassonne
(Ampliaciones Y Reproduciones MAS — ND Giraudon)

The fortified city of Carcassonne occupies a site used for defensive purposes
from Roman times. Its present form is largely a result of construction of
the thirteenth and fourteenth centuries. This impressive monument takes
maximum advantage of the site. The principal line of fortifications consists
of inner and outer walls reinforced at intervals by round towers. Until
the advent of cannon such a town remained almost impregnable.

Palazzo Vecchio, Florence
1298-1314
(Alinari Art Reference Bureau)

The Palazzo Vecchio, begun in 1298 after the plans of Arnolfo di Bambio, was designed as the city's town hall, a function it still performs. The palazzo retains an overall fortress-like character well suited to a city periodically torn apart by internal strife. In the slender tower hung the bell that called the Florentines to the defense of their city.

Doge's Palace, Venice
1309-1424
(Alinari Art Reference Bureau)

The palace, built according to the designs of Giovanni and Bartolomeo Buon, provides a grand testimony of the proud position of Venice as a great trading community whose commerce was protected by the supremacy of her navy. The columned and pointed arcades supporting horizontal bands of tracery and a patterned brick facade is a Venetian adaptation of Middle Eastern decorative motifs.

Chateau, Blois
Wing Built by Louis XIII and Completed in 1503
(Wayne Andrews)

By the end of the fifteenth century, seige guns had made fortified castles
obsolete. Rulers could therefore afford to build more comfortable and open
residences, trusting to men at arms and guns to protect them instead of
heavy walls. The elegance of this French royal chateau was the result;
and inside wooden panelling and numerous fireplaces helped to make the
chill of winter more bearable.

and plaster. Houses of several stories were constructed, since it was important to keep the circuit of the town walls to a minimum in order to make defense more sure.

3) Literature. Literary expression took a wide variety of forms. In the twelfth century the study of Latin classics was avidly pursued, and a number of writers began to model themselves on the style and grammar of the ancient writers. Perhaps the most learned student of the classics was John of Salisbury (d. 1180). In the following century literary study was eclipsed by the study of logic and philosophy, and it was left to the humanists of the fourteenth and later centuries to return to the Latin literary classics with a new enthusiasm.

The medieval Church conducted its services and administration in Latin, but the Latin used was not the same language that had been spoken by Cicero. Grammatical simplification and extensive shifts in vocabulary maintained it as a living language. Latin was the sole language of learning, and every educated man was able to write and speak Latin as a second tongue. Poetry, both religious and secular, was written in medieval Latin. A number of great hymns which are still sung were written during this time, chief among them being the *Stabat Mater* and the *Dies Irae*. In sharp contrast, secular Latin poetry, usually called Goliardic verse, celebrated the joys of wine, women and song, sometimes in a quite pagan spirit.

Latin was, of course, not the ordinary everyday speech of the peoples of western Europe. In France, Spain and Italy the popular speech had evolved from classical Latinate speech. In Germany, Scandinavia and England it derived from earlier Germanic tongues. Under medieval conditions, endless variations of local dialect arose, and it was only by a gradual process that new literary languages were formed. The crystallization of the modern European languages did not occur until long after the thirteenth century, and to this day local dialects remain very much alive in most European countries.

An abundant literature in the vernacular tongues has survived from medieval times. Four general types may be distinguished: the epic, lyric, romance, and fabliaux. Epic poetry stemmed from pagan Germanic tradition. Presumably the deeds of gods and heroes were recited in medieval banqueting halls long before the versions of such tales which we possess came to be written down. The Anglo-Saxon poem, *Beowulf* (tenth century), the Norse sagas (twelfth century), and the Icelandic *Eddas* (thirteenth century) preserve a strong pagan coloring despite the fact that they were written down in Christian times. The *Niebelungenlied*, *Song of Roland* and *Poem of the Cid*, written in German, French and Spanish respectively, belong to the same general tradition, but stem from more deeply Christianized milieux. All three, in the versions which we possess, were written down in the late twelfth or early thirteenth centuries.

A quite different literary tradition was created by the Provençal troubadours, authors of graceful lyrics in praise of fair women. About the end of the eleventh century troubadours appeared at the courts of nobles in southern France, and their poems came to be much admired. Indeed it became a proper accomplishment for a nobleman to be able to write such poems himself. Troubadour poetry followed highly elaborate metrical and rhyme conventions. The poems were designed to be sung to the accompaniment of a lute or other stringed instrument, and it is possible (though not certain) that the art arose in imitation of Arabic models which existed close by in Spain. The Albigensian crusades early in the thirteenth century had the effect of dispersing troubadour poets all over Europe, where their skill in versification was widely imitated and provided a stimulus to new departures. The lyric traditions of all modern European literatures stem in great part from this Provençal origin.

A third and very popular form of vernacular literature was the romance. Whole cycles of romances based upon the legends of King Arthur and his knights were elaborated for the entertainment of noble families. Other cycles clustered around the figures of Charlemagne and Alexander the Great. The code of chivalry and Christian knighthood was embodied in these romances, which also drew upon the Provençal tradition of courtly love.

The three forms of literature mentioned above appealed primarily to the aristocracy. A quite different literature arose among the bourgeois classes —the fabliaux. These were tales, in verse or prose, which often had a satiric twist to them. The stories of Reynard the Fox, partially a burlesque of the knightly romances, had such an origin.

Very little trace of peasant literature has come down from the thirteenth or earlier centuries. Undoubtedly folk tales were passed from mouth to mouth among the peasantry, but it was not until a later age that they were written down.

Two notable histories were written in the vernacular. Geoffroy de Villehardouin (*c.* 1150–1212), a French nobleman, wrote a vivid, if rather simpleminded, account of the Fourth Crusade and the capture of Constantinople. He was himself a leading actor in the events he recorded. Another French noble, Jean de Joinville (1224–1317), a close friend and a companion of St. Louis of France, wrote his memoirs of the saintly king. They provide an intimate account of Louis' reign, from which both the king and Joinville emerge as very likable human beings.

4) Music. Music continued to develop a growingly complex polyphonic counterpoint during the twelfth and thirteenth centuries. The troubadour poets were musicians too, and elaborated instrumental accompaniments for their singing. In sacred music the organ was sometimes used as accompaniment for singing; but moralists frequently opposed the use of instrumental music in churches. Musical instruments remained relatively simple, and purely instrumental music was not created until several centuries later.

5) Education. The meager content of early medieval learning was enormously enhanced during the twelfth and early thirteenth centuries by the translation of numerous Greek and Arabic books into Latin. Jewish scholars and translators played a very important role in opening the learning of the Arabic world to the West. Jews regularly maintained family, religious and trading connections across Moslem-Christian frontiers, and were able to act as intermediaries between the two civilizations. Translation was systematically conducted at the Norman court in Sicily during much of the twelfth century, and Spain, too, became the seat of a school of translators. Much Greek philosophical writing was thus made available to western scholars by the beginning of the thirteenth century. In addition, many Arabic works, both original and commentaries on Greek texts, were translated. Classical *belles lettres* were, however, largely neglected by the medieval translators, partly at least because of their deep tincture of paganism. The impact of Greek and Arabic learning on the west was tremendous, and provided the immediate stimulus for the intellectual achievements of the thirteenth century.

The seven liberal arts together constituted the equivalent of modern primary and secondary education. Grammar meant the acquisition of mastery of Latin as a written and spoken language; rhetoric was reduced mainly to the conventions of letter writing; but logic, as embodied in Aristotle's *Organon*, and the Arabic and Christian commentaries upon it, was very carefully and thoroughly studied. Indeed logic tended to swallow up and eclipse other branches of study, particularly in the thirteenth century, when it became a prerequisite for the more advanced courses in law and theology.

The quadrivium underwent a similar expansion. Arithmetic came to be studied with the help of Arabic numerals—a vast improvement over the clumsy notation of Roman antiquity. For geometry, Euclid's *Elements* was the standard textbook; for astronomy, Ptolemy's *Almagest*. Music did not mean singing and instrumental performance, but rather a study of harmonics and proportions, and was regarded as a branch of mathematics. Augustine's *De Musica* was much used as a text book for this study.

After mastering the seven liberal arts a medieval student was prepared for more advanced professional study. Three faculties arose: law, medicine and theology. Law had two branches: the study of Roman law, as embodied in Justinian's code, and the study of canon law. About 1140 a monk named Gratian codified the canon law in a book (*Decretum*, or as it was officially entitled, *Concordance of discordant canons*) which quickly became a standard text. Changes in canon law were incorporated into a number of later codes, drawn up by various popes in imitation of Justinian's code of Roman law. Training in Roman and canon law became a highly useful preparation for a career in government service, for both kings and popes found legal minds useful, especially since lawyers could employ the absolute principles of Roman law to justify extension of royal power.

Medicine was studied through translations of the works of Galen and the Moslem Avicenna. It never attained the status or importance of law or theology, and no strikingly new ideas or techniques were developed by medieval doctors.

Theology in the medieval educational system enjoyed the highest honor and was considered the queen of the sciences. After Aristotle's philosophical works had been translated (by the beginning of the thirteenth century), the study of theology was generally conducted with the help of the terminology and method of the Philosopher, as medieval scholars called Aristotle. The general effort of the theologians was to justify by reason the tenets of Christian faith; or when this seemed impossible, at least to prove that reason did not contradict faith. Theology thus became a powerful support to Christian dogma, and its study prepared men for ecclesiastical careers as preachers and teachers, and, to a lesser extent, as administrators in the Church.

6) Philosophy and Theology. The development of medieval theological philosophy or philosophical theology (for the two are inseparable) started when a few individuals began to try to examine rationally the theological doctrines of the Church. Berengar of Tours (998–1088), for instance, said: "It is a part of courage to have recourse to dialectic in all things, for recourse to dialectic is recourse to reason, and he who does not avail himself of reason abandons his chief honor, since by virtue of reason he was made in the image of God." Berengar's reason, however, led him to doubt the transformation of the bread and wine of the sacrament into the body and blood of Christ, and he was compelled to withdraw his opinions.

Early controversy turned on the question of the reality (realism) or unreality (nominalism) of universals—whether such concepts as Man, Church, Sin had any existence apart from individual exemplars. Roscellin of Compiègne (d. *c.* 1121) was perhaps the most prominent defender of the nominalist position; his principal opponent was Anselm of Bec (1033–1109), who audaciously tried to prove by reasoning, the truth of such key Christian doctrines as the Atonement.

The most famous and influential of the early theologians was Peter Abélard (1079–1142). For us he is one of the most highly individualized of medieval men owing to the fact that his own account of his life has been preserved, as well as several of his letters to Héloise, a pious and beautiful woman with whom he fell violently (and disastrously) in love. Abélard's teaching career was a brilliant one. As much as any one man, he made the nascent University of Paris the leading seat of theological study in Europe. By systematically collecting conflicting data from the works of the Church Fathers in a book called *Sic et Non* (Yes and No), he showed the necessity for rational harmonization of conflicting Christian authorities. Peter Lombard (*c.* 1100-60), one of Abélard's pupils, undertook such a work about the middle of the twelfth century. His book of *Sentences* provided the model for most later theological works. In it he gathered conflicting statements from Christian authorities on points of doctrine, then proceeded by the use of logical distinctions to try to reconcile them and arrive at an authoriatative and defensible conclusion.

The recovery of the complete Aristotelian corpus, and of Moslem commentaries upon Aristotle's works, exercised a tremendous influence on the theologians of the west during the second half of the twelfth century. At first Church authorities tried to forbid the study of Aristotle, fearing that his paganism would corrupt students' minds. But this effort was unavailing. Instead, a series of scholars set about the task of fitting Aristotle, and the rest of Greek and Arabic learning, into a Christian framework. Their efforts created scholastic philosophy, so called because it was propounded and studied in schools—i.e., in the universities.

Albertus Magnus (1193-1280) and his pupil Thomas Aquinas (1225-74) were the two principal scholars who devoted themselves to this effort. Both were Dominicans and taught at the University of Paris. Albertus Magnus wrote a long series of commentaries on Aristotle's writings, in the course of which he covered almost all aspects of medieval learning. He distinguished natural from revealed truth, and succeeded in reconciling Aristotle with Christianity by accepting Aristotle's method and most of his conclusions in the realm of natural truth, beyond which, he argued, lay the higher truths of revelation which did not conflict with, but concerned matters unknowable by, natural reason.

St. Thomas Aquinas accepted and developed this distinction. He did not limit himself to commentaries on Aristotle, but using Aristotelian terms and logic he systematically arranged and painstakingly discussed all the principal questions of Christian theology and ethics. His greatest work, the *Summa Theologiae* (Summary of Theology), first considers under each question the difficulties and apparently contrary opinions of authorities, then advances carefully reasoned statements of correct doctrine, and finally refutes or escapes the difficulties listed at the beginning by making appropriate distinctions. The *Summa* succeeded in dealing with nearly all of the points which medieval theologians had brought under discussion. It soon came to rival Peter Lombard's *Sentences* as a standard theological textbook; and in 1878 it was recognized by the Roman Catholic Church as the most authoritative statement of doctrine.

The distinction which Albertus Magnus and Aquinas drew between revealed and natural truth marked the beginning of a separation between theology and philosophy. Within the sphere of natural truth, they regarded human reason as sovereign, and a good, reliable guide. Thus a large segment of human knowledge and speculation was separated from revelation, and the way opened for a relatively independent development of philosophy and science.

The Aristotelian rationalistic tradition was not, however, the only intellectual stream of the thirteenth century. Mysticism, drawing upon Platonic and Neo-Platonic sources, also flourished, and found its major intellectual defenders among the Franciscans. Perhaps the most notable mystic was St. Bonaventura (1221–74) who was a contemporary of Aquinas at the University of Paris. In England, at the University of Oxford, Robert Grosseteste (Big Head, d. 1253) and his pupil, the Franciscan friar Roger Bacon (*c.* 1214–94), belonged to the same tradition, but turned their attention chiefly to mathematical and what we would today classify as scientific questions, seeking to achieve by such study a fuller understanding of God's works and a path to the Divinity.

7) Natural Science. In the twelfth and thirteenth centuries, science was not distinguished as a separate intellectual discipline from theology and philosophy. Moreover, the majority of the philosophers were centrally interested in theological issues and tended to rest content with the authority of Aristotle and other Greek and Arabic writers when it came to understanding the physical world. Many of the technological inventions of the age—such things as windmills, rudders, mechanical clocks, windowglass, horse collars—were invented by craftsmen who had little if any acquaintance with learned theory. Some of these inventions were of fundamental importance: the windmill and the horse collar, for instance, enlarged the power resources available to western men very substantially.[3]

The learned men of Europe nevertheless were not entirely neglectful of the physical world. Roger Bacon wrote a treatise on optics, and knew the magnifying properties of lenses. He also dabbled in chemistry, and may have invented an explosive mixture similar to or identical with gunpowder. Another remarkable individual with an interest in the natural world was the Emperor Frederick II. His troubles with the papacy and his familiarity with Arabic and Byzantine culture (resulting from his residence in

[3]Horses move faster than oxen and thus can plow more land in a given time or haul a cart further. With the general introduction of the collar in the twelfth century it became possible for the first time to harness horses efficiently, and gradually they replaced oxen as the principal draught animals.

Sicily) led him to develop a distinctly sceptical bent of mind in matters of religion. He gathered a number of distinguished men of learning at his court, and himself wrote a book on falconry in which he discussed the question of how birds flew and demonstrated an exact knowledge of avian anatomy.

Alchemy and astrology, both derived from the Arabs, were eagerly pursued despite the disapproval of the Church, which regarded such activities as verging dangerously on black magic. The crust of superstition which surrounded these studies made much of the theory idle, yet both served to familiarize men with an ever wider range of natural phenomena.

3. THE WANING OF THE MIDDLE AGES (1270–1500)

---

    a. Introductory
    b. Economic Changes
        1) Agricultural
        2) Town Life
        3) Technology

    c. Expansion of Europe
    d. Political Changes
        1) The Political Overthrow of the Papacy
        2) France and England
        3) Germany
        4) Italy
        5) Other parts of Europe

    e. Cultural Growth
        1) Italian Renaissance
            a) Literature
            b) Art
            c) Science and Philosophy
            d) The Renaissance Ideal

        2) Culture in Northern Europe
            a) Literature
            b) Art
            c) Thought
            d) Religion

---

a. Introductory

The period from the end of the thirteenth century to the beginning of the sixteenth was one of general confusion in Europe. The balance between local and universal political institutions which had existed in the twelfth and thirteenth centuries was upset by the rising power of national monarchies; yet the various kings were not sufficiently powerful to eradicate papal power on the one hand, nor the power of the feudal nobility on the other. At the beginning of the fourteenth century the papal hope of establishing a universal rule throughout Latin Christendom was quite decisively destroyed, and no unifying political force arose in Europe to take the place which the popes had vacated. Instead, a long struggle between France and England, beginning in 1338, absorbed the attention of the two most powerful kingdoms until 1453. This absorption created something of a power vacuum in other parts of Europe. City states in Italy and a miscellaneous collection of princely, ecclesiastical and city states in Germany engaged in a series of vastly complicated political maneuvers. The result was that the common thread of political history, which the activities of the papacy provided in earlier times, disappeared as the numerous individual states of Europe became engrossed in local struggles and problems.

The fragmentation of European politics was matched by seemingly contradictory economic trends. On the one hand, the rapid growth of towns came to an end in the most developed part of western Europe, and continued mainly on the margins. In the older urban centers, the fourteenth and fifteenth centuries saw the differentiation of classes, and the development of a sizeable proletariat, often sunk in debilitating poverty. Yet against these facts one must set the continued improvement in technology (signalized by such basic inventions as printing, guns and gunpowder, and the development of larger seagoing ships), and the rise of fairly large-scale capitalism which was able to expand economic production and exploit new techniques.

Even Europe's expansion shows contradictory trends. In the east the Ottoman Turks conquered the Balkan peninsula, captured Constantinople, and pushed back the political dominion of Italian cities such as Venice from most of the Levant. On the other hand, new discoveries, along the Atlantic coast of Africa, resulted just before the end of the period in the opening of the sea route to India by Vasco da Gama (1497–98). Five years earlier Columbus had made his even more famous discovery of America.

Similar contrariety pervades the development of European culture. In Italy the movement known as the Renaissance gathered way about the middle of the fourteenth century. The brilliant achievements of the Italian cities in art, literature and thought impressed men throughout Europe. Yet simultaneously there flourished a tradition of Christian mysticism, which in many respects was antithetically opposed to the increasingly pagan attitudes of the Italian renaissance.

The period may be regarded as one of transition from the localism combined with universalism which had characterized the twelfth and thirteenth centuries, to the era of national states and cultures which began to emerge in the sixteenth century. Such an age may be regarded with equal propriety as the waning of the Middle Ages, as it has here been called, or the dawn of modern times, as others have often chosen to denominate it.

b. Economic Changes

1) Agricultural. In the fourteenth and fifteenth centuries, the manorial organization of agriculture remained predominant in Europe and there was little change in technique. In the west serfdom continued to decline as landlords commuted traditional services to money payments. But in parts of Europe, particularly in eastern Germany, lords availed themselves of favorable political conditions and of the property concepts of Roman law to extend their rights over the land at the expense of the peasantry. In extreme cases, lords were able to reduce formerly free peasants to the status of hired laborers working on capitalistically organized estates. The decay of peasant rights was especially pronounced in eastern Germany where large-scale grain farming for export grew in importance. Thus in the fourteenth and later centuries, the regions of eastern Germany where peasants had earlier enjoyed special privileges became the stronghold of a peculiarly oppressive serfdom.

In many parts of Europe there were unmistakable signs of peasant unrest. A series of peasant revolts, some of them very violent and suppressed even more violently, broke out in the course of the fourteenth century. The Black Death (bubonic plague), which ravaged most of Europe (1346–8) and killed perhaps as much as a quarter of the whole population, caused a temporary dislocation of all economic relationships. For a few years labor was scarce and wages rose, to the benefit of the poor in town and country; but this advantage was temporary.

2) Town Life. Despite gild regulations designed to keep all members on an approximately equal plane, individual merchants and entrepreneurs succeeded during the fourteenth and fifteenth centuries in achieving wealth far above that of their fellows. Some occupations particularly favored this differentiation. Mining, for instance, could not easily be carried on without large preliminary expenditures. As a result, it became one of the earliest strongholds of capitalistic enterprise. Long distance trade, similarly, required capital for ships and cargo; successful trade also brought large profits. Thus inter-regional trade also became a preserve for men with large capital at their command.

While some grew rich, others found life in the towns increasingly difficult. Many towns in western Europe ceased to grow or grew only slowly after about 1300; and the Black Death partially depopulated nearly all urban centers about the middle of the century. It was no longer easy for apprentices to pass into the ranks of masters of the craft. Entrance fees made it increasingly difficult for a man to save enough from his wages as a journeyman to enter the gild. Thus a town proletariat formed—men who spent their entire lives as wage earners, working for masters of the gilds.

In some cases, particularly in the textile trades, gild masters themselves sank to a dependent status. Large-scale capitalists adopted the practice of supplying the working capital—i.e., the wool, flax or linen—to the spinners, weavers or fullers, who manufactured it at piece rates. In some towns, however, these practices were prohibited by gild regulations; and to escape such limitations, it became increasingly common for capitalists to employ workmen who lived in the countryside, where gilds had no jurisdiction. This practice is called the domestic or putting-out system of industry. The growing prevalence of the domestic system accounts in part for the slowing down of town growth in such regions as Flanders. Instead of concentrating in towns, industry migrated to the countryside under the management of comparatively large-scale merchants and capitalists. It should be noted that this development of capitalistic industry was mainly confined to articles which entered into inter-regional trade. The uncertainties of a distant market, which an individual weaver or spinner could in no way cope with, required an entrepreneur who had larger capital resources. Hence the capitalistic organization of such trades contributed to their stability and expansion, even though individual workmen undoubtedly were frequently subjected to exploitation, and could never hope to rise far.

Another realm in which capitalism developed was banking. Banking originated partly from the inter-regional clearing of balances,[4] and partly from dealings with governments. The Italian bankers, who took an early lead, founded their fortunes in no small part on financial activities performed on behalf of the papacy. Loans to governments, tax collection on behalf of governments, special mineral and other concessions from governments, all contributed to the enrichment of bankers who became indispensable to most European rulers as a source of ready cash. Banking and commercial and industrial capitalism were of course closely linked. Great banking families such as the Medici of Florence or the Fuggers of Augsburg combined industrial and commercial loans with large-scale operations on behalf of the governments of Europe.

Despite the cessation of rapid town growth in the most developed parts

---

[4]Merchant A in Bruges owed merchant B in Florence; while merchant C in Florence owed merchant D in Bruges. Instead of shipping coin, it became usual to cancel one debt against another; so that merchant A paid merchant D, and merchant C paid merchant B. Such clearances were arranged by bankers who drew a commission on the deal.

of Europe, along the frontiers towns sprang up and flourished during the fourteenth and fifteenth centuries. In northern and eastern Germany, for instance, a large number of towns—Hamburg, Lübeck, Stralsund, and others—rose to new prominence and wealth. They associated themselves into the Hansa (i.e., League). This organization came to control the Baltic Sea, and carried on successful naval campaigns against Denmark for control of the straits at its mouth. In central Germany towns such as Augsburg and Nuremberg entered upon a period of unexampled prosperity; and further east Prague, Cracow, Vienna, Budapest and other towns became flourishing commercial, industrial and intellectual centers.

As the scale of inter-regional trading increased, and as the economic interdependence of widely separated districts became more pronounced, phenomena analogous to modern booms and depressions began to appear. Thus in the fourteenth century the failure of an Italian banking house (due to the English king's repudiation of his debts) had repercussions all over Europe, and induced financial panics and credit stringency in every country in Christendom.

3) Technology. Technological invention continued to make rapid strides. Many kinds of power-driven machinery were devised, depending on wind or water, which used geared wheels, cams, and transmission shafts. The spinning wheel, involving the use of a belt-driven spindle, was probably developed during the fourteenth century; and once understood, the use of belts made possible a much more efficient transmission of power then cumbrous wooden drive shafts had previously allowed.

The compass was first widely adopted as an aid to navigation after 1300. Instruments for determining approximate latitude were also developed, based upon the principle of measuring the altitude of certain clock stars for which tables were constructed. Accurate determination of longitude, however, remained beyond the powers of navigators until the eighteenth century, for it depended on the construction of highly accurate clocks. Shipbuilding made steady progress. Larger and more seaworthy vessels were built with closed decks and with "castles" for defense and living quarters fore and aft. The net result of these various improvements was to make possible long ship voyages out of sight of land. Mariners were no longer afraid to venture on the open seas, and a series of explorations into the Atlantic led to the discovery of the Canary islands and the Azores in the fourteenth century, and of the sea route to India and to the Americas in the fifteenth.

Military technology, too, made great strides. The elaboration of armor resulted in the complete encasement of the knight in cunningly designed armor plate. But such armor was in a measure self-defeating, for it seriously reduced the mobility of the knight, who became entirely helpless when unhorsed, unable even to rise to his feet. Yet heavy armor was made necessary by the improvement of missile weapons, in particular the cross bow and the long bow, which, in the hands of Italian and English infantry respectively, won numerous battles. The introduction of gunpowder and artillery in the fourteenth century did not at once work decisive changes in military technique, for at first guns were unreliable, and did more damage by scaring horses than in any other way. Artillery was, however, of some effect in sieges, though it was rivaled by catapults until the seventeenth century. By 1500 hand guns had been invented, but it was more than a hundred years before infantry armed with such guns became a decisive element on the battlefield.

The expanded employment of metal for military and other uses led to a series of improvements in mining and metallurgy. Particularly in Germany, techniques for draining and ventilating mines were developed in order to permit mining at greater depths. Ore furnaces were enlarged, and bellows, sometimes run by waterpower, were applied to increase the temperature of the flame. Coal mining, especially in England, became common, but coal was used mainly for heating dwelling places, since various chemical impurities made it unsuitable for smeling iron.

Printing with movable type and the manufacture of paper were undoubtedly two of the most influential of late medieval inventions. Paper manufacture was probably introduced into Europe in the thirteenth century, but became common only later. The art of paper-making was borrowed from the Arabs, who in turn acquired the skill from the Chinese. Printing, too, may have been stimulated by reports of Chinese printing; but the definitive invention of movable type seems to be properly credited to various craftsmen in Mainz, of whom John Gutenberg was the most important. About 1456 Gutenberg printed a Bible which is counted as the earliest typeset book. The importance of printing and paper-making was very great. Books became relatively cheap, learning became accessible to a much wider circle of the population than could be the case when a single hand-copied volume might cost as much as a peasant's farm. The gap between intellectual leaders and the population at large could be narrowed and the rate of diffusion of new ideas and techniques could be correspondingly increased. The use of woodcuts for illustrations and maps was almost of equal importance for such fields as medicine, botany, geography and engineering, where an accurately reproduced drawing could do more than endless words to make the meaning clear.

By the fifteenth century Europe had definitely surpassed the Classical world in the sphere of technology, and Europeans had begun to exhibit the mechanical inventiveness which was to become a peculiar mark of their civilization. The success of Europeans in technology was partly stimulated by expanding contacts with such far-off parts of the earth as

China and India. Partly, too, it should be recognized that there had never been as much retrogression in the sphere of technology as there had been in other aspects of Classical civilization, so that the west, inheriting a substantial body of technical achievements, had a head start over the ancient Greeks and Romans.

c. Expansion of Europe

Technological development was both a cause and a consequence of European expansion. New techniques made transport and exploration easier; at the same time new contacts stimulated Europeans to adopt and adapt new skills and inventions. Political events in the thirteenth century made contact with China much easier. Led by Genghis Khan (*c.* 1162–1227) the Mongols conquered a vast territory in Asia, and under his successors a strong, centralized government was extended from the Pacific coast of China to the frontier of western Christendom in Poland. Within the Mongol empire, effective communications were maintained. As a result it became far easier for strangers from the west to acquire information about distant parts of Asia. About the middle of the thirteenth century missionary diplomats visited the court of the Mongol Khan; between 1260 and 1295 a remarkable family of Venetian merchants, the Polos, actually made their way to China. Upon his return Marco Polo wrote an account of his travels, which had taken him not only to China but to India as well. His book presented a fascinating story of the wonders, wealth and strange pagan ways of the peoples of Asia. Many of his contemporaries disbelieved what Marco Polo told them, but modern scholars find his book to be generally truthful. The gradual break-up of the Mongol empire and the destruction of the trading cities of Central Asia by Tamerlane (d. 1405) made commercial connections between China and Europe more and more difficult in the fourteenth and fifteenth centuries; but the very obstacles that arose to the use of overland routes constituted a stimulus to the search for sea paths to the fabulous Orient—a hope which lay behind the voyages of both Vasco da Gama and Columbus.

Portugal took an early lead in the voyages of exploration. A series of expeditions, equipped by the king of Portugal, explored the African coast during the fifteenth century. Trade with central Africa (the Guinea coast) in slaves, gold and ivory amply repaid the Portuguese, but they pressed steadily onward in the hope of reaching India. In 1482 the mouth of the Congo river was discovered; in 1486 Bartholomew Diaz rounded the Cape of Good Hope; and in 1497 Vasco da Gama reached India and initiated an enormously profitable trade in spices, calico and other products of the East. In 1500 Portuguese vessels sailing for India accidentally discovered the Brazilian coast; but this discovery of a new continent in the West had been anticipated by Christopher Columbus, who, sailing under

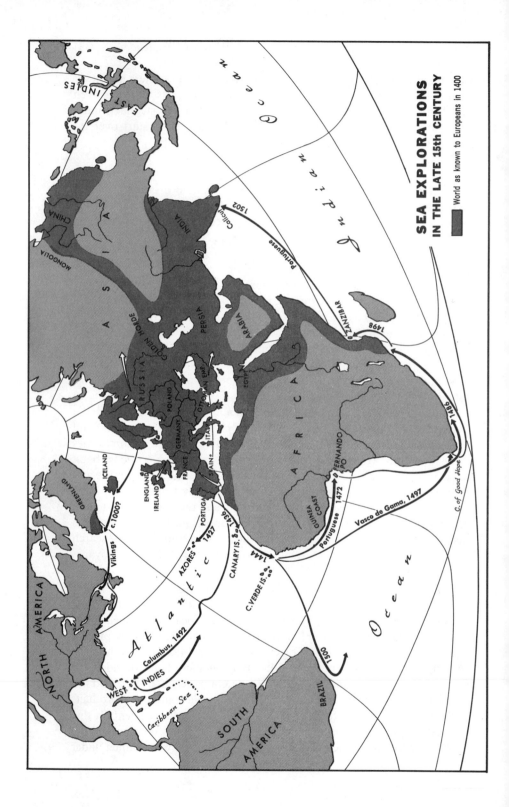

**SEA EXPLORATIONS
IN THE LATE 15th CENTURY**

■ World as known to Europeans in 1400

the Spanish flag, had in 1492 discovered some of the islands of the Caribbean. Believing them close to the Asian coast, he named them the Indies.

The eastward expansion of Germany did not cease. In 1229 the crusading Order of Teutonic Knights, having been driven out of the Holy Land,
undertook the conquest of one of the few remaining pagan tribes of the
Baltic region, the Prussians. Fifty years of fighting ended with the near
extermination of the Prussians, and the settlement of Prussia by German

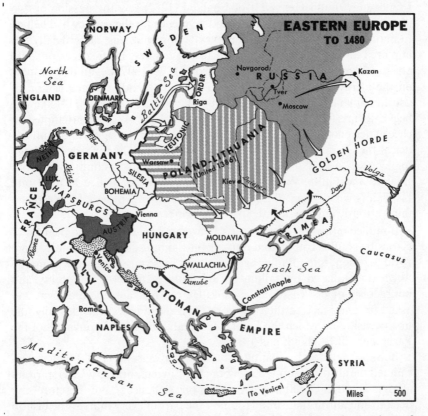

colonists. Further east and north along the Baltic coast, other orders of
German-speaking knights conquered Latvia and Esthonia, where they
reduced the natives to the status of serfs. The military and colonial expansion of Germany under the leadership of the Teutonic Knights came to an
end in the fifteenth century, when Poland and Lithuania, united under a
common king, attacked and defeated the Germans at Tannenberg in 1410.
Later in the century the Poles succeeded in reducing the lands held by the
Teutonic Knights in Prussia to the status of a Polish fief. Yet the rise of
Poland as an effective national state was accomplished only by imitation
of German institutions. Large numbers of Germans, and especially of

Germanized Jews, settled in Poland and Lithuania, where they constituted the backbone of the bourgeoisie, and were accorded special privileges by the Polish kings. As a result, from the fifteenth century, Poland became the largest single center of Jewish population in Europe.

d. Political Changes

1) The Political Overthrow of the Papacy. The death of St. Louis of France (1270) and Henry III of England (1272) saw the passing of two kings whose personal devoutness and reverence for the papacy had helped to maintain the fabric of papal universal power at least superficially unimpaired through the most of the thirteenth century. Their successors were not so scrupulous. In England, Edward I (1272–1307) began to levy taxes on the clergy despite papal opposition, and forbade the acquisition of additional lands by the Church. Philip IV of France (1285–1314) likewise began to tax the clergy. Pope Boniface VIII (1294–1303) attempted to check such encroachment of royal government on the rights and immunities of the Church. By his bull *Clericis laicos* (1296), he forbade the clergy to pay taxes to secular rulers. This at once precipitated a conflict with both Edward and Philip. Within a year the pope was compelled to moderate his claims when King Philip stopped all export of money from France, thus seriously cutting into the papal revenues.

Boniface returned to the contest five years later, forbidding the trial of clerics by secular courts, and once again claiming clerical immunity from royal taxation. King Philip, against whom these measures were primarily directed, retaliated by calling an assembly of the clergy, nobility and bourgeoisie of his kingdom in 1302. He put his cause before them and asked for and received their support. (This meeting was, incidentally, the first occasion on which the Estates General, the French equivalent of the Parliament of England, met.)

Boniface reacted by issuing a bull, *Unam sanctam* (1302) which proclaimed the absolute supremacy of the pope in temporal as well as spiritual affairs. The bull concluded with a famous sentence: "We therefore say, declare and affirm that submission on the part of every man to the bishop of Rome is altogether necessary for salvation."

But events quickly showed where real power lay. The French government organized a defamation campaign against Boniface and demanded his trial before a general council of the Church. Not content with such verbal warfare, an official of the French government arrested Boniface at the small Italian town of Anagni in 1303 with the help of a group of the pope's Italian enemies. The incident at Anagni stands as a symbol of the decay, just as the incident at Canossa stands as a symbol of the rise, of the political power of the medieval papacy. The pope's arrest precipitated a great scandal, and after a few days Boniface was released, a broken man.

He died soon afterward, and with him died the dream of a universal papal monarchy.

In 1305, two years after Boniface's death, a Frenchman was elected pope. Instead of going to Rome, he took up residence at Avignon, a town just outside the border of the French kingdom, on the Rhone river (1309). Moreover the new pope absolved Philip of all blame for the attack on Boniface, and, by appointing new cardinals from among the French clergy, he made the papacy in effect a captive of the French government. Succeeding popes were always careful not to antagonize the king of France. In effect, the papacy at Avignon and the monarchs of France and England struck a bargain whereby each supported the other in the congenial task of extracting larger and larger taxes and other payments from the bishops and lower clergy.

For more than seventy years, the popes remained in Avignon, absent from their episcopal see at Rome. This in itself was a grave scandal in the eyes of pious Christians, and tended to deprive the popes of their prestige as heirs to the universalist traditions of Rome. New heresies arose to plague the unity of the Church, and national or local governments were not always willing to cooperate with agents of the papacy in suppressing such movements.

The question of the right of the Church to hold property became a burning issue when a group within the Franciscan order of friars, the Spirituals, reasserted and extended St. Francis' doctrine of poverty. The Avignon popes declared the doctrine of apostolic poverty—that Christ and the apostles had owned no property—to be heretical; and when some of the Spiritual Franciscans refused to accept the papal ruling, they were subjected to persecution. In England, echoes of this controversy stimulated an Oxford professor, John Wiclif (d. 1384), to develop radical views. He questioned the rightfulness of ecclesiastical possession of property, and also challenged such doctrines as the Petrine supremacy and transubstantiation. He sponsored the earliest translation of the Bible into English, and began to emphasize the authority of the Scripture as superior to that of the Church and the priesthood. In 1377 the pope declared Wiclif heretical. Despite the pope, he attracted numerous followers, known as Lollards; but persecution by the royal government gradually repressed the movement.

From England, however, Wiclif's ideas spread to Bohemia through the medium of Czech students who studied at Oxford. John Hus (d. 1415) an eloquent preacher, espoused Wiclif's doctrines, and won a numerous following among the common people. The Hussite movement was in part a Czech national reaction against German domination of ecclesiastical and official positions, a fact which made the movement all the more formidable.

The fiscal policies of the Avignon papacy were very generally criticized by educated and devout men. Sale of church offices became quite open, and the pressing financial needs of the popes led to the invention of a variety of new taxes and fees which were levied on the lower clergy. The sale of indulgences (which were believed to replace penitential good works, but did not remit sin *per se*) was also developed by the Avignon popes as a supplement to their other income. These and like practices offended many earnest Christians, and the demand for Church reform became steadily greater.

Most reformers believed that the only way the papacy could be made to mend its ways was by assembling a general Council of the Church. They went further, and argued that the popes had in fact usurped the ecclesiastical sovereignty which rightfully belonged to the bishops and other prelates gathered together in a council.

The fate of the papacy in the last quarter of the fourteenth century gave a great impetus to ideas such as these. In 1377 Pope Gregory XI finally abandoned Avignon and went to Rome, where he died in the following year. The ensuing election was a troubled one. The populace of Rome demanded an Italian pope, and the cardinals reluctantly yielded by electing Urban VI. But they soon repented, and with the approval of the French government, the cardinals met a second time, declared the earlier election void, and elected a second pope, a Frenchmen. Thus began the Great Schism. Urban VI proceeded to appoint a new College of Cardinals, and lived in Rome, while the French pope took up residence at Avignon. Each pope anathematized the other; when they died their respective successors maintained the breach. The support of Europe was divided according to whether the local government was friendly or hostile to France.

Efforts to negotiate an agreement for the election of a single pope came to nothing; in 1409 a number of cardinals, from both papal camps, united to call a general council at Pisa in the hope of settling the dispute. But the council succeeded only in electing a third pope. This absurdity resulted in a second effort to end the schism by conciliar action. This time the council was summoned jointly by pope number three and by the German emperor, Sigismund. It met at Constance in 1414, promptly quarreled with its papal sponsor, and when he departed, the Council proceeded to act as the sovereign body of the Church, supported by the secular power of the emperor.

The Council of Constance faced three major problems: to check heresy, to reform the Church, and to choose a new pope who would be able to win general support and end the schism. To combat heresy, the council condemned Wiclif's opinions, and sentenced John Hus to death at the stake. Toward Church reform less was accomplished. Decrees were promulgated which recommended various reforms and provided for the periodic assemblage of councils. The Council, was, however, able to secure the abdication of two of the three popes who had claimed the office when it met, and managed to deprive the third of all political support so that he could safely be neglected. A new pope was then elected (1417) who commanded the support of all western Christendom.

Yet the Council of Constance had not solved all the major problems facing the Church. In particular, the execution of John Hus did not end heresy in Bohemia. When the papacy and the emperor tried to suppress the Hussites by proclaiming a Crusade against them, the Bohemian heretics were able to repulse their attackers. This military failure played a considerable part in setting the atmosphere for a second important council, the Council of Basel (1431-49). The Council of Basel quarreled with the pope almost from the start, but was able to assert its leadership despite papal opposition, especially in the matter of coming to a diplomatic settlement with the moderate wing of the Hussite movement. But when the thorny question of Church reform was raised again, the council broke into quarrelsome groups, and moderate men began to gather under the banner of the pope, who in 1438 called a rival council at Florence. The remnant of reformers at Basel made the mistake of raising a rival pope; but this echo of the Great Schism was altogether unpopular, and from that time onward the Council of Basel lost prestige. It was not formally dissolved until 1449, but long before that the principle of conciliarism had been discredited, and the pope emerged triumphant as the head of the Church. (Cf. p. 364 for a summary of conciliar theory.)

This papal victory largely annulled the reforming efforts of earlier years. Various papal practices continued to offend many devout men; but the hierarchy of the church took little cognizance of such feeling until compelled to do so by the explosion of the Reformation movement. The popes became immersed in Italian politics, and some distinguished themselves as patrons of art and letters. Their religious leadership of Europe was weakened by sometimes scandalous personal behavior, and by the manner in which spiritual weapons were freely used to forward the temporal interests of the papacy.

The vicissitudes through which the papacy passed in the fourteenth and early fifteenth centuries resulted in the loss of the dominating political position throughout Western Christendom which medieval popes had won, and seriously compromised papal control over what had earlier been considered purely ecclesiastical matters. More and more, clergymen were becoming subject to the political and economic control of local secular governments, and, especially in France, the idea of a national church within the framework of the universal Church began to emerge.

2) France and England. The consolidation of the French and English national states was hampered during the fourteenth and fifteenth centuries

by the outbreak of the Hundred Years' War (1338–1453) and by a series
of revolts and civil wars, which afflicted first France and then England.
The Hundred Years' War was largely fought by mercenary companies,
which, when a campaign was not in progress, ravaged the French countryside. Thus, although organized fighting was intermittent, punctuated
by long periods of truce and inactivity, the war was very destructive to
France.

HUNDRED YEARS' WAR — 1338-1453

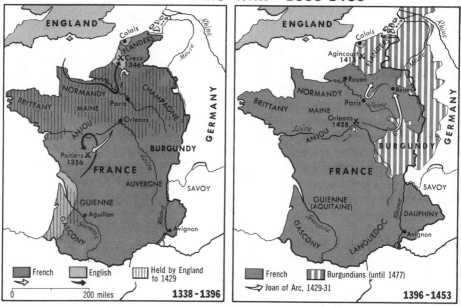

When the direct Capetian line died out in 1328 the Valois family as-
cended the French throne, despite the fact that the king of England,
Edward III, claimed through his mother to be the nearest heir. Ten years
later, in 1338, a quarrel over Flanders led Edward to advance his claim
again, and in the following years a series of English expeditions invaded
France. English archers won brilliant victories at Crécy (1346) and
Poitiers (1356) against French knights, on the strength of which the
English were able to occupy a large part of France. By 1380, however, the
French monarchy had recovered lost ground and almost succeeded in
driving the English out of France; but this success was nullified by the outbreak of civil war between French noble factions during the long reign of
the insane King Charles VI (1380–1422). This invited fresh intervention
by the English. Accordingly, in 1415 Henry V of England invaded France
again, and at Agincourt won a third notable victory for English arms.

The accidents of marriage and inheritance had meanwhile resulted in the creation of a powerful Burgundian state, lying partly within France, partly within the empire. It was ruled by a branch of the French royal family, but the dukes of Burgundy were not content to remain vassals of their neighbors. Instead they dreamed of creating a third kingdom between France and Germany which would extend from the Low Countries to the Jura mountains along the west bank of the Rhine. Between 1415 and 1435 the Burgundians cooperated with the English, and succeeded in establishing the English king Henry V in Paris, where they recognized him as legitimate ruler of France.

Into this situation the catalytic personality, Joan of Arc, projected herself. Inspired by visions, she conceived it to be her duty to drive the English from France. Although she was only a peasant girl, she made her way to the court of the heir to the French throne and inspired his troops with enough of her own pious confidence to permit them to relieve the city of Orleans, which the English had besieged. Then she conducted the dauphin to Reims, where he was crowned King of France in 1429. She was captured by Burgundians the next year, handed over to the English, and after a trial by the Inquisition was convicted of heresy and burnt at the stake in 1431. Nevertheless Joan had saved the French monarchy at a time when it seemed to have reached an almost hopeless debility.

In 1435 the Burgundians abandoned their alliance with the English. Slowly the French king was able to build up a strong and relatively efficient army, which in the following years drove the English out of France, save for the town of Calais. By 1453 the last English positions in Gascony had been taken, and France was once more united under a single monarch.

The Burgundian state, however, remained strong, and it was not until 1477 that the French king had the satisfaction of seeing the last duke of Burgundy killed in battle, and was able to seize possession of most of the French fiefs he had held. The rest of the Burgundian territories, including the rich provinces of the Low Countries, went to the Hapsburg family through marriage with the heiress of the last duke.

The effect of the Hundred Years' War on France was profound. The ravages of soldiers and the general disorder which reigned for so many years persuaded the Estates-General to delegate the power of taxation to the royal government (1439). Thereby the way was paved for the development of an absolute monarchy, since a king who had unquestioned rights of taxation was able to support a standing army with which local opposition could usually be overcome. The war also stimulated a more definite sense of nationality, for Frenchmen came to fear and hate the English foreigners. A third outcome of the war and the collapse of the Burgundian state was the consolidation of the whole of France under the rule of the king. Some great fiefs, notably Brittany, retained a certain independence under collateral branches of the royal family, but they too in the following generations were reincorporated into the kingdom, and subjected to the direction of a growing central bureaucracy.

The internal development of England stands in contrast to that of France, for the representative institutions, which in France were undermined by the necessities of the war, gained in power during the same period in England. The difference arose partly from the fact that the Parliament of England had developed earlier than had the Estates General of France. Parliament originated from the feudal custom of periodically calling together the royal vassals (the barons) in order to talk things over and to settle disputes among the royal vassals or between the king and any of his vassals. During the thirteenth century the barons were frequently at odds with the king, trying constantly to resist the encroachment of royal power on their old rights. The Magna Carta stood as the principal monument of baronial opposition to the king. Disputes over its application were frequent, and a number of baronial risings occurred later in the century.

About the middle of the thirteenth century the leader of one such rising, son and namesake of the Albigensian crusader Simon de Montfort, called representatives of the towns and of the lesser landholders of the shires into consultation along with the barons. This precedent was accepted by Edward I (1272–1307) who in 1295 summoned the so-called Model Parliament. In addition to the barons and the upper clergy, two representatives from each borough (i.e., from each town with a royal charter) and two knights (i.e., lesser landholders) from each shire were summoned to meet in Parliament.

The major reason for calling these representatives of the lower ranks was the king's constant need of money. By calling together representatives of the towns and of the lesser landholders the king could negotiate with them for grants of special taxes, and in general he could try to secure their support for various undertakings of the royal government. The long wars in France necessitated frequent appeals for additional taxes; and the custom gradually established itself for the knights and burgesses to meet together in the House of Commons, while the barons came to constitute the House of Lords. Since the Commons represented the majority of the taxpayers, their power over matters of taxation was gradually recognized as preeminent. Grants were made for limited periods of time or for specific purposes, thus necessitating frequent recourse by the royal government to fresh parliamentary assemblies. In 1399 the Lancastrian house usurped the throne, and their shaky title to royal power made the Lancastrian kings doubly cautious not to offend Parliament.

The English crown was not entirely dependent on Parliamentary grants, since the king enjoyed an income from his private estates, from fees paid to royal courts and from various customary levies on exports, the sale of licenses, etc. From the king's point of view, Parliamentary grants were simply a convenient way of increasing the royal revenue. Extraordinary exactions and fiscal manipulations were sometimes resorted to, but in general they caused more trouble and excited more opposition than did a tax to which Parliament had assented.

The development of English governmental institutions underwent a serious interruption when in 1455 intermittent civil war broke out between the rival families of Lancaster and York. In the course of the fighting many old baronial families were exterminated, so that when the Wars of the Roses (as the struggle is called) ended in 1485, the feudal organization of England had largely been broken up. Parliament, too, during these years had become the plaything of rival factions, and its powers and organization were seriously compromised. As a result, the first of the Tudors, Henry VII (1485-1509), was able to establish something very close to absolute monarchy. Parliament did not disappear, but it became a more or less passive instrument of the royal will.

English administrative and judicial machinery underwent notable expansion throughout the fourteenth and fifteenth centuries. Manorial, feudal and ecclesiastical courts lost most of their jurisdiction to the growing system of royal courts, which administered the common law. Older forms of taxation, such as scutage, were dropped, and new sources of income, notably export and import duties, replaced them.

The area under English administration also expanded. Edward I conquered Wales and briefly controlled most of Scotland, but his successor could not hold the latter. Resistance to the English in the first part of the fourteenth century did much to create a Kingdom of Scotland, whose institutions and culture came to be modelled on European and English forms. A part of Ireland, too, acknowledged English sovereignty from the time of Henry I.

3) Germany. In 1273 a petty nobleman, Rudolph of Hapsburg, was elected Holy Roman Emperor, but did not trouble to go to Rome to be crowned. Nor did he seek to make the royal power effective through all Germany, but instead he founded the fortune of the Hapsburg family by gaining possession of Austria. His descendants remained in control there until 1918. The kingship of Germany did not rest permanently with the Hapsburg house after Rudolph's time. The German princes tried to avoid electing a powerful ruler as king, and shifted the royal title from one family to another at frequent intervals.

With each election, new rights were guaranteed to the princes, who within their various states steadily built up a more and more absolute power. In 1356 the procedure of imperial election was specified by the so-called Golden Bull. It established seven electors—three archbishops and four secular princes—chosen from the most powerful rulers of Germany. Lesser princes, representatives of the free towns, and even individual "imperial knights" were represented in an Imperial Diet, which met at irregular intervals to consider general questions; but the Imperial Diet had no definite powers, and had no means of enforcing its decisions on all the German princes and states.

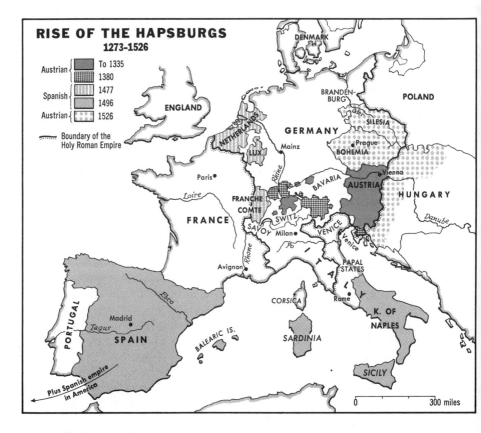

Individual kings of Germany played a part in the general European scene, and it was a German emperor, Sigismund, who in 1414 cooperated in summoning the Council of Constance which ended the Great Schism. Yet in general, the power of the German king or emperor was scarcely greater than what his private possessions conferred upon him.

By 1438 the Hapsburg family had risen to a leading place in Germany largely through a series of fortunate marriages. The power of the Hapsburgs was such that they were again able to secure election to the imperial title, and from that time until 1806 the emperors were nearly always chosen from the Hapsburg family. In 1477 marriage into the Burgundian house added the Low Countries to the Hapsburg possessions; and in 1496 another marriage with the heiress of Spain prepared the way for the addition of Spain to the Hapsburg inheritance, an addition which carried with it sovereignty over the New World.

These great increases in Hapsburg territory were matched by some losses. In 1291 some of the Swiss cantons banded together to resist their Hapsburg overlord. During the next two centuries conflicts between the Swiss and the Hapsburgs were chronic, ending only in 1499 when the independence of the Swiss was recognized by the emperor. It was not, however, until 1648 that Switzerland was formally recognized as a sovereign power by the other states of Europe.

4) Italy. The weakness of the emperors in the fourteenth and fifteenth centuries made it possible for small city states to achieve full sovereignty in Italy. The northern part of the peninsula came to be divided between numerous competing cities, of which Venice, Milan and Florence were the most powerful. Wars were frequent, and were fought by mercenary soldiers who were generally more interested in living to fight another day than in winning a crushing victory for their employers. Individual mercenary captains were sometimes able to seize control of the city which had hired them; and miniature despotisms became common as a result. The despots' rule was often uncertain, with danger of assassination, poisoning or revolution constantly at hand.

Florence retained a precarious republican government until 1434, when practical control of the city came to rest in the hands of the Medici family. The Medici kept republican forms but, through their wealth and an obedient political machine, managed to control the city effectively from behind the scenes. Venice, too, retained its medieval form of government—a narrow oligarchy of wealthy merchant families. They managed to make their city a power not only in Italy but throughout the Adriatic and in the Levant as well. During the long residence of the popes at Avignon (1304–78) the Papal States in central Italy fell prey to numerous local adventurers, and it was not until the end of the fifteenth century that papal rule was effectively reestablished there by the notorious Cesare Borgia, illegitimate son of Pope Alexander VI (1492–1503). Further south, the old Norman kingdom of Sicily had fallen on evil days following the accession of Charles of Anjou (1266). In 1282 the island of Sicily revolted from his harsh rule, and a branch of the Aragonese ruling family seized power. Thereafter there were two kingdoms of Sicily, one on the mainland of southern Italy, the other in the island itself. The wealth and culture which had distinguished the Norman kingdom was gradually dissipated, and the two Sicilies became a backwater of European life.

The wealth of the Italian cities, their bitter quarrels and internal social

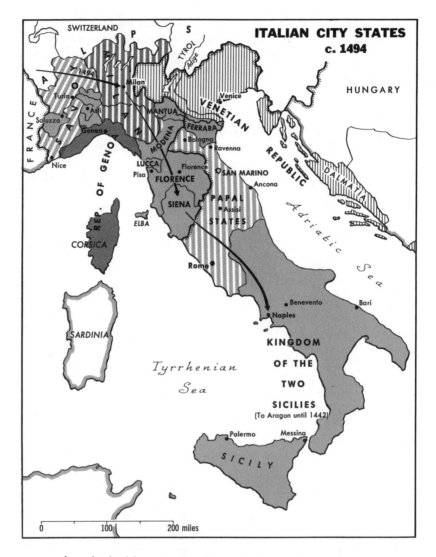

ITALIAN CITY STATES
c. 1494

SWITZERLAND

TYROL

HUNGARY

Milan

1494

Turin

Asti

VENETIAN

Venice

Saluzzo

MANTUA

Genoa

REP. OF GENOA

MODENA

FERRARA

Bologna

REPUBLIC

DALMATIA

Nice

Ravenna

FRANCE

LUCCA

Florence

SAN MARINO

Pisa

FLORENCE

Ancona

Adriatic

SIENA

PAPAL

Assisi

ELBA

STATES

CORSICA

Rome

Sea

Benevento

Bari

Naples

SARDINIA

KINGDOM

Tyrrhenian

OF THE

Sea

TWO

SICILIES

(To Aragon until 1442)

Palermo   Messina

S I C I L Y

0   100   200 miles

antagonisms invited intervention by the larger national states which had
formed in France and Spain during the fifteenth century. In 1494 Charles
VIII of France invaded Italy, and easily overrode the scattered military
resistance which was offered to him. This invasion marks the effective end
of the sovereignty of the Italian states. Thereafter Italy became a bone of
contention between French, Spanish and Austrian rulers; and the various Italian states, including the Papal States, became playthings of greater
powers. This change in political scale, resulting from the emergence of
powerful and well-consolidated nation states in France, Spain and

England, has been taken by many historians as the beginning of modern times.

5) Other parts of Europe. By the end of the fourteenth century the expansion of Western Christendom on the European continent was nearly complete. Scandinavia, the Baltic states, Poland, Lithuania and Hungary constituted its northern and eastern frontiers. Beyond lay Russia to the northeast, still subject to Mongol rulers, and in the southeast was the newly-formed Ottoman empire. Both these states were in large measure heirs of Byzantium, and their religion, customs, political institutions, and culture mark them off as belonging to a distinct civilization. Only in the eighteenth and nineteenth centuries did Western European civilization begin to penetrate these regions.

To the southwest, however, European expansion continued until 1492, when the Moors were driven from their last stronghold in southern Spain. The various Christian states of the Spanish peninsula were gradually amalgamated by conquest and marriage until by the end of the fifteenth century only two remained: Portugal and Spain. Portugal took a leading part in the overseas expansion of Europe, but its restricted territory in Europe itself prevented it from rising to the first rank among the powers of the continent. Spain, however, almost from the date of its formation in 1479, as a result of a marriage between Ferdinand of Aragon and Isabella of Castile, took a leading place among the states of Europe. Its inherent strength was enormously enhanced in the following century by the wealth which poured in from the gold and silver mines of the Americas. As a result, during most of the sixteenth century Spain was the greatest power of Europe.

e. Cultural Growth

1) Italian Renaissance. During the fourteenth and fifteenth centuries, the cities of Italy were the scene of a vigorous artistic and intellectual life. Beginning about the middle of the fourteenth century a number of men discovered a new enthusiasm for the literary works of the classical world; and from literature admiration for classical models passed over to art and architecture, and even colored the religion of a few enthusiasts. The rediscovery of the greatness of the classical world was considered by the men of the time to be a return to true civilization after a long twilight of Gothic barbarism and scholastic logic chopping. More recently historians have minimized the contrast between Italian culture of the renaissance and medieval achievements. Instead of "The Renaissance," scholars have come to speak of a series of renaissances, from the time of Charlemagne onward. But the fact remains that Italy became the cultural leader of Europe and the scene of innovations in literature, art and philosophy during the fourteenth and fifteenth centuries, which, under the stimulus of pagan classical models, largely broke away from the Christian tradition of earlier centuries.

a) Literature. Dante Alighieri (1265–1321) was at once the literary summator of the intellectual life of the thirteenth century and the herald of new literary departures. In his vernacular works, Dante more than any other single figure crystallized literary Italian, making the Florentine dialect standard for subsequent Italian writers. His greatest work, the *Divine Comedy*, recounted Dante's imaginary travels through Hell, Purgatory and Heaven. In the course of his journey Dante met the leading figures of history and learned from them the secrets of the whole universe. In addition, he encountered numerous prominent men of affairs from his own time, and was thus able to voice his judgment of contemporary society and events, frequently in no uncertain terms. (Dante predicted, for example, the early arrival of Pope Boniface VIII in Hell.) The poem has been frequently compared with the *Summa Theologiae* of St. Thomas Aquinas for the completeness with which it expresses a medieval view of the world.

In addition to the *Divine Comedy*, Dante wrote sonnets addressed to Beatrice, a Florentine lady whom he loved and idealized, although he spoke to her only once. The influence of Provençal models on his verse form and subject matter is obvious; yet Dante infused his sonnets with religious mysticism and symbolism quite alien to the lighthearted Provençal poets.

Dante also wrote a number of works in Latin prose. In one he defended the use of the vernacular for literary composition; but the most famous is his defense of the empire against the papacy, *De Monarchia*. This treatise arose in part from the unhappy political experiences of Dante's life. As a young man he embarked upon a political career in his native Florence, but in 1302 a factional revolution drove him into exile, where he remained for the rest of his life. He had belonged to the antipapal faction, and could never forgive the popes for helping to bring about his banishment.

Petrarch (1304–1374), another Florentine who spent his life in exile, like Dante wrote sonnet sequences in praise of a fair lady whom he scarcely knew named Laura. His sonnets were more sensuous, and, despite the fact that Petrarch was in Holy Orders, less religious than Dante's. Perhaps for these very reasons we can more easily understand and admire his sonnets. They were widely imitated by later poets, and established the sonnet as an enduring literary form. In later life Petrarch professed disdain for the vernacular, and devoted himself to a study and criticism of the literary works of pagan Latin writers. He thus became one of the earliest humanists, i.e., men who preferred to study things human rather than divine, literature rather than theology. In his numerous Latin works,

Petrarch tried to model his style on Cicero and Seneca. As others followed him in this pursuit, the living language of medieval Latin gradually fell into disrepute, and Latin became what it is today, a dead language, bound by strict grammatical rules and hampered by a limited vocabulary.

Petrarch was driven always by a consuming desire for fame and was intensely conscious of his own individuality—two characteristics he shared with later figures of the Italian renaissance. Yet at the same time he could never entirely renounce belief in the Christian virtues of humility and selflessness. Frequently he reproached himself with sins and shortcomings. Thus he may be considered as a transitional figure between medieval and renaissance points of view. The same may be said of Petrarch's contemporary, Giovanni Boccaccio (1313-75). Despite the fact that his fame rests on the *Decameron*—a collection of quite irreligious but amusing and frequently bawdy stories—Boccaccio was much troubled by an ambivalent attitude toward Christianity, and in his old age seriously thought of entering a monastery.

Later Italian poets did not equal Dante and Petrarch in vernacular composition; instead humanistic study attracted a growing number of enthusiasts. An impassioned search for new manuscripts of classic authors was initiated. After about the middle of the fifteenth century, knowledge of Greek became common among Italian scholars. Thereafter, a new generation of scholars were able to rediscover the works of Greek literature as Latin literature had been rediscovered earlier.

New schools for the study of humanistic literature were established in several Italian towns; and a good humanistic education came to be a prerequisite for service not only in the government of a city like Florence, but even in the papal chancery itself. Rich merchants and princes held scholarship in high honor. Many humanists lived on pensions supplied by such men. Some of the popes, too, distinguished themselves as patrons of scholars, poets and artists, despite the irreligious quality of much of their work.

Admiration for the works of pagan literature helped to weaken the Christian feeling of many humanists. Some of them invoked the pagan gods in their writings, in imitation of Vergil and Homer. A few abandoned Christianity entirely, openly professed irreligion and criticized the Church and its officials in bitter terms. The most famous of the humanists who broke with Christian tradition was Lorenzo Valla (1405-1457). By a scholarly criticism of the Donation of Constantine he proved that document to be a forgery. He also denied apostolic authorship of the Apostles' Creed, and regarded the Bible as a work of purely human authorship.

A similar critical and worldly spirit was evidenced in the writings of Niccoló Machiavelli (1469-1527). He was well educated in the humanist tradition, and, like Dante, entered upon a political career in Florence. But a revolution put him out of office and forced his retirement. During the rest of his life Machiavelli spent his time reading the Latin classics and mulling over current Italian political events. The results of his reflections were embodied in a book of *Discourses on Livy*, and in the more famous *Prince*. In addition he wrote a *History of Florence* and a small book on the *Art of War*. Machiavelli's political reflections bear a certain analogy to the effort of renaissance artists: to describe men as they are, not as they ought to be. Yet Machiavelli was a stout Italian patriot, and hoped to see Italy strong and united, able to face France and Spain on equal terms.

b) Art. The weakening of Christian attitudes and feelings which can be detected in Italian literary development was also reflected in the history of art. At the beginning of the fourteenth century, Giotto (*c.* 1276–1336) painted with surpassing skill in a fully Christian spirit. Less than two centuries later, admiration for classical art and literature, coupled with a more sensuous interest in the world around him, led Alessandro Botticelli (1444–1510) to paint his famous *Birth of Venus*. Anyone who looks first at Giotto's series of frescoes depicting the life of Christ, and then turns to Botticelli's masterpiece, cannot miss the transformation which had come over Italian minds during the interval.

The technique of painting made rapid progress during the renaissance. In general, renaissance painters strove to achieve accuracy above all else. Giotto marks a stage in this effort, for his figures are more life-like than those of earlier painters. Tommaso Guidi Masaccio (1401–1428) introduced the use of shading to suggest three-dimensionality in his figures; and about 1435 Leon Battista Alberti (1404–1472) described a method for calculating perspective mathematically. Therewith a new technique for organizing a picture became possible. Later painters experimented extensively and enthusiastically with linear perspective, and also studied aerial perspective—that is, the use of color variations, shadow and blurring to suggest distance. To improve the accuracy of their painting, some artists studied anatomy, botany and physics. Leonardo da Vinci (1452–1519) is the most famous such artist-scientist. His *Notebooks* contain a multitude of suggestions and ideas for technical inventions and scientific experiments in addition to matters more closely related to the problems of painting.

Like humanistic scholars, artists were held in high respect during the Italian renaissance. Rich patrons supported them, and cities, churches, monasteries commissioned special works. The popes in Rome and the Medici family in Florence were the most lavish and tasteful art patrons of the age.

It should be pointed out that the apex of Italian renaissance painting came at the very end of the fifteenth century and during the sixteenth when

RENAISSANCE ART

Between 1300 and 1500 in Italy, and above all in Florence, artists developed a technique of painting that defined the European or Western art style for the following four hundred years. The key innovation was the discovery of geometrically accurate linear perspective. This allowed a two dimensional surface to appear as though it were a window opening on three dimensional space. The illusion of visual experience this permitted satisfied a drive for realism or optical accuracy that, until the twentieth century broke with this ideal, distinguished modern from medieval painting.

"Faith" from the series, *The Seven Virtues*. **Giotto**
Circa **1306. Arena Chapel, Padua**
(Alinari Art Reference Bureau)

Giotto was the first famous Italian painter to break with medieval conventions. By use of shading, he gave his figures a solid, three dimensional appearance, as is well illustrated by the manner in which "Faith" seems here to be stepping out from the background. Yet the central idea of the painting, to personify an abstract Christian virtue, remained thoroughly medieval.

A Scene from the life of St. Peter Showing the Distribution of Money to the Poor. Masaccio.
1422-27. Santa Maria del Carmine, Brancacci Chapel, Florence
(Alinari Art Reference Bureau)

A century after Giotto flourished, Florentine painters were ready to take on more ambitions compositions, in which distant and close-up figures and scenes were related more or less coherently in a single illusory space. Yet careful inspection will show that the perspective lines of this painting do not yet all converge upon a single disappearing point, with the result that the architectural background does not look quite "right" to our camera-trained eyes.

Funeral of St. Stephen. Fra Filippo Lippi.
Circa 1450. Cathedral, Prato
(Alinari Art Reference Bureau)

Only a generation later, Italian artists had mastered the rules of geometric
perspective, and could now faultlessly organize vast illusory space
and crowds of figures into a single coherent three dimensional scene.
In addition, realism of details, especially facial details, gave a picture such
as this topical interest, for individual Florentines could recognize
themselves or their friends in Fra Filippo Lippi's brushwork.

Birth of Venus. Sandro Botticelli
1480. Uffizi Gallery, Florence
(Alinari Art Reference Bureau)

Botticelli's use of a pagan theme represented a different kind of break with
medieval artistic conventions. Pagan nudity was shocking to many, and
the painting itself suggests Botticelli's eagerness to get Venus covered
up as soon as possible.

Mars and Venus United by Love. Paolo Veronese
***Circa* 1580**
(Metropolitan Museum of Art, Kennedy Fund, 1910)

A century after Botticelli unveiled his Venus, Italian painters were fully at
home with nude human bodies. Allegorical scenes, like this, made
senuous pleasures increasingly explicit. Such works were intended for the
private homes of wealthy and cultivated Italian gentlemen. Public display of
such a work would still have shocked the less sophisticated lower classes.

Arnolfini Wedding. Jan van Eyck
1434
(National Gallery, London)
Inset Showing Detail of Mirror

North of the Alps, European painters were slower to learn the technique of
linear perspective. Hence Jan van Eyck still commits "errors" in the way he
aligns the floor boards of this interior scene. Yet the realism of his painting, the
skill with which he suggests different textures of fur, cloth, and flesh and the
illusion of light diffusing through the window all show how much this
Flemish painter shared with the Italians of his age. The extraordinary elaboration
of detail (witness the reflection in the mirror, here enlarged), on the other
hand, had no parallel in Italy.

Adam and Eve. Albrecht Duerer
1504. Engraving
(Courtesy, Museum of Fine Arts, Boston, Stephen Bullard
Memorial Fund)

As a result of a youthful trip to Italy, Duerer for the first time brought the
fully developed Italian perspective techniques to the attention of artists
north of the Alps. This work, however, illustrates a different side of his
achievement. It is an engraving and was printed in multiple copies, thus taking
advantage of the new technical possibilities opened to artists by the
invention of printing. Secondly, in theme and style this engraving might
be described as a pagan rendition of a Biblical scene. Such a close interplay
between sacred and secular was uncommon in Italy, where sacred painting
was in public view in churches and pagan sensualism was reserved
for private dwelling places.

Children's Games. **Pieter Brueghel the Elder**
1560
(Kunsthistorisches Museum, Vienna)

Brueghel here offers us a precise record of children's games as played in
sixteenth century Flanders. He was the first European painter to
portray common things and everyday happenings; and he founded a
school that preferred such scenes to the religious, classical, and historical
subjects with which earlier painters had usually dealt.

Lorenzo de 'Medici. **Andrea del Verrocchio**
1488
(National Gallery of Art, Washington, D.C.,
Samuel H. Kress Collection)

Ruthless realism pervades this extraordinary portrait of Lorenzo de 'Medici.
The tightly closed lips and intense stare convey the ambitious and
ruthless character of this man.

David. Donatello
1430-33. National Museum, Florence
(Alinari Art Reference Bureau)

Italian renaissance painters were emancipated from the tyranny of the ancients
by the fact that no paintings survived from classical times. Sculptors were
not so free. As the cult of antiquity took hold among the cultured upper
classes of Italy, numerous surviving Roman statues set a standard
and model for their art.

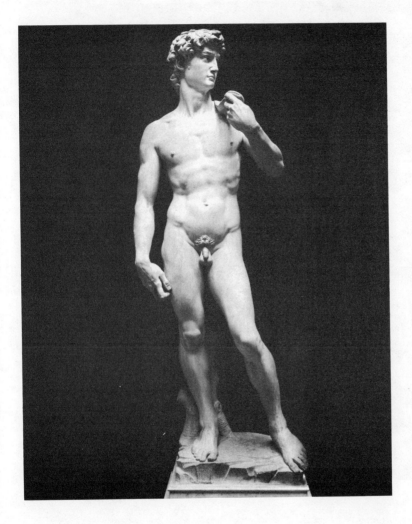

David. Michelangelo
1501-3. Academy, Florence
(Brogi Art Reference Bureau)

These two statues of David, made by Donatello and by Michelangelo at an
interval of just seventy years, show how successfully classical models
could be imitated, especially through recovery of skill in portraying accurate
anatomical detail.

***Christ Praying.* Till Riemenschneider
1499-1505. Rothenburg**
(Bildarchiv Foto Marburg Art Reference Bureau)

In northern Europe the impact of Roman sculpture was not felt until
much later. Hence Riemenschneider carved this panel, elaborating
medieval cathedral sculptural styles, at exactly the same time that Michelangelo
was working on his *David*. Riemenschneider's preoccupation with minute
detail closely resembled the work of contemporary painters
in northern Europe.

Leonardo da Vinci, Raphael (1483–1520), Michelangelo (1475–1564) and Titian (1477–1576) were active. In this, as in other fields, the periodization adopted in this *Handbook* fails to fit comfortably.

While painting was perhaps the most brilliant branch of renaissance art, new styles of sculpture and architecture also developed. Andrea Pisano (*c.* 1270–1348) and Lorenzo Ghiberti (1378–1455) both worked on elaborately modelled bronze doors for the baptistry of Florence. Their work showed little direct imitation of ancient models. Donatello (1386–1466) however, revived the classical idea of statuary on a pedestal independent of architectural setting. In his later work he definitely imitated Roman models, even to the point of clothing an Italian condottiere in Roman armor. The classic influence was also manifest in the work of later renaissance sculptors, of whom Michelangelo was the greatest.

Renaissance architects developed a new style, based on Roman motifs. Palatial private dwellings, churches and public buildings alike were built with classic colonnades and pilasters. The use of domes became especially characteristic of renaissance public building. The earliest example was the dome of the cathedral of Florence, planned by Filippo Brunelleschi (1377–1446); the largest and most magnificent was that of St. Peter's in Rome, which was planned by Lazzari Bramante (*c.* 1444–1514) and Michelangelo.

c) Science and Philosophy. The close connection between art and natural science in the mind of Leonardo da Vinci has already been mentioned. The emphasis which artists put upon fresh and minute observation certainly helped to free inquiring minds from excessive reverence for written authorities; yet in general no great advances in scientific theory were made by Italians until after the renaissance had passed its peak.

In philosophy, a number of scholars eagerly espoused Platonism and Neo-Platonism, partly at least, in reaction to the predominance of Aristotelianism among their medieval predecessors. The principal center of philosophic study was at Florence, where the Medici family founded the Florentine Academy in imitation of Plato's Academy.

d) The Renaissance Ideal. With the Italian renaissance a new ideal of human perfection achieved conscious definition. Old Christian virtues— humility, patience, loving kindness—were put aside. Men came to value life in the world, and to glory in it. Individual fame and distinction became a goal to be striven for, perhaps above all else; versatility and grace of mind and body were cultivated while specialization was accounted beneath the full dignity of man. It was an ideal which required leisure for its approximation and consequently an aristocratic one, though the aristocracy was not one of birth so much as of talent and of money.

A book which sums up much of the renaissance ideal is *The Courtier* by

Baldassare Castiglione (1478-1529). It is a book of manners, describing the talents and accomplishments which a cultivated man should possess. Castiglione emphasized the value of a humanistic education, a ready wit, a strong and graceful body, and a diplomatic tongue skilled to say the right thing to the right person at the right time. As a sort of Emily Post, this book and others like it helped to shape the character of court life and courtly manners both in Italy and elsewhere in Europe for several centuries.

2) Culture of Northern Europe. By the end of the fifteenth century, Italian cultural leadership was acknowledged by men throughout Europe. Prior to that time, Italian influence had been only sporadic. Yet even at the height of the influence of the Italian renaissance, the culture of the rest of Europe retained a somewhat different timbre. North of the Alps, the revival of classical antiquity never penetrated as fully as it did in Italy; and the Christian impress and religious interest inherited from earlier ages remained correspondingly stronger.

a) Literature. The fourteenth century marks an important stage in the development of both English and French as literary languages. In England, until the fourteenth century the feudal classes generally spoke Norman-French, while humbler persons spoke various dialects developed from the Germanic tongues of the Angles and Saxons. As time passed, a gradual amalgamation took place between French and Germanic speech, until a new language, English, was formed. Yet there remained wide variations, depending on locality and social class.

Two well known writers of the fourteenth century illustrate this divergence. William Langland, whose dates and career are both uncertain, wrote *Piers Plowman* in the form of a dream allegory. Langland's work is notable among medieval works of literature for its sympathy with the hard lot of the peasants. The language of *Piers Plowman* is equally interesting. Its verse form derived from Anglo-Saxon alliterative models, and the diction shows relatively little admixture of French and Latin.

Geoffrey Chaucer (*c.* 1340-1400), on the other hand, shows clearly the interpenetration of French, Latin and Anglo-Saxon elements in his grammar and diction. He was a Londoner, son of a prosperous wine merchant and a minor figure in the royal bureaucracy, who, as part of his official duty, went on diplomatic missions to France, the Low Countries and Italy. Thus he came to be familiar with the culture of these countries, and made numerous translations into English from French and Italian works of literature. His masterpiece, the *Canterbury Tales*, reflects Chaucer's wide culture, for it consists of a collection of tales in verse, many of which were borrowed (and transformed) from Boccaccio and other continental writers. The freshness and vigor of Chaucer's language, his evident joy in the bright world around, and his unforgettable pen portraits of the pilgrims on their way to Canterbury in the *Prologue*, make his poem one of the great works of English literature.

The translation of the Bible into English, carried through under the sponsorship of John Wiclif (see p. 335) foreshadowed the stateliness and vigor of the later King James version, which was, in fact, partly modeled on the Wiclif Bible.

In France individual authors comparable to Langland and Chaucer did not arise. Nonetheless, the dialect of Paris gradually began to assert itself as the language of literature. The lyric poet, François Villon (1431–c. 1489), one of the first Parisian bohemians, wrote in a sometimes humorous, sometimes plaintive vein of his reckless and violent life. His poems are reminiscent of the Goliardic verse of earlier centuries, but the fact that he wrote in French rather than in Latin may be taken as an index of the progress of the vernacular.

In Germany and other European countries no literary figures of first rank arose in the fourteenth century. In the fifteenth century, however, humanism penetrated from Italy into northern Europe and found an especially fertile field in the German cities of the Rhineland and in the Low Countries.

b) Art. Gothic construction continued to be elaborated in northern Europe, and indeed many of the greatest cathedrals, begun in the twelfth and thirteenth centuries, were not finally completed until the fourteenth or fifteenth centuries. In addition, a monumental secular architecture in modified Gothic style was employed for the construction of city halls and similar buildings in prosperous towns such as Bruges and Ghent.

Painting, as in Italy, took on stature as one of the major arts, particularly in Flanders, where the brothers Hubert (*c.* 1370–1426) and Jan van Eyck (*c.* 1385–1440) painted with a meticulous and charming attention to detail. Roger van der Weyden (*c.* 1400–1464) and Hans Memling (*c.* 1430–1494) carried on the tradition of the Van Eycks, and were particularly successful in portraiture and interior scenes. None of the weakening of Christian piety, which can be detected in Italian painting of the century, was manifest in the work of the Flemish painters; and indeed, Italian painting had little influence in Flanders until the sixteenth century.

c) Thought. Scholasticism did not come to an end with the thirteenth century. Long after logic chopping became the butt of Italian humanists, the study of theology and law remained the staple of university education and the prerequisite of an ecclesiastical career. Two English Franciscans, Duns Scotus (*c.* 1270–1308) and William of Ockham (*c.* 1300–1349) were the leading figures of a new scholasticism which challenged the rationalism of Aquinas, doubting the power of intellect to reach the truths of what

Aquinas called "natural theology." The result was a widening of the distinction, already made by Aquinas, between theology on the one hand and science and philosophy on the other. William of Ockham also became a prominent opponent of papal claims to political power, and helped to promote the conciliar movement.

d) Religion. The degradation of the papacy in the fourteenth century and the prevalence of corruption throughout the Church obviously created new problems for serious and devout Christians. Three major intellectual movements reacted in different ways to these conditions: conciliarism, mysticism, and Christian humanism.

The political failure of conciliarism has already been sketched; (pp. 337) but in spite of its inability to reform the Church, the movement stimulated a number of significant books of political theory. The anti-papal political writings of Dante and William of Ockham have already been mentioned. Another notable pair were Marsiglio of Padua (1270–1342) and John of Jandum (d. 1328), both ex-professors of the University of Paris, who collaborated to write *Defensor Pacis* (Defender of the Peace). This book has become famous as one of the earliest statements of a thoroughgoing theory of representative government. The authors argued that sovereignty could arise legitimately only from a delegation of powers made to a ruler by elected representatives of the general population. Theirs was not, however, a democratic theory, since they considered that representatives were naturally designated by their high birth and wealth.

Such theorizing both reflected and helped to support the development of national representative institutions, although it should be pointed out that only the English Parliament long survived as a significant element in political life, and its roots were far more in feudal and tax relationships than in bookish theories. Bookishness was indeed one of the serious weaknesses of the whole conciliar movement. When theory impinged on practical politics, as it did at the councils of Constance and Basel, university professors played a leading, but in the long run, ineffective part. Most notable among them was Jean Gerson (1362–1428), chancellor of the University of Paris and one of the moving spirits of the Council of Constance.

Mysticism, too, developed new prominence in the fourteenth and fifteenth centuries, especially in Germany and the Low Countries. Meister Eckhardt (*c.* 1260–1327), Thomas à Kempis (*c.* 1380–1471), and many other devout and pious men strove by contemplation to rise to communion with God. For such men, the corrupt state of the Church, however deplorable, could be neglected since the individual believer had a direct, personal path to God that did not require priestly mediation. Such a reaction to the problems of the times won wide response. *The Imitation of*

Christ edited by Thomas à Kempis, a book of private devotions and contemplation, was and remains one of the most popular books of religion ever written. This and other writings helped to spread mystical ideas widely among both clergy and laity. A semimonastic order, the Brethren of the Common Life, was established in the Low Countries in the fourteenth century. Through their schools and efforts at intensification of religious experience the Brethren did much to spread mystical piety and humanistic learning through a wide circle, especially in the Dutch provinces.

Following the failure of conciliarism to secure reform of the Church, intellectual leadership passed from the universities to individual scholars who were deeply influenced by the humanism which had developed in Italy. Jacques LeFèvre d'Etaples (*c.* 1450–1537), John Reuchlin (1455–1522), Thomas More (1478–1535) and, most influential of all, Desiderius Erasmus (*c.* 1466–1536) were all ardent students of the classics; but they differed from many of the Italian humanists in their continuing concern with religion. Through numerous books, disseminated widely by means of the printing press, they criticized the follies, superstitions and abuses which had grown up around the Church. Erasmus prepared a carefully collated Greek text of the *New Testament*. The result of his work was to cast doubt upon the accuracy of St. Jerome's Latin translation of the Bible (The Vulgate), which had so long served as the fundament of theology and canon law. In learned notes on the text, Erasmus took pains to attack a number of medieval interpretations of the Scripture which he regarded as erroneous.

Conciliarism, mysticism and Christian humanism all three contributed in their various ways to the Protestant reformation: conciliarism by attacking the papal monarchy and insisting upon the active role of laymen as well as ecclesiastics in matters of Church government; mysticism by emphasizing the possibility of individual approach to God without the mediation of priests; and humanism by a rationalistic and often biting criticism of persistent abuses in the Church. A vague discontent with the Church was certainly rife; and when the reunited papacy returned to Rome, became entangled in Italian politics, and failed to take reform seriously, the way was prepared for Luther to bring the latent discontent to a boil.

e) Natural Science. The exploration of far parts of the world was accompanied by an expansion of knowledge of geography, botany, and zoology. Cartography made very considerable progress, so that fairly accurate maps of the Mediterranean and other much traveled seas came into existence. The rotundity of the earth was admitted long before Columbus; although most men believed the size of the earth to be much smaller than was the case.

Astrology and alchemy continued to be studied, with a constant improvement in techniques for measurement, location, manipulation, and description of stars and chemicals. At the University of Paris a school of physicists modified some of the Aristotelian doctrines as to the nature of motion and of space. But none of the Parisian doctors equaled the fame and enigmatic genius of Nicholas of Cusa (1401-64), who adumbrated new concepts in mathematics, physics and astronomy which were to bear fruit in later centuries. He emphasized the relativity of observer and observed and the paradoxical union of opposites in infinity; but while some of his remarks may be interpreted as preparing the way for a Copernican view of the universe, Nicholas of Cusa did not himself make any specific and clear applications of his general (and predominantly mathematical and metaphysical) principles to the physical world.

Suggestions for Further Reading for Part III, B

Cambridge Economic History of Europe. Vol. 1. *The Agrarian Life of the Middle Ages.* Rev. ed. New York: 1966. Vol. 2. *Trade and Industry in the Middle Ages.* Cambridge: 1941.

Cambridge Medieval History. Vols. 7-8. Cambridge: 1926-36.

Adams, H. *Mont-Saint-Michel and Chartres.* Washington: 1904.

Baron, Hans. *The Crises of the Early Italian Renaissance: Civic Humanism and Republican Liberty in an Age of Classicism and Tyranny.* Princeton: 1966.

Bloch, Marc. *Feudal Society.* Chicago: 1960.

Blum, Jerome. *Lord and Peasant in Russia from the Ninth to the Nineteenth Century.* Princeton: 1961.

Bryce, J. *The Holy Roman Empire.* Rev. ed. London: 1913.

Cantor, Norman F. *Medieval History: The Life and Death of a Civilization.* New York: 1963.

Cantor, Norman F. *The Medieval World 300-1300.* New York: 1968.

Cheyney, E. P. *The Dawn of a New Era, 1250-1453.* New York: 1936.

Coulton, G. G. *Life in the Middle Ages.* New York: 1930.

Coulton, G. G. *Medieval Panorama: The English Scene From Conquest to Reformation.* Meridian Books.

Coulton, G. G. *The Medieval Scene: An Informal Introduction to the Middle Ages.* Cambridge: 1959.

DeWulf, M. *Philosophy and Civilization in the Middle Ages.* Dover Edition.

Douglas, David C. *William the Conqueror: The Norman Impact upon England.* Berkeley: 1964.

Evans, J. *Life in Medieval France.* Rev. ed. London: 1957.

Ferguson, W. K. *Europe in Transition 1300-1520.* Boston: 1963.

Gilson, E. *The Spirit of Medieval Philosophy.* New York: 1936.

Gilson, E. *Reason and Revelation in the Middle Ages*. New York: 1938.

Haskins, C. H. *The Normans in European History*. New York: 1966.

Haskins, C. H. *Renaissance of the Twelfth Century*. Meridian Books.

Haskins, C. H. *The Rise of Universities*. Cornell University Press Paperbacks.

Huizinga, J. *The Waning of the Middle Ages*. Anchor Books.

Kern, F. *Kingship and Law in the Middle Ages*. Oxford: 1939.

Lea, H. C. *History of the Inquisition*. 3 vols. New York: 1888.

McIlwain, C. H. *Growth of Political Thought in the West*. New York: 1932.

McKeon, R. P. *Selections from Medieval Philosophers*. 2 vols. New York: 1929.

Morison, S. E. *Admiral of the Ocean Sea*. Signet Books.

Myers, A. R. *England in the Late Middle Ages*. Pelican Books.

Oman, C. W. C. *The Art of War in the Middle Ages*. Rev. ed. London: 1924.

Painter, S. *French Chivalry: Chivalric Ideas and Practices in Medieval France*. Cornell University Press Paperbacks.

Painter, S. *A History of the Middle Ages, 284–1500*. New York: 1953.

Painter, S. *Rise of the Feudal Monarchies*. Ithaca: 1951.

Panofsky, E. *Gothic Architecture and Scholasticism*. Meridian Books.

Pirenne, H. *Economic and Social History of Medieval Europe*. Harvest Books.

Pirenne, H. *Medieval Cities*. Anchor Books.

Powers, E. *Medieval People*. Anchor Books.

Randall, John H. *The Career of Philosophy: From the Middle Ages to the Enlightenment*. New York: 1962.

Riasanovsky, Nicholas V. *A History of Russia*. New York: 1963.

Ross, J. B. and McLaughlin M. M. eds. *The Portable Medieval Reader*. New York: 1949.

Runciman, S. *A History of the Crusades*. 3 vols. Cambridge: 1951–54.

Sarton, G. *Introduction to the History of Science*. 2 vols. Washington, 1927–31.

Stenton, D. M. *English Society in the Early Middle Ages*. Pelican Books.

Stephenson, C. *Medieval Feudalism*. Cornell University Press Paperbacks.

Taylor, H. O. *The Medieval Mind*. 2 vols. Rev. ed. London: 1930.

Ullmann, Walter. *The Individual and Society in the Middle Ages*. Baltimore: 1966.

Waddell, H. *The Wandering Scholars*. Anchor Books.

Warren, W. L. *King John*. New York: 1961.

Wilkins, Ernest H. *Life of Petrarch*. Chicago: 1961.

Novels

Bowen, Marjorie. *The Leopard and the Lily*. New York: 1909.

Doyle, Sir Arthur. *The White Company*. New York: 1890.

Doyle, Sir Arthur. *Sir Nigel*. New York: 1906.
Druon, Maurice. *The Iron King*. New York: 1956.
Druon, Maurice. *The Poisoned Crown*. New York: 1957.
Druon, Maurice. *The Strangled Queen*. New York: 1957.
Druon, Maurice. *The Royal Succession*. New York: 1958.
Druon, Maurice. *The She-Wolf of France*. New York: 1961.
Duggan, Alfred. *Knight with Armour*. New York: 1951.
Duggan, Alfred. *Leopards and Lilies*. New York: 1954.
Duggan, Alfred. *Devils' Brood*. New York: 1957.
Duggan, Alfred. *The Cunning of the Dove*. New York: 1960.
Eliot, George. *Romola*. London: 1863.
Feuchtwanger, Lion. *The Ugly Duchess*. New York: 1928.
Hugo, Victor. *The Hunchback of Notre Dame*. London: 1833.
Johnston, Mary. *Admiral of the Ocean Sea*. Boston: 1922.
Lamb, Harold. *Durandal*. New York: 1931.
Lang, Andrew. *A Monk of Fife*. London: 1895.
Llewellyn, Richard. *Warden of the Smoke and Bells*. New York: 1956.
Lofts, Norak. *The Lute Player*. New York: 1951.
Lofts, Norah. *Town House*. New York: 1959.
Macpherson, Annie W. *The Fourteenth of October*. New York: 1952.
Myers, Henry. *Our Lives have just Begun*. New York: 1939.
Oldenbourg, Zoe. *The World is not Enough*. New York: 1948.
Oldenbourg, Zoe. *The Cornerstone*. New York: 1955.
Pargeter, Edith. *Heaven Tree*. New York: 1960.
Peacock, Thomas L. *Maid Marian*. New York: 1905.
Rolfe, Frederick W. *Don Tarquinio*. London: 1905.
Scott, Sir Walter. *Ivanhoe*. London: 1821.
Scott, Sir Walter. *The Betrothed*. London: 1885.
Shelley, Mary. *The Fortunes of Perkin Warbeck*. London: 1830.
Trease, Geoffrey. *Snared Nightingale*. New York: 1958.
Undset, Sigrid. *Kristin Lavransdatter*. New York: 1929.
Vidal, Gore. *Search for the King*. New York: 1950.
Waddell, Helen J. *Peter Abelard*. New York: 1933.
Warner, Sylvia T. *The Corner that held Them*. New York: 1948.

Chronological Table for Part III, B: Western Christendom

Revival of Civilization

910	Foundation of Cluny.
911	End of Carolingian dynasty in Germany.
911	Normandy granted to Normans under Hrolf.
919–1024	Saxon dynasty in Germany.

936–973	Otto I, king of Germany.
955	Otto defeated Hungarians at Lechfeld.
*962	Otto I crowned Roman Emperor.
987	End of Carolingian dynasty in France; Hugh Capet, first king of Capetian dynasty (987–1328).
1016–1035	Canute king of Denmark and England.
1024–1125	Salian dynasty in Germany.

The High Middle Ages

1056–1106	Henry IV, German king and emperor.
1059	Synod of the Lateran; establishment of College of Cardinals.
1059	Papal alliance with Normans of Apulia and Calabria.
*1066	Battle of Hastings; Norman conquest of England.
1073–1085	Pope Gregory VII (Hildebrand).
*1077	Penance of Henry IV at Canossa.
1091	Norman conquest of Sicily completed.
*1096–1099	First Crusade.
1122	Concordat of Worms.
1138–1254	Hohenstaufen dynasty in Germany.
1142	Death of Abélard (b. 1079).
1147–1149	Second Crusade.
1152–1190	Frederick Barbarossa, German king and emperor.
1153	Death of Bernard of Clairvaux (b. 1090).
1154–1399	House of Plantagenet (Angevin) in England.
1154–1189	Henry II, king of England.
1162–1227	Genghis Khan, Mongol ruler.
1170	Death of Thomas à Becket.
1176	Battle of Legnano.
1180–1223	Philip Augustus, king of France.
1183	Peace of Constance between Frederick Barbarossa and the Lombard cities.
1189–1199	Richard I, Coeur de Lion, king of England.
1189–1192	Third Crusade (Frederick Barbarossa, Richard I, Philip Augustus).
1190–1197	Henry VI, German king and emperor.
*1198–1216	Pope Innocent III.
1199–1216	John king of England.
1202–1204	Fourth Crusade.
1204–1261	Latin Empire in Constantinople.
1209–1213	Albigensian Crusade.

1211–1250	Frederick II, German king and emperor.
1214	Battle of Bouvines.
*1215	Magna Carta.
1215	Fourth Lateran Council.
1221	Death of St. Dominic (b. 1170).
1226	Death of St. Francis (b. 1182).
1226–1270	Louis IX, king of France (St. Louis).
1228–1229	Sixth Crusade (Frederick II).
1229	Beginning of Conquest of East Prussia by Teutonic Knights.
1231	Privilege of Worms (Regalia transferred to German princes).
1241	Battle of Liegnitz (in Silesia); farthest advance of Mongols into Europe.

Waning of the Middle Ages

1272–1307	Edward I, king of England.
1273–1291	Rudolph of Hapsburg, German king and emperor.
1274	Death of St. Bonaventura (b. 1221).
1274	Death of St. Thomas Aquinas (b. 1225).
1285–1314	Philip IV the Fair, king of France.
1291	Fall of Acre (last Crusaders' stronghold in Holy Land).
1291	Foundation of Swiss Confederation.
*1294–1303	Pope Boniface VIII.
1295	Model Parliament.
1296	Bull *Clericis laicos.*
1302	Bull *Unam sanctam.*
1305–1378	The popes in Avignon.
1314	Battle of Bannockburn: Scottish autonomy secured.
1321	Death of Dante Alighieri (b. 1265).
1328	End of Capetian dynasty in France; house of Valois 1328–1589.
1336	Death of Giotto (b. *c.* 1276).
*1338–1453	Hundred Years' War.
1346	Battle of Crécy.
1347–1349	Black Death in Europe.
1354	Ottoman Turks first invaded Europe.
1356	Golden Bull defined electoral system for Empire.
1356	Battle of Poitiers.
1374	Death of Petrarch (b. 1304).

1378–1415	The Great Schism; rival popes in Avignon and Rome.
1381	Peasants' Revolt in England.
1384	Death of John Wiclif.
1399–1460	House of Lancaster in England.
1400	Death of Chaucer (b. *c.* 1340).
1405	Death of Tamerlane (Timur) (b. 1369).
1410	Battle of Tannenberg; Poles defeated Teutonic Knights.
1414–1417	Council of Constance; restoration of papacy to Rome.
1415	Hus burnt at the stake.
1415	Battle of Agincourt.
1431	Joan of Arc burnt at the stake.
1431–1449	Council of Basel.
1434	Cosimo de Mecici got control of Florence.
1438	Austria, Bohemia, and Hungary first united under a Hapsburg ruler.
*1453	Conquest of Constantinople by the Ottoman Turks.
1455–1485	Wars of the Roses.
1456	Bible printed by Gutenburg.
1461–1485	House of York in England.
1462–1505	Ivan III, the Great, of Russia; threw off Mongol rule 1480.
1477	Burgundian possessions divided between France and Austria.
1479	Aragon and Castile united under Ferdinand and Isabella.
1485–1603	House of Tudor in England.
1486	Cape of Good Hope rounded by Portuguese explorers.
1492–1503	Pope Alexander VI.
1492	Fall of Granada, last Moorish stronghold in Spain.
*1492	Discovery of America by Columbus.
1494	Invasion of Italy by Charles VIII of France.
1497	India reached by Vasco da Gama.
1500	Discovery of Brazilian coast by Portuguese.
1519	Death of Leonardo da Vinci (b. 1452).
1520	Death of Raphael (b. 1483).
1527	Death of Machiavelli (b. 1469).
1535	Death of Thomas More (b. 1478).

1536	Death of Erasmus (b. *c*. 1466).
1564	Death of Michelangelo (b. 1475).
1576	Death of Titian (b. 1477).

C. The Modern World, 1500–Present

The geographical discoveries, the diffusion of printing, the rise of national states, and the breakup of the religious unity of Western Christendom worked great changes in the economic, political and intellectual life of Europe. In the eyes of most historians these changes have justified a distinction between medieval and modern European history. Various dates have been proposed to mark the transition: 1453 when Constantinople was captured by the Turks and the Hundred Years' War came to an end: 1492 when Columbus discovered America; 1494 when the French invaded Italy and initiated a long struggle for the control of that peninsula between France and Spain; 1517 when Luther nailed his 95 Theses to the door of the castle church in Wittenberg, and others. It should be needless to emphasize that there was no definite break; that great movements such as the Renaissance, the Reformation, the rise of capitalism and of national states all had a history long before 1500 and continued to operate as living forces long afterward. Any date must needs be arbitrary, and the round number, 1500, seems as good as any.

1. Reformation and Religious Wars, 1500–1660

    a. Expansion of Europe
    b. Economic Developments
       1) Economic Impact of the Discoveries
       2) Development of Capitalism
       3) Technology

    c. Politics and Religion
       1) The Empire of Charles V
       2) Religious Reformation
          a) Introduction
          b) Lutheranism
          c) Calvin and the Reformed Churches
          d) The Anglican Church
          e) Radical Protestant Sects
          f) Roman Catholic Reform
       3) Religious and Dynastic Wars

---

a. Expansion of Europe

Following the voyages of Vasco da Gama and Christopher Columbus, European sailors and soldiers rapidly explored the new realms which so suddenly opened before them. In the Americas, Vasco Nuñez de Balboa discovered the Pacific Ocean by crossing the Isthmus of Panama in 1513; and between 1519 and 1522, ships commanded by Fernando Magellan set out from Spain, rounded Cape Horn, and sailed home across the Pacific and Indian oceans, thus circumnavigating the globe for the first time. These discoveries were soon followed by conquest. Under the command of Hernando Cortez a small body of Spanish soldiers subdued the Aztec state in Mexico (1518–1521); and eleven years later Francisco Pizarro duplicated the feat by conquering the Incas of Peru.

Upon Columbus' return from his voyage to America, a quarrel broke out between Portugal and Spain, for the Portuguese thought that Columbus had been poaching on their special preserves. The matter was brought before the pope, who suggested a division of the world between the two powers; and in 1494 a treaty between Spain and Portugal specified that the meridian 370 leagues west of the Cape Verde islands would divide their respective spheres. This settlement gave all of the American continents to Spain except for a part of Brazil, and assigned the Far East to the Portuguese. Other European countries were excluded, and the Spanish and Portuguese made every effort to enforce their monopoly.

In the Far East the Portuguese were as active as were the Spanish in the New World. They set up trading stations in India; pressed eastward to the spice islands (East Indies) and into the Pacific, where they met the Spanish in the Philippines (discovered by Magellan). The first Portuguese explorer reached China in 1513; and by 1557 merchants had induced local Chinese officials to authorize regular trade and to allow them to reside at Macao, a peninsula near Canton. Northern Australia was discovered early in the sixteenth century, and Japan was first visited by Portuguese ships in 1542.

Other European countries were attracted by the wonderful wealth which these discoveries brought Spanish and Portuguese traders and adventurers, and tried to win a share for themselves. In 1497 an English expedition discovered Cape Breton island, and in 1534 Jacques Cartier explored the Gulf of St. Lawrence on behalf of the French. But these northern lands were not very attractive. Gold could not be found, and for many years the English were only interested in finding a passage to the Far East through the Arctic north of Canada. Not until 1607 was the first successful English colony in Virginia undertaken, and in the following year the French began their settlement of Canada. The gradual success of these colonies, especially the English ones, established a new type of European expansion. Instead of exploiting native inhabitants (as did the Spanish and Portuguese), the English and French established a modified replica of European society in the New World at the cost of the gradual destruction of native society.

The Dutch, too, entered relatively late onto the imperialist scene, but in the first half of the seventeenth century they were able to force their way into the Far East, displacing the Portuguese from the most lucrative trading regions. Dutch activity in the New World (New York) and in the Caribbean was also considerable. Together with English pirates, slave traders and privateers they made great inroads upon Spanish commerce and compelled the Spaniards to fortify and defend their American coastline.

Thus in an amazingly short time Europeans were able to explore most of the world and seize for themselves trading privileges in areas where they were not able or did not trouble to impose their political rule. European improvements in navigation and military technique made this rapid expansion possible. The expansion also demanded a spirit of daring endurance and reckless adventure which Europeans manifested abundantly. Their success initiated an interaction between European civilization and the civilizations and cultures of all the rest of the world which has been and remains one of the peculiar marks of modern times.

b. Economic Developments

1) The Economic Impact of the Discoveries. One consequence for Europe of the discoveries and conquests of the early sixteenth century was a great influx of precious metals. Vast amounts of gold and silver were plundered from the Aztecs and Incas; and large-scale mining enterprise was speedily organized by the Spaniards to keep the stream of precious metals flowing. The sudden increase in the amount of precious metal in circulation devalued gold and silver in all Europe. Prices rose correspondingly.

The resulting inflation severely wrenched established and customary economic relationships. As prices rose, persons whose income was more or less fixed inevitably suffered; and, as it happened, the most important class which was so circumstanced was the landed nobility. Most rents and dues had been converted to fixed money payments during earlier centuries; and the landed nobles now found their income losing much of its purchasing power. Wage earners also suffered, for, as usual, wages lagged behind rising prices. Trading and manufacturing capitalists profited most. They were able to increase their wealth vastly, benefiting by rising prices, expanding markets, and the development of new tastes for tropical and American goods (e.g., tea and tobacco) among Europeans. Thus the discoveries worked to improve the status of the bourgeoisie in general, and the upper bourgeoisie in particular. Bourgeois gain was feudal loss; and the weakening of the economic power of the feudal nobility helped to prepare the way for the establishment of absolute monarchy in most European states.

The development of overseas trade also displaced the economic center of Europe. The Italian cities, which had occupied a strategic place as middlemen between west and east during earlier centuries, were now cut off from the main lines of trade. The Portuguese (and later the Dutch) tapped the trade with India, China and the spice islands at its source, thus cutting the age-old route up the Persian Gulf or Red Sea and overland to the eastern Mediterranean coast. In consequence, a relative economic decay of the Italian cities set in, although for a time Italian bankers remained influential owing to the earlier accumulation of capital in the peninsula.

Spain and Portugal were not, as might have been expected, the principal beneficiaries of the new wealth. Lisbon, Cadiz and other ports of the Iberian peninsula did indeed become great entrepôts for the trade of all the world; but it was Dutch and, to a lesser degree, English and French merchants who distributed the products of the East and of America to the European continent. European goods, which were needed to support the new imperial ventures and to provide the means of trade with such politically independent parts as China and India, were also produced mainly in northern Europe.

Actually, the great stores of gold and silver that flooded into Spain worked economic damage in the long run. Prices rose more sharply in Spain than elsewhere; moreover a large proportion of the precious metal came into the hands of the government, and was used to support fleets and armies that operated, for the most part, outside of Spain. The glorious opportunities offered by the plunder and administration of the New World, and by mercenary service in the royal army in Europe, helped to divert Spanish energies from commercial and industrial pursuits. The expulsion of Jews and Moriscos (converted Moslems) from Spain, undertaken in the name of religion, also weakened the artisan and mercantile classes of the country substantially. Spain therefore lagged behind other parts of Europe in the development of industry, and, for all her gold, became by degrees relatively unproductive and therefore poor in comparison with the economically more active societies of northern Europe.

2) The Development of Capitalism. New opportunities for overseas trade were opportunities only for men with sufficient money to equip ships for a long voyage. Thus full exploitation of the new economic possibilities required the assemblage of relatively large masses of capital. Some individual merchants were sufficiently wealthy to be able to engage in such enterprise by themselves; but the custom of pooling capital among a number of partners, which had been common in the Middle Ages, was usually preferred, since a man with shares in twenty different ships was less likely to lose everything from shipwreck or a disastrous voyage than if he had used the same sum of money to equip a single vessel. At first partnerships were usually formed for a single voyage and were dissolved upon its completion; later the associations became more permanent, until eventually joint stock companies arose and speedily came to dominate overseas trade.

Companies had several advantages over private ventures and partnerships. Often a joint stock company was able to secure special rights from its home government, and indeed it became usual for governments to grant monopolies of trade in a given region to companies formed for the purpose. Thus in England companies for trade with Russia (The Muscovy Company), the eastern Mediterranean (The Levant Company), the Far East (The India Company), America (The Merchant Adventurers of Virginia) and others were granted royal patents of monopoly in their respective spheres during the sixteenth and seventeenth centuries.

Two other advantages of joint stock companies should be mentioned. First, the savings of numerous individuals could be mobilized to support overseas trading ventures through the device of negotiable stock. This meant that the scale of European operations in the far corners of the world could be raised to a far higher level than would have been the case if only men who had the personal knowledge and skill required to conduct long range trade had supplied capital for the ventures. Second, the legal permanence of the companies made it possible for them to undertake large-scale and long range projects for facilitating trade. The Dutch East India Company, organized in 1602, was a pioneer in this line. It speedily became very prosperous, and took on many governmental functions in the East Indies. Governors, armed merchant vessels and even armies sent out by the Company were able to displace the Portuguese from most parts of the Far East during the early part of the seventeenth century.

In other spheres of economic activity, capitalism had a less free field. The medieval gild organization of industry remained in existence in nearly all towns, and gild regulations designed to prevent the concentration of control in a few hands obstructed the free development of capitalist industry. Nevertheless individual men of wealth made constant inroads; the domestic system of industry became more common; and some branches, especially mining (where large amounts of capital were necessary for the construction and maintenance of mines) expanded the scale of capitalistic organization.

Agriculture was the stronghold of the older economic order. In most of Europe manorial organization remained much as it had for centuries. Serfdom was unusual in the west, although in backward districts serfs continued to exist. Relics of old obligations remained everywhere in the form of various and sometimes burdensome payments which the peasant farmers owed to their landlords. In eastern Europe, however, serfdom remained in full operation; and in countries such as Russia and Rumania, serfdom analogous to, though not identical with, the serfdom of western Europe was actually extended and consolidated during the sixteenth and seventeenth centuries.

But even in agriculture, capitalistic enterprise made some headway. In England, for example, a number of landlords enclosed the fields, i.e., built fences and drove the peasants off the land in order to convert it to sheep pasture. The reason for this was that the demand for wool increased steadily until it became possible to make more money by raising sheep than by raising grain and other crops. In some other parts of Europe similar changes occurred, but on a small scale. Even in England enclosures affected only a small proportion of the cultivated land prior to the eighteenth century.

Banking continued to develop in importance and scale of operation. Italian bankers gradually lost their preeminence, and by the middle of the seventeenth century Holland had taken the place formerly occupied by Italy as the principal banking center. Commercial and industrial loans attracted more and more capital, while loans to governments and kings (which had absorbed a very large proportion of banking capital in the Middle Ages), became relatively, though not absolutely, less important. This meant, in effect, that economically productive use of capital became more widespread. With this transformation, the social stigma which had been attached to the taking of interest in the Middle Ages lost its basis in economic facts. Capitalism more and more became an engine for the expansion and increase of wealth.

Relations between the states of Europe and capitalists became very close. Governments depended on bankers for loans; governments also granted concessions, monopolies and special privileges to various trading and industrial enterprises. Yet the state did not always favor the capitalist class. Efforts were made to protect the poor by governmental action. In England, for example, Queen Elizabeth's government enacted a poor law which required local parishes to levy taxes for the support of indigent persons. Another statute regulated wages with the intent of maintaining some sort of balance between social classes.

Nevertheless, merchants and capitalists were the ones who benefited most from governmental policies. Most European states strove to increase the national wealth by fostering trade and shipping. Efforts were made to insure a favorable balance of trade, so that bullion would accumulate within the country where it could serve as liquid capital for the support of warlike and other enterprises. Real wealth and the possession of gold were often confused, and government regulations were frequently designed to assure a maximum accumulation of precious metal.

By degrees the regulation of economic activity passed from local city governments to royal, nation-wide governments. This enlarged the effective economic units, and removed or circumvented numerous restricting regulations which had been inherited from medieval gilds and towns. The change also acted to strengthen the national governments enormously, bringing royal officials into intimate and important contact with large groups of the population. Similarly, state regulation gave a much larger scope to capitalists, who became more consciously than ever the most active supporters of royal power. Only in England toward the end of the period here under consideration did conflict between the bourgeoisie and the royal government begin to manifest itself; elsewhere in Europe monarchs were generally able to establish absolute rule with the moral and financial support of the commercial and capitalist classes.

Regulation of the economy by national governments according to the principles here suggested is called mercantilism. As time passed, regulations increased in number and complexity, and sometimes hindered rather than helped economic development. This phenomenon, however, became significant only in the eighteenth century.

3) Technology. Between 1500 and 1660 the beginnings of an extremely fruitful interaction between scientific theory and technological practice began to manifest itself. Gerard Mercator (1512–94), for example, developed a mathematical system for map projection which made great circle sea routes appear as straight lines—a great convenience to navigators; the lore of mining and metallurgy was systematically gathered together by a German scholar who called himself Agricola (1490–1550); and both optical lenses and optical theory were greatly improved so that the invention of such instruments as the microscope and the telescope became possible.

In the sphere of military technology, guns and gunpowder gradually came into their own. Naval strategy came to depend on cannonades and upon maneuvering to make cannon fire maximally effective. On land, musketry, firing by volleys, was introduced as an effective military arm by the Swedish king, Gustavus Adolphus, during the Thirty Years' War (1618–48). Shipbuilding and navigation improved with new and more accurate maps, studies of ocean currents and prevailing winds, larger and more seaworthy ships. The Dutch devised something close to mass production of ships, building them with standard parts and using mechanical devices such as wind-driven saw mills. Mining technology continued to improve, and the depth and size of mines increased. Coal mining, especially in England, where a shortage of wood became serious in the seventeenth century, became important, but only where mines were located close to navigable water, for coal was too bulky to be transported overland for more than a few miles. Metallurgy, too, developed a new scale of production. Forges were designed where cannon weighing several tons could be cast successfully.

c. Politics and Religion

1) The Empire of Charles V. By 1500, strong national states had already developed in part of western Europe, to wit, in Spain, France and England. As the century progressed, the power of these national governments constantly increased, and a new nation, the Dutch, appeared as a major force on the political and economic scene. Yet much of Europe was not nationally organized. The sprawling territory of the Holy Roman Empire was divided among hundreds of states; and the Italian peninsula was divided into more than a dozen fully independent governments. The political history of the period from 1500 to 1648 may be viewed as a record of the enhancement of the power of national states at the expense of the European areas which were not nationally organized.

Early in the sixteenth century, the major axis of European politics turned upon the rivalry between the Valois kings of France and the Hapsburgs, whose scattered territories included Austria, the Low Countries, Sardinia, Sicily, and Spain. Charles V, who came into this magnificent inheritance in 1519, spent almost the whole of his reign at war with France. The major theater of warfare was Italy, where the French were able to assemble shifting alliances aimed against the Hapsburg power. England managed to stand aside from the Valois-Hapsburg rivalry, and used the respite to gather economic strength.

A second problem which constantly harassed Charles V was the threat of Ottoman encroachment on his Austrian possessions. The Turkish danger persuaded Charles, two years after his accession, to entrust his brother Ferdinand with the rule of Austria and neighboring lands. Ferdinand was only partially successful in resisting the Turks. They extinguished the

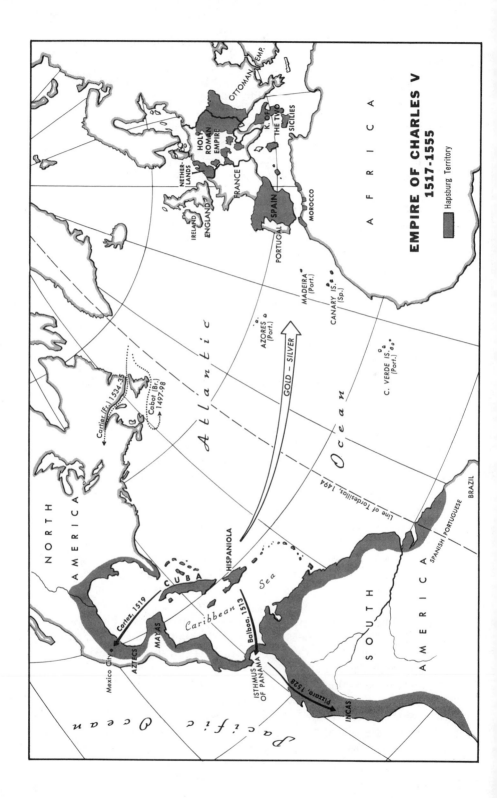

EMPIRE OF CHARLES V
1517–1555

▨ Hapsburg Territory

OTTOMAN EMP.

HOLY ROMAN EMPIRE

K. OF THE TWO SICILIES

NETHER-LANDS

FRANCE

IRELAND

ENGLAND

SPAIN

PORTUGAL

MOROCCO

A F R I C A

MADEIRA (Port.)

AZORES (Port.)

CANARY IS. (Sp.)

C. VERDE IS. (Port.)

GOLD – SILVER

A t l a n t i c

O c e a n

Line of Tordesillas, 1494

Cartier (Fr.) 1534-35

Cabot (Br.) 1497-98

N O R T H

A M E R I C A

Mexico City

AZTECS

MAYAS

CUBA

HISPANIOLA

Cortez, 1519

Caribbean Sea

Balboa, 1513

ISTHMUS OF PANAMA

Pizarro, 1528

INCAS

S O U T H

A M E R I C A

SPANISH

PORTUGUESE

BRAZIL

P a c i f i c O c e a n

independent kingdom of Hungary in 1526 (Battle of Mohacs). Three years later they besieged Vienna, but withdrew without capturing the city. The military strength of the Ottoman Turks was then at its height, and they remained undefeated by European arms until 1571 (Lepanto).

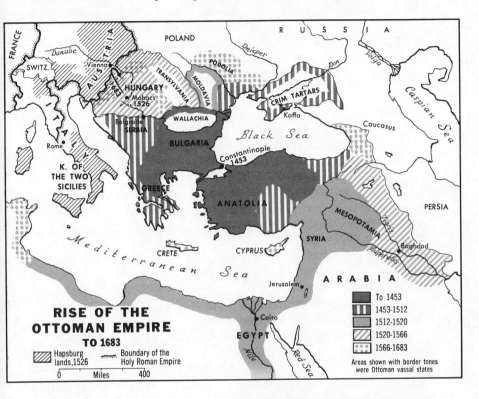

RISE OF THE OTTOMAN EMPIRE
TO 1683

| | Hapsburg lands, 1526 |
| | Boundary of the Holy Roman Empire |

0 Miles 400

	To 1453
	1453-1512
	1512-1520
	1520-1566
	1566-1683

Areas shown with border tones were Ottoman vassal states

The internal problems of Germany ranked third among the issues which Charles V faced. Even when Martin Luther began to stir up religious excitement and was convicted of heresy, the Emperor was too busy with his other struggles to devote more than sporadic attention to the new problems which Lutheranism created in Germany. It was only when the French and the Turks left him free that Charles V could think seriously of dealing with the Lutheran movement and with the German princes who supported it. As it happened, no such moment came until after the Lutherans had become firmly established in many of the German states.

Yet in retrospect it appears that the movement initiated by Luther in 1517 was of at least equal importance with the Hapsburg-Valois contest for supremacy in Italy. During the following hundred years and more politics were vastly complicated by religious issues. To dynastic and national rivalries, religious animosities were added; and Europe came to be divided between Roman Catholic and Protestant states. The early political success of the Reformation depended in good part on the distraction which constantly drew the attention and effort of Emperor Charles V from the internal and religious affairs of Germany; it depended also on the peculiar political constitution of the Holy Roman Empire which left almost complete sovereignty in the hands of numerous local princes and rulers. These political facts must be born in mind when one tries to understand the early history of the Protestant movement.

2) Religious Reformation

a) Introduction. Agitation for reform of the Church was almost as old as Christianity. Throughout the Middle Ages devout sons of the Church had rivaled heretical sects in denouncing the abuses and venality of the clergy. During the fourteenth, fifteenth and early sixteenth centuries the stream of criticism ran particularly strong; but the official hierarchy of the Church did little to meet the attacks which were leveled against it by heretics such as Wiclif or by Christian humanists like Erasmus. Pent-up discontent thus found explosive expression when a professor at an obscure German university, Martin Luther, boldly challenged the propriety of some of the Church's practices. Luther speedily enlarged the scope of his attack, and convinced himself and many others that the Church needed a thorough reformation which would restore it to the original purity of apostolic times. The religious excitement which Luther stirred up stimulated others to go far beyond him in the radical character of the reforms which they advocated and practiced.

Yet for nearly a generation efforts continued to be made to heal the breach which thus appeared in the unity of Western Christendom. The early reformers clung to the idea of a catholic (i.e., universal) Church; and within the Roman Church a group of earnest men arose who hoped by diplomacy both to reform the Church and to bring the Protestants back within the fold. When this attempt failed, a more militant and anti-Protestant spirit of reform gained ground within the Roman Catholic Church which, colliding with the uncompromising spirit of the Protestants, produced a long series of religious wars, culminating in the Thirty Years' war in Germany.

b) Lutheranism. Luther's father intended him to become a lawyer; but while at the University of Erfurt, young Martin Luther (1483–1546) suddenly changed his plans, and instead entered a monastery and became a priest. In 1508 he was transferred to Wittenberg, where he became a professor of theology at the newly-founded university. Despite an outwardly placid and successful academic career, during the next few years Luther lived in mental torment. He could not convince himself that he was worthy of salvation. The more he pursued ascetic practices and sought to

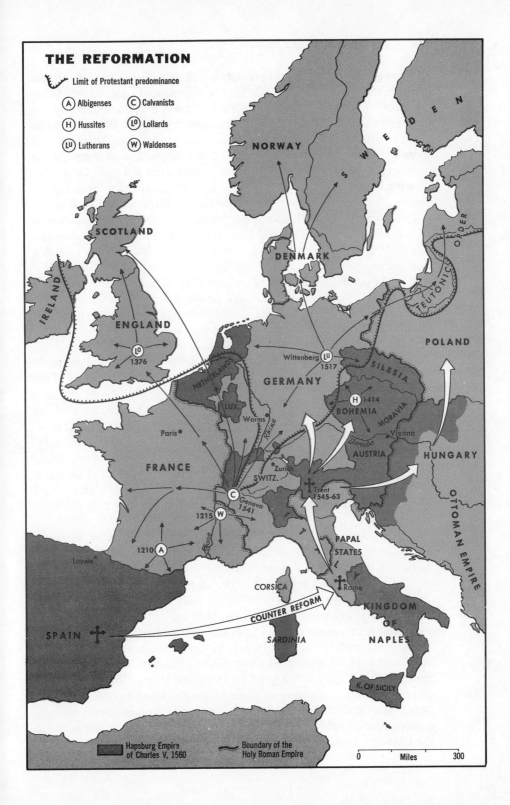

THE REFORMATION

Limit of Protestant predominance

- (A) Albigenses
- (H) Hussites
- (LU) Lutherans
- (C) Calvinists
- (LO) Lollards
- (W) Waldenses

NORWAY

SWEDEN

DENMARK

SCOTLAND

IRELAND

ENGLAND

(LO) 1376

NETHERLANDS

LUX.

Worms

Paris

FRANCE

Zurich

SWITZ.

Geneva 1541

(C)

(W) 1215

1210 (A)

Loyola

SPAIN ✝

TEUTONIC ORDER

Wittenberg (LU) 1517

GERMANY

SILESIA

(H) 1414

BOHEMIA

MORAVIA

Vienna

Danube AUSTRIA

Trent 1545-63 ✝

POLAND

HUNGARY

OTTOMAN EMPIRE

Rhine

Rhone

ITALY

PAPAL STATES

Rome ✝

CORSICA

SARDINIA

KINGDOM OF NAPLES

K. OF SICILY

COUNTER REFORM

Hapsburg Empire of Charles V, 1560

Boundary of the Holy Roman Empire

0   Miles   300

perform good works, the more vividly he felt that his sins outweighed his merits in the eyes of God. Then in 1515 he experienced a great relief. Reading Paul's *Epistle to the Romans,* he was suddenly illuminated by the phrase: "The just shall live by faith." Luther found in St. Paul's words an answer to the problem which had been troubling him, for he interpreted them to mean that salvation depended not on good works, nor on the merit of the individual person, but was instead a free gift from God, Who gave it to those who had faith in Him. In a word, salvation (or as Luther commonly called it, justification) depended on faith, and on faith alone.

This doctrine solved Luther's own personal problem: with faith (and he had faith) he was saved. But there were certain logical consequences. The fasts, ceremonies, even the sacraments of the Church were, in such a view, unnecessary to salvation, and might even be positively harmful if men relied upon them instead of seeking after faith. The importance of a consecrated priesthood to mediate between man and God became secondary, since the individual Christian could, with the help of the Divine revelation contained in the Bible, seek after faith and find it for himself with the help and friendly guidance of other sincere Christians. Thus, as a result of his own personal struggle for salvation, Luther found himself advocating doctrines which undermined the whole structure of the medieval Church.

These revolutionary implications became clear to Luther only by degrees. In 1517 a preacher of indulgences arrived in a town near Wittenberg, selling remittance of penance, either in this world or in Purgatory, to any who would buy. Luther, freshly inspired by his views of the central importance of faith, felt that such trafficking in the penalties of sin was a caricature of true Christian behavior. Accordingly he posted Ninety-Five Theses on the church door of Wittenberg, challenging the whole theory of indulgences.

Luther's theses immediately stirred up a tremendous public reaction. Many Germans were distrustful of the sale of indulgences (which had indeed been thoroughly commercialized) and felt that the whole structure of the Church needed reform. A series of public debates forced Luther during the next two years to develop the more radical implication of his doctrine of justification by faith. By 1520 he had recognized the gap separating his theological views from those of the Roman Church, and in a series of pamphlets (of which the three most important were *Address to the Christian Nobility of the German Nation, The Babylonian Captivity of the Church,* and *The Liberty of a Christian Man*) he explained his views on Church reform, on the proper place of the sacramental system, and on justification by faith. These pamphlets and Luther's other activity aroused a widespread controversy in Germany. Many discontented men flocked to the Lutheran banner, bringing with them widely divergent views.

In 1521 Luther appeared before the Emperor Charles V and representatives of the pope at a meeting of the Imperial Diet, held at Worms. Accused of heresy, Luther refused to recant and was accordingly declared a heretic and an outlaw. But Luther's condemnation by the emperor and by the pope did not bind the German princes. The Elector of Saxony, one of the most powerful rulers of Germany and Luther's immediate political sovereign, took the reformer under his protection. For a year Luther hid in one of the elector's castles, and while in hiding he translated the New Testament into German. A few years later, with the help of some colleagues, he translated the Old Testament also. Luther's *Bible* did for the German language what Dante's poems had done for Italian: it fixed the literary medium for generations to come. Since Luther rested his case against the pope on the authority of the Bible, reading and meditating upon the Bible became of central importance among his followers.

During the next few years different groups which had originally rallied around Luther's cause broke off one by one. Humanists such as Erasmus could not sympathize with the recklessness and doctrinaire quality of Luther's position. When Luther set about revising public worship and doctrine in accordance with his understanding of Scripture, many radicals felt that he did not go far enough and separated themselves from the Lutheran cause. Numerous divergent ideas were current among these groups, of which the so-called Anabaptists were the most prominent. They found their following mainly among the poor of town and country and in some cases espoused egalitarian and other socially revolutionary doctrines. The year 1525 marks a decisive turning point. In 1524–25, large numbers of peasants in central and southern Germany, stirred up partly by Luther's religious agitation, rebelled against their landlords. Luther was shocked to discover that the Christian liberty which he had preached was interpreted by these peasants as applicable also to economic and social life, and in rage he wrote a bitter pamphlet urging that they be put down without mercy.

A part of Luther's anger arose from the fear that the peasant revolt would discredit his religious movement in the eyes of the princes and upper classes of Germany. His repudiation of the revolt prevented such an outcome; indeed the net effect of the emperor's opposition and of the defections which Luther's cause suffered between 1521 and 1526 was to make Lutheranism largely dependent on the support of territorial princes and of the upper middle classes of the German towns. The princes had much to gain, for when Luther summoned them to reform the Church he opened the door for the confiscation of most Church property by the state, and for the establishment of far reaching control over ecclesiastical government by secular rulers. The bourgeoisie of the towns found Luther's assertion of the individual's direct access to God attractive; they shared his sense of German nationalism and his indignation at the sight of Italian clerics wringing good money out of credulous Germans; and they sympathized with Luther's rejection of asceticism in favor of an ideal of self discipline and Christian devotion in ordinary everyday occupations.

After his break with the papacy had become clear, Luther was faced with the problem of establishing a church which would accord with his interpretation of the Scripture. In general, Luther retained whatever elements of the medieval Church he felt were not contrary to the Bible. Thus he eliminated compulsory confession, celibacy of the clergy, monastic orders, veneration of saints, and he reinterpreted the Eucharist, denying any miraculous powers to the priests who performed the service. In most, but not in all, Lutheran Churches the episcopate was also abolished.

During Luther's lifetime his movement spread through about half of Germany, mainly in the north. Princes claimed the right to determine the religion of their subjects, so that the conversion of a German prince came to mean the conversion of the inhabitants of his state. During the same years, Lutheranism spread beyond Germany into Scandinavia, but found no permanent root elsewhere in Europe.

The spread of Lutheranism in Germany disturbed the Emperor Charles V, but his wars with France and with the Turks prevented him from giving much attention to the protestant German princes until 1546. By then he found the new religion too firmly entrenched to be extirpated by the force at his command. As a result in 1555 a peace was concluded (Peace of Augsburg) which recognized the right of each German prince to choose between Lutheranism and Roman Catholicism, and to impose the religion of his choice on his subjects.

c) Calvin and the Reformed Churches. Echoes of the great religious upheaval in Germany traveled through all parts of Europe, and Luther's doctrines found responsive minds in many countries. In Switzerland, Huldreich Zwingli (1484–1531) was stimulated by his own religious experience and by the success of the Lutheran movement to begin a reformation of the Church in Zurich. Zwingli won over the majority of the city council and initiated the Swiss reformation. His principles differed from Luther's mainly on the doctrine of the Eucharist, which Zwingli held to be commemorative of the Last Supper, whereas Luther believed that the body and blood of Christ were really present in the bread and wine.

From Zurich, Zwinglian reform spread to neighboring Swiss towns, and penetrated into adjacent parts of France and Germany. But not all the Swiss welcomed religious innovations, and the "forest cantons" stood fast by their old faith. War broke out, and in 1531 Zwingli was killed in battle. A peace was concluded soon after which left each of the Swiss cantons free to maintain the religious status quo.

The activities of Zwingli and of many other earnest reformers, of whom the most eminent and influential was a Frenchman, John Calvin (1509-64), resulted in the establishment of a number of "Reformed" churches in various parts of Europe. Calvin's theology was widely accepted by these churches, and they are often called Calvinistic as a result. The Reformed churches constitute the second great branch of Protestantism on the European continent, differing from Lutheranism on a number of doctrinal points, and in matters of church organization.

John Calvin was a highly educated man, familiar with the classics and trained in law. Soon after he had completed his legal education, however, he became convinced by a study of the Bible and of numerous religious writers that the Roman Catholic Church was in error. He thereupon left France, fearing persecution as a heretic, and took up residence in the Swiss town of Basel. There Calvin completed the first edition of his *Institutes of the Christian Religion* (1536), a book of theology in which he set forth in lucid and systematic fashion the doctrines he had come to believe. The book was extensively expanded in later editions, and became the most comprehensive and systematic statement of Protestant theology. In the latter years of Calvin's life he established a powerful moral ascendancy over the Swiss reform movement, and spread his influence widely through all parts of Europe from the city of Geneva, where he made his home after 1541.

Calvin accepted many of Luther's ideas for the reform and purification of the Church, but there were some points of difference. Calvin put his doctrine of the Eucharist into a slightly different form; and he emphasized the predestination of God more than Luther had done. Luther had, to be sure, accepted the doctrine of predestination—that some men are saved and others damned according to the inscrutable will of God; but the matter had never seemed of central importance to him as it did to Calvin. Indeed, the dominant theme of Calvin's theology was the greatness, grandeur and glory of God and the weakness, sinfulness and helplessness of mankind. Salvation, he argued, was possible only through faith; but man was as powerless to achieve faith by his own efforts as he was to avoid sin. Thus God awarded saving faith to some, while abandoning others to the eternal suffering in Hell which their sins merited.

Such a doctrine of predestination might seem to encourage men to adopt a sort of passive fatalism; yet the opposite was the case. Calvinists developed a tremendous moral earnestness, and strove to establish godly morality by example where they were a minority, and by legal force where they attained political power. Geneva, under Calvin's leadership, became a closely organized theocracy. Dissent was rigorously suppressed. The ministers and elders of the churches disciplined public and private morals and relied upon the city government to punish stubborn offenders against their code of ethics and principles of theology.

In matters of church organization and the conduct of services Calvin was more radical than Luther. Calvinist churches were organized, according to what Calvin regarded as Scriptural precedent, without bishops. Instead ministers and a board of elders (or presbyters—hence Presbyterian) managed each separate congregation of the faithful. Representative assemblies, in which both ministers and laymen took an active part, decided general questions. Everything for which Scriptural precedent could not be found was rejected from Calvinist services. Thus among the seven sacraments of the medieval church, only baptism and the Eucharist were retained; and preaching, Bible reading, and the singing of psalms replaced the more elaborate ritual of the medieval Church.

In France, England and in the Rhinelands, Calvinism won the adherence of numerous townsmen; but in these countries Calvinists always remained a minority of the total population. In Holland, however, Calvinism became dominant in the course of the sixteenth century; and in Scotland, the accidents of politics and the fiery preaching of John Knox (1505–72) converted the kingdom to Calvinist reform. In eastern Europe Calvinism achieved temporary success also, especially in Hungary and Poland; but the Roman Catholic counter offensive in the late sixteenth and early seventeenth century resulted in the reconversion of these countries to Catholicism, with the exception of a part of eastern Hungary, where Calvinism remains strong to this day. The influence of Calvinism on other Protestant churches was also great, especially in the Anglican Church.

d) The Anglican Church. In England the development of Protestant religious agitation was gradual. It was not because of popular conviction or powerful preaching that the English government broke away from communion with Rome. Rather it was a matter of royal wishes and high politics. King Henry VIII of England (1509–47) was married to a Spanish princess, Katherine of Aragon; but after eighteen years, lacking a male heir, he decided to have the marriage annulled. He applied for papal authorization on the ground that Katherine, as widow of his elder brother, could not by canon law be married to him. The pope found himself in an awkward position. Henry's marriage had been made possible in the first place only by a special papal dispensation, and the pope did not wish to cancel what his predecessor had sanctioned. Still more, the Hapsburg Emperor Charles V put pressure on the pope to prevent the annulment. (Katherine of Aragon was his aunt.) In this circumstance, the pope delayed announcing a decision until Henry impatiently made Parliament declare him to be the head of the English Church, and secured from Archbishop Cranmer ecclesiastical sanction for the annulment of his marriage.

Henry's action eventually (1538) led the pope to excommunicate him; meanwhile Henry was able to persuade Parliament to pass the Act of

Supremacy in 1534. This act severed all relationships with the papacy, and put the English church under the king alone. In later years of his reign, Henry VIII confiscated the land owned by monasteries in England and sold most of it to his political supporters and to newly rich merchants and townsmen. But in matters of doctrine and church organization he remained a thorough conservative until his death in 1547.

The ease with which King Henry VIII broke with Rome was in large part due to widespread discontent among Englishmen against various papal practices. From the time of Wiclif in the fourteenth century religious views somewhat similar to those propounded by reformers on the continent had been rife in England. After 1534 sympathy with Protestant ideas mounted. The Prayer Book, which prescribed the rituals of worship, was twice revised during the reign of Edward VI (1547–53); and in 1552 it was given a definitely Protestant form. When Queen Mary (1553–58) came to the throne, she tried to restore Roman Catholicism in England, but her pro-Spanish policy (she was the daughter of Katherine of Aragon and the wife of Philip II of Spain) was widely unpopular. Under her successor, Queen Elizabeth (1558–1603), English patriotism and Protestantism came to be closely linked.

Elizabeth not only restored a Protestant form of Prayer Book, but also adopted an enduring definition of Anglican doctrine—the Thirty-Nine Articles, which were enacted into law by Parliament in 1563. Belief in these articles was declared to be binding on all clergymen in the Kingdom; but on critical points the articles were phrased with sufficient ambiguity to allow a wide variety of interpretation. As a result, widely differing Protestant groups were able to remain within the Anglican Church. Radical reformers were not satisfied with such a compromise. Towards the end of Elizabeth's reign organized groups of nonconformists (i.e., persons who did not conform to the religion established by the state) arose. The majority of them were strongly influenced by Calvinism, and were generally known as Puritans. During the first half of the seventeenth century Puritans increased in numbers and influence, and they became the prime movers in the resistance to the Stuart kings who succeeded Elizabeth.

e) Radical Protestant Sects. The religious excitement generated by the reformers led to the rise of prophets and preachers, who founded numerous and widely varying sects. Such sects set out, like Lutheranism and Calvinism, to return to primitive and uncorrupted Christianity. But views as to what primitive Christianity had been differed widely. In general, the sects emphasized the Bible and the experience of emotional conversion. They distrusted all attempts at systematic church government and discipline, and sometimes took on overtones of social revolution. They were persecuted by Protestant and Roman Catholic authorities alike.

The Anabaptists (from whom contemporary Baptists indirectly des-
cend) have already been mentioned. Other groups which have endured to
the present include the Mennonites of Holland, who practiced a radical
pacifism; Congregationalists of England, who were predominantly Calvinist in theology but rejected Calvin's presbyterian form of church
government, and Socinian Unitarians, who denied the doctrine of the
Trinity. The following of these and of other sects was relatively small in
the sixteenth and seventeenth centuries, but their ideas were frequently influential on the larger body of Protestants.

f) Roman Catholic Reform. At first the Protestant movement did not
arouse any very profound reaction among the leaders of the Roman
Catholic Church. The popes were enmeshed in international politics, and
far from cooperating with Emperor Charles V to suppress Lutheranism,
they fought against him. Nevertheless, a growing number of influential
Roman Catholics began to press for reform, hoping to satisfy their own
religious standards and at the same time check the spread of Protestantism. In 1534, when Paul III ascended the papal throne, such reformers
gained considerable influence over the papacy; but Paul III was not whole-
heartedly in their favor, for some of the reformers revived the fourteenth
century appeal to the authority of a general council of the Church as
superior to that of the popes themselves. Moreover, the lines between
Protestants and the reform party within the Roman Catholic Church were
not at first clearly drawn, for on both sides there were men who hoped to
see the whole Church purified and reunited.

By degrees the separation between Roman Catholic and Protestant
churches and theology became definite and hopes of bridging the chasm
between them disappeared. This development was accompanied by a
transformation of the reform movement within the Roman Catholic
Church. Reformers adopted a militant and uncompromising spirit, and
strove to strengthen and purify the Roman Catholic Church in order to
combat the spread of Protestantism, and where possible to reconvert
Protestants to the old doctrines.

The new spirit was clearly evident at the Council of Trent, which Pope
Paul III convened toward the end of his pontificate. The Council held a
number of sessions between 1545 and 1563, interrupted by long recesses.
The Council specifically recognized papal supremacy. Thus one of the
long-standing disputes in the matter of Church government was settled.
The supreme authority of the pope over the Roman Catholic Church has
never since been challenged. On questions of reform, the Council forbade
the sale of Church offices, and entrusted the papacy with the supervision
of the behavior of high ecclesiastical officials to assure a more faithful
fulfillment of their religious functions. Under Paul III and his successors,

appointments to Church positions were given to more devout and pious men, and by degrees the moral and intellectual quality of the hierarchy was greatly improved.

In matters of doctrine, the Council of Trent faced the Protestant challenge by reaffirming numerous theological tenets which had been called into question by the reformers. The most telling point which Protestants had made was the lack of Biblical authority for many of the practices of the medieval Church. This criticism the Council of Trent met by asserting that ecclesiastical tradition had an equal authority with the Bible as a basis for ritual and doctrine.

The decisions and resolutions of the Council of Trent were carried out by the papacy. The most effective instrument which the popes found for carrying through the reform of the Church and for countering Protestant preaching and teaching was a new religious order, the Jesuits, or, more properly, the Society of Jesus. The Society of Jesus was established by St. Ignatius of Loyola (1491–1556), a Spaniard. As a young man he had embarked upon a military career, but while recovering from a wound, he underwent a religious conversion and decided to devote the rest of his life to serving as a soldier of the Church. He gathered a number of similarly minded persons around him while studying theology at the University of Paris, and in 1540 the pope authorized him to form them into the Society of Jesus. The members of the Society took a special vow of obedience to the

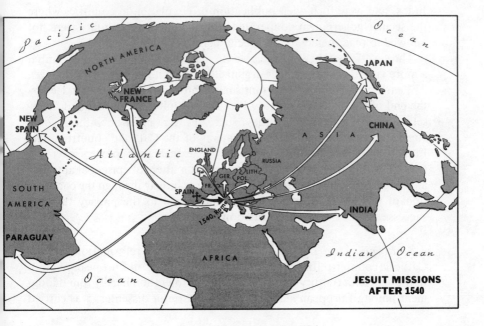

JESUIT MISSIONS
AFTER 1540

pope, and were organized on military lines, completely subject to the decisions of their superiors. They increased rapidly in numbers, and by means of a rigid training became, as it were, shock troops at the disposal of the papacy.

Jesuit missionaries became active in Europe, where they succeeded in reconverting Poland and other areas of eastern Europe to Catholicism, and were largely instrumental in preventing Protestantism from making further headway in Germany and elsewhere. At the same time, the Jesuits initiated a great burst of missionary enterprise in the Far East and among the Indians of America. Jesuit schools, established in many parts of Europe, became the best of the day; and Jesuits took an active part in high politics, acting as advisers and confessors to Catholic princes of Europe. Members of the newly founded order played a prominent part in the deliberations of the Council of Trent, acting as strenuous and effective advocates of papal prerogatives.

Various other innovations helped to assure the Roman Catholic Church of the faith and loyalty of its members. Catechisms were developed and taught to children so that the doctrines of the Church became clearer to them. In addition, the Inquisition was revived, and heretics were sought out and punished with the help of Catholic rulers. The Inquisition was active principally in Spain and Italy, where it succeeded in almost extirpating heresy. Still another device was the Index of prohibited books, which the Council of Trent first drew up, and which was later maintained currently. Books judged to be of heretical content were placed upon this Index, and were forbidden publication or circulation in countries where the secular government cooperated with the papacy. Catholics were not allowed to read them without special permission.

The net effect of these changes was to make the Roman Catholic Church a more vigorous and stronger organization than it had been for centuries. The early expansion of Protestantism was brought to a halt, and indeed by the end of the sixteenth century Protestants quite generally found themselves on the defensive. Yet these successes were not won without some concessions to the national governments of the Catholic countries. The French and Spanish kings were able to extend their powers over the Church within their respective kingdoms in matters of episcopal appointment, taxation, etc. As a matter of fact, it was largely through the cooperation of the secular rulers who remained loyal to the papacy that the successes of the Catholic reformation were won.

3) Religious and Dynastic Wars. The Protestant reformation and the Catholic counter-reformation had a powerful effect on European politics. In the sixteenth century the idea of religious toleration hardly found lodgment among European statesmen. Persecution of dissenters was carried through with varying degrees of thoroughness by every government. Each ruler tried to assure the religious uniformity of his subjects, and religious dissent was looked upon as equivalent to treason. In international relations, something approximating an ideological division of Europe between Protestant and Catholic camps therefore developed. In nations where religious minorities existed, Catholics tended to look to the great Catholic power, Spain, for moral and practical support; and Protestants tended equally to look abroad for help to England, Holland or Sweden.

Yet it is easy to exaggerate the influence of strictly religious considerations on international politics. Early in the sixteenth century the pope and the Most Catholic King of France allied themselves with the Moslem Turks in order to fight the Catholic Emperor Charles V; and a century later the French government, under the direction of Cardinal Richelieu, became a most potent ally of the Protestant princes of Germany in their struggle against the Catholic German Emperor. For a few decades however, during the second half of the sixteenth century, while the Catholic reform movement was at its height and while Spain was the most powerful state of Europe, religious considerations did loom large in determining the wars and alliances of European states.

The political history of Europe between 1500 and 1660 centered around the Hapsburg family. Three phases may be distinguished. (a) Until 1559 the Valois kings of France engaged in a long contest with the Hapsburgs for control of Italy. After sporadic wars and tortuous diplomacy this struggle ended with the treaty of Cateau-Cambresis (1559) by which the French government abandoned its ambitions in Italy. (b) During the next forty years France ceased to be a strong power, since internal wars between Protestant and Catholic parties paralyzed the government. The Hapsburg possessions were divided into a Spanish and an Austrian branch and the former took the leading place in European international politics. England and Holland became the principal opponents of the Spanish Hapsburgs and were able to win important successes against Spanish ships and armies. (c) A third phase opened when religious peace was reestablished in France in 1598, and the French monarchy emerged a second time as the principal European rival of the Hapsburgs. In 1618 war between Catholics and Protestants broke out in Germany, and gradually spread to involve nearly all the continent. When peace finally came to Germany (1648), France had clearly displaced Spain as the greatest power of Europe, and the peace between France and Spain in 1659 sealed the new relationship.

a. The first of these three phases has already been touched upon. It need only be added here that the Hapsburg victory in 1559 resulted in the establishment of Hapsburg predominance in Italy which lasted until past the middle of the nineteenth century. First under Spanish and then under

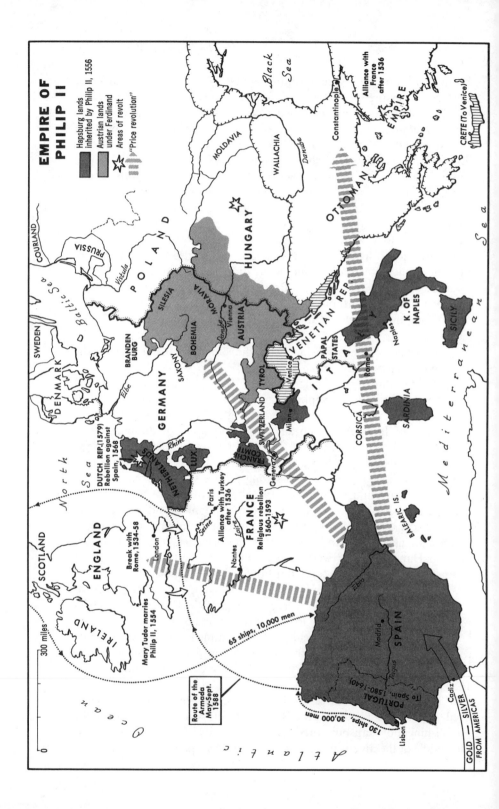

EMPIRE OF PHILIP II

- Hapsburg lands inherited by Philip II, 1556
- Austrian lands under Ferdinand
- ✩ Areas of revolt
- "Price revolution"

Black Sea

Constantinople

OTTOMAN EMPIRE

Alliance with France after 1536

CRETE (To Venice)

MOLDAVIA

WALLACHIA

Danube

HUNGARY ✩

Vienna

POLAND

COURLAND

PRUSSIA

Vistula

SWEDEN

DENMARK

BRANDEN BURG

SILESIA

MORAVIA

BOHEMIA

SAXONY

AUSTRIA

TYROL

VENETIAN REP.

Venice

PAPAL STATES

Rome

ITALY

K. OF NAPLES

Naples

SICILY

Mediterranean Sea

North Sea

GERMANY

Elbe

Rhine

DUTCH REP. (1579) Rebellion against Spain, 1568

NETHERLANDS

LUX.

SWITZERLAND

FRANCHE COMTÉ

Geneva

Milan

CORSICA

SARDINIA

BALEARIC IS.

SCOTLAND

IRELAND

ENGLAND

Break with Rome, 1534-58

London

FRANCE

Religious rebellion 1560-1593 ✩

Paris

Seine

Loire

Nantes

Alliance with Turkey after 1536

Mary Tudor marries Philip II, 1554

300 miles

65 ships, 10,000 men

Route of the Armada May-Sept. 1588

Ebro

Madrid

SPAIN

Tagus

PORTUGAL (to Spain) 1580-1640

Lisbon

Cadiz

130 ships, 30,000 men

Atlantic Ocean

0

GOLD — SILVER FROM AMERICAS

Austrian dominion, Italy underwent economic, political and cultural decline. The prolonged fighting in the first half of the fifteenth century and the shift in trade routes did much to destroy Italian wealth; the helplessness of Italian states as against the national monarchies of Europe made many Italians lose their self-confidence; and the Catholic reformation inhibited or repressed many characteristic expressions of Renaissance culture. Thus Italy by degrees lost the leading place it had held earlier, and by the end of the seventeenth century had sunk to secondary rank culturally as well as politically.

b. Spain was the predominant European power between 1559 and 1598. When Emperor Charles V abdicated in 1556 he divided his extensive possessions between his son, Philip II of Spain (1556–98), and his brother Ferdinand. Philip inherited Spain, the Low Countries and the Hapsburg possessions in Italy; while Ferdinand assumed the imperial title and took over formal sovereignty of the Hapsburg lands in Germany which he had ruled on behalf of his brother since 1522. In this division, the German or Austrian branch of the Hapsburg family received by far the smaller share. The imperial title meant little, and Austria was scarcely a first class power. Philip, however, succeeded his father as the most powerful ruler of Europe. Spain was at the apogee of its strength, controlling a vast empire in the New World. In addition, Philip had married Mary Tudor, Queen of England (1553–58), and could thus exert some influence on English affairs.

Philip's political preponderance in Europe was enhanced by the weakening of the French monarchy. Protestantism had made considerable progress in France, spreading especially among the bourgeois of the towns, many of whom were attracted to Calvinism. Thus arose a wealthy and influential group which opposed the Catholic monarchy for religious reasons. They were known as Huguenots. Two other factors entered into the situation. A series of sickly brothers succeeded one another on the throne of France, and it became increasingly probable that they would leave no direct heir. This opened a question of succession, for the nearest collateral line, the Bourbons, were Huguenots. Finally, the French nobility was restless under the monarchy, and welcomed opportunities for rebellion. The consequence was that France came to be divided into rival leagues, led by nobles and identified respectively with the Catholic and Protestant religious cause. A number of civil wars broke out which came to an end only in 1593 when Henry IV, the first of the Bourbon kings of France, abandoned his Protestantism in order to secure the loyalty of the majority of his subjects. Five years later, in 1598, he issued the Edict of Nantes, establishing limited toleration for the Huguenots of France. By this religious settlement, a relatively stable internal peace was established in France, and the French government became once more a strong power on the international scene.

French weakness did not however result in a lack of serious opposition to Spain elsewhere in Europe. Philip II was himself a devout and indeed a fanatical Catholic, and he pursued his international policies partly with an eye to extirpating heresy. The application of this policy, coupled with attempts to impose new taxation on the prosperous merchants of the Low Countries, led in 1568 to the outbreak of revolt against Spain in the northern Dutch provinces. Long and bitter fighting ensued, but the best efforts of the Spanish soldiers did not succeed in reconquering the revolted provinces, which in 1579 formed themselves into a federation known as the Dutch Republic. During the course of the long war with Spain, Calvinism made steady headway among the Dutch, and became in time the religion of the majority. Thus the struggle took on the qualities of a religious war, and the eventual Dutch success came to be viewed as a victory for Protestantism. In 1609 a truce was concluded which effectively established the independence of the Dutch Republic; but the new state was not formally admitted to the circle of European nations until 1648.

Philip had trouble with England also. While his wife, Mary, was queen, England returned to communion with the papacy; but when Mary died without children, and her half-sister Elizabeth came to the throne in 1558, England once more severed relations with Rome and in so doing came into opposition to Spain. Elizabeth was able to secure a more or less satisfactory religious settlement within England; and at home her administration remained strong. But abroad Elizabeth had to face a complicated situation. She did not marry, and therefore had no direct heir. Mary Stuart, queen of Scotland, was the nearest relative; but she was a Catholic. Consequently Philip of Spain and the Catholic party in France hoped and plotted for Mary's accession to the throne of England.

In addition to the question of the succession to the throne, there were other points of friction between Philip and Elizabeth. The Spaniards supported the Catholic Irish in rebellions against the English (who had claimed but not exercised sovereignty over Ireland since the time of Henry II). After prolonged campaigning, English troops succeeded in conquering all of Ireland, and for the first time brought that island fully under the control of the English crown. On the high seas, English pirates attacked Spanish treasure ships with the connivance of the English government; and, in addition, the English extended some help to the Dutch in their revolt against Philip's authority.

Thus when Mary of Scotland fled from the wrath of her Scottish subjects and took refuge in England (1568) she was not warmly received. Elizabeth imprisoned her; and at length executed her when it appeared that plots to place Mary of Scotland on the English throne threatened Elizabeth's life. Philip thereupon declared war, and sent a great fleet (The Invincible Armada) to invade English in 1588. It was defeated by a combination of bad weather and English seamanship, and very few of the Spanish ships succeeded in returning to their home ports. During the following years the English took the offensive on the sea, harried

THIRTY YEARS' WAR
1618–1648

→ Foreign intervention in Germany

⇨ Counter reformation

Hapsburg lands, 1648

TREATY OF WESTPHALIA

▦ To Sweden

▦ To Brandenburg

▧ To France

⁓ Boundary of the Holy Roman Empire

SWEDEN

DENMARK

Baltic Sea

PRUSSIA

Vistula

POLAND

Lübeck
Hamburg
BREMEN
POMERANIA

BRANDENBURG

UNITED NETHERLANDS

SP. NETHERLANDS

BRUNSWICK

Stadtlohn

Elbe

X Breitenfeld
1631

SILESIA

Oder

GERMANY

Rhine

Prague
BOHEMIA
1618

Mainz
PALATINATE

Paris

1635

Danube

Munich
BAVARIA

Vienna

HUNGARY

AUSTRIA

FRANCE

FRANCHE COMTÉ

SWITZERLAND
(Independent)

TYROL

SAVOY

PIEDMONT

MILAN

VENETIAN

Venice

REPUBLIC

Rhone

Po

ITALY

PAPAL STATES

0   100   200 miles

SHAPERS OF THE MODERN WORLD

Dante
Seventeenth Century. Copper
Engraving by John Stradanus
(The Bettman Archive)
Dante and his conception of earth,
hell, and paradise.

Shakespeare
(The Bettmann Archive)
Title-page of the first collected
edition of Shakespeare's plays,
printed in London, 1623.

Nicolaus Copernicus
1473-1543
(The Bettmann Archive)

Erasmus of Rotterdam
1523. Hans Holbein the Younger
(Das Kunstmuseum Basel
Amer bach-Kabinett 1662)

Henry VIII, King of England
1491-1547. After Painting by
Hans Holbein
(The Bettmann Archive)

Charles V
Painting Attributed to Francois
Clouet
(The Bettmann Archive)

Calvin
(The Bettmann Archive)

Martin Luther
Painting by Lucas Cranach
(Alinari Art Reference Bureau)

René Descartes
Painting by Franz Hals
(The Bettmann Archive)

Galileo
Painting by Sustermans
(The Bettmann Archive)

Oliver Cromwell
Painting by Samuel Cooper
(The Bettmann Archive)

Sir Isaac Newton
Painting by Riley
(The Bettmann Archive)

the Spanish Main (i.e., the Caribbean) and even sacked the great Spanish port of Cadiz two years before Philip died. The war dragged on until 1604, when the new king of England, James I, son of Mary of Scotland, made peace.

c. Despite Philip II's failures in Holland and England, Spain remained apparently the strongest power of Europe at the turn of the century. It was not until the latter years of the Thirty Years' War (1618–48) that France definitely supplanted Spain as the chief power of Europe.

The occasion for the Thirty Years' War was a revolt in Bohemia against the Hapsburg rulers of that country. The revolt was not successful for long, but it touched off hostilities which soon spread to nearly every German state, and eventually involved most of the nations of Europe. During the first years of the war, a league of Catholic German princes, cooperating with the Hapsburg emperors, took the offensive against their Protestant opponents. First Denmark (1625) and then Sweden (1630) intervened on the Protestant side. By 1635 the Hapsburg emperor of Germany was ready to make a compromise peace; but the French, whose policy was then directed by Cardinal Richelieu, made haste to intervene in the hope of defeating the Hapsburgs more thoroughly. Throughout the war in Germany, the Spanish branch of the Hapsburg family assisted the Catholic cause in Germany—or, more accurately, assisted the Austrian Hapsburg cause. Thus when France entered the war, fighting took place not only in Germany, but in Italy and the Pyrenees as well.

At length, in 1648, the Peace of Westphalia brought the war in Germany to an end. (The war between France and Spain dragged on until 1659.) The treaty gave France and Sweden control of important territories within the Holy Roman Empire; the independence of Switzerland and of Holland was formally recognized; and Calvinists were accorded equal rights with Lutherans and Catholics within Germany. These terms in themselves were not the most significant result of the Thirty Years' War. Its most enduring marks on Europe were the devastation, depopulation and impoverishment of Germany, the defeat which the Spanish and Austrian Hapsburgs had suffered, and the victory which French diplomacy and arms had won.

Indeed, the Peace of Westphalia together with the peace concluded eleven years later between France and Spain (peace of the Pyrenees) may be taken to mark the end of a period of Spanish predominance in European politics and the beginning of a period of French predominance. From the early seventeenth century until 1870 France was, by and large, the most powerful state on the continent of Europe, whereas the once mighty Spanish kingdom and empire languished. Hence, Spain's European possessions in Italy and the Netherlands became the prey of other states early in the eighteenth century, and nearly all of Spain's possessions overseas were lost in the nineteenth.

4) Internal Political Development of the Leading European States

a) Continental States. Between 1500 and 1660 most European states saw a steady growth in the power of the central government, which took the form of absolute hereditary monarchy. Representative assemblies, which had been inherited from the Middle Ages, steadily lost ground; and a centralized bureaucracy, drawing its personnel largely from the bourgeoisie, enforced the royal will. The role of the state expanded. One consequence of the Reformation was to make the church, both in Catholic and Protestant countries, more thoroughly subject to the control of secular governments. Simultaneously, state intervention in economic matters expanded into new fields, as has already been indicated. And at the same time the business of government—tax collection, justice, police—increased in bulk and complexity. The great powers of the continent began to maintain standing armies of professional soldiers who were paid regular salaries and equipped with all the paraphernalia of war. The feeling of nationalism was stimulated as local institutions and peculiarities tended to wither away under the more nearly uniform systems of government established by the monarchies. Opposition to the royal government on the part of descendants of old feudal families was largely overcome; and the royal government remained effectively unchallenged, supported by the bourgeois classes of the towns.

Various parts of Europe differed from this over-all pattern in greater or less degree. In Germany, of course, it was not the central government of the emperors, but the local governments of the princes which underwent the consolidation which has been sketched. The same was true of Italy, with this additional modification: the Italian states remained for the most part under the influence of foreign powers, and lived as their clients and dependents. In Spain the role of the bourgeois classes in support of the monarchy was not as great as in France; but the Spanish monarchy found compensating strength in the gold from American mines and in its control over the Spanish church.

The outbreak of religious wars in France (1562–98) temporarily checked the consolidation of the royal power. Moreover, when Henry IV brought the wars to an end, he did so by conceding to the Huguenots the right to erect and maintain a number of fortified places within the kingdom. Thus something like a state within a state arose. Opponents of the royal government therefore tended to rally to the Huguenot camp. This situation seemed intolerable to Cardinal Richelieu, minister to Louis XIII (1610–1643). He attacked the Huguenots in their fortresses, and after a siege, the principal Huguenot strong point, La Rochelle, was captured in 1628. Thereafter royal absolutism was almost unchecked. New administrative officers—the intendants—were created to govern France in the name of the king; and after 1614 the Estates-General ceased to meet. To be sure, between 1648 and 1653 armed revolts broke out against the king's power; but the Fronde, as this rebellion was called, was supported by diverse and mutually incompatible groups, and its failure merely confirmed and extended royal absolutism in France.

Switzerland and the Dutch Republic must be excepted from the general description above. In Switzerland, local institutions, varying from canton to canton, remained in full force, and the country was governed on a rather loose federal and republican basis. The Dutch Republic was unique at the beginning of the seventeenth century in that its political life was largely directed by prosperous merchants and manufacturers. The Dutch government was a federation of seven provinces, among which the province of Holland was by far the richest and most influential. An assembly, the States-General, deliberated on matters of common interest, while executive authority was vested in a Stadtholder. Conflict between the Stadtholder and the States-General was more or less chronic during the seventeenth century. The Stadtholder was supported by landed proprietors and by the more conservative elements among the bourgeoisie. By the middle of the eighteenth century the Stadtholder had won the upper hand. The office became hereditary in the house of Orange, and Holland became a monarchy in all but name. Thus in a sense the political evolution of the Dutch Republic conformed to, but lagged behind the general pattern of European development; for in Holland, too, a central and semimonarchical power eventually consolidated itself at the expense of representative institutions.

   b) The Puritan Revolution in England. Under the Tudors (1485–1603) royal absolutism and centralization prevailed in England in much the same fashion as on the continent. The throne was almost always able to control

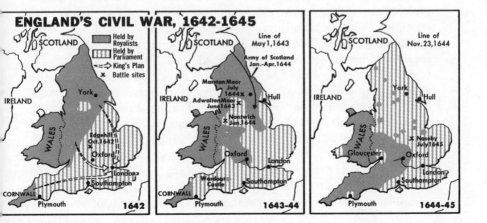

ENGLAND'S CIVIL WAR, 1642-1645

Parliament; and indeed Parliament became little more than a rubber stamp. The nobles in the House of Lords were too weak, and the knights and burgesses in the House of Commons were too much in sympathy with royal policy to resist proposals made by ministers of the crown.

During the first half of the seventeenth century however, when the French monarchy was recovering step by step from the crisis of the religious wars, a contrary development occurred in England. A change in dynasty, which brought the unpopular Stuart kings to the throne, helped to weaken the position of the English monarchy. When Queen Elizabeth died in 1603 the nearest heir was the son of Mary of Scotland. James I (1603–25). James had stayed behind as king of Scotland when his mother fled to England in 1568. Thus when he inherited the English throne the two kingdoms were united under his person, and for the first time peaceful contact between them became common. Scotland, however, remained a separate kindom, with laws and a Parliament of its own.

James Stuart was an intelligent man, but tactless and pedantic. He delighted to instruct his subjects in questions of political theory, and advanced the claim to rule by Divine Right. Such theories were being used to justify the new powers of the French monarchy, and accorded ill with the traditional role of Parliament in English Government. Furthermore, the doctrine that the king could make law by his own independent act ran contrary to the tradition of the English common law. When James' son and successor. Charles I (1625–49). attempted to assess new taxes and otherwise change the established laws of England, he succeeded in turning the lawyers and a large number of country landholders against him. They saw the liberties of Englishmen and the security of their property endangered by the new principles which Charles professed and followed.

An even more powerful opposition to the Stuart kings arose as a result of the royal government's effort to secure religious uniformity in England. The definition of Anglican doctrine which had been made in Queen Elizabeth's reign committed the established Church of England to Protestantism, but left room for very considerable differences of interpretation. During the first four decades of the seventeenth century, however, the religious compromise which Elizabeth had been able to maintain became more and more precarious. On the one hand, growing numbers of Englishmen, especially those who lived by trade and industry, came under Calvinistic influence. Such persons were called "Puritan" because they wished to purify the established Church from doctrines and practices which they thought were ungodly and "popish." Some Puritans remained within the Church of England; others separated themselves from that communion and set up congregations of their own. There was no definite agreement among Puritans as to what exact form of Church government and discipline should be established. Yet thousands, perhaps tens of thousands of serious and devout men came to feel that God's will required a new and more thorough reformation of the English Church.

The Puritan spirit collided head on with the policy of the Stuart kings and their servants, the bishops of the Church of England. Especially after William Laud became Archbishop of Canterbury in 1633, a determined effort was made to enforce uniformity in doctrine and in worship upon all the parishes of England; and some of Laud's doctrines and his emphasis upon ceremonial in church services seemed to the Puritans to be a plain violation of true religion.

Thus from the beginning of his reign Charles I had to face a serious opposition which drew its strength partly from political, legal and economic quarrels and partly from religious disputes. The opposition found voice and focus in the House of Commons, which, as it had been from medieval times, was elected by burgesses of certain privileged towns and by landowners in the shires of England. Unfortunately for the royal cause, Charles found it impossible to govern without cooperation from the House of Commons. The royal income was inadequate to keep the administration going without grants of taxes from Parliament; but the Parliaments which Charles summoned were uniformly unwilling to make such grants to the King unless he would first redress their grievances, i.e., abandon administrative and religious policies to which the Commons objected. In the face of such demands, Charles was driven to subterfuge, then to defiance. From 1629–40 he governed England without Parliament, attempting to create an efficient, powerful absolutism on the continental model.

Discontent in England became intense and widespread, yet if Charles had not attempted to impose the English Prayer Book upon the Scots, an explosion might have been averted or at least postponed. But in 1637 the King made his fatal mistake. He ordered the Scottish Church (which since the days of his grandmother, Mary Queen of Scots, and of John Knox, had been Presbyterian in its government and Calvinist in its doctrine) to conform to the ritual of the Anglican Church. This precipitated revolt in Scotland, and the king, chronically short of money at best, was quite unable to find funds with which to raise an army capable of suppressing the rebels. In the hope of securing a grant of fresh taxes, Charles summoned Parliament again in 1640. But the English burgesses and gentry were in no mood to meet Charles' requests. Those among them who were Puritans found much to sympathize with in the rebellion of their Scottish neighbors, whose religion so much resembled their own. When the mood of Parliament became evident, Charles dismissed it (May, 1640). The Scots then marched into northern England and stopped their invasion only when the King promised them a subsidy sufficient to pay their soldiers until further negotiations could lead to a definite settlement.

Once again Charles was desperate for money, and fell back upon the hope of finding help from an English Parliament. Accordingly he summoned a new Parliament (the Long Parliament) which met in November 1640. In spite of the Scottish invasion, the members of the new House of Commons were no more ready to grant taxes to the King than before. First they wished to assure themselves that no future effort to govern without Parliament could succeed. They therefore devoted their attention to punishing some of the ministers of Charles' government who were held responsible for the illegal acts of the preceding eleven years. Accordingly, Charles' leading minister, the Earl of Strafford, was tried and executed; and Archbishop Laud was imprisoned. The special courts which the King had used to enforce his will upon the Kingdom were abolished, and an act requiring triennial meetings of Parliament became law. After these pressing grievances had been attended to, Parliament voted a special poll tax to pay off the Scottish army, which then returned home.

Measures such as these won the support of the overwhelming majority of the members of the House of Commons, and secured the sometimes grudging assent of the House of Lords. But when it came to questions of religion, agreement could not be attained so easily. A bill to abolish bishops "root and branch" was introduced in May, 1641, but only the more extreme Puritans (Presbyterians and Independents) were prepared to alter the traditional organization of the Church of England so radically. The bill did not pass; but the debate on it showed that the Parliamentary opposition to King Charles was no longer united. The King attempted to exploit this split by appointing some of the moderate Parliamentary leaders as his ministers.

Charles seemed on the point of taming Parliament when a new emergency struck. In October, 1641, the Irish revolted and slaughtered several thousand Protestants who were living in Ireland. This event had tremendous repercussions in England, where religious dispute and tension was already acute. Charles required an army to put down the revolt; but Parliament was totally unwilling to grant the moneys necessary for fear that Charles would use such an army not only to overthrow the Irish Catholics but to impose absolutism on England as well. The dilemma was similar to that of the previous year when the Scots had been in revolt; and as before the Parliament preferred first to make sure of its ground at home before attending to the outside threat.

Accordingly, in November, 1641, after a long and close debate, the House of Commons passed by a majority of only eleven votes what was called the Grand Remonstrance. This document was a long list of all the demands for change which the Puritan party in Parliament supported; and although the Remonstrance was couched in deferential language, its substance was revolutionary. If Charles had yielded, the Remonstrance would have established something close to Parliamentary sovereignty.

But the King refused; and in the first six months of the following year England drifted toward civil war. Many of the more moderate members of the House of Commons and a majority of the members of the House of Lords rallied to the side of the King, quietly absenting themselves from the meetings of Parliament. But this did not deter the remaining members of the House of Commons from passing an act which deprived the King of command of the army (March, 1642). Charles declared the act illegal and began to rally soldiers to his headquarters in York. Parliament did likewise from its seat in London; and after some further fruitless negotiation, the King declared Parliament traitorous. Hostilities began in August, 1642.

In general, the religious conservatives supported the King, although some of them distrusted his absolutist ambitions. The main strength of the royalist (Cavalier) party lay in northern and western England, the parts of the country least affected by economic innovation. Parliament, on the other hand, found its support mainly in the towns and in south eastern England; and its supporters were mostly Puritans of one shade or another—men who felt that further reformation of the Church of England was necessary.

It is possible to distinguish five phases through which the revolution passed during the next sixteen years.

1. From 1642–46 the struggle lay between Cavalier and Roundhead (as the supporters of Parliament were contemptuously dubbed because they cut their hair short). After some initial defeats, Parliament reorganized its forces under the effective leadership of Oliver Cromwell, a country gentleman of stern Puritan convictions; and with the help of Scottish Presbyterians, the "New Model Army" defeated the royalist forces utterly.

2. From 1646–48 the victorious Parliament and its Army faced the problem of what to do with their newly-won power. The most insoluble problem was how to reform religion. A majority of the members of the House of Commons wished to establish a presbyterian form of Church government, and with the help of some Scottish divines they drew up the Westminster Confession of Faith to define the new basis of religion and church government. But Presbyterianism was not to the taste of the more radical Independents, who wished to allow each congregation to manage its own affairs. Independents were a small minority in Parliament, but Cromwell belonged to that persuasion and a majority of the soldiers and officers of the Parliamentary army likewise came to feel, as Milton said, that "new presbyters were but old priests writ large." Indeed more radical religious ideas had gained ground in the ranks of the army. Inspired prophets and preachers, some of them common soldiers, advanced a wide variety of doctrines; and these sectarian religious ideas frequently involved equally radical social and economic views. Such radicals were called "Levellers," since in general they wished to equalize the political

rights of all Englishmen. Some of them also advocated a more equable redistribution of land.

3. From 1648–51 the confusion of opinions among the victorious Parliamentary party opened the door to a renewal of civil warfare. This time Cromwell's army was pitted against both King and Presbyterians, both of whom now rested their main military hope on the Scottish army. But when the Scots invaded England, Cromwell was able to defeat them (1648), and his victorious army determined to bring the King to trial. The majority of the House of Commons was not prepared for such radical proceedings. A detachment of soldiers therefore stationed itself at the door of the House to exclude Presbyterians and others who opposed the army's policy. Only about 60 members of the original (1640) House of Commons remained after this purge, and in fact the Rump Parliament (as the remnant was called) had lost all independence of action. Power rested openly in the hands of the army, and the army was now free to deal with King Charles I. who was executed in January. 1649.

The execution of a lawful (even though unpopular) King was a shocking thing to most Englishmen; and in both Scotland and Ireland attempts were made to establish the authority of the king's son and namesake, Charles II. But Cromwell's army was more than equal to any force that could be brought against it. After swift campaigns, both Ireland and Scotland were subdued. By the end of 1651 all open, organized resistance to the army had been suppressed. But this second victory merely brought forward once more the difficult problem of how to establish lawful government and reformed religion; a problem all the more perplexing for the victors because only a tiny minority of the whole population of England sympathized with their religious and political views.

4. From 1651–58 Cromwell and the army tried a series of experiments in constitution-making. In 1653 the Rump was dissolved by Cromwell in person; next a nominated Parliament (Barebone's Parliament) chosen from among reliable "saints" adhering to the Independent sect was instituted. This body resigned its powers into Cromwell's hands, and at the end of 1653 a group of army officers drew up a new Instrument of Government which declared Cromwell to be Lord Protector of the Commonwealth of England, Scotland and Ireland. Cromwell was accorded large powers, but was supposed to govern with the advice of a council. Moreover the instrument of government accorded sole power to assess taxes to an elected Parliament.

Cromwell speedily found himself in a position like that King Charles had formerly occupied: elected Parliaments quarreled with him and refused to recognize the authority of the Instrument of Government. Cromwell, however, had command over an army as Charles had never had, and as long as he lived his power could not be seriously shaken by merely

Parliamentary objections. During these years, foreign wars with the Dutch, French, Spaniards and Portuguese kept part of the army busy and victorious. In addition Cromwell maintained a considerable garrison scattered through England, Scotland and Ireland. Many of the functions of local government were entrusted to the officers who commanded these garrisons. In spite of a policy of religious toleration for all forms of Protestantism, Cromwell's government became a thinly disguised military dictatorship.

5. Cromwell's death in 1658 at first threatened the renewal of disorders, since his son and successor, Richard Cromwell, lacked the prestige and personality to keep ambitious generals and restless Parliaments in check. An almost universal repugnance to military dictatorship and a growing distaste for the religious enthusiasms which had originally fired the Puritans led, in 1660, to the restoration of the original Parliament of 1640: that is, as many of its members as still survived reassembled long enough to call new elections. The newly elected Parliament summoned Charles II to the throne, but only after he promised an amnesty and undertook to respect the limitations upon the royal authority which had been established by the acts of the Parliament in 1640, before the outbreak of civil war.

From one point of view, the Puritan revolution of 1640–60 may be called the last of the reformation wars of religion; from another, it may be regarded as the first modern revolution—a precursor of the American, French and Russian. Certainly it combined elements of both. Although Cromwell and his fellows were mainly concerned to assure godly religion, the long-run significance of the revolution they carried through lay not so much in the religious as in the political sphere, for it was the example of the English Parliament which upheld the idea of representative government and constitutional monarchy in an age of absolutism; and the English Parliamentary system of government was later to provide the model for numerous experiments and changes in the political institutions of other European (and non-European) countries in the nineteenth and twentieth centuries.

d. Culture

1) General Trends. The sixteenth century saw the spread of Italian renaissance ideas and ideals to much of northern Europe. Particularly in Spain and in England notable literary development occurred in the vernacular; and in all countries the study of the classics was eagerly pursued. The religious excitement of the reformation and counter-reformation tended to divert energy and attention away from art and literature during the latter part of the sixteenth and early seventeenth centuries. In England, for example, the Puritans closed the theaters in which Shakespeare's plays had been presented, and destroyed some works of art as smacking too much of idolatry. In reaction to religious austerity and bigotry, the beginnings of a new spirit of religious toleration (or even indifference) became manifest; but the full development of this attitude waited for the eighteenth century. Natural science made notable advances, especially in the fields of astronomy, mathematics, physics and medicine. The differentiation of national cultures became pronounced. This reflected the extended use of vernacular languages, the increasingly national organization of religion, and the developing spirit of national patriotism.

The impact upon the European imagination of the great discoveries was enormous. A vast new world, filled with amazing wonders—glittering wealth, peculiar animals and plants, strange peoples and stranger customs—opened before the eager eyes of the European public. Vast numbers of travel books and descriptions of far places were printed to satisfy this curiosity. Moreover, Europeans were in the comfortable position of being able to feel superior to all that they discovered. Their military and economic prowess were such as to overwhelm opposition in most parts of the earth. Even the rich and ancient civilization of Asia seemed to most Europeans far inferior to their own.

The discoveries also contributed to a profound revolution in the general intellectual outlook which took place in the course of the seventeenth century. During the first centuries of European development, the authority and prestige of ancient authors, both Christian and pagan, was immense; and much, perhaps most, intellectual activity took the form of glossing and interpreting the writings of such authorities. But by the seventeenth century it became clear that the ancients were not infallible: indeed it was borne in upon many reluctant minds that neither the Church fathers nor the pagan Greeks and Romans had actually known as much about the world as enterprising Europeans had discovered in their own time. The superiority of modern to ancient learning and letters became a subject of controversy in such countries as France and England in the seventeenth century; and by degrees the moderns had the best of the battle.

The idea of scientific and technological progress has become so familiar and so much a matter of course in our own time that it is difficult to recover in imagination the excitement generated by the conviction that unprecedented knowledge and power had been won by the living generation. The world came to seem like an open book, to be studied afresh and critically; men began to look forward to the further improvement of knowledge, not backward toward the intellectual authority of the past; and, willy-nilly, men were forced more and more to rely upon their own powers as the only available means for the pursuit of truth.

It would be easy to exaggerate the rapidity with which this intellectual revolution occurred. Religious controversy, turning upon the interpretation of the Bible, and classical study, directing men's enthusiasm to the literature of the ancient world, were the dominant intellectual concerns for the overwhelming majority of educated men in the sixteenth and early seventeenth centuries. Yet the attitudes suggested above were also present; and the thought of a few individuals laid the groundwork for the general acceptance of the idea of progress and of the superiority of the modern age to all others— an acceptance which came with the eighteenth century, and which has constituted a distinguishing mark of European cultural life down to the present day.

2) Literature. In Italy, two poets revived the epic: Ludovico Ariosto (1474–1533) with *Orlando Furioso* and Torquato Tasso (1544–95) with his *Jerusalem Delivered.* These Italian poems influenced the writing of Edmund Spencer (1552–99) in England (*The Faery Queen*) and Luis Vaz de Camoens (1525–80) in Portugal, whose epic account of the Portuguese discoveries, the *Luciads*, not only established Portuguese as a literary language, but became a focus of Portuguese patriotism, and was an important factor in preventing that country from being culturally absorbed by Spain.

Italian models also influenced much of the English lyric poetry of the Elizabethan age. The sonnet, for example, was introduced into England from Italy and quickly became a popular verse form. John Donne (1573–1631), the leading "metaphysical" poet, was not strikingly Italianate, but the youthful poetry of John Milton (1608–74) was steeped in the classicism that had originated centuries before among the Italian humanists. Milton's greatest work, *Paradise Lost,* set out to justify God's ways to man by recounting the Christian epic of Adam's fall from grace. Written in his later years, it reflected the religious preoccupation and verbal mastery which made him one of the leaders of the Parliamentary cause in the Civil War, and for some years a sort of Foreign Secretary to Cromwell.

Secular drama developed in Italy, Spain, France and England, derived in part from medieval mystery and miracle plays, in part from efforts to revive classic forms of art. In Italy the effort to imitate the classics rather stifled native drama by making it unduly artificial; the same was true of France until after the period here under consideration. In Spain however a vigorous drama arose. The most famous (and incredibly prolific) Spanish playwright was Lope de Vega (1562–1635). A similar dramatic efflorescence came to England, where Christopher Marlowe (1564–93), William Shakespeare (1564–1616), Ben Jonson (1573–1637) and numerous others wrote plays in a wide variety of forms—tragedy, comedy, farce, masque, patriotic history, etc.

A number of famous prose works should be mentioned. English prose was permanently influenced by the cadences and vocabulary of the Authorized (or King James) Version of the Bible, prepared by a committee of scholars, and completed in 1611. In Spain, Miguel Cervantes (1547–1616) wrote *Don Quixote*, a satire on human life in general and upon the extravagances of chivalrous romances in particular. The French version of Calvin's *Institutes of the Christian Religion* was an important milepost in the development of the modern French literary language; a distinction incongruously shared with the unrestrained and gusty satire, *Gargantua and Pantagruel* written by François Rabelais (c. 1494–1553). French prose was taken up where Rabelais left it by the essayist Michel Eyquem de Montaigne (1533–92). The quiet, balanced judgment which Montaigne constantly evinced has excited admiration ever since. In matters of religion, Montaigne had a rather sceptical bent of mind; and he steadily recommended a moderate and reasonable life according to the laws of nature. Many of his essays foreshadow ideas and attitudes which became popular only a century and more after he wrote. Finally, Italian prose may be represented by the autobiography of Benvenuto Cellini (1500–1571), an artist, soldier, and braggart, whose self-portrait permits a vivid glimpse of the individualism and versatility of men of the Italian renaissance.

Latin remained the usual language of scholarship, and numerous humanists continued to compose works of literature, satire and social or religious criticism in Latin. Of such works, Sir Thomas More's *Utopia* (1516) and Desiderius Erasmus' *Praise of Folly* (1509) were among the most famous.

3) Art. With the sixteenth century, renaissance architecture and painting developed a more decorated and elaborate style which is known as baroque. The baroque style flourished especially in the parts of Europe and America under Spanish and Jesuit influence. But even in these lands, the convolutions of baroque art were rivaled by a severer Palladian tradition descending from the work of Andrea Palladio (1516–80).

Italian painting continued the tradition of earlier renaissance masters, developing toward a more violent, dramatic style. Venice became the most flourishing center of painting, with Paul Veronese (1528–88), and Tintoretto (real name Jacopo Robusti, 1512–94). In Spain Domenico Theotocopuli (c. 1548–1625), a native of Crete and known usually as El Greco (i.e., the Greek), exhibited a remarkable and very powerful blending of Byzantine and Italian renaissance styles in his painting. The greatest strictly Spanish painter was Diego Velasquez (1599–1660), who, as official court painter, produced faithful likenesses of the thoroughly unprepossessing Spanish royal family.

The tradition of Flemish art, which had achieved greatness in the fifteenth century with the Van Eyck brothers, was carried on in the sixteenth century by Pieter Brueghel (c. 1530–1600). His vigorous scenes of peasant life show little trace of Italian influence. Later painters of the Low

Countries, such as Peter Paul Rubens (1577–1640) and Anthony van Dyck (1599–1641) were, on the contrary, strongly under the spell of Italian renaissance art. In Holland, however, a vigorous and extremely prolific group of painters continued to carry on an independent tradition. Rembrandt van Rijn (1606–69) and Jan Vermeer (1632–75) were the two greatest figures of the Dutch school. Their paintings are characterized by realistic portrayal of the solid comfort of Dutch middle class life, and by a remarkable mastery of light and shading in interior scenes.

A distinct German school of painting developed during the sixteenth century. Its great figures were Matthias Grunewald (*c.* 1475–1530), Albrecht Dürer (1471–1528), Hans Holbein (1497–1543) and Lucas Cranach (1472–1553). Dürer, Holbein and Cranach were all engravers and makers of woodcuts as well as painters. Italian influence is perceptible in their works, but a distinct German element, derived from medieval miniature painting, is also apparent.

4) Music. With the improvement of musical instruments, music designed mainly or solely for instrumental performance came to be written. The organ had been known throughout the Middle Ages; but its design and range were improved, and new instruments such as the harpsichord, violin and trombone were introduced during the sixteenth century. Secular music (madrigals and lute songs) were reduced to written notation instead of being transmitted by ear as they had been earlier. A close connection existed between lyric poetry and music, so that many Elizabethan poems which are merely read today were originally intended to be sung.

The greatest composer of the age however was a church musician, Giovanni da Palestrina (*c.* 1524–94). He combined organ with choral music in a stately and effective manner. His music finally reconciled the Roman Catholic church to the use of instruments in its services in place of the earlier plainsong. The religious oratorio originated in Italy during the sixteenth century; and early in the seventeenth century secular operas became highly popular. Luther's hymns and Calvinist psalms, set to simple but sometimes powerful music, established the musical standards for Protestant services.

5) Natural Science. During the sixteenth and early seventeenth centuries, students of natural science largely emancipated themselves from the authority of the classic authors. Improved instruments and methods of mathematical notation, careful observation and logical argument proved the ancients wrong on a number of important points. The geographical discoveries and the progress of astronomy compelled men to reorient themselves drastically in the natural world. Jerusalem no longer appeared to be the center of the earth as it had to medieval men; and the earth itself became merely a minor planet in the Copernican system of astronomy. This shift in mental perspective dawned upon the generality of men only slowly, and its full impact upon inherited religious ideas and attitudes was scarcely developed until the eighteenth century.

a) Astronomy. Nicholas Copernicus (1473–1543), a Polish priest, was the first modern astronomer to argue that the earth was not the center of the universe, but was a planet, revolving around the sun. His hypothesis was supported by mathematical calculations, but the observations on which he based his deductions were not very accurate, and in details his theory was erroneous—for example, Copernicus thought that the orbits of the planets were circular rather than elliptical.

Careful observation of the heavens by Tycho Brahe (1546–1601) accumulated more acurate information; and with the help of Tycho Brahe's tables of planetary motion Johannes Kepler (1571–1630) was able to improve upon the Copernican hypothesis, recognizing the elliptical motion of the planets, and devising three mathematical formulae which described the movements of the planets accurately. Galileo Galilei (1564–1642), with the help of a telescope which he devised, was able to disprove the Aristotelian theory of the perfection of the heavens by discovering irregularities on the moon and sunspots on the sun. He also discovered such celestial phenomena as the rings of Saturn, and the moons of Jupiter. His defense of the Copernican theory, coupled with an aggressive attack on Aristotelian doctrines, led Galileo's enemies to bring him to trial before the Inquisition; and in his old age he was for a short time confined to prison and compelled to renounce his teachings.

An important result of astronomical research was the reform of the calendar. In 1582 Pope Gregory XIII approved a readjustment of the calendar, skipping ten days to bring it back in accordance with the astronomical year. According to the Gregorian calendar every fourth year is a leap year, except for those ending in double zero but not divisible by 400. (Thus the year 1900 was not a leap year, but 2000 will be.) This calendar reform was adopted in Roman Catholic countries at once, and at later dates by Protestant nations. In such countries as Russia, however, the calendar was not reformed until the Bolshevik revolution, so that dates in Russian history are frequently written doubly, as 25 October/7 November, 1917, the date of the Bolshevik seizure of power.

b) Mathematics. Mathematical symbols in use today, such as signs for plus and minus, square root, decimal points and multiplication brackets, came into general use during the sixteenth century. Their simplicity immensely facilitated mathematical calculation. Helped by the improvement in mathematical notation, a rapid development took place. Girolamo

Cardano (1501–76) learned how to solve certain kinds of quadratic equations; John Napier (1550–1617) invented logarithms; René Descartes (1596–1650) broke down the age-old distinction between algebra and geometry by developing analytic geometry; Blaise Pascal (1632–62) worked out a number of theorems dealing with probability; and these were only a few of the many men who were actively at work in expanding, generalizing and increasing the power of mathematical analysis during the sixteenth and early seventeenth centuries.

c) Physics. Galileo conducted a number of important experiments in mechanics and dynamics, recognized that sound was transmitted as an undulation of the air, and disproved a number of Aristotelian doctrines. His most famous experiment, of course, was dropping cannon balls of different weights from the top of the leaning tower of Pisa in order to prove that they fell with equal velocity, despite Aristotle's statement that speed of falling bodies depended on their weight. The nature of air came to be better understood. Evangelista Torricelli (1608–47), one of Galileo's students, invented the barometer and measured air pressure with it; a German, Otto von Guericke (1602–86), developed a method for pumping air from a closed space, and invented the "Magdeburg spheres" as a vivid method of demonstrating air pressure.

d) Medicine. The traditional authority of Galen as a guide to medical theory and practice was spectacularly challenged by Paracelsus (real name, Theophrastus Bombast von Hohenheim, hence the English word bombast, *c.* 1490–1541) when he prefaced lectures on medicine by publicly burning copies of Galen's work. His own theories were a strange mixture of empiricism, Neo-Platonic mysticism and magic, but he did add some valuable new drugs to the medical pharmacopeia. The careful dissection of corpses, introduced into medical practice by Andreas Vesalius (1514–64), likewise helped to discredit Galen's authority, since Galen had used pigs for his anatomical studies and as a result had made some obvious errors which Vesalius was able to correct. Ambroise Paré (*c.* 1517–1590) introduced a similarly empirical attitude into surgery, abandoning a number of Galen's time-honored principles, such as treating "like with like," which surgeons had interpreted as requiring the use of boiling oil to cure the burn of gunpowder. Paré adopted the practice of sewing up arteries instead of cauterizing them, and made other innovations on the basis of his observations of the effect which various treatments had on patients. William Harvey (1578–1657) laid the foundation for modern physiology by his discovery of the circulation of the blood. He did not, however, arrive at a satisfactory explanation of how the blood passes from arteries to veins, since he could not see the capillaries.

6) Religious Thought. Religious questions dominated the thought of most men during the age of the reformation and religious wars. The major lines of Protestant theology have already been sketched. Successors elaborated the principles of Luther and Calvin into something akin to a new scholasticism. Lutheranism did not develop any important new doctrines after the time of Luther himself; but Calvinism split between strict followers of Calvin and Arminians, who, following the teaching of a Dutch theologian, Arminius (1560–1609), modified the Calvinistic theory of predestination. Roman Catholicism, too, developed an active and strangely parallel theological controversy between orthodox Catholics and followers of Cornelius Jansen (1585–1638). Jansenists emphasized conversion and personal piety, and their opponents, among whom the Jesuits were the most active, accused them of teaching Calvinistic predestination. The Jansenist controversy reached its high point in the second half of the seventeenth century; and Jansenism was finally crushed only in the eighteenth century.

The extremism and intolerance of all religious parties began to yield by degrees to more moderate and sometimes sceptical or indifferent religious attitudes. Montaigne was one of the earliest spokesmen of such a viewpoint; and an organized group, the "politiques," appeared during the latter stages of the wars of religion in France. In England, Lord Herbert of Cherbury (1593–1648) advocated a "natural" religion, based upon reason and the common sense of all mankind, Christian and heathen alike. He was one of the forerunners of deism, which became fashionable in the eighteenth century.

Yet one must not exaggerate the importance of rationalist and sceptical thought. The intensity of religious passion was as great among the highly educated as it was among ignorant persons, and only a few individuals held themselves aloof from the religious conflicts of the age. Moreover, superstition continued to flourish and even took on new virulence. For example, belief in witchcraft intensified, and the detection and punishment of witches became almost a mania in various parts of Europe, both Protestant and Catholic, during the sixteenth and seventeenth centuries. Many persons were accused and executed on the charge of witchcraft, often on the flimsiest sort of evidence.

7) Philosophy and Political Theory. In the sixteenth century, philosophers as distinct from theologians were few and far between. The speculations of Giordano Bruno (1550–1600) were unsystematic and semipoetic in their expression. He was a mystic and pantheist, deeply impressed by the concept of infinity; and his disregard of traditional Christian doctrine resulted in his being burnt at the stake in Rome as a heretic. Francis Bacon (1561–1626), Lord Chancellor of England, was of a very different philosphical mould. His *Novum Organum* attempted to set forth a new system of inductive logic which he hoped would replace that of Aristotle. Bacon was particularly notable for his confidence in the possibility of the advancement of knowledge, and his vision of improvements that would result from systematic application of newly acquired knowledge to the mechanic arts.

The rapid development of mathematics in the seventeenth century made a profound impression upon philosophers such as René Descartes (1596–1650) and Baruch Spinoza (1632–77). Indeed. Descartes' metaphysical and cosmological theories, have often been taken to mark the beginning of distinctively "modern" philosophy. His willingness to doubt everything and his effort to proceed by mathematically rigorous logical deduction from clear and distinct primary ideas cleared away (or discarded) much of the older tradition of philosphy which had been closely wedded to Christian doctrine and revealed truth. Spinoza, like Descartes, attempted to model his philosophical argument upon mathematics; but it is not his method so much as the moral grandeur of his pantheistic image of a universe bound by immutable law that has made his philosophy an ever-living stimulus to later generations.

The concept of "natural law," applicable both to inanimate objects and to the relations of men was one that found growing support in the seventeenth century. In proportion as faith in revealed religion weakened, natural law seemed to offer a new basis for social and political institutions; and such an attitude could easily be reconciled with a watered down version of the religious tradition of Europe by attributing the establishment of natural law to God.

Two political theorists exemplified the role of natural law in seventeenth century thought. Jean Bodin (1530–96) argued that an absolute monarchy was the best form of human government, but at the same time insisted that the monarch must obey natural law. Hugo Grotius (1583–1645) wrote a famous book *On the Laws of War and Peace* in which he attempted to find a natural and yet lawful basis for relations between states.

Figures like these represented an intellectually radical wing. The spate of political pamphleteering thrown up as a by-product of the Puritan revolution in England showed how strong Christian ideas remained; and even though some of the writers propounded democratic and even socialistic doctrines, they did so on an intellectually traditional basis, finding their inspiration and authority mainly in the Bible and Christian authorities, not from any new-fangled light of natural reason.

Suggestions for Further Reading for Part III, C–1

The New Cambridge Modern History. Vol. 2. *The Renaissance 1493–1520.* New York: 1957.

Bainton, R. H. *Here I Stand. A Life of Martin Luther.* Mentor Books.

Bainton, R. H. *The Reformation Era.* Princeton: 1956.

Bainton, R. H. *The Reformation of the Sixteenth Century.* Beacon Paperback.

Berenson, B. *Italian Painters of the Renaissance.* Meridian Books.

Blum, Jerome. *Lord and Peasant in Russia from the Ninth to the Nineteenth Century.* Princeton: 1961.

Boehmer, H. *Martin Luther: Road to Reformation.* Living Age Books.

Bowen, Catherine D. *The Lion and the Throne: The Life and Times of Sir Edward Coke (1552–1634).* Boston: 1957.

Burckhardt, J. *The Civilization of the Renaissance in Italy.* London: 1944.

Caspar, Max. *Kepler.* New York: 1959.

Cassirer, E; Kristeller, P. O; and Randall, J. H. eds. *The Renaissance Philosophy of Man.* Phoenix Books.

Cellini, Benvenuto. *Autobiography.* Modern Library.

DeRoover, R. *The Rise and Decline of the Medici Bank.* Cambridge, Mass: 1963.

Elliott, J. H. *Imperial Spain 1469–1716.* New York: 1964.

Erikson, Erik H. *Young Man Luther.* New York: 1958.

Geyl, Pieter. *The Netherlands in the Seventeenth Century.* New York: 1961.

Gilmore, M. P. *The World of Humanism, 1453–1517.* New York: 1952.

Hall, A. R. *The Scientific Revolution, 1500–1800.* Beacon Press.

Holborn, Hajo. *A History of Modern Germany: The Reformation.* New York: 1959.

Huizinga, J. *Erasmus and the Age of Reformation.* Torchbooks.

Hunt, R. N. C. *Calvin.* London: 1933.

Jedin, H. *A History of the Council of Trent.* London: 1957.

Lindsay, T. M. *A History of the Reformation.* 2 vols. New York: 1950 1st ed. 1906–7.

Mattingly, G. *The Armada.* Boston: 1959.

Mattingly, G. *Renaissance Diplomacy.*

McNeill, J. T. *The History and Character of Calvinism.* New York: 1954.

Ogg, David. *Europe in the Seventeenth Century.* New York: 1960.

Origo, I. *The Merchant of Prato.* London: 1957.

Parry, J. H. *The Age of Reconnaissance.* Cleveland: 1963.

Parry, J. H. *The Spanish Seaborne Empire.* New York: 1966.

Penrose, B. *Travel and Discovery in the Renaissance.* New York: 1956.

Petrie, Sir Charles. *Philip II of Spain.* New York: 1963.

Randall, John H. *The Career of Philosophy: From the Middle Ages to the Enlightenment.* New York: 1962.

Ranke, L. von. *The History of the Popes in the 16th and 17th Centuries.* London: 1896.

Ranke, L. von. *History of the Reformation.* London: 1905.

Riasanovsky, Nicholas V. *A History of Russia.* New York: 1963.

Ridley, Jasper. *Thomas Cranmer.* New York: 1962.

Santillana, Giorgio de. *The Crime of Galileo.* Chicago: 1959.

Stone, Lawrence. *The Crisis of the Aristocracy, 1558-1641.* New York: 1965.

Tawney, R. H. *Religion and the Rise of Capitalism.* Mentor Books.

Taylor, H. O. *Thought and Expression in the 16th century.* 2 vols. London: 1920.

Trevelyan, G. M. *England under the Stuarts.* 15th ed. New York: 1930.

Troeltsch, E. *The Social Teachings of the Christian Churches.* 2 vols. New York: 1950.

Troeltsch, E. *Protestantism and Progress.* London: 1912.

Weber, M. *The Protestant Ethic and the Spirit of Capitalism.* London: 1930.

Whitehead, A. N. *Science and the Modern World.* Mentor Books.

Williamson, J. *The Tudor Age.* London: 1953.

Woodward, W. H. *Studies in Education during the Age of the Renaissance.* Cambridge: 1906.

Novels

Blackmore, R. D. *Lorna Doone.* New York: 1874.

Cervantes, Saavedro, Miguel de. *Don Quixote.*

Defoe, Daniel. *Memoirs of a Cavalier.* London: 1720.

Gogol, Nikolai V. *Taras Bulba.*

Hewlett, Maurice. *The Queen's Quair.* New York: 1904.

Irwin, Margaret. *Young Bess.* New York: 1944.

Kaye-Smith, Sheila. *Superstition Corner.* New York: 1934.

Lewis, Janet. *The Wife of Martin Guerre.* New York: 1941.

Lewis, Janet. *The Trial of Soren Quist.* New York: 1947.

Lofts, Norah. *Afere was a Man.* New York: 1936.

Macpherson, Annie W. *The Player's Boy.* New York: 1953.

Mann, Heinrich. *Young Henry of Navarre.* New York: 1937.

Mann, Heinrich. *Henry, King of France.* New York: 1939.

Manzoni, Alessandro. *The Betrothed.* London: 1875.

Mason, A. E. W. *Fire Over England.* New York: 1936.

Payne, Robert. *Roaring Boys.* New York: 1955.

Radcliffe, Ann. *The Mysteries of Udolpho.* New York: 1931.

Vigny, Alfred V., comte de. *Cinq-Mars.* London: 1847.

Walpole, Hugh. *The Bright Pavillions.* New York: 1940.

Chronological Table for Part III, C–1: Reformation and Religious Wars

1509–1547	Henry VIII, king of England.
1513	Discovery of the Pacific Ocean by Balboa; Portuguese explorers reach Canton.
*1517	Luther's 95 Theses.
1518–1521	Conquest of Mexico by Cortez.
1519	Death of Leonardo da Vinci (b. 1452).
1519–1556	Charles V, German king and emperor (king of Spain since 1516).
1519–1522	First circumnavigation of the globe (Magellan).
1520	Death of Raphael (b. 1483).
1520	Luther's *Liberty of a Christian Man*.
1521	Luther before the Diet of Worms.
1524–1525	Peasants' War in Germany.
1527	Sack of Rome by Charles V's army.
1527	Death of Machiavelli (b. 1469).
1529	Siege of Vienna by the Turks.
1531	Death of Zwingli (b. 1484).
1531–1533	Conquest of Peru by Pizarro.
1533–1584	Ivan IV, the Terrible, of Russia.
1534	Act of Supremacy; Henry VIII head of English Church.
1536	Death of Erasmus (b. *c.* 1466).
1540	Papal sanction for Society of Jesus (Jesuits).
1543	Death of Copernicus (b. 1473); publication of his *De Revolutionibus*.
1545–1563	Council of Trent.
1546	Death of Luther (b. 1483).
1549	*Book of Common Prayer*.
1555	Religious Peace of Augsburg.
1556	Death of St. Ignatius of Loyola (b. 1491).
*1556–1598	Philip II, king of Spain.
*1558–1603	Elizabeth, queen of England.
1559	Peace of Cateau-Cambresis (French abandon claims in Italy).
1562–1598	Religious Wars in France.
1563	The 39 Articles (doctrinal basis of Anglican Church).
1564	Death of Michelangelo (b. 1475).
1568	Beginning of revolt against Spain in the Low Countries.

1571	Battle of Lepanto: naval defeat of the Turks.
1572	Massacre of St. Bartholomew in France: death of John Knox (b. 1505).
1579	Union of Utrecht (Dutch Republic established).
1582	Gregorian reform of calendar.
1588	Spanish Armada.
1589–1792	House of Bourbon in France.
1589–1610	Henry IV, king of France.
1598	Edict of Nantes—limited toleration for Huguenots in France.
1600	Founding of English East India Company.
1602	Founding of Dutch East India Company.
1603–1625	James I, King of England.
1607	Founding of Jamestown in Virginia.
1608	Founding of Quebec by the French.
1611–1632	Gustavus Adolphus, king of Sweden.
1613–1917	House of Romanoff in Russia.
1614	Last meeting of French Estates General.
1616	Death of Shakespeare (b. 1564).
1616	Death of Cervantes (b. 1547).
*1618–1648	30 Years' War—ended by Peace of Westphalia.
1625–1649	Charles I, king of England.
1626	Death of Francis Bacon (b. 1561).
1630	Death of Kepler (b. 1571).
1637	Descartes' *Discourse on Method*.
1640	Meeting of the Long Parliament.
1640	Death of Rubens (b. 1577).
*1642–1648	Civil War in England.
1642	Death of Galileo (b. 1564).
1649	Execution of Charles I.
*1649–1660	Commonwealth in England.
1658	Death of Oliver Cromwell (b. 1599).
1658	Peace of the Pyrenees between France and Spain.
*1660	Restoration of monarchy in England (Charles II).
1660	Death of Velasquez (b. 1599).
1674	Death of Milton (b. 1608).

2. Absolutism and Aristocracy, 1660–1789

a. Introductory

Except in England, Holland and Switzerland, European states were ruled, between 1660 and 1789, by monarchs who claimed God-given absolute power; and the practical administration of government in England and Holland as well as in other European countries, rested very largely in the hands of privileged groups of men of wealth. High positions in the administration, army and church were largely, though not entirely reserved for members of noble families; while the ordinary mass of subjects was without any effective voice in government and was regarded by the ruling groups as more or less passive material for their manipulation.

Conditions of course varied considerably from country to country. In France and most Catholic countries the clergy constituted a privileged class alongside of the nobility, and the Church continued to be a powerful landowner. In Protestant countries the upper clergy were closely tied to the aristocracy, but church lands had been largely confiscated during the Reformation. Moreover the manner in which the noble and ruling class was recruited varied considerably from country to country, as did the degree of active supervision which the nobles exercised over their land and over local government.

The economic life of the period was even more diverse. In England the beginnings of the industrial revolution manifested themselves toward the end of the eighteenth century; but agriculture remained, even in England, by far the most important economic pursuit. State control of the economy —mercantilism—reached its fullest development in the latter part of the seventeenth century; during the eighteenth a number of theorists attacked the principle of artificial regulation of trade and industry; and in some countries regulations were allowed to lapse or were simplified in the direction of laissez faire.

Culturally, the age was one of cosmopolitanism, of increasing indifference to traditional religion, of confidence in reason and natural law, and of optimism and belief in progress. French cultural leadership displaced Italian; but toward the end of the eighteenth century the beginning of revolt against French "classicism" became evident in Germany and in Great Britain with the advent of what has been called "romanticism."

b. Economic Growth

1) Agriculture. The age-old manorial relationships underwent gradual and cumulative change in the seventeenth and eighteenth centuries; but strong traces of medieval rural life remained in most parts of Europe until after the French Revolution. Particularly in central and eastern Europe, cooperative cultivation remained common; but in western European countries the inefficiency of manorial techniques, the inconveniences which arose from the scattering of strips, and the new possibilities opened up by expanding urban markets all acted to reduce the amount of land which remained under the traditional form of cultivation. Sometimes the members of a village community were able to come to an agreement with their landlord by which the land was parcelled out among the peasants in consolidated blocs. In other cases, especially in England, the landlords were able to carry through enclosure (as the process was called) without the consent of the villagers, and often to their detriment. Moreover as new land was reclaimed for agricultural purposes it was divided into separate farms and rented out to individual tenants. In general, the further east in Europe, the more conservative farming methods remained, while the two centers of agricultural improvement were Holland and England. Thus in countries such as Austria and Poland manorial agriculture prevailed until about the middle of the nineteenth century; and in Russia something analogous to manorial agriculture remained predominant until 1917.

The agricultural situation in France on the eve of the Revolution was neither progressive as in England nor stable as in eastern Europe, but was, as events proved, potentially explosive. Relatively few French manors continued to function as in medieval times. The lords had nearly all withdrawn from active cultivation of the demesne land, becoming passive receivers of rents and dues who contributed little or nothing to the agricultural management of the land. In many parts of France scattered strips had been consolidated into separate farms; but the tenants of such farms were still subjected to a wide variety of rents and dues which had descended from manorial times, and which often no longer corresponded to practical relations—as when a peasant was required to pay a fee for grinding his flour at the lord's mill even though the lord in question no longer maintained a mill for the peasants to use.

The rise of prices, the growth of urban populations and improvement of transport stimulated an ever increasing spread of commercial agriculture. In the most prosperous commercial and industrial areas of Europe, a very considerable percentage of the total population came to be concentrated in towns, dependent on purchase of their food. London, for example, had a population of about 700,000 in 1700, and this amounted to about a tenth of the total population of England. After 1760 England ceased to be able to raise sufficient food for its population and began to import grain from eastern Germany, Ireland and other places, despite the fact that English farming was then the most efficient and productive of Europe. In Holland, it has been estimated that more than half of the Dutch population pursued urban occupations at the beginning of the eighteenth century. But England and Holland were exceptional. In Europe as a whole the vast majority of the population remained on the land, and, particularly in eastern regions, subsistence farming remained common.

In regions where the old manorial regulation of agricultural processes broke down, important innovations in technique were introduced. Holland was the leader in the elimination of the wasteful fallowing of land. The Dutch discovered that various grasses and leguminous crops could be planted after a field had been under grain for one or two years. This had a double advantage. The nitrogen content and fertility of the soil could be increased through the activity of bacteria which cluster on the roots of legumes like alfalfa or vetches. Simultaneously, weeds could be kept down by cutting the green growth before seeding. This in turn produced good cattle feed, and allowed the farmer to keep his animals stabled for all or most of the year, thus conserving their manure for use on the fields. It thus became possible to crop land continuously, and still maintain or even improve its fertility.

From Holland these new techniques were introduced into England during the latter part of the seventeenth century. Improving landlords adopted them widely during the following century. Turnips, used for cattle feed, became an important crop in England, and since they required repeated cultivation, it became possible to eliminate undesirable weeds from a field more thoroughly than had ever been feasible before. Systematic selective breeding of farm animals produced startling results. The size and strength of draught animals was greatly increased; this, and the fact that with the new fodder crops animals could be easily maintained over the winter, meant that a single plow team could do as much work as several had done in the Middle Ages. The design of farm implements was also improved. All-metal plows were introduced in England in the eighteenth century as well as a variety of horse-drawn cultivators. By these means, tillage was greatly improved. In addition, the development of drainage works allowed the reclamation of extensive fen and swamp land in Holland and also in England.

A wave of enthusiasm for agricultural improvement swept over England in the eighteenth century. Experiments with all sorts of crops, machines, fertilizers, rotations, breeds of animals and varieties of seed were systematically pursued. Magazines which described the latest achievements were widely circulated, and no less a person than King George III (1760–1820) prided himself in the appellation "Farmer George" which he used as a pseudonym when writing to agricultural journals about the latest experiments he had carried out on his farm.

Agricultural improvement was facilitated in England by the fact that Parliament authorized numerous compulsory enclosures, carried through by the landlords. Large farms of several hundred acres, owned by men who had sufficient capital to try new crops and methods of tillage, became the usual operating unit. Elsewhere in Europe these conditions did not obtain, and agricultural technique lagged behind. In France, for example, the royal government usually resisted efforts made by landlords to enclose an old manor, being anxious to protect the rights and property of small peasant farmers. But the peasants generally lacked both the capital and the knowledge needed for agricultural improvement. As a result, open fields and unimproved common lands remained far more general in France than in England. A numerous peasantry provided potential strength for French armies, but most of the peasants were very poor and often resented paying rents to absentee landlords who took little or no part in the management of their estates.

2) Technology and Industry. Agricultural improvement was facilitated by the more careful design of farm implements. In other branches of economic activity, especially in industry, technological advances were of even greater importance. During the seventeenth century Holland was in most respects the leader of Europe in technology and industry as well as commerce; during the eighteenth, France and England took over first place; and toward the end of the century England established a preeminence which lasted through the first half of the nineteenth century.

It is impossible to mention more than a few of the technological inventions of the period. The construction of canals and of roads was of fundamental importance. Holland pioneered canal construction in northern Europe, building on Italian precedent (where the canal lock had been invented in the seventeenth century). The major river systems of France were linked by canals during the later part of the seventeenth century; in England, where the indented coastline made the need less pressing, canal building on a large scale waited until the eighteenth century. All-weather roads were introduced only after the middle of the eighteenth century when engineers such as John Macadam (1756–1836) and Thomas Telford (1757–1834) discovered that a gravelled and raised road-bed could assure passage for wheeled vehicles the year round. French roads were the best of Europe by the end of the eighteenth century.

A number of precision instruments were invented or improved, paving the way for theoretical advances in science on the one hand and for practical improvements in machinery on the other. Christian Huygens (1629–95) invented the pendulum clock which could measure time with greater accuracy than before; and in 1736 John Harrison invented the marine chronometer—a clock which was minutely accurate even on a wave-tossed ship. This solved a long-standing navigational problem by permitting measurement of longitude through a comparison of local sun time (discovered by sighting with a sextant to find when the sun reached its apex at noon) with Greenwich time (kept by the chronometer). Another important precision instrument was the thermometer, developed in Italy about 1654, and much improved by Gabriel Fahrenheit (1686–1736), whose temperature scale is widely used today.

In military technology, the infantryman armed with a muzzle-loading gun came into his own during the seventeenth and eighteenth centuries. Battles were won and lost largely on the strength of the discipline of infantry formations, which performed the movements of marching, loading and firing at the sergeant's command and in unison. The "drill" of contemporary armies is a survival from these eighteenth-century methods of fighting. Fortification made considerable strides. To counter the improvement of artillery, earthen ramparts were used to protect masonry walls; and the walls themselves became elaborate emplacements for artillery. In field battles, however, difficulties of transport usually prevented artillery from coming into play, and it was not until the time of Napoleon that heavy guns became sufficiently mobile to keep up with marching infantry.

The most important innovations in industrial technology were made in England. Two industries were especially affected: mining and metallurgy, and textile production. Mining was greatly stimulated in England when Parliament passed an act in 1688 establishing the rights of the surface owner to sub-soil minerals. This provided a powerful incentive for land-lords to develop mines, since a successful mine could be expected to bring in a handsome income. A second stimulus to mining was the growing shortage of wood, which became serious in England during Tudor times. Coal could be substituted for most fuel purposes; and England was fortu-nate in possessing numerous coal fields adjacent to navigable water which made cheap and widespread distribution of coal possible. The resultant increase in the scale of coal mining can be seen in the following annual pro-duction figures:

1550—about   200,000 tons
1700—about   3,000,000 tons
1800—about 10,000,000 tons

Such an expansion required deeper mines; and deeper mines in turn re-quired pumps for draining sub-soil water from the shafts.

It was in connection with the problem of pumping water from mines that the steam engine was invented. In 1706 Thomas Newcomen devised a very clumsy and inefficient engine which pumped when the condensation of steam in a cylinder created a partial vacuum. Between 1765 and 1769 James Watt radically improved the design of Newcomen's engine by using the expansive power of hot steam to drive the piston instead. A few years later the new steam engines came into use as prime movers for textile fac-tories when Watt invented a satisfactory means for translating the reci-procating movement of the piston into rotary motion.

The importance of the steam engine as a convenient, cheap, and easily controlled source of power can hardly be exaggerated. It was no longer necessary to locate industrial works on mountain streams where dams and water wheels could supply power to move machinery; instead a nearby supply of coal became the major determinant of the location of heavy in-dustry. This involved a widespread geographical shift of population and production, and made the coal fields of Europe major centers of popula-tion. But these effects came only gradually; and it was not until the nine-teenth century that the full impact of the steam engine on industry was felt, even in England.

Early in the eighteenth century a method for smelting iron with coke was discovered by Abraham Darby (about 1709). (Raw coal contains chemicals which make it unsuitable for smelting.) This meant that England was no longer dependent on dwindling charcoal supplies for iron produc-tion. At first however the process was kept as a family secret, and it was not until after about 1750 that the use of coke for smelting became general. As the technique spread, it increased the demand for coal still further, and made iron cheaper.

Iron manufacture underwent other important improvements. In 1784 Henry Cort introduced a process for making malleable wrought iron on a large scale with the use of "puddling furnaces" and power-driven rollers. The resulting product was far superior to brittle cast iron for almost every purpose. Steel remained prohibitively expensive for most uses, since it still had to be manufactured from wrought iron by handicraft methods.

A serious and persistent problem in the eighteenth century was the difficulty of manufacturing accurate metal parts. Standardization of machinery was scarcely known, and parts had to be worked over by skilled mechanics with file and chisel in order to make them fit. This difficulty almost prevented Watt's steam engine from achieving success, since it required accurate fitting of the piston to the cylinder. A major step in solving this difficulty was taken when Henry Maudsley invented a lathe in 1794 which could cut metal accurately to a thousandth of an inch.

Technical invention in textile manufacture was equally revolutionary. A series of inventions (John Kay's flying shuttle, 1733; James Hargreave's spinning jenny, 1770; Richard Arkwright's spinning frame, 1769; Samuel Crompton's spinning mule, 1779) mechanized the processes of spinning. Mechanical looms were more difficult, and in spite of the invention of a power loom by Edward Cartwright as early as 1785, it was not until about 1850 that fully satisfactory power looms supplanted weaving by hand. As these machines were adopted, textile production came to be transformed from a domestic occupation, carried on within the home by means of small spinning wheels and looms, into a factory industry, which used first water, and later steam as a source of power. Throughout the eighteenth century most textile machines were built of wood; only at the very end of the century did the developments in metallurgy begin to affect textile manufacture, as steam engines and metal machine parts came more and more into use.

One must guard against assuming that the date of invention marks the date at which a machine or technological process came into general use. Restrictive patents sometimes delayed the adoption of an improved design; sometimes manufacturers kept improved methods secret from rivals. Moreover, many machines were defective at first, or could only produce coarse, low-grade goods. One should also remember that the major inventions took place in England, and spread only slowly to other European countries. The English government and English manufacturers at first tried to maintain a monopoly of new techniques, forbade the exportation of machinery, and tried to prevent skilled workmen from emigrating.

Another factor which slowed down the spread of new techniques was the survival of old gild regulations, and (more important in the eighteenth century) the existence of elaborate production codes, tariffs and state-guaranteed monopolies which mercantilist statesmen had set up to foster new and protect old industries. These regulations often served to protect uneconomic and technologically backward enterprises. England, in this as in other respects, was advantageously situated. In the course of the Puritan revolution the royal right to grant monopolies had been challenged; and in later decades English judges adopted the principle that trade and industry ought to be open to all who wished to enter upon those pursuits. Thus nearly all gild and royal monopolies were swept away within England. After the union with Scotland (1707) Great Britain became by far the largest area within Europe where trade was free from local tariffs, tolls and monopoly rights.

Up until about 1780, at the very end of the period here under consideration, French industry, measured by the value of its product, came near to keeping pace with British development. In one sense this did not mean a real equality of wealth, since French population (about 24 million by 1789) was more than twice as great as the population of Great Britain. French industry also tended to specialize in articles of fine manufacture—such things as silk cloth, porcelain chinaware, etc. This partly reflected the demand of the French court for luxuries; partly the fact that France did not have such abundant coal and iron deposits as Great Britain. French industry differed from British in another important respect. Government regulation, subsidy and control were far more pervasive in France than in England. Such supervision probably helped the growth of French industry in the seventeenth and early eighteenth centuries; but government rules tended to become obstacles to the introduction of new techniques at the very time when the English made their most rapid progress in the latter part of the eighteenth century. Other parts of Europe followed French rather than English industrial patterns, but, with the exception of the Low Countries, lagged considerably behind.

Thus while the beginning of what has been called the Industrial Revolution antedated 1789, it was only a beginning. Europe remained predominantly agricultural until long after the outbreak of the French Revolution; and the society of the eighteenth century was in no sense predominantly industrial.

3) Commerce. Improvement of the means of transport within Europe and improved communications with the Americas, Africa and the Far East contributed to a steady growth in the bulk and value of trade. English and French colonies in North America and the islands of the Caribbean became increasingly important. Sugar, tobacco and cotton were the major crops of the islands and the southern mainland; iron, timber, and furs came from New England and Canada. Until the end of the eighteenth century, the trade with the islands of the Caribbean and with the southern colonies was by far the more valuable to European nations—a fact which is illustrated by the settlement at the end of the Seven Years' War, when the French government thought the island of Martinique more valuable than all Canada.

Labor for the plantations of the New World was supplied mainly by slaves, brought from Africa by European shippers. Slavery never established itself in Europe proper, although the type of serfdom that received legal sanction in eighteenth-century Russia differed only slightly from the chattel slavery of the New World.

In the Far East the eighteenth century saw the establishment of French and British power in India. After scattered fighting, however, the British were able to drive the French from nearly all of India, and the East India Company imposed its political control on a large portion of that subcontinent. Tea and cotton cloth were the two principal imports from India, and they became at least as valuable as the imports of spices from the East Indies, which remained almost a Dutch monopoly.

A third area in which French and British commerce competed was in the Spanish colonies of Central and South America. At the beginning of the eighteenth century, the French supplied a majority of the European goods which South Americans needed; after 1713 the British secured trading concessions from Spain and gradually took over a dominant place in South and Central American trade.

Internal trade and inter-regional specialization within Europe grew at the same time. It is impossible to give any figures for such commerce, much of which was never recorded. But records of overseas trading companies do exist, and from them it has been calculated that the trade of Europe with other continents quadrupled in value during the eighteenth century.

4) Capitalism, the Factory System and Banking. As town gilds continued to decay, capitalism made further progress in industry. Mining and commerce, old capitalist strongholds, came to be almost entirely capitalistically organized. In parts of England, where power machinery came into use, factories sprang up to house the new machines. The development of factories meant that the owner or his manager was able to exert a far more rigorous control over the workmen. The relative freedom of the hand worker to set his own hours of labor vanished; and with it some of the skill and rewards of craftsmanship. Until the introduction of steam power, however, factories were not clustered together in great manufacturing towns, for they had to be located along streams, where dams or waterfalls could supply the motive force for the machinery. Thus the industrial city was a phenomenon of the nineteenth century. Cities of the eighteenth century continued to be administrative, mercantile and handicraft rather than industrial centers.

Factories remained exceptional until the nineteenth century. They were almost unknown in most countries; and even in England, many trades were quite unaffected by the new form of industrial organization. Handicraft industry, carried on in small workshops, sometimes dependent on an outsider for the supply of working capital, remained the usual form of production.

The development of joint stock companies, which had been a conspicuous characteristic of the seventeenth century, suffered a considerable setback in the early years of the eighteenth. Speculative booms in stock had developed even in the seventeenth century; but in the years 1718–20 an unprecedented fever of speculation came to both England and France (the South Sea Bubble, so-called). It led to an equally unprecedented crash. This experience tended to discredit joint stock enterprises, and legal changes in both France and Britain actually prohibited private companies from taking the form of limited liability joint stock enterprises. As a result, the new industrial plants which began to arise in England during the second half of the century were owned and managed by individual entrepreneurs or by partnerships.

Two new developments in banking may be mentioned. In medieval and early modern times, governmental borrowings were considered as personal debts contracted by the king; and a new ruler quite often saw fit to repudiate any outstanding obligations his predecessor had left unpaid. Interest rates were of course correspondingly high. By the end of the seventeenth century this concept had been replaced in the more advanced European countries by the idea that debts were owed impersonally by the government as such; in other words national debts were invented. Holland and England, where the royal power was relatively small, took the lead in developing the idea of a national debt; and partly as a consequence, the Dutch and English governments were able to borrow money at lower interest rates than could other states. In time of war or other extraordinary emergency, this proved a tremendous advantage.

A second important development was the increasing use of banknotes. The issuance of promissory notes against specie holdings of a bank was not new; but the scale on which such notes were issued, and the confidence which people came to have in them had a novel effect, since the superior convenience of paper currency led by degrees to the supercession of coinage for most large transactions. Even in the Middle Ages bankers had discovered that it was possible to issue more promissory notes than there was metal in the bank, since not everyone was likely to demand payment at once. This opened up the possibility of expanding or contracting the paper currency at will, and introduced a new element into the business cycle. Currency expansion and contraction helped to make bigger and better booms and sharper depressions.

The establishment of the Bank of England in 1694 marks an important step in both these developments. The Bank was originally organized by a group of private financiers in order to handle the national debt; and Bank of England banknotes came to have a sort of standard value in Great Britain against which notes issued by other banks were measured.

5) The State and Economic Life. Mercantilist theories continued to inspire the economic policies of most European states in the seventeenth and eighteenth centuries. Two general ways in which the state influenced economic relations may be distinguished. First, every state required revenue, and required it in growing amounts as the expenses of administration and particularly of war mounted. Secondly, nearly every state tried to improve its international balance of payments by fostering home trade and industry. Regulations, monopolies, tariffs and various state-owned enterprises were set up with this end in view.

The tax policies of the European states defy any broad description. In general, the various revenue devices which had been inherited from former times were maintained; and new taxes were invented more or less haphazardly. France, for example, was divided into numerous tariff areas so that goods transported within the country had to pay frequent tolls. Special excise taxes were imposed on articles like salt; there were in addition poll taxes, income taxes, land taxes, license fees, and others. Taxes were by no means uniform for the entire kingdom, but varied from province to province and even from town to town. Nor were they applied equally to all social classes, the nobility and clergy being exempt from some taxes, and managing to escape the full burden of others.

Other European countries labored under similarly confused tax systems. In Great Britain, however, as a result of its medieval inheritance, taxation was far more uniform throughout the country; and the fact that the central government maintained a far less complex bureaucracy and did not support a large standing army made the total tax burden considerably lighter.

Taxation and measures designed to improve the international balance of payments were of course closely intertwined. Protective tariffs, for example, yielded revenue and at the same time helped home industry; the same was true of grants of monopolies to particular companies, which paid various sums to the government in return for their privileged status.

Some governmental acts, however, can definitely be attributed to a wish to promote home industry and trade apart from direct fiscal returns. In England, Cromwell's government introduced the Navigation laws designed to protect and extend English shipping. After the restoration, Corn laws, which encouraged export of grain when prices were low and prohibited it when they were high, were introduced and gradually elaborated. Such laws reflected the interests of the merchants and the landowners of England, who were able, through Parliament, to make the government help or protect their economic interests.

In France and most other continental countries, the desires of private citizens played only a minor role in fixing governmental economic policies. Royal ministers and officials more often took the lead, and, wishing to encourage some particular line of industry, to build up a strong merchant marine, to improve the road system, or to accomplish some other end, they made regulations which they hoped would induce or compel men to act accordingly. Thus Jean Baptiste Colbert (d. 1683), minister under Louis XIV, prescribed minutely the standards of quality and even the processes of manufacture for French cloth in the hope that a uniform and high-quality product would win for France good markets in all the world. In some instances Colbert went beyond regulation, and set up government-owned factories.

A field in which government regulation was particularly active was colonial trade. The colonies were regarded as sources of wealth for the mother country, and in general no outsiders were allowed to trade with them. Moreover, colonial competition with home industry was discouraged or forbidden. But the relation was not altogether one-sided. In North America, for instance, the British subsidized the production of indigo; and the raising of tobacco in England was forbidden, thus assuring the colonies a monopoly of that lucrative crop.

It is difficult to estimate the effect which these and similar government regulations had on the development of economic life. Smuggling and evasion of governmental rules were common, so that one can never assume that laws on paper did in fact govern economic relationships. Yet it would also be rash to assume that regulation did not produce at least some of the desired results. Certainly France under Colbert made rapid progress in trade and industry and it was not until after government regulations came to be administered by less capable men than he that the mercantilist system of France began to show serious flaws.

Toward the end of the eighteenth century, however, economic theorists began to doubt the beneficial effect of government regulation. The rule of nature, it was argued, would improve upon any human regulations, and would assure a harmony between the selfish interests of individuals and the general good. In France a school of laissez faire economists arose about the middle of the eighteenth century; and in Great Britain, Adam Smith published his famous book, *The Wealth of Nations*, in 1776. Adam Smith's arguments in favor of free trade were impressive; in addition important commercial and industrial interests in England and in France found certain government regulations increasingly inconvenient. In England the government responded by allowing regulations to lapse or by abolishing them. In France, however, the government was far less responsive to pressure from the bourgeoisie, and it was left for the revolution to sweep away numerous regulations which that class found distasteful or obstructive.

c. Politics

1) International

a) French Preponderance, 1660–1713. Spain, once the strongest power of Europe, had not been a party to the Peace of Westphalia, which ended the Thirty Years' War. Fighting dragged on with France until 1659, when the Spanish government found itself compelled to make peace. For the next half century, France remained preeminent in Europe. Louis XIV (1643–1715) conceived the ambition of extending the French boundaries to "natural frontiers"—that is to the Rhine; the Alps and the Pyrenees. He had succeeded in reaching the Pyrenees in 1659, and spent most of the rest of his long reign in trying to reach the Rhine. A series of wars resulted, and provoked a series of European coalitions designed to resist Louis' plans. At first Holland was the principal antagonist. But the Dutch could hardly match the power of France, and in the first part of his reign Louis was able to annex some territory along his northern and eastern frontier. After 1688, however, England took over leadership of the coalition, and thereafter the French were unable to win major successes.

Toward the end of Louis XIV's reign the royal house of Spain died out, and he was able to place one of his grandsons on the Spanish throne. This precipitated a long war (1701–14) which came near to exhausting France. The war ended with a compromise. The French candidate retained the Spanish throne, but lost control of all the former Spanish possessions in Europe which were distributed among the various powers which had fought against the French. The peace settlement of 1713–14 marked the end of unquestioned French predominance on the continent. The coalition, headed by Great Britain and Austria, had come near to defeating France; and the treaties (Utrecht 1713; Rastadt and Baden 1714) which ended the war were drawn in such a way as to strengthen the enemies and rivals of France.

The peace settlement awarded control of most of the former Spanish possessions in Italy to the Austrian Hapsburgs (Naples, Sardinia and Milan); and in addition the Austrians became rulers of the former Spanish Low Countries (subsequently known as the Austrian Netherlands and later as Belgium). Austria thus fell heir to the lion's share of the former Spanish possessions in Europe, and became a much stronger power than

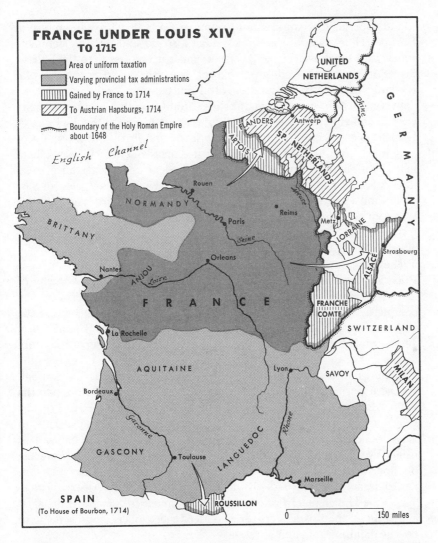

FRANCE UNDER LOUIS XIV
TO 1715

- Area of uniform taxation
- Varying provincial tax administrations
- Gained by France to 1714
- To Austrian Hapsburgs, 1714
- Boundary of the Holy Roman Empire about 1648

English Channel

UNITED NETHERLANDS

GERMANY

FLANDERS   Antwerp

ARTOIS

SP. NETHERLANDS

Rhine

Meuse

Metz

LORRAINE

Strasbourg

ALSACE

Rouen

NORMANDY

Reims

BRITTANY

Paris

Seine

FRANCE

ANJOU

Loire

Orleans

Nantes

FRANCHE COMTE

SWITZERLAND

La Rochelle

AQUITAINE

Lyon

SAVOY

MILAN

Bordeaux

Garonne

GASCONY

LANGUEDOC

Rhone

Toulouse

Marseille

SPAIN
(To House of Bourbon, 1714)

ROUSSILLON

0   150 miles

had formerly been the case. Successful wars against the Turks (1682–99 and again 1714–18) extended Austrian possessions throughout Hungary and into the northern Balkan peninsula during the same period. Thus an Austrian imperial state arose in south central Europe.

Unlike France or England, Austria was not a national state. Germans, Hungarians, Italians, Czechs, Croats, Serbs, Rumanians, and still other peoples were united under the Hapsburg crown. National and linguistic diversity was fully matched by diversity of institutions. Indeed the Austrian state was only held together by the common allegiance various kingdoms, duchies, marks, counties, etc., owed to the Hapsburg ruler, and by a vague imperial sense of mission to uphold Catholic Christian culture in Europe. Thus Austria was not so much a single state as a collection of states; and the power of the Austrian emperor was less than the bulk of his territories would lead one to expect. Nevertheless, after the Peace of Rastadt, Austria stood second only to France on the continent.

In comparison with Austria, the states around which Italy and Germany were to unite in the nineteenth century were small indeed. Yet the Peace of Utrecht marks the promotion of both Savoy and Prussia to the status of kingdoms. The duke of Savoy was awarded the island of Sicily as his share in the spoils of the Spanish empire; and with Sicily went the medieval royal title. A few years later, he gave Sicily to the Austrians in exchange for Sardinia, and changed his title accordingly to King of Sardinia. The new kingdom of Sardinia was the largest independent Italian state; and except for the Papal States in central Italy it was almost the only state in Italy which was not subject to foreign control.

The Peace also made the former Elector of Brandenburg "King in Prussia." Brandenburg originated as an eastern mark of the duchy of Saxony, and the earliest margraves carved out a state for themselves by conquering various Slavic tribes which inhabited the region. In 1415 the Hohenzollern family came into possession of the Mark of Brandenburg, and slowly through succeeding generations added to their territories until by the end of the Thirty Years' War they had become second only to the Hapsburgs among German rulers. Various territories scattered through northern Germany were in their possession, and along the Baltic coast the Hohenzollerns held East Prussia as a fief of the Polish crown. In 1713 the Peace of Utrecht added one more patch of territory in western Germany to their dominions, and recognized the growing power of the Hohenzollern rulers by according them the royal title. Since Prussia lay outside the boundaries of the Empire, and could not be regarded as in any way subject to the control of the Holy Roman Emperor (i.e., of the Austrian Hapsburgs) the Hohenzollern ruler chose to call himself "King in Prussia"— and soon all the various territories under Hohenzollern control came to be called, indiscriminately, Prussia.

The British share of the booty distributed at Utrecht took the form of overseas acquisitions. From France the British took Nova Scotia and Newfoundland; from Spain, Gibraltar, and a valuable trading concession which gave British ships a monopoly of the slave trade with the Spanish colonies and a limited right to trade in other goods with Spanish possessions in the New World.

b) The Balance of Power, 1713–1789. From 1713 to 1789 no one European power dominated international politics. The tangled diplomacy and fighting of the period may be conceived as revolving around two general issues: first, the drastic readjustment of power in central and eastern Europe which resulted from the decline of Sweden, Poland and Turkey; and second, the struggle between France and England for colonial supremacy in India and in America.

i) Readjustment in Central and Eastern Europe. During the seventeenth century Sweden had created a Baltic empire; but when Prussia and Russia began to organize powerful, centralized and militaristic states, the Swedes found themselves unable to defend their extensive possessions against these neighbors. Poland suffered an even more drastic fate. It disappeared from the map of Europe at the end of the eighteenth century as a result of the weakness of the central government and the aggression of Russia, Prussia and Austria. The Ottoman empire, which had for several centuries been a serious military threat to the West, began to undergo a complicated process of internal decay during the late seventeenth and subsequent centuries. Like the Swedes and the Poles, the Turks became unable to defend their possessions from the assault of their neighbors, Russia and Austria.

Thus the stage was set in eastern Europe for a rapid shift in the balance of power. Three states profited: Austria, Prussia and Russia. The first two have already been briefly described; it remains to introduce the Russians onto the European scene.

The Russian state had been founded in the ninth century by Scandinavian vikings, known as Rus. They ruled over a Slavic population, and in the course of a few generations were absorbed into it. Christianity and some of the culture of Byzantium penetrated into Russia in the tenth century; in the thirteenth the Mongols, under one of the successors of Ghengis Khan, conquered all but one of the numerous Russian principalities into which the original state had been divided. The Mongols did not destroy native institutions, and for the most part contented themselves with collecting tribute money. At length, in 1480, Ivan III, prince of Moscow (1462-1505), formally repudiated subjection to the heirs of the Mongol power by withholding tribute payments. In the following century, Ivan IV, the Terrible (1533-84), carried through a drastic reorganization of the state, overthrowing the power of the boyar (noble) families, and establishing himself as an autocrat. In an act that asserted a fictitious continuity with imperial Byzantium, Ivan IV crowned himself Czar, i.e., Caesar. Subsequent Russian rulers regularly took this imperial title. At the beginning of the next century the growth of the Russian empire was threatened by internal troubles and by the intervention of the Poles; but in 1613 the first Romanoff Czar was elevated to the throne, and he succeeded in driving back the Polish invaders.

When Peter the Great (1682-1725) became czar, he inherited a vast but undeveloped land, where Byzantine and Asiatic traditions far outweighed the small influence which European traders and artisans had come to exercise. Peter, a man of enormous energy and ruthless will, determined to make Russia a state which could compete on equal terms with the great powers of Europe. He realized vividly that the first step in such a direction must be the creation of an army; and that before a Russian army could be successful in battle against European forces, he must be able to equip and train it according to European methods.

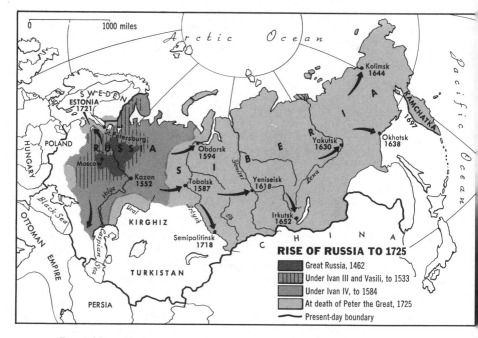

RISE OF RUSSIA TO 1725

- Great Russia, 1462
- Under Ivan III and Vasili, to 1533
- Under Ivan IV, to 1584
- At death of Peter the Great, 1725
- — Present-day boundary

Peter himself visited western Europe in order to study the techniques and manners of western men, and throughout his reign promoted in every way he could the spread of European influence to Russia. He imported large numbers of technicians to help him train soldiers and create the necessary factories in which guns, ammunition and all the various require-ments of an army and navy could be manufactured. In some of his efforts he succeeded surprisingly. By the end of his reign, for instance, Russia produced more iron than England did (though not more than Sweden or Germany); and some of Peter's factories were larger than anything known in the West when measured by the number of persons employed. In some of his other efforts, Peter came close to absurdity, as when he personally cut off the beards of his courtiers to make them into Europeans, or com-manded the ladies of the court to abandon their customary semi-oriental seclusion and, wearing European dresses, try to imitate the behavior of a French drawing room.

Nevertheless, the wholesale Europeanization of Russia which Peter initiated from the top did gradually take effect among the upper classes. Russian noblemen became familiar with the French language and with the latest ideas of the French *philosophes*. Their clothes, their manners and some of their ideas came to be European. But the great majority of the Russian peasants were serfs, and their masters sometimes bought and sold them like slaves. The land was cultivated by village communities, which were known as *mirs*. Towns were relatively small and few, and the bourgeois class, which exercised so much influence in western Europe, was of very minor importance in Russia.

Two changes did, however, affect the Russian population as a whole. One was the gradual development of a centralized bureaucracy which brought the power of the czar into the Russian countryside. In Peter's time, the shortage of trained officials was a tremendous handicap, and he relied extensively upon foreigners, even using prisoners of war to administer his empire. Gradually this shortage was overcome, and a good post in the government came to be the primary goal of most educated Russians.

The other novelty which affected the general mass of the Russian population was the organization of a conscript army. Indeed, the central aim of Peter's reforms was the construction of a powerful army, and he succeeded very well. Each village was required to send a quota of men to serve in the army; they were trained by European drillmasters, equipped with European weapons, and sent to fight against European and Turkish soldiers. When it came to battle the Russians from the first acquitted themselves well.

Peter fought a series of campaigns against the Swedes, and by 1721 he succeeded in defeating them. He annexed Esthonia and an area around the head of the Gulf of Finland, where a new capital, St. Petersburg, was erected in what had previously been a desolate marsh. St. Petersburg was a "window on Europe" for the new Russian state, and became, far more than Moscow, a European city.

Peter's successors continued to pursue, though with less energy, his policy of Europeanization. By far the most successful of them was Catherine II (1762–96). During her reign. the kingdom of Poland was dismembered in three successive partitions (1772, 1793, 1795) and Russia got the largest part. Wars with the Turks led to the annexation of the Crimea, and campaigns in the south east led to the extension of the Russian frontier across the Volga and into the Caucasus.

Prussia shared with Russia in the dismemberment of both the Swedish empire and the kingdom of Poland, and emerged by the end of the eighteenth century one of the great powers of Europe. Prussia's rise was very largely the work of her kings, and especially of Frederick II (1740–86), or as he is usually called, Frederick the Great. When Frederick came to the Prussian throne he inherited a very frugal and admirably efficient state. His father had devoted the rather slender resources of his kingdom to building up an army; and in the very year of his accession Frederick used that army to seize from Austria the province of Silesia. Frederick's action helped to precipitate a general European war (War of the Austrian Succession, 1740–8) in which France and some lesser powers joined with Prussia in attacking Austria. When peace was made, it confirmed the Prussian acquisition of Silesia, but made few other changes in the map of Europe.

Frederick's success displeased the French; and the Austrian government was eager to get revenge. As a result, the long standing rivalry between Hapsburg and French monarchs was patched up, and in 1756 Austria and France united to attack Prussia. Russia too joined in the fray, and Prussia was left without a single ally on the European continent. Great Britain, however, had been fighting France in America since 1754, and came to Frederick's aid with subsidies and a few troops. The odds certainly seemed desperate, but for six years the Prussian armies were able to stand off their three enemies, winning several brilliant victories and losing some

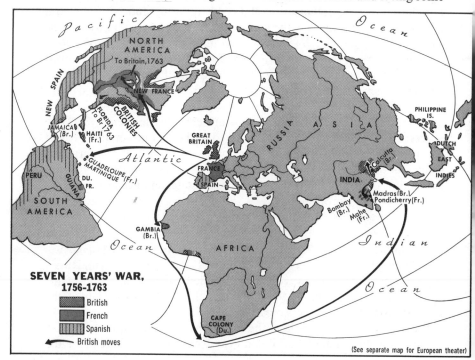

SEVEN YEARS' WAR, 1756–1763

■ British
■ French
▥ Spanish
← British moves

(See separate map for European theater)

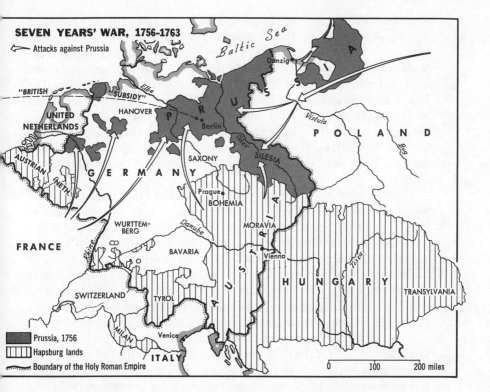

SEVEN YEARS' WAR, 1756-1763
← Attacks against Prussia

Baltic Sea, Danzig, "BRITISH SUBSIDY", UNITED NETHERLANDS, HANOVER, Elbe, P R U S S I A, Berlin, Vistula, Bug, P O L A N D, AUSTRIAN NETH., G E R M A N Y, SAXONY, Oder, SILESIA, Prague, BOHEMIA, WURTTEM-BERG, Danube, MORAVIA, A U S T R I A, Tisza, FRANCE, Rhine, BAVARIA, Vienna, H U N G A R Y, TRANSYLVANIA, SWITZERLAND, TYROL, MILAN, Venice, ITALY

■ Prussia, 1756
▦ Hapsburg lands
▬▬ Boundary of the Holy Roman Empire

0   100   200 miles

hard fought fields. In 1762 Peter III came to the Russian throne, and, reacting violently against the policies of his predecessor, made a generous peace with Frederick. France, too, had suffered numerous defeats overseas in the war with Great Britain and wanted to make peace. Consequently the Austrians were compelled to give up hope of recovering Silesia, and a treaty was concluded in 1763, bringing the Seven Years' War to a close.

The Seven Years' War was the hardest fought and most decisive of any eighteenth-century war. Prussia had suffered tremendous devastation — Berlin, the capital, had twice been occupied by Russian troops, and almost every part of Frederick's kingdom had been fought over. Yet the Prussians emerged successful, with the reputation of being the best soldiers of Europe; and Prussia established itself as one of the great powers of the continent. From 1763 there were thus five great powers: Russia, Prussia and Austria in central and eastern Europe, and France and Great Britain in the west. This remained, with many shifts of relative importance, the alignment of Europe until 1918.

ii) Franco-British Rivalry Overseas. By 1714, Holland had followed Spain and Portugal into relative eclipse as a great colonial power. Yet some important regions of the colonial world remained in the possession of each of these states. The Spanish and Portuguese colonies in Central and South America looked impressive on a map, but, more and more, the trade with those regions passed into the hands of British merchants, and with the trade passed most of the economic advantages of possession. The Dutch imperial possessions in the East Indies and elsewhere were rather more valuable to the mother country, for Dutch ships continued to ply the high seas, and the spice trade remained concentrated in Dutch hands. But the days of Dutch imperial expansion passed with the seventeenth century. Thereafter the field was left to be disputed between France and England.

The two principal regions in which British and French colonial enterprise came into conflict were North America and India. Each time fighting broke out in Europe after 1688 France and Great Britain found themselves on opposite sides; and their conflict was fought out not only on the continent of Europe, but on the high seas and in the colonies as well. The decisive war was the Seven Years' War, 1756-63, or, as it is known in American history, the French and Indian War, 1754-63 (for fighting broke out in America two years before it did in Europe.) By the Peace of Paris, which ended the struggle, the French lost both Canada and India.

A chance for revenge came when the American colonies revolted against Great Britain in 1776. In 1778 France declared war on the British, and was joined by Spain (1779) and Holland shortly afterwards (1780). Thus a powerful coalition of rival colonial nations faced the British. With the cooperation of the American army under George Washington, they were able to administer a series of defeats to their common enemy. By 1783 the British were ready to yield. The peace secured American independence, and retroceded various colonial areas to France and Spain. Despite these losses, however, Britain remained the strongest single colonial power and the most active mercantile nation of Europe. India remained in the British sphere of influence, and so did Canada and Nova Scotia to the north of the newly formed United States of America (1789).

2) Internal Political Organization of the Leading European Nations. Absolute monarchy remained the typical form of European government, until the outbreak of the French Revolution in 1789 challenged the ideas and institutions of the "Old Regime." In most European states, it came to be a recognized legal principle that what the king willed was law, and the right of subjects to share in control of government policies was not admitted.

The use which the various kings and emperors made of their theoretical prerogatives was of course severely limited in practice by inherited traditions of government, and by the human limitations of the monarchs. No one man could begin to cope with all the concerns of an eighteenth-century government. Kings had to depend on their servants, the bureaucrats and ministers, to make innumerable decisions which, taken together, constituted most of the reality of government. Thus Divine Right of kings, really meant the unchecked power of government officials. Obviously, the efficiency of such governments depended on who the officials were, how they were chosen, and how promoted. Much depended on a handful of men at the top—the king and his ministers who headed the principal departments of government. A vigorous and energetic ruler was able to impress his will on all branches of the government; on the other hand a ruler who was more interested in the pleasures of court life than in the arduous work of administration simply allowed the governmental machine to drift along in its own haphazard fashion.

a) Governmental Reorganization in Central and Eastern Europe. During the eighteenth century, a number of rulers arose in central and eastern Europe who tried vigorously to reform, reorganize and increase the efficiency of their governments. Some of their policies professed to apply principles of contemporary social theory; hence they are known as "Enlightened Despots." They strove to centralize government, to make institutions uniform in the various parts of their domain, to encourage the arts and sciences, to reduce or eliminate internal barriers to trade and industry, and in general to strengthen and enlarge their states. Frederick the Great (1740–86) was the most successful of these rulers; Catherine II of Russia (1762–96) and Joseph II of Austria (1780–90) emulated him.

Catherine's policies continued the Europeanization of Russia which had been initiated by Peter the Great. At the beginning of her reign she faced a problem of securing herself in power, for she was by birth a German princess and her only claim to the Russian throne was through her marriage with the Czar, whom she deposed soon after she had married him. Consequently Catherine found it expedient to make generous concessions to the Russian nobility. She released them from the duty of serving the state (which had been theirs since the time of Ivan the Terrible) and confirmed and extended their legal power over the peasant serfs of Russia. She professed enlightened ideas as to a ruler's duties toward subjects, but did little to help any class save the nobility.

In Austria, the confusing multiplicity of local institutions and rights, which resulted from the piecemeal manner in which the Hapsburg possessions had been acquired, struck Joseph II as a terrible incubus upon the efficiency of the state and, into the bargain, an offense against rational principles. During his short reign he tried hard to unify the Austrian dominions and to make his government more efficient. But local opposition was stubborn, and the outbreak of the French revolution in 1789 helped to discredit radical efforts at change. His reforms were thus only partially effective, and Austria entered upon the nineteenth century without achieving any real internal unity.

The Prussian administration was, like the Prussian army, the envy of Europe. Its efficiency dated back to the seventeenth century, when Frederick William, the Great Elector (1640–88), had nursed his scattered provinces, devastated like the rest of Germany by the Thirty Years' War, back to economic prosperity, and had centralized their administration in Berlin. During the eighteenth century the tradition of paternalistic efficiency, parsimony and thoroughness were continued. In particular, appointment and promotion in the Prussian service depended on passing written examinations that tested knowledge needed for efficient performance. This device assured a far higher general level of competence among Prussian officials than was usually found in other European governments. With their aid, Frederick the Great carried through numerous public works, attracted settlers from all parts of Europe, and through the usual devices of a mercantilist state did what he could to encourage trade and industry. It was under Frederick the Great, and with his active encouragement, that potatoes first became an important crop in Germany. This plant, a native of South America, throve in the sandy soils and cool climate of Prussia. Its widespread cultivation enormously enlarged the food resources of that kingdom and permitted a relatively great growth in population.

b) French Absolutism. The history of the internal government of France stands in contrast to that of the newer and more easterly states. During the first part of Louis XIV's reign many of the policies which later distinguished the enlightened despots were pursued. Colbert painstakingly fostered the welfare of French merchants and industrialists; and another minister, the Marquis of Louvois, expended a similar care on the French army. Louis himself exhibited an enormous industry in matters of government, and personally supervised his ministers. Under such administration, as we have seen, France rose to first rank among European powers.

The latter part of Louis' long reign was not so fortunate. Powerful coalitions blocked the success of his foreign policies, and the resultant long and difficult wars damaged the internal prosperity of France. Moreover, with the death of Colbert (1683) and Louvois (1691), Louis' most capable ministers disappeared, and the aging king did not replace them with men of equal caliber. Religious bigotry led Louis to embark upon persecution of the Jansenits and the Huguenots; and in so doing he succeeded in driving from his kingdom many industrious and skilled families. Huguenot refugees helped notably to build up Prussian industry, and brought new artisan skills to England.

Under Louis XV (1715-74) the relaxation of the efficiency of the French government continued unchecked. Efforts to alter or reform institutions were abandoned; a routine and often corrupt administration hindered rather than helped economic development; and public criticism multiplied. French commerce and industry nevertheless continued to grow at a rapid pace through most of the eighteenth century; but the effect of this growth was simply to make the middle class more and more discontented with the public administration to which they were subjected.

The major grievance of the middle classes was that a small number of nobles and high ecclesiastics enjoyed special privileges from which they were excluded. Many nobles drew pensions from the king; and all nobles were exempted from certain taxes. The high posts of government and of the army were reserved for men of noble birth, and promotion often depended more on acquaintance at court than on merit. Many nobles and some of the high clergy led a frivolous life at the royal court in Versailles, attending the ceremonial gatherings around the person of the king, and conspiring in polite drawing-rooms for the favors of fair ladies and the perquisites of governmental office or pensions. This state of affairs seemed to many a good bourgeois to be both unjust and irrational.

In addition there were other grievances. The administration of justice was sometimes erratic, for the king had the power to arrest anyone without giving any reason and imprison him as long as he wished. There was no uniform system of law in France. Each of the provinces which had been united during the late Middle Ages to make the French kingdom retained many of the laws and peculiar institutions which had prevailed there before. Some uniformity was assured by the fact that France was divided into administrative districts under intendants—a reform which had been carried through by Cardinal Richelieu at the beginning of the seventeenth century. But in the eyes of the critical middle class, these officials were tyrants rather than defenders of the public good. In the early seventeenth century, intendants and the royal judges had been recruited mainly from the middle class, and a career in government service was more or less open to talent. By the eighteenth century, however, the corps of high government officials had become a nearly closed caste—the *noblesse de robe*—which was only slightly less privileged than were the descendants of the medieval feudal class—the *noblesse d'épée*.

The survival of traces of the medieval manorial system constituted another important grievance, and made the peasants of France side with the discontented bourgeoisie. The chaotic tax system and the unequal incidence of taxation were likewise resented by both peasants and townsmen; and the gradual obsolescence of many of the government's economic regulations exacerbated the impatience of large numbers of the king's most wealthy subjects.

The discontent of the majority of Frenchmen was voiced by numerous writers and publicists, who called themselves *philosophes*; but the agitation made little impression on the ruling circles of France until financial crisis compelled reorganization of the governmental system. The cost of foreign wars was of prime importance in bringing the government to the verge of bankruptcy, for the inefficient credit and tax system did not allow for easy expansion of government income to meet extraordinary emergencies. Efforts to impose new taxes were resisted by some of the king's own officials, especially by the judges of the so-called *Parlements*; and the central administration lacked the ruthlessness to beat down such opposition, supported, as it was, by an active public opinion.

When Louis XVI came to the throne in 1774 he made some half-hearted attempts to bring order out of the chaos into which French administration had fallen. A reforming minister, Anne Robert Jacques Turgot, was appointed to wrestle with the problem of finances; but his proposals stirred up a storm of opposition among the nobles of the court and among high officials of the government, and Louis weakly surrendered by dismissing Turgot after only twenty months in office. A new minister of finance, Jacques Necker, succeeded in keeping the government solvent by means of loans and a mild policy of retrenchment; but he too stirred up the enmity of powerful circles in the court, and was dismissed in 1781. Thereafter the government's finances went from bad to worse. The expenses of the war with Britain (1778–83) and help sent to the American revolutionists emptied the treasury. A series of makeshifts failed to relieve the financial difficulties of the government, and in 1789 as a last resort Louis XVI agreed to summon a meeting of the Estates-General in the hope that it would be able to solve the government's financial problems. Instead, the Estates-General initiated the French revolution.

c) British Constitutional Monarchy. Unlike the states of continental Europe, representative institutions, derived from medieval times, remained powerful in England in the seventeenth century. The course of the Puritan revolution has already been sketched. Parliament took a leading part in the early stages of that movement, and in the years 1640–1 had passed a series of laws which severely limited the royal prerogative. When Charles II (1660–85) was restored to the throne of his father, he promised to abide by the laws which Parliament had promulgated in those years. With the restoration, widespread reaction against Puritanical religious zeal swept over the English people. The Anglican church was re-established as a state church, and men's minds very generally turned away from religious to other concerns.

The English aristocracy, among whose ranks were included many recruits from the mercantile class, came to dominate political life. Parliament controlled the central government, and Parliament represented the landed gentry and the wealthy classes of the towns. Local government was largely in the hands of squires and burgesses, who acted as local magistrates and usually served without pay. Thus the English government was able to dispense with a paid, professional bureaucracy such as administered the governments of continental European states. Suspicion of royal power was never entirely allayed. Parliament was generally careful to make money grants to the king only for specific purposes, and often made them contingent upon the king's assent to some new piece of legislation. Legislation thus came to reflect the interests of the gentry and merchants of England. Other groups in the population, including the king and the king's court, could exercise only indirect influence by winning the support of members of Parliament.

Neither Charles II nor his successor, James II (1685–8), liked the limitations that Parliament imposed on the royal power. Toward the end of his reign, Charles fell into difficulties with parliament and ruled for four years without it. A revival of religious antagonism came when the heir to the throne, James, openly espoused Roman Catholicism. A group in Parliament tried to exclude him from the line of succession. This group, which came to be known as the Whigs, failed to gets its way, since a majority of the Parliament (the Tories) feared renewal of revolutionary disturbances if the hereditary principle were undermined. From the debate over James II's accession dates the division of Parliament into two fairly definite and more or less permanently organized parties. The present-day Conservative Party of Great Britain is descended from the Tories of the seventeenth century, and the Whigs survive as the Liberal Party.

James' religious and political policies soon deeply disturbed both Whigs and Tories. He overrode Parliamentary decisions by suspending laws and statutes, and began to appoint Roman Catholics to high positions in the army and the government. His foreign policy, too, was unpopular, for James was subservient to the French king, Louis XIV, at a time when French empire-builders and merchants were beginning to compete actively with the English in the colonial regions of the world. When a son was born to James, discontent reached the boiling point, for now it appeared that the succession would not pass to James' Protestant daughters Mary and Anne, but would remain in Catholic hands.

The result was a conspiracy in which the Whigs took the leading part. Mary's husband, William of Orange, was invited to come from Holland. When he landed in England in 1688 supporters flocked to him and James fled to France. A hastily assembled Parliament offered the crown jointly to William and Mary, but was careful to draw up a new set of conditions— the Bill of Rights—which the new monarchs accepted. By the provisions of the Bill of Rights, Parliament became, definitely and beyond dispute, the sovereign authority in the government of England, with sole powers to assess taxation and to authorize the maintenance of an army.

The expulsion of James II is often referred to as the Glorious Revolution. Despite the fact that it was almost bloodless (there was a movement in Ireland to support King James, but at the Battle of the Boyne, 1690, the Irish forces were crushed and Protestant ascendancy was assured for the following hundred years) the Revolution of 1688 marked a decisive step toward constitutional monarchy and parliamentary government.

The accidents of dynastic inheritance promoted and profoundly influenced the further development of England's peculiar governmental institutions in the following three generations. William of Orange was mainly interested in foreign policy, and he eagerly mobilized the resources of his new kingdom to resist the aggressive plans of Louis XIV. As we have seen, England's intervention against France was of decisive importance on the international scene. But the consequences for English home politics were equally decisive. William was in general quite content to leave the administration of England to Parliament. He adopted the practice of appointing Whig ministers to conduct his government when there was a Whig majority in Parliament, and Tory ministers when there was a Tory majority. From William's point of view, such an arrangement simply avoided troublesome friction with the Parliament; but the effect of such a practice was to extend Parliamentary control over the executive branch of the government.

William and Mary had no direct heirs, and so the throne passed to Mary's younger sister, Queen Anne (1702–14). During her reign, the kingdom of Scotland was united with that of England to form Great Britain. Since 1603 the two kingdoms had been in personal union under the Stuart kings, but (except under the Commonwealth) separate Parliaments and other institutions of government had been retained. In 1707 parallel acts in the Scottish and English Parliaments resulted in the merging of the two Parliaments, and England and Scotland were declared to be one kingdom. Ireland, although subject since the days of Queen Elizabeth to the English crown, remained separate with its own Parliament and laws until 1800.

When Queen Anne died in 1714, Parliament passed over the hereditary claim of James II's son and offered the crown to a remote cousin of the Stuart house, the Elector of Hanover, who became King George I (1714–27). George I and his Son, George II (1727–60) were German princes, and neither of them ever learned to speak English fluently. Like William of Orange, their major personal interest lay in their ancestral possessions on the continent, and they were quite willing to leave the administration of their British kingdom to Parliament.

Since George I could not understand English, he generally absented himself from meetings of his ministers. Consequently the ministers (or Cabinet, as they were collectively called) came to conduct meetings and decide policies by themselves; and the king regularly approved what they had done. In the course of time this precedent came to have a binding force, until the British king became little more than a figurehead.

During the first two Hanoverian reigns the office of prime minister came into existence. For many years Sir Robert Walpole was able to maintain the support of Parliament. He won the confidence of George I and George II to such a degree that they entrusted him with the selection of the royal ministers, whose appointments were simply ratified by the king. Walpole retained his unique position for more than twenty years (1721–42); and his preeminence came to be recognized in popular speech by according him the title of prime (i.e., first) minister. His career was long enough to create a fairly firm precedent for the practice of choosing the royal ministers through a prime minister. In time it became a principle of British government that the king should call upon the leader of the majority party in Parliament to form a cabinet, and the king's power to choose "his" ministers became little more than a formality.

Thus almost by accident arose the Cabinet system of government, a system which had the advantage of a remarkable flexibility, permitting changes in public opinion and in the strength of parties to be registered almost automatically by appropriate changes in the administration of the government. One should not assume, however, that the British government represented all the people of Great Britain in the eighteenth century. Parliamentary franchise was very limited. There were no uniform voting rules in the boroughs, but in general only a few of the inhabitants of towns had the right to vote for their borough representatives; and a property qualification for voting for the "knights of the shire" meant in effect that the gentry controlled the county elections. Moreover Walpole and others discovered that Parliamentary elections could often be manipulated by bribery. Shifts in the centers of population were not reflected by changes in the distribution of Parliamentary seats after the time of Charles II, so that a number of almost depopulated towns ("rotten boroughs") retained the right to send two representatives to Parliament, while new towns, no matter how large they might be, were unrepresented. A consequence was that quite a number of Parliamentary seats came to be controlled by a handful of electors, or even by a single great landowner, who could intimidate or bribe the voters to make them choose whomever he wished. Thus, British government became oligarchic in fact and a constitutional monarchy in form during the seventeenth and early eighteenth centuries.

George III (1760–1820) had been brought up in England and was English rather than Hanoverian in his interests and sympathy. He was not content to remain a figurehead, but took an active part in Parliamentary affairs. During the early part of his long reign he tried, with very considerable success, to establish a king's party in Parliament, and to govern rather than merely to reign. The failure of the royal policy in the North American colonies, and the reverses of the American War of Independence helped to discredit George's active participation in government; but the fact that he became intermittently insane during his latter years did even more to establish the precedent that the king of England reigns but does not rule.

Sentiment for reform began to develop in Great Britain just as in France in the latter part of the eighteenth century. After the failure of the war with the colonies, a reform party demanded readjustment of representation in Parliament to make it coincide more accurately with the distribution of population. But before such efforts met with any success the outbreak of the French revolution discredited all attempts at change, and for the following forty years no important departures were made in governmental organizations.

Perhaps the most salient contrast between the political life of Great Britain and that of France in the eighteenth century was the difference in the role played by the upper and middle classes. In England, the actual business of local government was largely handled by squires and burgesses, and the policies of the central government generally reflected the interests of the landed and commercial classes. In France governmental policies and administration were controlled mainly by a court clique and by a more or less self-perpetuating bureaucracy, both of which groups had fallen out of touch with the great majority of the Frenchmen.

The membership of the aristocracy of Great Britain, too, differed from that of France. In England there was a much closer tie between commerce and landownership: many individuals after making a fortune in trade acquired respectability by purchasing an estate and setting themselves up as landed gentlemen. Conversely, many landowners put a part of their capital into commercial and industrial enterprises. In France, on the other hand, pride of ancestry and disdain for commercial pursuits was much more firmly established among the aristocracy; it was more difficult for self-made men to win entrance into the charmed circle of the nobility; and in the few cases where new men succeeded in arriving, they hastily cut off their degrading ties with commercial or industrial activities. Consequently the French aristocracy tended to sink to the level of a parasite upon society as a whole; while its privileges and frivolity exposed it to the envy and attacks of intellectual leaders and of the middle class in general.

These differences help to explain why revolution broke out in France and not in England. To such differences should be added the social impact of Methodism in England. The Methodist religious revival of the late eighteenth century, like the Franciscan movement of the thirteenth century, adapted traditional religious organization to a new social mileu: in this case, to the rising industrial towns of England. Methodism not only inculcated submission to constituted authority and faithfulness in the walk of life to which it had pleased God to assign each individual; it also had the effect of diverting the energy and organizing capacity of the English working classes (among whom Methodism found its principal supporters) into a religious channel. The further fact that, once revolution had broken out in France, patriotism and conservatism came to be equated in many English minds, also acted as a powerful brake against political change.

d. Culture

The term classicism has been used to describe the predominant forms of literature, art and music of the late seventeenth and early eighteenth centuries; and romanticism has been used to describe changes which began to manifest themselves in these same fields toward the end of the eighteenth century and which continued to develop in the first decades of the nineteenth. It is very difficult to pin down the exact meaning of such terms; and they are at best inadequate to describe the ever growing diversity of Europe's cultural expression. Yet many critics believe they can detect a vague common denominator between the poetry of Pope, the plays of Racine, the music of Mozart, and the painting of Reynolds which may be called classicism. Optimism, rationality, moderation, cosmopolitanism and polish with just a touch of artificiality—all these are in some degree characteristic of the classicism of the first half of the eighteenth century. In contrast, romanticists valued feeling, self-expression, inspiration, liberation from traditional artistic forms, and frequently looked to the medieval and local or national past with admiration and a new interest.

New scientific theories which had an enormous impact on men's thinking were advanced during the seventeenth and eighteenth centuries; rapid progress in material technology and increase in wealth contributed toward a sense of optimism, if not of complacency, and confirmed a growing belief in progress. Conviction that human reason was able to cope with the problems of the world gained a wide acceptance, and traditional religious beliefs were profoundly modified or rejected by an influential group of intellectual leaders, especially in France.

Another important aspect of European culture in the eighteenth century was the rise of Vienna as a great cultural center. What Paris was to the western parts of Europe, Vienna became to central and south eastern Europe after about 1699, when victorious wars against the Turks changed the Hapsburg capital from a frontier town into the center of a great empire. It was mainly to Italy that the Austrian (and Hungarian) nobles turned for instruction when they became interested in art, architecture, and music; and it was scarcely before 1750 that native Austrians emancipated themselves from Italian tutelage.

SHAPERS OF THE MODERN WORLD

Montesquieu
(The Bettmann Archive)

John Locke
(The Bettmann Archive)

Voltaire
Bust by Houdon
(The Bettmann Archive)

Jean Jacques Rousseau
Portrait by De La Tour
(The Bettmann Archive)

This development, centering in Vienna, recapitulated a pattern of cultural development which had existed in France (and Western Europe generally) about two centuries earlier. At the beginning of the sixteenth century, Frenchmen were almost as much under the sway of the Italian renaissance as Austrians came to be in the first decades of the eighteenth century: and it is not without foundation to imagine the cultural history of modern Europe as having been fertilized by two great streams flowing northward from Italy over the western and then over the eastern Alpine passes, first to France, and later into Austria. To be sure, local variations were always important, and Italian models were regularly modified when imitated under northern skies. But the degree to which there was a uniformity of European culture in the early centuries of modern history can best be understood as a consequence of the common stimulus men of all European countries found in the achievement of the Italian Renaissance. When the art forms which had originated in Italy or found stimulus from Italy were abandoned, or so transformed as to become scarcely recognizable, the uniformity of European culture disappeared, to be replaced by national cultures and even by individualistic art forms. The progressive fragmentation of Europe's tradition along these lines is one way to interpret the cultural history of the nineteenth century.

1) Literature. Under Louis XIV French language and literature became a model for most of continental Europe. A group of savants standardized and purified the French language by compiling a dictionary which was completed in 1694. Until near the close of the eighteenth century words which did not appear in the Dictionary were barred from *belles lettres*. One consequence was (and remains) a clarity and precision which no other European language equals; another was a limited vocabulary and a lack of plasticity in French literary expression. Nevertheless, modern French dates from the efforts of the Dictionary writers to define the language.

The three giants of classical French literature were Pierre Corneille (1606–84), Moliere (real name Jean-Baptiste Poquelin 1622–73) and Jean Racine (1639–99). Corneille and Racine were tragedians, and their plays were strongly influenced by Greek and Latin models. Molière, on the other hand, wrote comedies, and drew his characters and plots largely from contemporary French life. Taken together, the three dramatists occupy a place in French literature which may be compared to that of Shakespeare in English; they are *the* classic French authors, and study of their works constitutes an important part of French education to the present day.

Lesser writers of the age of Louis XIV include Jean de la Fontaine (1621–95) who wrote a book of fables in which, through the mouths of beasts, he portrays and whimsically satirizes human foibles; Bishop Bossuet

(1627-1704), author of numerous sermons, theological tracts and of a *Universal History*; and Nicholas Boileau (1637-1711), a poet and literary critic.

During the eighteenth century the prestige of French literature remained preponderant in Europe. In the hands of a man like Voltaire (real name François Arouet, 1694-1778) *belles lettres* became a mouthpiece for a radical philosophic offensive against what he regarded as superstition and injustice. Voltaire was deeply impressed by the scientific achievements of Newton and others, and did much to popularize Newtonian physics on the continent. He believed that an application of reason and good will could solve most of the problems of society; and had nothing but scorn and biting mockery for organized religion which he regarded as a stronghold of superstition and bigotry. He was not, however, a systematic philosopher; he was rather a man of letters who valued a telling phrase above logic or perfect consistency.

The bulk and variety of Voltaire's literary output was tremendous. He tried his hand at epic poetry, tragedy, history, as well as the philosophical journalism and satire for which he is most remembered. Voltaire exercised a very great influence on his own generation. He conducted an extensive correspondence with many of the rulers and intellectual leaders of Europe, advising both Frederick the Great and Catherine of Russia on the governance of their kingdoms, for instance. His attacks on religion kept him from the good graces of the French court through most of his life, but his books and pamphlets were read all over Europe, and in his old age he was recognized as the leading European man of letters.

Voltaire was not alone in his literary assault upon established institutions and religion. Religious scepticism had been expressed by Pierre Bayle (1647-1706) before Voltaire's time. Among his contemporaries, Denis Diderot (1713-84), Jean Le Rond d'Alembert (1717-83) and Baron d'Holbach (1723-89) may be mentioned. D'Alembert and Diderot organized and edited an extremely ambitious work, the *Encyclopédie*, in which the latest discoveries and theories of natural and social science were explained by leading authorities. The *Encyclopédie*, published between 1751 and 1766, not only summarized the scientific knowledge of the eighteenth century and provided an impressive statement of a cautiously rationalistic outlook upon religion and society, but also became a model for later works of reference of which the *Encyclopedia Britannica*, first published in 1771, is the most famous.

English literature, almost alone in Europe, was not overshadowed by the French. Poets like John Dryden (1631-1700) and Alexander Pope (1688-1744), dramatists like William Congreve (1670-1729) and Richard Sheridan (1751-1816), journalists like Joseph Addison (1672-1719) and Daniel Defoe (1660-1731), historians like Edward Gibbon (1737-94) and David Hume (1711–76), the satirist Jonathan Swift (1667–1745), the lexicographer and critic, Samuel Johnson (1709–84), the biographer, James Boswell (1740–95), and numerous others maintained a rich and varied output. The novel, which was to become the most popular literary vehicle of the nineteenth and twentieth centuries, developed in England during the eighteenth century. Samuel Richardson (1689–1761) was a pioneer in the new literary form, but *Tom Jones* by Henry Fielding (1707–54) is, at least to modern taste, the first really satisfactory English novel.

In the latter part of the eighteenth century, classicism was supplanted among a growing circle of English writers by romanticism. The change can be detected in the poems of Thomas Gray (1716–71), and was much stimulated by the publication of Thomas Percy's *Reliques of Ancient English Poetry* in 1765 and of James Macpherson's *Ossian*, between 1760 and 1763. The first was a collection of popular folk ballads; the second pretended to be a translation of an ancient Scottish poem, but was in fact Macpherson's fabrication. Both these books, particularly *Ossian*, exerted a wide influence not only in England but on the continent as well.

In France romanticism found little foothold prior to the French revolution; but in Germany men's minds began to turn away from French, Greek and Latin models to the folk poetry and traditions of the German peoples. A revival of German literary activity had begun with the work of Gotthold Ephraim Lessing (1729–81). Lessing was a classicist who strove to go directly to the Greeks for his inspiration, rather than taking classicism at second hand from the French as earlier German writers had tended to do. But a new note was struck, and struck with a new enthusiasm by Johann Gottfried Herder (1744–1803). He reacted strongly against classicism in general, and against French cosmopolitanism and rationalism in particular. He believed that only by rooting itself deeply in the traditions of the nation could German, or any other literature, flourish. Accordingly, he became an ardent student of German folklore, customs and language.

Herder exercised considerable influence over two of the giants of German literature: Johann Wolfgang von Goethe (1749–1832) and Johann Friedrich von Schiller (1759–1805). Goethe's greatest work was the poetic drama, *Faust* but he also wrote poems, novelettes and was also something of a scientist. Schiller wrote several plays as well as essays and poems. Herder, Goethe and Schiller together managed to dispel the dominance which French literary example had earlier enjoyed in Germany. A literature which used the German language and which could stand comparison with the works of the best French and British writers emerged in the second half of the eighteenth century, bringing to an end a long period of literary stagnation which followed the Reformation. The rise of German literature was at once a symptom and a cause of the further development of German cultural (and eventually of German political) nationalism.

2) Art. Public buildings, especially palaces for kings and nobles, were erected in large numbers during the seventeenth and eighteenth centuries. The great palace at Versailles, erected for Louis XIV, was the most magnificent example of the architectural taste of the age; and both the Emperor of Austria and the King of Prussia later imitated the French example with similar palaces of their own. In the eighteenth century a more delicate and ornate style, the roccoco, came into favor; and toward the end of the century a reaction in the direction of simplicity and pure "classic" lines took place. In England, the most famous architectural monument of the age was St. Paul's Cathedral, London. It was built on a monumental scale, and its general plan resembled St. Peter's of Rome.

The social prominence of courts and aristocracy was also apparent in the development of painting. A self-consciously "grand manner" was cultivated by artists who painted portraits and court scenes for their aristocratic patrons. Antoine Watteau (1684–1721), Thomas Gainsborough (1727–88) and Joshua Reynolds (1723–92) were among the most fashionable painters of their time who served such a public. Francisco Goya (1746–1828) painted similarly for the Spanish court and aristocracy in its days of decadence; but he was stirred by the events of the Napoleonic period, when the Spaniards carried on a bitter guerrilla war against the French, to make some very powerful war pictures depicting French brutality. Landscape painting was developed as a distinct form of art by artists like Jacob van Ruysdael (*c.* 1628–82), Meindert Hobbema (1638–1709), Nicholas Poussin (1594–1665) and Claude Lorrain (1600–1682).

The minor arts–the making of furniture, fine chinaware, candelabra and knicknacks of all sorts—flourished under the patronage of the aristocratic classes. Names of furniture makers like Thomas Chippendale (1717–79) and George Hepplewhite (d. 1786) are still remembered since the styles they originated are imitated in many drawing rooms today. Sèvres, Dresden and Wedgewood pottery works all were founded during the period, and styles of chinaware originated then are still with us.

3) Music. Opera, which had originated in Italy early in the seventeenth century, developed an increasing popularity during the latter part of that century. Other countries began to imitate the Italians. Jean Baptiste Lully (1632–87) introduced opera in France; and Henry Purcell (1658–95) did the same in England. Early opera was a highly conventionalized art, consisting of long arias which were often ill-joined together. Christoph Willibald Gluck (1714–87) for the first time brought music and words, instrumentation and voice together into a single artistic whole, so that modern opera largely descends from his achievement.

The manufacture of musical instruments was notably improved during the late seventeenth century. The violin, for example, was perfected by a

ART IN THE SEVENTEENTH AND EIGHTEENTH CENTURIES

The widening variety of European society found its mirror in the art of the seventeenth and eighteenth centuries. The familiar gap between Italian and northern painting traditions remained, yet both shared in a more conscious effort to achieve dramatic and surprising effects. In addition, the deliberate stateliness of royal palaces, bitter satire and social criticism, sweet playfulness and eager exploitation of new techniques like porcelain manufacture all found expression in visual forms.

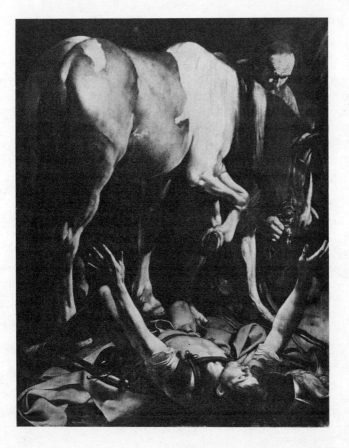

Conversion of St. Paul. **Caravaggio**
1601-2. Cherasi Chapel in Santa Maria del Popolo, Rome
(Alinari Art Reference Bureau)

During the period of the Counter-Reformation, the Roman Catholic Church
employed artists such as Caravaggio to dramatize the doctrines of the
Church. Caravaggio preserves here the sensational moment when Paul was
suddenly blinded and fell down from his horse. An earlier painter
might well have chosen a more contemplative theme from Paul's life.
Caravaggio heightened the moment through his dramatic use of light
and shadow. The highly foreshortened figure of Paul serves to
draw the viewer into the picture and make him almost a participant
in this supernatural event.

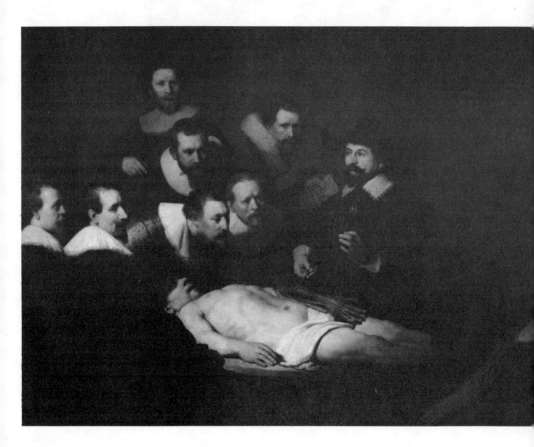

The Anatomy Lesson of Dr. Tulp. Rembrandt
1632
(Royal Picture Gallery, Mauritshuis, The Hague)

Dutch art of the seventeenth century reflected the interest and tastes of
a prosperous and energetic Protestant middle-class society. The Dutch
burgher had little time to appreciate the exploits of classical heroes and had
no use for showy church art. He preferred realistic paintings for interior
decoration and particularly appreciated portraits. The Anatomy Lesson
shows a group of sober and self-assured Dutchmen listening intently to their
teacher, Dr. Tulp, who is demonstrating the attachments of the tendons
that control the fingers. The theme of this picture suggests the
growing interest in natural science during the seventeenth century.

The Surrender of Breda. **Diego Velazquez**
1634-35. Prado, Madrid
(Ampliaciones y Reproducciones MAS)

The Spanish painter, Velasquez, here commemorates one of the victories won
by the Spaniards in their long and bitter war against the Dutch. The difference
of costume dramatizes the difference of nationality; and the devices
Velasquez used to concentrate attention upon the two central figures —
blurring the background and suppressing distracting detail — enhance the
significance of the gesture whereby the defeated Dutch commander offers his
conqueror the key to the surrendered city.

David. Gian Lorenzo Bernini
1623. Borghese Gallery, Rome
(Alinari Art Reference Bureau)

The contrast between this statue of David and those that issued from the hands
of Donatello and Michelangelo typifies the departure baroque artists made
from the work of their predecessors. The effort to catch the drama of
the passing moment, to express the heights and depths of passion, to explore
the limits of the human potentiality —these were the marks of baroque style.
It is a striking fact that the contrast between High Renaissance sculpture
and the baroque is remarkably similar to the differences between Greek classical
and Hellenistic sculpture. This may partly be due to direct imitation; but it
is also the case that when once the technical problems of accurate
representation of human proportions had been fully solved; the sculptors
of the Baroque and of the Hellenistic ages had little to do but experiment
with extreme, dramatic postures and suggestions of violent movements.

Honey-licking Putto. Joseph Anton Feuchtmayer
Circa 1750. **Pilgrimage Church, Birnau**
(Hirmer Verlag München)

This chubby, charming cherub utterly lacked the grandeur traditionally
associated with European sculpture. As a wall decoration in a church, it
utterly lacked traditional sanction of any kind. The artist, in short, was using
his technical virtuosity to arrest the attention of his viewers by deliberately
violating conventions of his art.

This transformation from the baroque to the rococo style suggests both the
softening of manners and a trifling with ennui among Europe's upper
classes on the eve of the overthrow of the Old Regime.

Palace of Versailles, Garden Facade
1661-1756
(Wayne Andrews)

The palace at Versailles, originally conceived as a hunting lodge, was quickly
expanded at the command of Louis XIV into a building project on a
scale unapproached before and unequalled since. The enormous expanse of
the palace is enhanced by its extensive park setting. The great wealth
of the kingdom and absolute power of the monarch are superbly symbolized
by the palace. The building of the palace also served a definite social function
in the process of consolidating royal power and making it absolute.
The palace was so vast and sumptuous that it could attract and accomodate
all the leading families of France. The nobles who flocked to Versailles
came under the close scrutiny of the king; and in competing for royal favor,
they lost their former sense of independence.

Versailles, Hall of Mirrors
1678-84
(Alinari Art Reference Bureau)

Oberes Belvedere, Vienna
1721-23
(Wayne Andrews)

Blenheim Palace
1705-20
(Wayne Andrews)

The size and magnificence of Versailles established a model for other rulers and
princes to imitate in other parts of Europe. The two palaces illustrated here
however were erected by private persons rather than by ruling princes.
The Belvedere Palace in Vienna was built by Prince Eugene, the
famous general; Blenheim palace in England was erected for Eugene's
partner in war against the French, the Duke of Marlborough. The
monumental scale of these two structures symbolizes the fact that in both
England and Austria the high nobility preserved far greater wealth
and independence vis-à-vis the king and central government than was
possible in France under the jealous eye of the "Sun King."

"Audience of the Legate," History of the King Tapestries 1662
(Conservation du musee de Versailles)

The ritualized patterns of court life under Louis XIV are here portrayed in needlework. The king, seated and wearing a hat — both signs of rank — receives a legate from the Pope who reads the Pope's message to the king while the other courtiers stand around in hope of catching the king's eye.

The tapestry itself was one of a series recording King Louis' grandeur. They were all products of the Gobelin manufactury established by the state to produce wall decorations for the king's use and as gifts for foreign dignitaries. The lavish expenditure of skill and time that went into the needlework of such a tapestry were never equalled before or since in Europe.

Mme. de Pompadour. Francois Boucher
Circa 1755. Collection Maurice de Rothschild
(Bulloz)

The growing importance of women in eighteenth century society is superbly
expressed by Boucher's *Mme. de Pompadour*. Longtime mistress to Louis
XV, her good will was recognized as the real avenue to royal favor.
She is shown reposing amidst a gorgeous array of delicate textures which set
off her powdered beauty.

The Picnic after the Hunt. **Nicolas Lancret**
1740
(National Gallery of Art, Washington, D.C.,
Samuel H. Kress Collection)

French upper classes, tired of dancing attendance on the king at court,
could always take to the countryside and hunt — or better yet,
picnic in open air where the formality of manners might
be somewhat, but not too much, relaxed.

Italian Comedy in Verona. **Marco Marcola**
1772
(Art Institue of Chicago)

A wider spectrum of society could afford to attend the theater for amusement
and recreation. This painting shows a theater set up in the midst of the
ancient Roman arena at Verona. A comedy akin to Punch and Judy shows
seems to be in progress while the audience scrambles for seats, gossips,
and seems in general more interested in watching one another
than in anything happening on stage.

"Le souper fin" from *Monument du Costume.* Jean Moreau the Younger
(Art Institute of Chicago)

Large Porcelain Plate from the Bruehl "Swan" Service. Johann Joachim Kaendler, Modeller
1738-41. Meissen
(Art Institute of Chicago)

The eighteenth century was a time when many of the elegancies of household furnishings that still find place in private houses first came into existence. Such details as chandeliers, table cloths, stuffed furniture, side tables, and porcelain ware were known mainly among the nobles and the rich in the eighteenth century. Their patterns of luxury consumption set a standard which lasted with ups and downs until the present.

"The Pillaging of a Farm," *The Miseries of War.* Jacques Callot
1633
(Art Institute of Chicago)

Callot who personally experienced the horrors of the Thirty Years' War in his
native Alsace, deliberately used his art to publicize the inhumanity of war.
In the scene of "The Hanging," a priest gives the last rites to those about to
die. The other scene shows innocent inhabitants being subjected to violence,
rape, and murder by a troop of ruthless soldiers.

These are etchings from a larger collection on related themes. They were
intended for comparatively wide distribution, since large numbers of copies
could be made with only slight loss of accuracy or precision.

la les beaux exploits de ces cœurs inhumains   L'vn pour auoir de l'or, inuente des supplices, Et tous d'vn mesme accord commettent mechamm
r̃auiagent par tout rien ne chappe ̃a leur mains   L'autre à mil forfaicts anime ses complices ;   Le vol, le rapt, le meurtre, et le violement.

a fin ces Voleurs infames et perdus ,   Monstrent bien que le crime (horrible et noire engeance)   Et que c'est le Destin des hommes vicieux
me fruits malheureux a cet arbre pendus   Est luy mesme instrument de honte et de vengeance,   Desprouuer tost ou tard la iustice des Cieux .

"The Hanging," *The Miseries of War.* Jacques Callot
1633
(Art Institute of Chicago)

Scenes from series entitled *An Election*. William Hogarth
"An Election Entertainment" and "Canvassing for Votes."
***Circa* 1754**
(Trustees of Sir John Soane's Museum, London)

The English painter, William Hogarth, here lampoons parliamentary elections
as conducted in the mid-eighteenth century. In the scene above, voters are wined
and dined to the point of insensibility to prepare them for the polls. In
the scene at the right, the voter coyly accepts money from representatives
of each of the rival parties while the lower classes riot in the background.

"Scene III, Orgy" *The Rake's Progress.* **William Hogarth**
Circa **1734**
(Trustees of Sir John Soane's Museum, London)

This scene from Hogarth's series *The Rake's Progress* is entitled "Orgy." As
with his political lampoons, Hogarth seems good humored in his burlesque
of the follies he attacked, and loads his canvas with details that allow
a vivid glimpse of tavern life in eighteenth century London.

Execution of May 2, 1808. **Francisco de Goya**
Prado, Madrid
(Ampliaciones y Reproducciones MAS)

Late in life, the Spanish painter Goya witnessed the French invasion of his
native land ordered by Napoleon in 1808. His reaction of horror and anger
found expression in this painting, which shows a French firing squad
executing a group of citizens from Madrid — accused, no doubt, of guerrilla
actions against the French. Such a painting captured the renewed ferocity
of politics and war that came with the French revolution and the
harnessing of popular feeling to political programs pioneered so successfully
by the French revolutionary leaders.

number of Italian craftsmen, of whom Antonio Stradivari (1644–1737) was the most famous. Johann Sebastian Bach (1685–1750) and others worked out the mathematical and mechanical principles of a stringed keyboard instrument which could be used to play in different keys—the well-tempered clavier, as Bach called it. The modern piano is descended from instruments such as Bach's. These and other improvements were reflected in the steady enrichment of instrumental music. New forms—sonata, concerto, symphony—were developed for instrumental performance. Their names reflect their Italian origin.

But the greatest names of eighteenth-century music were German: George Frederich Handel (1685–1759), Johann Sebastian Bach (1685–1750), Wolfgang Amadeus Mozart (1756–91), and Franz Josef Haydn (1732–1809). Differences in their individual styles cannot be adequately described here, and a label must suffice: Handel, Bach, Haydn, and Mozart were the principal figures of the "classical" as against the "romantic" style of music which appeared in the first years of the nineteenth century with the works of Ludwig van Beethoven (1770–1827).

4) Mathematics and Natural Science. The rise of mathematics, which had been such a prominent feature of the intellectual history of the early seventeenth century, did not cease after 1660; but mathematics lost some of its preeminence as a result of the development of physics and chemistry. The former was, in fact, very largely applied mathematics, for men of Sir Isaac Newton's generation (1642–1727) regularly strove to reduce physical laws to mathematical formulas, and were strikingly successful in the attempt.

In the field of pure mathematics, the principal achievement was the development of the infinitesimal calculus. Newton and Gottfried Wilhelm Leibnitz (1646–1716) independently worked out the principles of calculus, using different systems of notation. Leibnitz' notation, with minor modification, is the one used today.

The power of mathematical reasoning when applied to the analysis of physical phenomena was illustrated by the work of Christian Huygens (1629–95) when he succeeded in reducing the motion of a pendulum and the motion of waves to mathematical description. (A by-product of Huygen's theoretical work was the invention of reliable pendulum clocks.) Newton, in a similar fashion, was able to describe the motion of bodies by three laws capable of mathematical expression; laws which were able to account for and even to predict the behavior of bodies on earth and in the heavens alike. Such a simplification of the apparent diversity of natural phenomena almost dizzied the mind. A new universe, regulated by simple, rational and mathematical laws opened before men's startled gaze. The confidence in natural law, which had already become widespread in the most advanced intellectual circles before 1687 (when Newton's *Philosophiae Naturalis Principia Mathematica* was published), received a powerful new support. Many came to feel, with Alexander Pope:

"God said: 'Let Newton be, and all was light.'"

Popularizers quickly arose who undertook to explain how the motion of the planets and the fall of an apple alike illustrated the universal principle of gravitation. Newton also initiated spectral analysis of light by using a prism to break sunlight and starlight into their component colors. During succeeding generations, other astronomers and physicists worked out details of Newton's gravitational theory and found numerous new illustrations of it. The greatest of Newton's successors was Pierre Simon Laplace (1749–1827) who was able to calculate with great refinement the gravitational relations of the solar system, taking into account the perturbations of orbits which arise from third bodies—e.g., the sun's effect on the moon's orbit round the earth.

Modern chemistry, as distinct from the capricious theories of alchemists, took its rise with the careful experiments and observations of Robert Boyle (1627–91), Henry Cavendish (1731–1810), Joseph Priestley (1733–1804) and Antoine Lavoisier (1743–94). Lavoisier was particularly notable for his careful and exact measurements, as a result of which he propounded the theory of the conservation of matter, regardless of changes in chemical state. He was also the first to interpret combustion as a rapid form of oxidation.

The development of biology and medicine was enormously assisted by the invention of improved microscopes which permitted the human eye to discover details of anatomy and physiology. Microscopes also opened up a new world of unicellular plants and animals. Comparative anatomy was studied by George Louis Leclerc de Buffon (1707–88) and the likenesses he discovered led him to suggest that different species were related to one another, although the authority of *Genesis* prevented him from doubting the separate creation of each species. Classification of plants and animals was systematized by a Swedish scholar, Carl von Linné or (as he is usually called) Linnaeus, (1707–78). His method of classification is still used by botanists.

It should be emphasized that the new theories and discoveries mentioned above provide only a small sample of the total bulk of the scientific work that was done in the seventeenth and eighteenth centuries. A widespread enthusiasm for science spread through all parts of Europe. Scientific societies, such as the Royal Society of England (founded in 1662), became gathering places for curious experimenters of all sorts, and journals published by such societies provided a means for the dissemination of new ideas and information. The prestige of great scientists such as Newton came to be immense. Despite his humble birth, he was knighted by Queen

Anne, and was buried with great pomp in Westminster Abbey where kings had preceded him.

5) Philosophy and Social Theory. The prestige of natural science and the practical achievements of the scientists worked a great change in the general intellectual outlook of the age. The success of men like Newton in bringing very diverse phenomena under a common law led more and more individuals to place high confidence in the capacity of the human reason to cope not only with physical nature but with human nature as well. Many men, impressed by the simplicity in apparent complexity which the law of gravitation revealed, argued that the Creator of the universe was a master mathematician who, having set the stars in their courses, refrained from further interference in the working of the laws of motion which He had ordained. This metaphysical view is known as deism. Deists denied the possibility of Divine intervention in mundane affairs, and scoffed at miracles as the inventions of the credulous and of self-interested priests.

As for human nature, the enlightened thinkers of the eighteenth century believed that it, too, was an open book for reasonable men to read—a book which had, however, been sadly smudged and blotted in times past. But in the clear light of reason, human nature was seen to be fundamentally good and everywhere the same. Bad institutions and deceitful or ignorant leaders had twisted and corrupted the natural goodness of men to produce the society of the age; but a rational reorganization of institutions seemed entirely possible and highly to be desired. Not only did man seem good, but the men of the Enlightenment believed that they could detect certain natural rights which all men inherited simply because they were men. Life, liberty and property were generally recognized as natural rights; some added equality to the list.

History came to be viewed, in Gibbon's phrase, as a record of the miseries, crimes and follies of mankind; but in that record there appeared a slow, halting but unmistakable progress. Reason, to optimistic eyes, seemed to be winning new victories every day; a new age of enlightenment had dawned and mankind seemed on the point of emerging from a long night of superstition and ignorance. All that remained was to eliminate the remnants of bygone times: in particular, to men like Voltaire, that meant the destruction of the Church. Once all such obstacles had been removed, nothing would any longer prevent a rational reorganization of society and the inception of an age of general happiness when the natural goodness of men would prevail.

Such a paraphrase is really a parody. Many men held some of the opinions sketched above; few would have subscribed to them all, or at least would have modified and qualified the language, as cannot be done in a short summary. Yet beliefs such as these did come to be held by an important body of men in many different countries. France was the center of such teaching, and Voltaire was its most eminent propagandist. He and others convinced not only members of the middle class (who had most to gain from a change in institutions) but also many nobles, officials and even some kings. Frederick the Great of Prussia and Catherine of Russia, for example, prided themselves on being "enlightened"; and several other rulers also accepted some or all of the new ideas. Reason, Nature and Science were all invoked by the philosphers of the Enlightenment to give evidence for the correctness of their views; and it was a bold or stupid man who could neglect such authorities.

More formal philosophy, dealing with metaphysics and epistemology, also fell under the spell of natural science. The mathematician, Gottfried Wilhelm Leibnitz (1646–1716), like Descartes before him, attempted to construct a cosmological and metaphysical system which would take account of the new discoveries of physics, and yet preserve the elements of traditional Christianity. But Leibnitz could not satisfy every critic, and persistent disagreements among philosophers more and more directed attention to the problem of how men can know anything certain at all. John Locke (1632–1704) cast doubt on the possibility of achieving universally valid knowledge in his *Essay Concerning Human Understanding*; Bishop George Berkeley (1684–1753), David Hume (1711–76) and Immanuel Kant (1724–1804) all took up the same issue, pointed out new difficulties in the way of achieving certain knowledge, and, in varying fashions, tried to solve the problems they and their predecessors had raised.

In general philosophers became increasingly sceptical of the possibility of universally valid knowledge. Descartes and Leibnitz had been able to reason out complete (and incompatible) systems of cosmology, psychology, and metaphysics; Hume, on the other hand, denied that the human mind was capable of achieving any certainty in these realms of speculation. Immanuel Kant stands as a sort of bridge between eighteenth- and nineteenth-century philosophy. He conceded to Hume that the nature of things in themselves remains unknowable, but believed that a careful examination of the structure of the human mind made it possible to arrive at necessary and universal truths concerning all possible objects of sense perception. He thus stands as the summator of the critical philosophy of the eighteenth century, and was at the same time the founder of the school of German idealism which dominated the philosophic thought of the early nineteenth century.

As the Enlightenment undermined traditional religion, political theorists were impelled to seek a new basis for sovereignty and political authority. If one believed that the Deity did not intervene at will in the affairs of men, Divine Right by which monarchs had earlier claimed to rule, became mere usurpation. This difficulty was met by Thomas Hobbes

(1588–1679). In his book *Leviathan* (1651), he defended absolute monarchy by assuming the existence of a social contract between ruler and ruled which assigned absolute powers to the monarch in order to curb the natural bestiality of men.

In any theory of a social contract, everything must depend on the supposed terms of the agreement between the sovereign and his subjects. By assuming different contractual terms a political theorist could support limited monarchy or even revolution. Thus, in the mind of John Locke the social contract was used to justify the Glorious Revolution of 1688 by which a would-be absolute, but undeniably legitimate, monarch had been driven from his throne. Locke argued that the social contract did not accord absolute powers to the sovereign, but entrusted him with the headship of government simply in order to safeguard the natural rights of men. Thus if a ruler failed to fulfill his duty and did not respect natural rights, his subjects quite properly should unite to overthrow him.

Locke's ideas and the example of the British government had a powerful effect upon numerous Frenchmen, who, as the eighteenth century wore on, saw their own government defeated abroad, and mismanaged at home by theoretically absolute but practically incapable monarchs. Charles Louis de Secondat, Baron de Montesquieu (1689–1755), was one of the first to praise British governmental institutions. He thought he detected in the British constitution a separation of executive, legislative and judicial powers; and argued that such a separation, with resultant checks and balances, was the best guarantee against tyranny and injustice. Although Montesquieu admired British political institutions, he did not think them a universal panacea for disordered constitutions elsewhere. He argued that different political institutions were required to fit varying geographical and social conditions. Montesquieu's political theory was a major element in the thinking of the American politicians who framed the Constitution of the United States.

Voltaire was another Frenchman who praised British institutions highly, and frequently drew unflattering comparisons between his own country's absolutism and British constitutional monarchy. However, the most influential political theorist of the eighteenth century, Jean Jacques Rousseau (1712–78), thought almost as ill of British as of French government. In his book, *The Social Contract*, published in 1762, Rousseau advanced a democratic theory of sovereignty. The social contract, he argued, had been made not between a ruler and the ruled, but among the general body of the people, who, by an act of will, associated themselves into civil society, adopted laws and established institutions of government. Such a contract could be changed at will, and if a government failed to satisfy the people over whom it ruled, then the people had reason to change the government in any way they saw fit.

Rousseau had a warm confidence in the essential goodness of mankind. He urged a return to nature and an abandonment of the artificiality of the salon. In a novel, *Emile*, he sketched a system of education which would preserve the natural goodness of children by allowing relatively free expression of their inclinations. In all his works, Rousseau exhibited a depth of feeling which was alien to the rationalistic, sceptic, mocking tradition of Voltaire, but which won for him a wide audience and many enthusiastic followers. More than any other single man's, his ideas, phrases, and catchwords dominated the thinking and speaking of the leaders of the French revolution.

The influence of men like Locke, Voltaire and Rousseau on the thought and action of educated men was pervasive. They, and numerous others, popularized new ideas which justified drastic political and social reform or even revolution. In other fields of thought, too, theory was able to exercise a direct influence on men's practice. Economists, of whom Adam Smith (1723–90) in Scotland and a physiocratic (i.e., rule of nature) school in France were the most influential, argued convincingly that governmental control over economic activity was harmful; that if human nature, inspired by enlightened self interest, were allowed free scope, production and exchange would automatically find their most efficient form. Such doctrines were never accepted universally and unquestioningly, yet the arguments of economists did play a part in weakening and reducing the scope of mercantilist supervision of economic life in the latter part of the eighteenth century.

In the field of law, Sir William Blackstone (1729–80) tried to bring rational order to the confusion of customary English law and make the study of law scientific. Cesare Beccaria (1738–94) in Italy tried to make law humane. Jeremy Bentham (1748–1832), during his long life, argued and worked for legal reform according to rational utilitarian principles and was able to influence many changes in English law.

In the field of education, too, Johann Heinrich Pestalozzi (1746–1827), a Swiss schoolmaster, reformed teaching methods in the light of his faith in human goodness and rationality.

6) Religion. Despite the prevalence of deism, materialism and even atheism among intellectuals of the eighteenth century, it should be emphasized that the great majority of Europeans remained at least nominal Christians, and many individuals and groups cultivated piety and charity seriously and devoutly.

Personal piety and religious feeling manifested themselves in a series of new religious movements: Quakerism, Pietism and Methodism among Protestants; Quietism and Jansenism among Catholics. All of these movements, in their various ways, emphasized personal, inner religious experience as opposed to ceremony and formality.

George Fox (1624–91), the founder of the Society of Friends, popularly called Quakers, was a mystic whose inner experience led him to discount the outward signs and ceremonies of traditional religion completely. The sect he founded became particularly notable for its resolute and radical rejection of participation in war. Pietism flourished mainly in Germany; but unlike the Quakers or Methodists it did not lead to the establishment of a new sect. Instead, a personal attitude of piety, and a vigorous rejection of the refinements of theological disputation which had hardened into a sort of neo-scholasticism, characterized the teaching of men like Philip Jacob Spener (1635–1705), the founder of the movement. German pietist influence was important in shaping the life of John Wesley (1703–91) who initiated an analogous shift in emphasis within the Anglican Church. Wesley's impatience at the indifference and opposition he met with among Anglican clergymen gradually led to a separation of the methodists (as his followers were called) from the general body of Anglicans, although the definitive establishment of a separate Methodist church organization did not come until after Wesley's death. Methodists emphasized inner conversion as the key to all religion, and found their main support among the poor of the new industrial towns of England and in the frontier communities of the United States.

The movement known as Quietism originated with the teachings of a Spanish priest, Miguel de Molinos (1640–96). He believed that the soul's salvation required not only the sacraments of the Church, but also a mystic indwelling of God. In 1687 his doctrines were declared heretical, Molinos was imprisoned, and the movement died out by degrees.

Jansenism has already been described. (See p. 416.) It gathered headway in France in the latter part of the seventeenth century, when a brilliant group of Jansenists (of whom the mathematician Blaise Pascal was one) gathered around a convent at Port Royal near Paris. Heated polemic between Jansenists and orthodox Catholics led the king to close Port Royal in 1709; and in the course of the following decade Jansenism was forcibly put down.

Another noteworthy development within the Roman Catholic Church was the suppression of the Jesuit Order. The Jesuits aroused the hostility of the rulers of France, Spain and Portugal by their intervention in political affairs, their zeal in persecuting groups such as the Jansenists, and by their extensive commercial activities, which did not always conform to the laws of the countries in which the Jesuits were domiciled. As a result of the demands of these monarchs, the Order was suppressed by the pope in 1773. Many Jesuits found refuge in Russia and Prussia, and the Order continued to exist in disguise in these and some other parts of Europe until the pope once more extended it official recognition in 1814.

Suggestions for Further Reading for Part III, C–2

The New Cambridge Modern History. Vol. 5, 6, 7, 8 (New York: 1961–67).

Anderson, M. S. *Eighteenth Century Europe 1713–1789*. New York: 1966.

Becker, C. L. *The Heavenly City of the 18th Century Philosophers*. New Haven: 1932.

Blum, Jerome. *Lord and Peasant in Russia from the Ninth to the Nineteenth Century*. Princeton: 1961.

Bruford, W. H. *Culture and Society in Classical Weimar 1775–1806*. Cambridge: 1962.

Buchan, J. *Oliver Cromwell*. London: 1934.

Burtt, E. A. *The Metaphysical Foundations of Modern Science*. Anchor Books.

Bury, J. B. *The Idea of Progress, an Inquiry into its Origin and Growth*. London: 1921 (also in Dover publications).

Butterfield, H. *Origins of Modern Science*. London: 1949.

Clarendon, E. H. *History of the Rebellion and Civil Wars in England*. 1702–04 (many later editions).

Clark, G. N. *Science and Social Welfare in the Age of Newton*. Oxford: 1937.

Cobban, Alfred. *A History of Modern France*. Vol. 2. Baltimore: 1960.

Cromwell, O. *Writings and Speeches*. ed. by Abbott, C. W. 2 vols. 1937–39.

Defoe, D. *The Complete English Gentleman* (reprinted). London: 1890.

Defoe, D. *The Complete English Tradesman*. London: 1732.

Dorn, Walter L. *Competition for Empire 1740–1763*. New York: 1940.

Gardiner, S. R. ed. *The Constitutional Documents of the Puritan Revolution*. 1625–1660. 3d ed. Oxford: 1906.

Geyl, P. *The Revolt of the Netherlands (1555–1609)*. London: 1932.

Geyl, P. *The Netherlands Divided, 1609–1648*. London: 1936.

Gierke, O. von. *Natural Law and the Theory of Society*. Beacon Books.

Godechot, Jacques. *France and the Atlantic Revolution of the Eighteenth Century 1770–1799*. Glencoe, Ill: 1965.

Guehenno, Jean. *Jean-Jacques Rousseau*. New York: 1966.

Halsband, Robert. ed. *The Complete Letters of Lady Mary Wortley Montagu*. 2 vols. New York: 1965–66.

Hazard, Paul. *The European Mind 1680–1715*. Cleveland: 1963.

Hazard, Paul. *The European Mind in the Eighteenth Century*. Cleveland: 1963.

Heckscher, E. F. *Mercantilism*. London: 1957.

Herr, Richard. *The Eighteenth Century Revolution in Spain*. Princeton: 1958.

Holborn, Hajo. *History of Modern Germany*. Vol. 2. *1648–1783*. Boston: 1964.

Kliuchevskii, V. O. *History of Russia.* 4 vols. London: 1911–26.

Koyré, A. *From the Closed World to the Infinite Universe.* Harper Torch-books.

Macaulay, T. B. *The History of England from the Accession of James II.* 5 vols. London: 1848–61 (also in Everyman's Library).

Mahan, A. T. *The Influence of Sea Power on History, 1660–1783.* Boston: 1890.

Ogg, David. *Europe in the Seventeenth Century.* New York: 1960.

Ogg, David. *Louis XIV.* Rev. ed. New York: 1967.

Palmer, Robert R. *The Age of the Democratic Revolution: A Political History of Europe and America, 1760–1800.* 2 vols. Princeton: 1959, 1964.

Plumb, J. H. *Sir Robert Walpole.* 2 vols. Boston: 1956, 1961.

Rothkrug, Lionel. *Opposition to Louis XIV: The Political and Social Origins of the Enlightenment.* Princeton: 1965.

Scoville, W. *The Persecution of the Huguenots and French Economic Development, 1680–1720.* Berkeley: 1960.

Shackleton, Robert. *Montesquieu: A Critical Biography.* New York: 1961.

Singer, C. ed. *A History of Technology.* Vol. 3. 1500–1750. Oxford: 1957.

Smellie, K. B. *Great Britain since 1688: A Modern History.* Ann Arbor: 1962.

Stavrianos, L. S. *The Balkans since 1453.* New York: 1958.

Taine, H. A. *Ancient Regime.* New York: 1876.

Tocqueville, A. de. *The Old Regime and the French Revolution.* Anchor Books.

Trevelyan, George M. *The English Revolution 1688–1689.* New York: 1938.

Wedgwood, C. V. *Cromwell.* New York: 1966.

Wedgwood, C. V. *The Thirty Years' War.* London: 1938.

White, R. J. *Europe in the Eighteenth Century.* New York: 1965.

Whitehead, A. N. *Science and the Modern World.* Mentor Books.

Willey, B. *The Seventeenth Century Background.* Anchor Books.

Wilson, Arthur M. *Diderot: The Testing Years, 1713–1759.* New York: 1957.

Wolf, John B. *The Emergence of the Great Powers, 1685–1715.* New York: 1951.

Wolf, John B. *Louis XIV.* New York: 1968.

Novels

Barker, Shirley. *Swear by Apollo.* New York: 1958.

Dickens, Charles. *Barnaby Rudge.* London: 1849.

Doyle, Sir Arthur Conan. *Micah Clarke.* London: 1888.

Dumas, Alexandre. *The Three Musketeers*. Boston: 1888.
Falkner, J. Meade. *Moonfleet*. London: 1898.
Feuchtwanger, Lion. *Power*. New York: 1926.
Feuchtwanger, Lion. *Proud Destiny*. New York: 1947.
Fielding, Henry. *The History of Tom Jones, a Foundling*. London: 1749.
Gilbert, Rosa M. *O'Loghlin of Clare*. London: 1916.
Goldsmith, Oliver. *The Vicar of Wakefield*. London: 1766.
Lewis, Janet. *Ghost of Monsieur Scarron*. New York: 1959.
Orczy, Baroness Emmuska. *The Scarlet Pimpernel*. New York: 1920.
Sabatini, Rafael. *Captain Blood*. Boston: 1922.
Scott, Sir Walter. *Waverley*. London: 1845.
Scott, Sir Walter. *Old Mortality*. London: 1846.
Scott, Sir Walter. *Bride of Lammermoor*. London: 1858.
Scott, Sir Walter. *The Heart of Midlothian*. London: 1858.
Stevenson, Robert L. *Kidnapped*. New York: 1886.
Stevenson, Robert L. *Treasure Island*. London: 1886.
Stevenson, Robert L. *The Master of Ballantrae*. New York: 1889.
Stevenson, Robert L. *David Balfour*. New York: 1892.
Thackeray, William Makepeace. *The Memoirs of Barry Lyndon, Esq*. New York: 1871.
Thackeray, William Makepeace. *The History of Henry Esmond, Esquire*. New York: 1879.
Undset, Sigrid. *Madame Dorathea*. New York: 1940.

Chronological Table for Part III, C–2: Absolutism and Aristocracy

1640–1688	Frederick William, the Great Elector of Brandenburg.
1643–1715	Louis XIV, king of France.
*1648	Peace of Westphalia.
1650	Death of Descartes (b. 1596).
1659	Peace of the Pyrenees.
1660	Death of Velasquez (b. 1599).
*1660	Restoration of monarchy in England (Charles II, 1660–1685).
1662	Foundation of Royal Society in England.
1662	Death of Pascal (b. 1632).
1669	Death of Rembrandt (b. 1606).
1673	Death of Molière (b. 1622).
1679	Death of Hobbes (b. 1588).
1682–1725	Peter the Great of Russia.

1683	Second Siege of Vienna by the Turks; turning point of Ottoman power.
1684	Death of Corneille (b. 1606).
1685	Revocation of Edict of Nantes.
1687	Newton's *Principia*.
*1688	Glorious Revolution: William III and Mary in England.
1688–1697	War of the League of Augsburg against France.
1689	Bill of Rights.
1694	Charter of Bank of England.
1699	Death of Racine (b. 1639).
1701–1714	War of the Spanish Succession.
1703	Founding of St. Petersburg.
1704	Death of Bossuet (b. 1627).
1704	Death of Locke (b. 1632).
1707	Union of England and Scotland.
c. 1709	Invention of coking process.
*1713	Peace of Utrecht.
1714–present	House of Hanover in England; since 1917 renamed Windsor; (George I 1714–1727).
1715–1774	Louis XV, king of France.
1716	Death of Leibnitz (b. 1646).
1720	Bursting of South Sea Bubble.
1727	Death of Newton (b. 1642).
1733	Invention of flying shuttle.
1740–1786	Frederick II, the Great, of Prussia.
1740–1748	War of Austrian Succession
1744	Death of Alexander Pope (b. 1688).
1750	Death of Bach (b. 1685).
1753	Death of Bishop Berkeley (b. 1684).
1755	Death of Montesquieu (b. 1689).
*1756–1763	Seven Years' War (French and Indian War).
1760–1820	George III, king of England.
1762	Rousseau's *Social Contract*.
1762–1796	Catherine II of Russia.
1769	Invention of spinning frame (Arkwright).
1769	Patent for James Watt's steam engine.
1770	Invention of spinning jenny.
1772	First Partition of Poland.
1774–1692	Louis XVI, king of France.
*1775–1783	War of American Independence.
1776	Adam Smith's *The Wealth of Nations*.
1776	Death of Hume (b. 1711).

1778	Death of Voltaire (b. 1694).
1778	Death of Rousseau (b. 1712).
1779	Invention of spinning mule.
1780–1790	Joseph II of Austria.
1781	Death of Lessing (b. 1729).
1784	Invention of puddling process for production of malleable iron.
*1789	Summoning of Estates-General in France.
1791	Death of Mozart (b. 1756); death of John Wesley (b. 1703).
1793	Second Partition of Poland.
1795	Third Partition of Poland.
1803	Death of Herder (b. 1744).
1804	Death of Kant (b. 1724).
1805	Death of Schiller (b. 1759).
1832	Death of Goethe (b. 1749).

3. LIBERAL, NATIONALIST AND INDUSTRIAL EUROPE, 1789–1914

a. *Introductory*
b. *Economic Changes: Technology and Applied Science*
  1) *Population Growth*
  2) *Scientific Agriculture*
  3) *Improvements in Transport and Communication*
  4) *Industrial Technology*

c. *The Organization of Economic Life*
  1) *Agriculture*
  2) *Organization of Industry*
  3) *Banking and Finance*

d. *European Politics, 1789–1914*
  1) *French Revolution and Napoleon, 1789–1815*
    a) *Introductory*
    b) *The Liberal Phase*
    c) *Girondin Control and Factional Struggle*
    d) *The Jacobin Supremacy*
    e) *Reaction and Consolidation*
  2) *Revolution vs. Reaction 1815–1871*
  3) *Internal Development of Major European countries, 1815–1871*

a. Introductory

The history of Europe between 1789 and 1914 may be regarded as dominated by two factors: the spread and transformation of industrialism from Great Britain where it first assumed modern forms, and the spread and transformation of the liberal, democratic ideals for society and politics which were first given practical expression by the American and French revolutions. The nineteenth century was a time of thitherto unparalleled social change. The daily lives of the majority of the population of Europe were deeply affected by economic and political innovation, and a confusing flood of new ideas welled up on all sides to compete for the attention, and in some cases for the loyalty, of men's minds.

The most distinctive characteristic of economic development was an increasingly systematic application of scientific theories to technological processes. The result was a tremendous expansion in the productivity of both agriculture and industry. But rapid technological change required extensive new social adjustments. The rise of labor unions, cooperative societies, and an expansion of governmental services and functions were among the most important means by which social adjustments to new technological conditions were made. The growth of corporations, holding companies, and horizontal or vertical industrial combinations were also important adjustments to the new complexity of economic production.

The political history of the nineteenth century is closely intertwined with economic changes, for new or newly strengthened economic groups in the population of various European countries were able to exert important pressure on governments. The demands which the rising classes made on their governments were largely derived from the French revolution. The famous revolutionary slogan, Liberty, Equality and Fraternity may be translated into the language of the nineteenth century as liberalism, socialism and nationalism—the three political movements which attracted men's loyalties in varying degree from 1815 to 1914. Resistance to political change was of course always present; but the defenders of the old pre-revolutionary regime generally had no very positive political program, and by degrees were compelled to yield or to adjust to acceptance of at least some of the revolutionary attitudes. In general, conservative groups found nationalism by far the most attractive of the revolutionary triad; and after about 1850 nationalism grew more and more preeminent and tended, especially in central Europe, to eclipse liberalism and to undermine socialism.

Three major periods of political history may be distinguished. From 1789 to 1815 European politics was dominated by the explosive force of the French revolution. Napoleon's final overthrow in 1815 inaugurated a new period during which the ideas and ideals of the French revolution combated conservatism, and in the process suffered important changes in their emphasis and formulation. This period lasted, roughly, from 1815 to 1871, by which time nationalism and socialism were well defined movements, while liberalism (except in Great Britain) had suffered important setbacks. The third period extended from 1871 to 1914. It was distinguished by growing national rivalries, by a renewed imperialist expansion into Africa and Asia, by a more or less stable establishment of democratic governments in western Europe, and by the development of revolutionary or semirevolutionary democratic-socialist movements in central and eastern Europe.

The cultural history of Europe is much more difficult to describe. During the eighteenth century there remained a more or less real unity to European culture, for the ideas of the Enlightenment were cosmopolitan and overrode national barriers. It is of course true that only a minority in any country sympathized with the Enlightenment, but despite that, the "enlightened" minority was culturally the most active, and succeeded in setting a more or less common stamp on all Europe.

With the nineteenth century such a cultural community broke down. At the beginning of the century romanticism attained a new popularity in nearly every country; but romanticism encouraged each nation to treasure its own peculiar past and to go its own way. Romantics went further and deliberately cultivated self-expression: individual artists, authors, thinkers strove to be unique and personal. Natural science traveled a quite different path, and remained international and impersonal. The continued progress of science and its manifest successes in explaining and controlling the physical world made a deep impress on most men's thoughts, and had some effect on art.

The variety of national and individual expression in literature, art and thought, which the romantic movements specially cultivated, makes any general statement about European cultural development in the later nineteenth century almost impossible. All that this *Handbook* can do is list a few of the more famous and influential individuals and schools.

b. Economic Changes

The development of elaborate power-driven machinery and the concentration of industry into factories, which had begun in England in the latter part of the eighteenth century, and which spread to favored parts of the European continent during the nineteenth century, has often been called the Industrial revolution. In fact the changes were extended over many years and affected different regions at different periods of time, so that some historians have recently preferred to deny that there was ever such a thing as *the* Industrial revolution, and have substituted the concept of an uninterrupted spread of mechanization to new geographical areas and to new industries throughout the past two hundred years. Yet, recognizing this blurring of the concept, it still seems possible to take a longer time scale and think of an industrial revolution which has extended from about 1780 to the present in time, and has spread from the midlands of Great Britain (where it mainly originated) to many parts of the inhabited globe. Certainly when measured by the effect industrial change has had on the ordinary life of the people of the world it deserves the name of revolution. In any case, whether one uses the term or not, what matters is to have a reasonably accurate conception of what has so far occurred.

The major fact is this: men have systematically and deliberately begun to apply the theories of natural science to the processes of economic production. Acceptance of the idea that techniques were subject to a constant modification and improvement in the light of scientific experiment and theory did not come at once. Industrial inventions of the eighteenth century, for instance, were made mostly by craftsmen and entrepreneurs who had little if any acquaintance with natural science. During the nineteenth century, however, this ceased to be the case. Schools for engineers arose where theory and practice were brought together; and theoretical scientists began to pay more and more attention to the practical problems of industry and agriculture. Landmarks in this process of bringing theory and practice together were discoveries such as Humphry Davy's safety lamp for coal mining (1815), the experiments of Michael Faraday with electricity which resulted in the invention of the dynamo (1831) and Justus von Liebig's chemical analysis of plants, which led to the introduction of chemical fertilizers (1840). It was not, however, until near the end of the nineteenth century that large industrial corporations adopted the practice of maintaining scientific staffs for the purpose of conducting industrial research. The electrical and chemical industries, relative newcomers, were pioneers in this development.

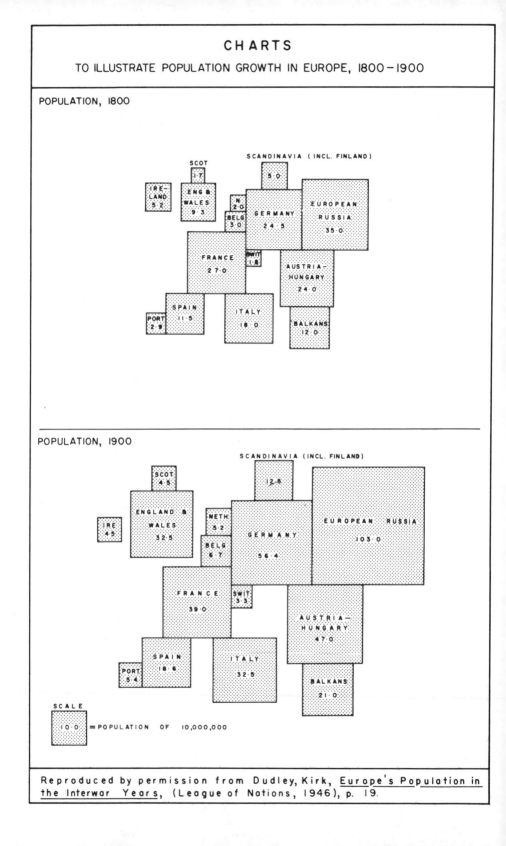

CHARTS

TO ILLUSTRATE POPULATION GROWTH IN EUROPE, 1800 – 1900

POPULATION, 1800

SCANDINAVIA (INCL. FINLAND)
5·0

SCOT
1·7

IRE—LAND 5·2

ENG & WALES 9·3

N. 2·0

BELG 3·0

GERMANY 24·5

EUROPEAN RUSSIA 35·0

FRANCE 27·0

SWIT 1·8

AUSTRIA—HUNGARY 24·0

PORT 2·9

SPAIN 11·5

ITALY 18·0

BALKANS 12·0

POPULATION, 1900

SCANDINAVIA (INCL. FINLAND)
12·5

SCOT 4·5

ENGLAND & WALES 32·5

NETH. 5·2

IRE 4·5

BELG 6·7

GERMANY 56·4

EUROPEAN RUSSIA 103·0

FRANCE 39·0

SWIT 3·3

AUSTRIA—HUNGARY 47·0

PORT 5·4

SPAIN 18·6

ITALY 32·5

BALKANS 21·0

SCALE

10·0 = POPULATION OF 10,000,000

Reproduced by permission from Dudley, Kirk, Europe's Population in the Interwar Years, (League of Nations, 1946), p. 19.

The major phenomena which accompanied or resulted from the application of scientific theory to technological practice may be listed as follows: (1) rapid growth in population; (2) marked increase in agricultural productivity; (3) revolutionary facilitation of transport and communication; (4) an equally revolutionary elaboration of industrial technology. The cumulative impact of these changes provoked drastic social readjustments. The organization of agricultural and industrial production was altered; governmental regulation of economic relations was expanded; governmental services to the population increased; and workingmen and farmers combined into labor unions and cooperative societies in order to protect and promote special interests.

1) Population Growth. With the opening of the nineteenth century fairly reliable population statistics for most parts of Europe became available. In 1800 the population of all Europe stood at about 187 millions; a hundred years later it had increased to about 401 million, despite the fact that nearly 60 million persons emigrated overseas during the century, and other hundreds of thousands migrated from European Russia into Siberia.

Population growth was not uniform in all parts of Europe. (See chart.) In general, the populations of northern Europe grew the most rapidly. The population of Great Britain and Russia approximately tripled and that of Germany more than doubled during the nineteenth century, whereas France only added about forty-four per cent to hers.

Within the various countries, there were important shifts in the centers of population. With the improvement of transport, the local availability of food ceased to be the major determinant of population distribution as had always been the case before. Instead, proximity to coalfields became a major factor in fixing the location of dense populations, since it was easier to bring even so ponderous a raw material as iron ore to the fuel supply than it was to transport fuel to other raw materials. As a result, in Great Britain the coal-rich midlands of England and the lowlands of Scotland became the site of the major new industrial towns; on the continent, an irregular belt of coalfields extending from Belgium through the middle Rhineland and eastward into central Germany became the center of vast agglomerations of population.

It would be wrong to assume that population growth was directly dependent on industrialization. The growth of Russian population was a growth of a peasant farming population, not of industrial workers; the same was true in Ireland (to 1845), and in eastern and southern Europe generally. It is not even correct to say that increased economic opportunity was the sole factor in increasing European population during the nineteenth century; indeed in some parts of Europe (notably Ireland) the growth of population was associated with a deterioration of the economic standard of living, resulting from excessive subdivision of small farms. This phenomenon became far more widespread in the twentieth century, when southern Italy and the part of Europe which lay east of a line drawn between St. Petersburg and Trieste suffered definite lowering of the standard of living while population continued to grow as before.

One of the major causes for the rapid growth of European population was the improvement of medical knowledge and practice which checked and in some countries almost eliminated a number of diseases such as smallpox, typhus, typhoid and diphtheria. Inoculation against smallpox was developed by an English doctor, Edward Jenner (1749–1823) in the 1780's and was made public in 1796. Louis Pasteur (1822–95) in France and Robert Koch (1843–1910) in Germany developed other vaccines and innoculations; and they, with others, detected the bacterial origin of several common diseases, thus making possible effective control of epidemics through public sanitation and quarantine. In surgery, Joseph Lister (1827–1912) applied new antiseptic techniques to reduce the danger of infection. These and many other improvements in medicine resulted in a marked lowering of the death rates in all European countries; and since birth rates remained as high as they had been earlier, when disease had regularly decimated the population, population grew with unprecedented rapidity throughout the nineteenth century. Only toward the end of the period did a lowering of the birth rate manifest itself in countries such as Great Britain and Germany, with a consequent slackening of the rate of population growth. The French birthrate declined somewhat earlier, a fact reflected in the failure of French population to grow proportionately to the populations of neighboring countries in the nineteenth century.

2) Scientific Agriculture. Despite the rapid growth of population, the continent of Europe, taken as a whole, remained self sufficient for food until about 1870. Some nations, most notably Great Britain, had begun to import large quantities of food in the late eighteenth century; but this was counterbalanced by the opening up of new areas, mainly in eastern Europe, for commercial agriculture, especially for grain farming. Simultaneously, new crops, chemical fertilizers, improved methods of cultivation, better selection of seed and of animal breeds, and improved crop rotations all united to increase food production in western Europe.

Two new crops played an important role. During the Napoleonic wars, potatoes became of first importance in all parts of Europe which were climatically suited to them. Primarily it was the north European plain, especially its eastern reaches in Germany, Poland and Russia, where potatoes thrived. In these regions cereals gave rather low yields, and the potato roughly quadrupled the number of calories that could be produced per acre. Sugar beets, too, were introduced during the Napoleonic wars, and became a crop of first rank in the second half of the century, especially in Germany. The beets not only yielded sugar for human consumption, but the tops and the residue after sugar had been extracted provided a valuable cattle food.

Europe's agricultural production was also enlarged by the use of chemical fertilizers. A German chemist, Justus von Liebig, announced in 1840 his discovery that plants require specific chemicals for their growth. He and numerous disciples taught the need for chemical analysis of soils to discover what might be lacking. Then, by adding appropriate fertilizers, soil fertility could be maintained indefinitely, regardless of what crops were planted. As a result of Leibig's work, chemical fertilizers were widely adopted by the farmers of Europe in the second half of the nineteenth century.

Another important factor in increasing agricultural output was the introduction of improved machinery. Drain tiles, invented in 1845, made cheap and effective drainage of land possible and eliminated the need for plowing high ridges, which had previously been the rule in wet fields. The invention of the horse-drawn reaper by Cyrus McCormick, an American, made possible a notable increase in grain production per man; but its greatest effect was reserved for the American prairies, since in most parts of Europe farms were not large enough to make reapers and similar machinery economical. The McCormick reaper was patented first in 1834, but it underwent subsequent improvement and was not commercially successful until the 1850's.

Particularly toward the end of the nineteenth century, when European countries were all exposed to the competition of grain grown overseas, dairying and intensive market farming became more important. Denmark's development of the dairy industry was especially successful; but other European farmers too began to depend increasingly on the production of perishable dairy and market garden products which could be sold profitably in the industrial towns.

These improvements in agricultural technique were not made uniformly throughout Europe. England (until 1870), Germany, Holland, Belgium and Denmark were all in the forefront of agricultural improvement; other countries lagged behind by various degrees. Eastern Europe was relatively backward. Potatoes in the northern and maize in the southern parts of eastern Europe did add to the food resources of those regions; but the techniques of scientific farming were, generally speaking, not adopted. Age-old fallowing of fields continued to be usual in most of Russia, for example, until the twentieth century; and the same was true of the Balkan peninsula and of many parts of Austro-Hungary. It is true that Russia and Rumania began to export considerable quantities of wheat to western Europe after the middle of the nineteenth century. However, the ability to export was not due to any notable improvement of agricultural technique, but rather to the fact that new land was broken to the plow, while pastures or woodlands were correspondingly reduced in extent. Thus while total food production rose very greatly in eastern Europe, production per acre and per man remained low in comparison with the standards of western European countries. Among the Latin peoples of western Europe a variety of social obstacles (stubbornly conservative peasants in France, and absentee landowners in Italy and Spain who were not interested in agricultural techniques or their improvement) prevented these countries from sharing to the full in the advances which were made elsewhere.

3) Improvements in Transport and Communication. A mere list of the principal inventions which facilitated transport and communication during the nineteenth century will serve to show the revolutionary character of the changes that took place. The steamship, railroad, automobile, and airplane were all invented before 1914; so were the telegraph, telephone, radio, public post office, rotary presses and the typewriter.

Roads and canals underwent a steady improvement in most European countries during the latter part of the eighteenth and the early nineteenth centuries. Public post chaises had reduced the traveling time between London and Edinburgh to forty-four hours by 1835 instead of the 14 days it had taken early in the eighteenth century. In 1830 the first successful steam railroad was opened; but it was not until the 1840's that railroads came to link the major cities of Great Britain together. Higher speeds and cheaper haulage were the result: by the 1850's the time between London and Edinburgh had been cut to twelve hours. Railroad building on the continent was begun almost as soon as in Great Britain. Belgium led the way, followed by France and Germany. By 1870 western Europe was covered with a fairly dense railroad network; during the following three decades extensive railroad construction was undertaken in eastern Europe, the Balkans and Russia. In 1903 the Trans-Siberian line running all the way to Vladivostok on the Pacific coast was completed.

The consequences of railroad construction were profound. Cheap and rapid overland transport became available not only for persons and light freight (which was all that had been possible earlier), but for bulky articles such as ore, coal and wheat as well. Inland iron and coal fields which had previously been only partially exploited owing to difficulties of transport became the seats of prosperous industry. Commercial agriculture could spread widely, since remote villages came to be only as far from urban markets as the nearest railway station. The railroads helped to bind nations together by facilitating movement of goods and people; they came also to play a crucial military role as the Prussian general staff proved in 1866 during the Austro-Prussian war.

The first successful steamboat was built by Robert Fulton in 1807; but for many years steamboats were confined to short runs, and clung for the most part to sheltered waters. Machinery was clumsy and used so much coal that only relatively short trips could be made without refueling. However, combination sailing and steam vessels reduced the time required for Atlantic crossings to two weeks by 1838, and in 1840 regular steamship service, with scheduled runs, opened between Liverpool and Boston. By 1850 the steamship had ousted sailing vessels for carrying passengers and mail across the Atlantic and on shorter ocean voyages; but until about 1870 engines and coal took up so much hull space that sailing vessels remained superior as freight carriers for the longer ocean hauls. By 1870, however, the design of marine engines had been improved, and coal consumption had been reduced; even more important, the size of ships had been greatly increased by the introduction of iron (1839) and then of steel (1879) hulls. These improvements left ample cargo space, and made the steamship a carrier of the world's intercontinental commerce. It was not, however, until about 1890 that steam vessels definitely supplanted sailing ships for the longest ocean runs where convenient coaling stations could not be found, e.g., between Australia and England.

Communication was revolutionized no less drastically than transport. In 1840 Rowland Hill introduced the public penny post in Great Britain. Other countries soon followed the British lead in setting up public postal services; and in 1875 an international postal agreement was concluded by which reciprocal postal privileges were granted by the various public post offices of the world. Electric telegraphy became a practical possibility after 1844 when Samuel Morse first demonstrated his invention. The possibility of instantaneous telegraphic communication was rapidly translated into reality. The first commercial telegraph company was formed in 1846; by 1851 submarine cables linked Great Britain with a telegraph network on the continent, and in 1866 a cable was successfully laid across the Atlantic. The telephone was invented by Alexander Graham Bell in 1876, but it became an important means of communication only slowly. Radio on the other hand was adopted for wireless telegraphy very quickly after the first transmission by Guglielmo Marconi in 1895. The automobile and the airplane, however, hardly became more than curiosities in Europe before 1914. The bicycle, first widely adopted after 1870, was of far more importance for ordinary Europeans.

The typewriter, without which modern business administration and government would be inconceivable, was invented in 1872 but only gradually supplanted handwritten records. More important for the nineteenth century was the development of the popular newspaper. Rotary presses solved the problem of rapid mass printing. By the 1850's popular journalism established itself in Great Britain, and public opinion, sometimes whipped up by irresponsible reporters, began to play a new role in political life. (The British participation in the Crimean war, 1854–56, was in part the result of a popular patriotic hysteria, created mainly by newspapers.)

The net effect of these and other improvements in transport and communication was to unite the whole world as never before into a single interacting whole. The price of tea in London or of wheat in Chicago came to influence decisions made in very distant parts of the world; and the public statements of diplomats and of government ministers came to be known almost instantly not only to other governments but to the public at large. Diplomacy could no longer be conducted in the atmosphere of an exclusive club any more than the business man in Canton, Bombay or New York could neglect what was happening on the exchanges of Europe. Great movements of population became easy. The tide of overseas emigration reached unprecedented heights with the establishment of ocean-going steamships; and the Russian migration into Siberia increased enormously with the opening of the Trans-Siberian railroad.

The augmentation of transport and communication facilities opened up new occupations and enlarged markets for coal, iron and steel as well as for a host of other products. Industrial advances made possible many of the improvements in transport; and they in turn created a new demand for industrial products. International trade expanded enormously. Between 1815 and 1914 the value of European international payments increased about twentyfold; and the scale of internal exchanges within countries presumably grew in proportion.

Another consequence of the revolution in transport and communication was the rapid opening of landlocked areas to European exploitation, most notably in North America, Africa, the Middle East and China. The rapid development of areas like the American middle west and central Europe, too, was enormously facilitated by the railroad and steamship which connected these inland areas with the markets of the world.

4) Industrial Technology. Nineteenth century industry was based primarily upon coal and iron. Ever new uses were found for these two materials. Prior to about 1830 machine technology had been mainly confined to the textile (especially cotton) industry and to mining and metallurgy. After 1830 machinery was invented which mechanized a host of other traditional trades—shoe making, sewing, flour milling, brewing, gun making, etc. In addition, the progress of technology created new industries of fundamental importance. The chemical, electrical and petroleum industries were perhaps the three most important newcomers. They as well as older trades all depended on the steady refinement of machine tools which were used to manufacture machinery itself. In particular, improved lathes and other devices permitted engineers to build machines with interchangeable parts according to standard models. This meant an enormous economy in repair and upkeep.

In the field of metallurgy, the major change was the cheapening and consequent widened use of steel. The inventions of Henry Bessemer (1856) and William Siemens (perfected 1865) made possible large-scale manufacture of steel for the first time. Steel thereupon replaced iron for most industrial, military, and household uses. Until 1878 iron ores which contained phosphorus could not be made into steel since the Bessemer and Siemens processes did not remove phosphorus. In that year, however, Sidney Gilchrist Thomas developed a lining for steel furnaces which absorbed phosphorus from the molten metal successfully. This discovery had important effects in Europe, for it made the extensive iron ore deposits of Lorraine, which contained phosphorus, available for steel manufacture. By 1894 Germany had become the leading steel producer of Europe, since Lorraine ore and Ruhr coal could now be brought together to make steel.

The chemical industry has so many ramifications that it is difficult to give any satisfactory account of it. Gas for illumination was introduced in 1807; in the 1850's chemists explored the structure of coal tars (a by-product of coke manufacture), and a great variety of useful products were synthesized from them—analine dies, aspirin, saccharine, high explosives, asphalt, ammonia, lubricating oils, and many more. Commercial production of acids and alkalis, used in a very wide variety of industrial processes, made great strides about the middle of the nineteenth century; and at its end, rayon was first synthesized. The invention of dynamite by Alfred Nobel in 1867 did much to revolutionize mining and warfare, for a high explosive which was powerful and yet safe to handle could be employed for blowing up either rocks or men.

Petroleum had been known as a curiosity from Babylonian times, but it was only in the latter part of the nineteenth century (and at first in the United States) that it became of prime economic importance. Lubrication for high speed machinery was almost as important as the fuel uses to which petroleum was put in diesel and gasoline engines. By the end of the century oil had proved its superiority to coal as a fuel for ocean-going vessels, being easier to handle and store, and at the same time providing more power per unit of bulk. The variety of chemical by-products from the refinement of petroleum was comparable to the number and usefulness of the by-products of coal tar.

Electricity, too, had been known for many centuries, but a better understanding of electrical phenomena and practical applications of electric power came only in the nineteenth century. Michael Faraday discovered electrolysis, whence developed electroplating of metals to prevent rust or to make an attractive finish. He also devised an electric motor in 1831, but it was not until the 1870's that improvements in design made electric motors an important source of power. In 1879 Thomas Alva Edison patented an improved incandescent bulb, and in succeeding decades electric light replaced gas and kerosene illumination in most cities. Electric power began to be applied to a growing number of machines and the efficiency of long distance transport of electric current was notably increased. However the full impact of electricity was only beginning to be felt in 1914.

In addition to these major developments, hundreds of thousands of other improvements and new inventions created an ever-growing efficiency of machine production. Nearly every trade was affected by mechanization; only a few luxury and highly skilled occupations remained handicrafts. The flow of machine-produced goods lowered some prices, and greatly expanded the range of commodities available for ordinary consumption. A rising standard of living thus became a technological possibility. A series of readjustments in the social organization of economic life helped, by the end of the century, to make a rising living standard a reality for most Europeans.

c. The Organization of Economic Life

1) Agriculture. Scientific agriculture and efficient utilization of the land usually required changes in traditional forms of land tenure. In nearly all of western Europe and some parts of eastern Europe scattered strips were consolidated into fields, the routine of manorial agriculture was broken and individual farmers were thus freed to plant what crops they wished. The process of consolidation of holdings was a difficult one, since someone could usually make out a claim to be hurt by the exchange of land which consolidation required. But various laws were passed by European governments by which consolidation was made mandatory if a certain number of the members of a village asked for it. Communal control over land-use survived only in Russia and some Balkan countries in 1914.

Two sharply contrasted forms of agricultural organization emerged from the consolidation of holdings. In Great Britain and in northeastern Germany large estates of several hundred acres became the dominant type of land unit. The Parliament which authorized consolidation of holdings in Great Britain was peculiarly favorable to the big landholders, since they were the class mainly represented in Parliament. As a result, during the late eighteenth and early nineteenth century many small farmers either left the land and swarmed into the rising industrial towns or became hired agricultural laborers, working on large farms. In eastern Germany large-scale farms had existed even in the late Middle Ages, and they remained characteristic of the trans-Elban regions of Germany down to 1945.

In other parts of Europe, however, circumstances were more favorable to small cultivators. In some cases the governments protected the peasant farmers, regarding a stalwart peasantry as a source of military strength and social stability. This was the case, for instance, in Austria. In some cases the landlords were mostly absentees who were not interested in farming for themselves, and were quite content to accept rents from peasant occupants. This was generally the case in Italy and in Mediterranean regions as a whole. In France and the Low Countries, the events of the French revolution had a decisive effect, transferring full ownership of the land for the most part to small peasant farmers. In western Germany, a similar transfer occurred— stimulated after 1848 by the policies of the governments of the south German states.

At the beginning of the French revolution serfdom persisted in a few remote parts of France, and became increasingly common as one moved eastward in Europe. All servile obligations were abolished by the revolution inside France, and in the neighboring territories by Napoleon. In Prussia, serfdom was abolished in 1810; in Austria in 1848; in Russia in 1861. Such abolition meant first of all removal of various legal disabilities under which serfs had previously existed. Secondly, it meant a division of the land between landlord and ex-serf according to various principles laid down differently by each government concerned. Except in Prussia, where the junkers had managed commercial farms for generations, the effect of emancipation was in the long run to transfer the majority of the land to peasant ownership, for most landlords both in Austria and in Russia found it easier to sell off bits and pieces of their land than to try to farm it for themselves with hired labor. Furthermore, government policy often favored the distribution of land to peasants, particularly toward the end of the nineteenth century and at the beginning of the twentieth. Rich agricultural areas such as the mid-Danubian plain in Hungary, and the chernozom soils of the Ukraine and the lower Danube (Rumania) were exceptions, for in such regions landlords generally found it profitable to cultivate their land and were able to employ hired labor. These were the areas where a large surplus of grain was raised to supply the cities of western Europe.

The perfection of the steamship as an oceanic freight carrier in the 1870's brought overseas agricultural competition home to European farmers. In Great Britain, the government was committed to free trade, and made no attempt to protect British farming. The result was disastrous for British agriculture. Great areas which had been among the best cultivated in Europe were turned into deer parks or pastures, or else abandoned. On the continent governments universally took steps to protect farmers by establishing tariffs on agricultural imports. Nevertheless agricultural prosperity was threatened in Europe by the lowering of world grain and meat prices, Russia, Rumania and other European grain-exporting countries found it increasingly difficult to compete with American and Australian grain on the only market which remained wide open: the British.

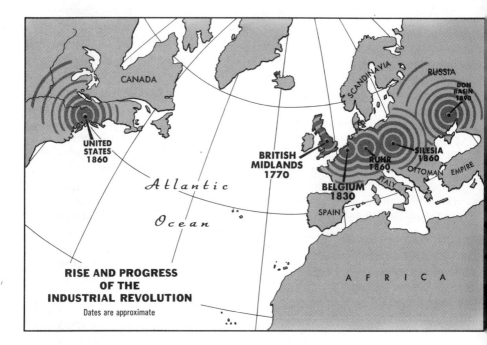

2) *Industry*. With the proliferation of power driven machinery, the factory became the predominant form for the social organization of industry. Handicrafts and domestic production were replaced by degrees; but it is easy to exaggerate the rate at which the shift took place. Until near the end of the nineteenth century cutlery, for example, was still mainly produced in small shops where light machines and skilled workmen turned out a better product than could be made by mass production. The further east in Europe, the stronger was the survival of handicrafts so that, for example, probably more than half of Russian industrial production in 1914 (measured by value) was produced by handicraft methods.

In general, it was not until after 1830 that factories and mass production spread from the textile and metallurgical industries to others. It was about the same date that heavy machine industry first established itself on the continent of Europe. Belgium was the first country to follow the British example. France lagged considerably behind, lacking extensive coal and iron deposits. Germany was handicapped by the survival of small states, each with its own tariff barriers to trade. The formation of a tariff union—

the Zollverein—which included most of the German states (1834) removed that obstacle; the construction of railroads in the 1850's and 1860's solved a second problem—the lack of cheap and efficient inland transport. By 1870 Germany was therefore able to become a first class industrial power, rivaling Britain. By the end of the century, German industry had surpassed the British in most respects, so that Germany stood first in Europe in industrial capacity and organization. The industrialization of Russia began on a fairly large scale about 1890, but Russia remained predominantly agricultural in 1914 and had to import many vital manufactured products. Across the Atlantic, the United States emerged, like Germany, as a powerful industrial nation by about 1890. Japan also burst upon the scene in the decade before World War I as an industrial (and military) power of key importance in the Asian Far East.

A persistent difficulty in the early stages of industrialization was the problem of finding sufficient capital. The abuses to which joint stock companies could be put by unscrupulous promoters had been illustrated as early as 1720; and in 1825 a panic in Britain once again wiped out hundreds of companies which had been formed on joint stock principles for the exploitation of mines in South America and elsewhere. This debacle helped to bring about a number of legal changes in Great Britain, extending from 1844 to 1861, as a result of which the modern corporation, with a legal personality and limited liability for its investors, was brought into being. The new legal form for business enterprise was quickly adopted by numerous old and new industrial enterprises. Partnerships and individual firms which had characterized the first stages of the industrial revolution in Great Britain were generally superseded by limited companies, or in American parlance, by corporations. Other European countries modified their laws more or less along the British lines within the next few years. The advantages of the corporation were numerous. As a legal person, it could enter into contracts, sue and be sued, and enjoy all the privileges of the law. In addition, passive investors, who did not expect to take any share in the management of the corporation, could contribute their savings to industry (by purchasing stocks) without risking, as had been the case under earlier laws, responsibility for all the debts of the company if it should go bankrupt. The flow of capital into industry was thereby facilitated, and the over-all pace of industrial capital formation steadily increased.

As the century progressed, the size of corporations tended to grow. Great industrial aggregations were formed with the intention of controlling more fully the market (horizontal combinations) or the supply of raw materials and sale of products (vertical combinations). Germany was particularly active along these lines, for the German government tolerated and even encouraged the formation of cartels (horizontal combinations) which divided the market between competing concerns and often set minimum prices as well. During the decades immediately preceding World War I, international cartels were formed in some businesses, notably in oil and chemicals.

The effect of cartels and vertical combinations has been much disputed by economists and politicians. The intention of the men who formed them was to assure a greater stability to prices and profits by reducing competition and eliminating middle-men. In some cases there is reason to suppose that such organizations did increase the efficiency of production, especially in industries which required a very heavy capital investment. In other cases the cartels seem to have worked chiefly to maintain a higher rate of profit than could otherwise have been attained, and, by eliminating competition, checked technological improvement.

The role of governments in controlling industry was of prime importance. In the nineteenth century one may distinguish two general attitudes, typified by the policies of the British government at one extreme and of the German government (before 1871, the Prussian government) at the other.

Industry in Great Britain had grown up piecemeal, and when mechanization of the textile and metallurgical industries started in the eighteenth century no one foresaw the eventual development of a predominantly industrial society. Britain lacked an extensive centralized bureaucracy, and the economic ideas which were most current assured men that the enlightened self-interest of individuals would in the long run work to the general good. As a result, the British government did as little as it could to intervene in economic relationships.

Laws against combinations of workingmen were passed by Parliament in 1799, largely stimulated by fear of radicalism which might spread from the French revolutionary example; and these laws were not repealed until 1824. By degrees the miserable conditions of work in early factories and the slums which arose in the mushrooming industrial towns began to excite the attention of humanitarians and reformers. Parliament was, however, very reluctant to interfere in the contractual relationship between employer and employee. The first laws regulating factory conditions applied only to women and children in textile factories, and were not very effective since no system for enforcement was provided. In 1833, a new law was passed which established factory inspectors whose duty it was to report violations of the regulations; in 1847 a ten hour law was passed which limited work for women and children to ten hours (and by so doing effectively limited men's work also since the factory necessarily worked as a unit and could not continue operation without women and children). These laws all applied only to textile factories; in later years regulation of working hours and conditions were slowly extended to other industries.

By the first decade of the twentieth century, government boards had been established to fix minimum wages for most industries and in 1911–12 compulsory unemployment and sickness insurance were organized by the state. In this rather piecemeal fashion the British government by slow degrees came to recognize a responsibility for the working conditions and welfare of industrial employees, and restricted the power of employers.

The British government pursued a similar policy of laissez faire, within practicable limits, in matters of tariff and state ownership. Protective tariffs were whittled away during the first half of the nineteenth century under the pressure of economic theory and the demands of industrialists who hoped to sell their products abroad, and realized that foreign countries could buy only if they could export goods to Great Britain in return. The most notable landmark was the repeal of the Corn Laws in 1846, which ended the protection of British agriculture by the state.

New creations of the industrial revolution such as railroads and public utilities were allowed by the British government to pass under the control of private companies. Even such matters as sewage disposal and water supply were at first not regarded as falling within the proper sphere of government; but by degrees the obvious and pressing needs of the growing industrial towns resulted in alteration of this attitude. In 1835 a law was passed facilitating the formation of new local governments in places where great towns had formed, and town authorities gradually accepted responsibility for sanitation systems, water mains, parks, and other amenities of urban life.

In Germany, traditions of government were different from those of Great Britain. The Prussian bureaucracy had been famous throughout Europe for its efficiency since the days of Frederick the Great; and military considerations, which played almost no part in British industrialization policy, were always present in the minds of the directors of the Prussian government. As a result, when the industrial revolution began to make headway in Germany, after about 1850, officials played a far more active role than was the case in England.

Protective tariffs to defend infant industries from overwhelming British competition were established by the state, beginning in 1834. When railroads were constructed in Prussia, it was with the help of the state, which guaranteed interest on capital invested in them and promised new railroads a monopoly of certain routes. Thus much of the wasteful duplication of facilities which had distinguished British (and American) railroad construction was avoided.

Military considerations also influenced the construction of the railroad net in Germany. The German general staff realized the potential usefulness of railroads for moving troops and supplies, and military advice played an important part in determining the layout and density of railroad construction. The majority of German railroads were built by private companies; but before 1914 most of the mileage had come to be owned and operated by the German states themselves. This gave government officials a powerful lever over the whole economy. Differential freight rates were used to encourage some industries, notably the steel industry, which required the transport of iron ore from Lorraine to the Ruhr coalfields. The planning and control which Prussia and the other German states exercised over the construction and operation of railroads made them the most efficient in Europe. The railroads enormously strengthened Germany both militarily and economically, and their management by the state gave a very real centralized direction to the whole German economy.

In dealing with the labor problem, the German government was similarly emancipated from the qualms which had restricted British official intervention. Between 1883 and 1889 a comprehensive series of laws instituting social insurance and regulating hours and conditions of labor were passed, which at the time were far more sweeping than similar legislation in any other country.

The economic policies of other European states fell somewhere between the extremes represented by Great Britain and Germany. Some European states, especially those of the Balkans, were, however, in no real sense masters of their own economic development. They were semicolonial areas, where the capital for mines, railroads and whatever industry existed came mostly from abroad. Foreign capitalists were usually able to secure concessions from the local governments which were designed not in the interest of the country concerned but to assure a maximum return to the capitalists. The same was in some degree true of Russia before 1914.

Adjustment to industrialization was not confined to the efforts of industrial managers and governments. The workingmen themselves began to take steps to organize unions which could both defend their interests in negotiations with employers and perform various other functions—e.g., provide insurance, burial benefits, etc. The early history of the trade union movement was a stormy one, since laws in nearly every country forbade combinations. Moreover, workingmen did not have a favorable political position and so were generally unable to make their wishes felt in governmental circles. Early unions, too, were deeply influenced by socialist theory. Robert Owen (1771–1858), for example, the moving spirit behind the first effort to erect a national trade union movement in Great Britain (1833–34), conceived of labor unions as a means for regenerating society as a whole. These facts tended to direct labor activity into revolutionary political channels on the one hand, and into utopian projects for establishing ideal communities on the other.

It was not until the second half of the nineteenth century that less ambitious but more successful unions arose in Great Britain. They were organized along craft lines—metal workers, transport workers, etc.—and limited their efforts mainly to securing better working conditions and wages by means of negotiation and strikes. Many unions also carried on insurance programs, collecting dues from their members and in return providing benefit payments in case of sickness, strikes, unemployment or death. Skilled and semiskilled workmen were unionized first; by the end of the century the less skilled trades—dock workers and coal miners, for example—were also unionized.

During the course of the nineteenth century a series of reforms of the franchise (1832, 1867, 1884) resulted in the introduction of almost complete manhood suffrage in Great Britain. As a result, the laboring classes of the population became an important and powerful political group. This fact did not at once lead to the organization of a special workingman's party, since there were many trade union leaders who felt that it was better to stay out of politics and concentrate on economic betterment through wage and hour negotiations. In 1893, however, a small group, influenced by socialist principles, organized the Independent Labour Party. Beginning in 1900 this party combined with other groups to found the Labour Party. Its strength grew rapidly, but not until after the First World War did it equal either of the traditional political parties of Great Britain—the Liberal and the Conservative.

On the continent of Europe socialism gained a stronger hold on the minds of the working classes than in Great Britain. Until about 1860 labor organizations were of small significance; and until near the end of the century unions constantly had to struggle against the power of governments which outlawed or tried to suppress them. One consequence of this struggle was to give a more political cast to continental labor unions; and the majority of them, especially in Germany, rallied under the banner of Marxian socialism, and supported socialist political parties. By degrees, however, the revolutionary ardor of unions decreased as Marxian doctrine was reinterpreted, and as rival unions arose to compete with the dominant Marxian ones. At the same time the hostility of European governments was gradually mitigated. In 1884 legal discriminations against unions were removed in France; Germany followed suit in 1890, and even Russia made unions legal in 1906.

In France and Italy syndicalism competed with Marxian principles for the loyalty of the workingmen. Syndicalists expected a general strike to bring about a fundamental reorganization of society—the termination of capitalist control of industry, and the establishment of workers' control and management instead. In the Rhinelands and elsewhere Catholic labor unions achieved some success also. Their leaders sought to make medieval guild organization of industry a model for reform of nineteenth century capitalist patterns of industrial organization. In Russia a wide variety of revolutionary doctrines were in circulation, but until the first years of the twentieth century it was mainly intellectuals, not workingmen, who espoused revolution.

A different sort of adjustment to industrial conditions was represented by the cooperative movement which originated in 1844 in Rochdale, a small town of Lancashire. From very humble beginnings, centering around the management of a store whose ownership was kept in the hands of its customers, the cooperative movement branched out in all directions, undertook manufacture and distribution of a wide variety of consumer goods and became a significant element in the retail and consumers' goods business. Cooperative organization was also adopted in other European countries. The fact that in most continental countries small farmers predominated in the countryside opened the possibility of farmers' cooperatives. Cooperative marketing and purchasing at wholesale rates saved middlemen's profits for the farmers; and in countries such as Denmark cooperatives became the dominant element in the entire economy, since they conducted the main business of the nation's farmers.

3) Banking and Finance. The growth of commerce, the constantly increasing need for capital in industry, and the close integration of all economic processes which industrialization brought in its train, meant that banking and financial policies came to exert a profound influence as coordinators and in some degree as controllers of the entire economy. During the Napoleonic wars the British government discovered the possibility of maintaining an industrial economy on paper money. But this was regarded as a temporary and dangerous expedient. In subsequent years payment of specie on demand was resumed, and after 1871 all European countries adopted gold as their currency standard. Until the depression of the 1930's gold remained the basis of most European and world currencies, although states sometimes suspended gold payment in time of emergency.

A more important phenomenon was the export of capital from Europe, especially from Great Britain and France. Loans to foreign governments and investment in private enterprises located abroad began to be made on a large scale after the Napoleonic wars. The export of capital gained momentum throughout the century as the investors of one country after another accumulated a surplus of capital at home and entered foreign markets. In general loans were of two kinds: those which financed some sort of industrial enterprise, mine or plantation, and those (made mostly to governments) which were used for some economically nonproductive purpose. Loans of the first type were frequently of benefit to both parties. The industrialization of the United States and of Germany was greatly facilitated, for example, by the export of British capital to those countries, which meant that the rate of American and German industrial expansion was not limited to what could be financed by the savings of the local population. Unproductively used loans to governments, on the other hand, frequently brought on the bankruptcy of the borrowing government, whereupon indignant investors were sometimes able to mobilize the diplomatic and military force of their home governments to extract repayment or compel economic reorganization of the defaulting country. Thus export of capital served in some instances as an opening wedge for the extension of political control. The Middle East and the Balkans were the principal areas in which defaulted loans led to large-scale political intervention by European governments in the nineteenth century.

The formation of great industrial combinations and cartels in the later decades of the nineteenth century was accompanied by the extension of banking and financial control. Holding companies and other devices were invented in order to secure centralized financial direction of a wide variety of manufacturing enterprises; and mergers of competing companies were carried through by financial manipulations. This development concentrated great power in the hands of a relatively few men, often bankers, whose decisions were not always wise and sometimes hindered technological efficiency or ran counter to the general interests of society as a whole. The entrepreneur, thoroughly familiar with the technical aspect of manufacture, and also acquainted with labor and other conditions in his factory, was more and more replaced in positions of economic power by men whose tie with industry was purely financial, and who measured industrial success by studying balance sheets. Yet at the same time, centralized financial control served to coordinate the activities of diverse factories and was able to achieve a certain stability in production which might otherwise have been lacking.

d. European Politics, 1789–1914

1) The French Revolution and Napoleon (1789–1815)

   a) Introductory
   b) The Liberal Phase
   c) Girondin Control and Factional Struggle
   d) The Jacobin Supremacy
   e) Reaction and Consolidation

a) Introductory. The French revolution burst upon most Frenchmen and upon all Europe as a great surprise. Institutions, ideas, attitudes which had arisen in the course of centuries were discarded or radically modified within the period of a few months; and a nation which had been unsuccessful in most of its wars of the eighteenth century found new strength and a revolutionary enthusiasm so great that the French armies were able to withstand and overcome the military opposition of nearly all Europe.

Such rapid and unexpected developments were accompanied by a great confusion within France. Groups with widely differing political loyalties arose, and for a few years civil war was superadded to foreign. Opinions and political groupings shifted with kaleidoscopic rapidity. The radicals of one year became conservatives of the next; and under the pressure of foreign and domestic dangers, a reign of terror was introduced which brought one group of political leaders after another, as well as thousands of private citizens, to the guillotine.

In other European countries there were persons who sympathized in varying degrees with the aspirations and deeds of the French revolutionaries; but reaction against their principles and practices united the governments and most of the ruling classes of Europe. Yet in self defense, it proved necessary for the other European states to adopt some of the French innovations; and in the territories which France conquered and annexed, revolutionary principles of social and political organization were imposed. Thus when in 1815 the European powers were finally able to restore the legitimate king of France, they did not find it possible to restore the status quo of 1789, even though they tried in some respects to do so.

Four principal phases of the French revolution may be distinguished: (1) a liberal phase, May, 1789–August, 1792, during which absolutism was replaced by constitutional monarchy; (2) a moderate republican phase, August, 1792–June, 1793, during which a political group known as the Girondins tried to stabilize a bourgeois republic at home and conduct revolutionary war abroad; (3) a radical republican phase, June, 1793–July, 1794, during which a political group called the Jacobins organized France for successful foreign war and tried to establish a Republic of Virtue at home; (4) a prolonged period of reaction and consolidation, July, 1794–1814. The period of reaction and consolidation was itself complicated and passed through various phases, but for our purposes here the whole period of the Directory (1795–99), Consulate (1799–1804) and Empire (1804–14) may be regarded as a time when the more radical aspirations of revolutionary leaders were discarded and the changes which had been made during the first phase of the Revolution were incorporated into more or less stable institutional forms.

b) The Liberal Phase, May, 1789–August, 1792. Dissatisfaction with the government of France had mounted through the eighteenth century, and when Louis XVI's ministers found themselves in growing financial difficulties nearly every group in the population resisted the efforts of the royal government to impose new taxes. Theoretically the king was absolute and had the legal right to assess and collect taxes as he saw fit; but in fact the monarchy was not able to impose its will without at least the passive acquiescence of the French people. When Louis' ministers proposed new taxes, judicial bodies known as Parlements refused to register the royal decrees, i.e., refused to acknowledge them as law enforceable in the courts. The Parlements, especially the Parlement of Paris, thus became popular champions against absolutism, despite the fact that their members were royal officials.

In 1787 the King summoned an Assembly of the Notables in the hope that representatives of the nobility and of the higher clergy would agree to heavier taxation of their property. But the Notables were not willing, and the effort came to nothing. Meanwhile excitement mounted in France. Numerous pamphlets urged government reform. The demand for a revival of the old medieval representative body, the Estates General, became widespread. This body had not met since 1614. It had then been composed of representatives of the three "estates" of the realm—that is, the clergy, the nobility, and the commoners. The representatives of each estate had met and voted separately. Obviously such an arrangement gave the clergy and nobility a decisive preponderance, and when in August, 1788, the king decided to summon the Estates General, the question of how that body would be organized became a burning one. Members of the commons (or Third Estate) were not satisfied with the old medieval distribution of power, and found effective spokesmen for their wishes in the Abbé Sieyès and others. After some indecision, the royal government agreed that the representatives of the Third Estate should equal in number the representatives of the other two orders combined.

When the Estates General assembled at Versailles in May, 1789, details of procedure had not, however, been settled. In particular the king had not committed himself on the all-important question of how the representatives would vote, whether by head (in which case the double representation of the Third Estate and the fact that some of the clergy and nobility sympathized with a sweeping reform program would have given a majority to advocates of reform) or by order (in which case the conservative majorities among the clergy and nobility would have assured a maintenance of the status quo with perhaps a few modifications). The royal government at first tried to dodge this issue, but the representatives of the Third Estate refused to organize themselves as a separate chamber, and invited the clergy and nobility to join them in a common National Assembly. They had a powerful moral support from the nation at large. When the elections to the Estates-General were organized, the voters had been asked to write down instructions for their delegates. These instructions (cahiers) reflected a widespread and organized agitation for fundamental reform;

and it was the cause of thoroughgoing reform to which the delegates from the Third Estate pledged themselves.

Such insubordination on the part of the Third Estate seemed dangerous to some of the king's advisers, and on June 20 the room in which the Third Estate had been meeting was locked up and put under military guard. The king's intention was to call a special meeting of the Estates General on June 22 to lay down the law as to how voting would take place; but the delegates of the Third Estate had not been informed of the royal intention. When they found themselves locked out, they concluded that some foul plot was afoot. A defiant spirit swept through the clamoring representatives. They moved into an indoor tennis court nearby and solemnly swore never to disband until a constitution had been established for France. This "Oath of the Tennis Court" marked an important step in the development of the incipient revolution. The Third Estate's representatives had in effect denied the king's power to dismiss them and had affirmed their intention of establishing a constitution which would put an end to royal absolutism.

Louis XVI was by nature vacillating and weak-willed; moreover he sympathized with some of the demands for reform. Consequently the revolutionary Oath of the Tennis court did not stir the king to decisive action. Louis tried to insist upon separate meeting and voting by order; but in succeeding days individual members of the clergy and nobility began to attend the meetings of the representatives of the Third Estate; and on June 27 the king yielded and ordered all three estates to sit together and vote by head. Thus the Estates General became transformed into the National Assembly, and the supporters of thoroughgoing reform won a decisive advantage.

Some court circles were not willing to yield so easily, and Louis vacillated between them and more liberal advisers. In July the king began to gather troops at Versailles, and it was suspected that he or some of his courtiers were contemplating a forcible dissolution of the National Assembly. This suspicion took on new plausibility when the liberally-minded Controller General of Finance, Jacques Necker, was dismissed (July 11). The result was to stir the people of Paris to wild excitement A makeshift committee, representing the sections into which Paris had been divided for elections to the Estates-General, usurped the government of the capital, and ordered the citizens to organize a National Guard to protect their liberties and keep order. On July 14 an angry crowd, looking for arms with which to equip the new National Guard, attacked the Bastille, a royal fortress and prison in the heart of Paris. After a few hours' siege and some bloodshed, the Bastille surrendered. The violent action of the people of Paris frightened the king. The next day he appeared at a meeting of the National Assembly to announce that he had reinstated Necker and ordered his troops to leave Versailles.

The capture of the Bastille came in later years to be celebrated as the birthday of the Revolution. It did indeed mark a further step. The populace of Paris had for the first time decisively entered the political scene. The Commune, as the revolutionary government of the city was called, thenceforth constituted a distinct center of power, which, supported by the city mobs, was often able to force the king and even the National Assembly to yield to its will.

The revolutionary establishment of the Commune in Paris was widely imitated in provincial towns and cities. The old governmental machine lost its hold over many parts of France and new revolutionary authorities seized control. In the countryside the peasants took the law into their own hands. Excited by news of great events in Paris, they rebelled against their landlords, refused any longer to pay rents and dues, and wherever possible destroyed the records in which their obligations were officially written down. Some manor houses were burnt and a few nobles killed by angry peasant crowds.

When news of these peasant uprisings reached the National Assembly, debate shifted to the question of what should be done about them. On the night of August 4–5 a remarkable excitement swept over the Assembly. One after another, amid scenes of wild enthusiasm, nobles, clergy, and representatives of town corporations arose and solemnly resolved to abolish old rights and privileges. During the following days these resolutions were transformed into legislation which magniloquently claimed to "completely abolish the feudal system." Actually this was an exaggeration, for while the equality of all ranks of citizens before the law was affirmed, it was also decreed that the peasants should continue to pay tithes to the clergy and rents to the nobles until some method of redeeming these obligations had been decided upon by the Assembly. This decision actually had little effect, for in most localities the peasants continued to destroy the records of their obligations and refused to pay dues and rents which they had previously owed to the noble landowners.

During the next two years the National Assembly remained in session. Its avowed aim was to establish a constitution for France, but it was frequently distracted from this task by governmental crises which demanded immediate action. The most important crisis was financial. Tax income decreased during the first few months of the revolution, and the government became insolvent. In November, 1789, the National Assembly decided to meet this problem by confiscating the lands belonging to the Church in France, and issued a paper currency, the *assignats*, which were to be redeemed as the land was sold. The issuance of assignats, however, proved such an attractive solution to the financial difficulties of the government that they were issued in sums far exceeding the value of the confiscated land, even when the lands of the king and of nobles who had fled from France (the émigrés) were also confiscated. As a result the *assignat* currency underwent drastic inflation, and by 1795 had become worthless.

This financial expedient had two important consequences. On the one hand, the inflation of currency meant a corresponding rise in prices, which worked hardship on wage earners, especially those who lived in towns and had to buy their food. This fact acted as a constant goad to the revolutionary ardor of the Paris proletariat, who blamed their sufferings on the secret machinations of enemies of the revolution. This helped to make Paris and other great towns primary strongholds of radicalism.

The second, and far more enduring consequence was the widespread transfer of property which resulted from the extensive confiscations and resale of land. At first much of the confiscated land was bought by speculators, mainly townsmen, but by degrees they resold to peasant farmers who thus came into full and free possession of most of the land of France. As a result, from the time of the revolution until the 1940's France remained predominantly a land of small farmers. During the years of the revolution itself, the transfer of property had the important consequence of binding the majority of the peasants to the revolutionary cause, for they feared that a restoration of the old system of government would also mean a restoration of their newly acquired possessions to their former owners.

Confiscation of Church lands, however attractive as a financial expedient, raised the question of how the clergy was to be supported. The National Assembly answered this question by adopting a series of measures collectively entitled the Civil Constitution of the Clergy (July, 1790). By these laws, the state undertook to pay fixed salaries to members of the clergy. In addition, the boundaries of dioceses were shifted to correspond with changes made in the political subdivision of France; and, most radical of all, the Assembly decreed that in the future all priests, bishops and other religious officials would be elected by the citizens of the appropriate district. This meant that Protestants, Jews and free thinkers would have the right to a voice in the selection of the clergy. Such a possibility scandalized most Catholics. Six months after the Civil Constitution had been adopted, the pope condemned it and anathematized its authors. A consequence was that the clergy of France came to be divided between those who accepted the new arrangement (the juring clergy) and those who refused to do so (the non-juring clergy). Moreover it became difficult for good Catholics to support the revolution when once issue had been joined with the papacy, and a serious division at once appeared among Frenchmen—a division which still plays a prominent part in French politics.

Another major problem which the National Assembly had to face was its relation to the king. Louis was surrounded by persons who detested what the National Assembly was trying to do. A particularly powerful influence over the weak-willed king was exercised by his queen, Marie Antoinette. She was the sister of the emperor of Austria and did not delay in appealing to her brother for support against the revolutionaries. By degrees Louis was won over to the queen's point of view, and he too entered into correspondence with many of the leading sovereigns of Europe, seeking their support against any further diminution of his royal power.

Suspicion of the queen was strong among the people of Paris, and when in October, 1789, a temporary shortage of bread aroused them to action, a mob straggled out to Versailles and demanded that the royal family and the National Assembly return with them to Paris. After much confusion and some violence, the king agreed to accompany the crowd back to the capital city. A few days later the National Assembly followed him to Paris.

From this time onward the power of the Paris populace over the National Assembly increased, since it became much easier to pack the galleries and to organize impressive mass demonstrations when that body was close at hand in the city and not twenty miles away at Versailles. King Louis' attitude also underwent a decisive change. He began to feel himself a prisoner of the revolution, and all his initial sympathy with reform vanished. The Civil Constitution of the Clergy was especially repugnant to him, for the king was personally a very devout man. For the time being he found himself powerless, and was driven to fall back upon a policy of systematic duplicity—accepting the decisions of the National Assembly in public, while plotting in private to escape from Paris and overthrow the revolutionaries.

In the midst of revolutionary excitement, the National Assembly by degrees worked out the details of a constitution. As early as August, 1789, the Assembly had adopted a Declaration of Rights of Man and the Citizen which was intended as a general statement of political principles and became a preamble to the finished constitution. The Declaration asserted that all citizens were free and equal in rights, and listed the cardinal rights of man as liberty, property, security, and resistance to oppression. Moreover the nation was declared to be the source of all political authority.

In an age when such phrases have been worn nearly threadbare, and when liberal principles are usually taken more or less for granted, it is difficult to grasp the revolutionary character of such pronouncements. Old rights of kings, clergy and nobility were boldly thrown into the discard, and "the people" were elevated to a new dignity as the source of political authority. Such ideas were intoxicating to erstwhile subjects of an all powerful monarch. The principles of the revolution were fervently espoused by thousands of men and women. New phrases spread rapidly from lip to lip. The slogan Liberty, Equality, Fraternity came into use as a summation of the new system of government. To many it seemed that at

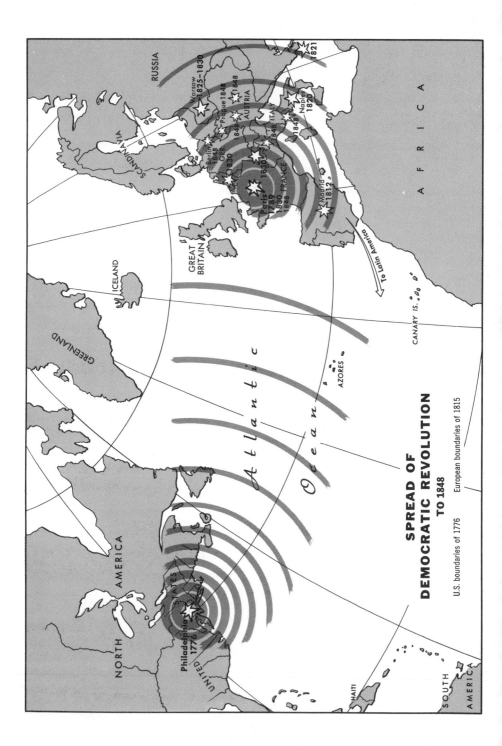

SPREAD OF
DEMOCRATIC REVOLUTION
TO 1848

U.S. boundaries of 1776   European boundaries of 1815

NORTH AMERICA

UNITED STATES

Philadelphia 1776

HAITI

SOUTH AMERICA

GREENLAND

ICELAND

GREAT BRITAIN

Atlantic Ocean

AZORES

CANARY IS.

To Latin America

SCANDINAVIA

RUSSIA

Warsaw 1825-1830

Prague 1848

Berlin 1848

GER. 1830

AUSTRIA 1848

ITALY 1848

1821

Naples 1820

Paris 1789 1830 1848

FRANCE 1830 1848

Madrid 1812

AFRICA

long last Reason and Justice had triumphed, and that the enlightened principles which had been taught by the philosophes for more than a generation would finally be put into practice.

When the members of the National Assembly came to translate their revolutionary principles into a constitution, however, they found it prudent to restrict the meaning of equality and fraternity very considerably. There was no problem in the minds of the majority about sweeping away old abuses and confusions. The special legal status of clergy and nobility were abolished, and in that sense all citizens became equal. But in other respects equality was not established. Two classes of citizens were distinguished: active and passive. Active citizens were those who paid taxes above a certain amount, and they alone could vote or bear arms. A higher property qualification was imposed for legislators and office holders; and a system of indirect election was established to cushion still further the impact of this cautious approach toward democracy.

The constitution of 1791 divided authority over the central government between a Legislative assembly and the king. The Legislative assembly was assigned control of taxation, the right to impeach ministers or call them to account, and a supreme appellate jurisdiction. It was thus in possession of essential sovereign powers. But its legislative power was limited by a suspensive veto entrusted to the king, who could postpone but not prevent the passage of laws which displeased him. In addition, the king had the right to choose ministers to head the executive branch of the government, and appointed diplomats and army officers.

The local government of France was reorganized and decentralized. All old subdivisions were swept away and new administrative units, the departments, were set up instead. Administrative districts, judicial organization, and the dioceses of the Church were all made to coincide with the new departmental boundaries. Events soon made almost the whole of the constitution invalid; but the division of France into departments has lasted to the present day.

Before the constitution had been completed, Louis XVI and the royal family made an attempt to escape from Paris in disguise (June, 1791). But the king was recognized, the coach in which the fugitives were traveling was stopped at the little village of Varennes, and they were compelled to return ignominiously to Paris. The apparent disloyalty of the king to the new order raised a serious question for the constitution-makers of the National Assembly, for they were proposing to entrust him wth quite substantial powers. However, there seemed no alternative, since republican principles excited only horror among most of the members of the National Assembly. Consequently when the king signified his willingness to accept the constitution he was taken at his word, and elections were organized under its provisions. When this had been done, on September 30, 1791, the

National Assembly adjourned; on the following day the new Legislative Assembly convened.

To all appearance the Revolution was over. The king had accepted a drastic reorganization of the French government, nobles and clerics had been reduced to the status of ordinary citizens, the peasants had gained effective—if not legal—emancipation from old manorial obligations, and the middle class had secured predominant voice in the control of government. Thus the most important discontented groups in the French population had more or less achieved their goals. The inherited complex of inefficient, duplicating and unmanageable political institutions had been swept away and a logical, simple system of administration had been substituted.

But at the extremes of the social scale the deeds of the National Assembly failed to please. Members of the aristocracy and upper clergy had fled from France to neighboring countries where they busied themselves with plans to stir other European governments and dissatisfied elements in France to action against the new order. The king and his immediate circle were in the thick of this plotting. At the other extreme, the working classes of the greater towns, and especially of Paris, had little to show for their activity on behalf of the revolution. A law (Law of La Chapelier, passed June. 1791) forbade workingmen's associations in restraint of trade and imposed severe penalties for disturbances of the peace or even for threats of strikes. Moreover, the inflation of the *assignat* currency brought a rapid rise in prices, and, as always, wage earners suffered.

The discontent of the Paris proletariat was in some measure shared by the lower middle classes who could not always meet the property qualification for active citizenship. Their dissatisfaction was given voice and organization by a number of radical intellectuals and professional men who felt that the revolution had stopped short of its goal, and had failed to eliminate the last vestiges of privilege. Republican democracy and a more vigorous suppression of the enemies of the new order were the main elements in the radical program. Among the most prominent radical leaders were Jean Paul Marat (1743-93), a doctor turned journalist; Georges Jacques Danton (1759-94), a lawyer and powerful orator; and Maximilien Robespierre (1758-94), another lawyer turned politician.

These and numerous other fanatical young men won prominence during the first two years of the Revolution as extreme revolutionists. Danton and Marat founded a political club, the Cordeliers, in 1790; Robespierre belonged to a similar organization, the Jacobin club, which he came to dominate after 1791 when its more conservative members withdrew. These clubs, especially the Jacobin club, created a network of corresponding societies in provincial towns and villages. Itinerant orators and a constant exchange of letters between Paris and these local clubs took on the character of a most effective propaganda machine. When the Jacobins came to power, the provincial clubs usurped some of the functions of local government, keeping a careful eye on the political orthodoxy of officials.

In 1791, however, it was principally the Parisian populace which responded to the exhortations of the Cordeliers and Jacobin spokesmen. Nor were the activities of the political clubs limited to talk. When crucial issues arose, the clubs, in cooperation with the Commune, developed a regular system for calling out the populace for defense of their liberties. Demonstrations and organized intimidation of members of opposing political groups were systematized; and since the only police force in Paris, the National Guard, sympathized with the revolution, organized crowds had free run of the city. Not until 1795 were effective means found for checking the impetuous and radical Paris populace.

When the Legislative Assembly met in October, 1791, it faced a highly unstable situation in France and abroad. Sporadic antirevolutionary outbreaks had begun in the Vendée and neighboring districts; the Paris populace was actively discontented; and the king and the émigrés were engaged in treasonable correspondence with the rulers of Austria, Prussia, and other states. The Assembly itself was divided into three sections: the Feuillants, who hoped to keep things as they were and make the constitution a success; the Girondins, more radical, some of whom were theoretical republicans, but who at the same time distrusted the Paris mobs, and favored only gradual and constitutional changes in government; and finally, the largest group of all, men who belonged to neither organized extreme but shifted back and forth between.

At first the Feuillants were the strongest group; but within a few months the Girondins had won over the support of a majority of the Legislative Assembly. Two factors helped them. On several occasions King Louis used his suspensive veto to prevent acts of the Assembly from becoming law. This raised the suspicion that the king did not really wish to make the new government a success, and was merely using his legal powers to sabotage public action. Secondly, deteriorating diplomatic relations with Austria and Prussia led to a declaration of war by the French on April 20, 1792. Since it was the Girondins who had most actively advocated war, they were able to profit from the wave of patriotic enthusiasm which swept the nation.

However, when actual campaigning began patriotic enthusiasm proved to be not enough. Offensive efforts were thrown back, and French armies were compelled to retreat inside home territory. These reverses stimulated wild excitement in Paris. The people came to believe (quite correctly) that the king and queen were plotting with the nation's enemies, and on August 9-10, 1792, Danton and others organized a rising which put an end to the constitutional monarchy. The Paris crowd attacked the palace of the

Tuileries and the royal family had to seek safety in the building where the Legislative Assembly held its meetings. Despite reluctance on the part of many of the members of that Assembly, the shouts and threats of the mob persuaded them to suspend the king, abrogate the constitution, and summon a new National Convention to draw up a better, more workable instrument of government.

The rising of August, 1792, brought more radical ideas and leaders to the fore. Under their pressure the Legislative Assembly abolished all payments to prerevolutionary landlords, giving peasants and other purchasers of land full legal possession. Another manifestation of the new radicalism was secularization of marriage, and legalization of divorce. These were among the most important and enduring changes wrought by the revolution; altering fundamental patterns of land ownership and family legal relationships.

The failure of the constitution of 1791 under the pressure of foreign war, popular excitement and the king's betrayal marks the end of the first phase of the French Revolution. It is worth remark, however, that most of the permanent work of the revolution was accomplished during the two and a half years when the National Assembly held its sessions. Nearly all the inherited institutions of the Old Regime had been overthrown, never to be restored; and the liberal, nationalistic and democratic ideas which were to guide subsequent political innovation had been clearly expressed, even though the particular institutions established by the constitution of 1791 were ephemeral. The later, more radical, phases of the revolution were in a sense a mere episode. When reaction came in 1794 nothing remained of the Republic of Virtue of which Robespierre had dreamed; but the achievements and principles of the first phase of the revolution were neither undone nor abandoned.

c) Girondin Control and Factional Struggle, 10 August, 1792—2 June, 1793. Between August 10, 1792, when the king was suspended from office, and September 21, when the National Convention assembled for the first time, it seemed that the revolution was about to be overthrown. The Austrian and Prussian armies continued to advance, and within France royalists and reactionaries hoped and worked for a return to the old régime. But the energy of Danton in Paris, and the measures which the Legislative Assembly had taken to call all patriots to arms, staved off disaster for the revolutionary cause. Early in September, Paris crowds attacked the prisons where persons suspected of sympathizing with the old régime had been incarcerated, and massacred many hundreds of them. This act of terrorism was matched by strenuous steps to reform and equip the army. As a result, on the day before the Convention assembled, the French repulsed a Prussian army at Valmy; and from that time onward the revolutionary armies were by degrees able to shift to the offensive.

Theoretically, the Convention was elected by universal manhood suffrage although only a small proportion of the eligible voters took part in the election. When it met, the lines of the political spectrum had shifted definitely to the left. The Girondins, who had been the radicals of the Legislative assembly, were the conservatives of the Convention. Jean Pierre Brissot (1754–93) became their most prominent leader. The mathematician and philosopher Marie Jean Antoine, Marquis de Condorcet (1743–94) and General Charles François Dumouriez (1739–1832) were also associated with the Girondins. On the radical extreme of the Convention were the Jacobins, fewer than the Girondins, but led by fanatical and capable men such as Robespierre, Lazare Carnot (1753–1823) and Louis de Saint-Just (1767–94). Danton occupied a curious position, closely associated with the Jacobins and like them dependent on the support of the Paris crowds, but unwilling to embark upon an all-out attack on the Girondins. His efforts to soothe party strife proved unavailing, despite the fact that an absolute majority of the Convention belonged to neither of the extremes, but shifted its vote from one to the other as circumstances dictated.

The issues between Girondins and Jacobins were not always clear. Personal rivalries entered powerfully into play; and trumped up charges were leveled by both groups against their opponents. One palpable difference lay in the fact that the Girondins depended on the support of the provinces while the Jacobins drew support directly from the populace of Paris. In general the Girondins were a bit more conservative, distrusted the proletariat, and aspired to establish a republic in which men like themselves, drawn from the professional and mercantile classes, would govern France. The Jacobins on the other hand had full confidence in the virtues and capacities of the ordinary man in the Paris street, and dreamed of a thoroughly democratic republic.

The first problem which faced the Convention was what to do with the king. At the very first meeting (September 21) the deputies voted to abolish royalty, and a few days later they declared France a republic. The king was brought to trial before the Convention on the charge of treason. Evidence was easy to discover, and King Louis was therefore quickly condemned and executed for treasonous correspondence with the enemy.

Meanwhile French armies under General Dumouriez had invaded the Austrian Netherlands (Belgium). Other armies had conquered Savoy and some of the principalities of the Rhineland. Wherever French arms were successful, revolutionary régimes were set up, often with the support of a considerable number of the local inhabitants. These successes encouraged the Convention to promulgate a decree offering "fraternity and aid to all peoples who shall wish to recover their liberties" and another which promised to treat as an enemy everyone who wished to "maintain, recall, or treat with a prince and the privileged classes." (November and December, 1792.) These propaganda decrees constituted a gage of battle thrown in the face of all the monarchs of Europe. The execution of Louis XVI in January, 1793, added fresh provocation, and nearly every European government became convinced that some strange madness had come to France which would have to be cured by force.

Consequently, at the beginning of 1793 a coalition of Austria, Prussia, Great Britain, Holland, Spain and Sardinia was formed to combat the French revolutionaries. The allied armies were able to reoccupy Belgium and once again invaded France. Simultaneously serious revolt broke out in the Vendée, where Catholic peasants resisted the efforts of the Republic to draft them for military service, and formed a number of irregular bands which for several years waged a persistent guerrilla war and threatened the internal security of the Republic.

These reverses fanned the bitterness of the quarrel between Girondins and Jacobins. Each accused the other of secretly working to restore monarchy. When the Girondin general, Dumouriez, deserted to the enemy in April, 1793, the Jacobins accused all the Girondins of being equally untrustworthy. The Girondins replied that the Jacobins, through their extreme policies and the agitation which they organized among the people of Paris, were undermining the strength of the Republic from within and exacerbating the hostility of foreign enemies.

Party strife did not entirely prevent the Convention from making headway on what was theoretically its main task: the drafting of a new constitution for France. But in addition to planning a future constitution, the Convention took a number of important steps to meet the crisis which was threatening the Republic. A levy of 300,000 soldiers was decreed in March and deputies from the Convention were sent out "on mission" to see that the levy was carried through. Their powers were later extended to cover most aspects of local administration. Roving deputies on mission from the Convention became in the ensuing months one of the principal means by which the policies of the Convention were enforced in the provinces. A special Revolutionary Tribunal was also set up to try persons accused of treason; and in April, 1793, a Committee of Public Safety was created to control the day to day administration of government. Finally, in May a maximum price law was passed (despite the opposition of the Girondins) in an effort to halt the ever-rising cost of living.

The net effect of these measures was to establish the machinery for a strongly centralized government; but as long as the Girondins remained predominant in the Convention and were able to place their sympathizers in most of the key positions, a moderate, and in the eyes of the Jacobins, a half-hearted policy was pursued. Bitterness between the two parties steadily mounted. The Jacobins fell back upon their power over the Paris mob, and used it to cow the Convention, since packed galleries could shout down speakers they disliked and cheer their champions to the skies. The sessions of the Convention consequently became more and more disorderly, and some of the Girondins proposed transferring their meeting place to some other spot where they would be immune from the pressure of Paris.

The struggle culminated at the beginning of June, 1793, when the Paris crowds, after presenting petitions for the exclusion of a number of Girondin leaders from the Convention (on the ground that they were obstructing patriotic measures), besieged the Convention until its members agreed to grant the crowd's demand. Accordingly the Girondin leaders were expelled, and the Jacobins inherited leadership of the Convention.

During their tenure of power, the Girondins had been able to accomplish little. Perhaps their most significant contribution to the revolution was the note of military missionary enterprise which they injected into revolutionary policy. As long as their general, Dumouriez, was successful in Belgium, the Girondins remained stout advocates of stability at home and revolutionary war abroad. It was a formula which was to play a big role in the later stages of the revolution, and might be taken as the epitome of Napoleon Bonaparte's early policy. But in 1793, when the French armies were in retreat and insurrection in the rear was growing day by day, the Girondin policy was not enough. Heroic and violent measures were required to safeguard the Republic, and only the Jacobins were ruthless and radical enough to carry them through.

d) The Jacobin Supremacy, June 2, 1793—July 28, 1794. For a few weeks after the Girondin leaders had been expelled from the Convention, the Jacobin power over that body was not entirely secure. Some Girondin deputies had fled to their native districts and tried to stir up revolt against the Convention; and it was partly to meet this danger that the Jacobins hastily completed a constitution and promulgated it in 1793. The assassination of Marat in July by Charlotte Corday, a young girl who was vaguely associated with the Girondins, helped, ironically, to make the Jacobin position secure, for such a deed seemed to justify the strong measures which had been taken against their Girondin enemies. In the succeeding weeks the personnel of the Committee of Public Safety and of the Revolutionary Tribunal was changed, and Jacobin leaders assumed control over these bodies. Systematic terror against the enemies of the Republic was instituted; the Constitution of 1793, after having been accepted by a plebiscite, was suspended until the conclusion of peace; universal military conscription was decreed; and a sweeping mobilization of the economic resources of the nation was organized in order to supply the newly mobilized soldiers. More comprehensive price maximums were set; a capital levy bolstered government finance; a law of suspects entrusted summary powers to revolutionary courts; deputies on mission were required to report regularly to the Committee of Public Safety and were given almost unlimited powers to deal with local obstacles to revolutionary action; and a centralized police force, directed by a Committee of General Security, was organized.

The effect of these and other measures was to vivify a strong centralized administration. The threads of power centered in the hands of the Committee of Public Safety, and Robespierre was preeminent among its members. Something close to total mobilization for war and for the revolution was accomplished; and despite the manifold confusion of the time, and the rise of new factions among the members of the Convention, French armies were once more able to turn the tide and drive back the Austrian, Prussian, Spanish, and British invaders, all of whom had found lodgement on the soil of France in the hectic days of 1793. By July, 1794, French armies were once more on the Rhine; Belgium and the left bank had been conquered, and the coalition of European powers was in full retreat. Young and brilliant generals, systematized supply, numerical superiority on the battlefields, and an enthusiastic revolutionary spirit all contributed to these amazing successes.

But the removal of pressing foreign danger unleashed fresh factional quarrels among the revolutionaries. In October, 1793, Brissot and some other leading Girondins were executed. The remnants of the Girondin party sought safety by hiding from the Jacobin police. This was, however, only the beginning of the bloodletting. By the end of 1793 the Jacobins who controlled the Convention found themselves in a position very like that which faced the Girondins when the Convention opened. A new radical wing had formed among the populace of Paris—the Enragés, led by Jacques Roux—which criticized the Jacobins for not being truly revolutionary. The major issue was an economic one. Leaders of the Enragés demanded more sacrifices from the rich, and, in particular, more stringent laws against profiteering and hoarding. But unlike the Girondins, the Jacobin leaders were now in command of a powerful machine for suppressing dissent, and were willing to use it. As a result, in January, 1794, the leaders of the Enragés were arrested and executed.

This did not, however, end criticism from the left. A new group, centering around the figure of Jacques Hébert, a journalist who had won great influence in the Paris Commune, took up the cry against the rich. Hébert and his followers further distinguished themselves by converting many of the churches of Paris into Temples of Reason. At the same time, opposition gathered on the right. Danton and others began to agitate for a relaxation of the Terror, which instead of waning as the foreign danger receded was actually stepped up.

The number of persons executed by the Jacobins is difficult to estimate, and was greatly exaggerated at the time by horrified enemies of the Revolution. The total seems to have been about 5,000 in Paris and other thousands in the provinces. Many distinguished persons were killed, including Marie Antoinette, the former Queen, Condorcet, the mathematician and philosopher, Lavoisier, the chemist, and others. Many were executed on very flimsy evidence. Possession of soft hands or of fine clothes was sometimes enough to prove a man's aristocratic leanings—one consequence of which was a change in the style of men's clothing from the knee breeches of the eighteenth century to the long trousers of the "sans-culottes." The Jacobin leaders did not pretend that all the executed were guilty, but argued that occasional miscarriages of justice were unavoidable and that summary trials and severe punishments were necessary in order to safeguard the revolution from its many enemies both at home and abroad.

With the fading of foreign danger, the major justification for the Terror was removed. But the Jacobins were not willing to give up the power which the Revolutionary Tribunal concentrated in their hands, as Danton seemed to wish; nor were they willing to allow Hébert and his followers to criticize them as half-hearted revolutionaries. Consequently first Hébert (March, 1794) and then Danton (April, 1794) were arrested, condemned and executed. The Committee of Public Safety, with Robespierre as its spokesman and most prominent figure, appeared to be supreme.

Robespierre used his influence to try to establish a Republic of Virtue in which sound institutions, sound education and sound religion would create unparalleled human happiness. He devoted part of his attention to the establishment of a new cult of the Supreme Being, and drove Hébert's cult of Reason from the churches of Paris. But Robespierre felt that before Virtue could reign supreme, it was necessary to detect insincere patriots who mouthed the words but did not share in the reality of republican virtue. Such a program frightened many members of the Convention who were not sure that they would measure up to the standards of Virtue which Robespierre prescribed.

Robespierre also toyed with ideas of further economic reform. He was troubled by what he regarded as the lack of patriotism and virtue among the rich, and considered (at least in some moods) the possibility of extending equality from the political to the economic sphere. Even though Robespierre does not appear ever to have definitively made up his mind on this question, the fact that he was considering reapportionment of property was known. Most members of the Convention feared any such extension of revolutionary principles.

Thus when Robespierre was at the very apex of his power, he succeeded in alienating many of the deputies. When a dispute developed among the members of the Committee of Public Safety, dividing that powerful body into two hostile factions, the latent fear and distrust of Robespierre suddenly boiled to the surface. At a tumultuous meeting of the Convention he was impeached on July 27 (or, by the revolutionary calendar which had been instituted in 1792, on 9 Thermidor—hence the Thermidorian reaction), and was imprisoned pending trial. His faithful supporters among the leaders of the Paris Commune released him from prison during the night; but before they had time to summon the populace of Paris to the rescue, a small force acting in the name of the Convention broke into the City Hall, arrested Robespierre a second time, and executed him a few hours later.

Robespierre's overthrow had been engineered by a coalition between members of the Committee of Public Safety, who wished to continue the Terror and maintain their power, and members of the Convention, who feared that Robespierre's plans might endanger their own existence or property. There was no immediate or clear intention of altering the organization of the government; but in fact the fall of the man who had become a symbol of the Terror and of the whole Jacobin policy brought on a reaction. Within a few months the Jacobins' power over the Convention disintegrated; the surviving Girondin members were readmitted, and the extraordinary concentration of power in the hands of the Committee of Public Safety was brought to an end. Thus Robespierre's execution marks a decisive turning point. Instead of passing to ever more radical phases, the revolutionary tide began to recede.

During this third period of the Revolution two rather contrary efforts were simultaneously put forth: on the one hand the successful military mobilization of the full resources of France; on the other, Robespierre's unsuccessful effort to inaugurate a reign of virtue. The centralization of provincial government and the military mobilization remained in force after the reaction set in and constituted permanent consequences of the Jacobin rule. On the other hand everything that justified the Terror and the centralization of power in the eyes of a man like Robespierre was abandoned after Thermidor. Revolutionary idealism waned, and men generally ceased to aspire to a perfect society. Instead supporters of the revolution were more concerned with keeping the advantages which they had already secured.

Although the Republic of Virtue was not realized, several important steps were taken by the Jacobins to consolidate and stabilize the new order of society. The metric system of weights and measures proved a vast improvement on previous irrational confusion; and plans for a systematic code of law and for a national public school system presaged the later accomplishments of Napoleon. But perhaps the most significant consequence of the Jacobin rule was the enhancement of national patriotism which came as a result of the systematic and incessant propaganda which

Jacobin agents organized everywhere in France. The common people were told that the government was theirs, and that they were sovereign; revolutionary principles and French nationalism tended to be confused, and annexation of neighboring regions was soon felt to be a logical consequence of revolutionizing them. Thus the French frontiers were extended to the Rhine following the military successes of 1794, and the dream of Louis XIV seemed to have been fulfilled. By degrees revolutionary ardor and enthusiasm (which had been distinctly internationalist at first) was converted into something very like the same old French drive for "natural" frontiers. To other nations, the spirit of the revolution seemed to differ from the ambitions of earlier French kings only in being more formidable.

e) Reaction and Consolidation, 1794–1815. The men who overthrew Robespierre in 1794 had no idea of abandoning the revolution, and most Frenchmen agreed with them. But they did feel, generally, that the revolution had gone far enough within France, and were prepared to abandon the plans and proposals for yet further innovation which Robespierre and other Jacobins had been nourishing. In particular, the majority of the Convention was tired of being coerced by the Paris mob; and when in 1795 the Parisians rose (under the influence this time of royalist propagandists) in order to demonstrate against some recent decisions of the Convention, a young artillery officer, Napoleon Bonaparte (1769–1821) was called upon to protect the legislators. He did so most effectively by firing a "whiff of grapeshot" into the advancing crowd. From that time onward the Paris populace ceased to play a leading role in political affairs, and the middle class majority of the Convention felt free to draw up a constitution, which, like that of 1791, guaranteed political preponderance to men of property by means of a restricted franchise. This constitution, completed in 1795, placed the executive power in the hands of five Directors. The Directory governed France until 1799.

But abroad, the policy of the government after Thermidor was as revolutionary as it was conservative at home. The French armies, organized in the white heat of revolution, continued to win victory after victory. In 1795 Spain and Prussia withdrew from the war. Holland became a republic under French protection. In 1797, after a brilliant campaign in Italy, Napoleon Bonaparte compelled the Austrians to make peace, and only Great Britain remained at war with the victorious French. The next year Napoleon persuaded the Directory to equip an army and send it to Egypt under his command. The expedition was successful at first, despite precarious communications with the homeland. Napoleon's victories in Egypt soon came to stand out in high relief against a series of failures which beset the Directory at home.

In 1798 a new coalition (the Second) was formed by Britain, Austria and

Russia. In the following year the armies of the coalition were able to defeat the French in Italy and Switzerland and once more threatened the borders of France itself. At home the government of the Directory was discredited by unblushing corruption and by the fact that public order had not been very successfully maintained. Royalist and reactionary plots were rife; and on the extreme left a conspiracy formed under the leadership of François Babeuf (1760–97). Babeuf advocated public ownership of all land in order to establish economic as well as political equality. The conspiracy came to nothing and Babeuf was arrested and executed; but his ideas became one of the sources for the later development of socialism.

Failure in war and the threat of disturbances at home seemed to indicate that the Republic was in need of a stronger and more resolute rule. Napoleon saw this as his opportunity. When news of French reverses in Italy reached him, he hastily left Egypt and within a month of his arrival in France organized a *coup d'état* (1799). Napoleon first established himself as supreme military commander and First Consul of the Republic, and then drew up a new Constitution (the Consulate) and submitted it to ratification by plebiscite. The theory of popular sovereignty was retained in the phrases of the new constitution, but the reality of power rested in Napoleon's hands. He not only commanded the armies, conducted administration at home and diplomacy abroad, but also proposed all laws, which were then accepted or rejected by an intricately designed set of legislative chambers.

Napoleon speedily justified the faith which the French people had shown in him when they overwhelmingly ratified the new system of government. Once again he invaded Italy and defeated the Austrian armies. Russia had already withdrawn from the war; Austria made peace in 1801 and Great Britain followed suit in the next year (Treaty of Amiens). For the first time since 1792 France was everywhere at peace and everywhere victorious.

Napoleon's brilliant successes were due in part to his personal qualities. He was a great general, who knew how to choose efficient officers and how to win the devotion of his soldiers. He built on the military tradition of the French revolutionary armies, and developed further the tactics which had been evolved by others before him. The chief technical innovation Napoleon made in warfare was his greater use of field artillery. Lighter field guns, which could keep pace with marching infantry, instead of bogging down several miles behind the lines of battle, could usually be brought into play even before the infantry engaged. Until his opponents imitated French guns, and began to employ them in similar numbers, Napoleon's armies had a decisive advantage, quite apart from the additional edge in numbers and enthusiasm which general conscription and revolutionary feeling secured for the French.

As a young artillery officer, Napoleon had sympathized with the Jacobins, and when he became the ruler of France he claimed to be a true son of the revolution. Formal deference was paid to popular sovereignty even when Napoleon assumed the title of Emperor, and all his changes of the constitution were submitted to plebiscite for ratification. But Napoleon was more interested in order than in liberty, and almost from the start his rule was despotic.

In one respect Napoleon broke with the revolutionary tradition. The religious policy of the successive revolutionary bodies had resulted in a deep division of France between Catholics and revolutionists. Napoleon sought to heal this fissure in French society by entering into negotiations with the pope. In 1801 he reached an agreement (Concordat) which governed the relation between the French government and the papacy until 1905. By the Concordat of 1801 the pope recognized the loss of Church property in France and admitted Napoleon's right to nominate bishops, whom the pope then installed in office. Salaries were to be paid by the state. Catholicism was recognized as the religion of "the majority of Frenchmen," but was not accorded any legal monopoly. Actually Napoleon subsidized other religious groups from state funds.

In most other respects, Napoleon retained and systematized the work of the revolution. A code of law, which the Convention had begun to draw up, was brought to completion—the Code Napoleon. In its provisions the enduring changes wrought by the revolution were spelled out in detail, and a logical, relatively simple system of law was brought into operation in all parts of France, and in all regions which French armies conquered as well. A national public school system was established, and all educational institutions were brought under the supervision of a central administrative body called the University of France. Numerous public works were constructed, and a vigorous administration checked graft and speculation among public officials and maintained the solvency of the government. Control of currency and financial policy was vested in the Bank of France, organized in 1800.

Local government was strictly centralized. The departments were placed under prefects whom Napoleon appointed; and all towns of over 5000 inhabitants were headed by mayors appointed in the same way. A central police force was created to keep order in all the large towns and keep tabs on real and suspected political enemies of the régime. A rigorous censorship of newspapers prevented opposition from achieving any public expression.

A few royalists and a fringe of Jacobins remained dissatisfied, but Napoleon succeeded in winning the support of the great majority of the French population. The First Consul had brought peace, order and glory; and if revolutionary liberty had been curtailed, the equality of all classes before the law and the fraternity of patriotism had been retained and consolidated. In 1802 a grateful nation conferred the Consulship on Napoleon for life; two years later, after still more splendid victories, he was crowned Emperor of the French.

In 1803, scarcely more than a year after peace had been signed, Great Britain declared war again. The immediate issue was the British refusal to surrender Malta (as they were bound to do by the treaty of Amiens). The underlying and more important causes for the renewal of hostilities, however, were British suspicion of Napoleon's effort to restore a French empire in Louisiana and Haiti, and the activities of the French government in Holland, Italy and Switzerland, where Napoleon was setting up puppet states. For several months after the renewal of war, Napoleon busied himself with preparations for an invasion of England; but when British subsidies and diplomacy raised a Third Coalition against the French (Austria, Russia, Sweden and, later, Prussia) he diverted his armies to meet his continental foes. In a series of brilliant victories (Ulm, Austerlitz, Jena, Friedland) Napoleon defeated all his land enemies. By 1806 he was supreme on the continent. He used his power to reduce Austria and Prussia to the level of second-rate powers by taking from them large slices of territory. With the Russians he came to an agreement (Tilsit) by which Europe was in effect divided between Czar Alexander I (1801–25) and the Emperor of the French.

On the sea, however, the British won a decisive victory at Trafalgar (1805), and Napoleon thenceforth abandoned his hope of challenging British naval supremacy or of invading England. Instead he resorted to an economic blockade (the Continental System), hoping to bring the "nation of shopkeepers" to terms by ruining British trade.

Between 1806 and 1812 Napoleon used his power to reorganize the state system of Europe. The borders of France were enlarged and at their greatest extent included Holland and the North Sea coast of Germany at one extreme and the Illyrian Provinces (along the east coast of the Adriatic Sea) at the other. Moreover he ringed France round with satellite states. Italy was completely under French control. Some territories (including Rome itself) were annexed to France; the rest of the peninsula was divided between a kingdom of Italy of which Napoleon made himself king, and a kingdom of Naples, entrusted to one of his relatives. Napoleon tried to reduce Spain to similar dependency after 1808, but was not successful for long.

Napoleon's most lasting territorial changes were made in Germany. With the cooperation of some of the larger German states, Napoleon suppressed several hundred of the small principalities, free cities and ecclesiastical states into which Germany had been divided for centuries. He also united the German states adjacent to France into a Confederation of the

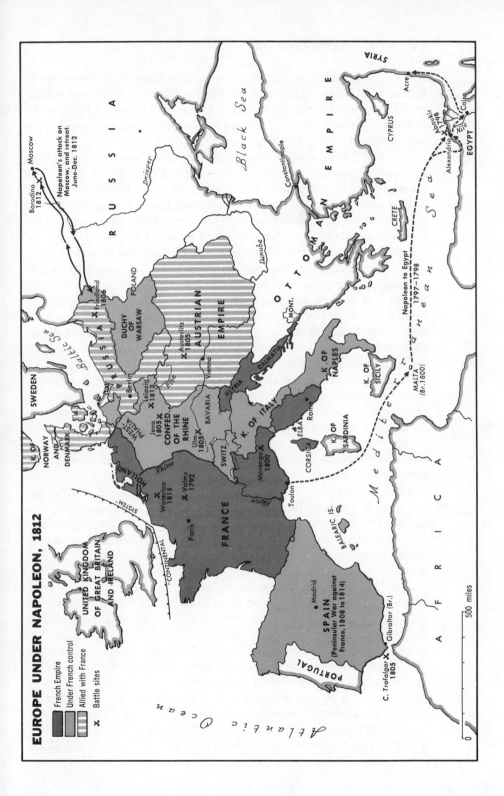

EUROPE UNDER NAPOLEON, 1812

French Empire

Under French control

Allied with France

x   Battle sites

SWEDEN

NORWAY AND DENMARK

K. OF SWEDEN

UNITED KINGDOM OF GREAT BRITAIN AND IRELAND

Baltic Sea

PRUSSIA   x Friedland 1806

DUCHY OF WARSAW

POLAND

RUSSIA

Napoleon's attack on Moscow, and retreat. June–Dec. 1812

Borodino 1812   Moscow

Dnieper

Black Sea

Constantinople

OTTOMAN EMPIRE

SYRIA   Acre

Cairo

Aboukir 1798

Nile

Alexandria

EGYPT

CYPRUS

CRETE

Napoleon to Egypt 1797–1798

MALTA (Br. 1800)

Mediterranean Sea

AUSTRIAN EMPIRE

x Austerlitz 1805

Vienna

Danube

Berlin

Leipzig x 1813

Jena 1805 x

WEST. PHALIA

CONFED. OF THE RHINE

Elbe

BAVARIA

Ulm 1805 x

SWITZ.

ILLYRIA

DALMATIA

MONT.

K. OF NAPLES

K. OF SICILY

K. OF ITALY

Rome

ELBA

CORSICA

K. OF SARDINIA

Marengo x 1800

HOLLAND

Rhine

x Waterloo 1815

x Valmy 1792

Paris

FRANCE

Rhône

Toulon

BALEARIC IS.

SPAIN (Peninsular War against France, 1808 to 1814)

Madrid

PORTUGAL

C. Trafalgar x 1805

Gibraltar (Br.)

"CONTINENTAL SYSTEM"

AFRICA

Atlantic Ocean

500 miles

Rhine, and in north central Germany created a new kingdom of West-phalia, ruled by one of his brothers. Finally, territory taken from Prussia and Austria was formed into a Grand Duchy of Warsaw—a rump of the former kingdom of Poland which had been wiped from the map during the last quarter of the eighteenth century.

French influence in all of these dependent areas was very strong. Re-forms of government and society were carried through on the French model, roads and other public works were built, and a familiarity with the leading ideas of the French revolution was acquired by many segments of the population. In Germany and Italy the new order was not unpopular at first, and it was only after Napoleon had suffered military defeat that he lost the support of the new states which he had established in those regions.

But French reform and example were two-edged weapons. Further east in Europe, statesmen were impelled to imitate many things which the French had done in order to make themselves strong to resist further French agression. Prussia and Austria, smarting under defeat, began an extensive reorganization of their governments and military establishments, supplementing long service professional troops with conscript armies like the French. Great Britain, too, despite economic difficulties caused by Napoleon's blockade, remained supreme on the sea, and fanned every spark of discontent. In Russia, the admiration which Czar Alexander had conceived for Napoleon when first they met in 1806 gradually cooled. Alexander found that Napoleon was not willing to give him a free hand to conquer the decaying Ottoman Empire; and he also discovered that the blockade of British goods, to which he had reluctantly agreed, seriously hurt the Russian economy.

All these factors worked to undermine the supremacy which Napoleon had won. But perhaps the most significant element in his eventual down-fall was the stimulus to nationalism which the French example provided for all the peoples of Europe. Germans and Italians began to feel that if France could be strong, united and powerful their countries could and should be so too; and the presence of French troops, who lived off the country, helped to stimulate a detestation of the foreign conquerors not only among the ruling classes (who had hated and feared the French from the first) but among the common people as well. Thus the resistance to Napoleon gradually transformed itself from an effort of governments to an effort of whole peoples united behind their governments. In such wars the French revolutionary élan was countered, and eventually surpassed by the patriotic enthusiasm of their opponents.

It was above all else in Spain and in Prussia that the new sense of nationalism weakened Napoleon's position. In 1808 Napoleon persuaded the Spanish king to abdicate and turn over his throne to one of Napoleon's brothers. This transaction stirred the Spanish people to revolt, and a long and bitter guerrilla war ensued (the Peninsular War, 1808–14). A British expeditionary force under Sir Arthur Wellesley (later Duke of Wellington) came to the aid of the rebels, and the British and Spaniards between them were able to keep up a running battle against the French occupation troops until Napoleon's final downfall.

Something close to revolution, conducted from the top, came to Prussia between 1807 and 1813. Serfdom was abolished and many of the liberal principles of the French revolution were written into law. Most important of all, a new army was carefully and painstakingly trained; and a spirit not only of Prussian but of German nationalism was cultivated.

In Austria efforts at reform were hampered by the fact that in the polyglot empire of the Hapsburgs nationalism could not be a consolidating force. Consequently reform was generally limited to military matters. In 1809 the Austrians completed a reorganization of their army, and once again took the field against Napoleon. In two hard fought battles the Austrians inflicted great losses on the French, but in the end were compelled once more to make peace and surrender still more territory. In 1810 the proud Hapsburgs even agreed to sanction the marriage of the emperor's daughter to the upstart ruler of France.

It was not until 1812 that military defeat caught up with Napoleon. In that year he invaded Russia in order to punish the Czar for having lifted the blockade against British goods. The march to Moscow and Napoleon's dismal retreat in the dead of winter are too well known to require description. Napoleon's defeat in Russia stirred Prussia to attack; a fever of national patriotism swept Germany and other German states soon followed the example set by the Prussians. A new coalition arose, this time including Russia, Prussia, Great Britain and Austria. After many battles, of which the "Battle of the Nations" near Leipzig was the greatest, Napoleon was driven back inside France and compelled to abdicate (April, 1814).

The victorious coalition restored the brother of Louis XVI as king of France. (He took the title Louis XVIII since royalists considered Louis XVI's son to be Louis XVII even though he had never reigned.) A diplomatic congress was assembled at Vienna to settle the future of Europe. Negotiation at the Congress did not proceed smoothly. The great powers seemed near to splitting up over the question of what to do about Poland and Saxony. This situation, and widespread dissatisfaction in France, persuaded Napoleon to leave the island of Elba (where the powers had given him a miniature state to govern) and land once more in France. Napoleon did indeed rally the French nation behind him; but he had miscalculated the reaction of the European powers. They promptly buried their differences and took the field together against the renewed danger. In June 1815, Napoleon marched to meet an allied army under the Duke of

Wellington. Battle was joined near the village of Waterloo in Belgium, and after a hard day's fight the French army was routed. Four days later Napoleon abdicated for the second time. He surrendered himself to the commander of a British warship, and, without setting foot on dry land, was transported to the desolate island of St. Helena in the South Atlantic. There he died in 1821.

Napoleon's overthrow did not mean the obliteration of his work. The restored Bourbon dynasty did not even try to reestablish the institutions of the Old Régime; and in other parts of Europe too it was found impossible to set things back as they had been before French armies and French ideas had penetrated the length and breadth of the continent.

Only in Great Britain and in Russia had French influence failed to operate powerfully. A stout conservatism seized upon British ruling circles almost from the beginning of the French revolution, and as the long war dragged on, British patriotism became identified with resistance to innovoation and acceptance of established institutions. The control of the landed aristocracy and of the wealthy commercial classes over the government was thus confirmed; and what sporadic discontent existed among workmen and farmers was easily kept down. The Napoleonic wars had another important consequence for Great Britain. The needs of the navy and army provided an extraordinary market for the products of British workshops; and war-induced inflation brought high profits to industrialists. Thus industrialization proceeded, as it were, under forced draft; and while continental nations were suffering the devastation of war, Great Britain advanced in wealth and productivity until British industry and commerce far excelled that of any other European country.

Russia experienced only faintly the shock of revolutionary ideas. The war of 1812 certainly helped to create a stronger national feeling, but the majority of the population was too uneducated to be susceptible to other aspects of the French revolutionary program. Yet among a few army officers, and in Poland (which was largely annexed to Russia by the peace settlement) the ideas of the French revolution did find receptive ground. The Russian revolutionary tradition of the nineteenth century took its origin from these groups.

2) Revolution vs. Reaction, 1815-1871. After Napoleon's downfall the rulers of every European country were anxious to safeguard things as they were and above all wished to prevent any recurrence of the revolutionary disturbances which had kept Europe in turmoil for twenty-five years. But there were many persons, especially among the middle classes, who admired the revolution and hoped to be able to establish the revolutionary principles of liberty, equality and fraternity firmly in all Europe. The years between 1815 and 1871 saw an almost incessant struggle between

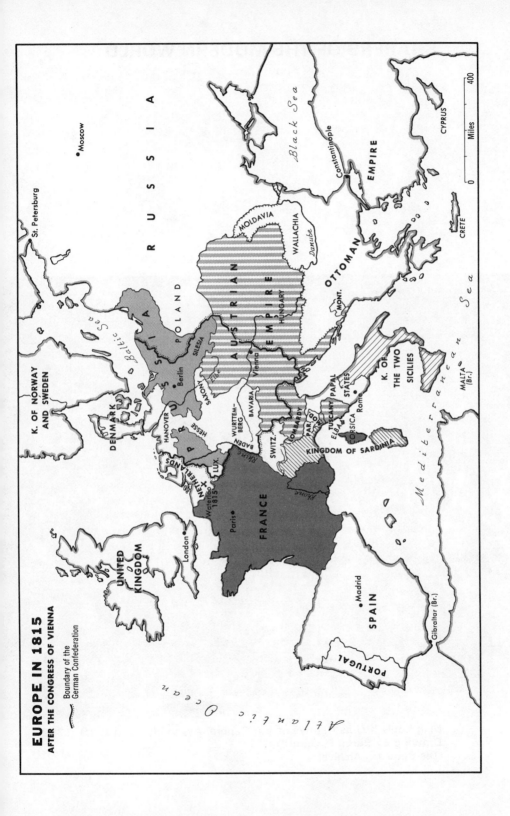

EUROPE IN 1815
AFTER THE CONGRESS OF VIENNA

····· Boundary of the
German Confederation

Atlantic Ocean

UNITED
KINGDOM

London●

K. OF NORWAY
AND SWEDEN

St. Petersburg●

R U S S I A

Moscow●

DENMARK

Baltic Sea

P R U S S I A

POLAND

Berlin●

SILESIA

SAXONY

HANOVER

HESSE

WÜRTTEM-
BERG

BADEN

BAVARIA

NETHERLANDS

LUX.

Waterloo
1815

Paris●

FRANCE

SWITZ.

Rhine

Rhone

AUSTRIAN

EMPIRE

Vienna●

HUNGARY

MOLDAVIA

WALLACHIA

Danube

MONT.

OTTOMAN

EMPIRE

Constantinople●

Black Sea

LOMBARDY

PARMA

MODENA

TUSCANY

PAPAL
STATES

Rome●

ELBA

CORSICA

KINGDOM OF SARDINIA

K. OF
THE TWO
SICILIES

Mediterranean Sea

CRETE

CYPRUS

MALTA
(Br.)

SPAIN

Madrid●

PORTUGAL

Gibraltar (Br.)●

0   400

Miles

SHAPERS OF THE MODERN WORLD

King Louis XVI as Captive of the General Assembly, August 10, 1792
Drawing by Baron F. Gerard
(The Bettmann Archive)

Napoleon I
(The Bettmann Archive)

Robespierre
Anonymous Painting
(The Bettmann Archive)

these two groups; but as the years passed conservatives yielded ground, and their opponents split into fairly distinct segments: nationalists, bourgeois liberals, and socialists.

The Congress of Vienna, which had been interrupted by Napoleon's return from Elba, resumed its sessions after his final defeat, and proceeded to redraw the map of Europe. The twin principles of restoration and legitimacy guided and assembled statesmen of Europe in reestablishing old dynasties and boundaries. France was given generous terms, partly to make the restoration of the Bourbons more palatable to the French public, and partly as a result of the skillful diplomacy of Charles Maurice Talleyrand (1754–1838). (Talleyrand, one-time bishop of Autun, had abandoned his clerical career to take a leading part in the revolution, but he changed sides in time to become the main diplomatic representative of the restored Bourbon king at the Congress of Vienna.)

But the map of Europe was not restored to its prerevolutionary shape. Some of the changes which Napoleon had made were quite agreeable to the leading powers at the Congress; in particular, the consolidation of the petty German states was allowed to stand. A new German Confederation, in which Austria took the leading place, linked the thirty-eight separate German states which were allowed to survive by means of an ineffective standing Diet. Another consideration which modified the principle of restoration was the desire of the powers to erect stronger states along the French borders in order to prevent any revival of French military aggression. Consequently, Holland was strengthened by the incorporation of Belgium; Prussia was given extensive territories in the Rhineland; and Sardinia was enlarged by the addition of Genoa. The other Italian states, except the Papal states, were put under the rule of members of the Austrian Hapsburg family—a form of compensation for the cession of Belgium, and for Austrian losses in Poland. The long and difficult dispute over the disposal of Poland and Saxony was resolved by awarding most of Poland to Russia, compensating Prussia with most of Saxony, and Austria with Italian lands. Great Britain as usual picked up overseas possessions by annexing Malta, South Africa, part of Guiana and some other lesser colonial territories.

The problem of future maintenance of peace exercised much of the attention of the assembled diplomats. On the initiative of Czar Alexander I, a Holy Alliance was concluded between the rulers of Russia, Prussia and Austria by which the respective sovereigns agreed to conduct their governments according to Christian principles and to "remain united by the bonds of a true and indissoluble fraternity" in order "on all occasions and in all places to lend each other aid and assistance." The king of Great Britain was invited to join the Holy Alliance but declined to do so on the ground that he lacked the constitutional powers to fulfill its provisions.

The impressionable Czar of Russia took the Holy Alliance seriously; but the other rulers and ministers of Europe felt that such high principles had little place in practical international politics.

On a more practical plane, therefore, the four great powers—Austria, Russia, Prussia and Great Britain—formed a Quadruple Alliance by the terms of which periodic congresses were to be called to discuss outstanding problems, to preserve peace, and to take steps to maintain the status quo should it be threatened by revolutionary disturbances in any part of Europe. Within a few years France, too, was admitted to the Concert of Europe, as this arrangement was sometimes called.

The leading spirit in creating the Concert of Europe was Prince Metternich (1773–1859), chief minister of the Austrian empire. He was able to dominate Austria, Italy and Germany between 1815 and 1848; and the period is often called the era of Metternich. His major preoccupation was to prevent any further outbursts of revolutionary disturbance. To achieve that end he tried to strengthen conservative elements everywhere, and to repress liberalism wherever it seemed to threaten the established order.

Flaws soon developed in the system which had been set up at the Congress of Vienna. Revolutions broke out in various European states against restored rulers, and the Spanish colonies of South America revolted from Spain. The British government was not willing to use force to suppress some of these movements, and as a result Great Britain gradually dissociated itself from the European concert. The Greek revolt against the Turks (1821–30) provided a particularly difficult diplomatic problem for the conservative statesmen of Europe. Liberal and religious sympathy with the Greeks, combined with the ambitions of the great powers to extend their control over the decaying realm of the Ottoman Turks, eventually led to Russian, British and French intervention on behalf of revolutionaries against their lawful rulers in 1827.

Thus the Concert of Europe had already been badly strained when revolution broke out again in France, in July, 1830. The legitimate king fled and Louis Philippe, the "citizen king," ascended the throne. News of the July revolution in Paris stirred liberals in Belgium to rise against the Dutch; and in Italy and Germany revolutionary movements manifested themselves. Further east, Poland became the scene of a rising aginst the Russians. But France under her new bourgeois government was not prepared to come to the aid of revolution elsewhere; and in central and eastern Europe the revolts were suppressed. Only in Belgium did the rising succeed. The great powers agreed to recognize the independence of the new state and found a king for the Belgians from the German princely house of Saxe-Coburg.

In the generation after 1830 industrialism began to make rapid progress on the continent. The accompanying shifts in wealth and population gave new impetus to revolutionary aspirations. The middle class and an increasing group of proletarians aspired to an active part in government. Socialist movements, aflame with the vision of a new and more egalitarian society, arose in France and elsewhere, splitting off from the main liberal revolutionary movement. A second differentiation in the revolutionary movement arose as a result of political disunity of the peoples of Germany, Italy and Poland. In these regions, many persons felt that national unification must come first and foremost, so that in some minds (though not in all) nationalist aspirations began to eclipse the liberal and egalitarian elements of the revolutionary tradition.

These growing differences were brought into relief by the events of 1848. Once more revolution broke out in France; Louis Philippe was deposed, and a republic proclaimed. The French example was echoed by revolutionary movements in Germany, Italy and Austria. In France republicans and socialists had cooperated to overthrow Louis Philippe, but once in power they quarreled, and after some months the socialists were repressed by force. A new constitution, prescribing universal manhood suffrage, was drawn up, and Louis Napoleon (1808–73), nephew of the great Napoleon, was elected president of the Second Republic.

In Germany the revolution of 1848 seemed successful at first. An assembly met at Frankfurt in order to draw up a new constitution for a united and liberal Germany; but the delegates found themselves facing insoluble difficulties. Republicans quarreled with advocates of constitutional monarchy, and the question of whether or not to include Austria (with its extensive non-German possessions) was a second stumbling block. When the Prussian king refused to accept an invitation made by the Frankfurt assembly to become emperor of all Germany, practical hope of success vanished and the revolution petered out, leaving German liberals disheartened and disillusioned.

One important result of the revolution was, however, allowed to stand. In the first days of upheaval the king of Prussia had granted his subjects a constitution which provided for the creation of a representative assembly. Its powers were ill-defined, and the monarchy retained control of the army and administration. Nevertheless, the existence of a representative body provided Prussian liberals with a forum in which to voice their opinions, and made it possible for many to hope that Prussia might in time become a genuinely constitutional monarchy. When absolutism was restored in Austria, Prussia seemed the only hope for liberals; and as national unification began to loom ever larger in their minds as a necessary prerequisite of any further reform, the hopes of bourgeois revolutionists began to turn more definitely toward Prussia, the only rival Austria need fear for primacy among the German states.

In Austria the outbreak of revolution in 1848 brought about the downfall of Metternich, but it did not in the end destroy Metternich's system. The revolutionists were hopelessly divided against one another by divergent nationalistic aspirations, so that the central Austrian government found it possible to play one national group off against the other. Serfdom was abolished; and this act had the effect of separating the peasants of the empire from the bourgeois leaders who hoped to establish some sort of liberal government. In Hungary, however, patriotic feeling united practically all the politically active groups in the nation against the Hapsburgs. Fearing that the contagion might spread to Poland, Russian troops intervened. With Russian help the Austrian emperor was able to reestablish absolutism.

Austrian recovery implied the defeat of the revolutionary movement in Italy. At first, most Italian states had rallied behind the leadership of the kingdom of Sardinia in an effort to throw off Austrian control. But there were serious differences among the insurgent Italians. The question of the future status of the Papal States was a particularly thorny problem. During the first weeks of the revolution the pope expressed sympathy for the movement; but when a Roman republic was proclaimed the pope set his face resolutely against this threat to the age-old political independence of the papacy. Consequently the issue of what to do about the Papal States became critical for those Italians who hoped to see their country united and strong.

Even before the Hapsburg government had repressed the revolution at home, Austrian armies defeated the king of Sardinia and reestablished control over all the states which had been awarded to the Hapsburgs in 1815. Despite the defeat which Sardinian armies had suffered, that kingdom emerged after 1849 as the one hope for the national unification of Italy. The king had granted a constitution, and his successor did not withdraw it after the failure of the revolution. Republican schemes for the unification of Italy had been discredited by the failures of 1848–49, so that, more and more, nationalistic Italians turned toward Sardinia in much the same fashion as Germans began to look toward Prussia. In both countries, Austria appeared as the arch-enemy of liberal and nationalistic reform.

To sum up, 1848 was doubly significant. In central Europe the revolutionary confidence in the effectiveness of popular action had been discredited. If any part of the revolutionary program were to be made a reality, it seemed necessary to find support from existing states, i.e., from Sardinia and Prussia. Such a step meant at least a temporary renunciation of the more liberal aspirations which revolutionists had previously nurtured; but many felt that national unification must come first and believed that liberal reform could wait.

Equally significant for the future was the split between socialism and liberalism which events in France had made evident. Karl Marx (1818–83) and his colleague Friedrich Engels (1820–95) published the *Communist Manifesto* in 1848 on the eve of the revolution, and thereafter devoted themselves to agitation on behalf of an international socialist revolutionary movement. It was many years before international socialism became an important political element in any European country; but from 1848 onward the latent antagonism between liberal and socialist ideals became clear and definite. The appearance of a more radical social revolutionary doctrine probably played a part in persuading the middle classes of Germany and Italy to abandon some of their liberalism and concentrate instead on striving for national unification.

The consequences of this realignment of forces in European politics were not slow to manifest themselves. Louis Napoleon, inspired by the example of his illustrious predecessor, carried through a *coup d'état* in 1851 and established a second French Empire, assuming the title of Napoleon III. As heir to the Napoleonic tradition, Louis Napoleon aspired to play a leading role in international affairs and at the same time considered himself a patron of liberalism and of good revolutionary causes. It was not long before Napoleon III found occasion to act. In 1854 a quarrel over the protection of the Holy Places in Palestine gave the Russians an excuse for war against Turkey. France, Great Britain and Sardinia came to the defense of the Turks, and sent their armies to the Crimea, where, despite considerable mismanagement, they won several victories. In 1856 Russia made a humiliating peace, agreeing to demilitarize the Black Sea coast and to give up claims to special rights in Turkey. This defeat had important consequences for internal Russian development which will be touched upon below. (See pp. 551–52.)

Napoleon III's next foreign adventure was in Italy. Since the defeat of 1848–49 the kingdom of Sardinia had undergone a far-ranging reorganization under the capable leadership of Count Camillo di Cavour (1810–61) who consciously and deliberately worked for the unification of all Italy under Sardinian leadership. Sardinia's participation in the Crimean war had been motivated by a desire to win powerful friends, and at the peace conference Cavour dramatically demanded redress of Italian grievances against Austria. Two years later, in 1858, Cavour succeeded in coming to an understanding with Napoleon III. In return for French help against the Austrians, Cavour agreed to cede Nice and Savoy to France. With this secret agreement to strengthen him, it was easy for Cavour to pick a quarrel with Austria, and when the war began Napoleon III made good his promise of intervention. In two battles the French and Italian forces defeated the Austrians, but before the peninsula had been completely liberated, Napoleon withdrew and made peace.

Austria's defeats stirred the Italians to take matters into their own hands.

Popular risings in a number of states, and a famous filibustering expedition headed by Giuseppe Garibaldi (1807–82), resulted in the unification of all the states of Italy under the king of Sardinia, except for the Papal States (where a French force protected the pope's possessions) and Venetia, where the Austrians remained entrenched. In 1866 Venetia was added to the Italian kingdom as a result of the defeat of Austria by Prussia; and in 1870 the unification of Italy was completed by the annexation of the Papal States. Until 1929 the Italian government remained at odds with the popes, who refused to recognize the loss of the territory which had been governed for so long by the successors of St. Peter. The clerical issue thus became and has remained of key importance in Italian politics.

But the most significant change in the European balance of power in the nineteenth century was the unification of Germany under the leadership of Prussia. In 1861 William I came to the Prussian throne and in the next year he appointed Otto von Bismarck (1815–98) as first minister. The king and his minister defied the efforts of the Chamber of Deputies (which had been established by the constitution of 1848) to restrict credits for the enlargement of the Prussian army; but this defiance of liberal principles was counterbalanced by more and more open support of German nationalistic aspirations.

The steps by which the unification of Germany was brought about were carefully contrived by Bismarck. In 1864 he joined with Austria to seize Schleswig and Holstein from Denmark; Bismarck then quarreled with Austria over the disposal of these provinces and in a six weeks war utterly routed the Austrian army (1866). This led to the annexation of Venetia by the new kingdom of Italy; and to renewed friction among the peoples of the Austrian empire, which was resolved only when the Austrians recognized the autonomy of Hungary in 1867. Thereafter the Hapsburg state became a double monarchy, Austria-Hungary.

But more important, the war of 1866 made Prussia supreme in Germany. All the German states except those of the south—Bavaria, Würtemberg, Baden and Hesse-Darmstadt—joined with Prussia in a new North German Confederation. The Confederation had a common legislative body—the Reichstag—representing the population directly, and an upper chamber—the Bundesrat—representing the princes of the constituent states. The king of Prussia was president of the Confederation, and controlled the federal military forces and foreign policy. Prussia's new power seemed ominous to Napoleon III, and it was not difficult for Bismarck to stir up war with France as a means of completing the unification of Germany by associating the south German states with the Confederation. Bismarck was able by some rather unscrupulous diplomacy (he published a secret telegram in an edited form that made the French feel that they had been insulted) to make Napoleon appear to be the aggressor; and as

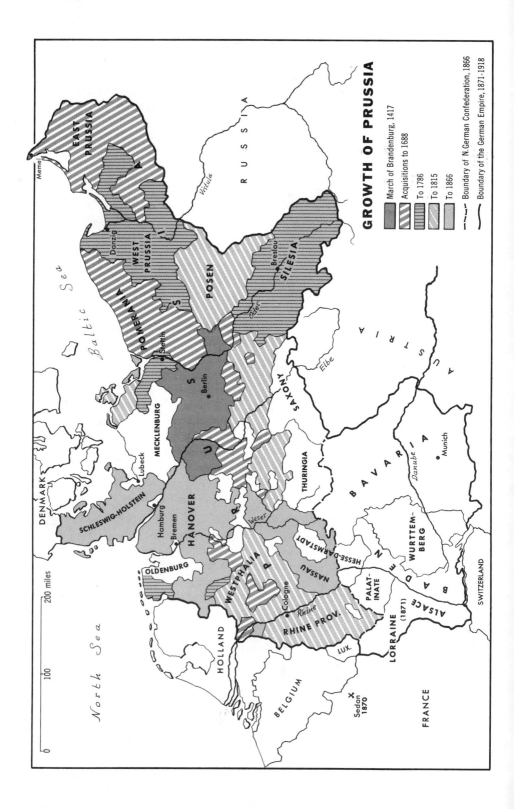

GROWTH OF PRUSSIA

March of Brandenburg, 1417
Acquisitions to 1688
To 1786
To 1815
To 1866

— — — Boundary of N. German Confederation, 1866
———— Boundary of the German Empire, 1871-1918

North Sea

Baltic Sea

Memel

DENMARK

SCHLESWIG-HOLSTEIN

Lübeck

MECKLENBURG

Danzig

WEST PRUSSIA

EAST PRUSSIA

POMERANIA

Stettin

Berlin

POSEN

RUSSIA

Vistula

Breslau

SILESIA

Oder

SAXONY

Elbe

THURINGIA

AUSTRIA

Hamburg

Bremen

HANOVER

Weser

OLDENBURG

HOLLAND

WESTPHALIA

Cologne

Rhine

HESSE-DARMSTADT

NASSAU

RHINE PROV.

LUX.

BELGIUM

PALAT-
INATE

WÜRTTEM-
BERG

BADEN

BAVARIA

Munich

Danube

SWITZERLAND

ALSACE

LORRAINE
(1871)

Sedan
1870

FRANCE

200 miles
100
0

Bismarck had calculated, the south German States joined with the troops of the North German Confederation to fight the French. War broke out in 1870. To the surprise of nearly all Europe, the German armies were easily victorious. Napoleon III and a large French army were captured at Sedan, and the Germans pressed onward to besiege Paris. The city held out against the Germans for a few months, but had to surrender in January 1871.

A few days before Paris surrendered the German princes assembled at Versailles to proclaim William of Prussia the Emperor of Germany. The southern German states adhered to the new German Empire which superseded the North German Confederation. Four months later, defeated France made peace and ceded the provinces of Alsace and Lorraine to the newly formed German state.

Thus by 1871, nationalist aspirations, together with the statecraft of Cavour and Bismarck, succeeded in reorganizing the map of central Europe. Two new nations had achieved statehood through the unification of smaller, previously existing states. Further east in Europe, nationalism had a quite contrary effect. In the regions controlled by the Austrian, Russian and Ottoman empires, national feeling worked to break up existing large states into smaller units. For the next fifty years the submerged nationalities of eastern Europe continued to struggle against foreign rule. Their efforts constituted an important disturbing element in European politics; and, indeed, the First World War originated from just such a conflict in the Balkan peninsula.

3) Internal Development of Major European Countries, 1815-1871. The internal development of the major states of western and central Europe has already been suggested sufficiently in the above discussion of international relations. Two important states, however, stood rather apart from the general development of the continent: Great Britain to the west and Russia to the east.

In Great Britain reaction against the French revolution waned slowly. The landed and commercial oligarchy which had guided Britain against Napoleon retained its control of Parliament and of the government until 1832, when a rising tide of agitation, the play of party politics, and the liberal convictions of some members of the ruling class led to a drastic reapportionment of Parliamentary seats in order to make them correspond more accurately to the distribution of population. The Whig (or as it was now coming to be called, the Liberal) party led the agitation for reform; and much of the support for the measure came from the industrialists of unrepresented new towns such as Manchester. In 1832 franchise provisions were made uniform for all the nation; and the new law had the effect of admitting the middle and professional classes to voting privileges.

In the ensuing three decades the reformed Parliament carried through a widespread transformation of English law, making the legal and governmental organization of Great Britain more rational, individualistic, and in many cases more efficient than before. Taken together, these reforms did for Britain what the revolutionary legislative bodies had done for France earlier: most of the legal privileges and antiquated peculiarities of the aristocratic régime of the eighteenth century were removed, and a more egalitarian and systematic body of law was put into operation. The effect of these reforms, which were very deeply influenced by the utilitarian philosophy of Jeremy Bentham (1748–1832) and his followers, was to give individual persons and private capital freer scope, and to make the middle class supreme in English politics.

But in the years after 1832 the workingmen of Great Britain found that they had gained little or nothing, despite the fact that many of them had pinned great hopes on the reform of Parliament. As a result, widespread agitation for a completely democratic suffrage arose. The movement, known as Chartism, took legal forms, hoping to persuade Parliament to change the suffrage by monster petitions and demonstrations. In the same years, Robert Owen headed an ambitious attempt to organize nation-wide trade unions. Both these efforts failed to gain immediate success; and after 1846 when the repeal of the Corn laws led to a significant lowering of the price of bread, working class discontent and agitation declined. Even the outbreak of revolution on the continent in 1848 failed to provoke more than faint echoes in Great Britain. By the 1850's a new burst of prosperity, promoted by rapid railway construction in Britain and in other parts of the world, helped to reduce the bitterness of political conflict. Factory regulation by the government, humanitarian legislation, and the other adjustments to industrialism which have been mentioned above (pp. 508–9) also played a part in reconciling the industrial workingmen to their lot.

The growing confidence of the British ruling classes in the loyalty of the workingmen was strikingly illustrated when in 1867 Benjamin Disraeli (1804–81), leader of the Conservative party, introduced and passed a bill in Parliament which extended the franchise to the urban workmen. This move was designed as a shrewd bid for political support for the Conservative (former Tory) party. Disraeli thought that the workingmen of the towns would vote against the party which most of their employers supported—the Liberal; and would in gratitude, if nothing else, support the party which had given them the right to vote. A few years later (1884), William Ewart Gladstone (1809–98), leader of the Liberal party, returned the compliment by enfranchising agricultural laborers, who might be expected to vote against the Conservative party to which most of their landlord employers belonged. Thus, partly as a by-play of party politics, the franchise in Great Britain was progressively extended until something near to universal manhood suffrage had been established.

In this fashion British institutions were adjusted to the democratic theories which had originated with the French revolution. Yet the political leadership of the aristocracy and the upper middle class was not overthrown. British ruling groups showed great flexibility in assimilating newcomers and in domesticating new ideas without breaking the continuity of Parliamentary institutions and government. As a result the periodic revolutions and the resort to occasional violence which characterized French politics and the political life of nearly every other continental country were avoided in Britain. By the mid-nineteenth century the old aristocratic régime had been transformed piecemeal and by legal procedures into a new liberal régime.

Russia stood at the other extreme. Czar Alexander I (1801–25) toyed with liberal and enlightened ideas when first he came to the throne, but accomplished little before a growing antipathy to Napoleon and all things French transformed him into a pillar of reaction. His brother and successor, Nicholas I (1825–55), was equally reactionary. At the time of his accession a revolt broke out (the Decembrist movement) led by some army officers who had been influenced by the liberal ideas of the French revolution. It was suppressed and its leaders executed. Another revolt in Poland, in 1830, confirmed Nicholas in his hatred of liberalism; and the Czar's government tried hard to root out all centers of disaffection by means of secret police.

The defeats which Russia suffered in the Crimean war (1854–56) shocked the Russians, who remembered their brilliant successes against Napoleon. The new Czar, Alexander II (1855–81), was convinced that Russia's defeats had been caused by a failure to keep pace with European political and social development. The government therefore embarked on a program of reform. Serfdom was abolished in 1861. New institutions of local government based on a limited representative system (zemstvos) were established three years later. Alexander projected other reforms—of education, and of the judicial system—and relaxed the severity of press censorship somewhat; but in 1863 another Polish uprising turned his sympathies away from any further efforts to transform the existing order.

The strands of Russian opinion in the nineteenth century were rather different from those common in the West. Many intellectuals associated themselves with a Slavophil movement, which rejected all imitation of European society and lauded the primitive virtues of the Russian soul and the Russian peasant. The novelist Feodor Dostoievsky (1821–81) became a prominent member of this group. On the other hand a student generation espoused nihilism—a sweeping denial of all conventional values, moral or political—and devoted itself to radical and often merely negative criticism. Between the extreme of glorification of all things

Russian and the other extreme of nihilism, were groups which in various ways reflected the influence of European ideas—although European ideas nearly always suffered a change in the Russian climate of opinion, because so many of the presuppositions of European social and political thought could not be transferred to the Russian scene where a different history had produced different institutions, habits and sensibilities.

Individuals who wanted to make Russia over according to the liberal patterns of European states were called "westernizers"; but very few Russians were "westernizers" consistently throughout their lives. Alexander Herzen (1812-70), for example, in early life was an enthusiastic liberal and ardent admirer of France; but in middle life, when he visited France and England as an exile from Russia, he became disillusioned with western ways, and developed a peculiar personal compound of anarchism and Slavophilism. Despite his hatred of the Czarist government, he enthusiastically welcomed Alexander II's liberation of the serfs; but when the Czar turned his back on further reform, Herzen and others like him were bitterly disappointed.

Most reformers and revolutionaries in nineteenth-century Russia exhibited a fluctuation between the poles of Slavophilism and westernizing similar to Herzen's. During the 1860's and 1870's a group of *Narodniki* (i.e., People-ists) arose who hoped to transform Russia by enlightening the peasantry. They tried to act as missionaries of a new and better society by going to the villages and preaching to the peasants. But their efforts met with small success. Russian peasants were suspicious of their efforts and were profoundly attached to age-old ways of village community life.

Revolutionary movements such as these have a peculiar interest in view of the later history of Russia; but it should be noted that in the nineteenth century only a tiny fraction of the population was touched by radicalism, while the vast majority remained ignorant peasants. Disaffection toward the oppressive government was doubtless widespread, but its organized expression was confined to a small group, mainly intellectuals, who dared to risk the attentions of the police and the dangers of execution or exile to Siberia.

4) European Alliances, 1871-1914. Industrialism grew at an accelerated tempo after 1871, especially in Germany, which within a few years of the formation of the German empire became the leading industrial as well as the leading military state of Europe.

The military and economic rise of Germany worked a fundamental change in the European political balance. As long as Bismarck remained Chancellor of the new German state, his skillful diplomacy, playing upon long-standing rivalry between France and Britain, and between Russia and Britain, kept potential enemies of Germany separated. At the same time he was able to form alliances with Austria (1879) and Italy (1882), and he maintained friendly relations with Russia.

Bismarck's dominance on the continent was made easier by the fact that the other great powers of Europe were engaged in imperialistic rivalries overseas. France and Great Britain were frequently at loggerheads over Africa, the most notable crises coming in 1882, when the British asserted control over Egypt, and in 1898, when rival French and British expeditions met one another in the Sudan at Fashoda. A similar tension existed between Great Britain and Russia. In central Asia, the two powers intrigued against one another in Afghanistan and Persia; and in the Near East, Russia, Austria, and Great Britain indulged in a three cornered contest for influence and control over the Ottoman empire.

The situation in the Balkan peninsula was further complicated by the development of fiery nationalism among the Balkan peoples themselves. Greeks, Serbs, Rumanians, Bulgars, Albanians, and Turks, each in turn began to awake to European ideas of national self determination during the course of the nineteenth century; and each people developed the ambition to create a new or enlarged state which would embrace all fellow nationals. Such ambitions were, of course, mutually conflicting; yet the various Balkan nationalities were able to find champions for their cause among the interested great powers. In 1877 the Russians declared war on Turkey on behalf of the Bulgars, and the next year victorious Russian armies were able to impose a peace which created a "Big Bulgaria" (San Stephano). But the British and other European nations were opposed to such an apparent increase in Russian influence in the Balkans, and after some rather heated diplomatic negotiation, a congress of diplomats met at Berlin in 1878. The Congress of Berlin altered the boundaries of Bulgaria in Turkey's favor—a victory for the British; and Austria established a protectorate over Bosnia and Herzegovina, two Ottoman provinces in the western Balkans. The Congress also marked the beginning of a more active German penetration of the Balkan peninsula, first economically, and later politically. The result of German activity in the Ottoman empire was to make the Turks shift (by about the turn of the century) from dependence on Great Britain to dependence on Germany.

Not only in the Near East, but in Africa, China and Oceania as well, German traders and German diplomats began to rival the older imperial powers. Germany's entrance upon an imperialist career had the effect of provoking a fundamental change in the European balance of power, for the appearance of a newcomer had the effect of bringing together the other imperial nations. Their rivalries and mutual suspicions were gradually compromised and overcome, so that during the first decade of the twentieth century a new and powerful grouping of France, Russia and Great Britain came to be arrayed against the Germans and their allies.

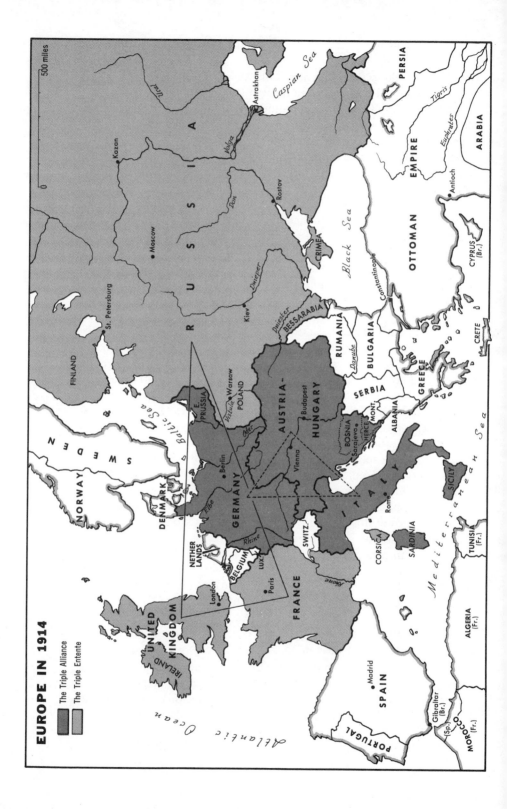

EUROPE IN 1914

The Triple Alliance

The Triple Entente

500 miles

0

NORWAY

SWEDEN

FINLAND

Baltic Sea

St. Petersburg

Moscow

Kazan

Volga

Astrakhan

Caspian Sea

R U S S I A

Ural

Don

Rostov

Dnieper

Kiev

Dniester

BESSARABIA

CRIMEA

Black Sea

DENMARK

E.
PRUSSIA

POLAND

Warsaw

Vistula

Oder

Elbe

Berlin

GERMANY

Rhine

NETHER-
LANDS

BELGIUM

LUX.

SWITZ.

AUSTRIA-
HUNGARY

Budapest

Vienna

BOSNIA

HERCE.

Sarajevo

MONT.

SERBIA

ALBANIA

RUMANIA

Danube

BULGARIA

GREECE

Constantinople

OTTOMAN
EMPIRE

CRETE

CYPRUS
(Br.)

Antioch

Tigris

Euphrates

ARABIA

PERSIA

Mediterranean Sea

ITALY

Rome

SARDINIA

CORSICA

SICILY

TUNISIA
(Fr.)

Rhone

FRANCE

Paris

London

UNITED
KINGDOM

IRELAND

Atlantic Ocean

SPAIN

Madrid

PORTUGAL

Gibraltar
(Sp.) (Br.)

MOROCCO
(Fr.)

ALGERIA
(Fr.)

This new turn of events became particularly evident after William II (1888–1918) came to the German throne. In 1890 Bismarck was dismissed from his post as Chancellor, and the young Emperor undertook personally to direct the German government. William was determined to make his mark on history, and was deeply impressed by the arguments of Admiral Mahan in favor of sea power. Consequently, he determined to build up a powerful German navy that could rival the British on the high seas; and at the same time he began to extend vigorous support to German imperial plans, especially in Turkey.

The effect of his policies was to bring together a powerful coalition opposed to Germany. Against the Triple Alliance of Germany, Austria and Italy, which Bismarck had formed, there arose the Triple Entente— France, Russia and Great Britain. The formation of the Triple Entente was a difficult matter, for it required compromises to regulate the powers' respective "spheres of influence." Such compromises were not always easy to achieve. In 1894 France and Russia formed an alliance without difficulty; the French-British compromise came only after prolonged negotiation, and even then the British were not willing to sign a definitive treaty binding them automatically to warlike action. Consequently all that was achieved was an understanding—an *entente cordiale* in the language of diplomacy (1904). Three years later a settlement of disputed claims in central Asia and in the Near East brought Great Britain and Russia together in a similar entente.

Thus from 1907 onward Europe was divided: Germany, Austria and Italy faced France, Russia and Great Britain. The balance of power between the two groups was very nearly equal, and any slight alteration produced tremors throughout the entire state system of Europe. The consequence was that periodic crises arose which more than once threatened war. In 1905 and again in 1911 the German government intervened in Morocco, where the French government was busy extending and consolidating a protectorate. Both these acts engendered much bad feeling, but were settled peacefully.

In the Balkan peninsula a crisis arose in 1908 as a consequence of the annexation of Bosnia and Herzogovina by Austria. The little Balkan state of Serbia had long aspired to fall heir to these provinces of the Ottoman empire, and looked to Russia, the great Slav power, to help in the realization of this ambition. But in 1908 Russia was unable to come to Serbia's aid, for the Russians had just suffered a humiliating defeat at the hands of the Japanese (1904–5) and the government felt that it needed time for military reorganization and reestablishment of internal stability. In 1912 another Balkan crisis arose as a consequence of the successful war which the Christian states of that peninsula (Serbia, Montenegro, Bulgaria and Greece) fought against the Turks. The delicate balance of power between the great states of Europe was affected by the division of spoils, for the Serbs and Montenegrins were attached to Russia and so to the Triple Entente, whereas the Bulgars (who had quarreled with their Russian protectors) leaned toward Austria and so were connected with the Triple Alliance. This crisis, too, was surmounted without general European war. Even when the victors quarreled over the spoils and a second Balkan war broke out (1913) that pitted Serbia, Greece, Rumania and Turkey against Bulgaria, prompt capitulation on the part of Bulgaria forestalled any widening of the disturbance.

Each time one or the other of the great powers backed down in a crisis, its leaders resolved not to do so again—resolved also to prepare militarily so that a further diplomatic setback need not be endured. Consequently a growing arms race developed among the major powers. When the Germans began to build a navy, the British decided to outbuild them; when a new and more efficient type of warship—the dreadnaught—was introduced, both Germans and British decided to build more of them than the other did. On land a similar rivalry developed. The size of standing armies was increased by prolonging the period of training to which conscripts were subjected; and the decisions of one government came to be tied to the decisions made by a rival.

Thus the stage was set for the outbreak of World War I. The actual occasion was almost trivial: in June, 1914, the heir to the Austrian throne was assassinated at Sarajevo in the recently annexed province of Bosnia. The Austrian government accused the Serbs of complicity in the crime, demanded satisfaction, and when their demands were not wholly met, the Austrian armies mobilized and marched against Serbia. But this time the Russians were resolved not to give in, as they had done in 1908, and came to Serbia's aid against the Austrians. Thereupon the whole chain of alliances was brought into operation. Germany came to Austria's help; France and Great Britain joined with Russia; and, to the surprise and bewilderment of many, in the early days of August, 1914, almost all Europe found itself engaged in a bitter war which had originated with a political assassination in an obscure Balkan town six weeks earlier.

5) Internal Development of the Major European Countries, 1871-1914. In the latter part of the nineteenth century, European political and social institutions showed a rather definite gradation from the liberalism of such western countries as France and England, through the semi- or pseudo-constitutional monarchies of Germany and Austro-Hungary in central Europe, to the autocracy of Russia in the east. This pattern reflected the impact of the French revolution and of the industrial revolution, an impact felt most strongly and earliest in western Europe, more weakly and more tardily in eastern Europe.

For more than forty years after 1863 (when a Polish revolt dissuaded Czar Alexander II from carrying reforms any further) Russian internal development was, as it were, frozen by the fear that any change would simply precipitate violent revolution. Particularly after 1881, when a secret and extremist revolutionary group succeeded in assassinating Czar Alexander II, official policy became stern repression of all overt dissent and refusal to consider changes in established institutions. There was, however, a significant economic development: industry, much of it financed from western Europe, made rapid progress in Russia, especially after 1890; and the building of a rail net during the same decades opened up still further prospects for economic advancement.

Reactionary government and rapid economic change both contributed to the development of revolutionary sentiment in Russia. In the 1880's Marxism first found Russian followers and advocates, among whom George Plekhanov (1857-1918) was the most prominent; and in 1903 Lenin (real name, Vladimir Ilitch Ulianov, 1870-1924) founded the Bolshevik party by splitting with more moderate Marxian socialists. Other revolutionary groups took form about the same time: for example, the Socialist Revolutionaries who placed their faith in the socialistic traditions of the peasant village community, and the Constitutional Democrats, who wished Russian government to follow the patterns of west European constitutional monarchy.

Yet none of these groups and parties was able to win more than a tiny numerical following, however widespread the latent discontent against the established régime may have been. That discontent was widespread was proven in 1905, when the defeats suffered by Russian armies in war against Japan discredited the government, and provided an occasion for widespread popular risings. These were put down, partly by force, partly by concession; for the Czar established a representative assembly. the Duma, in the hope of disarming the opposition and strengthening his government. The revolution of 1905 permitted extreme radical groups, such as the Bolsheviks, to emerge from their illegal underground into the public arena for a few months; but after 1907 changes in the franchise and renewed governmental repression once again drove the Bolsheviks and other revolutionary groups underground, where they remained until a new crisis, provoked by the strain of World War I, brought Lenin and his fellow Bolsheviks into the center of the political stage.

The Czarist government had to face another very difficult problem in the decades before 1914: the nationalities which had been incorporated into the Russian Empire in earlier times became increasingly restless, and an official policy of "Russification" only exacerbated the ill feeling between such groups as Poles, Finns, Ukrainians, Georgians, etc. and the Great Russians who constituted the preponderant element in the Empire.

The Austro-Hungarian monarchy was disturbed by an even more complex and difficult nationalities problem. In 1867 the Hungarians had won a wide degree of autonomy. This inspired other nationalities, especially the Slavic peoples who owed allegiance to the Hapsburg crown, with ambitions to achieve autonomy of their own, or even complete independence. The problem was especially acute on the southern frontier of the

Austro-Hungarian monarchy, for in that direction Serbs and Croats could turn their eyes across the border toward the little independent state of Serbia; and patriotic Serbs could equally look at their fellow nationals within the Austro-Hungarian state and dream dreams of a Great Serbia of the future which would unite all the speakers of the Serbo-Croat language. The annexation of Bosnia and Herzogovina in 1908 was intended to close the door to such ambitions, shutting Serbia off from the Adriatic sea; but, as it turned out, this extension of the territory of the Hapsburg monarchy instead paved the way for the outbreak of World War I and for the disintegration of the imperial Austrian state.

The nationalities problem, which was so explosive in eastern and south-central Europe, ceased, after 1870, to be a major axis of political life in the western nations. To be sure, French patriots could not forget Alsace and Lorraine, which had been ceded to the German Empire in 1871, but for the time being there were other issues to engage the minds of French politicians, and the patent military weakness of the French when pitted against a united Germany meant that the hope of "revanche" had to be put off into an indefinite future.

The German Empire which had been proclaimed at Versailles in 1871 was a federation of twenty-five states, each with its own form of government. The constitution drawn up under Bismarck's supervision left numerous functions to these states, but assured effective predominance to Prussia, which was by far the largest and most powerful member of the new Empire. The Imperial government was directed by a Chancellor, who was responsible only to the emperor. In addition, there was a Reichstag elected by universal manhood suffrage, and a Bundesrat, composed of representatives of the rulers of the component German states. New laws and taxes had to be approved by both bodies. Under Bismarck's leadership a number of important laws were passed which greatly strengthened the imperial government. A uniform legal code was adopted for all Germany, an Imperial Bank was organized, and the system of military conscription was made uniform throughout the Empire.

Between 1871 and 1883 Bismarck engaged in a conflict with the Roman Catholic Church, trying to make the Church in Germany more national. After 1878 however he made peace with the papacy in order to be free to combat the rising socialist movement. The German Social Democratic Party had been established in 1875 through a union of Marxists and other socialist groups. It rapidly gained influence over the workingmen of Germany and became by far the largest and best organized socialist party in Europe. Bismarck tried to cut the ground from under socialist agitation by a program of social legislation, but his efforts were not very successful. The Social Democrats continued to grow in numbers and became the largest single party in the Reichstag. But in proportion as the socialists gained in numbers they modified their radicalism, and when the decisive test came in 1914 the German Social Democratic party, like nearly all other European socialist groups, supported the German war effort and proved by their acts that national loyalties were stronger than socialist internationalism.

In France the defeat of 1870–71 led to the establishment of a republic— the third of French history. Just after the German victory a revolutionary rising took place in Paris, inspired mainly by socialists. The Paris Commune of 1871 repudiated the authority of a National Assembly which had been gathered together at Bordeaux after Napoleon III's capture at Sedan. The result was a short but sanguinary civil war. Paris was besieged again, and French troops overthrew the Commune. This event crushed the French socialist movement for nearly a generation, and led to the breakup of the First International which Marx and others had organized in 1864.

But the victorious National Assembly was itself divided between republicans, and three sorts of royalists—Legitimists (i.e., supporters of the Bourbons), Orleanists (i.e., supporters of the Orleans family to which Louis Philippe had belonged), and Bonapartists. The factions could not agree, but established a republic on an interim basis. The temporary stopgap gradually became permanent despite the recurrent agitation of monarchists, clericals and others who disliked the new regime. Between 1894 and 1899 France was profoundly agitated by the Dreyfus case. Captain Alfred Dreyfus (1859–1935) was a Jew, unjustly condemned on the charge of betraying military secrets to Germany. The efforts of the novelist Emile Zola (1840–1902) and others uncovered evidence of Dreyfus' innocence, and showed that a royalist Catholic clique in the army had shielded the real culprit. This discovery produced a widespread shift in French opinion and helped to bring a Republican-Socialist coalition government to power in 1899. Thereafter the republican form of government became relatively secure, despite numerous shifts in cabinets and in party alignments in the Chamber of Deputies.

British political development between 1871 and 1914 revolved largely around two issues: the Irish question and the labor question. Ireland had been incorporated into Great Britain in 1800; but the Irish (as distinct from the Anglo-Irish, who were mostly landlords) resented British control, and began to agitate for redistribution of the land, and for political autonomy. The problem was complicated by a religious issue. The Irish were Catholics; but in northern Ireland a substantial minority of Scotch-Irish Protestants clung stoutly to the British connection because they feared Catholic domination of the island. Irish representatives in the British Parliament were frequently able to make their wishes felt by holding the balance of power between Liberal and Conservative parties. As a result during the latter part of the nineteenth century some of the Irish demands were gradually realized. Land was extensively redistributed to former tenants, and the Anglo-Irish landlords lost most of their influence in the island. But feeling remained bitter until after the outbreak of World War I; and it was not until 1922, following an abortive revolt, that southern Ireland was granted political autonomy and became a dominion within the British empire.

The labor question took a new form in 1893 when the Independent Labour Party was organized to represent the interests of the workingmen directly. The new party did not at once win much success. Despite Disraeli's clever calculations, the Liberal party had come to depend to a considerable degree on workingmen's votes and adopted policies more and more favorable to them. From 1905 to 1915 Liberal Cabinets held power with the support of Irish Home-rulers and Labour members of Parliament. The Liberals used their power to institute sickness, accident and unemployment insurance for workmen, and to make the laws more favorable to labor unions. High taxes, including a graduated income tax, financed these social services; and despite the bitter opposition of the Conservatives, the House of Lords was deprived of its power of absolute veto over legislation.

Thus by 1914 the politics of both France and England had come to be dominated by parties which drew their major numerical strength from the lower classes, particularly from the working populations of the towns; and in Germany the Social Democrats, with a similar popular base, had become the most numerous party, although the constitutional setup of the German Empire did not give them more than a consultative voice in determination of official policies. It seemed to many that an age of democracy and progress was at hand; that the productivity of machines and a more just distribution of the wealth which machines produced would in time assure an abundant life for all. International rivalries and recurrent diplomatic crises disturbed some minds; but to many persons it seemed that the economic interdependence of all the great nations of the world, and the suicidal consequences of battles fought with the instruments of destruction which science and engineering had developed, would prevent any wholesale outbreak of war. To these sanguine expectations, the events of 1914 came as a shattering blow.

6) Imperialism, 1871–1914. European overseas expansion continued at an accelerated pace between 1871 and 1914. Most of Africa was parceled out among European nations, with France and Britain seizing the major shares. In central Asia the British pushed the frontier of their Indian possessions northward and the Russians pressed their empire southward until only a thin strip of Afghanistan separated the two from one another. In China European powers competed for concessions, gaining extraterritorial rights over various ports, rights to construct railroads, and other

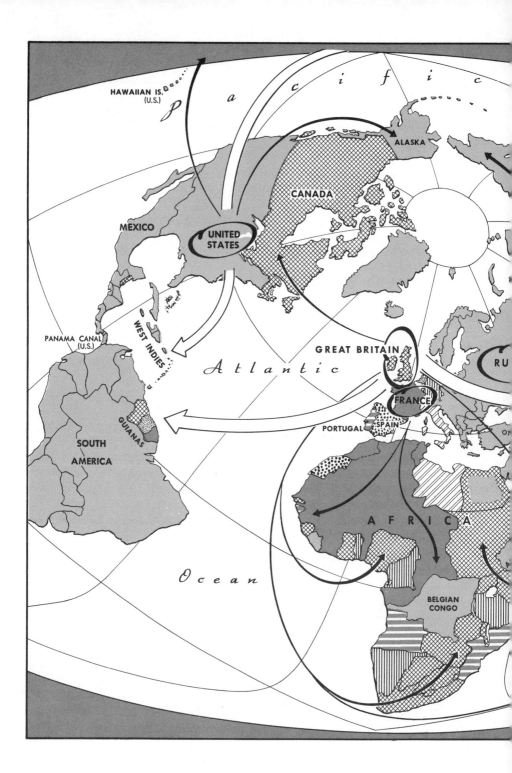

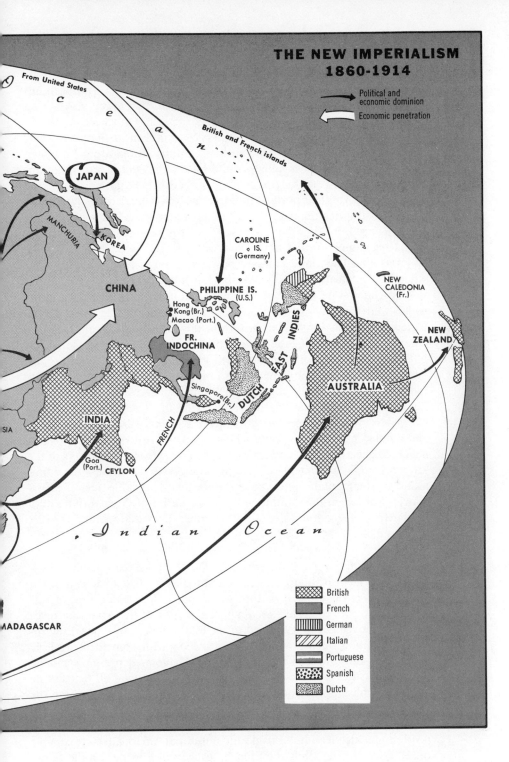

THE NEW IMPERIALISM
1860-1914

→ Political and economic dominion

⇨ Economic penetration

From United States

British and French islands

JAPAN

MANCHURIA

KOREA

CHINA

CAROLINE IS. (Germany)

NEW CALEDONIA (Fr.)

PHILIPPINE IS. (U.S.)

Hong Kong (Br.)
Macao (Port.)

FR. INDOCHINA

EAST INDIES

DUTCH

NEW ZEALAND

Singapore (Br.)

FRENCH

AUSTRALIA

INDIA

Goa (Port.)
CEYLON

SIA

Indian Ocean

MADAGASCAR

British
French
German
Italian
Portuguese
Spanish
Dutch

economic advantages. In the Near East and the Balkans, European imperialism took financial forms. The governments of Turkey, Egypt, and
the Balkan states (which had won their independence at various times between 1817 and 1878) fell into debt and became little more than playthings
for the rival ambassadors and business groups representing European
powers. Only Japan was able to stand off the pressure of European imperialism. In 1854, an American admiral, Matthew Perry, compelled the
Japanese to open their ports to trade. In the following decades Japan succeeded in adopting many of the industrial and military techniques of the
western world. By 1894 the Japanese were strong enough to imitate Europeans by making war on China and wresting Korea from Chinese cóntrol.
In 1904–5 the new-found Japanese power was compellingly demonstrated
when Japan defeated the Russians in Manchuria.

A special and peculiar evolution occurred in those British possessions
which were largely inhabited by European settlers. After some disturbances in Canada, limited self-government was accorded to the Canadian
colonies in 1840; in 1867 the various provinces united into the Dominion
of Canada and additional rights of self-government were extended to the
new Confederation. The Canadian example was later used as a pattern for
the establishment of self-governing Dominions in Australia (1901), New
Zealand (1907) and South Africa (1909). Thus the British Empire fell into
two parts: crown colonies, governed from Britain by appointive officers;
and dominions, where the only representative of British authority was a
governor-general whose powers were little greater than the powers of the
king in Britain. Sentiment was the principal bond which held the dominions to Great Britain; but it proved to be a fairly reliable tie in the First
World War, when the dominions came to the aid of Great Britain both
militarily and economically although their immediate interests were
scarcely at stake.

7) Developments in the Americas, 1789–1914. By a remarkable coincidence, George Washington was inaugurated as the first President of the
United States on the day before the Estates General of France was
scheduled to convene. Thus the final stabilization of the American revolutionary movement that had led to the establishment of a new English-
speaking nation on the North American continent coincided precisely
with the beginning of the French revolution. The coincidence was symbolic
too, for the success of the American colonies in throwing off British rule
and in establishing a republican government that claimed to draw its
"just powers from the consent of the governed," in the words of the
Declaration of Independence (1776), was an important stimulus to French
revolutionary leaders. If the crude and untutored Americans were capable
of self government, surely the French, teachers of Europe and the world,

were also capable of managing their own affairs and ought to be allowed to do so—or so it seemed to many eager and impatient Frenchmen in 1789.

While Europe became embroiled in a whole generation of wars provoked by the impact of French revolutionary ideas and practices upon the states and peoples of the Old World, peoples of the New World for the most part stood aside. Yet it was Napoleon's effort to take over Spain in 1808 that gave decisive impetus to Latin American movements for local self government. By 1821 almost all of the former Spanish American colonies had made good their independence. Ideals derived from both the French revolution and from the United States played a part in inspiring the Latin American revolts; but after 1821, the reality of popular self government was seldom attained in Latin America. Instead various self appointed cliques, often military juntas, took power.

The Roman Catholic Church had been very powerful in all the Spanish colonies. It possessed much land and had controlled education and dominated most other aspects of culture. Some of the revolutionaries were bitterly anticlerical. A central issue for most of the newly independent countries therefore became what to do about limiting (or defending) the powers of the church. Neither the clericals nor their opponents were usually willing to abide by election results in trying to settle the argument. Defenders of the Church were in principle—and usually also in practice—opposed to the doctrine of popular sovereignty anyway and therefore felt justified when they could in overturning election results by *coup d'état*. Nor were the defenders of popular sovereignty very consistent: they regularly overlooked the inert Indian peasant communities that constituted a majority of the population of many Latin American lands. Yet the possibility of an Indian rising was never far from their minds. Paraguay, for example, became a militarized Indian state after 1816, more or less permanently at odds with all its neighbors; and in other lands the danger of provoking peasant revolt and waking the sleeping Indian giant by proclaiming too loudly the sovereign rights of the people often became apparent. Mexico had a particularly stormy history of Indian-white relationships, and not until 1911, did a successful revolution bring Indian elements more or less effectively into the political arena of that country. Elsewhere the Indians remained effectively excluded from active political life until after 1914.

Yet, in spite of frequent *coups d'état* and the unstable rule of self appointed cliques and dictators, the countries of Latin America increased rapidly in population and some, like Argentina and Chile, became important producers for the world market. Argentine grain competed with grain from the United States and Canada; and Chilean copper and nitrate (derived from guano deposits on the desert shores of the north) were of key importance for European and world markets before 1914. Less dramatic but unmistakable economic and technical advances occurred in the other countries of Latin America. Brazil, for example (which became independent of Portugal in 1822 but remained a monarchy until 1889) developed large-scale coffee and rubber production to supplement the older sugar economy of the country. Only in the Caribbean, did European empires persist. Yet here too there were independence movements. Thus, Haiti broke away from France during the Napoleonic period; and Cuba and Puerto Rico broke away from Spain in 1898, but only with help from the United States of America to the north.

The economic development of Latin America, though substantial, lagged far behind what took place in the English-speaking parts of the New World. As the wheat lands of the prairie provinces were occupied by settlers, the Dominion of Canada became a major agricultural exporter. But the giant of the New World was, of course, the United States. By pushing ever westward, first the Appalachians and then the Rocky mountain barriers were overcome, and a territorially vast nation, with enormous agricultural and, from about 1870, also great industrial wealth, arose. European capital and European emigrants were both of vital importance in hastening the development of the United States; but politically the United States took little part in affairs on the other side of the Atlantic after 1812, when a brief war with Great Britain ended indecisively.

The disengagement of the United States from foreign entanglements in the nineteenth century was possible largely because the British government acquiesced in the Monroe Doctrine (1823), whereby President James Monroe declared that any European intrusion upon the New World would be looked upon as an unfriendly act. During the Civil war (1860–65) however, the French sent an expeditionary force to Mexico in hope of propping up the throne of the Emperor Maximilian, a Hapsburg archduke who had been invited into Mexico by one of the feuding factions of that land. But the expedition proved a failure and French troops were soon withdrawn.

By far the most serious crisis of United States history came from embittered sectional conflict, centered around the question of slavery. When the southern states attempted to withdraw from the Union in 1860 and formed their own confederation, war broke out. It lasted until 1865, when the superior manpower and above all the industrial resources of the northern states allowed President Lincoln's armies to win a crushing victory. Legal emancipation of the slaves did not, however, lead to very effective equality for the Negroes of the United States, who remained a poor, ignorant and for the most part rural population, concentrated, as before, in the southern states.

The Civil war, justified for many northerners by the moral necessity to suppress slavery, confirmed popular belief in the superior righteousness and virtue of the American way of life. Freedom, equality, republican government together with hard work, thrift and Yankee ingenuity reaped a rich reward indeed in the second half of the nineteenth century. The population and material resources of the United States shot upward decade after decade, until by 1914 it had become a great world power, inexperienced and untried perhaps, but so big and rich as to outweigh any single European state. When during World War I, the survival of British imperial power, behind which the United States had grown so great, seemed in question, American resources were thrown into the fight—at first by sale of supplies to the Allies, and then (1917) more directly and massively by full-scale participation in the war itself. With World War I, the adolescent phase of United States history can be said to have come to an end. The European state system, out of which the United States had sprung, and from which it had deliberately isolated itself during most of the nineteenth century, reached out and engulfed its offspring in 1917. Even more dramatically, Russia launched her Communist revolution in that same year, so that not one but two giant states, flanking old Europe on the east and on the west, abruptly assumed leading world roles, thereby shouldering aside the states of western Europe which for more than two centuries had dominated not only the European but the world scene.

e. European Culture, 1789–1914

1) Art. Between 1789 and 1914 numerous architectural styles derived from different periods of the past were simultaneously employed and modified. Toward the end of the nineteenth century technological advance in construction methods—mainly the use of reinforced concrete and steel girders for the building frame—made taller buildings possible; and some architects strove to make their buildings functional—that is, to make the artistic effect of the building depend upon the disposition of its structural elements.

Until about 1875 the traditions which had originated in the Italian Renaissance continued to dominate painting. During the last quarter of the century, however, a fundamental shift began to occur when leading painters abandoned the perspective conventions which had been established by renaissance artists. Instead shapes and colors were distorted in new ways; sometimes two or more points of view were placed simultaneously upon the canvas; or successive moments were suggested by multiple portrayals of what could at least be interpreted to be a single object. Symbolism and abstraction were freely employed by some painters; others resorted to a conscious primitivism.

Art critics distinguish various schools: classic, romantic, Barbizon, impressionist, post-impressionist and others. In this *Handbook* it is impossible to give such terms any meaning, since it is only by looking at paintings

MODERN PAINTING

Beginning in the last quarter of the nineteenth century, European painters began to break away from the fundamental frame for their art that had been established by the painters of the Italian Renaissance a full four hundred years earlier. This created what is commonly called modern art. No new binding conventions emerged to supercede the rejected techniques of perspective and the ideal of illusionistic painting. Instead, artists strove to be original, even at the risk of becoming unintelligible; and schools of art, sharing or exploiting some new device or trademark, rose and fell with great rapidity. Such nervous innovation and stylistic instability seems an accurate mirror of the larger uncertainties and indecisions that characterize the most recent decades of European and world history.

Old St. Lazare Station, Paris. **Claude Monet**
1877
(Art Institute of Chicago)

As the industrial revolution rose up through the presently dissolved older
structures of European society, so the impressionistic painter, Monet,
here adheres to the familiar perspective frame but allows visual details to
dissolve into blotches of color. Yet through a remarkable alchemy, his
multicolored splotches of paint create an impression of light struggling through
an atmosphere clouded with smoke and steam.

On the Terrace. **Auguste Renoir**
1881
(Art Institute of Chicago)

The dominion of the European middle class stood near its apogee when Renoir
painted this idyllic picture. While the face and figure of mother and child
are clear enough, Renoir dissolved all the details of the background into a
swirl of light and color — charming, fresh and delightful as a pattern in
its own right quite apart from anything it portrays or represents.

Madame Cézanne in a Yellow Armchair. Paul Cézanne
1890-94
(Art Institute of Chicago)

Cézanne was not trying to paint a visually accurate portrait of his wife here.
He felt free to simplify forms by skipping details (notice, for example,
the unfinished look of the upholstery). Like the impressionists, he was moving
away from the ideal of imitating three-dimensional visual experience,
preferring to treat line, color, and composition as aspects of a work of art,
to be manipulated by the artist to achieve the effect he desired.

The Day of the God. Paul Gauguin
1894
(Art Institute of Chicago)

Gauguin, who viewed modern society and culture as corrupt, sought refuge from
European civilization in Polynesia. Strongly influenced by the simple patterns
of primitive art, he developed a style of flat decorative designs. In *The Day
of the God,* Gauguin has transformed an idyllic south island scene into
a brilliant and arresting pattern of shapes and colors.

With such a painting, repudiation of traditional European techniques reached
a breaking point. A revolutionary phase in the history of art began.

I and the Village. Marc Chagall
1911
(Collection, The Museum of Modern Art, New York,
Mrs. Simon Guggenheim Fund)

Freed from traditional rules for visual representation of realistic images,
artists were able to explore conscious and unconscious psychic imagery. The
result was "surrealist" painting. Surrealists deliberately set out to penetrate
the more-than-real subjective world by transcending the limits of
ordinary spatial relationships, falling back on the freer juxtapositions of
memory and dreams. Here Chagall treats the Russian village in which he
grew up in a fashion such as to create a sweet yet vaguely ominous
portrait of the past.

Departure. **Max Beckmann**
1932-35
(Collection, The Museum of Modern Art, New York)

Expressionist art conveys the rigors and excitement of life through simplification of line and form reinforced by the use of strong colors. Beckmann painted *Departure* shortly before Hitler's campaign against degenerate art drove him into exile. The tryptich form is itself an echo of Christian usage, and the themes Beckmann chose — hope and peace in the center flanked by hellish scenes of suffering and violence — also echoes traditional religious art.

Christ Cutting Down the Cross. Orozco
1934
(By permission of the Trustees of Dartmouth College)

An angry, violent Christ threatening destruction to a corrupt world harked
back explicitly to traditional themes of Christian art. Yet Orozco was
proclaiming the overthrow of all tradition and was not reaffirming
the Christian apocalypse.

These two works from the depression years of the 1930's express the
artists' anger and distress at the course of public events. They may also be
read as expressions of the perils of repudiating, and the impossibility
of restoring, old faiths and traditional limitations — whether in styles
of art or in styles of politics.

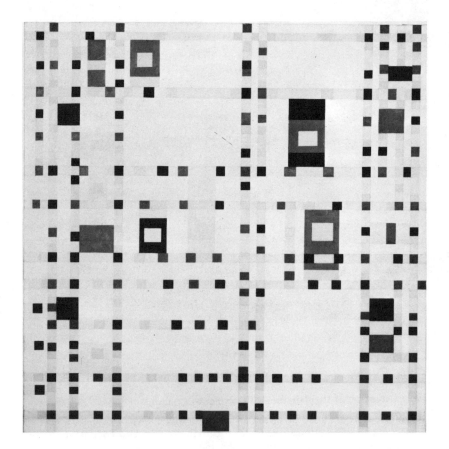

Broadway Boogie Woogie. Piet Mondriaan
1942-43
(Collection, The Museum of Modern Art, New York)

***Grayed Rainbow.* Jackson Pollock**
1953
(Art Institute of Chicago)

Abstract art carried repudiation of the illusionistic ideal of painting to
its logical conclusion by making the painting complete in itself, representing
no outside object or state of mind. Yet within this seemingly limited
frame, wide differences proved possible as these two examples show. The
geometric precision of the one and the drips and dribbles of the
other stand at opposite poles, yet both create pleasing and entrancing patterns.

and comparing one with another that the names acquire significance. A few outstanding painters can, however, be attached to the "schools" as follows: Classicists: Jacques Louis David (1748–1825), Jean Auguste Ingres (1780–1867). Romanticists: Eugene Delacroix (1799–1863), Joseph Mallord William Turner (1775–1851), John Constable (1776–1837). Barbizon: Camille Corot (1796–1875), Jean Francois Millet (1815–75). Impressionists: Edouard Manet (1832–83), Edgar Dégas (1834–1917), Claude Monet (1840–1926), Pierre Auguste Renoir (1841–1919). Post-impressionists: Paul Cézanne (1839–1906), Vincent Van Gogh (1853–90), Henri de Toulouse-Lautrec (1864–1901), and Paul Gaugin (1848–1903). But in addition to these there were individuals who defy classification, of whom Honoré Daumier (1808–79) may be mentioned. From such a list as this the remarkable dominance of France and indeed of Paris in the history of nineteenth- (and twentieth-) century painting may be inferred. Artists migrated to Paris from all over Europe, and were deeply influenced by the ideas and examples of Parisian painters.

2) Literature. Individuality among writers was cultivated as assiduously as among artists, and the same difficulty in making worth while generalizations consequently holds. Since literature is inevitably tied intimately to language, there was no single dominating center as there was for painting. Rather literature was national, and varied considerably from country to country.

English poets of the nineteenth century include William Wordsworth (1770–1850), Samuel Taylor Coleridge (1772–1834), George Gordon, Lord Byron (1788–1824), John Keats (1795–1821) and Percy Bysshe Shelley (1792–1822) who are usually grouped together as romantics. Later in the nineteenth century Robert Browning (1812–89) and Alfred, Lord Tennyson (1809–92) were the most widely admired of the "Victorian" poets. The novel was the most popular of all forms of literature. Sir Walter Scott (1771–1832), Charles Dickens (1812–70) and Thomas Hardy (1840–1928) were among the principal novelists whose works were and are still widely read.

French literature passed through a period of relative inactivity during the revolutionary and Napoleonic periods; or perhaps it would be more correct to say that *belles lettres* were largely eclipsed by political pamphleteering. Beginning about 1820, however, Victor Hugo (1802–85) began to write "romantic" novels and poems. Stendhal (real name, Marie Henri Beyle, 1783–1842), Honoré de Balzac (1799–1850), Gustave Flaubert (1821–80), Guy de Maupassant (1850–93), Emile Zola (1840–1902) and Anatole France (1844–1924) were among the most distinguished novelists and story tellers of the later part of the nineteenth century. Flaubert, Maupassant and Zola are often called "realists" in contradistinction to the romanticism of earlier writers. French poets include Alfred de Musset (1810–57), Charles Baudelaire (1821–67), Stéphane Mallarmé (1842–98), Paul Verlaine (1844–96), and Arthur Rimbaud (1854–91). Musset wrote in a romantic vein, strongly under the influence of Byron; Mallarmé, Verlaine and Rimbaud are often called "symbolists," and all three were strongly influenced by Baudelaire's poetry. Mention should also be made of François-René de Chateaubriand (1768–1848), whose book, *The Genius of Christianity* contributed to a revival of the intellectual respectability of religious belief in the early part of the nineteenth century; of Jules Michelet (1798–1874) one of the first and most passionate historians of the French revolution; and of Charles-Augustin de Sainte-Beuve (1804–69) and Hippolyte Taine (1828–93), literary critics and historians.

No such commanding literary figures as Schiller and Goethe arose in Germany in the nineteenth century. Nevertheless, the poets Heinrich Heine (1797–1856) and Rainer Maria Rilke (1875–1926), the novelist, Gottfried Kellar (1819–90) and the novelist and dramatist Gerhart Hauptmann (1863–1946) achieved an international reputation.

In Russia, the nineteenth century saw the rise of a powerful literature which has won the admiration of all the West. Alexander Pushkin (1799–1837) made the Russian language for the first time a vehicle for great poetry; he was followed by a distinguished group of novelists: Nicolai Gogol (1809–52), Ivan Turgenev (1818–83), Feodor Dostoievsky (1821–81), Count Leo Tolstoy (1828–1910), Maxim Gorky (1868–1936); and by the dramatist and short story writer, Anton Chekov (1860–1904).

A handful of writers from the smaller European countries should also be at least mentioned, since European culture was not a monopoly of the Great Powers. The passionately patriotic poetry of Adams Mickiewicz (1798–1855) did much to keep Polish nationalism alive during the generations when there was no independent Polish state. In contrast, the works of the Italian poet, Giosue Carducci (1835–1907), of the Norwegian playwright Hendrik Ibsen (1828–1906) and of the Swedish playwright and novelist August Strindberg (1849–1912) were concerned mainly with personal and private relationships. Ibsen, particularly, stirred acute controversy by writing "realistic" drama in prose, thus breaking with the heroic and poetic traditions of the European stage. His example was widely imitated in other countries in the twentieth century.

3) Music. During the nineteenth century musical composers adopted a more and more elaborate instrumentation; compositions became more complex and often longer as well. Orchestras were increased in size, and musical instruments were improved or new ones invented. The modern piano, for example, was not perfected until the early years of the nineteenth century. Frédéric Chopin (1810–49) and Franz Liszt (1811–86), both piano virtuosos, composed pieces designed to exploit the versatility of the new instrument, and between them gave the piano its current musical eminence. Another line of technical development was the introduction of new harmonies which led toward the end of the century to experiments with new or modified musical scales by Claude Debussy (1862–1918) and others.

The music of the nineteenth century is often called romantic. Certainly many nineteenth-century composers tried to make their music more emotional than had been usualy in earlier times; some tried to express their own feelings, other sought to suggest scenes or states of mind through music. The development of national schools drawing themes partly from folk songs, was a musical reflection of the growing nationalism of the time. Edvard Grieg (1843–1907) in Norway and Anton Dvorak (1841–1904) in Bohemia may be cited as examples of such national music; so may the Russian composers, Modest Moussorgsky (1835–81), Piotr Tschaikovsky (1840–93), and Nicholas Rimsky-Korsakov (1844–1908).

The greatest musicians of the century, however, cannot well be fixed within the limits of any label, and it seems best simply to list a few of the most famous names: Ludwig van Beethoven (1770–1827), Giuseppe Verdi (1813–1901), Richard Wagner (1813–83), Johannes Brahms (1833–97), and Gustav Mahler (1860–1911).

4) Natural Science. Between 1789 and 1914 natural science achieved a new dignity, almost reverence. Particularly in Germany, special research laboratories and institutes were founded for the scientific investigation of the natural world. The rise of German natural science turned largely upon the career of Alexander Humboldt (1769–1859). Humboldt was primarily a student of geography and natural history, but his interest embraced all fields of science and his personal prestige in Germany came to be immense. His principal successor as spokesman, organizer and public representative of natural science in Germany was Hermann Ludwig Ferdinand von Helmholtz (1821–94). He was primarily a physicist, but his formulation of the theory of the conservation of energy was only an incident in his entire career. More than any other single man he established scientific research institutes in Germany, institutes whose resources far exceeded those of comparable institutions in other European countries and helped to put Germany in the forefront of all branches of scientific research in the latter part of the nineteenth century. French and English science, by comparison, tended to rest upon individual work, often pursued in connection with established universities whose funds for support of natural science were limited.

Some of the consequences of the progress of science for technology and economic activity have already been discussed (see pp. 495–504). What interests us here is rather the consequences of scientific theories upon men's thinking and general attitude toward the world.

Mathematics continued to generalize its theorems. In the nineteenth century mathematicians broke through Euclidean presuppositions as to the nature of space to develop a variety of non-Euclidean and more generalized geometries. Nicholai Lobatchevski (1793–1856), working in the isolation of the University of Kazan on the Volga, first suggested the possibility of a geometry based upon non-Euclidean axioms in 1826. Georg Friedrich Bernhard Riemann (1826–66) was able to develop theorems applicable to Euclidean and various non-Euclidean systems of geometry alike. Jules Henri Poincaré (1854–1912) a third great mathematician, worked so abstrusely as to defy description here.

Until almost the end of the nineteenth century physics retained the base which Newton's mechanics had provided. New experiments, measurements and calculations worked out in detail a theory of energy and a theory of matter. Matter and energy came to be regarded as fundamentally distinct constituents of physical nature. Here are a few highlights in the nineteenth-century development of physics. In 1798 Benjamin Thompson, Count Rumford (1753–1814) first suggested that heat was a form of motion; later experiments by James Joule (1818–89) and others showed the equivalence of heat with chemical, electrical, and kinetic energy and their interchangeability under certain conditions. James Maxwell (1831–79) in 1873 further expanded the concept of energy by suggesting that light was only part of an electro-magnetic spectrum of radiant energy which included X-rays (discovered by Wilhelm von Roentgen in 1895) at one extreme and infra-red radiation at the other.

The theory of matter evolved in a similar fashion, bringing new and apparently diverse phenomena under a common theoretical formulation. John Dalton (1766–1844) suggested early in the century that all matter was composed of atoms; Count Amadeo Avogadro (1776–1856) demonstrated that gases were composed of molecules. For some years there was confusion between atoms and molecules but by degrees the present distinction between the two came to be established. Between 1869 and 1871 Dmitri Mendeleyev (1834–1907) arranged the elements in his famous periodic table, showing certain recurrences in chemical behaviors. A theoretical explanation of this phenomenon was supplied by the work of Joseph Thomson (1856–1940) and Hendrik Lorenz (1853–1928). With others, they built up a picture of the atom as consisting of a nucleus and rings of planetary electrons.

But electrons were at the same time a fundamental unit of electricity. Thus at the end of the nineteenth century, theories of matter and of energy in a sense converged upon the electron. But some aspects of the behavior of electrons proved baffling to physicists. In 1912 Max Planck (1858–1947) added another difficulty by suggesting that radiant energy, too, was made up of particle-like units which he called "quanta." Still another problem was how to account for the phenomena of radio-activity—the spontaneous emission of very high frequency radiation by certain elements such as uranium and radium. Radio-activity had first been observed by Henri Becquerel (1852–1908) in 1896.

At the end of the nineteenth century, therefore, physicists studying subatomic particles and radiant energy faced a series of problems which Newtonian physics seemed incapable of explaining satisfactorily. In addition, astronomers had observed certain minute discrepancies in the orbit of Mercury. In 1905 Albert Einstein (1879–1955) rose to this great challenge by propounding a theory of relativity. His paper of 1905 was later supplemented by a second in 1915, and by a book published in 1929. Generally speaking, the theory of relativity broke down the antithesis between matter and energy, which had seemed basic to physicists of the nineteenth century, and allowed for the possibility of their mutual convertibility. In addition, the Newtonian framework of space and time was abandoned. Space and time, like matter and energy were viewed as mutually varying aspects of a single whole. An indefinite number of space-times, each relative to a particular body or to an arbitrarily chosen point of reference, replaced the infinite and uniform space and time of Newtonian mechanics.

The revolution in fundamental concepts which Einstein (assisted by the efforts of many other physicists) brought about was as drastic as the revolution Newton had wrought in the seventeenth century. Throughout the eighteenth and nineteenth centuries it had been possible to visualize the world as an exceedingly ingenious machine, understandable by ordinary men, even if terrifyingly vast and alarmingly empty. But after the work of Einstein and his colleagues a new and much stranger world arose to confront men's minds—a world of relativity and quanta, where waves and particles became indistinguishable and where space and time had to be converted into multiple space-times; a world, moreover, which could only be described by complex mathematical formulae and could neither be adequately explained in words nor visualized accurately by the ordinary human mind.

Indeed the new world of physics was so alien to everyday human experience as to have little effect upon popular thought. The development of biology and of psychology had a much more direct and disturbing impact upon the public mind. When Charles Darwin (1809–82) in his book *The Origin of Species* (1859) argued that new species of plants and animals had evolved as a result of natural selection and the survival of the fittest, a great controversy immediately arose in Great Britain and elsewhere. Darwin's theory contradicted the account of creation in Genesis; and what was even more disturbing, it seemed to imply a world in which aggression, violence and destruction of rivals were the only means to assure survival. Thus the ethical inheritance of the western world seemed to be an error; and there were men who drew the full logical consequences of such "Darwinism" to justify European imperialism and to propound racial theories of history. Darwin himself was concerned only with the origin and interrelations of species, and did not draw any general philosophical conclusions from his theories. In a second famous book, however, he traced the *Descent of Man* from the great apes, thereby adding fresh fuel to the controversy.

Later developments of biology, notably the theory of the continuity of germ plasm (August Weisman, 1834–1914), cast doubt upon the inheritance of acquired characteristics, which some biologists had assumed to be the basis of evolution; yet evidence that evolution, however controlled or caused, had in fact occurred, continued to accumulate until by the end of the nineteenth century nearly all biological scientists accepted some sort of theory of evolution.

While evolution seemed to many persons to undermine traditional morality, others found it possible to take an optimistic view. They regarded morality as an evolutionary product which might have a positive survival value, and argued that progress—biological, material and social —was the law of the universe. Belief in human progress had come to be widely accepted in the eighteenth century; Darwinism and the continued development of science, medicine (see p. 498) and technology provided powerful support to the conception in the nineteenth century, so that most men (so far as they reflected on the matter at all) came to believe in the irresistible march of progress toward some far and indiscernible but definitely desirable goal.

During the first decades of the twentieth century psychology leaped into the public eye much as biology had fifty years earlier. The theories of Sigmund Freud (1856–1939) were the most controversial and the most discussed. He stressed unconscious mental processes and sexuality; and his analysis of the human psyche cast doubt upon the belief in human rationality and benevolence. The full impact of Freudianism, and of other schools of irrational psychology, however, did not reach the general public until after World War I.

The net effect of new theories in physics, biology and psychology was curiously paradoxical. Human reason and habitual concepts of the world were overthrown; yet it was the human reason which performed the act of dethronement, and, in recognizing its own limits, perhaps became the more powerful. The more minutely they were studied, the greater became the mysteries of the world and of man.

5) Social Science. Two major stands may be discerned in the development of social science in the nineteenth century. On the one hand, the conspicuous success of natural science inspired some men to try to apply similar methods to the study of human society. On the other, a strong sense of the past and of the strength of perculiar institutions and of historical circumstance to shape social conduct developed during the nineteenth century, partly in reaction against the hasty generalization and *a priori* reasoning which had often characterized social theory in the eighteenth century.

Sociology, in the mind of Auguste Comte (1798-1857), who invented the term, was an effort to create a science of society as sure and certain as physics seemed in his day. Herbert Spencer (1820-1903) was another man who attempted to import the methods of physical science into the study of society. On the other hand, such figures as Henry Maine (1822-88) and Max Weber (1864-1920), were more acutely conscious of the historical dimension of human affairs, and never divorced their social theory from the matrix of history, with all its irritatingly accidental, particular and local qualities.

The development of economics showed even more clearly an interplay between abstract scientific reasoning and historical study. The "classical" economists of the early nineteenth century tended to assume as a basis for their arguments such concepts as "perfect competition" and the "economic man"; and they frequently vested their conclusions with an aura of absolute certainty and universal validity. Among the most distinguished were T. R. Malthus (1766-1834), whose book on *Principles of Population* excited much controversy as a result of his conclusion that the growth of population always tended to outrun the means of subsistence; David Ricardo (1772-1823), who worked out a theory of rent and of wages; and John Stuart Mill (1806-73), who systematized the doctrines of his predecessors in his book *Political Economy*.

Even in the early nineteenth century, however, the doctrines of these economists were challenged. In Germany, Friedrich List (1789-1846) denied that free trade was always and everywhere desirable, pointing out that competition from established industrial centers might sometimes inhibit the development of infant industries. About the middle of the century a new group of statistical economists arose in England who attempted to abandon *a priori* argument in favor of careful measurement of what actually happened in economic affairs. William Stanley Jevons (1835-82) was a leader of this school; and Alfred Marshall (1842-1924) tried, with very considerable success, to combine the new data so assembled with the older theoretical framework into a new and more exact science. He and others introduced the concept of "marginal utility" upon which most subsequent theoretical economics has been based. Toward the very end of the nineteenth century Thorstein Veblen (1857–1929) suggested that purely economic motives and such concepts as the "economic man" were indefensible abstractions, artificially detached from the tangled matrix of human behavior and desires—a criticism of classical economics which tended to bring anthropology, sociology and history all into play as helps to the understanding of economic phenomena.

Systematic study of primitive human societies commenced about the middle of the nineteenth century. Lewis Henry Morgan (1818–81), Edward Tyler (1832–1917), and James Frazer (1854–1941) were the principle pioneers.

Another new and closely related field which opened up in the nineteenth century was archaeology. After Jean Champollion (1790–1832) discovered the key to decipherment of Egyptian hieroglyphics, a new avenue to an understanding of ancient Egyptian civilization lay open. Mesopotamian cuneiform script was deciphered soon after; but the most dramatic archaeological discovery was the uncovering of a pre-Greek civilization in Crete and Troy as a result of excavations conducted by Heinrich Schliemann (1822–92) and Sir Arthur Evans (1851–1941). Other finds from neolithic and paleolithic sites gradually permitted archaeologists to piece together a picture of the slow emergence of civilized societies from long ages of primitive life.

The lengthening of the historical time scale as a result of the labors of archaeologists was matched by an enrichment of detailed knowledge about the historical past of European and also of non-European peoples and states. In the early years of the nineteenth century a school of "scientific" historians arose in Germany. The greatest figure among them was Leopold von Ranke (1795–1886). He and his pupils did much to revolutionize the writing of history by insisting upon a much more thorough examination of sources than had been undertaken before. Vast collections of source material were made available to historians by systematic publishing of half forgotten documents; but it often happened that in proportion as more information about the past was gathered, the effort to interpret and generalize about the past was abandoned. Thus, for example, Lord Acton (1834–1902), one of the most learned historians of his own or any other time, never was able to write the great history of liberty which he projected as his life work, being overwhelmed by the mass of evidence which seemed relevant to the undertaking. Other historians, less ambitious, were able to produce famous histories dealing with limited periods: for example, Theodor Mommsen's (1817–1903) history of the Roman Republic; Hippolyte Taine's (1828–93) account of the Old Regime in France; Frederick William Maitland's (1850–1906) studies of medieval English institutions, etc.

One of the major uses to which historical study was put in the nineteenth century was to provide a base for the growing sense of nationalism. National histories were written in great numbers. Wherever a nationality found itself without a state of its own, one of the first tasks nationalistically minded intellectuals set themselves was to investigate the past glories of their ancestors.

A sphere in which historical study had a particularly important effect on general opinion was the criticism of the Bible and reconstruction from its pages of what seemed to accord with the historian's conception of probability and possibility. David Friedrich Strauss (1808–74) was a pioneer in the "higher criticism" of the Bible; Ernest Renan (1823–92) was the most widely read. The higher critics based their conclusions on careful textual examination of the Bible, and tried to reconstruct the elements from which the Bible had been put together. In general, they regarded miracles and other supernatural occurrences as myths, and tried to reconstruct the historical figure of Jesus along purely human dimensions.

6) Philosophy and Political Theory. The philosophic problem of assimilating and organizing the flood of new information and of fresh scientific theories was staggering. Different philosphers followed very divergent paths in their efforts to synthesize knowledge and belief into a comprehensible whole. The problem of epistemology, which had been inherited from the eighteenth century, remained prominent, and men were not wanting who denied the whole possibility of philosophical truth, and urged the abandonment of metaphysics for practical facts which alone could be verified. Auguste Comte (1798–1857), indeed, elaborated his "positive" philosophy from such a principle, and in his old age tried to found a new religion of humanity which could do away with theology and metaphysics.

More influential for the century as a whole was the philosophy of Georg Wilhelm Friedrich Hegel (1770–1831). He denied any distinction between reason and reality; argued instead that reason (or Idea or Spirit) unfolds itself in human experience and in history and can be comprehended by individual human minds only through a study of development and change. He suggested that the Spirit moved in a definite fashion—from thesis, through antithesis to a synthesis which incorporated the seeming contradictions of thesis and antithesis into a new and higher whole; and the synthesis then in its turn became a thesis for the renewal of the process. Hegel's prestige in his own day was immense, and his thought stimulated other philosophers through the nineteenth century and continues to do so to the present. Hegel's most famous pupil was Karl Marx (1818–83). He claimed to have "stood Hegel on his head"; that is, he adopted the Hegelian dialectical process (thesis, antithesis, synthesis) and applied it to the material world of technology and economic relations. In addition to

Hegelianism, Marx was strongly influenced by the French tradition of humanitarianism and rationalism, and by English economic theory, especially by David Ricardo. Karl Marx was, of course, more influential as the founder of a political movement which both predicted and worked to bring about social revolution than as an abstract philosopher.

The progress of natural science in measuring, predicting and controlling physical phenomena led some philosophers to deny the existence of any reality other than matter in motion. Ernst Haeckel (1834-1919) was one of the most extreme materialists, attempting to explain psychological and all other phenomena as the result of moving particles of matter. Darwin's theory of organic evolution stirred others to generalize his theory by creating philosophies which viewed all aspects of the world as an evolutionary product. Herbert Spencer (1820-1903) was among the most influential of these.

Despite their many differences, Comte, Hegel, Marx, Spencer and even Haeckel were all confident of the possibility of achieving a rational understanding of the world and of humanity. This possibility was denied by a number of philosophers who may conveniently be lumped together as antirationalists. Arthur Schopenhauer (1788-1866) proclaimed that blind will was the essence of the universe and of man; Friedrich Nietzsche (1844-1900) saw the will to power as the core of human psychology and advocated its ruthless pursuit, regardless of customary or legal restraints, by those who dared and were able to become "supermen." A very different sort of antirationalism was propounded by Henri Bergson (1859-1941), who spoke of an *élan vital* which guided and impelled a never ceasing evolution and which could be apprehended only by intuition and instinct, not by reason.

In the narrower realm of political theory, John Stuart Mill (1806-73) developed and defended a philosophically rounded theory of democratic liberal government; but the steady modification of his thought as he grew older—from the utilitarianism which he inherited from his father, James Mill (1773-1836), through liberal laissez faire toward what he called socialism—makes it impossible to identify his thought with any particular doctrine or to sum it up in a phrase.

Radicalism took numerous forms. During the first half of the century, "utopian" socialists like Robert Owen (1771-1858), Louis Blanc (1811-82), and anarchists like Pierre-Joseph Proudhon (1809-65) aspired to bring about a transformation of society by a change in institutions, and particularly by alteration of property relations. They hoped to effect the change by peaceful persuasion and by example. During the second half of the century, Marxian socialism overshadowed the "utopians," but anarchism (Michael Bakunin, 1814-76) and syndicalism (Georges Sorel, 1847-1922, during a part of his life) continued to dispute the ground with

Marxians. After the death of Marx (1883), splits developed within the Marxian movement itself. Eduard Bernstein (1850–1932) was the most prominent of the Marxian "revisionists" who began to deny the inevitability of violent revolution as a preliminary step to the victory of the proletariat.

Authoritarianism and a rejection of democracy were not without intellectual advocates. Auguste Comte and Friedrich Nietzsche shared a dislike for the common herd and a distrust of its political capabilities. Vilfredo Pareto (1848–1923) and Georges Sorel, in some of the phases of his thought, may also be mentioned as political theorists who argued that power must always rest in the hands of an élite, and who consequently scorned democracy.

7) Religion. The early years of the nineteenth century saw a notable revival of Christianity, partly in reaction against the irreligious enlightened doctrines of the eighteenth century which had helped to produce the French Revolution. In France the writings of François-René de Chateaubriand have already been mentioned. In England, a movement known as evangelicalism helped to vitalize the Anglican church and spread piety among the upper classes. William Wilberforce (1759–1833), whose long agitation in Parliament led to the abolition of the slave trade in 1807, was one of the most prominent leaders of the evangelical movement. Friedrich Schleiermacher (1768–1834) in Germany and Soren Kierkegaard (1813–55) in Denmark played a similar role on the continent of Europe inasmuch as they attempted to rehabilitate the intellectual and emotional power of Christianity.

On the other hand, militantly anti-Christian doctrines never disappeared. Comte's positivism and Marx's dialectical materialism have already been mentioned. A third influential anti-Christian religious thinker was Ludwig Andreas Feuerbach (1804–72) who developed the doctrine, sometimes called religious humanism, according to which all religions are to be understood as projections upon the universe of strivings and ideals generated in the human mind. Darwinism, anthropological studies of primitive religion, and the investigations of historians into the development of religious ideas and practices, led many peoples to view Christianity and other religions as an evolutionary product of social experience. Such views were sometimes associated with a rejection of Christian doctrine; but others, while accepting the gradual development of religious belief and practice as an historical fact, yet believed that Christianity was a uniquely valuable and profoundly helpful product of past human experience.

During the second half of the nineteenth century these various strands of opinion offered a profound challenge to established Christian belief. The challenge was met in various fashions. The Roman Catholic Church emphatically reasserted its traditions and refused all compromise with "modernism." In 1864 Pope Pius IX issued a *Syllabus of Errors* in which liberal and individualistic doctrines were condemned; in 1869-70 a general council assembled at the Vatican, reaffirmed the pope's stand, and proclaimed the doctrine of papal infallibility in matters of faith and morals. Under Leo XIII (1878-1903), the Roman Catholic Church embarked upon a more positive program, supporting the organization of Catholic labor unions, cooperative societies, and political parties. But, under Pius X (1903-14) the Church hierarchy was purged of a group of "modernists" who had tried to assert that dogma was not immutable but had evolved, and who argued that the value of the Church lay not in its Divine origin so much as in its social utility.

Protestant churches reacted to the trends of thought current in the nineteenth century in divergent ways. Some asserted the literal inspiration of the Bible, and rejected Biblical criticism and organic evolution as contrary to the Word of God. In contrast to these "fundamentalists," others tried to reconcile religion with science and placed especial emphasis on the moral teachings of Christianity. Such modernists accepted the mythological interpretation of many passages in the Bible, and regarded Jesus as a specially inspired man whose ethical example and teaching had a supreme value. In some Protestant churches, most notably in the Anglican, a group arose which emphasized ritual far more than had been customary in earlier Protestantism. In the 1830's a small but influential group of students and teachers at Oxford University started the so-called Oxford Movement. The Oxford movement emphasized the importance of the Church as a source of religious authority, superior to individual judgment and coordinate with the Bible. Such teachings led some of the most prominent leaders of the Oxford movement to join the Roman Catholic Church. John Henry Newman (1801-81), later Cardinal Newman, was the most prominent such convert. His career excited widespread controversy in England.

Through early modern times Jews had lived a segregated life in most European countries. They were subject to special laws which frequently recognized a more or less autonomous Jewish community. The major center of Jewish population was in Poland; but substantial communities existed also in Germany, and smaller ones in most other European countries. During the eighteenth and nineteenth centuries, the progress of liberal ideas, a decline of religious bigotry, and the unwillingness of rulers to brook the rivalry of autonomous semigovernmental organizations led to a gradual breakup of the Jewish communities and the emancipation of Jews from the legal restrictions which had previously been put upon them. Segregation in ghettos ceased to be compulsory, although long habit and

SHAPERS OF THE MODERN WORLD

AXIAL FIGURES OF THE NINETEENTH CENTURY

**Otto von Bismarck
Painting by Hader**
(The Bettmann Archive)

Camillo Cavour
(The Bettmann Archive)

Charles Robert Darwin
(The Bettmann Archive)

Dmitri Ivanovitch Mendeleyev
(The Bettmann Archive)

Karl Marx
(The Bettmann Archive)

Sigmund Freud
(The Bettmann Archive)

Nikolai Lenin
(The Bettmann Archive)

Albert Einstein
(The Bettmann Archive)

592   III. European Civilization

a continuing popular prejudice often acted to maintain something very like ghettos, especially in the areas where Jews were numerous.

The breakdown of legal restrictions had a consequence of inducing many Jews to abandon some of the distinctive ceremonials and peculiarities of dress which had earlier distinguished them from the majority of their fellow citizens. Such an abandonment of tradition led to a split in Judaism between orthodox and reformed. In the course of the nineteenth century many European Jews came to adhere to reformed synagogues or to abandon formal attachment to their religion entirely.

In the latter part of the nineteenth century antisemitism began perceptibly to increase. It was given an intellectual formulation by Houston Stewart Chamberlain (1855–1927) and others who based their arguments not on religious grounds, but on racial doctrines. Partly in reaction to "racial" antisemitism, and partly in imitation of the nationalism which swept all Europe, some Jews began to aspire to the establishment of a national home for themselves in Palestine. The most prominent early advocate of Zionism, as the movement was called, was Theodore Herzl (1860–1904).

In general it seems fair to say that among intellectuals religion in its various traditional forms lost ground during the nineteenth century. Agnosticism, scepticism and atheism became more widespread. In Catholic countries anticlericalism was strong among liberals, republicans and socialists, partly as an inheritance from the doctrines of the French revolution, and partly as a result of the predominantly conservative activities of the Roman Catholic hierarchy in politics. Yet the majority of the population of every European country continued to profess Christianity, and theological and moral teachings of the various churches continued to influence many minds profoundly.

Suggestions for Further Reading for Part III, C–3

Cambridge Economic History of Europe. Vol. 7. *The Industrial Revolutions and After: Incomes, Population and Technological Change*. New York: 1965.

New Cambridge Modern History. Vol. 9. *War and Peace in an Age of Upheaval 1793–1830*. New York: 1965; Vol. 10. *The Zenith of European Power 1830–1870*. New York: 1960; Vol. 11. *The Era of Violence*. New York: 1960.

Ashton, T. S. *The Industrial Revolution, 1760–1830*. London: 1948.

Blake, Robert. *Disraeli*. New York: 1967.

Brinton, C. *A Decade of Revolution, 1789–1799*. New York: 1934.

Briggs, Asa. *The Age of Improvement*. London: 1959.

Brogan, D. W. *France under the Republic: The Development of Modern France, 1870–1939.* New York: 1940.

Cameron, Rondo. *France and the Economic Development of Europe, 1800–1914: Conquests of Peace and Seeds of War.* Princeton: 1961.

Carr, Raymond. *Spain 1808–1939.* New York: 1966.

Clapham, J. H. *Economic Development of France and Germany, 1815–1914.* Cambridge: 1921.

Clapham, J. H. *An Economic History of Modern Britain.* 2d ed. London: 1938.

Clough, Shepard B. *The Economic History of Modern Italy.* New York: 1964.

Cobban, Alfred. *Edmund Burke and the Revolt against the Eighteenth Century: A Study of the Political and Social Thinking of Burke, Wordsworth, Coleridge, and Southey.* New York: 1960.

Cole, G. D. H. *A Short History of the British Working Class Movement, 1789–1925.* London: 1925.

Cole, G. D. H. and Postgate, R. *The British Common People, 1746–1938.* New York: 1939.

Croce, B. *History of Italy, 1871–1915.* Oxford: 1929.

Deane, Phyllis. and Cole, W. A. *British Economic Growth, 1688–1959: Trends and Structures.* New York: 1967.

Eyck, E. *Bismarck and the German Empire.* London: 1950.

Fay, S. B. *The Origins of the World War.* 2 vols. 2d ed. New York: 1966.

Gershoy, L. *The French Revolution.* Rev. ed. New York: 1964.

Geyl, P. *Napoleon, For and Against.* New Haven: 1949.

Guérard, Albert. *France: A Modern History.* Ann Arbor: 1959.

Halévy, E. *The Growth of Philosophical Radicalism.* Beacon Paperbacks.

Halévy, E. *History of the English People.* Rev. ed. 6 vols. London: 1949–52.

Hobsbawm, E. J. *The Age of Revolution, 1789–1848.* Cleveland: 1962.

Holborn, Hajo. *History of Modern Germany.* Vol. 2. 1648–1840. New York: 1964.

Hughes, H. Stuart. *Consciousness and Society: The Reorientation of European Social Thought, 1890–1930.* New York: 1958.

Jelavich. Charles and Barbara. eds. *The Balkans in Transition: Essays on the Development of Balkan Life and Politics since the Eighteenth Century.* Berkeley: 1963.

Kohn, H. *The Idea of Nationalism.* New York: 1944.

Landauer, Carl. *European Socialism: A History of Ideas and Movements of Power.* Vol 1. *From the Industrial Revolution to the First World War and Its Aftermath.* Vol. 2. *The Socialist Struggle against Capitalism and Totalitarianism.* Berkeley: 1959.

Langer, W. L. *European Alliances and Alignments, 1871–1890.* New York: 1931.

Langer, W. L. *The Diplomacy of Imperialism, 1890–1902.* New York: 1935.

Latourette, Kenneth S. *Christianity in a Revolutionary Age: A History of Christianity in the Nineteenth and Twentieth Centuries.* Vol. 2. *The Nineteenth Century in Europe: The Protestant and Eastern Churches.* New York: 1959.

Lefebvre, G. *The Coming of the French Revolution.* 1789. Vintage Books.

Lefebvre, Georges. *The French Revolution: From Its Origins to 1793.* New York: 1963.

Lefebvre, Georges. *The French Revolution from 1793–1799.* New York: 1964.

Mantoux, P. *The Industrial Revolution in the 18th Century.* Rev. ed. London: 1948.

Markham, Felix. *Napoleon.* New York: 1966.

Mariott, J. *The Evolution of the British Empire and Commonwealth.* London: 1939.

Masur, Gerhard. *Prophets of Yesterday: Studies in European Culture 1890–1914.* New York: 1961.

Mathiez, A. *French Revolution.* New York: 1928.

Moore, Barrington Jr. *Social Origins of Dictatorship and Democracy: Lord and Peasant in the Making of the Modern World.* Boston: 1966.

Mosse, George. *The Crisis of German Ideology: Intellectual Origins of the Third Reich.* New York: 1964.

Palmer, Robert R. *Twelve Who Ruled.* New York: 1958.

Palmer, Robert R. *The Age of Democratic Revolution.* 2 vols. Princeton: 1959, 1964.

Pelling, Henry. *A History of British Trade Unionism.* New York: 1963.

Pflanze, Otto. *Bismarck and the Unification of Germany: The Period of Unification 1815–1871.* Princeton: 1963.

Pinson, K. S. *Modern Germany, Its History and Civilization.* New York: 1966.

Pulzer, P. G. *The Rise of Political Anti-Semitism in Germany and Austria.* New York: 1964.

Rose, J. H. *Life of Napoleon.* 2 vols. 8th red. ed. London: 1922.

Rudé, George. *Revolutionary Europe 1783–1815.* New York: 1964.

Schmitt, B. E. *The Coming of the War, 1914.* New York: 1930.

Seton-Watson, Hugh. *The Russian Empire, 1801–1917.* New York: 1967.

Stearns, Peter. *European Society in Upheaval: A Social History since 1800.* New York: 1967.

Stern, Fritz. *The Politics of Cultural Despair: A Study in the Rise of the Germanic Ideology.* Berkely: 1961.

Stewart, J. H. *A Documentary Survey of the French Revolution.* New York: 1951.

Taylor, A. J. P. *The Struggle for Mastery in Europe, 1848–1918.* Oxford: 1954.

Thompson, D. *The Third and Fourth Republics.* London: 1952.

Thompson, J. M. *Napoleon, His Rise and Fall.* Oxford: 1952.

Treitschke, H. Von. *History of Germany in the 19th Century.* 7 vols. London: 1915–19.

Trevelyan, G. M. *History of England.* Vol. 3. Anchor Books.

Veblen, T. *Imperial Germany and the Industrial Revolution.* New York: 1915.

Wallace, D. M. *Russia.* London: 1877.

Wolf, J. B. *France, 1815 to the Present.* New York: 1940.

Woodward, E. L. *Age of Reform* (Oxford History of England). Oxford: 1938.

Novels

Austen, Jane. *Pride and Prejudice.* London: 1813.

Balzac, Honore de. *The Chouaus.* Boston: 1896.

Bennett, Arnold. *The Old Wives' Tale.* London: 1908.

Beyle, Marie Henri (Stendhal). *The Charterhouse of Parma.*

Beyle, Marie Henri (Stendhal). *The Red and the Black.*

Bronte, Charlotte. *Jane Eyre.* New York: 1848.

Bronte, Emily. *Wuthering Heights.* New York: 1848.

Conrad. Joseph. *The Nigger of the Narcissus.* London: 1897.

Crosbie, W. J. *David Maxwell.* London: 1902.

Dickens, Charles. *Oliver Twist.* London: 1838.

Dickens, Charles. *Nicholas Nickleby.* London: 1839.

Dickens, Charles. *David Copperfield.* London: 1850.

Dickens, Charles. *Little Dorrit.* London: 1857.

Dickens, Charles. *A Tale of two Cities.* London: 1859.

Dickens, Charles. *Hard Times.* New York: 1883.

Dumas, Alexander. *The Count of Monte Cristo.* London: 1888.

Eliot, George. *Adam Bede.* New York: 1859.

Eliot, George. *Middlemarch.* New York: 1872–3.

France, Anatole. *The Gods are Athirst.* London: 1913.

Forester, C. S. *The Gun.* Boston: 1933.

Giono, Jean. *Horseman of the Roof.* New York: 1954.

Hugo, Victor. *Ninety-Three.* Boston: 1900.

Lagerlof, Selma. *Gosta Berlings Saga.*

Lampedusa, Giuseppe D. *The Leopard.* New York: 1960.

Llewellyn, Richard. *How Green was my Valley.* New York: 1940.

Mann, Thomas. *The Beloved Returns.* New York: 1940.
Sabatini, Rafael. *Scaramouche.* Boston: 1921.
Stevenson, Robert L. *St. Ives.* New York: 1934.
Thackeray, William Makepeace. *Vanity Fair.* London: 1848.
Trollope, Anthony. *Phineas Finn.* London: 1869.
Webb, Mary. *Precious Bane.* London: 1924.
Wilkins, William V. *And So—Victoria.* New York: 1937.

Chronological Table for Part III, C–3: Liberal, Nationalist and Industrial Europe

*1789	Opening of Estates-General in Versailles. Capture of Bastille (July 14).
1789–1791	National Assembly.
1790	Civil Constitution of Clergy.
1791	Constitution of 1791 in France.
1792–1795	National Convention.
1792–1797	War of the First Coalition (against France).
1792	France a republic.
1793	Constitution of 1793 in France.
*1794	Execution of Robespierre.
1795–1799	Directory in France.
1798–1799	Napoleon Bonaparte's Egyptian expedition.
1798–1801	War of the Second Coalition (against France).
*1799	Napoleon Bonaparte's *coup d'état* (eighteenth of Brumaire).
1799–1804	Consulate in France.
1801–1825	Alexander I of Russia.
1802	Treaty of Amiens (between France and England; broken in 1803).
1803	Louisiana Purchase.
1804	Death of Kant (b. 1724).
1804–1814	Napoleonic Empire.
1805–1807	War of the Third Coalition (against France).
1805	Battles of Trafalgar and Austerlitz.
1806	Death of Pitt, the Younger (b. 1759).
1806	End of Holy Roman Empire.
1807	Robert Fulton's steam boat.
1807	Abolition of slave trade in British Empire.
1808–1814	Peninsular War.
1809	Napoleon's war against Austria.
1810	Abolition of serfdom in Prussia.
1810–1826	Revolts of the Spanish-American colonies.

1812–1814	War of 1812 (between Great Britain and U.S.A.).
*1812	Napoleon's Russian campaign.
1813	Battle of Leipzig.
1814	First abdication of Napoleon.
*1814–1815	Congress of Vienna.
*1815	The Hundred Days; battle of Waterloo; second abdication of Napoleon.
1821	Death of Napoleon Bonaparte (b. 1769).
1821–1830	Greek War of Independence.
1823	Monroe Doctrine.
1824	Repeal of Combination Acts in Great Britain.
1825–1855	Nicholas I of Russia.
1825	Steam locomotive demonstrated in England.
1825	Decembrist revolt in Russia.
1827	Death of Beethoven (b. 1770).
1830	Beginning of French conquest of Algeria.
*1830	July Revolution in France; revolutions in Belgium, Germany, Italy, Poland.
1830	Opening of Liverpool-Manchester railroad.
1831	Kingdom of Belgium.
1831	Death of Hegel (b. 1770).
1831	Invention of dynamo (Faraday).
*1832	Great Reform Act in England.
1832	Death of Goethe (b. 1749).
1833	Abolition of slavery in British colonies; Factory Act.
1834	Formation of *Zollverein* (German customs union).
1834	Invention of McCormick reaper.
1836–1848	Chartist movement in England.
1837–1901	Victoria queen of England.
1839–1842	Opium War: free trade for Westerners in China.
1844	The Rochdale Pioneers.
1844	Invention of electrical telegraph (Morse).
*1846	Repeal of Corn Laws in Great Britain.
1847	Ten Hour Law in Great Britain.
*1848	*The Communist Manifesto.*
*1848	February Revolution in France; revolutions in Germany, Austria, Italy, Hungary.
1851	The Great Exhibition in London (Crystal Palace).
1851	*Coup d'état* of Louis Napoleon (Napoleon III, 1852–1870).

1854	Perry in Japan.
1854–1856	Crimean War.
1855–1881	Alexander II of Russia.
1856	Development of Bessemer process.
1858	Transfer of government of India to the Crown from the East India Company.
1859	Darwin's *Origin of Species.*
1859	Austro-Sardinian War.
*1861	Kingdom of Italy.
*1861	Abolition of serfdom in Russia.
1861–1865	Civil War in U.S.A.
1864–1876	First Socialist International.
1864	Bismarck's war with Denmark over Schleswig-Holstein.
1866	Transatlantic cable.
1866	Austro-Prussian War.
1867	Urban workers enfranchised in Great Britain.
1867	North German Confederation.
1867	British North America Act (Canada a dominion)
1869	Opening of Suez Canal.
1869–1870	Vatican Council.
*1870–1871	Franco-Prussian War.
1870–1940	Third French Republic.
1870	Rome becomes Italian capital: completion of Italian unification.
1871–1918	Second German Empire.
1871	Paris Commune.
1873	Death of J. S. Mill (b. 1806).
1875	Purchase of controlling bloc of Suez canal shares by Great Britain.
1876	Invention of telephone (A. G. Bell).
1876	Victoria crowned Empress of India.
1877	Russo-Turkish War.
1878–1903	Pope Leo XIII.
1878	Congress of Berlin.
1879	Alliance between Germany and Austria.
1881–1894	Alexander III of Russia.
1882	Beginning of British control of Egypt.
1882	Triple Alliance (Germany-Austria-Italy).
1883	Death of Marx (b. 1818).
1884	Rural workers enfranchised in Great Britain.
1888–1918	William II of Germany.
1890	Dismissal of Bismarck.

1894	Franco-Russian alliance.
1894–1917	Nicholas II of Russia.
1894	War between Japan and China.
1895	Invention of wireless telegraphy (Marconi).
1898	British conquest of Sudan; Fashoda incident.
1899–1902	South African War (Boer War).
1901	Commonwealth of Australia.
1901–1910	Edward VII of England.
1902	Anglo-Japanese alliance.
1903	First successful airplane flight (Wright brothers).
1904–1905	Russo-Japanese War.
1904	Entente Cordiale between England and France.
*1905–1907	Revolution and agrarian disturbance in Russia.
1905	Independence of Norway.
1905	Einstein's Special Theory of Relativity.
1905	First Morocco Crisis.
1907	Anglo-Russian Entente.
1907	Dominion of New Zealand formed.
1908–1909	Bosnian Crisis.
1909	Union of South Africa formed.
1911	Second Morocco Crisis; annexation of Tripoli by Italy.
1911–1912	Chinese revolution.
1912	Formulation of quantum theory by Max Planck.
1912–1913	Balkan Wars.
1914	Opening of Panama Canal.
*1914–1918	First World War.

4. AN ERA OF WARS AND REVOLUTION: 1914 TO 1969

a. Introductory

Two world wars and a number of social revolutions—semi, pseudo, and real—dominated the history of Europe and the world after 1914. These upheavals profoundly affected economic life. The waste of war expenditures helped to destroy the hegemony which western Europe exercised over the world economy during the nineteenth century. Peripheral countries, most notably the United States of America and the Union of Soviet Socialist Republics, became leading industrial states, and most of the separate nation states of western Europe sank to secondary rank. Social conflicts within, and age-old rivalries among the nations of Europe further weakened the political and economic power of the old center of European civilization.

The emergencies of war, depression and cold war were met with varying degrees of success by extension of the power of the state over economic relationships so that some economists have come to speak of neo-mercantilism in the twentieth century. Technological progress continued. Vistas of drastic future change resulting from the release of atomic energy, the uses of computers, and a host of less dramatic but cumulatively very important technical improvements become compellingly and sometimes distressingly apparent.

Perhaps the most basic change since 1914 was the loss of European autonomy. For about 1000 years, from the inception of European civilization until the twentieth century, European development had depended primarily upon the interplay of institutions, techniques, ideas, events and personalities indigenous to Europe; and beginning with the sixteenth century, the power and splendor of European civilization had permitted Europeans to stamp their imprint deeply upon other peoples and regions of the earth. Since 1914, on the contrary, European history has more and more reflected the impact of forces coming from outside Europe. The rise of the United States and of the Soviet Union to world power was one aspect of the change. The revolt of the non-European peoples of the world against European political and economic control was another. The vogue of primitive art, of American jazz and of American movies, and the widespread revulsion against traditional forms of artistic expression in Europe itself may perhaps be taken as indices of an analogous transformation in the sphere of culture; but it would be wrong to suppose that the decay of European cultural leadership has so far been anything like as drastic as the decay of European political and economic supremacy.

b. Economic Changes, since 1914

Two long and destructive wars, fought largely on European soil, contributed powerfully to the relative economic decline of western Europe. Destruction of life and of wealth, dissipation of capital investments abroad, the rise of discontent in colonial areas dominated by European powers, and, most important of all, the development of powerful industrial states outside of western Europe combined to reduce the preponderance which Great Britain, Germany and France exercised in the world economy before 1914. All of these changes were accelerated or caused by the two world wars. But after 1957, when the European Common Market began to operate, western Europe experienced a prolonged economic expansion that did much to restore Europe's economic strength and self-confidence.

Between the wars (1918–39) the relatively small size of western European nations interfered with the full development of the resources of the continent as a whole. Tariff barriers, governmental policies designed to make each state as nearly self-sufficient as possible, interruption of easy communication by national frontiers, the mutual hostilities and suspicions which divided one European nation from another, all acted as obstacles to the rational exploitation of the economic resources of the continent. Two other internal factors acting as a brake upon European economic life may be mentioned: (1) in many countries social antagonism between economic classes made free cooperation between them difficult and directed energy and attention into more or less futile political contests; and (2) many European nations suffered from obsolescence of machinery and of methods of manufacture when compared with the machinery and practices of newer industrial areas such as the United States.

Yet one should not exaggerate the economic weakening of western Europe. Although individual countries were surpassed by the new industrial giants, America and Russia, the continent taken as a whole still rivalled the economic production of either, and surpassed each in many respects.

Perhaps the most serious economic difficulty which faced western Europe during the interwar period was the problem of markets. The major nations of the west were peculiarly vulnerable. Large concentrations of

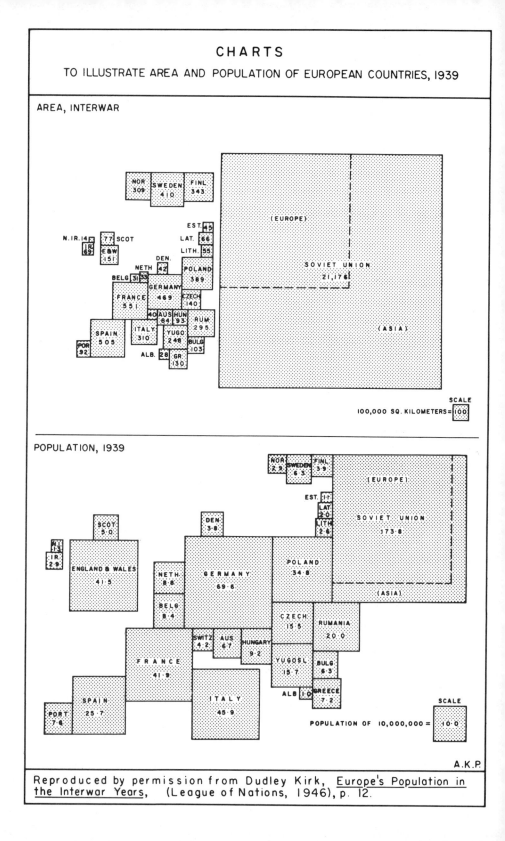

CHARTS

TO ILLUSTRATE AREA AND POPULATION OF EUROPEAN COUNTRIES, 1939

AREA, INTERWAR

NOR 309 | SWEDEN 410 | FINL 343

N.IR. 14 | IR 69 | 77 SCOT | E&W 151

EST. 45 | LAT. 66 | LITH. 55

NETH | DEN. 42 | POLAND 389

BELG 31 | 33

FRANCE 551 | GERMANY 469 | CZECH 140

40 | AUS 84 | HUN 93 | RUM. 295

SPAIN 505 | ITALY 310 | YUGO 248 | BULG 103

POR 92

ALB. 28 | GR. 130

(EUROPE)

SOVIET UNION 21,176

(ASIA)

SCALE
100,000 SQ. KILOMETERS = 100

POPULATION, 1939

NOR 2.9 | SWEDEN 6.3 | FINL 3.9

(EUROPE)

EST. 1.1 | LAT 2.0 | LITH. 2.6

SOVIET UNION 173.8

SCOT 5.0

N.IR. 1.3 | IR. 2.9

DEN. 3.8

ENGLAND & WALES 41.5 | NETH. 8.8 | GERMANY 69.6 | POLAND 34.8

BELG. 8.4

(ASIA)

CZECH 15.5 | RUMANIA 20.0

SWITZ 4.2 | AUS 6.7 | HUNGARY 9.2

FRANCE 41.9 | YUGOSL. 15.7 | BULG 6.3

ALB. 1.0 | GREECE 7.2

SPAIN 25.7 | ITALY 45.9

PORT 7.6

SCALE
POPULATION OF 10,000,000 = 10.0

A.K.P.

Reproduced by permission from Dudley Kirk, _Europe's Population in the Interwar Years_, (League of Nations, 1946), p. 12.

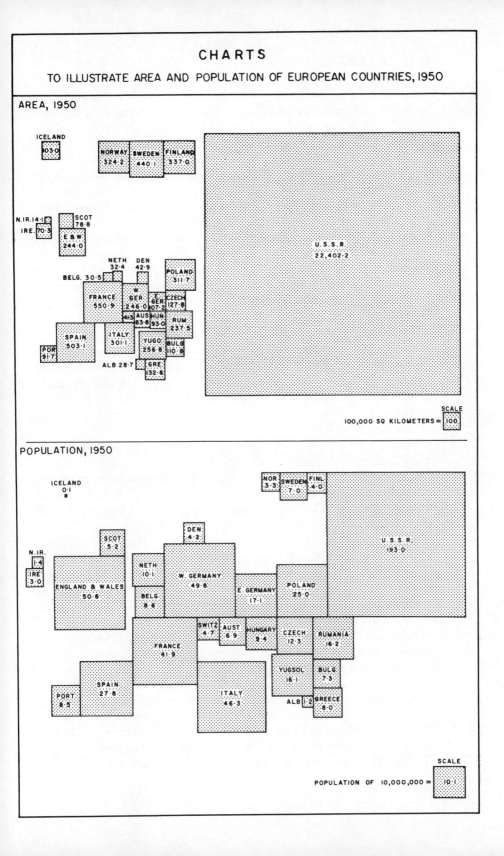

population required import of food and raw materials which could only be paid for by export of manufactured goods. But the areas of the world which in the nineteenth century were content to remain suppliers of food and raw materials more and more have undertaken to build up industry for themselves, and have shut out European competition by tariff barriers. After World War I this trend became quite evident, and the leading industrial nations of Europe were able to balance their international payments only by drawing on income from capital invested abroad. During World War II most European capital invested abroad was dissipated, so that this resource was no longer available, and western European nations became partially dependent on governmental grants made by the United States to make good their trade deficits.

The relative decline of European economic power did not result in a cessation of population growth, although the rate of growth in western countries declined considerably. The population of Europe was about 401 million in 1900; by 1950 it had increased to about 589 million. With the exception of the Netherlands, however, most of this growth occurred in eastern and southern Europe, where industrialization had made the least progress. (See chart.) In many countries, especially in the Balkans, and in eastern parts of Poland and Czechoslovakia, the growth of population was associated with a decline in the standard of living due to subdivision of small peasant farms.

Until the 1950's major improvements in technology usually found a more eager reception in the United States and in Russia than in western Europe itself, although some industries, especially those demanding special skills on the part of the workmen, remained more advanced in Europe than elsewhere. Production of chemicals and of optical instruments are two examples of such industries. After 1914, devices such as the automobile, airplane and radio, which had been invented before the outbreak of World War I, began to have a great economic (and military) importance. New chemical processes were developed with great rapidity, and the use of synthetic materials replaced natural products for many uses—textiles like rayon and nylon; synthetic rubber; plastics in place of wood or metal, etc. Oil and gasoline were used on an ever increasing scale; the same was true of electricity. Coal lost a part of its nineteenth-century prominence as a source of power to these newcomers. Iron, which had been of prime importance in the nineteenth century, was likewise challenged. Aluminum became important for light-weight construction; at the same time innumerable steel alloys produced new metals suited to special purposes.

The elaboration of devices for calculation and record keeping—the typewriter, adding machines, calculators, computers and many others—was of fundamental importance in making possible the extension of governmental and corporation control over economic activity. In factories, a new degree of efficiency was introduced into many types of manufacture by the establishment of assembly lines, with concomitant minute specialization of work.

All these and many other technological improvements may soon be dwarfed by the possibilities of atomic energy. The release of a portion of the energy locked in matter created a new and very powerful military weapon (1942, 1945); more recently atomic piles have been constructed to provide energy for electrical generators. Older limits upon available power were thereby removed, with long range consequences for mankind that can only be surmised.

The two world wars acted as a powerful stimulant to technological innovation. War emergencies were equally decisive in promoting changes in the control and organization of economic relations. During the First World War (1914–18) state control over the economy of every European country was greatly expanded in order to assure the production of munitions, distribution of food and other necessities, and the maximal utilization of manpower. After the war ended, most of these controls were withdrawn, but for several years the aftermath of the war remained all-pervasive in the form of inflation, economic dislocation and suffering.

Russia's development was, of course, peculiar in the sense that after 1917 a revolutionary Marxist party controlled the country. Yet the fluctuations of Bolshevik economic policy bore a notable resemblance to the developments of western Europe. Thus the abandonment of "war communism" in 1921 may be compared to the relaxation of war-time economic controls which occurred somewhat earlier in western Europe; and the inaugurations of wholesale state planning with the Five Year plans (beginning 1928) preceded and exceeded, yet bore a certain likeness to, the reassertion of governmental control over economic processes which began in western European countries with the depression of 1930–37.

After 1933, when Adolf Hitler took power in Germany, a new impetus to governmental control over economic affairs was felt in every European country. Hitler used his position to rearm Germany, and in doing so induced a sort of prosperity: at the least he brought an end to massive unemployment by putting the German industrial plant to work on state contracts. As the menace of German rearmament became clear, other European nations (including Soviet Russia as well as France and Britain) launched rearmament programs of their own, and in doing so extended or confirmed the power of the state over economic processes. One may, indeed, consider this extension of state control over the economy as an application in peace time of the techniques which had been developed during World War I.

World War II (1939–45) precipitated a much more thorough application of governmental economic regulation. During the first years of the war, the Germans were able to exploit most of the European continent to support their military forces, and many of the old restrictions on economic activities which had been created by national states were over-ridden. German defeat resulted in the reestablishment of national governmental control over national economies in the western part of Europe; but in the regions occupied by the Russians or brought under Communist governments it appears that national control was modified by the overriding power of the Russian government itself. In both eastern and western Europe the abandonment of governmental controls over the economy was partial, and came more slowly than it had after World War I. In some countries, most notably in Great Britain, strong socialist parties came to power committed to a policy of government control over economic relations on a permanent peacetime basis.

The post World War II years did not witness the sort of fumbling and confusion in economic matters that had characterized the years after World War I. This time, the damages done to European society and economy were so great that no one could suppose that things would come back to "normal" of their own accord, as the British and American governments had hoped and expected in 1918. Instead, large-scale planning was obviously needed. Immediate post-war emergency relief was handled by UNRRA (United Nations Relief and Rehabilitation Administration). When its efforts proved inadequate, the United States and most of the nations of western Europe collaborated in a European Recovery Program (1948-52). This program was usually referred to as the "Marshall Plan," in honor of General George C. Marshall, United States Secretary of State, who made the initial proposal. It delivered large quantities of American capital and goods to the participating European nations, including defeated Germany. Moreover the separate national plans of each country were supposed to key in with the plans of others to produce a Europe-wide program of investment and development.

The practical result was a resounding success. European recovery leaped forward so that prewar levels of economic activity were soon far surpassed. Moreover, the habit of cooperating across national frontiers proved so rewarding that permanent organizations for trans-national economic management were set up: first the Iron and Coal Community (1950) and then the European Common Market (1957). Of the major west European powers, only Britain remained outside the Common Market. Partly as a result, British economic life lagged conspicuously behind the achievements of the continent.

In eastern Europe, the Russians set up a rival economic association among the communist states. Planned investment within each country and exchanges of commodities and credits among the communist states led to remarkable increases in industrial production, and rapid over all economic development in eastern Europe. It seems, nevertheless, that the pace of west European expansion in the postwar decades, 1949–69, surpassed the development of eastern Europe, perhaps mainly because the westerners started from a more advanced industrial base, and used the mechanisms of the market to allocate scarce resources more sensitively than was done in the east, where inefficient producers and hoarding of scarce materials and of manpower were common.

Behind the extraordinary economic successes of the post World War II years lay two important changes in industrial organization and management. One was mainly the work of the British economist, John Maynard Keynes (1883–1946), who developed a theory of how to manage credit and money in an industrial economy so that government and financial managers could even out the boom and bust patterns that had been so distressing in the inter-war years. In particular, new theoretical insights derived from Keynes' work, make recurrence of the situation prevailing in the 1930's unlikely, when idle and hungry men confronted idle machines and unsold goods, and no one knew what to do about it.

Secondly, deliberate invention has been so well organized, and substitute materials and processes have become so numerous, that older determinants for the location of industry have ceased to be as important as previously. An educated, skilled work force and a supply of really top flight engineering talent is now perhaps mere important to many industries than is convenience of access to any particular kind of raw material. With the widespread shift to atomic generators as a source for electrical energy that occurred in the 1960's, it has even become true that supplies of fuel are ceasing to be tied closely to geography. Since in such reactors a few pounds of uranium can produce vast amounts of power, where the uranium happens to come from is a trifling factor in the cost of the power it produces.

The tendency, therefore, is to permit practically any land to become the seat of complex technology and industry, so long as the human population has the requisite skills and social organization. This has had the effect of giving Europe a fresh lease on economic prosperity. Even the loss of colonial territories has meant little or nothing for European economic processes. If anything, political independence simply shifted the costs of administration to local peoples and freed European manpower and materials for other purposes. Decaying mineral resources, especially of coal and iron, have ceased to matter very much. The quality of European skills and training establishments assures a continued supply of competent personnel for economic as well as other forms of activity; and the advantages the United States and Russia both enjoyed, when Europe was divided by tariff barriers into a number of comparatively very small segments, was neutralized by the success of the European Common Market after 1957.

The world's largest mass market no longer lies in America or Russia but in western Europe, where more people with a high standard of living are gathered together within a single tariff system than anywhere else in the world. Such an upshot of two devastating world wars would have seemed incredible in the 1930's, and testifies to the continued vitality of European society.

c. Political Development of Europe, 1914 to 1953

1) World War I, and the Peace Settlement. Austro-Hungary declared war on Serbia on July 28, 1914. Within a week the alliance system of Europe resulted in the intervention of Russia, France and Great Britain on the side of Serbia, and of Germany on the side of Austria. Italy, although a member of the Triple Alliance, and so allied with Germany and Austria, did not join in the war immediately, declaring that the terms of the alliance did not apply because the Austrians were fighting aggressively. The battles between Serbia and Austria quickly became a minor aspect of the war; major combat centered in northern France (the Western Front) and over a wide belt of territory lying between Germany, Austria and Russia (the Eastern Front).

The Germans were the best prepared of any of the belligerents and until near the end of the war were able to keep the military initiative in their hands for the most part. The initial German plan was to concentrate against France, and after administering a knockout blow, to turn eastward to deal with the Russians. This plan came near success. During the first weeks of the war German armies penetrated far into France, and reached the Marne river, about thirty miles from Paris. Between September 5 and 12, however, the French managed to stop the German advance (the first Battle of the Marne), and during the ensuing weeks, the Germans withdrew some miles and both sides began to dig in, building elaborate trench systems, which, when resolutely defended, proved almost unpassable. The result in the West was nearly four years of trench warfare. Efforts by either side to break through proved very costly—more than a million casualties were suffered at Verdun and the Somme in 1916—but always fell short of decisive success.

The war in the east remained much more mobile. While the Germans were invading France during the first weeks of the war, the Russians advanced into East Prussia. This persuaded the German General Staff to withdraw some forces from the Western Front and rush them to the east, where, at the end of August, 1914, the Russian advance was halted (Battle of Tannenberg) and the Russians were compelled to withdraw from German soil.

It is not necessary to describe the various campaigns and offensives which were launched during the following years. Two general tendencies

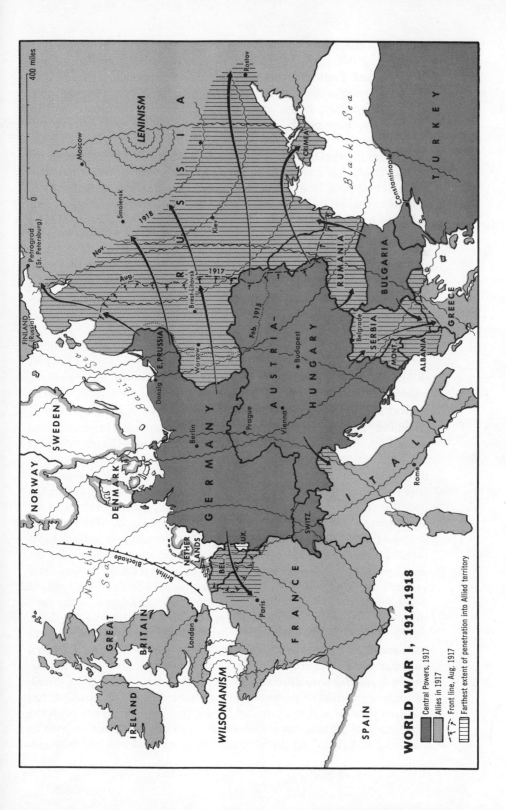

400 miles

LENINISM

Moscow

Smolensk

1918

Nov.

Petrograd
(St. Petersburg)

Aug.

FINLAND
(Russia)

Rostov

Crimea

Black Sea

TURKEY

Constantinople

Kiev

1917

Brest-Litovsk

Feb. 1915

BULGARIA

RUMANIA

SERBIA

Belgrade

MONT.

ALBANIA

GREECE

R U S S I A

E. PRUSSIA

Danzig

Warsaw

AUSTRIA-

HUNGARY

Budapest

Berlin

Prague

Vienna

SWITZ.

G E R M A N Y

Baltic Sea

SWEDEN

DENMARK

NORWAY

I T A L Y

Rome

NETHER-
LANDS

BEL.

Lux.

Paris

F R A N C E

North Sea

British Blockade

GREAT
BRITAIN

London

IRELAND

WILSONIANISM

SPAIN

WORLD WAR I, 1914-1918

Central Powers, 1917

Allies in 1917

Front line, Aug. 1917

Farthest extent of penetration into Allied territory

may be noted. First, the British instituted an economic blackade against Germany which was rigorously enforced, even in defiance of provisions of international law. In the long run the blockade had an important effect in weakening Germany by cutting off some necessary raw materials and by reducing the food supply which was needed to maintain the German population in good fighting and working condition. Germany retaliated by attempting to blockade Great Britain with submarines. But this weapon was never wholly effective, and had the unfortunate effect for Germany of helping to precipitate the intervention of the United States in the war. This brings us to the second general tendency: the spread of the war to involve other countries. Both sides strove by all means at their command to find additional allies. The result of military action, diplomacy, propaganda and threats was to bring Belgium (1914), Italy (1915), Rumania (1916), the United States (1917), and Greece (1917) into the war on the side of the Allies; while Turkey (1914) and Bulgaria (1915) associated themselves with the Central Powers. Outside of the European continent, Japan and some of the countries of Central and South America also declared war on the Central Powers, although they took little part in the actual combat.

In 1917 the strain of the war, the incompetence of the Czarist government, and widespread discontent among Russian soldiers and civilians resulted in the collapse of the Russian armies. During the first two years of the war, Russian armies had fought well, despite lack of adequate military equipment and occasional bad generalship. Ground won at great cost of human life against the Austrians was lost again when German generals and reinforcements arrived to strengthen the Austrian armies; and a deep distrust of their government gradually took firm hold on the majority of Russian minds. Revolutionary undercurrents had been strong among the people of Russia for more than a decade; in 1917 the discontent and the revolutionary impulse came suddenly to the surface. In March of that year the Czar abdicated and a provisional government was formed. Eight months later, after the Provisional Government tried to reorganize the army and resume offensive operations, a second revolution occurred and brought the Bolsheviks to power (November, 1917). Peace, immediate peace, was a part of the Bolshevik program; and before the end of the year, the new revolutionary government signed an armistice (Brest-Litovsk).

This victory made it possible for the Germans to concentrate most of their forces on the Western Front. In the spring of 1918, they launched a last offensive. For several weeks the German armies were able to advance, and in July, 1918 they once again reached the Marne river. But German manpower and military resources were almost exhausted by the effort, and the arrival of large contingents of American troops in France, with the psychological lift that the assurance of American participation gave to battle-weary French and British troops, turned the tide. In July the Allies began a counteroffensive, and the Germans were compelled to retreat all along the Western Front.

Meanwhile success was coming to the Allied armies in other theaters of war. Bulgaria capitulated in September, 1918; Turkey followed suit in October; Austro-Hungary began to break up into various new national states, and the Imperial Hapsburg government officially withdrew from the war on November 3. A week later, on November 11, Germany too signed an armistice. Emperor William II had abdicated two days before.

Thus after four years and three months of fighting and the death of nearly ten million combatants, the war came to an end. It had been the most costly and hardest fought war of history, involving the mobilization of nearly all resources—human, material and financial—for the war effort, and a deep disruption of peacetime relationships. Famine and disease were rife in central and eastern Europe during the latter stages of the war and in the first years after the armistice; and in Russia and Turkey, disturbances connected with internal revolutions maintained war conditions until 1922.

The Peace Conference which met in Paris (January, 1919–June, 1920) was dominated by three figures: Woodrow Wilson, President of the United States, David Lloyd George, Prime Minister of Great Britain, and Georges Clemenceau, Premier of France. There were serious differences among the three men, in particular between Wilson and Clemenceau. Wilson hoped to bring permanent peace to the world by creating a League of Nations and by establishing democratic governments based on the principle of self-determination of peoples everywhere in Europe (if not in the world). Clemenceau, on the other hand, was interested in preventing the recovery of German military strength, and hoped to be able to wring from Germany reparation for the damage which had been done to France during the war. Lloyd George generally stood between his two colleagues: like Clemenceau, he wanted reparations, but he tended to sympathize more with the idealistic hopes of President Wilson than did the French premier.

These conflicts were supplemented by the numerous and frequently incompatible claims which smaller nations advanced before the Peace Conference. Italian demands for the annexation of the Dalmation coast were particularly troublesome. Secret treaties had promised the Italians a generous slice of Austrian territory, and it was on this basis that the Italian government had entered the war on the Allied side. But the promises of the secret treaties violated the principle of self-determination which President Wilson had enunciated as the basis of a just and durable peace, and he set his face resolutely against their fulfilment. As a result, the Italian delegates withdrew from the Peace Conference, and in the end the frontier between the new state of Yugoslavia (formed around the prewar Serbia by the addition of Croatia, Slovenia, and Montenegro) and Italy was

EUROPE AFTER WORLD WAR I

— Boundaries after 1923

Territories in 1914:
- Russia
- Germany
- Austria-Hungary

NORWAY

SWEDEN

FINLAND

RUSSIA

Helsinki

Leningrad

Oslo

Stockholm

ESTONIA

Moscow

GREAT

North
Sea

Baltic Sea

LATVIA

IRELAND

DENMARK

LITH-
UANIA

BRITAIN

NETHER-
LANDS

Danzig

E.
PRUSSIA

London

BELGIUM

Berlin

Warsaw

GERMANY

POLAND

Paris

LUX.

Prague

CZECHOSLOVAKIA

FRANCE

Vienna

Budapest

SWITZ.

AUSTRIA

HUNGARY

RUMANIA

Bucharest

Black
Sea

Belgrade

Danube

SPAIN

ITALY

Adriatic Sea

YUGOSLAVIA

BULGARIA

Sofia

CORSICA

Rome

ALBANIA

GREECE

TURKEY

SARDINIA

Mediterranean

Athens

SICILY

ALGERIA

TUNISIA

CRETE

Sea

0   500 miles

LIBYA

EGYPT

settled by direct negotiation between the two countries. The Italians felt that they had been very shabbily treated by their erstwhile allies, and the failure of the Italian government to secure more favorable terms from the Peace Conference helped to discredit it in the eyes of the Italian public. This situation provided a significant stimulus to the rise of Fascism.

At the Peace Conference, a series of treaties were prepared for the signature of the defeated nations. The Treaty of Versailles was signed by a representative of the German government on June 18, 1919. It was a document of several hundred pages, but its main provisions may be summarized as follows. Germany was required to cede Alsace and Lorraine to France, territory in the east to the newly resurrected state of Poland, as well as smaller bits of territory to Denmark and Belgium. German colonies were all transferred to the jurisdiction of the League of Nations, which later assigned them to various powers to be administered as mandates pending the time when such regions could assume full independence. The German army was reduced to a maximum of 100,000 men; the navy was severely limited; and a belt of territory extending from the French border to a line 30 miles east of the Rhine was demilitarized. The west bank of the Rhine was to be occupied for fifteen years by allied troops as a guarantee of the fulfillment of the terms of the treaty. In addition, Germany was required to admit guilt for causing the war, and agreed to pay reparations of an unspecified amount to the victorious nations to make good the wartime destruction of civilian property in Allied countries. Nearly all Germans regarded the Versailles treaty as unfairly punitive. The socialist government which came to power in Germany after the abdication of the Emperor signed only upon threat of resumption of war.

The Treaty of Saint-Germain with Austro-Hungary (signed September 10, 1919) was even more drastic in the sense that the old Hapsburg empire was entirely broken up. A small Austrian state and a small Hungarian state were formed; but the largest part of the former Austro-Hungarian Empire was portioned out to Czechoslovakia, Rumania, Poland, Yugoslavia, and Italy. Treaties with Bulgaria (Neuilly) and Turkey (Sèvres) made other changes in frontiers, prescribed reparations and limited the armaments of the defeated nations. The treaty with Turkey was not enforced, however, for a Turkish nationalist movement repudiated the terms, and, after several years of fighting, succeeded in winning a new and more favorable settlement (Lausanne, 1923).

In numerous details the frontiers drawn by the peace treaties disregarded the Wilsonian principles of self-determination. The men who drew the boundaries were interested in rewarding friends and punishing enemies; they were also inspired by a fear of the revival of German power, and so strove to build up strong states on the German frontier that would be capable of checking any resurgence of German strength. On numerous occasions President Wilson tried to mollify the severity of the terms imposed upon the defeated nations, and he won some concessions. But, in general, Wilson yielded, and put his main reliance upon the League of Nations, which he hoped would be able in future years to adjust some of the faults of the peace treaties. The Covenant of the League of Nations had been incorporated as a part of the Versailles Treaty and of the other treaties of peace, and the new international organization met for the first time in the fall of 1920. But it met without the United States, for the Senate refused to ratify the Versailles Treaty, very largely because ratification would commit the United States to membership in the League and so limit American sovereignty. Two other conspicuous absentees were Germany and Bolshevik Russia. The Germans neither wished nor were asked to join the League; and the Bolsheviks were then actually at war with the leading powers of the League.

Despite their effort to end the war with Germany, the Bolsheviks had not been allowed to remain in unchallenged control of Russia. A number of counter-revolutionary "white armies" formed in 1918; and Germany, France, Great Britain, the United States and Japan all at different times and in varying degrees lent aid to the counter-revolutionary forces. The Bolsheviks for their part were eagerly awaiting the outbreak of international socialist revolution, which they confidently expected to come as a result of the war. They had no thought of joining the League, which they regarded as an association of predatory capitalist governments.

In the westernmost portions of the Russian empire, the counter-revolutionaries met with some success. A tier of new states was formed largely or entirely from former Russian territory: Finland, Esthonia, Latvia, Lithuania and Poland. Until 1921 the Bolsheviks remained at war with white armies and with forces raised by some of these new states. By 1921, however, white armies had been driven from nearly all of the areas of the Czarist Empire which were inhabited by Russian-speaking populations, and the Bolshevik government decided to make peace and recognize the independence of the new states which had arisen along the former western frontier. The last treaty was that with the Poles, signed in March, 1921 (Treaty of Riga).

The absence of the United States, Russia and Germany from the League meant that it fell under the dominance of France and Great Britain. Under the leadership of these nations, President Wilson's hope of establishing the League as an effective world organization proved vain. France indeed put relatively little faith in the League of Nations from the beginning, and set about creating a net-work of alliances with Poland, Czechoslovakia, Yugoslavia, and Rumania aimed at maintaining the new settlement of Europe. Against these powers were arrayed a much weaker grouping of "dissatisfied" nations: Italy, Hungary, Bulgaria, and Austria.

Germany and Russia, potentially far more powerful, were also not satisfied with the new order of Europe; but until the 1930's internal problems
kept them from taking a primary place on the international scene. Under
Gustav Stresemann, who directed German foreign affairs from 1923–
1929, Germany embarked upon a policy of conciliation, and was able to
secure the abrogation of some of the more galling provisions of the
Versailles Treaty. During the same years, the Bolsheviks were struggling
with the problem of rebuilding a nearly shattered society. They did not
take a very active part in official diplomacy, for they regarded all bourgeois
governments as their natural enemies, and tended to rely on revolutionary
movements to undermine and eventually to overthrow the established
régimes of Europe and elsewhere.

2) War-Born Revolutions. World War I brought revolution to most of
Europe. The violence and character of the revolutions varied from country to country, being most drastic in Russia and less so in other nations of
central and eastern Europe. Only the three major revolutions can be
separately described here: the Russian, the Italian and the German.

It should, however, be pointed out that the establishment of new nation
states in central and eastern Europe, as a result of the disruption of the
Austro-Hungarian, Russian and (to a much lesser degree) German Empires, involved something resembling social revolution. In the Baltic states,
Poland, Czechoslovakia, Rumania and Yugoslavia new men rose to positions of political and economic power, displacing the old official, land-
owning and managerial classes. To be sure, the shift took place under the
banner of national self-determination, and national patriotism bound together different classes among the formerly submerged nationalities of
eastern Europe; yet because the topmost social positions had formerly
been pre-empted in large degree by Austrians, Hungarians, Russians and
Germans, the establishment of these new national states did resemble
social revolution. This was especially the case with respect to land ownership. In the years immediately after 1918, great estates were broken up in
most of the east European countries and apportioned to the peasantry.
Since great estates, owned mostly by noble families, had been characteristic of these regions before 1918, the scale and significance of the
change was very great. Only in Hungary, in some parts of Poland, and in
eastern Germany did the prewar landed aristocracy succeed in maintaining
its position, and even in these cases, did so with difficulty.

In the victorious nations of western Europe the prestige of victory tended
to bolster the established order. Yet even in the west the immediate postwar years were a time of social unrest and revolutionary ferment. The
general strike in Great Britain in 1926 was the most dramatic expression
of this spirit, but it was by no means the only one. Wilsonian liberalism and

Marxian socialism were both, in their different ways, revolutionary when applied to the Europe of 1918; and the two challenges to the old order, one issuing from the United States, the other from Bolshevik Russia, unsettled European society more profoundly than any comparable movements after World War II succeeded in doing.

   a) The Bolshevik Revolution and the Communist Régime in Russia, 1917–1941

---

   i)   Peculiarities of Russian Society
   ii) Bolshevik Seizure of Power
   iii) War Communism and Civil War
   iv) NEP and Intra-Party Disputes
   v)   Five Year Plans
   vi) Foreign Policy, 1917–1939

---

   i) Peculiarities of Russian Society. Regular contact between Russia and western Europe dated only from the sixteenth century, and despite all that had been done by Peter the Great (1682–1725) and his successors, Russian society remained very different from that of western Europe. Up to 1917, towns remained relatively few and most of them were small. Class divisions familiar in western Europe did not fit the Russian scene very well, and it is most profitable to think of the town population of Russia as divided between officials and non-officials, realizing that the former performed many functions which were left to private hands in Western countries, and enjoyed a high social prestige. In the countryside, the division was between landowners and peasants; but in most parts of Russia, the peasantry was organized into a peculiar and distinctive organization, the *mir*. The *mir* was the unit of local taxation, and performed many functions of local government; but what made it unique was the custom of periodically redividing the land among the members of the association, each peasant family having a right to a share proportionate to the number of working hands it could muster. Within the *mir*, obviously, concepts of property in land, familiar in the west for centuries, were absent. Most Russian peasants felt strongly that private landownership (represented for them by the nobles' estates which had been withdrawn from communal cultivation only in 1861 in connection with the abolition of serfdom) was unjustified.

   The workingmen of the towns were recruited almost entirely from peasant families, and many of them continued to maintain membership in the *mir* into which they had been born and to which they continued to owe tax obligations. The men working in a particular factory found it natural to recreate the informal organization of the *mir* in their new environment, and in periods of excitement proceeded to set up soviets (i.e., councils) to discuss and decide what should be done. These soviets functioned quite as did the village assembly which conducted the business of the *mir*; and the soviets constituted a ready-made instrument for revolutionary action when a determined leadership could be provided for the separate soviets of each factory or (under the conditions of 1917) of each army unit. It was largely because the Bolsheviks were able to avail themselves of the network of soviets which had sprung spontaneously into being in the confused days of 1917, that a tiny number of professional revolutionaries was able to rise to power in Russia; and just because the internal organization and "staying power" of the soviets was very weak, the Bolsheviks were able, once in control of police and army, to disregard and even to repress further manifestations of discontent which took a "soviet" form.

ii) The Bolshevik Seizure of Power. The outbreak of war in 1914 constituted a serious crisis for the international socialist movement. Marxist parties had formed a Second International in 1889, but when hostilities commenced in 1914, one after another the socialist parties of the European nations came to the support of their national governments. Socialist internationalism proved to be hollow indeed. A few small groups, however, clung steadfast to their theoretical principles. Lenin and the Bolshevik party were among those who opposed "imperialist war" and urged the conversion of international into civil war, i.e., a war of proletarians against the bourgeoisie. During the first three years of the war, however, Lenin had no opportunity to put his principles into operation. He was an exile in Switzerland, cut off from events in Russia by the difficulties of wartime communication.

Meanwhile in Russia confidence in the government reached a very low ebb. In March, 1917, strikes and street rioting broke out on a large scale in Petrograd (as the capital had been named after the outbreak of the war with Germany). Liberal members of the Duma seized upon the opportunity to demand responsible constitutional government; on March 11 the Czar declared the Duma dissolved, but the deputies decided to remain in session and elected a committee to lead the Duma in its struggle against the autocracy. During the same day, a city-wide soviet was formed among the workers of the Petrograd factories, and deputies from units of the army were invited to join it. After four days the Czar decided to yield. He recognized the Committee of the Duma as a Provisional government, and abdicated in favor of his brother, who, however, refused to accept the crown. Thus the Romanoff dynasty came abruptly to an end. Six days after his abdication, Nicholas II and his family were made prisoners. In 1918 they were executed.

The leaders of the Duma and of the Provisional government were mostly liberals; the Petrograd Soviet, on the other hand, speedily came under the influence of socialists and revolutionaries. An uneasy balance of power came to exist between the two. The Provisional government depended on the loyalty and obedience of the old governmental bureaucracy, and on the army. But these proved an inadequate support. The bureaucracy, police and army were thoroughly demoralized; and when the Provisional government persisted in trying to organize further campaigns against the Germans, the unpopularity of the war and the propaganda of the Bolsheviks effectively undermined its power. Soldiers deserted and went home in great numbers upon hearing rumors that the land was at last to be distributed among the peasants, for they wished to be on the scene and be able to assure themselves of their full share when the division took place.

Events in Petrograd moved rapidly. The original Provisional government (Prince Lvov's cabinet) speedily found itself unable to meet the crisis which it faced. Changes in personnel brought the more radical members of the Duma to the fore. Thus, Alexander Kerensky, a Socialist Revolutionary (though belonging to a moderate wing of that group) became the head of the Provisional government in July, 1917; but for all his eloquence he could not succeed any better than his predecessors in satisfying the demands of the people of Petrograd and the peasants of Russia. Plans for electing a constituent assembly to fix a permanent new form of government were repeatedly postponed, until, just before his overthrow, Kerensky ordered elections and set a date in January, 1918, for the meeting of a Constituent assembly.

In April, a little more than a month after the establishment of the Provisional government, Lenin arrived in Petrograd. He had been sent to Russia by the Germans, who hoped that he would be able to weaken or even cripple the Russian war effort by his agitation. In their calculation, the Germans were entirely correct. Within a day of his arrival, Lenin publicly proclaimed in his "April Theses" the necessity for fraternization between Russian and German troops in order to bring the imperialist war to a fittingly revolutionary end. Trotsky (real name Lev Bronstein, 1879–1940) returned to Russia from the United States a few weeks later and soon joined the Bolshevik party. He rapidly rose to a leading place, second only to Lenin.

Soviets analogous to that of Petrograd had meanwhile been formed in most provincial towns, and various revolutionary agitators established a fairly effective liaison between the local soviets and that of the capital. In June, the first All-Russian Congress of Soviets met in Petrograd. At this Congress the Bolsheviks were a small minority, while the Socialist Revolutionaries were by far the largest group. The Congress listened to speeches denouncing the war and the Provisional government; it also elected an

Executive Committee of 300 and a Praesidium of 10 to act as a sort of shadow government and coordinate the policies of the various soviets which had sprung into existence.

In July the Bolsheviks attempted to seize power by a *coup d'état*; but they were thwarted, and Lenin and other Bolshevik leaders went into hiding for a few months. In September the Provisional government faced the danger of a coup from the right. The effort came to nothing, but at the height of the scare the Provisional government fell back upon support offered by the Bolsheviks, who had organized a militia in the factories and working class districts of Petrograd—the Red Guards. The Red Guards were among the few military forces available to the Provisional government at the time; accordingly the Bolsheviks were forgiven for their earlier attempt to overthrow the government, the Bolshevik leaders came out of hiding, and soon exercised a much greater influence than before.

The new popularity of the Bolsheviks was demonstrated by the election of Trotsky as president of the Petrograd Soviet in October, 1917. He used his position to organize, with Lenin and others, a second *coup d'état*. The preparation for seizure of power was amazingly open and leisurely. On October 22 the Petrograd Soviet voted to organize a Military Revolutionary Committee; the next day the Central Committee of the Bolshevik party voted to make the organization of an armed insurrection the immediate task of the party. On November 2 actual preparation began— assemblage of units of the Red Guards and the establishment of a military chain of command. On November 5, the Provisional government made a belated effort to crush the rising, but Kerensky could find very few troops willing to obey his orders; and when, during the night of November 6–7, the Bolsheviks assaulted the governmental offices in the center of Petrograd they met with almost no opposition.

The reasons for Bolshevik success were many. The confusion and irresolution of Kerensky and other members of the Provisional government certainly helped; the contrasting firmness of will which Lenin exhibited and the discipline of the Bolshevik party were also of importance. But perhaps the most important reason of all was the fact that the Bolsheviks succeeded in voicing the major demands of the great majority of the Russian people in general and of the inhabitants of Petrograd in particular. Bolshevik propaganda was summed up in three words: Peace, Land and Bread—peace for the soldiers, land for the peasants and bread for the city dwellers. Such an appeal proved irresistible, and no other political group persistently and consistently advocated all three.

The success which the Bolshevik propaganda had met was demonstrated by the fact that when the Second All Russian Congress of Soviets met a few hours after the seizure of power (which had indeed been timed in part with this in mind) the Bolsheviks and their sympathizers from among the left-wing Socialist Revolutionaries had a majority. When the Congress assembled on the evening of November 7, it proclaimed the dissolution of the Provisional government, and declared itself to be the supreme political authority of Russia. In the provinces, local soviets followed the example of Petrograd and took over governmental functions. The remnants of the Czarist bureaucracy simply dissolved.

Meanwhile, in the capital, the Congress of Soviets elected a Central Committee to take over direction of the central government; and the Committee appointed a Council of People's Commissars to conduct actual administration. Lenin became chairman of the Council of Commissars, while Trotsky was appointed Commissar for foreign affairs, and Stalin was made Commissar for nationalities. The government declared itself a dictatorship of the proletariat, and set out to build a socialist society.

It is difficult to recover the breathlessness and excitement of the days when the Bolsheviks came to power. High idealism flamed in the face of brutal necessity. Despite the uncertainty of the situation in Russia, hope and confidence in a bright proletarian future were intense. Many believed that the evils of society were about to be destroyed forever. World revolution was expected speedily to establish a classless society in which exploitation of man by man would cease and there would be abundance and leisure for all.

But Marx and his followers had not prepared specific plans for the realization of the post-revolutionary socialist ideal. Not only did the Bolsheviks lack definite socialist blue-prints, but they also faced very difficult conditions in Russia—conditions which had brought about the successive fall of the Czarist and of the Provisional governments. Hunger was widespread in the towns. Many factories were closed or worked only part time due to shortages of raw materials. The army had nearly disintegrated, and so had the civil administration.

It should be stressed that the Bolshevik leaders during the first few years of their rule in Russia lived in almost daily expectation of the outbreak of world revolution. They confidently believed that the proletariat of the more developed industrial countries would revolt against capitalist exploitation and rally fraternally to the revolutionaries of Russia. This expectation helped to buoy up revolutionary hopes in the most difficult times when it looked to most others as though the Bolshevik government were about to collapse. The expectation of world revolution also had the effect of making every action of the Bolshevik government seem temporary, to be reconsidered, perhaps retracted, as soon as The Revolution had taken place, for then, it was expected, the wealth of western Europe and the absence of serious foreign danger would completely transform the situation within Russia. Such considerations helped to make easier the numerous compromises with revolutionary idealism Lenin made in the first years.

Between 1917 and 1941 Bolshevik rule passed through three fairly distinct phases. From 1917 to 1921 was a period of War Communism and civil war; from 1921 to 1928 was a period of recuperation and temporary retreat from communist principles of economic organization; and after 1928 came a period of rapid industrial expansion and the consolidation of state control over all aspects of the economy and, indeed, over most aspects of human life.

iii) War Communism and Civil War. The Bolshevik government set itself to translate its slogan Peace, Land and Bread into reality without delay. On the day following the seizure of power the Soviet Congress issued a proclamation to the world calling for an immediate armistice. At the same meeting the Congress issued a decree abolishing private ownership of land in Russia. Landlords' properties were simply confiscated without compensation. The problem of supplying bread to the towns was more difficult, and could only be met by a series of makeshifts throughout the period of war communism.

The Bolsheviks (or as we may now call them, the Communists, for the party name was officially changed in March, 1918) soon discovered that it was one thing to ask the warring nations of the world to make peace and another thing to get them to lay down their arms. The Russian armies had already disintegrated as effective fighting forces when the Bolsheviks came to power; as a result the Germans were able to advance deeper and deeper into the country. At the same time, anti-Bolshevik groups began to form centers of resistance in outlying regions of the Russian empire. Near anarchy prevailed in many provinces, particularly in the Ukraine.

After waiting vainly for the proletariat of Germany, France and Britain to respond to his plea and halt the war, Lenin reluctantly entered into direct negotiations with the German government. An armistice in December was converted into a peace by the Treaty of Brest-Litovsk, signed in March, 1918. By this treaty, Poland, Lithuania and Latvia were ceded to Germany; Finland, Esthonia and the Ukraine were set up as independent states; and other pieces of territory were ceded to the Turks and to the Rumanians. The loss of the most developed parts of the old Russian state was a severe blow to the new government; but worse was to come, for various groups of counter-revolutionaries began to form irregular armies in the south, north and east, so that by the fall of 1918 the territory under the control of the Communist government had shrunk to north central Russia.

The danger in which the Communist government found itself called forth a great effort. Trotsky became Commissar for war and proceeded to organize a new Red Army. Conscription was reinstituted, and the Red Army grew from about 330,000 men in August, 1918 (when Communist fortunes were near their lowest ebb) to 5,500,000 two year later. This was

the instrument which turned back the White forces (by 1920) and invaded and nearly succeeded in conquering the new Polish state which imprudently attacked the Communists in the same year. It was therefore not until 1921 that the revolutionary government succeeded in establishing the peace which it had promised.

The problem of land offered no such obstacles: the peasants took control and the Bolsheviks legalized their action. Yet the alliance between the peasantry and the Communists was not firm. To maintain the bare military necessities of industrial production the Bolsheviks had to find food to keep the urban population alive, and the Red Army, too, had to be fed. But under the chaotic conditions which the Bolsheviks inherited, and which became worse rather than better after their seizure of power, it was impossible to feed the towns without resort to force. This meant violent confiscation of grain and other foodstuffs from the peasants; and such confiscation stirred up numerous peasant revolts. What saved the Communists was the fact that the Whites did the same thing; and when offered a choice of evils, the peasants generally preferred the Bolsheviks, who at least were committed to dispossessing the landlords.

The Communists not only had to wrestle with problems connected with peace, land and bread but also faced the difficulties of reorganizing a government. By degrees new instruments of administration were created, and some of the features of the Czarist régime were reinstituted. On November 17, 1917, for example, just ten days after the revolution, the Bolsheviks restored press censorship; in December a new political police, the Cheka, was organized to safeguard the revolution and punish saboteurs; and the organization of the Red Army has already been noted.

In January, 1918, the long-awaited Constituent assembly met in order to reorganize the Russian government on a permanent and legal basis. It had been elected by universal suffrage, and arrangements for its convocation antedated the Bolshevik seizure of power. When the Assembly met, it turned out that the Bolsheviks had only a minority of sympathizers among its members. As a result, the Bolshevik members withdrew on the very day that the Constituent assembly met; and four hours afterwards armed guards dismissed the august body which had been ready to make a new constitution for the Russian state. The basis of Bolshevik government was not to be democratic—at least not in the western way. Instead proletarian dictatorship drew its legitimacy from the support of workers', soldiers' and peasants' soviets led and instructed by the Communist party.

In the first months after the Bolshevik seizure of power, a part of the Social Revolutionary party cooperated with the new rulers of Russia; but in July, 1918, an abortive rising on the part of some Social Revolutionaries ended the coalition. Thereafter the Communist party had a monopoly of legality. The Communists enforced their new position by systematic terror which lasted until 1921. By then victory was assured, and summary executions and purges were stopped, to be resumed briefly under Stalin in the late 1930's.

An important problem which had been inherited from Czarist days was the relationship between the Great Russians and the various other nationalities included within the boundaries of the Russian state. On the west, the sense of nationality among Finns, Esthonians, Letts, Lithuanians and Poles was well developed and quite antagonistic to the Russians; in Central Asia and the Caucasus the numerous nationalities of those regions were much less conscious of their corporate identity. The Ukraine stood midway between. The Bolsheviks at first proclaimed that any groups which so desired had the right to secede; but during the period of civil war such a principle was found to be impractical and in fact appeals to the "true" interests of the subject nationalities were used to justify the overthrow of nationalist groups which tried to avail themselves of their theoretical right of secession.

In 1923 a new constitution was promulgated. The state was renamed Union of Soviet Socialist Republics, and four Soviet Republics were set up: the Russian, Ukrainian, White Russian and Trans-Caucasian. During subsequent years a number of other republics were formed in Central Asia, and by 1940 the number of constituent republics in the Soviet Union had reached sixteen. Political autonomy of the separate Republics was largely fictitious, since Party organizations and the All-Union organs of government exercised a very powerful control, and on several occasions disloyal or troublesome Republics were suppressed. On the other hand, the Soviet government encouraged the development of non-Russian national and tribal cultures within the framework of Communist ideas.

Side by side with the official machinery of government there grew up another, and as it proved, more powerful instrument of control: the Communist Party organization. Before the revolution, the Bolshevik party had been a very small group whose members were mostly professional revolutionaries. The party had financed its activities in part by robberies of banks and of government moneys—an activity in which a young Georgian named Joseph Djugashvili (1879-1953) particularly distinguished himself. He later became better known as Stalin (i.e., steel).

Supreme direction of party activities was vested in a Central Committee on which Lenin was the dominating figure. The theory of party discipline was described as "democratic centralism." The main principle was this: free discussion should prevail within the party until a policy was officially decided at a Party Congress or by the Central Committee; but once a decision had been made, every Bolshevik was bound to follow the party line and support the party's policy no matter what doubts, reservations or opposition he might personally feel or later develop. By insistence on this principle, Lenin was able to create a powerful, disciplined instrument through which the policies of the Communist government could be and were carried out.

The relation between the Party and the government was at first unclear. As early as 1919, however, Lenin enunciated the principle that the Party should guide the Soviets, and as time passed the primacy of the Party organization became more and more definite. Communists were held responsible for seeing that things went well within a factory, in a village, in units of the army, etc., and if they detected an official performing his task slackly or corruptly it was a part of Communist duty to step in and correct the situation. Communists also acted as propagandists among the rank and file of the population, explaining the purposes and policies of the new government to ignorant peasants and to impatient workmen. Cells of the Communist Party were by degrees organized everywhere, in factories, city blocks, and villages.

Above such primary Party cells an elaborate Party hierarchy came gradually into existence. District and city Party units were subordinated to regional units, and regional units to Party organizations which comprised entire Republics. The highest level was the All-Union Party organization. At each level above the primary cells, there was a three-fold Party organization: representative and deliberative assemblies, executive bodies, and a secretariat with subordinate or associated special bureaus.

Only the organization on the All-Union level will here be described. The All-Union representative body was the Party Congress, elected by active Party members all over the Soviet Union on the basis of one representative for every thousand members. From 1918 until 1925 Party Congresses were held annually, and at some of them matters of policy were heatedly discussed. Thereafter Congresses became rarer, and deliberation resolved itself into propaganda on behalf of policies already decided upon by the top Party leadership.

The Party Congress elected a Central Committee. During the first years of the new régime the Central Committee of the Party exercised much effective sovereignty; but as time passed the Committee was enlarged (68 members in 1939) and its meetings, too, became rarer. Power passed instead into the hands of smaller bureaus, organized by, and theoretically responsible to, the Central Committee (and through it to the Party Congress). These bureaus were the Politbureau (which dealt with political questions), the Orgbureau (which dealt with matters of Party organization, personnel and discipline), and the Secretariat (which carried out the decisions of the other two bureaus).

The Secretariat was of peculiar importance. In 1920 Lenin decided to create a Secretary General of the Party who would occupy a seat on both the Politbureau and the Orgbureau in order to coordinate the decisions of those bodies. The Secretary was supposed to be the passive executive agent of the two bureaus, carrying out their decisions, choosing appropriate Party members for various tasks, etc. In May, 1922, Stalin became

Secretary General. Shortly thereafter, because of a cerebral hemorrhage, Lenin's leadership came to an end: by the time of Lenin's death in 1924, Stalin had established himself as the most powerful leader of the Party.

Thus the history of Party organization was one of rapid concentration of power at the top. In theory the Party Congresses were (and remain) supreme, representing the rank and file of Party members; and all committees and bureaus theoretically derive their power from the Congresses. But in fact Stalin was able to control the Congresses, and by virtue of the principle of Party discipline and "monolithic unity" his decisions and those of the Politbureau, Orgbureau and Secretariat were never publicly questioned after 1927.

As the Party machine was perfected, it became possible for the Communist Party to control the Soviets, which were in theory the source of governmental power. As a result, debates and decisions taken by the Soviets at all levels of the hierarchy became little more than a formal ratification of what the leaders of the Communist Party had already decided upon.

By 1921 the civil war had come to an end. The Communists were victorious in Russia, the Ukraine, Siberia and the Caucasus. On the other hand the expected world revolution had not materialized, even though the Russians had established a new Communist International (the Third) in 1919, and Communist armies had tried to reach German comrades by invading Poland in 1920. The failure of revolution abroad made it appear that Communism would have to maintain itself in Russia alone, at least for a time, without the help and fraternal support of richer countries of the West.

Yet within Russia the prospect was bleak. Peasants had quite generally reacted to government requisitions by ceasing to plant more land than was needed to maintain themselves and their families. In addition, two successive drought years struck the south, especially the Volga region. The result was a severe and widespread famine, followed as always by disease from which hundreds of thousands, if not millions, died. At the same time industrial production was at its lowest ebb and hunger or near starvation raged in the towns. This was the unhappy situation which led Lenin to introduce a New Economic Policy at the Eleventh Congress of the Communist Party in the spring of 1921. The implementation of this policy introduced the second major phase through which the Russian revolution passed: the period of NEP.

iv) NEP and Intra-Party Disputes, 1921–1928. The essential innovation of Lenin's New Economic Policy was a restoration of a limited freedom for personal pursuit of gain. This involved a retreat from the communist ideal, and many persons both inside and outside of Russia regarded the concessions which were made in 1921 as a sort of Russian Thermidor. Yet state control over the economy was never abandoned. What was done was to limit the amount of grain which peasants owed to the state in lieu of taxes, and allow them to trade any surplus they might have for whatever they could find. Correspondingly, workmen in factories were paid partly in kind and in proportion to the amount of work done. This opened up the possibility of barter between town and country; and a new class of traders (the NEPmen) appeared to carry on such trade. In addition, private enterprise was permitted free scope in some light industry, mainly handicraft. But the state retained a monopoly of foreign trade, and the "commanding heights" of the economy remained in governmental hands, i.e., banks, heavy industry, and the more important light industries.

The effect of the cessation of civil and foreign war and of the NEP was to bring about a gradual recovery of Russian economic life. By 1927 agricultural production was about what it had been in 1913 and industrial production was back to about 85 percent of the prewar level.

Such success might seem to have warranted the continuation of NEP indefinitely. But two factors worked against such an outcome. First, NEP represented a compromise with communist theory which many members of the Party felt could not be tolerated forever. The second factor which operated against the continuation of NEP was the outbreak of serious rivalries among the leaders of the Communist party. In 1924 Lenin died. While he was alive Lenin had been able to exercise personal ascendancy over the party which he, more than any other, had created.

Of his lieutenants, Trotsky was by far the most famous and popular. Trotsky had won world fame as the organizer of the Red Army; and his great gifts as a writer and orator had secured him a high place in the councils of the Party. But Trotsky suffered from temperamental weaknesses. He was often haughty and overbearing. The fact that he had not joined the Bolsheviks until 1917 made many old Party members resent his preeminence. And Trotsky was a Jew, a fact which exposed him to covert antisemitism. Moreover his point of view was international, and he tended to think of Russia primarily as a point of leverage for bringing on the world revolution. This attitude exposed him to covert nationalist attack.

When Lenin died, Stalin was a relatively obscure figure in the public eye, but a power in the Party. He had a record as an Old Bolshevik, and had taken part in the civil war as a subordinate (and not always an obedient subordinate) of Trotsky. In addition to his post as Commissar of Nationalities in the first Bolshevik government, Stalin had served as Commissar of Workers' and Peasants' Inspection (1919); and from 1917 he had been a member of the Party Politbureau. His later power was founded, however, on the post of General Secretary of the Party to which he was appointed in 1922.

Of the other Communist leaders who engaged in the dispute for power after Lenin's death only two need be mentioned here. Grigory Apfelbaum (1883–1936), commonly known as Zionoviev, had been a companion of Lenin's exile. He became head of the Third International when it was first organized (1919), and with Stalin formed a clique in the Politbureau which controlled the policies of the government during Lenin's last illness. Leo Rosenfeld (1883–1936), known as Kamenev, was the third member of the triumvirate which took over Lenin's position. He was, like Zinoviev, a companion of Lenin's exile, and a brother-in-law of Trotsky.

When Lenin died, the first anxiety of Stalin, Zinoviev and Kamenev was to prevent Trotsky from inheriting Lenin's place. In this they were successful; but Trotsky more or less publicly criticized their policies, and soon gathered around himself a "left opposition." As a result, in 1925 Trotsky was deprived of his post as Commissar of War. Meanwhile Zinoviev and Kamenev had quarreled with Stalin; and in June, 1926, they came to an understanding with Trotsky, joining him in the left opposition. The group prepared an elaborate statement of their platform and program for presentation to the Fifteenth Party Congress, schedule for December, 1927. But the program was never presented. On November 7, 1927, on the day of the tenth anniversary of the Bolshevik seizure of power, Trotsky and his supporters organized a demonstration against Stalin. The demonstration was broken up by police, and Trotsky and Zinoviev were at once expelled from the Party on the charge of having violated Party discipline. When the Fifteenth Congress met several hundred others were also expelled. Two years later, in 1929, the Soviet government exiled Trotsky from Russia. He continued to criticize Stalin from various lodging places abroad, until he was assassinated in Mexico by an agent of the Russian secret police in 1940.

v) Five Year Plans, 1928–1941. The defeat of Trotsky and the "left opposition" in 1927 seemed to assure a continuation of NEP. Yet that was not what happened. In 1928 the first five year plan was drawn up and adopted, and the Soviet government under Stalin's leadership embarked upon a program of rapid industrial expansion. Without enormous loans from abroad (which was the method which the prewar Czarist régime had used) the only way in which capital for industrial development could be found was to use taxation and price control to withdraw a portion of current production from consumption and use it instead for investment. This is what the first and subsequent five year plans accomplished. State monopoly of nearly all selling made it possible to mark up prices by any desired amount, and to use the profits so acquired to finance the building of new factories. Side by side with such financial planning and control went physical planning—a calculation of how much of every product would be needed for the planned achievements, and of the physical exchanges that would be necessary for the fulfillment of the plan. Still a third aspect of planning was the control of manpower. This was secured through the re-institution of a system of internal passports, and also by extensive use of compulsory labor.

The major economic production of Russia was agricultural, and, if resources were now to be devoted to building up industry, it was perforce from the peasants that a large share of the necessary means must come. The peasants' contribution to industrialization was three-fold: manpower was taken from farms and used for various construction or factory tasks; grain was taken from the peasants, and used to feed the factory and construction workers (as well as the administrative, police and army personnel); and, thirdly, agricultural products were sold abroad and the money realized was used to purchase machinery that could not be manufactured in Russia, to hire foreign engineers, etc.

A country divided into millions of separate farms could not easily be controlled for such purposes. Individual farmers could hide part of their produce, or might resort to the device of not planting enough seed to provide the necessary surplus. Consequently, the first Five Year Plan provided for the collectivization of a large proportion of the farms of Russia. The program of collectivization was pressed with full revolutionary enthusiasm, and in an amazingly short time (1930) nearly all the soil of Russia was portioned out among collective farms. Collectivization was not, however, carried through without loss. Many peasants, especially the more prosperous ones, did not want to pool their livestock, tools and land in a collective farm, and rather than do so, slaughtered their animals. Those who sabotaged the new agricultural organization, or who were accused of wanting to do so, were deported in great numbers, and were sent to compulsory labor in distant mines and forests at tasks for which free labor could not be found.

Collective farms had a number of advantages from the point of view of the government. It was a relatively easy administrative matter to collect from them a portion of the harvest for state uses, whereas to collect from millions of individual peasants was difficult. The use of machinery was facilitated, with corresponding saving of manpower which was needed for construction work. Moreover, agricultural experts could supervise the work on the collectives, and might in time improve farming techniques.

From the point of view of the peasants, however, the drastic and compulsory reorganization of traditional village life into collectives did not win wide support. The Government took a heavy proportion of the collectives' production in the form of taxes; peasant living standards remained very low; and from a peasant point of view the multiplication of accounting and administrative personnel within the collective farm unit meant "idle" mouths to feed from the common pool.

In the field of industry, the first Five Year Plan concentrated upon heavy construction. New mines were opened up, and factories for refining ore, making agricultural machinery, airplanes, machine tools, chemicals, etc., were built in great number. About one third of the national income was devoted to such expenditures. Inevitably the Russian people suffered a corresponding decrease in the quantity of consumption; but widespread public enthusiasm, whipped up by all the propaganda means at the command of the government, helped to sustain the morale of the population despite physical hardships. Collectivization caused famine in some parts of Russia in 1932–33, and the new factories did not immediately begin production of consumers' goods. Yet, in 1932, after only four and a half years, the first Five Year Plan was declared "overfulfilled," and a second one was prepared.

The Second Five Year Plan (1932–37) was originally designed to concentrate on building up consumers' goods industries; but the accession of Hitler to power in Germany in 1933 led the Soviet leaders to change their plans, and to divert the main effort from consumers' goods to heavy industry and armaments. The same emphasis characterized the Third Five Year Plan which was in operation when the Germans invaded Russia in 1941.

The net achievements of the five year plans was very great. A country which had been predominantly agricultural, and which had depended on foreign countries for the import of essential manufactured goods, was changed into a leading industrial producer, largely independent of foreign imports. The test of war from 1941 to 1945 proved the quality and quantity of Russian military production. But these successes were won at tremendous cost. The diversion of wealth to armaments meant a depression of the standard of current consumption. Until the 1950's there was little if any rise in the Russian standard of living; and some statisticians believe that between 1928 and 1941 it remained lower than in 1913.

The hardships and sufferings of the five year plans did not fail to find political expression. In 1934 one of Stalin's closest associates, Sergei Kirov, was assassinated; and his death provided the occasion for the arrest and trial of a number of prominent Communists who had been associated with various opposition movements. In addition a widespread purge of the Party was undertaken, and many thousands of malcontents were arrested and either shot or condemned to forced labor under conditions which often resulted in death. Something like the Terror of War Communism was revived. Two famous trials were held at Moscow in 1936 and in 1937 in which the Soviet government attempted to prove that Trotsky, Zinoviev, and several other famous leaders of the Bolshevik movement had engaged in conspiracy against the Russian régime and had even come into contact with the Nazi government in Germany, hoping to enlist Hitler's help against Stalin. An extraordinary aspect of these trials was that some of the accused confessed, although their confessions were certainly false on some points of detail.

In 1936 a new "socialist" constitution was adopted and has since remained in force. This constitution made several alterations in the Soviet hierarchy of government. The class basis of previous constitutions was abandoned, and the right to vote was accorded to everyone on equal terms, regardless of his class origin. Supreme power was in theory entrusted to a body known as the Supreme Soviet, divided into two parts, a Council of the Soviet Union, representing the population directly, and a Council of Nationalities, representing the various Republics, autonomous regions, national areas, etc., into which the territory of the state was subdivided.

The Constitution of 1936 was officially hailed as "the most democratic of the world." It was held to inaugurate the era of socialism, a stage on the way to ultimate communism (to be based on the principle: from each according to his ability, to each according to his need). Yet the political monopoly of the Communist Party was not relinquished. Every effort was made to secure unanimity in elections to the Supreme Soviet and in the votes of that body. Thus in spite of the changes brought by the Constitution of 1936, effective power remained with Stalin and a small circle of his advisers in the Party Politbureau and Secretariat.

vi) Foreign Policy 1917-1939. When the Bolsheviks came to power in Russia they expected the early outbreak of world revolution. This expectation lasted until about 1923, when the failure of Communist movements in Germany and elsewhere persuaded the rulers of Russia that capitalism had temporarily been stabilized. Yet belief in the ultimate arrival of a world revolution was never officially abandoned. The Soviet government consequently conducted its foreign policy on a double plane: one based upon official diplomatic relations with other nations of the world, and the other based upon revolutionary comradeship with, and, after about 1936, control over the Communist parties of other countries.

Until 1922 official diplomatic relations did not exist with any Western state, but in that year a treaty was signed with Germany, and gradually other nations recognized the Soviet Union and exchanged diplomatic representatives. The rise of Hitler to power in Germany (1933) created a new danger for the Soviet state, and the rulers of Russia reacted by seeking allies abroad. In 1934 the Soviet Union joined the League of Nations and tried to use that body to help ward off the threat of Nazi aggression. In 1935 the USSR signed a defensive alliance with France designed to serve the same end. But there was never any real confidence between the nations of the West and the Soviet Union. When the British and French capitulated to Germany and Italy at Munich (1938) Stalin decided that no trust could be placed in support from the capitalist west. Accordingly in 1939 the Russians and the Germans signed a "non-aggression" pact. A few days later Germany attacked Poland, thus beginning World War II.

Unofficial foreign relations with other Communist parties were carried on through the Third International or Comintern, established in 1919. Theoretically the Russian Communist Party was only one of several national parties all subordinated to the International, but in fact its power and prestige were so great in comparison with other Communist parties that the Comintern was dominated by Russia from the first. As time passed Russian control was consolidated and made more complete. At the beginning the various groups which associated themselves with the Comintern included radicals with diverse backgrounds, many of whom were not prepared to accept dictation from Moscow; but by degrees such leaders were purged as "factionalists," and new men, many of them trained in special revolutionary schools in Russia, came to control the Communist parties of the world. This development was completed only in the years immediately preceding the Second World War, and was much accelerated in connection with the purges of the Communist Party in Russia which occurred between 1936 and 1938.

b) The Fascist Movement in Italy. The failure of Italian diplomats to win extensive territorial gains at the Peace Conference of 1919 helped to discredit the government. Far more serious was the widespread outbreak of disorder, especially in the cities of the north. There revolutionary socialist parties (associated with the Third International) and a new Fascist party came into repeated conflict. Street brawls and riots became commonplace.

The Fascist party was founded in March, 1919, under the leadership of Benito Mussolini (1883–1945). Mussolini had been a socialist before the war, and his new party at first adopted a radical program which borrowed much from socialist and syndicalist theories. But in place of the internationalism which was traditional among socialist movements, Mussolini emphasized Italian nationalism, and proclaimed that war and violence were schools through which nations and individuals must pass on the way to greatness. Rather rapidly the elements of social radicalism faded from the Fascist program while the militaristic and nationalistic elements came to the fore. "Battalions of combat," equipped with clubs and firearms, systematically attacked socialists, broke up the print shops of unfriendly newspapers, and in general seized forcible control of the streets in Milan and other important towns.

By 1922 Mussolini had attracted to his party a fairly numerous following of adventurers, ex-soldiers, discontented intellectuals, etc., and had secured financial support from some businessmen and landowners. In

October of that year he announced a March on Rome. Fascist battalions entrained in Milan and elsewhere, arrived in Rome and took over the principal public buildings without meeting any effective resistance. The king was alarmed, but yielded to the *fait accompli* by asking Mussolini to become premier of the government.

When Mussolini first became the premier of Italy his party was a minority in the Chamber of Deputies, and his first cabinet contained no less than ten non-Fascists as against four members of his party. However, the new premier was able to wring a grant of special powers from the Chamber of Deputies, and took advantage of his position to put Fascists in key positions, while building up the strength of both the army and the Fascist battalions. The battalions continued to attack political opponents, and by degrees non-Fascist political parties were driven underground. Press censorship was instituted in 1924 and all opposition newspapers were suppressed in the following year. Non-Fascist labor unions were broken up in 1926; and by about 1927 Mussolini had succeeded in establishing himself as absolute master of Italy.

The new dictator of Italy used his power to reorganize the political institutions of the country on totalitarian lines. All rival political parties were made illegal, and the organization of the Chamber of Deputies was drastically transformed. After 1928, representation was not based upon geographical regions, but upon occupational groupings—an adaptation of syndicalist doctrine to Fascist use. A list of candidates was prepared under the scrutiny of the Fascist party, and voters could only choose between endorsing the list presented to them and casting a negative vote.

Changes in governmental machinery were accompanied by a steady expansion of the role of government in the economy. Extensive public works were carried through, and private capital was guided into channels approved by the state. Education was extended to many backward regions of the country on a greater scale than ever before; and systematic efforts were made to rally the entire Italian people behind the Fascist government and the Duce (i.e., leader).

Another important success for Mussolini was the accord he reached with the papacy in 1929. The pope recognized the loss of the Papal States and accepted sovereignty over a tiny area around the Vatican and St. Peter's. In return for this concession, Mussolini declared Roman Catholicism to be the "sole religion of the state," and undertook to pay clerical salaries from state funds. This agreement ended a long standing dispute between Church and state in Italy which had previously acted to divide the country into mutually mistrustful parts.

Abroad, Mussolini attempted during the 1920's to rival the power of France by fanning discontent in states dissatisfied with the peace treaties. Especially friendly relations were thus established with Austria, Hungary and Bulgaria; and Italy supported intrigues designed to disrupt the post-war state of Yugoslavia. Mussolini constantly glorified war and spoke of a revival of the ancient Roman empire. The rise of German military power after 1933 resulted in a temporary effort to improve relations between Italy and France; but in 1935, when Mussolini attacked Ethiopia and was denounced as an aggressor by the League of Nations, the friendship between Italy and France came to an end. Half hearted economic sanctions were imposed against Italy, but the French and British were not willing to risk war. They feared to see Mussolini overthrown, believing that such an event might bring communism to Italy or at least would create serious disturbance from which world war might result.

Thus the policy adopted by France and Great Britain succeeded in alienating Mussolini without succeeding in checking his attack upon Ethiopia. The result was a rapprochment between Italy and Germany. Prerequisite for this rapprochement was an agreement over Austria. In 1934, when the Nazis first tried to take over that country, Mussolini mobilized the Italian army on the frontier, and compelled Hitler to abandon the enterprise. In 1936 however, Hitler agreed to leave Austria independent and to refrain from making propaganda for the annexation of Austria to Germany. On this basis Italy and Germany became allies, forming what came commonly to be called the Axis.

The most conspicuous activity in which the new allies engaged during the next years was intervention in the Spanish civil war. Fighting broke out in Spain in 1936 when a group of army officers revolted against a left republican government which had come to power as a result of elections in 1936. With the help of arms and "volunteers" sent from Italy and from Germany, the rebels won the war (1939) and General Francisco Franco became dictator of Spain.

During the same years Germany succeeded in casting off the shackles of the Treaty of Versailles, and was able once again to build up a formidable military establishment. In 1938, despite the understanding of two years previous, the Nazis took over Austria. The next spring, as a sort of consolation prize, Mussolini moved troops into Albania, which had long been an economic dependency of Italy and had been ruled by a puppet government. This was Mussolini's last success in foreign policy. With the outbreak of World War II German power eclipsed the Italian; and indeed, the enterprises on which Italy embarked alone—war with Greece (1940–41) and fighting against the British in North Africa—were embarrassing failures for the Duce who had so long boasted of the new military prowess of the Italian nation. In the spring of 1941 German armies had to come to the rescue of the Italians in both Greece and North Africa. In July, 1943, a *coup d'état* overthrew Mussolini's government a few weeks before the Allied landings in Italy; but German paratroopers rescued the fallen dictator and he remained a German puppet in the part of Italy which German troops controlled until 1945.

c) The German Revolutions. Of all the countries of the world, Germany seemed the leading candidate for socialist revolution in the days immediately after World War I. Germany had a large proletariat and a strong and numerous Marxian party, the Social Democrats. Defeat in 1918 brought profound discredit to the imperial régime, serious impoverishment, and widespread social disorder. Indeed, a legal revolution did take place. After the Kaiser abdicated (November, 1918) an interim régime took over based in the old imperial Reichstag. As soon as possible, a constitutional assembly met in Weimar and established a new republican constitution for Germany. There was no legal continuity between Imperial Germany and the Weimar republic, and in this strict legal sense a revolution had therefore occurred. But in practice, the Social Democrats who from the beginning occupied the leading place in the new government, were half hearted revolutionaries. The leaders of the Social Democratic party had a long tradition of successful trade union and party work behind them, and had become administrators and parliamentarians. They had come to pin their faith on democracy and on the liberal institutions associated with democratic government. They were willing to postpone the transformations of property relations, called for by their socialist principles, until the operations of legal parliamentary government could bring such changes gradually and peacefully.

Such a frame of mind was barely capable of coping with the chaotic conditions of post war Germany. A powerful German Communist party, stimulated by the Russian example, attempted twice, in 1919 and again in 1923, to seize power by a *coup d'état*. On the extreme right, also, splinter groups and parties arose whose leaders were altogether unwilling to abide by the rules of democratic and parliamentary government. The National Socialist German Workers' Party, better known by the abbreviation Nazi, was one such group, founded in 1919. It soon came under the leadership of an obscure Austrian, Adolf Hitler (1889–1945), who had served as a corporal in the German army during the war.

Until 1923 the survival of the Weimar republic seemed often in doubt. Friction with France over the question of reparations payments led to a French invasion of the Rhinelands in 1923. Germans reacted by refusing to work in mines and factories for the benefit of the occupiers. As production slowed down, monetary inflation skyrocketed; and the whole financial structure of Germany collapsed, wiping out the savings of hundreds of thousands of middle class persons. This, more than the events immediately after the armistice, affected the temper and economic standing of social classes in Germany, bringing many professional and salaried people to a proletarian level. It was very largely from these dispossessed classes that the Nazis were able in later years to recruit their leaders and most fanatic followers.

The crisis of 1923 provoked a new flare-up of political violence in Germany. In that year the Communists made their second attempt to seize power; and Hitler also tried to imitate Mussolini by proclaiming a "putsch" in Munich. Neither effort was successful. Hitler and some other Nazi leaders were imprisoned for a few years, and Hitler used the enforced leisure of gaol to write *Mein Kampf* (My Battle), a book of autobiography and political doctrine which combined contempt for democracy, Jew-baiting and race mysticism into a turgid but heady brew. Like Mussolini, who provided something of a model for Hitler's first political adventures, the Nazis began as both a socialist and nationalist movement; but in proportion as he came nearer to power, Hitler tended to soft pedal socialist themes, and emphasized more his nationalist, antisemitic and anti-Bolshevik doctrines. Two other characteristics distinguished the Nazi movement. One of these was the leadership cult. Nazis fixed all authority upon the person of Adolf Hitler, who in some mystic way was supposed to embody the will of the German race in his person and would therefore provide the strong and resolute government which alone could throw off the shackles of Versailles and assure the future of the German people against all enemies. A second Nazi peculiarity was extreme antisemitism justified by the assertion that Jews were of a different race from true Germans and therefore natural rivals and indeed enemies.

After the crisis of 1923, a period of relative stability set in for the Weimar republic. International action brought a temporary settlement to the reparations problem; loans, mostly supplied from the United States, helped to stabilize German currency and a brief period of economic prosperity came to the harrassed people of Germany. But beneath the surface two great sores rankled. Nearly all Germans felt that the Versailles treaty was unjust, and many Germans felt impatient with a government which had accepted the Treaty (though not without protest) and which seemed incapable of securing real modification of its terms by peaceable negotiations. Denunciation of Versailles constituted one of Hitler's principal propaganda weapons in the political struggle of the early 1930's; and since he seemed to have the will to do something drastic about the hated treaty, his appeal was effective. The second weakness of the Weimar régime was the discontent of the impoverished professional and salaried classes, whose support of the Nazis has already been mentioned. In addition, there were powerful German groups, comprising aristocratic landowners, some industrialists, and such groups as the old officer corps, who looked back to the glories of imperial Germany with deep regret. Such conservative and nationalist groups disliked the Weimar régime, partly because a democratic and liberal government seemed weak—a government of talk rather than of deeds—and partly because they viewed the political leaders of the Social Democratic and other associated parties as social upstarts, whose political goals were subversive of the old order to which the conservatives wished to return.

Finally, the working classes of the industrial towns, upon whom the Social Democrats depended for their popular support, were by no means solidly committed to the Weimar government. A powerful Communist party continued to exist in Germany after 1923, and Communists agreed with Hitler in regarding the democratic and liberal constitution of Germany with the utmost contempt. In the critical years just before Hitler came to power, Communists directed their efforts against the Social Democrats in the hope of seizing power themselves: and by that policy certainly contributed something to Hitler's eventual success.

The half hidden weaknesses of the Weimar régime came into the open when the world depression, beginning in 1929, settled down upon Germany. Street demonstrations and riots increased in number, and all too clearly, the Government did not know what to do. Shifting coalitions between the Social Democrats and other parties floundered in the face of vast unemployment and street violence; and no firm majority in the Reichstag could be found to support any kind of stable government. Under such disturbed conditions both Communists and National Socialists throve, as can be seen from the following table:

NUMBER OF DEPUTIES ELECTED TO THE REICHSTAG

	Communists	Nazis
1930	77	107
1932	89	230
1932, fall	100	196

The second election in 1932 seemed to show that Hitler's movement had passed its peak. Some conservative and nationalist politicians concluded that it might be possible to use Hitler for their own purposes, by drawing upon the popular support of the Nazi movement to sustain their own exercise of power. The President of the Republic, Field Marshal Paul von Hindenburg therefore reluctantly agreed to appoint Hitler head of the German government.

Accordingly, when Hitler took power in January, 1933, the Nazis were a minority in the Reichstag and also in his first cabinet of ministers. This situation did not accord with Hitler's authoritarian principles. In March, 1933, he therefore called for new elections. The Nazi party machine was mobilized to secure the maximum possible number of votes for Hitler, and various laws were put into effect designed to limit the electioneering rights of opposition parties. As a result, the Nazis, together with a variety of smaller nationalist and reactionary parties, won a slender majority of the Reichstag (52 percent). When the Reichstag met, the delegates passed a law suspending the Weimar constitution and giving Hitler dictatorial powers for a period of four years.

Hitler used his new position to establish a totalitarian government. Institutions surviving from earlier times were suppressed; for instance the old German states were eliminated as political units and a new centralized, uniform administration was set up for all of Germany. Within a few days of his assumption of dictatorial powers, Hitler made the Communist party illegal, and a few months later other political groups were outlawed, giving the Nazi party a legal monopoly (July, 1933). Labor unions were suppressed, and new organizations, representing workers, employers and the government, were created to regulate wages and conditions of labor. The government extended its control over the economy with slight regard for the traditions of conventional "sound" finance. Large sums were appropriated for public works and for rearmament—which at first was carried on secretly, and became open only in 1935. By these means unemployment was rapidly reduced and prosperity was restored.

One of the most brutal aspects of the Nazi régime was its persecution of Jews. Government propaganda directed popular unrest against Jews. Antisemitic street riots and mob violence resulted. Legal discrimination and persecution followed. The attainment of German racial purity was enunciated as a goal of government policy.

In 1934 Hitler faced a crisis. Some among his followers felt that the socialist part of the party's program was being betrayed. The dispute was tangled with personal rivalries among high functionaries of the Nazi party, and in addition, jealousy existed between the regular army and the Nazi "private" army of Storm Troopers. The result of these, and perhaps of other strains within the Nazi party, was a purge in which several of the most prominent leaders of the Nazi party were summarily shot. A number of other figures prominent on the political scene before Hitler's rise were also executed. This demonstration of force helped to strengthen Hitler's position; when Hindenburg died in the same year, Hitler assumed the powers of the Presidency of the Reich, and was confirmed in his new dignity by a plebiscite. The result was to make Hitler the undisputed head of state. To mark the break with the Weimar régime, Hitler did not assume the presidential title but rested content with a new official appellation, Der Führer (i.e., leader), and called his government the Third Reich, (i.e., Third Empire—the first being the medieval Holy Roman Empire and the second, the German Empire of 1871-1918).

Hitler by degrees developed the full panoply of totalitarianism. Radio and press were thoroughly brought under government control; a secret

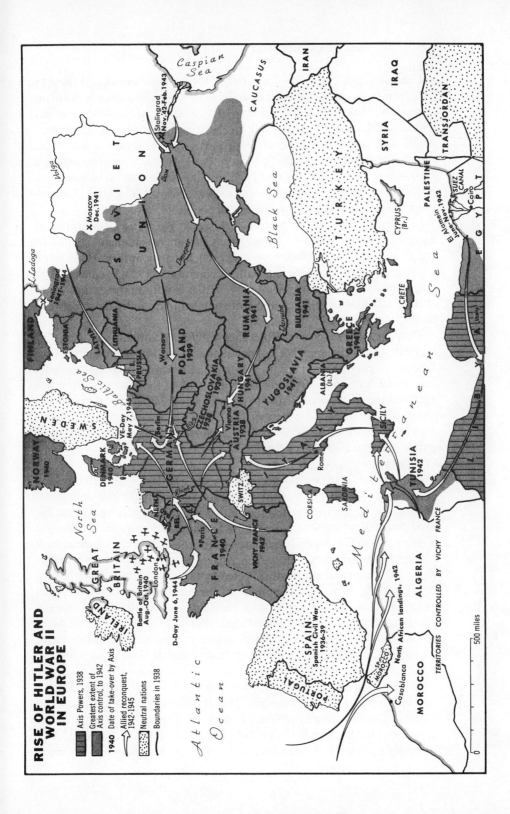

RISE OF HITLER AND WORLD WAR II IN EUROPE

Axis Powers, 1938

Greatest extent of Axis control, to 1942

1940 Date of take-over by Axis

Allied reconquest, 1942-1945

Neutral nations

Boundaries in 1938

0   500 miles

Caspian Sea

Volga

IRAN

IRAQ

Stalingrad Nov. 42-Feb. 1943

CAUCASUS

SYRIA

TRANSJORDAN

X Moscow Dec. 1941

S O V I E T   U N I O N

Don

T U R K E Y

PALESTINE

SUEZ CANAL

Cairo

L. Ladoga

Leningrad 1941-1944

Black Sea

CYPRUS (Br.)

El Alamein Nov. 1942

Suez

EGYPT

FINLAND

ESTONIA

LATVIA

LITHUANIA

Dnieper

RUMANIA 1941

BULGARIA 1941

GREECE 1941

CRETE

Danube

Baltic Sea

PRUSSIA

Warsaw

POLAND 1939

CZECHOSLOVAKIA 1938 1939

HUNGARY 1941

YUGOSLAVIA 1941

ALBANIA (It.)

A (Italy)

SWEDEN

VE-Day May 7, 1945

Berlin

Elbe

Vienna

AUSTRIA 1938

I T A L Y

SICILY

Mediterranean Sea

TUNISIA 1942

NORWAY 1940

DENMARK 1940

GERMANY

Rhine

SWITZ.

Rome

SARDINIA

North Sea

NETH.

BEL.

Paris

FRANCE 1940

VICHY FRANCE 1942

CORSICA

GREAT BRITAIN

IRELAND

Battle of Britain Aug.-Oct. 1940

London

D-Day June 6, 1944

ALGERIA

VICHY FRANCE

Atlantic Ocean

SPAIN Spanish Civil War 1936-39

PORTUGAL

Sp. MOROCCO

North African landing, 1942

Casablanca

MOROCCO

TERRITORIES CONTROLLED BY VICHY FRANCE

police (Gestapo) ferreted out political dissenters and consigned them to concentration camps for political reeducation or punishment which not infrequently resulted in death; a wide variety of financial and other manipulations concentrated foreign trade into channels approved by the government; and under the guise of Jewish persecution a very considerable transfer of property took place. Above all else, Hitler began to organize Germany for war, believing that only by military force could he secure the changes in frontiers which he regarded as necessary to secure "Lebensraum" (i.e., living space) for the German people.

In foreign affairs, Hitler met with successes as great and as unexpected as were his victories within Germany. German rearmament failed to create any decisive reaction among the French, partly at least as a result of the memory of the fiasco of the Ruhr occupation of 1923. Even when, in open defiance of the Versailles treaty, Hitler boldly marched into the Rhineland (1936), the French and British failed to do more than register diplomatic protests.

During the following years Hitler met with one diplomatic victory after another. In 1936 he came to an understanding with Mussolini and in the following years he helped secure victory for Franco in the Spanish civil war. In 1938 he annexed Austria, and in the fall of the same year he was able to compel France and British to agree to a dismemberment of Czechoslovakia. (Munich pact, September 19, 1938.) The following spring German troops occupied the remainder of Czechoslovakia, and its component parts—Bohemia, Moravia, and Slovakia—were made into German "protectorates."

It is obvious from this hasty account that once Hitler had risen to power in Germany he escaped from the restraints conservative and nationalist groups who had helped him to office attempted to impose upon him. He used them; they were unable to use him. In a limited sense, Hitler brought a revolution to Germany. New social elements took power, new ideas took hold upon the German people, violence flared briefly in 1934, and the former social order was profoundly affected by the militarization of the economy and the corresponding buildup of the armed forces. Yet the Nazi revolution, like that of 1919, was a partial affair. The turn-over was less complete than that wrought in Russia after 1917, and the Nazis never eradicated the influence of such powerful groups as the officers corps, whose tradition descended unbroken from imperial Germany.

3) France and Great Britain, 1919–1939. While revolution and semi-revolution swept over eastern and central Europe, the governments and social systems of France and Great Britain remained comparatively stable. Losses of wealth which both countries had suffered during the World War were not completely made good. In France a serious monetary inflation

SHAPERS OF THE MODERN WORLD

WORLD WAR II POLITICAL LEADERS

Franklin Roosevelt
(The Bettmann Archive)

Adolf Hitler
Photo, 1937
(The Bettmann Archive)

Winston Churchill
Photo, 1939
(The Bettmann Archive)

Joseph Stalin
(The Bettmann Archive)

kept the economy in an uproar until 1926 when new taxes were imposed to balance the budget. Britain suffered from the loss of some important prewar markets which had been taken over by the United States during the war years; also the decline in the demand for coal (resulting from increased use of oil and water power) brought severe depression to coal mining, which had been one of the nation's primary industries. Labor discontent simmered as a result of chronic unemployment, and even when Ramsay MacDonald, the head of the Labour Party, became Prime Minister of a coalition cabinet in January, 1924, conditions failed to improve. A dispute over wages for coal miners resulted in the calling of a general strike in 1926; the failure of the strike (and accusations against the Labor Party of being in close connection with the Russian Communists) helped to confirm the tenure of a Conservative cabinet which had taken over from MacDonald in October, 1924.

For three brief years, from 1926–29, prosperity came to France and Britain—partly as a result of the prosperity which American loans brought to Germany during the same period. But the depression of 1930 brought this period to a dismal end, and problems of unemployment once again beset the two nations. The stability of the French government was threatened by various groups which disliked or distrusted the republican form of government—Communists on the left, and a variety of semifascist and clerical groups on the right. In Britain no one seriously challenged the system of government, but, on the other hand, no one knew how to meet the economic crisis effectively.

The timid and short sighted foreign policies of the western democracies in the 1930's must be understood against this background of economic distress and internal weakness. Fear of war was very widespread and deepseated. Many persons felt that any concession to avoid war was worth while. In addition a good many Englishmen and some Frenchmen believed that there was at least a grain of justice on Hitler's side, and that the provisions of the Treaty of Versailles had been unfairly punitive. But as Hitler's appetite for new territory seemed to grow with the feeding, and as he broke his promises one after another, public opinion began to harden against any further concession. The Munich surrender of 1938 was received with initial relief, followed by serious regrets in both France and Britain. Both governments resolved not to yield again. As a result Britain and France extended guarantees to Poland by which they undertook to fight any attempt to violate the territorial integrity of that country.

Such a guarantee, combined with a similar promise made to Rumania, blocked further German expansion to the east. Hitler was faced with a choice; either to give up his ambitions or continue with his plans and risk war with France and Britain. Hitler chose the second path. His choice was certainly made easier by the treaty which the Russians concluded with him on August 23, 1939. A week later, on September 1, the German armies marched into Poland; and on September 3 Britain and France, in accordance with their promise to Poland, declared war on Germany. So began the Second World War.

4) World War II and Aftermath, 1939–1949. For nearly two years after the beginning of the war German armies met with continual and brilliant success. Poland was overrun in a matter of weeks; in the spring of 1940 France too was conquered, as well as Norway, Denmark, Holland and Belgium. After the surrender of France (June, 1940) Britain alone remained at war with the victorious Germans. But German efforts to prepare an invasion of England came to nothing, and Hitler decided to turn his arms against the only remaining powerful land force within his reach: the Russian Soviet state. The Germans attacked Russia on June 22, 1941, and at first met with very considerable success. But the initial year's campaign failed to capture Moscow or to paralyze Russian resistance, although many of the richest parts of the country were occupied by German troops. At the end of 1941 a decisive change occurred when the United States entered the war as a result of the Japanese attack on Pearl Harbor (December 7), followed by Germany's declaration of war on the United States (December 11).

The turning point came in the fall and winter of 1942–43. In November, 1942 American and British troops landed in North Africa, and by May 1943 succeeded in driving German forces from that continent and winning control of the Mediterranean. During the same period, from November to February, the Russians fought a great battle for Stalingrad, and were able to surround a large German army and force its surrender. Thereafter, German forces were everywhere on the defensive. The Russians gradually drove the invaders from the soil of the Soviet Union, and by the spring of 1944 were able to cross the old borders and pushed on into the Balkans, Poland and, before the end of 1944, had penetrated into parts of Germany itself. The Anglo-Americans invaded Sicily in July, 1943, and Italy in September of the same year; then in June, 1944, succeeded in crossing the English channel with a great force and by the end of 1944 had reached a line very close to the western German frontier. The Germans had been seriously weakened by air attack and by naval blockade, so that when the final offensives began in the spring of 1945 the Allies were everywhere victorious. Hitler killed himself, probably on May 2, 1945, in Berlin; and on May 8–9 the final act of surrender was signed.

The war against Japan came to its end soon thereafter. In the first years the great ocean distances of the Pacific made it very difficult for American forces to attack the Japanese; but by the end of 1943 new methods of amphibious warfare had been developed by the U.S. Navy. From that time onward it became possible to move across the Pacific by leaping from one island to another, moving forward as much as 1000 miles at a time. In October, 1944, a great naval battle fought near the Philippines (Battle of Leyte Gulf) destroyed a large part of the Japanese fleet. Thereafter Japan's warpower was rapidly sapped by naval and air blockade. Surrender came in August, 1945, before actual invasion of the Japanese home islands had begun. The final documents ending World War II were signed on September 2, 1946, six years and one day after hostilities had started.

The vast scale and genuinely world-wide character of World War II was unprecedented in history. The effectiveness with which Britain, Russia and the United States linked their separate national economic and military efforts into one vast whole was also without precedent. To be sure, military cooperation between Russia and the western allies was never intimate; but Anglo-American forces actually merged their field armies and fought under a single command. On the economic level, the operation of American Lend Lease assumed such a scale as to make the three war economies of Britain, Russia and the United States into an interdependent single whole. Social, economic and military planning on unprecedented scale was developed in each of the belligerent nations; and the leading peoples of the world succeeded in concentrating their collective energies and resources upon the waging of war as never before.

The Grand Alliance of World War II was held together first and foremost by common enmity against Hitler; but the policies and personalities of the three great war leaders, President Franklin D. Roosevelt (1882–1945), Prime Minister Winston Churchill (1874–1965) and Generalissimo Josef Stalin (1879–1953) must also be given credit for successful cooperation between governments that in fact had much to quarrel over. Periodic conferences (Tehran, November, 1943, Yalta, February, 1945, and Potsdam, July–August, 1945) between the three heads of government settled some disputes and papered over others during the course of the fighting; but once Hitler and the Japanese had been removed from the military scene, the Grand Alliance rapidly fell apart. Points of friction which had been glossed over during the war itself came to the forefront, and a thinly veiled struggle for power and influence in such countries as Poland, Germany and China soon degenerated into the aptly named "cold war." Between 1945 and 1947 the principal tension lay between Britain and Russia; but after 1947, when President Harry Truman (1884–   ) offered American support to Greece and Turkey against Communist threats, most of the world came to be divided between the United States and its supporters on the one hand and the Soviet Union with its dependencies on the other.

The new international organization which had been set up in 1945, the United Nations, was powerless to cope with such disputes between the

Great Powers. Effective action required unanimity among the permanent members of the Security Council, and such unanimity was almost unattainable when disputes between Russia and the West reached an acute stage. Nevertheless, the debates of the United Nations continued to be a prominent feature of international affairs. At United Nations headquarters in New York, the great powers and lesser ones engaged in rival propaganda and, behind the scenes, sometimes negotiated seriously with one another. When compared with the fate of the League of Nations, the new international organization at least lasted longer. The principal nations of the world (with the conspicuous exceptions of Germany and Communist China) continued to think membership worth while, and judged that appeal to the common opinion of the governments and peoples of the world through the United Nations was wise or else prudent. This in itself, constituted a slender but real restraint upon acts of national egoism.

The course of World War II demonstrated the vast power which both the United States and the Soviet Union could command. Although the war began in Europe, and for the first 18 months was fought between traditional European nation states, during the latter years of the war it was no longer nation states in the old European sense that found themselves locked in combat. Instead, vast trans-national organizations of power were constructed to fight the war. This was as true of Germany as of the Allies, for Hitler succeeded in organizing almost the whole resources of Europe to serve the Nazi war machine, just as the Russians organized the resources of their own vast territory, and just as the Americans and British organized the broad areas of the earth which they either ruled or influenced. Japan's war power, too, was drawn not only from Japan proper but from Manchuria and other regions conquered by Japanese arms in the course of the fighting.

The practical demonstration of what could be done to organize the manpower and resources of comparatively vast territories to serve a common purpose was one of the main breakthroughs of World War II. The second breakthrough of earlier limits on human action was the equally impressive demonstration of how existing levels of technology could be altered by deliberate decisions to devote ingenuity and engineering resources to discovering new devices and manufacturing methods. The Germans developed rockets and jet aircraft in this fashion, though both of Hitler's "secret weapons" came into operation too late to have much effect on the course of the war. The allies developed radar and the atom bomb by similar methods, along with a host of less dramatic devices like proximity fuses for shells. Both of these major breakthroughs continued to be important in the postwar period.

CENTRAL EUROPE
AFTER WORLD WAR II

- ··········· Boundaries after WW I
- ───── Boundaries after WW II
- Soviet Union and areas under communist control (Warsaw Pact)
- Iron Curtain
- NATO members

NORWAY

SWEDEN

FINLAND

Helsinki

Leningrad

ESTONIA

LATVIA

LITHUANIA

SOVIET

UNION

North
Sea

GREAT
BRITAIN

DENMARK

Baltic Sea

E. PRUSSIA

NETHERLANDS

Berlin

WEST GERMANY

EAST GERMANY

Oder

Neisse

POLAND

Warsaw

BELGIUM

Bonn

LUX.

Elbe

Prague

CZECHOSLOVAKIA

Rhine

Paris

BESSARABIA

FRANCE
(France withdraws
from NATO, 1967)

Vienna

SWITZ.

AUSTRIA

HUNGARY

Budapest

RUMANIA

Bucharest

Black
Sea

ITALY

Adriatic
Sea

Belgrade

YUGOSLAVIA
(Break with Stalin, 1948)

Danube

BULGARIA

SPAIN

CORSICA

Rome

Sofia

ALBANIA

BALEARIC IS.

SARDINIA

TURKEY

GREECE

Athens

Mediterranean Sea

SICILY

CRETE

ALGERIA

TUNISIA

MALTA

0   400 miles

5) Cold war and its Breakup, 1949–1975

The political history of Europe after 1949 is so closely interwoven with the history of the United States and the USSR, not to mention Africa, China, India and the Middle East, that the confines of this *Handbook* no longer fit. Generally speaking, international politics was deeply affected by a semisecret arms race, centered upon the design and improvement of atomic warheads and means for their delivery. At first, only the United States and Russia took part in this race; Great Britain dabbled and then, in effect, withdrew. But in 1958 France began to devote important resources to developing atomic weapons of its own, and in 1964 the Chinese, too, exploded their first "atomic device."

By 1956 or thereabout, it became clear both to the American and to the Russian government that the potential destruction that could be wreaked by atomic war, using hydrogen warheads (perfected between 1950 and 1956), was so great that all-out war was no longer an acceptable national policy. As this became clear to other nations, the two great powers' hold over their allies weakened. France began to defy the United States; Rumania, Poland and Yugoslavia did the same to the USSR; and from 1960 an open and bitter quarrel between China and the Soviet Union split the Communist world into rival segments. Complicated and shifting alignments, more like the old European balance of power, projected however to the world scale, began to transform the bi-polar world that had emerged in the immediate postwar years.

Between 1949 and about 1957, however, the "cold war" between the United States and its allies and the Russians and their allies dominated everything else. In 1949 mainland China became Communist; in the following year, a Communist régime in north Korea attempted (presumably with Stalin's approval) to unite the whole country under its control. The American government responded to these events by consolidating a military alliance with the states of western Europe (NATO—North Atlantic Treaty Organization) and by sending American troops and supplies to aid the south Korean government. The United Nations condemned north Korea as an aggressor; and a total of sixteen nations contributed greater or lesser military aid to the south Korean cause before the war came to an end. The Chinese, however, came to the aid of north Korea when victorious United Nations forces began to approach the Chinese-Korean border. Chinese troops caught the Americans by surprise, and drove the United Nations forces southward until the front nearly coincided with the 38th parallel from which the struggle had begun. The war ended, therefore, in stalemate and truce (1953).

The immediate postwar years also saw the rapid breakup of European empires in Africa and Asia. Britain withdrew from India, Burma and Ceylon in 1947; beginning in 1956 a very rapid transfer of sovereignty to local governments took place in all former British colonies of Africa, and the same policy prevailed in south east Asia and in the Caribbean— wherever a local political movement demanding independence could be discovered. France, the other great European colonial power, was at first reluctant to break off imperial ties. But a pair of nasty wars—one in Indo-China (1947–54) and one in Algeria (1954–62)—convinced the French that it would be impossible to hold their empire by force, and under the leadership of General Charles De Gaulle (recalled to power in 1958) the French, too, gave independence to their colonies in Africa and elsewhere. Belgium took the same course in 1960 by liberating the vast Belgian Congo.

As Europe's economic prosperity mounted with the success of the Common Market, the concern of Europeans for African and Asian lands diminished. Similarly, after Stalin's death (1953) and the end of the Korean war both the Russians and the Americans became more concerned about domestic problems than before. In Russia, the desire to improve standards of living seemed far more urgent than pursuit of world revolution. In the United States, Negro civil rights and other domestic issues also achieved fresh importance.

China, Egypt (where a military coup brought Gamal Abdel Nasser to power in 1954) and Cuba (where Fidel Castro led a Communist guerrilla movement to victory in 1959) remained as active centers of revolutionary aspiration and idealism; but they met with little success, for each had serious problems at home too. Only in Viet Nam did a Communist-led guerrilla movement meet with continued success in an effort to overthrow the government of the southern part of that land. United States support had helped to establish a separate south Vietnamese government after the cease fire agreements between the French and Vietnamese guerrillas (1954); and when that government seemed in danger, American troops and supplies were sent to try to stop the Communists from taking power. Major United States commitment to the struggle occurred only after 1964; but since the north Vietnamese Communists easily rallied support against white skinned invaders and were able to get large quantities of arms from Russia and China, the scale and duration of the war belied American official expectations. In time, a war on behalf of people in Viet Nam who showed no very definite signs of preferring Americans to their fellow countrymen became unpopular in the United States; but fear of a loss of prestige kept the struggle going until 1975, when American withdrawal was swiftly followed by Communist victory.

The other major trouble center of the world's international affairs was in the Middle East where three brief wars between the Jewish state of Israel (established 1947) and its Arab neighbors led to Israeli victory each time (1947, 1956, 1967). But each defeat only hardened the Arabs' determination to try again at some future time.

No thumbnail sketch of the recent internal political history of the European or world powers seems worthwhile here. Except in France, where there were two extra-legal changes of régime after World War II, Europe's political history between 1949 and 1969 was remarkably orderly, in Communist and non-Communist lands alike. The European nations' emphatic economic success perhaps explains this fact.

d. Culture

It would be absurd to try to describe the history of European culture since 1914 in this *Handbook*. Some names stand out: the painters Pablo Picasso (1881–1973) and Henri Matisse (1869–1954); the writers James Joyce (1882-1941), Marcel Proust (1871-1922) and Thomas Mann (1875-1955); the composers Paul Hindemith (1895-1963) and Sergei Prokofief (1891-1953); the philosophers Alfred North Whitehead (1881–1947) and Benedetto Croce (1866-1952); and the poet and critic Thomas Stearns Eliot (1888-1964); but we are still too close in time to these and the many other artists, writers and thinkers of the age to be sure of their long range standing in the tradition of western culture.

In the field of natural science, enormous amounts of new data have been gathered since 1914 in every field. Physics occupied the most influential role in the 1920's and 1930's, as men tried to comprehend and then adjust their mental grasp of the world to Einstein's theory of relativity. In the post-World War II decades, however, the most dramatic theoretical breakthrough came in biology with the deciphering of the chemical structure of the DNA molecule by James Watson and F. H. C. Crick (1953). This opened up a comparatively precise understanding of the mechanisms of inheritance, and suggested the possibility that scientists might in future learn how to alter heredity by deliberate manipulation of the DNA "codes." Such power over life processes and the patterns of organic evolution staggers the imagination, especially if such techniques should ever be applied to human beings.

In the social sciences, only the practical applications of economic theory as modified by the work of John Maynard Keynes (1883-1946) had any sort of comparable significance. Yet the increased scope of anthropological and historical understanding of the human adventure on earth and of man's diverse cultural systems and achievements may also have a cumulatively very great importance in shifting men's views of one another, especially across racial and cultural differentia. No single name stands out in these fields, though the anthropologists Bronislaw Malinowski (1884-1942) and Alfred Kroeber (1876-1960) and the historians Arnold J. Toynbee (1889–   ) and Marc Bloch (1886–1944) were among the most influential leaders of their respective disciplines.

A striking change came over the Roman Catholic Church under Pope John XXIII (1958-63). He allowed advocates of change within the Church to express their thoughts freely at an ecumenical council, Vatican II, that he summoned. Even more significant, perhaps, was the fact that at Vatican II and afterwards, the pope and other leading prelates of the Roman church entered into friendly relations with Protestant and Orthodox churchmen for the first time since the Reformation era.

A characteristic of recent times has been the effort by totalitarian states to control cultural expression in order to make artists, writers and thinkers serve political ends. In all countries the area of concensus among cultural leaders and among the population in general tended to shrink in the years after World War I, and totalitarian control may be regarded as an effort to restore consensus by compulsion and police methods. The effectiveness of modern propaganda and police in shaping the minds of ordinary men has been amply demonstrated by Fascist, Nazi and Communist governments; but it seems possible, perhaps probable, that such methods will lead to cultural sterility. Only time will tell.

Suggestions for Further Reading for Part III, C–4

Black, C. E. and Helmreich, E. C. *Twentieth Century Europe*. New York: 1952.

Borkenau, Franz. *The Communist International*. London: 1938.

Brogan, D. W. *France under the Republic: The Development of Modern France, 1870–1939*. New York: 1940.

Brzezinski, Zbigniew. *The Soviet Bloc: Unity and Conflict*. Cambridge, Mass: 1967.

Bullock, Alan L. *Hitler, a Study in Tyranny*. Rev. ed. New York: 1964.

Churchill, Winston S. *The Second World War*. 6 vols. Boston: 1948–53.

Cruttwell, C. R. M. *A History of the Great War, 1914–1918*. London: 1934.

Daniels, Robert V., ed. *A Documentary History of Communism*. New York: 1960.

Deakin, F. W. *The Brutal Friendship*. New York: 1963.

Deutscher, Isaac. *Stalin, A Political Biography*. New York: 1967.

Deutscher, Isaac. *The Prophet Armed: Trotsky, 1879–1921*. New York: 1954.

Deutscher, Isaac. *Prophet Unarmed: Trotsky, 1921–1929*. New York: 1959.

Deutscher, Isaac. *Prophet Outcast: Trotsky, 1929–1940*. New York: 1963.

Diebold, William. Jr., *The Schuman Plan: A Study in Economic Cooperation*. New York: 1959.

Eisenhower, Dwight. *Crusade in Europe*. New York: 1967.

Fainsod, Merle. *How Russia Is Ruled*. Cambridge, Mass: 1963.

Falls, C. *The Second World War: a Short History*. London: 1948.

Fischer, Louis. *The Life of Lenin.* New York: 1965.

Florinsky, M. T. *Russia: a History and an Interpretation.* 2 vols. New York: 1954.

Gathorne-Hardy, G. M. *A Short History of International Affairs, 1920–1939.* 4th ed. London: 1950.

Halle, Louis. *The Cold War.* New York: 1967.

Hazard, John. *The Soviet System of Government.* Chicago: 1968.

Hiscocks, Richard. *The Adenauer Era.* Philadelphia: 1966.

Hitler, Adolf. *Mein Kampf.* New York: 1937.

Jackson, Gabriel. *The Spanish Republic and the Civil War, 1931–1939.* Princeton: 1965.

Kennan, George. *Russia and the West under Lenin and Stalin.* Boston: 1961.

Keynes, John Maynard. *The Economic Consequences of the Peace.* London: 1920.

Kohn, Hans. *The Twentieth Century: a Midway Account of the Western World.* New York: 1949.

McNeill, W. H. *America, Britain and Russia: their Cooperation and Conflict, 1941–46.* London: 1954.

McNeill, W. H. *The Contemporary World.* New York: 1968.

Mayer, Milton. *They Thought They were Free.* Chicago: 1966.

Maynard, John. *Russia in Flux.* New York: 1948.

Meyer, Albert G. *Communism.* New York: 1960.

Meyer, Albert G. *Leninism.* Cambridge, Mass: 1957.

Moore, Ruth. *Niels Bohr: The Man, His Science and the World They Changed.* New York: 1966.

Mowat, Charles L. *Britain between the Wars.* Chicago: 1956.

Mumford, Lewis. *The City in History: Its Origins, Its Transformation and Its Prospects.* New York: 1961.

Nolte, Ernst. *Three Faces of Fascism: Action Française; Italian Fascism; National Socialism.* New York: 1966.

Pinson, Koppel S. *Modern Germany, its History and Civilization.* New York: 1954.

Rees, David. *The Age of Containment: The Cold War 1945–65.* New York: 1967.

Rauschning, Hermann. *The Revolution of Nihilism.* New York: 1939.

Reed, John. *Ten Days that Shook the World.* New York: 1919.

Roberts, H. L. *Russia and America, Dangers and Prospects.* New York: 1955.

Salvemini, Gaetano. *Under the Axe of Fascism.* New York: 1936.

Seton-Watson, Hugh. *The East European Revolution.* New York: 1950.

Seton-Watson, Hugh. *Eastern Europe between the Wars.* Hamden, Conn: 1962.

Seton-Watson, Hugh. *From Lenin to Malenkov: the History of World Communism*. New York: 1953.
Sherwood, Robert. *Roosevelt and Hopkins*. New York: 1948.
Shirer, William L. *Berlin Diary, 1934–1941*. New York: 1942.
Stalin, Joseph. *Leninism: Selected Writings of Joseph Stalin*. New York: 1942.
Taylor, A. J. P. *English History, 1914–45*. New York: 1965.
Thomas, Hugh. *The Spanish Civil War*. New York: 1961.
Trotsky, Leon. *The History of the Russian Revolution*. 3 vols. New York: 1933.
Wilmot, Chester. *The Struggle for Europe: History of World War II*. New York: 1952.
Wilson, Edmund. *To the Finland Station*. New York: 1940.

Chronological Table for Part III, C–4: An Era of Wars and Revolution

*1914–1918	First World War.
1917, March	"February Revolution" in Russia.
*1917, Nov. 7	"October Revolution" in Russia.
1917–1921	Civil War and "War Communism" in Russia.
1918, March	Peace Treaty of Brest-Litovsk.
1918, July	First Soviet Constitution.
1918, Nov. 11	Armistice ending World War I.
*1919–1920	Peace treaties of Versailles, St. Germain, Neuilly, Trianon, Sèvres.
1919	Establishment of Third (Communist) International.
1919–1933	Weimar Republic in Germany.
1919–1920	Polish-Russian War.
1920	First meeting of League of Nations.
1921–1928	NEP in Russia.
1922	Treaty of Rapallo (between Russia and Germany).
1922	Fascist "March on Rome."
1923	Occupation of the Ruhr by the French; Nazi Putsch; Communist uprising in Germany.
1924	Death of Lenin.
1924	First British Labor Cabinet.
1924	Dawes Plan.
1925	Locarno Treaties: rapprochement between Germany, France, Italy and Britain.
1926	General Strike in Great Britain.

1926	Admission of Germany to the League of Nations.
1928–1932	First Five-Year Plan in Russia.
1929	Beginning of the Great Depression.
1929	Lateran Treaties between the Pope and Mussolini.
1929	Young Plan: German reparations scaled down.
1930	Evacuation of Rhineland by occupation armies.
1932–1937	Second Five-Year Plan in Russia.
*1933	Seizure of power in Germany by Hitler.
1933	Germany resigns from League of Nations.
1934	Russia joins League of Nations.
1935	Conclusion of Franco-Russian alliance.
1935	Italian attack on Ethiopia.
1936	Remilitarization of Rhineland by Germany.
1936–1939	Civil war in Spain.
1936	German-Italian Pact ("Axis").
1936	New Soviet Constitution.
1938	Seizure of Austria by Hitler.
1938	Munich Agreement.
1939	Annexation of Czechoslovakia by Germany.
1939	German-Russian pact.
*1939–1945	Second World War.
1939, Sept. 1	German invasion of Poland.
Sept. 3	Declaration of war on Germany by Great Britain and France.
1940, Apr. 9	German invasion of Denmark and Norway.
May 10	German invasion of Belgium, Netherlands, Luxemburg.
June 22	Capitulation of France.
Oct. 28	Italian invasion of Greece.
1941, June 22	German invasion of Russia.
Aug. 14	Atlantic Charter.
Dec. 7	Pearl Harbor.
Dec. 8	Declaration of war by USA on Japan.
Dec. 11	Declaration of war by Germany and Italy on USA.
1942, Nov. 8	Landing of US forces in French North Africa.
Dec. 2	First controlled release of nuclear energy; step towards A-bomb.
1943, Feb. 2	Capitulation of German army at Stalingrad.
1944, June 6	Invasion of Normandy.
1945. Feb.	Conference at Yalta.
April–June	San Francisco Conference (United Nations Charter).

Apr. 12	Death of Roosevelt (b. 1882).
*May 7–9	German surrender.
July–Aug.	Potsdam Conference.
*Aug. 14	Japanese surrender.
1945	Death of Mussolini (b. 1883); death of Hitler (b. 1889).
1946 Jan.	First meeting of United Nations General Assembly.
1947	Truman doctrine; British accord independence to India and Pakistan.
1949	Chinese Communists win control of Chinese mainland; North Atlantic Treaty.
1950–1953	Korean war.
1953	Death of Stalin (b. 1879).
1956	Anti-Communist revolt in Hungary; Russian intervention.
1956	French–British–Israeli attack on Egypt for nationalizing the Suez canal. Halted by UN.
1957	European Common Market set up; ten-year transition period.
1957	Russians launch first artificial earth satellite (sputnik).
1959	Fidel Castro to power in Cuba.
1960	Quarrel between USSR and China made public.
1962–1963	Second Vatican Council.
1962–69, Oct.	Cuban missile crisis; USSR backed down.
1964	United States engaged in undeclared war in Viet Nam.
1967	Third Arab–Israeli war; victory for Israel.
1968	Apollo 8: USA sent three men around the moon.

Conclusion

If one tries to look back through time, and, as it were, take in at one glance the history of Western Civilization from its roots in the ancient Orient to the present, the first impression may be one of distress. So much confusion, so many wars, so many good intentions and warm ideals which have failed of realization. On the other hand, one may appreciate the toughness of human nature and society, which has on numerous occasions undergone great disasters and yet survived despite the crimes, follies and miseries of mankind.

In this *Handbook* there are two lacks which you as students should make an effort to supply from your own imaginations and collateral reading. One is the absence of any systematic effort to consider causes; the other is the absence of any adequate portrayal of the rich human variety of the past. By dealing with abstract generalizations and in trying to maintain a certain modicum of objectivity, an account of history such as this sacrifices much of the emotional appeal which history may and should have. Heroes and villains have existed in the past; and to know them, even pallidly through books—to share in imagination their hopes and fears, to kindle in admiration or recoil in horror from their deeds—this is an important way to extend one's private experience and to strengthen one's own moral judgments. Indeed, it is only by finding one's own heroes and villains in the past that knowledge of history may have its maximum effect upon one's own behavior. The same may be said of the effort to arrive at a causal understanding of the past: only with such an understanding can one's judgments of current problems be fully intelligent and informed. But it is impossible for anyone to state moral judgments which will win universal acceptance, and men have not arrived at any indisputable understanding of the causal connections which may control social development. Yet it is worthwhile to consider these problems and to make at least tentative personal judgments. Well reasoned beliefs as to the causal and moral lessons of history are the final flower of a study of the past; a flower which requires rich information and private reflection for its growth; a flower, moreover, which will undoubtedly vary in shape and color from person to person, since The Truth about history continues to elude human minds.

Index

657